D0283002

Iqaluit

Hudson Bay

Atlantic Ocean

ONTARIO

QUEBEC

Quebec City

ATLANTIC CANADA

St. John's

Ottawa

Montreal

Halifax

Toronto

0 km 500
0 miles 500

EYEWITNESS TRAVEL

CANADA

EYEWITNESS TRAVEL

CANADA

LONDON, NEW YORK,
MELBOURNE, MUNICH AND DELHI
www.dk.com

Produced by Duncan Baird Publishers, London, England
Managing Editor Rebecca Miles
Managing Art Editor Vanessa Marsh
Editors Georgina Harris, Michelle de Larrabeiti, Zoë Ross
Designers Dawn Davies-Cook, Ian Midson
Design Assistance Rosie Laing, Kelvin Mullins
Visualizer Gary Cross
Picture Research Victoria Peel
DTP Designer Sarah Williams

Dorling Kindersley Limited
Project Editor Paul Hines
Art Editor Jane Ewart
US Editor Mary Sutherland
Editor Hugh Thompson

Contributors
Bruce Bishop, Eric & Katharine Fletcher, Paul Franklin, Sam Ion, Ffion Llywd-Jones,
Helena Katz, Philip Lee, Cam Norton, Lorry Patton, Sandra Phinney, Geoffrey Roy,
Michael Snook, Donald Telfer, Paul Waters

Photographers Alan Keohane, Peter Wilson, Francesca Yorke

Illustrators Joanna Cameron, Gary Cross, Chris Forsey, Paul Guest, Claire Littlejohn, Robbie
Polley, Kevin Robinson, John Woodcock

Printed and bound by
South China Printing Co. Ltd., China

First American Edition, 2000
14 15 16 17 10 9 8 7 6 5 4 3 2 1

Published in the United States by DK Publishing, 345 Hudson Street,
New York, New York 10014

Reprinted with revisions 2002, 2004, 2006, 2008, 2010, 2012, 2014

Copyright 2000, 2014 © Dorling Kindersley Limited, London
A Penguin Company

Published in Great Britain by Dorling Kindersley Limited.

A catalog record for this book is available from the Library of Congress

ISSN 1542-1554
ISBN 978-1-46541-137-2

MIX
Paper from
responsible sources
FSC™ C018179

**The information in this
DK Eyewitness Travel Guide is checked regularly.**
Every effort has been made to ensure that this book is as up-to-date as possible at
the time of going to press. Some details, however, such as telephone numbers,
opening hours, prices, gallery hanging arrangements, and travel information are
liable to change. The publishers cannot accept responsibility for any consequences
arising from the use of this book, nor for any material on third party websites, and
cannot guarantee that any website address in this book will be a suitable source of
travel information. We value the views and suggestions of our readers very highly.
Please write to: Publisher, DK Eyewitness Travel Guides, Dorling Kindersley, 80 Strand,
London, WC2R 0RL, Great Britain or email travelguides@dk.com.

Front cover main image: Moraine Lake and Valley of the Ten Peaks, Banff National Park

◀ The dazzling fall foliage of Quebec's maple forests

Contents

The historic reconstruction of Fortress of
Louisbourg, Nova Scotia

Quebec

Moraine Lake in Banff National Park in the Rockies

Château Frontenac in Quebec City

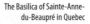
The Basilica of Sainte-Anne-
du-Beaupré in Quebec

INTRODUCING CANADA

GRAND TRUNK RAILWAY.

MAKE THE MOST OF CANADA

The following itineraries have been designed to include as many of the country's highlights as possible, while keeping long-distance travel to a minimum. First come three 2-day tours of Canada's most important cities: Toronto, Montreal, and Vancouver. These itineraries can be followed individually, or, in the case of Montreal and Toronto, included in a week-long provincial tour. Next come four 7-day tours, covering British Columbia and the Rockies, Ontario, Quebec, and the Maritime Provinces. Select, combine, and follow your favorite tours, or simply dip in and out and be inspired. Booking ahead for major sights is recommended.

British Columbia and the Rockies

Main map

0 kilometers   200

0 miles   200

Niagara Falls
Located on the border between Canada and the USA, the magificent Niagara Falls are visited by around 14 million people each year.

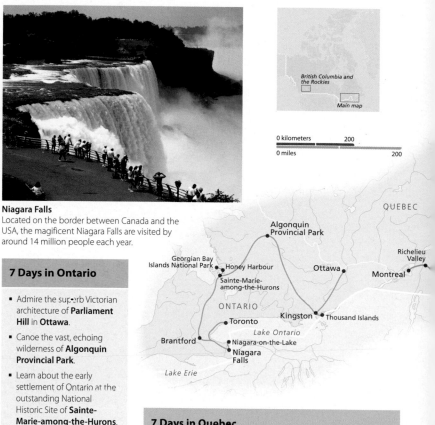

QUEBEC

Algonquin Provincial Park

Richelieu Valley

Georgian Bay Islands National Park   Honey Harbour   Ottawa   Montreal

Sainte-Marie-among-the-Hurons

ONTARIO   Kingston   Thousand Islands

Toronto   Lake Ontario

Brantford   Niagara-on-the-Lake

Niagara Falls

Lake Erie

7 Days in Ontario

- Admire the superb Victorian architecture of **Parliament Hill** in **Ottawa**.

- Canoe the vast, echoing wilderness of **Algonquin Provincial Park**.

- Learn about the early settlement of Ontario at the outstanding National Historic Site of **Sainte-Marie-among-the-Hurons**.

- Boat and hike through the beautiful scenery of **Georgian Bay Islands National Park**.

- Marvel at the magificent the thundering waterfalls of **Niagara Falls**.

- Saunter the streets of **Niagara-on-the-Lake** with its charming assortment of old timber houses.

7 Days in Quebec

- Explore the ancient streets of **Quebec City** and enjoy its fine riverside setting.

- Join the crowds at the mighty **Montmorency Falls** at the **Parc de la Chute Montmorency**.

- Linger at **Sainte-Anne-de-Beaupré**, Quebec's holiest place of pilgrimage.

- Take a whale-watching tour from the agreeable town of **Tadoussac**.

- Experience the rugged landscapes of the **Parc National du Canada Forillon**, at the tip of the **Gaspé Peninsula**.

- Investigate the vineyards of the **Richelieu Valley** near **Montreal**.

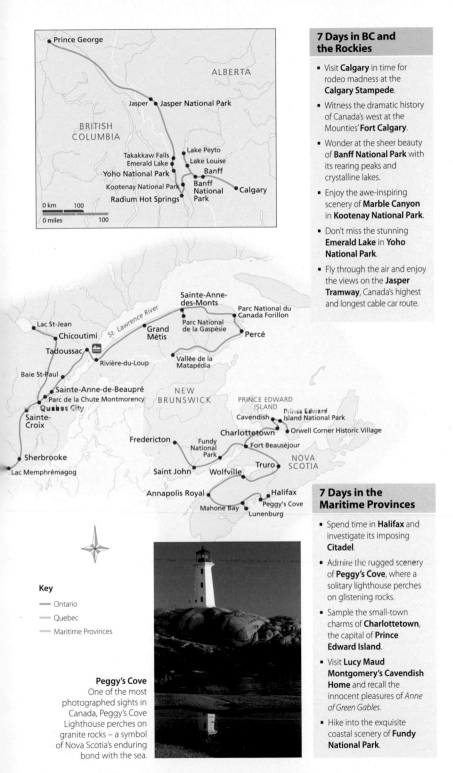

Prince George

ALBERTA

Jasper • Jasper National Park

BRITISH
COLUMBIA

Takakkaw Falls
Emerald Lake
Yoho National Park
Kootenay National Park
Radium Hot Springs

Lake Peyto
Lake Louise
Banff
Banff
National
Park

Calgary

0 km 100
0 miles 100

7 Days in BC and the Rockies

- Visit **Calgary** in time for rodeo madness at the **Calgary Stampede**.
- Witness the dramatic history of Canada's west at the Mounties' **Fort Calgary**.
- Wonder at the sheer beauty of **Banff National Park** with its rearing peaks and crystalline lakes.
- Enjoy the awe-inspiring scenery of **Marble Canyon** in **Kootenay National Park**.
- Don't miss the stunning **Emerald Lake** in **Yoho National Park**.
- Fly through the air and enjoy the views on the **Jasper Tramway**, Canada's highest and longest cable car route.

Sainte-Anne-des-Monts

Parc National du
Canada Forillon

St. Lawrence River

Lac St-Jean
Chicoutimi
Tadoussac

Grand
Métis

Parc National
de la Gaspésie

Percé

Rivière-du-Loup

Vallée de la
Matapédia

Baie St-Paul

Sainte-Anne-de-Beaupré
Parc de la Chute Montmorency
Québec City

Sainte-
Croix

NEW
BRUNSWICK

PRINCE EDWARD
ISLAND

Prince Edward
Island National Park

Cavendish

Charlottetown

Orwell Corner Historic Village

Sherbrooke
Lac Memphrémagog

Fredericton

Fundy
National
Park

Fort Beauséjour

Saint John

Wolfville

Truro

NOVA
SCOTIA

Annapolis Royal

Halifax

Mahone Bay

Peggy's Cove

Lunenburg

Key
— Ontario
— Quebec
— Maritime Provinces

Peggy's Cove
One of the most photographed sights in Canada, Peggy's Cove Lighthouse perches on granite rocks – a symbol of Nova Scotia's enduring bond with the sea.

7 Days in the Maritime Provinces

- Spend time in **Halifax** and investigate its imposing **Citadel**.
- Admire the rugged scenery of **Peggy's Cove**, where a solitary lighthouse perches on glistening rocks.
- Sample the small-town charms of **Charlottetown**, the capital of **Prince Edward Island**.
- Visit **Lucy Maud Montgomery's Cavendish Home** and recall the innocent pleasures of *Anne of Green Gables*.
- Hike into the exquisite coastal scenery of **Fundy National Park**.

2 Days in Toronto

Canada's economic power-house, Toronto has dozens of great hotels, first-class restaurants, and world-class museums.

- **Arriving** There are regular express buses from Toronto airport to downtown, 16 miles (27 km) away; the journey takes 40–70 minutes, depending on traffic.
- **Moving on** There are regular flights from Toronto to Vancouver, and trains, buses, and flights to Montreal.

The modern Toronto skyline on the north side of Lake Ontario

Day 1

Morning Begin a visit to **Toronto** at the **CN Tower** (*p176*), whose needle-like spire soars high above the city center, offering panoramic views over the lake and across Ontario; be brave and step onto the tower's glass floor. Then, walk to the **Toronto Dominion Gallery of Inuit Art** (*p178*), home to a small but superb collection of Inuit sculptures. Finish off the morning with a stroll along the harborfront and lunch in one of the cafés on **Queen's Quay** (*p175*).

Afternoon At **Fort York** (*p190*), see how Toronto began life as a British stockade garrisoned by a handful of Redcoats, before heading to the **Art Gallery of Ontario** (*pp182–3*), one of Canada's finest galleries, to sample the magnificent collection of art. Nearby is **Kensington Market** (*p184*), a boho shopping area celebrated for its cosmopolitan vibe and vintage fashion stores.

Day 2

Morning Start the day by exploring the **Royal Ontario Museum** (*p186*), whose huge collection features everything from massive totem poles to intimidating dinosaur skeletons. Then proceed to the **Bata Shoe Museum** (*p186*), featuring three whole floors of antique shoes and boots of every shape and description.

Afternoon Don't miss the wonderful ceramic collection exhibited at the **Gardiner Museum of Ceramic Art** (*p186*) and then be sure to visit **Casa Loma** (*p190*), an extravagant Victorian folly, which was built to resemble a medieval castle. Complete the day with a boat trip to the balmy **Toronto Islands** (*p192*, where cars are banned and the lake's breeze is welcomed by cyclists and beachgoers visiting the city's best beach at **Hanlan's Point** (*p192*).

> **To extend your trip...**
> Toronto is just two hours by car, train, and bus from the world-famous Niagara Falls, where you can spend a day exploring the famous natural wonder (*see the Ontario itinerary page 13, and pages 216–17*).

Gothic Revival façade of Sir Henry Pellatt's Casa Loma, Toronto

2 Days in Montreal

French-speaking Montreal is one of North America's finest cities.

- **Arriving** A shuttle bus covers the 13 miles (22 km) from Montreal airport to downtown; allow 40 minutes.
- **Moving on** There are regular flights from Montreal to Vancouver; trains, buses, and flights go to Toronto.

Day 1

Morning Introduce yourself to **Montreal's** varied charms at the city's finest church, the beautifully decorated **Basilique Notre-Dame-de-Montréal** (*pp116–17*). From here, stroll down to the **Centre d'Histoire de Montréal** (*p118*), where entertaining displays explore the history of the city, from Canadian origins up to today. Nearby, down on the river, be sure to visit the **Centre des sciences de Montréal** (*p118*), located on a former pier and crammed with collections on technology and engineering.

Afternoon Begin the afternoon with an easy ramble along the waterfront, where the old port – **Vieux-Port** (*p116*) – has been turned into a leafy park. After-wards, wander up into the heart of **Vieux-Montréal** (*pp114–15*), where the distinguished **Château Ramezay** (*p117*) is a charming, 19th-century copy of a French château. Nearby, **Sir George Etienne-Cartier National Historic Site** (p117) consists of two richly furnished Victorian houses on Rue Notre Dame, which is itself flanked by some of Montreal's most imposing old buildings.

Day 2

Morning Start the day with a promenade along **Rue Sherbrooke** (p126), which is liberally sprinkled with graceful old mansions, sturdy churches, and bijoux stores. Montreal's finest art gallery, the **Musée des Beaux-Arts** (pp122–3), which is famous for its collection of European paintings, is also on this street. Nearby, savor the bustling atmosphere of **Square Dorchester** (p123) and **Place du Canada** (p123), a splash of greenery in the heart of the city that is home to statues of famous Canadians of yesteryear. Afterwards, drop by the **Cathédrale Marie-Reine-du-Monde** (p126), whose attractive façade was inspired by St. Peter's Basilica in Rome.

Afternoon Wander the open, airy plaza of the **Place des Arts** (p119) before investigating the **Musée d'Art Contemporain de Montréal** (pp120–21), whose extensive collection of modern art runs from paintings and photographs to videos and installations. Afterwards, head to **Parc du Mont-Royal** (p127), a hilly slab of parkland, meadow, and wood with look-out points offering lovely views

back over the city. If the weather is good, clamber the steps up to the **Oratoire Saint-Joseph** (p127), Montreal's largest shrine, devoted to the Virgin Mary. Alternatively, head for the **Plateau Mont-Royal** (p119), the city's most atmospheric neighborhood, complete with bistros, bars, bookshops, and bazaars.

2 Days in Vancouver

Laid-back Vancouver is the quintessential west coast city, with an exquisite setting between the ocean and the mountains, and a scattering of show-stopping attractions.

- **Arriving** Vancouver airport is 8 miles (13 km) south of the city center, a journey covered by the SkyTrain in about 25 minutes.
- **Moving on** There are regular flights from Vancouver to Toronto and Montreal.

Day 1

Morning Explore Vancouver's lively **waterfront** (pp272–3), where boats bob in and out; the modern architecture of **Canada Place** (p272) provides a real aesthetic splash. Look out for the imposing **Waterfront Station** (p272) and the **Harbour Centre Tower** (p272), which offers expansive views. Head inland to **Vancouver Art Gallery** (p275), for its excellent Canadian art collection.

Afternoon Stroll through **Gastown** (pp272–3), with its vibrant street scene and cafés before heading into **Chinatown** (p274), stretching from Carrall to Gore streets. Stalls and storefronts crowd the pavements, offering Chinese delicacies. Recover in the **Dr. Sun Yat-Sen Classical Chinese Garden** (p274). Finish off the day with the inventive exhibits at **Science World** (p274).

Geodesic dome overlooking False Creek at Science World, Vancouver

Day 2

Morning Take a city bus to **Stanley Park** (p279), a slab of greenery that occupies a headland jutting out into English Bay. Hike through the woods, relax on the beach, or cycle the perimeter wall, but above all enjoy the views over city, sea, and mountain.

Afternoon Detour out to the **University of British Columbia Museum of Anthropology** (pp280–81) to examine the country's finest collection of Northwest coast native peoples' art. Exhibits include giant totem poles, ornate headdresses, and exquisite feast dishes. Allow a good couple of hours for the museum and afterwards, on the way back into the city center, stop at **Vanier Park** (p270), a lovely expanse of parkland.

> ### To extend your trip...
> Spend two days in Victoria, one of Canada's most beguiling towns, just two hours by ferry from Vancouver (see pp284–9).

Visitors taking in the 18th-century charm of Vieux-Montréal by horse-drawn carriage

Gondolas transporting visitors to and from Sulphur Mountain, Banff

7 Days in BC and the Rockies

- **Airports** Arrive and depart from Calgary airport.
- **Transport** A car is essential for this trip.
- **Booking Ahead** *Jasper National Park: Jasper Tramway*

Day 1: Calgary
Start your tour of the Rockies in **Calgary** *(pp296–7)*, a big and breezy city with a western feel. Calgary is famous for its rodeo, the "Calgary Stampede", but has much more to offer. Be sure to visit the **Glenbow Museum** *(p297)* with its wide-ranging collection of Canadian paintings, and **Fort Calgary Historic Park** *(p298)*, which features a restored Mounties' fort.

Day 2: Banff
With its fine mountain setting, **Banff** *(p307)* is a perfect introduction to the Canadian Rockies. Take the gondola up to the top of **Sulphur Mountain** *(p307)* for breathtaking views; drop by the **Cave and Basin National Historic Site** *(p307)* to learn about the town's colorful history; and relax at the **Upper Hot Springs Pool** *(p307)*.

Day 3: Banff National Park
Head west from Banff for a closer inspection of the white-tipped mountains, deep forests, crystal-clear lakes, and extraordinary glaciers that surround the town and punctuate **Banff National Park** *(pp304–7)*. Linger

at the turquoise waters of **Lake Louise** *(p307)*, delve into the depths of **Johnston Canyon** *(p305)*, and stroll off the highway to the well-signed vantage point overlooking **Peyto Lake** *(p306)*.

Day 4: Kootenay National Park and Radium Hot Springs
Drive the dramatic Kootenay Highway as it winds its way through **Kootenay National Park** *(p303)*. Stop at Paint Pots, for the short walk to rust-colored mineral springs, and pause at Marble Canyon, a plunging gorge with dramatic limestone shanks. Take a dip at **Radium Hot Springs** *(p303)*, a pocket-sized town also famous for its mineral springs.

Day 5: Yoho National Park
Begin your exploration of **Yoho National Park** *(pp308–9)* at Emerald Lake, a stunningly beautiful circle of water in the midst of glowering peaks. Sign up for a guided tour of the **Burgess Shale** *(p309)*, where the rock beds hold a remarkable collection of ancient fossils. Finish off the day with a detour to the impressive 833-ft (254-m) high **Takakkaw Falls** *(p309)*.

Day 6: Jasper National Park
No tour of the Canadian Rockies would be complete without a visit to **Jasper National Park** *(pp312–15)*. Sample the magnificent mountains surrounding the pretty little town of Jasper; enjoy the plunging ravine that

comprises **Maligne Canyon** *(p315)*; paddle the cool, green waters of **Pyramid Lake** *(p315)*; and relax in the **Miette Hot Springs** *(p315)*. Alternatively, drive and hike up to the Angel Glacier on **Mount Cavell** *(p315)*; or take the **Jasper Tramway** *(p312)*, Canada's longest and highest cable car, linking Jasper town with a vantage point 9,465 ft (2,885 m) above sea level.

Day 7: Prince George
Round off your tour by visiting **Prince George** *(p316)*, a bustling valley town and transport center at the junction of the Yellowhead Highway and Highway 97. Wander the town center, popping into its several art galleries, and investigate the intriguing **Fraser-Fort George Regional Museum** *(p316)*, whose excellent displays journey through the history of the town, from fur-trading station to tourist destination.

A waterfall coursing through the ravine at Maligne Canyon, Jasper National Park

Stunningly beautiful scenery at Yoho National Park in the Rockies

Trees turning to fall colors on the Thousand Islands, downstream from Kingston, Ontario

7 Days in Ontario

- **Airports** Arrive and depart from either Ottawa or Toronto airport.
- **Transport** Trains run daily between Ottawa, Kingston and Toronto. The journey from Ottawa to Kingston takes about 2.5 hours, and it's another 2.5 hours to Toronto. You will need a car to see inland Ontario.
- **Booking Ahead** Toronto: CN Tower, Casa Loma

Day 1: Ottawa
Start in the nation's capital, **Ottawa** (pp196–201), a bustling city with a superb range of hotels, restaurants, and sights. Prioritize three key attractions – **Parliament Hill** (p198), with its handsome Victorian buildings; the **Canadian War Museum** (p199), holding an unparalleled range of military artifacts; and the **National Gallery** (pp202–3), which boasts Canada's widest collection of paintings.

Day 2: Kingston and the Thousand Islands
Stroll through the old streets of **Kingston** (p204), a historic town with a fine collection of distinguished Victorian mansions, and admire nautical memorabilia at the **Marine Museum of the Great Lakes** (p205). Allow time for a cruise along the St. Lawrence River:

boat trips leave Kingston bound for the scenic **Thousand Islands** (p204).

Day 3: Algonquin Provincial Park
Begin your day at **Algonquin Provincial Park** (pp208–9), a vast forested wilderness latticed with lakes and rivers. Begin by driving along the Parkway Corridor (Hwy 60), the only road to cross the park, visiting the **Algonquin Gallery** (p208) and the **Algonquin Logging Museum** (p209) en route. Select one of the park's several lodges for an overnight stop.

Day 4: Algonquin Provincial Park (cont.)
Make an early start, hire the correct outdoors equipment, and explore part of the Algonquin Provincial Park by canoe – either under your own steam or with a guide.

The glass and granite building of the National Gallery of Canada, Ottawa

Day 5: Sainte-Marie-among-the-Hurons and Georgian Bay Islands National Park
Enjoy Ontario's prime historical attraction, **Sainte-Marie-among-the-Hurons** (pp224–5), a reconstruction of the Jesuit mission built in the heart of Huronia in the 17th century. Afterwards, head for the hamlet of **Honey Harbour** (p223), where you can take a water taxi to one of the pine-dusted islands of **Georgian Bay Islands National Park** (p223). Alternatively, take the ferry to **Beausoleil Island** (p223), which has a dozen hiking trails to match all abilities.

Day 6: Brantford, Niagara Falls, and Niagara-on-the-Lake
Detour to **Brantford** (p222), an attractive town with a selection of grand Victorian buildings. Drive out to the **Bell Homestead National Historic Site** (p222), the home of Alexander Graham Bell, the telephone pioneer. Heading southeast, aim for **Niagara Falls** (pp216–17), where two walls of water crash over the precipice – one on the American side, the other in Canada. Clouds of spray drift up and "Maid of the Mist" boats take tourists as near to the Falls as they dare. Travel on to **Niagara-on-the-Lake** (p212), a lovely town cocooned within lush gardens.

Day 7: Toronto
Pick from the Toronto itineraries on page 10.

The wild landscape of the Parc National du Canada Forillon, Quebec

7 Days in Quebec

- **Airports** Arrive and depart from Montreal airport.

- **Transport** Greyhound Buses serve many destinations around Quebec and there are regular trips between Montreal and Quebec City, with a journey of about 3 hours. A branch train line inches its way around part of the Gaspé Peninsula, but services are infrequent. A car allows for more flexibility.

Day 1: Quebec City
Start your tour of Quebec in **Quebec City** *(pp134–41)*, which occupies a delightful location on the banks of the St. Lawrence River. Wander the lovely old town: begin with the citadel and then explore the narrow cobblestone streets. Allow time for the **Musée de la civilisation** *(p137)*, and the extravagant **Fairmont Le Château Frontenac** *(p138)*.

Day 2: Quebec City excursion: Chicoutimi and Lac-Saint-Jean
Spend a day enjoying the environs of Quebec City. Drive to **Chicoutimi** *(p144)*, a sleepy town with a riverside setting. Continue onto **Lac-Saint-Jean** *(p145)*, a well-known beauty spot, where tiny villages hug the lakeshores amid spruce forests and rolling hills.

Day 3: Parc de la Chute Montmorency, Sainte-Anne-de-Beaupré, Baie-Saint-Paul, and Tadoussac
Head northeast from Quebec City along the St. Lawrence River. The first stop has to be the **Parc de la Chute Montmorency** *(p143)*. A mighty waterfall here marks where the Montmorency River crashes down into the St. Lawrence. Spend time in nearby **Sainte-Anne-de-Beaupré** *(pp142–3)*, Quebec's answer to Lourdes. Visit the church, a richly decorated structure built in the 1920s. Pushing on, take a break at **Baie St-Paul** *(p143)*, one of the prettiest coastal towns, and continue to **Tadoussac** *(p144)*, which offers whale-watching tours.

Day 4: The Gaspé Peninsula: the North Shore
Catch the ferry across the St.

Imposing Fairmont Le Château Frontenac, Quebec City

Lawrence River from St-Siméon to **Rivière-du-Loup** *(p147)* and stroll the town's attractive center. Take the road along the north side of the **Gaspé Peninsula** *(pp144–5)* with the river on one side and wooded hills on the other. Aim for the lush gardens at **Grand Métis** *(p148)* and the pretty hamlet of **Sainte-Anne-des-Montes** *(p149)*. Take a short hike in the **Parc National de la Gaspésie** *(p148)*.

Day 5: The Gaspé Peninsula: the South Shore
Pause at the tip of the Gaspé Peninsula to sample the landscapes of the **Parc National du Canada Forillon** *(p149)*. See small-town life at the village of **Percé** *(p149)*. Proceed to the scenic **Vallée de la Matapédia** *(p148)*, a rural haven noted for its fruit farms and maple syrup.

Day 6: The Eastern Townships
Experience rural Quebec at its most beguiling at the **Sainte-Croix** manor house *(p152)*. Enjoy small-town life in **Sherbrooke** *(p152)*, followed by a detour to the scenic **Lac Memphrémagog** *(p152)*, surrounded by historic villages and rolling hills. Finish the day by driving along the **Richelieu Valley** *(p152)* whose orchards and vineyards frame the approaches to Montreal.

Day 7: Montreal
Choose from the Montreal itineraries on pages 10–11.

7 Days in the Maritime Provinces

- **Airports** Arrive and depart from Halifax airport.
- **Transport** A car is essential for this trip.

Day 1: Halifax

In **Halifax** (pp94–5), the capital of Nova Scotia, make a beeline for the **Citadel National Historic Site** (p95), a fortress overlooking the city and the harbor. Then stroll down to the waterfront, Halifax's most atmospheric quarter and home to the elegant **Province House** (p95) and the intriguing **Maritime Museum** (p94).

Day 2: Peggy's Cove and Lunenburg

Don't miss the rugged shoreline running southwest of Halifax. Its surf-battered bays and coves are at their most beguiling at tiny **Peggy's Cove** (p93), with its solitary lighthouse perched on bleak granite rocks. Nearby, enjoy the small-town delights of **Lunenburg** (p92) with its cluster of attractive Victorian houses on a narrow, hilly peninsula.

Day 3: Mahone Bay, Annapolis Royal, Wolfville, and Grand Pré

Stroll the streets of **Mahone Bay** (pp92–3), a pretty place with a trio of old churches. Venture into the heart of Nova Scotia, where **Annapolis Royal** (p89) boasts fanciful Victorian houses and two old forts. Then savor the charms of gracious **Wolfville** (p89) and head to **Grand Pré National Historic Site** (p89), commemorating the Acadian settlers who were forced out by the British.

Day 4: Truro, Fort Beauséjour, and Charlottetown, PEI

Detour to **Truro** (p88) and watch the tidal bore as it rushes up the Salmon River. Enjoy wide views over the Minas Basin from the immaculately restored **Fort Beauséjour** (p88) and drive over the Confederation Bridge to **Prince Edward Island** (pp84–7). Admire the island's charming capital, **Charlottetown** (p87), and take in **Province House** (p87), the place where the "Fathers of Confederation" began the process of creating Canada from its component parts.

Day 5: PEI: Cavendish, PEI National Park, and Orwell Corner Historic Village

Explore the country roads of **Prince Edward Island** (PEI), where your first port of call should be **Cavendish** (p86), home to all things to do with *Anne of Green Gables*, including **Lucy Maud Montgomery's Cavendish Home** (p87). Proceed to the north shore of the island where **Prince Edward Island National Park** (p86) boasts wonderful sandy beaches. Finish the day by visiting **Orwell Corner Historic Village** (p87), a careful recreation of country life in the 19th century.

Historic Great George Street, Charlottetown, Prince Edward Island

Day 6: Fundy National Park and Saint John

Investigate **Fundy National Park** (p80), an area of wilderness nudging up to Fundy Bay, which has some of the mightiest tides on earth – reckon on a differential between low and high tide of around 49 ft (15 m). Take a coastal hike before moving on to the vibrant city of **Saint John** (p80).

Day 7: Fredericton

Spend at least a day in pretty **Fredericton** (p81), the capital of New Brunswick. Highlights include the outstanding **Beaverbrook Art Gallery** (p81) and a string of British military buildings dating back to the 19th century.

To extend your trip…
Day 8: Cape Breton Island
Head for the magnificent scenery of **Cape Breton Island** (see pp96–7). A must-see is the **Cape Breton Highlands National Park** (see p98). Take a break in pretty **Cheticamp** (see p98).
Day 9: Cape Breton Island (cont.)
Continue on the highway that circumnavigates Cape Breton Highlands National Park, pausing for a hike on one of the many trails. Press on to **Baddeck** (see p98), which is famous for its connections with Alexander Graham Bell.

The harbor at Peggy's Cove, near Halifax, Nova Scotia

Putting Western and Northern Canada on the Map

Canada lies at the northern end of the American continent and covers 9,970,610 sq km (3,849,652 sq miles). More than 70 percent of this area is uninhabited because of vast tracts of frozen wilderness in the north. In contrast, British Columbia boasts Canada's only temperate rainforest.

Melville Island

Parry Channe

Victoria Island

Holman

Cambridge Bay

Coronation Gulf

Paulatuk

Inuvik

Great Bear Lake

Norman Wells

Thelon

NORTHWEST TERRITORIES

Dawson City

YUKON

Yellowknife

Great Slave Lake

Dubawnt

Whitehorse

Watson Lake

Hay River

Fort Resolution

Fort Smith

97

Lake Athabasca

Fort Nelson

ALBERTA

Fort McMurray

BRITISH COLUMBIA

Fort St. John

SASKATCHEWAN

Athabasca

35

Prince Rupert

Haida Gwaii

Prince George

43

Saskatchewan

Prince Albert

Flin Flon

97

Edmonton

16

Saskatoon

Pacific Ocean

Red Deer

Yorkton

Banff

Calgary

Kelowna

Vancouver Island

Vancouver

1

Regina

Victoria

Seattle

90

Butte

Portland

15

UNITED STATES OF AMERICA

94

5

Salt Lake City

Denver

80

0 kilometers   400

0 miles   400

Key

≡ Expressway

▬ Major road

⋯ Minor road

— Principal rail routes

▬ International border

- - Provincial border

◀ Ships in Quebec Bay

Devon Island

Somerset
Island

Prince
of Wales
Island

Baffin Island

Mileage Chart

BANFF								
128 **80**	CALGARY			10 Distance in miles				
3039 **1889**	2911 **1809**	DAWSON CITY		**10 Distance in kilometres**				
253 **157**	146 **91**	1976 **1228**	RED DEER					
888 **552**	764 **475**	2526 **1570**	610 **379**	REGINA				
748 **465**	630 **391**	2297 **1427**	476 **296**	260 **161**	SASKATOON			
928 **577**	1057 **657**	1917 **1191**	934 **580**	2424 **1506**	1677 **1042**	VANCOUVER		
2513 **1562**	2385 **1482**	440 **274**	2188 **1360**	2871 **1784**	2614 **1624**	2697 **1676**	WHITEHORSE	
1464 **910**	1336 **830**	2942 **1828**	1186 **737**	888 **552**	829 **515**	3312 **2058**	3524 **2190**	WINNIPEG

NUNAVUT

Baker Lake

Rankin Inlet

Arviat

**Vancouver
and Environs**

West
Vancouver   North Vancouver
Vancouver   Port
                             Moody
               Burnaby   Coquitlam
Vancouver   Maple
International   New   Ridge
              Westminster
                          Surrey
Richmond

0 km   5
0 miles   5

Hudson
Bay   **QUEBEC**   Ungava
                          Bay

Churchill

MANITOBA

Thompson

Canada

GREENLAND

U.S.A   CANADA   See next
                    page

Belcher
Islands

James
Bay   U.S.A   Atlantic
                   Pacific   Ocean
Lake   Ocean   MEXICO
Winnipeg

ONTARIO

Albany
        Moosonee

Winnipeg

Thunder Bay

Lake
Superior
                North Bay
Sault Ste. Marie   Fredericton   Sydney
Minneapolis   St. Paul   Ottawa   Montreal
                     Lake   Saint John
                     Huron   Halifax
              Lake   Toronto
              Michigan   Lake
         London   Lake Ontario
Omaha   Windsor Erie Niagara   Boston
                         Falls
        Chicago
        Pittsburgh   New York

For map symbols *see back flap*

Putting Eastern Canada on the Map

Most of Canada's 30 million people live close to the US border, in a band that stretches from the east coast across to British Columbia in the west. Over 60 percent of all Canadians are concentrated in the southeast corner of the country, in the provinces of Ontario and Quebec. This is the heartland of Canadian industry, including electronics, hydro-electricity, lumber, and paper. The maritime provinces of Nova Scotia, New Brunswick, and Prince Edward Island are Canada's smallest, but the beauty of their landscapes attracts thousands of tourists each year. Newfoundland and Labrador is also known for its rugged charm.

MANITOBA

Hudson Bay

Cape Dorset

Ivujivik

Mansel Island

Île Avaqqutaq

Churchill

Nelson

Thompson

Flin Flon

The Pas

Lake Winnipeg

Yorkton

Red Lake

ONTARIO

Fort Sevem

Seven

Belcher Islands

Kuujjuarapik

Long Island

Chisasibi

Akiniski Island

Eastmain

Waskaganish
(Fort Rupert)

Albany

16

Winnipeg

1

Brandon

17

Nipigon

Hearst

11

Timmins

29

Thunder Bay

Wawa

17

Fargo

94

35

Duluth

Sault Ste. Marie

Sudbury

North Bay

117

94

Minneapolis

75

Lake Superior

Lake Michigan

Lake Huron

11

Ottawa

Rapid City

Sioux Falls

Toronto

Lake Ontario

Windsor

London

Lake Erie

Niagara Falls

Chicago

Indianapolis

Pittsburgh

Washington D.C.

70

U.S.A.

Richmond

Nashville

Charlotte

81

81

95

Toronto

North York

401

Scarborough

404

Eglinton

427

Rexdale

401

400

2

Pearson
International
Airport

York

East York

5

Toronto

Etobicoke

8

Billy Bishop
Toronto City
Airport

Lakeview

Lake Ontario

0 km   5

0 miles   5

Mileage Chart

CHARLOTTETOWN									
356 **221**	**FREDERICTON**								
239 **148**	473 **294**	**HALIFAX**							
1149 **714**	834 **518**	1003 **623**	**MONTREAL**						
1860 **1156**	1510 **938**	1925 **1196**	676 **420**	**NIAGARA FALLS**					
1339 **832**	1016 **631**	1456 **905**	200 **124**	536 **333**	**OTTAWA**				
954 **593**	598 **371**	1071 **665**	257 **160**	946 **588**	724 **450**	**QUEBEC CITY**			
1412 **877**	1267 **787**	1512 **939**	859 **534**	1569 **975**	1074 **667**	637 **396**	**SEPT-ILES**		
2794 **1736**	2471 **1535**	2910 **1808**	1654 **1028**	1521 **945**	1503 **943**	1963 **1220**	2613 **1624**	**THUNDER BAY**	
1689 **1049**	1366 **849**	1806 **1122**	549 **341**	137 **85**	399 **248**	809 **503**	1449 **900**	1384 **860**	**TORONTO**

10 Distance in miles
10 Distance in kilometres

Key

≡ Expressway
▬ Major road
⋯ Minor road
— Principal rail routes
▬ International border
- - Provincial border

Baffin
Island
✈ Iqaluit

Kangiqsujuaq

Péninsule
d'Ungava

Akpatok
Island

Kangirsuk

Gyrfalcon
Islands

Kuujjuaq

Nain

Schefferville

Réservoir de
Caniapiscau

Labrador

Churchill Falls   Happy Valley
Goose Bay

Labrador
City

QUEBEC   **NEWFOUNDLAND
& LABRADOR**

Laurentian Mountains

Sept-Iles

Natashquan

Chibougamau

138

Anticosti
Island

Gander

167

Chicoutimi   132   Gaspé

155

*Gulf of
St Lawrence*   *Newfoundland*

1

Quebec City

Moncton   Charlottetown

Montreal   Fredericton   Sydney

Channel-Port
aux Basques   St. John's

93

89

Halifax

Yarmouth

87

Boston

*Atlantic
Ocean*

New York

Philadelphia

0 kilometers   400
0 miles   400

Montreal and Environs

Laval   25

440   40   Anjou

13   15   Maisonneuve   20   25

Longueuil

Montreal

St-Laurent   St-Hubert

40   Côte
St-Luc   Verdun   Brossard

Pierre-Elliott-
Trudeau   20

Lachine   15

*Lac
St-Louis*

0 km   5
0 miles   5

For map symbols *see back flap*

A PORTRAIT OF CANADA

Blessed with ancient forests, rugged mountains, and large cosmopolitan cities, Canada is unimaginably vast, stretching west from the Atlantic to the Pacific and north to the Arctic Ocean. Around 20,000 years ago Canada was inhabited by aboriginal peoples, but by the 19th century it had been settled by Europeans. Today, the country is noted as a liberal, multicultural society.

In part, Canada's heritage of tolerance is a result of its conflict-ridden past. Two centuries of compromise was necessary to fully establish the country. Following fighting between the British and French armies in the 1750s, the British won control of the country in 1759. The self-governing colonies of British North America spent three years hammering out the agreement that brought them together as the Dominion of Canada in 1867. Newfoundland did not become part of the nation until 1949. Powerful regional differences, particularly between French- and English-speaking Canada, meant that

the country has had difficulties evolving a national identity. When Pierre Berton, one of Canada's most prolific writers, was prompted to define a Canadian he evaded the question, replying: "Someone who knows how to make love in a canoe."

The second largest country in the world, Canada has a surface area of 9,970,610 sq km (3,849,652 sq miles). Over 40 percent of the land is north of the treeline at 60° latitude; this extraordinarily hostile and sparsely inhabited wilderness is bitterly cold in winter, averaging -30°C (-22°F), and plagued by millions of insects in summer. Not surprisingly, most Canadians live in

The snow-laden rooftops of Quebec City overlooking the St. Lawrence River at dusk

◄ RCMP riding in Canada Day, Ottawa

the more temperate regions farther to the south. Of the country's 30 million inhabitants, more than 80 percent live within 200 kilometers (124 miles) of the US border.

Flora and Fauna

In the far north, the permafrost of the treeless tundra (or taiga) supports the growth of only the toughest flora, such as lichen, mosses, and a range of unusually hardy varieties of flowers and grasses. In spring and fall however, the tundra flora bursts into an impressive display of color. Animal life is abundant in this region, and includes the polar bear, arctic fox, wolf, seal, musk ox, and caribou.

Spring flower from the Bruce Peninsula

Farther south, the boreal or coniferous forest covers a wide band from Newfoundland in the east to the Yukon in the west. A variety of trees here, including spruce, balsam fir, and jack pine, provides a home for those animals most typically thought of as Canadian – primarily moose, beaver, lynx, and black bear. The beaver is Canada's national symbol. It was the European fashion for beaver hats that created and sustained the Canadian fur trade and opened up the interior to European settlers, paving the way for the growth of the modern nation.

In the east, deciduous forests containing the emblematic maple are populated by deer, raccoons, and mink. Across central Canada, the grasslands, known as the Prairies, house elk, gophers, and increasing numbers of buffalo.

British Columbia's temperate rain forests are rich in wildlife such as black tail deer, brown bear, and cougar. Rare orchids and ferns grow here, among towering cedars, firs, and spruce trees.

The First Nations

Although thought of as a new country, Canada's prehistory dates back about 20,000 years to the end of the first Ice Age. At that time there was a land bridge joining Siberia to Alaska; Siberian hunter-nomads crossed this bridge to become the first human inhabitants of North America, and over the succeeding centuries

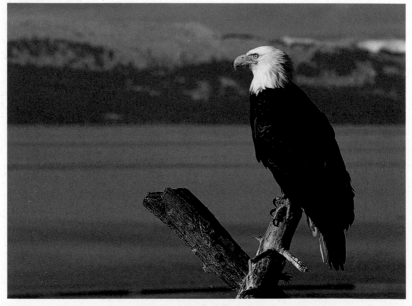
The bald eagle, a common sight around the Haida Gwaii archipelago in British Columbia

their descendants gradually moved south. Archaeological digs in the Old Crow River Basin in the Yukon have unearthed a collection of tools believed to date to this initial period of migration. These Siberian nomads were the ancestors of the continent's native peoples.

By the 16th century, Spanish, French, and Portuguese traders were the first Europeans to have close dealings with the aboriginal peoples of the Americas, whom they named "Indians" in the mistaken belief that they had reached India. The "Indian" appellation stuck, and the "Red" was added by British settlers in the 17th century when they met the Beothuks of Newfoundland, who daubed themselves in red ochre to repel insects. The native peoples of the far north were also given a name they did not want – "Eskimo," literally "eaters of raw meat." Given this history, it is hardly surprising that modern-day leaders of Canada's aboriginal peoples have rejected these names in favor of others: aboriginal, native Canadians, and First Nations are all acceptable, though the people of the north prefer Inuit (meaning "the people"). Included among Canada's native peoples are the Métis, mixed race descendants of aboriginal peoples and French-speaking European traders.

Inuit children at Bathurst Inlet, Nunavut

Society

The official languages of Canada are French and English, and the interplay between Canada's two largest linguistic and cultural groups is evident in the capital city of Ottawa, where every federal speech and bill has to be delivered in both languages. All packaging must also be bilingual. Canada's population is about 24 percent French Canadian, predominantly the descendants of French settlers who came to the colony of New France in the 17th and 18th centuries (see p49). Their English-speaking compatriots are largely descended from 18th- and 19th- century British immigrants.

Canada's reputation as a multicultural society began to be established in the 1800s, when successive waves of immigration, along with various settlement plans, brought people from all over the world to Canada. Today, perhaps the best way to experience this modern country's vibrant cultural mix is to visit its three largest cities – Toronto, Montreal, and Vancouver.

Government and Politics

Canada is a parliamentary democracy with a federal political system. Each province or territory has its own democratically elected provincial legislature headed by a Premier, and also sends elected

View from Centre Island's parks and gardens on Lake Ontario toward Toronto's CN Tower

Changing of the Guard outside Ottawa's Parliament Building

movement. Twice since 1980, the Quebecois have been asked to vote in referenda seeking their support to leave Canada and, although the electorate voted "No" both times, it was a close result. The issue of Quebec's relationship with the rest of Canada is still unresolved, and further political disputes seem inevitable.

Since the 1980s aboriginal politics has come to the fore with campaigns for constitutional, land, and mineral rights. The Assembly of First Nations has been at the forefront of the establishment of the Inuit homeland, Nunavut. Current issues include battles for self-government and land claims, as well as hunting and fishing rights.

representatives to the federal parliament in Ottawa. The House of Commons is the main federal legislature. The Prime Minister is the head of the political structure, as well as an elected member of the House of Commons where he must be able to command a majority. Bills passed in the Commons are forwarded to an upper chamber, the Senate, for ratification. At present, the Prime Minister appoints senators, although there is increasing pressure to make the upper chamber elective too. The nominal head of state is the British monarch, currently Queen Elizabeth II, and her Canadian representative is the Governor-General.

The ceremonial unveiling of the new Nunavut flag in 1999

In recent decades, the dominant trend in Canadian politics has been regionalism. The provinces have sought to take back power from the center, which makes it difficult for any one political party to win majority support in all parts of the country at once. The most conspicuous aspect of this process has been the conflict over Quebec, where there is a strong separatist

Canada has played its part in the major events of the 20th century, including both world wars, and today holds a prominent position in international politics. The country is a member of NATO and one of the Group of Eight (G8) countries, which, with the US, UK, Italy, Japan, France, Germany, and Russia, decide on world trade agreements.

Art and Culture

The vast and beautiful landscape of the country is a defining feature of Canadian culture. Outdoor pursuits such as hiking, skiing, and canoeing are high on the list of popular activities. Canadians are also great sports fans, and ice hockey, baseball, basketball, and Canadian football attract huge crowds of spectators, and foster deeply felt allegiances. In addition to their passion for sports, Canadians are also enthusiastic about the arts. This is the country that has produced internationally renowned classical pianist, Glenn Gould, and whose major cities possess well-respected orchestras. Canada has also produced more than its share of popular music stars, from ground breaking singer-songwriters such as Joni Mitchell and Neil Young to more middle-of-the-road artists such as Celine Dion, Bryan Adams, and Shania Twain. Canada's cosmopolitan culture also means that visitors are likely to find a wide choice of music in bars, cafés, and at the country's numerous festivals. All kinds of drama from Shakespeare to new writing can be seen at the renowned Stratford Shakespearean Festival, which is held in Ontario. Many Canadian artists have looked to the wilderness as a source of inspiration. The first artist to attempt to express a sense of national identity was Tom Thomson, with his distinctive, brightly colored landscapes of Northern Ontario. He influenced the country's most celebrated group of painters, the Group of Seven (see pp168–9), who evolved a national style of painting capable of representing Canada's wilderness, a theme developed by their contemporaries and successors, notably Emily Carr (see p286).

International rock star Alanis Morissette

Author Margaret Atwood, lauded worldwide

Canada's world-class museums and galleries represent the country's pride in its art collections: the outstanding Art Gallery of Ontario in Toronto (see pp182–3) has an extensive display of Group of Seven paintings, as well as Inuit art and cutting-edge contemporary art. Major contemporary Canadian artists on the international circuit include Janet Cardiff and Rodney Graham.

Among Canadian writers, there are distinguished practitioners in both English and French, and an impressive list of contemporary novelists includes such prize-winning authors as Margaret Atwood, Carol Shields, Michael Ondaatje, Jacques Poulin, Yann Martel, Alice Munro, and Germaine Guèvremont.

The Canadian film industry is thriving, with established directors such as David Cronenberg and Atom Egoyan continuing to create daring films. Barney's Version, a critically acclaimed 2010 adaptation of Mordecai Richler's 1997 novel, was set and shot in and around Montreal.

Behind Canada's flourishing cultural life, lies a pride in its history and cosmopolitan heritage, and an affection for the land's daunting beauty.

Toronto Maple Leaf legend Mats Sundin

Landscape and Geology

Canada is the second largest country in the world, covering an area almost as big as Europe. It was created from the world's oldest landmasses. The billion-year-old bowl-shaped Canadian Shield covers much of the country, dipping around Hudson Bay and rising to mountain ranges at its edges. The country is bordered by oceans on three sides, with a coastline 243,800 km (151,400 miles) long and an interior containing some two million lakes. Canada is well known for the diversity of its landscapes: from the frozen, barren north that descends to the mountainous west with its forest and wheat plains, through the wooded, hilly east, and the fertile lowlands of the southeast.

The Great Lakes region covers 3% of Canada's landmass, and comprises a fertile lowland bowl, vital to its agricultural economy.

The Interior Plains, including the prairies, are the principal wheat-growing areas of the country, and range southeast 2,600 km (1,600 miles) from the Cordilleras to the US border. The plains are divided into three huge steppes.

The Rockies and the Western Cordillera

This region is part of one of the world's longest mountain chains. In Canada, the Cordillera comprises the Pacific Coastal Mountains and forested basins. Graduated peaks and ridges reveal Ice Age erosion, as does the Columbia Icefield (see p314). The Rockies developed from continental plate movement, which began about 120 million years ago (see pp262–3).

Geographical Regions

Characterized by its variety, Canadian landscape falls into six main areas. The north of the country offers a landscape of tundra, with the far north ice-covered for much of the year. In the west and south, the warmer, fertile lands of the Cordillera and interior plains support the rural population. To the east, the Great Lakes area is an agricultural center. The vast Canadian Shield cradles the plains and rises to form the northern Innuitian region and the Appalachians in the south.

Innuitian Region and Arctic Lowlands

The Rockies & Western Cordillera

Canadian Shield

Interior Plains

Appalachians

Great Lakes

The Appalachians' rolling landscape is two-thirds woodland and covers both arable lowland areas and the highest peaks in Quebec. These are found on the Gaspé Peninsula, the outer mountain ring of the Canadian Shield highland. Most of the Appalachian mountain chain lies in the US. They are nature's barrier between the eastern seaboard and the continental interior lowlands.

The Canadian Shield, formed of the 1,100-million-year-old bedrock of the North American continent, is the core of the country. It spreads out from Hudson Bay for 5 million sq km (1.9 million sq miles). The center is scrub and rock, and rises to steep mountains around the rim.

The Innuitian region stretches northward from the Arctic Lowlands' modest height of 100–700 m (330–2,000 ft) above sea level to the peaks of the Innuitian mountain range, at their highest on Elles-mere Island at 2,926 m (9,600 ft). Vigorous glaciation for millenia has developed deep fjords, sharp peaks, and frost patterns on the earth. This region is rich in oil, coal, and gas.

Canada's Wildlife

By the time it emerged from the last Ice Age 10,000 years ago, Canada had developed a geography and climate that remains one of the most diverse on Earth. In the north, the Arctic weather produces a harsh, barren desert, in darkness for several months and frozen most of the year. By contrast, the country's most southerly province, Ontario, shares a latitude with northern California and offers fertile forests laced with rivers and lakes. In southern Canada, many varieties of wildlife flourish in the coniferous forest that covers the ancient rocks of the Canadian Shield. In the central plain are wheat-filled open prairies. From here, foothills lead to the Rocky Mountains, which gradually roll westward to coastal mountains and the balmy landscape of temperate rainforest along the Pacific coast.

The muskox is a gregarious herd animal and a remnant of the last Ice Age. Its thick topcoat of guard hair and undercoat of finer, fleecier hair keeps it warm even at –45°C (–50°F).

The Boreal Forest
The boreal forest extends from eastern Canada, across most of Quebec and Ontario, and into the northern parts of the prairie provinces. It consists of a mix of spruce, pine, birch, and aspen, and occurs mostly on the giant rock outcrop of the Canadian Shield *(see pp26–7)*. Dotted with thousands of lakes, it is a rich habitat for some of Canada's best-known wildlife.

The Prairies
Once referred to as a "sea of grass," the Canadian prairie is now predominantly agricultural in nature, specializing in growing wheat and other grains, and ranching prime beef cattle. While little original prairie wilderness remains, this is still a land of great open spaces that supports a surprising, often rare, wildlife population.

The timber wolf, or gray wolf, was hunted almost to extinction by 1950. It has now returned to the more isolated parts of its range in the boreal forest.

The pronghorn antelope is the last of its species to survive in North America. The fastest American mammal, it can reach speeds of over 75 km (47 miles) per hour.

The loon has a haunting call that rings out over northern lakes and is symbolic of the Canadian wilderness.

The bison now exists in only two remaining wild herds in Alberta and the Northwest Territories.

Canada's Sports Fish

From the northern pike and lake trout in the north to the walleye and smallmouth bass in the south, Canada is blessed with a large number of sports fish species. Some fish that are much sought after as sport in Europe (the common carp, for example) are regarded as "trash," or undesirable, in Canada, and exist in large numbers in lakes and rivers across the Canadian Prairies. The arctic char, plentiful in the far north, is also prized for its taste.

Fishing is one of Canada's most popular sports and is superbly supported by 37 national parks, each containing plentiful rivers and lakes.

Salmon migrating upriver provide an annual challenge for the keen sport fisherman. Canada has half the freshwater in the world, but deep sea angling can also prove rewarding.

The Rocky Mountains

The Rocky Mountains begin in the foothills of western Alberta and rise into British Columbia. Along with the Columbia Mountains and the coastal mountains, they form a unique environment that ranges from heavily forested lower slopes, through alpine meadows, to snow-covered rocky peaks. This habitat is home to some of the most majestic wildlife in Canada.

The Canadian Arctic

North of the 60th parallel of latitude, the forest yields to arctic tundra and rock. The tundra is mostly bare, and frozen year-round a few inches below the surface, the icy ground being known as permafrost. During the brief summer the top layer thaws, and the Arctic bursts into bloom. Even though the Arctic is a freezing desert with little moisture, wildlife flourishes.

The recurving horns of a mature male bighorn sheep, found in more remote spots of the Rockies, weigh as much as all its bones put together.

The great white polar bear spends most of its life alone, out on the polar ice pack, hunting for seals.

Canada's grizzly bear stands up to 2.75 m (8.8 ft) high and weighs up to 350 kg (800 lbs). It feeds on roots, berries, and meat.

The caribou is a North American cousin of the reindeer. Caribou in the arctic migrate with the season in herds of 10,000, heading north on to the tundra in spring, south into the forest during winter.

Multicultural Canada

Canada prides itself on its multiculturalism. The country has evolved a unique way of adjusting to the cultural needs of its increasingly diverse population. In contrast to the US's "melting pot," Canada has opted for what is often called the "Canadian mosaic," a model based on accepting diversity rather than assimilation. The origins of this tolerant and fruitful approach are embedded deep in Canadian history. Fearful of attack by the US in 1793, the British safeguarded the religious and civic institutions of their French-Canadian subjects in the hope that they would not ally with the Americans. This policy set the pattern of compromise that is now a hallmark of Canada. Citizens of British and French ancestry still make up the bulk of the population of 30 million, but there are around 60 significant minorities.

Young Inuit people in traditional dress huddled against the snow

Native Canadians

Today there are around one million Native Canadians, though national census figures usually break this group down into three sub-sections – aboriginals (750,000), métis (Indian and French mixed race 200,000), and Inuit (50,000). Of the million, about 60 percent are known as Status Indians, meaning they are officially settled on reserve land. However, over 40 percent of Status Indians now live away from reserve land, and only 900 of Canada's 2,370 reserves are still inhabited. These lands are home to 608 First Nations groups, or bands, which exercise varying degrees of self-government through their own elected councils. Since the 1970s, progressive councils have played a key role in the reinvigoration of traditional native culture. Most

non-Status Native Canadians are now integrated into the rest of Canada's population.

Rarely is the membership of a reserve descended from just one tribe. The largest band is the Six Nations of the Grand River, in Ontario, where the 19,000 inhabitants come from 13 groups including the Mohawk, Delaware, and Seneca peoples.

In the far north, where white settlers have always been rare, the Inuit have a small majority. A result of their self-determination was the creation of Nunavut, a semi-autonomous Inuit homeland comprising 349,650 sq km (135,000 sq miles) of the eastern Arctic, created officially in April 1999. Nunavut means "our land" in the Inuit language, and traditional skills of hunting and igloo-building have been reintroduced to this region.

British and Irish Canadians

Canadians of British and Irish descent constitute a large percentage of the country's population. The first English settlers arrived in the wake of the fleets that fished the waters off Newfoundland in the 16th century. Thereafter, there was a steady trickle of English, Scottish, Welsh, and Irish immigrants and several mass migrations, prompted either by adverse politics at home or fresh opportunities in Canada. Thousands of Scots arrived following the defeat of Bonnie Prince Charlie at Culloden in 1746, and the Irish poured across the Atlantic during and after the potato famine (1845–49). When the Prairie provinces opened up in the 1880s and at the end of both World Wars another large-scale migration took place.

These British and Irish settlers did much to shape Canada, establishing its social and cultural norms and founding its legal and political institutions. Canada's official Head of State is still the British monarch.

British poster of the 1920s promoting emigration to Canada

French Canadians

Canada's French-speakers make up about 20 percent of the total population, and are the country's second-largest ethnic group. They are mainly based in Quebec and New Brunswick, but other pockets thrive in other provinces. The French first reached the Canadian mainland in 1535 when Jacques Cartier sailed up the St. Lawrence River in search of a sea-route to Asia. Fur-traders, priests, and farmers followed in Cartier's footsteps and by the end of the 17th century, New France, as the colony was known, was well established. After the British captured New France in the Seven Years' War of 1756–63 *(see pp50–51)*, most French colonists stayed on as British subjects. The French-speakers maintained their own religious and civic institutions and a feeling of independence that has grown over time. Since the 1960s, the constitutional link between Quebec and the rest of the country has been the subject of political debate, with a strong minority of Quebecois pressing for full independence *(see p59)*.

German Canadians

Although there have been German-speakers in Canada since the 1660s, the first major migration came between 1850–1900, with other mass arrivals following both World Wars. On the whole, the English-speaking majority has absorbed the Germans, but distinctive pockets of German-speakers hold strong today in Lunenburg, Nova Scotia *(see p92)*, and Kitchener-Waterloo in Ontario *(see p222)*. The rural communities surrounding Kitchener-Waterloo are strongholds of the Amish, a German-speaking religious sect, whose members shun the trappings of modern life and travel around on horse-drawn buggies wearing traditional homemade clothes. German food and drink, especially its beer-making techniques, have added to Canadian cuisine. Ethnic restaurants in German areas still run on traditional lines.

Street scene in Chinatown, Toronto

Italian Canadians

The widespread Italian presence in Canada can prove hard to see, as, for the most part, all 600,000 immigrants have merged almost seamlessly with the English speakers. There are, however, exceptions; in Toronto, a large and flourishing "Little Italy" neighborhood delights both visitors and the city's epicurean residents. The first major influx of Italian Canadians came in the wake of the civil wars that disrupted Italy in the second half of the 19th century; another wave arrived in the 1940s and 1950s after World War II. Immigration continues into the 21st century, with two percent of Canadians today speaking Italian as their first language.

German beer stein

Chinese Canadians

During the 1850s, Chinese laborers arrived in Canada to work in the gold fields of British Columbia. Thereafter, they played a key role in the construction of the railroads, settling new towns and cities as their work progressed eastward. During this period the Chinese suffered much

brutal racism, including laws that enforced statutory discrimination.

Political uncertainties caused a flood of Chinese immigration just before the return of Hong Kong to China by the British in 1997. Most settlers chose Toronto, Montreal, and Vancouver. With the Chinese focus on keeping large families together, most new arrivals aim for an already established Chinese community. About half of all Canada's immigrants today come from Asia. Over two percent of the Canadian population claimed Chinese as their first language in the late 1990s.

Ukrainian Canadians

Although Ukrainians are a small fraction of the Canadian population, numbering less than three percent, they have had a strong cultural influence, especially in the Prairie Provinces where the cupolas of their churches rise above many midwestern villages. The first major wave of Ukrainian migrants arrived in the 1890s as refugees from Tsarist persecution. The Soviet regime and the aftermath of World War II caused a second influx in the 20th century.

Woman in native Ukrainian dress in Battleford, Saskatchewan

French Canada

Many Canadians are quick to point out that Canada's origins are more French than British, that the first European Canadians were explorers from France, and therefore called *canadiens*. French Canadians have had a centuries-long history of conquest and battle to preserve their language and culture, strongest in Quebec and parts of Atlantic Canada. This has left large parts of the country with a French cultural base that lives on in language, religion, and the arts. More recently, the French-Canadian struggle for recognition in the 20th century has left unresolved the issue of Quebec's independence.

The heart of French Canada is Quebec, a province many times the size of France. Here, 85 percent of people count French as their mother tongue. French is not just the language of food, folklore, and love; it is also the language of business, government, and law.

hearty. Meat pies are a specialty: *cipaille* comprizes layers of game meat under a flaky crust, and the more common *tourtière* has a filling made of ground beef spiced with cloves. Salmon pie, stews made with pigs' feet, and meatballs in a rich gravy are also typical. Desserts are rich; the Acadian *tarte au sucre* (sugar pie) is popular, as well as *pudding au chomeur* (literally "unemployed pudding"), an upside-down cake with a sweet, caramelized base of sugar baked into a rich batter.

Musician Felix Leclerc was a guardian of Quebec's folk music

Language

French is the joint official language of Canada, but it has mutated in much the same way that North American English has. *Canadiens*, especially those in the bigger cities, have adopted some anglicisms; modern English words relating to industries and trades introduced by English-speakers are favorites. Conversely, some words that have passed out of fashion in France survive here; Canada is one of the few places where a cart remains a *charette*, for example, instead of a *tombereau*, and the *fin-de-semaine* is the time to get away for some relaxation, rather than the now-universal *le weekend*. Young Quebecois in particular are also far more free in using the informal *tu*, than more formal *vous*, than their parents would perhaps consider polite.

Wide varieties exist in the quality and style of French spoken. The Paris-influenced intonation of Montreal's college-educated *haute bourgeoisie*, for example, is quite distinct from the rhythmic gutturals of the Acadian fishermen

of the Maritimes. Residents of Quebec's Saguenay-Lac-Saint-Jean region speak a hard, clear French that must sound very like that of their Norman forbears.

Over the years Quebecois have evolved a dialect called *joual*, which is informal, slangy, and peppered with anglicisms. It is also very colorful and viewed with a mix of pride and disdain. The accent may be hard for foreigners to follow.

Food

Canadiens have always considered themselves the epicures of Canada, and with some justice, enjoying the delights of the table more passionately than their English-speaking counterparts. Traditional food is rich and

Sugar pie, a traditional Acadian family dessert, served at celebrations

Music

Chansoniers are the troubadours of French Canada. Rooted in the traditional music of the first settlers, their haunting songs and simple melodies, such as the ballads of Felix Leclerc, might be melancholy or upbeat, but they are almost always romantic. These folk songs, accompanied by guitar, usually reflect optimism and a deep love for the land. Quebec *chansonier* Gilles Vigneault's *Mon Pays* has become a nationalist anthem for those seeking independence. Of course, French music is not confined to the traditional; there are several successful rock, pop, and independent bands. Acadia's singers are often *chansonières*, including Edith Butler and Angèle Arseneault vividly evoking the sadness and joy of life by the sea.

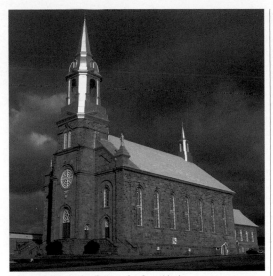
Traditional Catholic church in Cheticamp, Cape Breton Island

and Manitobans used the courts to force their provincial government to translate all Manitoba statutes into French.

This resurgence of national pride was felt most strongly in Quebec, where the charismatic and popular politician René Lévesque and his Parti-Québecois won the provincial election in 1976 and made outright separatism respectable. The party now regularly wins local elections and has so far held two referenda on independence. Both times Quebecois said no by the narrowest of margins, but the threat still dominates Canada's political life.

Symbols

The Quebec flag has a white cross on a blue background with a white Bourbon lily in each quarter. Acadians have created their own flag by adding a gold star to the French tricolor, which symbolizes *Stella Maris* (Star of the Sea), named after the Virgin Mary. The patron saint of French Canada is St. Jean Baptiste (St. John the Baptist); parades and parties mark his feast day on June 24. The celebrations take on a strongly nationalist style in Quebec, where the big day is called the *Fête National*. The provincial bird of Quebec is the snowy owl, and the flower remains the white lily, both of which flourish in the province.

Faith

The first French settlers were Roman Catholic, many very devout and zealous. The founders of Montreal, Paul Chomedy Sieur de Maisonneuve and Jeanne Mance, had hoped to create a new society based on Christian principles. Much of that devotion has evaporated in the modern age, especially in Quebec, which has one of the lowest church-attendance records in the country. Past fidelity has, however, left permanent monuments. Tiny French villages in Quebec and New Brunswick often have huge, stone churches with glittering tin roofs, gilding, and ornate interiors. Some parish churches in Montreal, like the magnificent Basilique Notre-Dame-de-Montréal *(see pp116–17)*, would pass for cathedrals in US cities.

Nationalism

There has been a nationalist strain to most *canadien* aspirations since the founding of Modern Canada. Quebecois entered the 1867 Canadian Confederation *(see p52)* only because French leaders persuaded them that the deal would preserve their faith and language. The 1960s and 1970s took the campaign into a new phase, with the aim being the independence of Quebec, as the politics of mere survival rose to the politics of assertiveness (with French President Charles de Gaulle adding his rallying cry *"Vive le Québec – libre!"* in 1966). Acadians in New Brunswick gained real political power to preserve their unique heritage, Franco-Ontarians fought for control over their own schools,

Quebec flag with Bourbon lilies

Demonstrators during referendum vote for independence of Quebec

Native Canadians

Most archaeologists believe that the first inhabitants of North America crossed from Siberia to Alaska around 25,000 years ago. These hunter-nomads came in search of mammoth and bison, the ice-age animals that constituted their basic diet. The first wave of migrants was reinforced by a steady trickle of Siberian peoples over the next 15,000 years, and slowly the tribes worked their way east and south until they reached the Atlantic and South America. Over the centuries, the descendants of these hunter-nomads evolved a wide range of cultures, which were shaped by their particular environment. In the icy north or across the barren wastes of Newfoundland, life was austere; but the fertile soils of Ontario and the fish-rich shores of British Columbia nourished sophisticated societies based on fishing and farming.

Europeans began to arrive in numbers during the 17th century. In Newfoundland, the first part of Canada settled by whites, interracial relations were initially cordial but soured when new settlers encroached on ancient hunting grounds. In a pattern repeated across the continent, the native peoples, many dying from European diseases, were driven to inhospitable lands.

The Iroquois

Spread along the St. Lawrence River and the shores of the Great Lakes, were the Iroquois-speaking tribes, among whom were the Mohawks, the Huron, and the Seneca. These tribes hunted and fished, but they also cultivated beans, pumpkins, squash, and corn, growing everything in abundance for a year-round food supply. This enabled them to live in large villages, often with several hundred inhabitants. Their traditional dwelling was the longhouse, built of cedar poles bent to form a protective arch and covered with bark. These settlements were all surrounded

by high palisades made of sharpened wooden stakes, a

Cornplanter, a 17th-century chief of the Seneca tribe

necessary precaution as warfare between the tribes was endemic.

An Iroquois-built longhouse

The Plains Peoples

War was also commonplace on the plains of southern Manitoba and Saskatchewan, where the majority Blackfoot tribe was totally reliant on the buffalo: they ate the meat, used the hide for clothes and tents, and filed the bones into tools. The first Blackfoot hunted the buffalo by means of cleverly conceived traps, herding the animals and stampeding them off steep cliffs (see p300). Originally, the horse was unknown to the native peoples of the Americas –

Indians on horseback hunting buffalo with arrows

their largest beast of burden was the dog – but the Spanish conquistadores brought the horse with them when they colonized South America in the 1500s. Thereafter, horses were slowly traded north until they reached the Canadian plains. The arrival of the horse transformed Blackfoot life: it made the buffalo easy to hunt and, with a consistent food supply now assured, the tribe developed a militaristic culture, focusing particularly on the valor of their young men – the "braves."

A Blackfoot camp, showing traditional homes

Peoples Of The Pacific Coast

The native peoples of the Pacific Coast were divided into a large number of small tribes such as the Tlingit and the Salish. The ocean was an abundant source

of food; with this necessity taken care of, they developed an elaborate ceremonial life featuring large and lively feasts, the potlachs, in which clans tried to outdo each other with the magnificence of their gifts. The peoples of this region were also superb woodcarvers, their most celebrated works of art being totem poles. Each pole featured a myth from the tribe's religion; magical birds and beasts mix with semi-human figures to tell a story in carved panels rising up the pole.

Totem pole in Stanley Park

Sqylax tribal celebration in British Columbia

The Inuit and the Peoples of the Northern Forests

Stretching in a band from Alaska to Greenland, the far north was home to the Inuit, nomadic hunters who lived in skin tents in the summer and igloos in the winter. Arctic conditions and limited food supply meant that they foraged in small family groups and gathered together only in special circumstances – during the annual caribou migration, for instance. To the south of the Inuit, and also widespread across modern-day Canada, were the tribes of the northern forest, including the

Naskapi, the Chipewyan, and the Wood Cree. These tribes were also nomadic hunters, dependent on fish and seal, or deer and moose. Successful hunters earned prestige, and the tribal priest (shaman) was expected to keep the spirit world bene-volent, but there was little other social organization.

An Inuit hunter by his igloo home

Inuit in Caribou parka, checking his harpoon

Paul Okalik, Nunavut's first Premier, at his inauguration

Native Canadian Issues

Since the 1960s, Canada's native peoples have recovered some of their self-confidence. A key development was the creation of the Assembly of First Nations (AFN), an intertribal organization that has become an influential player on the national scene. In the 1980s, the AFN successfully argued for a greater degree of self-government on the reservations and tackled the federal government on land rights, sponsoring a series of court cases that highlighted the ways the native population had been stripped of its territories. The AFN was also involved in the establishment of Nunavut (see p59), the homeland for the Inuit created in 1999 from part of the former Northwest Territories. By comparison with their white compatriots, Canada's native population remains, nonetheless, poor and disadvantaged. The rectification of historic wrongs will take decades, even assuming that the political will remains strong enough to improve matters.

Art in Canada

Inuit and other First Nations groups have produced art in Canada since prehistoric times: the Inuit carved wood or antler sculptures, and other native groups were responsible for works from rock paintings to richly decorated pottery. Early European immigrants, both French and English, generally eschewed native traditions and followed European forms. Throughout the 19th and early 20th centuries, artists traveled, to Paris, London, and New York to study European art. It was in the 1900s that painters sought to develop a distinctly national style. However, one consistent subject of Canadian painting is the country itself: a preoccupation with its lush forests, stately landscapes, and expanse of freezing northern wilderness. Today, Canadian art reflects a wide range of art movements, with native art in particular fetching high prices among collectors.

On the Saint Lawrence (1897) oil painting by Maurice Cullen

Painters in the New World

In the 1600s French settlers in Canada either imported religious paintings or commissioned stock subjects to adorn their new churches. Only Samuel de Champlain, the "Father of New France" *(see p49)*, stands out for his sketches of the Huron tribe. After the English conquest in the 1760s, art moved from religion to matters of politics, the land, and the people. Army officers, such as Thomas Davies (1737–1812), painted fine detailed works, conveying their love of the landscape. Artists such as Robert Field (1769–1819), trained in Neo-Classicism, which was prevalent in Europe at the time,

and became very popular, as did Quebec painters Antoine Plamondon (1804–95) and Théophile Hamel (1817–70). Cornelius Krieghoff (1815–72) settled in Quebec and was famous for his snow scenes of both settlers and natives. His contemporary, Paul Kane (1810–71), recorded the lives of the First Nations on an epic journey across Canada. He then completed over 100 sketches and paintings, of which *Mah Min*, or *The Feather*, (c.1856) is one of the most impressive *(see p44)*. During the 19th century, painters focused on the Canadian landscape. Homer Watson (1855–1936)

and Ozias Leduc (1864–1955) were the first artists to learn their craft in Canada. Watson said, "I did not know enough to have Paris or Rome in mind. … I felt Toronto had all I needed." His canvases portray Ontarian domestic scenes.

After Confederation in 1867, the Royal Canadian Academy of Arts and the National Gallery of Canada were founded in 1883. Artists could now train at home, but many still left to study in Paris. Curtis Williamson (1867–1944) and Edmund Morris (1871–1913) returned from France determined to revitalize their tired national art. They formed the Canadian Art Club in 1907, where new schools such as Impressionism were shown. James Wilson Morrice (1865–1924), Maurice Cullen (1866–1934), and Marc Aurèle de Foy Suzor-Coté (1869–1937) were key figures in this move toward modernity.

Modern Painters

Before World War I, Toronto artists criticized the influence of Europe and objected to the lack of a national identity in art. By the 1920s, the most influential set of Canadian artists, the Group of Seven *(see pp168–9)*, had defined Canadian painting in their boldly colored landscapes, such as A.Y. Jackson's *Terre Sauvage* (1913). Though he died before the formation of the Group, Tom Thomson is seen as a major influence. Three painters who came to prominence in the 1930s were influenced by the Group but had very different muses. Each artist was distinguished by a passion for their own province: David Milne (1882–1953), was known for his still lifes; LeMoine Fitzgerald (1890–1956) for his domestic and backyard scenes; and Emily Carr (1871–1945) *(see p286)* for her striking depiction of

Lawren S. Harris, painter (1885–1970)

Skidegate, Graham Island, BC, (1928) a later work by Emily Carr

the west coast Salish people and their totem poles. Carr was the first woman artist to achieve high regard. A writer as well as painter, her poem *Renfrew* (1929), describes her intense relationship with nature, which was reflected in her paintings:"… in the distance receding plane after plane… cold greens, gnarled stump of gray and brown."

The strong influence of the Group of Seven provoked a reaction among successive generations of painters. John Lyman (1886–1967) rejected the group's rugged nationalism. Inspired by Matisse, he moved away from using land as the dominant subject of painting. Lyman set up the Contemporary Arts Society in Montreal and promoted new art between 1939–48; even Surrealism reached the city.

Since World War II there has been an explosion of new forms based on abstraction. In Montreal, Paul-Emile Borduas (1905–60) and two colleagues formed the Automatists, whose inspirations were Surrealism and Abstract Impressionism. By the 1950s Canadian painters achieved international acclaim. Post-war trends were also taken up in Toronto, where The Painters Eleven produced abstract paintings. Today, artists work across the range of contemporary art movements, incorporating influences from around the world and from Canada's cultural mosaic. Experimental work by painters such as Jack Bush, Greg Carnoe,

and Joyce Wieland continues strongly in the wake of ideas from the 1960s. Canada now boasts a plethora of public and private galleries, and exceptional collections of 20th-century art.

Aboriginal Art

The art of the Inuit *(see pp330 31)* and the Northwest First Nations is highly valued in Canada. Pre-historic Inuit finds reveal beautiful objects, from sculpted figurines to carved harpoon heads, which were largely created for religious use. With the arrival of the Europeans the Inuit quickly adapted their artistic skills to make objects for sale such as sculptures made from ivory, bone, and stone. Today, Inuit artists such as Aqghadluk, Qaqaq Ashoona, and Tommy Ashevak are noted for their contribution to contemporary Canadian art,

especially their sculpture and wallhangings. The sculpture of the Northwest coast First Nations people is known worldwide, particularly the cedar-wood carvings of Haida artist Bill Reid (1920–98), the totem poles of Richard Krentz, and the Kwa Gulth Big House at Fort Rupert by Chief Tony Hunt.

Painters such as Norval Morisseau, Carl Ray, and Daphne Odjig cover a range of styles, from realism to abstract. Na-tive art celebrates the culture of its people, from their legendary survival skills, tales, and myths, to their land and the fight for its preservation.

Sculpture

European sculpture arrived in Canada with the French who created sacred figures to adorn their churches. Sculptors such as Louis Quévillon (1749–1823) carved decorative altarpieces as well as fine marble statues in Montreal. European traditions continued to dominate through the 19th century, and it was not until the 20th century that Canada's new cities began to require civic monuments. The façade of the Quebec Parliament was designed by Louis-Philippe Hébert (1850–1917).

Robert Murray's *Sculpture*

Native subjects were incorporated into much 20th-century sculpture, as were European styles including Art Nouveau and Art Deco. Since the 1960s, sculptors such as Armand Vaillancourt (b.1929) and Robert Murray (b.1936) have sought to develop a Canadian style. Modern materials and the influence of conceptual art inform the work of such current artists as Michael Snow. Their work can be seen not just in museums but also in commercial and civic buildings.

The late Haida sculptor Bill Reid

Literature and Music in Canada

As the Canadian poet the Reverend Edward Hartley Dewart wrote in 1864, "A national literature is an essential element in the formation of a national character." Much Canadian literature and music is concerned with defining a national consciousness but also reflects the cultural diversity of the country. Both English and French speakers have absorbed a variety of influences from the US, Britain, and France, as well as from the other nations whose immigrants make up the population. The Europeans' relationship with First Nations peoples has also affected the style and content of much Canadian fiction and poetry, as have the often harsh realities of living in a land of vast wilderness.

Stars of the popular 1934 film *Anne of Green Gables*

New Beginnings

Much of the earliest writing in Canada (between the mid-1500s and 1700s) was by explorers, fur traders, soldiers, and missionaries. French lawyer Marc Lescarbot's *Histoire de La Nouvelle France* (1609) is an early example of pioneer commentary and is a lively record of his adventures in Nova Scotia. After the English conquest of 1760, New France was subdued, but by the 19th century, French poets began producing patriotic poems such as *Le Vieux Soldat Canadien* (1855) by Octave Cremazie (1827–79), sparking a renaissance of poetry that continues today.

English writing was concerned with man's struggle with nature and life in the new world. *Roughing it in the Bush* (1852) by Susanna Moodie is a tale of struggles in isolated northern Ontario. British Columbia was the last region to be settled, and a captivating memoir is *A Pioneer Gentlewoman in British Columbia: the recollections of Susan Allison* (1876). Allison came from England to teach in the town of Hope and was the first European woman to make the dangerous journey across the Hope Mountains on horseback. Much 19th-century Canadian fiction romanticizes the past, such as William Kirby's (1817–1906) *Golden Dog* (1877), with its idealized view of 18th-century Quebec. Epic novels of the time focused on native lives and cultures, notably *Wacousta* (1832) by John Richardson (1796–1852). Archibald Stansfield Belaney (1888–

1938) took on a new identity as an Ojibway native named Grey Owl *(see p254)*, producing some of Canada's best-loved literature. *Pilgrims of the Wild* (1935) tells of his journey to find sanctuary for the over-hunted beaver. *The Adventures of Sajo and her Beaver People* and *Tales of an Empty Cabin* (1935–6) are laments for the wild and lost traditions.

Classics of the early 1900s deal with domesticity. These include *Anne of Green Gables* (1908) by L.M. Montgomery (1874–1942). Humorous writing was led by Stephen Leacock *(see p222)*, and Thomas Chandler Haliburton (1796–1865), a judge who created Sam Slick, narrator of *The Clockmaker* (1836). Painter Emily Carr's *A House of all Sorts* (1944) describes her days as a landlady.

Poetry

Early English language poets Standish O'Grady (1793–1841) and Alexander McLachan (1818–96) wrote verse that reflected a colonial point of view. The genre looked critically at an iniquitous motherland (England), while praising the opportunities available in the New World. Creators of a "new" Canadian poetry in the 1870s and 80s used detailed descriptions of landscape to highlight man's efforts to conquer nature. Two notable authors were Charles Mair (1838–1927) and Isabella Valancy Crawford (1850–1887).

By the 20th century the idea of the wilderness stayed at

Internationally renowned poet and songwriter Leonard Cohen

the center of Canadian poetry but was written in a sparer style that mirrored the starkness of the Group of Seven's landscape paintings *(see pp168–9)*. Robert Service's (1874–1958) popular ballads deal with history, and he is noted for his gold rush poems such as *The Spell of the Yukon* (1907) and the later *Rhymes of a Roughneck* (1950). John McCrae (1872–1918) wrote one of the most famous World War I poems *In Flanders Fields* (1915).

Modern English and French poetry now has a worldwide audience, with writers such as Anne Wilkinson, Irving Layton, Earle Birney, E.J. Pratt, Leonard Cohen, and Patrick Anderson, whose *Poem on Canada* (1946) looks at the impact of nature on European mentalities. The simple power of French writer Anne Hébert's poems, such as *Le Tombeau des Rois* (The Kings' Tombs) (1953) focuses on the universal themes of childhood, memory, and death. A postwar boom in poetry and fiction was fostered by the Canada Council for the Arts.

Canadian poet Robert Service in 1942

Native Canadian Writing

Despite a powerful oral tradition – where stories are both owned and passed down through families and clans – autobiography, children's books, plays, short stories, poetry, essays, and novels have been produced by Canadian native writers since the 19th century. One of the most popular autobiographies of this period was written by Ojibway native George Copway (1818–69). Titled *The Life, History, and Travels of Kah-ge-ga-ga-bowh* (1847), it had six editions in a year. The first book to be published by a native woman is thought to be *Cogewea, The Half-Blood* (1927), by Okanagan

author Mourning Dove (1888–1936). Another Okanagan novelist, Jeannette Armstrong (b.1948), published *Slash* in 1985. The struggles of a Métis woman in modern Canada are described in the best-selling autobiography of Maria Campbell in *Halfbreed* (1973).

Legend and political campaigning for native rights inform much aboriginal fiction, such as Pauline Johnson's *The White Wampum* (1895) and Beatrice Culleton's *In Search of April Raintree* (1983). The first Inuit work in English was *Harpoon of the Hunter* (1970), a story of coming of age in the northern Arctic by Markoosie (b.1942). One of Canada's top contemporary playwrights is Cree author Thompson Highway (b.1951), whose plays deal with the harsh reality of life on the reservations.

Modern Fiction

Since the 1940s, many Canadian writers have achieved international fame: Margaret Atwood (b.1939) is well known for her poetry, novels, and criticism, while Carol Shields (1935–2003) won the prestigious Booker Prize for *The Stone Diaries* in 1996. Mordecai Richler (1931–2001) and Robertson Davies (1913–95) are noted for their wry take on contemporary Canadian society. Many authors have reached a wider public through film adaptations of their books. Gabrielle Roy's *Bonheur d'Occasion* (1945) became 1983's *The Tin Flute*; a novel by W.P. Kinsella, *Shoeless Joe* (1982), became *Field of Dreams* in 1989; and the 1996 adaptation of Michael Ondaatje's

Michael Ondaatje, the acclaimed author of *The English Patient*

The English Patient (1992) won nine Oscars. There is a strong Canadian tradition of short-story writing, one master being Alice Munro (b.1931). Popular history is highly regarded; noted author Pierre Berton (1920–2004) wrote 40 books on the nation's history.

Music in Canada

Some of the biggest names in the music industry are Canadian. A strong tradition of folk and soft rock has produced such artists as Leonard Cohen, Kate and Anna McGarrigle, Joni Mitchell, and Neil Young. Other singer/songwriters who have continued the tradition of reflective, melodic hits include Alanis Morissette and k.d. lang; and the Cowboy Junkies and Shania Twain have their own takes on country music. Stars such as Celine Dion and Bryan Adams have made a huge impact in Europe and the US. In the classical sphere, orchestras such as the Montréal Orchestre Symphonique are world famous, as was the pianist Glenn Gould. Jazz is represented by the pianist Oscar Peterson (1925–2007), and every year Montreal hosts a famous jazz festival.

Legendary composer and folk singer Joni Mitchell

Sports in Canada

Canadians are avid sports fans, and most of the country's cities and towns offer visitors a chance to see year-round sports entertainment. Although the official national game is lacrosse – a First Nations game in which the ball is caught and tossed in a leather cradle on a stick – Canadians' greatest enthusiasm is for ice hockey. Baseball, basketball, and Canadian football (similar to the US game) are also big crowd-pullers. Major cities regularly attract international stars to world-class racing, golf, and tennis tournaments. Even small towns provide the chance to watch minor professionals, amateurs, and student athletes. For visitors who prefer participating in sports, Canada offers a broad choice of activities from skiing to golf, fishing, and hiking.

National ice hockey heroes in action during a league game

Ice Hockey

The popularity of ice hockey in Canada knows no bounds. Every town has a rink, and every school, college, and university has a team. The North American **National Hockey League** (NHL) was founded in 1917, and its principal prize, the Stanley Cup, was instituted in 1892 by Canadian Governor General, Lord Stanley. Today, the league has 30 teams, 6 of which belong to Canadian cities; the Montreal Canadiens, Calgary Flames, Edmonton Oilers, Toronto Maple Leafs, Ottawa Senators, and the Vancouver Canucks. Although most of the players in both the US and Canada are Canadian, there has been an influx of other nationalities such as Russian, American, and Swedish atheletes playing for the top teams. Renowned for its toughness, the game usually involves a skirmish or two among the players, which often means that this 60-minute game can last up to 3 hours. The season runs from October to April when the play-offs for the prestigious Stanley Cup begin.

Hockey stars such as Wayne Gretzky are national icons. He retired in 1999 after 20 years in the game, having captured 61 NHL scoring records.

Tickets to the major games can be hard to come by, and should be booked in advance. It is a good idea to contact the club's ticket lines, or book through **Ticketmaster**. Minor league and college games are easier to get into, and the University of Toronto and York, Concordia in Montreal, and the University of Alberta in Edmonton all have good teams. Tickets can be bought from the local arena, or direct from the administration center, and are usually a great bargain.

Baseball

Although baseball is seen as an American sport, the game also has a large following in Canada. There is one Canadian team that plays in the major leagues: the well-known **Toronto Blue Jays**, who won the World Series in 1992 and 1993. Baseball is played in the summer, and the season lasts from April to September (with play-offs through October). It can provide a great family day out, with beer, popcorn, an enthusiastic audience, and plenty of between-inning entertainment, to keep the less baseball-obsessed amused.

The Blue Jays take on their rivals in the Rogers Centre, an architectural marvel with a retractable roof *(see p177)*. Good tickets are easy to come by – just book a day or two in advance. Seats further back are almost always available on the day of the game. Seeing one of the minor league baseball teams can also be fun.

José Bautista ready to make a strike for the Toronto Blue Jays

Football

The Canadian version of football (not soccer) is noted for being a more exciting version of American football. Although the best Canadian players tend to move to the US for higher salaries, the game still attracts substantial home audiences. The Canadian Football League has two divisions of four teams who each play over the July to November season.

The games tend to attract a lively family crowd and are fun, especially around the Grey Cup final. Played on the last Sunday of November, the game is preceded by a week of festivities and a big parade in the host city. Football is also played at most universities, where a Saturday afternoon game makes for an entertaining excursion. The annual college championship game is called the Vanier Cup and is played at Toronto's Skydome and other arenas. Tickets are relatively easy to come by and are reasonably priced.

Basketball

What once was an American passion has now spread around the world to become one of the fastest growing international sports. The game was invented in the United States by a Canadian, Dr. James Naismith, and now enjoys huge popularity in his homeland. The **Toronto Raptors** play in the National Basketball Association, the top professional league in the world, against the likes of the Chicago Bulls, Boston Celtics, Los Angeles Lakers, and New York Knicks. The season lasts from October until late spring, and it is well worth a visit to Toronto's Air Canada Centre to watch one of their fast-paced games. Most of Canada's universities have teams, and although crowds tend to be smaller than those drawn by the professionals, the

competition is fierce and the atmosphere truly exhilarating, especially during the annual national championship tournament played each year in March.

Toronto Raptors versus the L.A. Clippers basketball match

Golf

Golf is an immensely popular participation sport in Canada, with more than 1,700 beautiful courses across the country, from the mountain courses in the west to the many rolling fairways of Prince Edward Island in the east.

The RBC Canadian Open, hosted by **Golf Canada**, is the biggest professional tournament on the golfing calendar each season in Canada. Held annually in July, it rotates between the country's best courses and draws large crowds of spectators to watch many of the world's greatest players. In 2014, it takes place at the Royal Montreal Golf Club. The LPGA's CN Canadian Women's Open is held annually in August.

Winter Sports

Famous for the plentiful snow and sunshine of its cold winters, Canada is one of the top places both to watch and participate in winter sports. Canadian resorts are less crowded than their European counterparts, and are set among some of the most dramatic scenery in the world.

DIRECTORY

National Hockey League
11th Floor, 50 Bay Street, Toronto. **Tel** (416) 981 2777.
W nhl.com

Ticketmaster
(for hockey games) **Tel** (416) 870 8000. W ticketmaster.ca

Baseball
Toronto Blue Jays
Tel Tickets: (416) 341 1234.
W bluejays.com

Football
Canadian Football League
110 Eglinton Avenue W., Toronto. **Tel** (416) 322 9650.
W cfl.ca

Basketball
Toronto Raptors Tel Tickets: (416) 815 5600. W raptors.com

Golf
Golf Canada
Tel (905) 849 9700.
W golfcanada.ca

Visitors can enjoy a range of winter sports options in resorts across the country, from Whistler in the Rockies to Mont Ste-Anne in Quebec. As well as downhill skiing, it is also possible to try snowboarding, snow-mobiling, dogsledding, or even heli-skiing on pristine snow (see p395).

Snowboarder descending a slope at speed in powder snow

CANADA THROUGH THE YEAR

Seasonal changes in Canada vary greatly across the country, but in general it is safe to say that the winters are long and cold and run from November to March, while spring and fall tend to be mild. British Columbia is the most temperate zone, with an average temperature of 5°C (40°F) in January. July and August are reliably warm and sunny in most places, even the far north, and most outdoor festivals are held in the summer months. There are plenty of events in winter, both indoors and out, some of which celebrate Canadians' ability to get the best out of the icy weather, especially activities such as dogsledding, snowmobiling, and ice-skating. A range of cultural events reflect the country's history, as well as its diverse peoples and culture.

Spring

March and April bring the country some of its most unpredictable weather, moving from snow to sunshine in a day. In the north this is a time for welcoming the end of winter, while farther south spring is the start of an array of fun festivals.

Dogsledding at Yellowknife's Long John Jamboree in spring

March

Long John Jamboree (late March) Yellowknife. A celebration of the arrival of spring, featuring dogsledding, snowmobiling, and delicious local foods.

April

Toonik Tyme (mid-April) Iqaluit. This week-long festival includes igloo building, traditional games, and community feasts.
Beaches Easter Parade (April) Toronto. This annual parade has become a popular spring institution. It follows a route along Queen St. E., between Victoria Park and Woodbine Avenue.
Shaw Festival (April–October) Niagara-on-the-Lake. Theater festival with classic plays by George Bernard Shaw and his contemporaries (see p212).

Summer

Warm weather across most of the country means that there is an explosion of festivals, carnivals, and cultural events, from May through August.

May

Canadian Tulipfest (mid-May) Ottawa. Colorful display of millions of tulips is the center-piece for a variety of events.
Stratford Shakespearean Festival (May–November) Stratford. World-famous theater festival featuring a range of plays from Elizabethan to contemporary works (see p215).
Shorebirds and Friends' Festival (late May) Wadena, Saskatchewan. Features guided bird-watching and tours of wildlife habitats.
Vancouver International Children's Festival (last weekend in May) Vancouver. Theater, circus, and music for children aged three and up.

June

Pride Week (early June) Toronto. A celebration of the gay community, featuring a fun, flamboyant parade.
Grand Prix du Canada (June) Montreal. Annual, weekend-long Formula One event.
Banff Summer Arts Festival (June–August) Banff. Two months of opera, music, drama, and dance.
Midnight Madness (mid-June) Inuvik. Celebration of the summer solstice, with parties under the midnight sun.
Mosaic – Festival of Cultures (first weekend in June) Regina. Cultural events from around the world.
Jazz Fest International (late June–July) Victoria. Jazz and blues musicians play in venues all over town.

Vividly colored tulips at Ottawa's spring festival, Canadian Tulipfest

Steer wrestling competition in the *Half Million Dollar Rodeo* at Calgary's Stampede

Red River Exhibition *(late June–July)* Winnipeg. A huge fair with many entertainments.

Festival International de Jazz de Montréal *(late June–July)* Montreal. Famous jazz festival with a number of free outdoor concerts.

Nova Scotia International Tattoo *(late June–July)* Halifax. There are 2,000 participants in one of the world's largest indoor shows.

July

Folk on the Rocks *(July)* Yellowknife. Inuit drummers, dancers, and throat singers perform here.

Klondike Days *(July)* Edmonton. Commemorates the city's frontier days.

Calgary Stampede *(mid-July)* Calgary. Ten-day celebration of all things western, including a rodeo *(see p298).*

Molson Indy *(mid-July)* Toronto. Indy car race held at Exhibition Place.

Quebec City Summer Festival *(second week)* Quebec City. Ten days of music and dance.

Just for Laughs Festival *(July)* Montreal. Twelve-day comedy festival with more than 600 comedians from around the world in venues across the city.

Canadian Open Tennis Championships *(July–August)* Montreal, Toronto. Major international tennis tournament.

Caribana *(July–August)* Toronto. One of the largest and livliest Caribbean celebrations in North America. The main event is the parade.

Antigonish Highland Games *(mid-July)* Antigonish. Oldest traditional highland games in North America, with pipe bands and dancing.

Ford race car at the Molson Indy meeting held in Toronto

August

Royal St. John's Regatta *(August 4)* St. John's. Noted as North America's oldest sporting event, features rowing races and a carnival.

Wikwemikong Powwow *(first weekend)* Manitoulin Island.

Ojibway native festival with a dancing and drum competition *(see p228).*

Folklorama *(early August)* Winnipeg. Multicultural festival of food, performance, and the arts.

Victoria Park Arts and Crafts Fair *(early August)* Moncton. Atlantic Canada's largest outdoor sale of arts, antiques, and crafts.

Festival Acadien de Caraquet *(early August)* Caraquet. Celebration of Acadian culture and history.

Halifax International Busker Festival *(second week)* Halifax. The best street entertainers from around the world.

Discovery Days Festival *(mid-August)* Dawson City. Commemorates Gold Rush days, with costumed parades and canoe races.

Fringe Festival *(mid-August)* Edmonton. Theater and live music with international performers in the historic Old Strathcona neighborhood.

Canadian National Exhibition *(August–September)* Toronto. Annual fair featuring spectacular air show, concerts, and a casino.

Folkfest *(mid-August)* Saskatoon. Saskatchewan's multicultural heritage celebrated in a variety of events.

Showjumping in the Masters equestrian event held in Calgary

Fall

Cool, but often sunny weather provides the best setting for the dramatic reds and golds of the fall foliage, which are mostly seen in the deciduous forests of the eastern provinces. In Ontario and Quebec, fall signals the end of the humid summer months and heralds crisp days that are perfect for participating in outdoor pursuits.

September
The Masters (first week) Calgary. Equestrian event with top international riders.
First People's Festival (September) Victoria. Three days of exhibitions, dancing, and a traditional native gathering known as the potlatch.
Toronto International Film Festival (September) Toronto. Movie stars and top directors attend this prestigious festival.

Niagara Grape and Wine Festival (mid-September) Niagara Falls. Vineyard tours, wine tastings, and concerts welcome the area's grape harvest.
Flambée des Couleurs (mid-September–October) Eastern Townships. Celebrations of glorious fall leaf colors.

October
Okanagan Wine Festival (early October) Okanagan Valley. Tours and tastings throughout the valley (see p321).
Oktoberfest (mid-October) Kitchener-Waterloo. Largest Bavarian festival outside Germany (see p222).

Traditional Bavarian costumes and music at the Oktoberfest

VANCOUVER

°C/°F	23/73		
	14/57	13/55	14/57
	5/41		7/45	6/43
0				0/32

	6 hrs	9 hrs	4 hrs	2 hrs
	90 mm	39 mm	172 mm	214 mm
month	Apr	Jul	Oct	Jan

TORONTO

°C/°F	27/81		
	17/63	15/59	
	12/54	7/45	
	3/37		
0			-1/30
			-8/18

	6 hrs	10 hrs	9 hrs	2 hrs
	66 mm	74 mm	41 mm	66 mm
month	Apr	Jul	Oct	Jan

Average daily maximum temperature
Average daily minimum temperature
Average daily hours of sunshine
Average monthly rainfall

Climate

This vast country has a variable climate, despite being famous for having long, cold winters. Most Canadians live in the warmer south of the country, close to the US border. Southern Ontario and BC's south and central coast are the warmest areas, while central and northern Canada have the coldest winters.

OTTAWA

°C/°F	27/81		
	14/57	13/55	
	10/50		
	0/32	3/37	
0			-6/21
			-16/3

	6 hrs	9 hrs	4 hrs	3 hrs
	69 mm	82 mm	67 mm	62 mm
month	Apr	Jul	Oct	Jan

MONTREAL

°C/°F	26/79		
	17/63		
	11/52	13/55	
	2/36	6/43	
0			-5/23
			-13/9

	5 hrs	8 hrs	4 hrs	3 hrs
	83 mm	98 mm	84 mm	87 mm
month	Apr	Jul	Oct	Jan

HALIFAX

°C/°F	23/73		
	14/57	14/57	
	9/48	7/45	
	1/34		
0			0/32
			-7/19

	5 hrs	8 hrs	5 hrs	3 hrs
	113 mm	94 mm	120 mm	140 mm
month	Apr	Jul	Oct	Jan

Celtic Colours *(mid-October)*
Cape Breton Island. International Celtic music festival held across the island.

Winter

Apart from coastal British Columbia, Canadian winters are long and cold with lots of snow. Events focus on winter sports, with some of the best skiing in the world available at such resorts as Whistler in British Columbia. The Christmas holidays are a time of fun activities to cheer everyone up in the midst of long, dark days.

November

Royal Agricultural Winter Fair *(early–mid-November)* Toronto. The world's largest indoor agricultural fair features the Royal Horse Show and the Winter Garden Show.
Canadian Finals Rodeo *(mid-November)* Edmonton. Canada's cowboy champions are decided at this event.
Winter Festival of Lights *(early November–mid-January)* Niagara Falls. Spectacular light displays and concerts.

December

Canadian Open Sled Dog Race *(December)* Fort St. John and Fort Nelson. Snow sports and family fun-days as well as dogsled races.

An illuminated display of Christmas decorations

Christmas Carol Ships Parade *(mid-December)* Vancouver. Boats are beautifully decorated with Christmas lights, and cruise Vancouver's waters.

January

Ice Magic *(mid-January)* Lake Louise. International ice sculpture competition.
Techni-Cal Challenge – Dog Sled Race *(mid-January)* Minden. Over 80 teams compete in international races.
Rossland Winter Carnival *(last weekend)* Rossland. Snowboarding contests, a torchlit parade, and lots of music and dancing.
Quebec Winter Carnival *(January–February)* Quebec. A famous canoe race across the

St. Lawrence River is just one attraction at these huge winter celebrations.
Jasper in January *(last two weeks)* Jasper. Winter festivities include skiing parties, races, and food fairs.
SnowDays *(January–early February)* Banff and Lake Louise. Variety of fun events, including skating parties, hockey tournaments, and barn dances.

February

Yukon Quest International Sled Dog Race *(February)* Whitehorse. Famous 1,600 km (1,000 mile) race from Fairbanks, Alaska to Whitehorse.
Nova Scotia Icewine Festival *(February)* throughout Nova Scotia. Celebrating the region's internationally renowned icewines.
Yukon Sourdough Rendevous *(February)* Whitehorse. A "mad trapper" competition and an array of children's events in this winter festival.
Frostbite Music Festival *(third weekend)* Whitehorse. Features a wide range of music from jazz to rock.
Calgary Winter Festival *(second week)* Calgary. Fun family activities, music, and feasting.
Festival du Voyageur *(mid-February)* Winnipeg. Celebration of fur trade history with an enormous street party.
Winterlude *(every weekend)* Ottawa. A wide array of activities including ice-skating on the Rideau Canal.

Two eagle ice sculptures at Ottawa's February festival, Winterlude

THE HISTORY OF CANADA

Canada is known for its wild and beautiful terrain, yet with the help of the aboriginal peoples, European settlers adapted to their new land and built up a prosperous nation. Despite continuing divisions between its English- and French-speaking peoples, Canada has welcomed immigrants from around the globe and is respected as one of the most tolerant countries in the world today.

Long before the first Europeans crossed the Atlantic in AD 986, the landscape we now know as Canada was inhabited by various civilizations. Tribes of hunters came on foot, walking across a land bridge that once joined Asia with North America as part of the ancient land mass of Laurasia.

These first inhabitants, now referred to as the First Nations, endured centuries of hardship and adaptation, eventually developing the skills, technology, and culture required to survive the rigors of life in Canada.

Early Survival

Across most of the country, from the Yukon to the Atlantic, there were two main groups of hunter-gatherers, the Algonquins and the Athapaskans. They lived in small nomadic bands, which developed birch bark canoes and snowshoes to travel across this vast land. Food and clothing were procured through fishing and animal trapping, traditions that gave Canada the lucrative fish and fur trades.

To the north of these two groups were the Innu people, who mastered life in the Arctic, being able to survive in a region of dark, ice-bound winters and brief summers. To the south, the Iroquois settled in forest villages where they lived in long-houses and grew corn as their staple crop.

On the western plains, other tribes depended on the bison for their livelihood, while communities living along the Pacific Coast relied on fishing and trading. Their towering totem poles indicated a rich culture and spiritual belief system.

The common bond between all the First Nations, despite their disparate lifestyles, was that they saw themselves as part of nature and not as its masters. They believed the animals they hunted had kindred spirits, and misfortune befell those who offended such spirits by gratuitous killing.

The generosity of the natives toward Europeans may have hastened their own downfall. As Canadian historian Desmond Morton points out: "Without the full… assistance of natives showing the Europeans their methods of survival, their territory, and their resources, the early explorers and settlers would have perished in even greater numbers and possibly abandoned their quest, much as the Vikings had done 500 years before."

9,000 BC Native peoples are living at least as far south as the Eramosa River near what is now Guelph, Ontario		**AD 986** Bjarni Herjolfsson, a Viking sailing from Iceland to Greenland, is the first European to see the coastline of Labrador				**1497** John Cabot's first voyage to North America

Viking ship c.980 AD

30,000 BC	**20,000 BC**	**10,000 BC**	**AD1**	**500**	**1000**	**1500**

30,000–10,000 BC Nomadic hunters arrive in North America across a land bridge from Asia

992 Leif "the Lucky" Ericsson visits Labrador and L'Anse aux Meadows, Newfoundland

1003 Thorfinn Karlsefni starts a colony in Labrador (Vinland) to trade with the natives, but it is abandoned two years later because of fighting with the hostile aboriginals

◀ *Mah-Min or The Feather,* **painting of an Assiniboine chief by Paul Kane c.1856**

The First Europeans

The Norse sagas of Northern Europe tell how Vikings from Iceland first reached the coast of Labrador in AD 986 and made a series of unsuccessful attempts to establish a colony here. Leif "the Lucky" Ericsson sailed from Greenland in 988, naming the country he found in the west Vinland after the wild grapes found growing in abundance there. Around 1000 AD Thorfinn Karlsefni tried to establish a Vinland colony. Thorfinn's group wintered in Vinland but sailed home to Greenland in the spring, convinced that a colony was impossible as there were too few colonists and the *skraelings* (aboriginals) were hostile. Remarkably, remains of this early Viking settlement were discovered in Newfoundland in 1963 *(see p75)*.

Italian navigator and explorer John Cabot

The English Invasion

In 1497, the Italian navigator John Cabot (1450–98), on the commission of King Henry VII of England, set sail aboard the *Matthew*, bound for America. On June 24, he found a sheltered place on Newfoundland. Here he went ashore with a small party to claim the land for England. He then went on to chart the eastern coastline before sailing home, where he was greeted as a hero.

In May 1498, Cabot sailed again with five ships and 300 men hoping to find the Northwest Passage to China. Harsh weather drove Cabot to relinquish his efforts and head south to Nova Scotia. Cabot then found himself sailing through a sea littered with icebergs. The fleet perished off the coast of Greenland, and English interest in the new land faded.

The French Arrival

Originally from the port of St. Malo, explorer Jacques Cartier (1491–1557) made his first voyage to Canada in 1534. He reached Labrador, Newfoundland, and the Gulf of the St. Lawrence before landing on

Map of the voyage of Jacques Cartier and his followers by Pierre Descaliers c.1534–41

1541 At the mouth of the Cap Rouge River, Cartier founds Charlesbourg-Royal, the first French settlement in America – it is abandoned in 1543

1567 Samuel de Champlain "Father of New France" born

1605 Samuel de Champlain and the Sieur de Roberval found Port Royal, now Annapolis Royal, Nova Scotia

1525   **1550**   **1575**   **1600**

1535 Cartier sails up the St. Lawrence River to Stadacona (Quebec City) and Hochelaga (Montreal)

Jacques Cartier

1608 Champlain founds Quebec City, creating the first permanent European settlement in Canada

1610 Henry Hudson explores Hudson Bay

Anticosti Island where he realized he was at the mouth of a great river. A year later, he returned and sailed up the St. Lawrence River to the site of what is now Quebec City, and then on to a native encampment at Hochelega, which he named Montreal. In 1543, Cartier's hopes for a successful colony died when, after a bitter and barren winter, he and his dispirited group returned to France. Seventy more years would pass before French colonists returned to Canada to stay.

Champlain, "Father of New France," fighting the Iroquois

The Father of New France

Samuel de Champlain (1567–1635) was a man of many parts – navigator, soldier, visionary – and first made the journey from France to Canada in 1603. While the ship that carried him across the Atlantic lay at Tadoussac, Champlain ascended the St. Lawrence River by canoe to the Lachine Rapids.

Champlain's 1605 attempt to found a colony at Port Royal failed, but in 1608 the seeds of a first tiny French colony at Quebec City were planted, with the construction of three two-story houses, a courtyard, and a watchtower, surrounded by a wooden wall.

The economic engine propelling Champlain was the fur trade. In its name he made alliances with the Algonquins and Hurons; fought their dreaded enemies, the Iroquois; traveled to Huron country, now central Ontario; and saw the Great Lakes. Champlain and the other Frenchmen who followed him not only established lasting settlements in the St. Lawrence Valley but also explored half a continent. They built a

"New France" that, at its zenith, stretched south from Hudson Bay to New Orleans in Louisiana, and from Newfoundland almost as far west as the Rockies. In 1612 Champlain became French Canada's first head of government.

Champlain's efforts also helped to create the religious climate that enabled orders such as the Jesuits to establish missions. But his work also laid the seeds of conflict with the English that would last well into the next century and beyond.

Hudson's last voyage

The Hudson's Bay Company

In 1610, English voyager Henry Hudson landed at the bay that still bears his name. The bay's access to many key waterways and trading routes ensured the fortunes of the fur trade. Founded in 1670, the Hudson's Bay Company won control of the lands that drained into the bay, gaining a fur-trading monopoly over the area. The company was challenged only by Scottish merchants who established the North West Company in Montreal in 1783. By 1821, these two companies amalgamated, and the Hudson's Bay Company remains Canada's largest fur trader to this day.

1648–9 The Iroquois disperse the Huron nation and Jesuit father Jean de Brébeuf is martyred during Iroquois raids on Huronia

Engraving of Iroquois

1702 French and British rivalries result in outbreak of Queen Anne's War

| 1625 | 1650 | 1675 | 1700 |

1629 British adventurer David Kirke captures Quebec, but it is returned to France in 1632

Raccoon pelt

1670 The Hudson's Bay Company is founded by royal charter and underwritten by a group of English merchants

1676 Population of New France swelled to 8,500 by settlers

Anglo-French Hostilities

Throughout the 18th century, hostilities between the French and English in Europe continued to spill over into the New World. By 1713, Britain ruled Nova Scotia, Newfoundland, and the Hudson Bay region and, after the Seven Years War in 1763, all of French Canada.

Anglo-French tensions were exacerbated by religion: the English were largely Protestant and almost all of the French Catholic. This resulted in the colony of Quebec being divided in 1791 into the mainly English-speaking Upper Canada (now Ontario), and majority French-speaking Lower Canada (now Quebec).

Taking advantage of the British conflict with Napoleon in Europe, the Americans invaded Canada in 1812. They were defeated by 1814, but the threat of another invasion colored Canadian history during much of the 19th century.

The Acadian Exodus
French-speaking Acadians were ruthlessly expelled from their homes by the British in the 1750s *(see pp66–7)*.

The Plains of Abraham, in Quebec, were the site of victory for the British over the French.

General Isaac Brock
Brock's heroic exploits during the War of 1812, such as the capture of an American post at Detroit, buoyed the spirits of the Canadian people.

United Empire Loyalists
The surrender of British General Cornwallis effectively ended the American Revolution (1775–83). A large number of United Empire Loyalists, refugees from the newly formed United States who remained loyal to the British crown, fled to Canada. They swelled the British population by 50,000.

The Seven Years War
The famous Battle of the Plains of Abraham in 1759 was the last between British and French forces to take place in Canada. The British launched a surprise assault from the cliffs of the St. Lawrence River at a site now known as Wolfe's Cove. Louis Joseph de Montcalm, the French commander, was defeated by General Wolfe and his army. Both generals were killed, and Quebec fell to the British. The war finally ended in 1763 with the Treaty of Paris, which ceded all French-Canadian territory to the British.

Louisbourg

The French fortress of Louisbourg on Cape Breton Island was built between 1720 and 1740, and was the headquarters for the French fleet until it was destroyed by the British in 1758. Today, the restored fortress is a popular tourist attraction with historically costumed guides (see pp100–101).

General Wolfe

The distinguished British soldier, shown here fatally wounded at the Plains of Abraham, preceded his 1759 victory in Quebec with the taking of the French fortress, Louisbourg, in 1758.

General Wolfe's forces sailed up the St. Lawrence River overnight, allowing them to surprise the enemy at Quebec.

French Rights

In 1774 the British government passed the Quebec Act, granting French-Canadians religious and linguistic freedom and giving official recognition to French Civil Law.

Wolfe's infantry scrambled up a steep, wooded cliff. They had to defeat an enemy post before the waiting boats of soldiers could join the battle.

1720	1740	1760	1780	1800

1743 The La Vérendrye brothers discover the Rocky Mountains

1755 Expulsion of the Acadians from Nova Scotia

1758 Louisbourg, the French fortress on Cape Breton Island, falls to the British

Sir Alexander Mackenzie

1793 Scottish explorer and fur trader Alexander Mackenzie crosses the Rockies and reaches the Pacific Ocean by land

1713 British gain control of Nova Scotia, Newfoundland, and Hudson Bay

1759 Wolfe defeats de Montcalm in the Battle of the Plains of Abraham

Medal for the British capture of Quebec 1759

1760 Montreal falls to the British

1774 The Quebec Act grants French colonists rights to their own language and religion

1812 The US at war with Britain until the Treaty of Ghent in 1814

A British Dominion

Twenty-five years after the War of 1812 ended in stalemate, violence of a different sort flared in Canada. The English wanted supremacy in voting power and to limit the influence of the Catholic Church. By 1834 the French occupied one quarter of public positions, although they made up three-quarters of the population. Rebellions in Upper and Lower Canada during 1837–38 were prompted by both French and British reformers, who wanted accountable government with a broader electorate. The response of the British Government was to join together the two colonies into a united Province of Canada in 1840. The newly created assembly won increased independence when, in 1849, the majority Reform Party passed an Act compensating the 1837 rebels. Although the Governor-General, Lord Elgin, disapproved, he chose not to use his veto. The Province of Canada now had "responsible government," (the right to pass laws without the sanction of the British colonial representative.)

The rest of British North America, however, remained a series of self-governing colonies that, despite their economic successes, were anxious about American ambitions. Such fears were reinforced by a series of Fenian Raids on Canadian territory between 1866–70. (The Fenians were New York Irish immigrants hoping to take advantage of French Canada's anti-British feeling to help them to secure independence for Ireland.) The issue of

Representatives meet in London to discuss terms of union

confederation was raised and discussed at conferences held from 1864 onward. Only by uniting in the face of this common menace, said the politicians, could the British colonies hope to fend off these incursions.

The new country was born on July 1, 1867. Under the terms of the British North America Act the new provinces of Quebec (Canada East) and Ontario (Canada West) were created, and along with Nova Scotia and New Brunswick became the Dominion of Canada. The new government was based on the British parliamentary system, with a governor-general (the Crown's representative), a House of Commons, and a Senate. Parliament received power to legislate over matters of national interest; defense, criminal law, and trade, while the provinces ruled over local issues such as education.

The Metis Rebellion

Following confederation, the government purchased from the Hudson's Bay Company the area known as Rupert's Land, which

Northwest rebel Louis Riel

1818 Canada's border with the United States is defined as the 49th Parallel from Lake of the Woods to the Rocky Mountains

1839 Lord Durham issues a report recommending the establishment of responsible government and the union of Upper and Lower Canada to speed the assimilation of French-speaking Canadians

1849 The boundary of the 49th Parallel is extended to the Pacific Ocean

1820 **1830** **1840** **1850**

1821 Merger of Hudson's Bay and North West Companies

1837 A general feeling that the government is not democratic leads to violent but unsuccessful rebellions in Upper and Lower Canada

1841 An Act of Union unites Upper and Lower Canada as the Province of Canada extended south and west inland for thousands of kilometers from Hudson's Bay. The Métis people (descendants of mostly French fur-traders and natives) who lived here were alarmed by the expected influx of English-speaking settlers. In 1869, local leader Louis Riel took up their cause and led the first of two uprisings. The Red River Rebellion was an attempt to defend what the Métis saw as their ancestral rights to this land. A compromise was reached in 1870 and the new province of, Manitoba was created. However, many Métis moved westward to what was to become the province of Saskatchewan in 1905.

Driving home the last spike of the Canadian Pacific Railroad, 1885

Riel was elected to the House of Commons in 1874 but, in 1875, he emigrated to the US. The government's intention to settle the west led the Métis of Saskatchewan to call Riel home in 1884 to lead the North-West Rebellion. It was short-lived. Defeated at Batoche in May, Riel was ultimately charged with treason and hanged in Regina on November 16, 1885.

Birth of a Nation

The defeat of the Métis and the building of a transcontinental railroad were crucial factors in the settlement of the west. British Columbia, a Crown colony since 1858, chose to join the Dominion in 1871 on the promise of a rail link with the rest of the country. The first train to run from Montreal to Vancouver in 1886 paved the way for hundreds of thousands of settlers in the West in the late 1800s. Prince Edward Island, Canada's smallest province, joined the Dominion in 1873.

In 1898, the northern territory of Yukon was established to ensure Canadian jurisdiction over that area during the Klondike gold rush (see pp54–5). In 1905, the provinces of Saskatchewan and Alberta were created out of Rupert's Land, with the residual area becoming the Northwest Territories. Each province gained its own premier and elected assembly. By 1911 new immigrants had doubled the populations of the new provinces.

For the time being, Newfoundland preferred to remain a British colony, but in 1949 it was brought into Canada as the country's tenth province.

The Metis People

The Métis people of central Canada were descended from native and largely French stock. Proud of their unique culture, this seminomadic group considered themselves separate from the rest of the Dominion. With their own social structure and lifestyle dependent almost entirely on buffalo hunting, they resisted integration. They responded to the unification of the country with two failed rebellions. The Métis won no land rights and were condemned to a life of poverty or enforced integration.

Métis hunt buffalo on the Prairie

Sir John MacDonald

1867 Dominion of Canada; Sir John A. Macdonald is Canada's first Prime Minister

1870 The Red River Rebellion is quashed by General Wolseley, and the the province of Manitoba is created

General Wolseley

1886 Gold found on the Forty-Mile River

1860

1870

1880

1866 The Fenians raid Canadian territory to divert British troops from Ireland

1855 Queen Victoria designates Ottawa as capital of the Province of Canada

Canadian Pacific

1885 Riel leads the North-West Rebellion. The Métis are defeated at Batoche, and Riel is hanged in Regina. The last spike of the transcontinental railroad is put in place

The Klondike Gold Rush

There had been rumors of gold in the Yukon since the 1830s, but the harsh land, together with the Chilkoot Indians' guarding of their territory, kept most prospectors away. Then, on August 16, 1896 the most frenzied and fabled gold rush in Canadian history started when George Washington Carmack and two Indian friends, Snookum Jim and Tagish Charlie, found a large gold nugget in the river they later named Bonanza Creek. For the next two years at least 100,000 prospectors set out for the new gold fields.

Only about 40,000 prospectors actually made it. Most took boats as far as Skagway or Dyea, on the Alaskan Panhandle, then struggled across the Coast Mountains by the White or Chilkoot passes to reach the headwaters of the Yukon River. From here boats took them 500 km (310 miles) to the gold fields. In all, the gold rush generated Can $50 million, although few miners managed to hold onto their fortunes.

Klondike Entrepreneur
Alex McDonald, a Nova Scotian with a canny business sense, bought up the claims of discouraged miners and hired others to work them for him. Known as "King of the Klondike," he made millions.

The stern`wheeler was a steamboat driven by a single paddle at the back.

Skagway, Alaska
The jumping-off point for the Klondike was the tent city of Skagway. There were saloons and swindlers on every corner, and gunfire in the streets was commonplace. The most famous con man was Jefferson Randolph "Soapy" Smith, who died in a shoot-out in 1898.

The Yukon River rises in British Columbia's Coast Mountains, winding for 3,000 km (1,900 miles) to Alaska.

The Mounties Take Control
The safety of the Klondike Gold Rush was secured by Canada's red-coated Mounties. Thanks to them, the rush was remarkably peaceful. A small force of 19 Mounties led by Inspector Charles Constantine were sent to the Yukon in 1895, but by 1898 there were 285, operating out of Fort Herchmer at Dawson.

Klondike Fever
The outside world learnt of the riches in July 1897, when miners docked in Seattle and San Francisco hauling gold. In no time, Klondike fever became an epidemic.

Dawson City
As the gold rush developed in the summer of 1897, the small tent camp at the junction of the Klondike and Yukon rivers grew to a population of 5,000. A year on it had reached 40,000, making Dawson City one of the largest cities in Canada.

Steamboats and other craft brought thousands of prospectors up the long Yukon River to Dawson, where the boats jostled for space at the dock.

Capturing the Mood
Even literature had a place in the Klondike. The gold rush inspired novels such as *Call of the Wild* (1903) by Jack London (shown here) and the 1907 verses *Songs of a Sourdough* by poet Robert Service.

Crossing the Yukon River
The ferocious Yukon River rapids in Miles Canyon smashed so many boats to splinters that the Mounties decreed that every boat had to be guided by a competent pilot. Experienced sailors could earn up to Can$100 a trip taking boats through the canyon. Past the canyon, only one more stretch of rapids remained before the Yukon's waters grew calmer all the way to Dawson City.

1896 George Carmack and two friends, Tagish Charlie and Snookum Jim, strike it rich on Bonanza Creek. Liberal Wilfred Laurier elected as the country's first French-Canadian prime minister

Klondike News 1898

1898 The Yukon is given territorial status, partly to assert British authority in the eyes of the Americans from neighboring Alaska

| 1896 | 1897 | 1898 | 1899 |

1897 Steamers from Alaska carry word of the strike to San Francisco and Seattle, setting off a frenzied gold rush

1899 Gold is discovered in Nome, Alaska, and Dawson begins to shrink as people leave to follow the new dream of riches farther west

New Optimism and Arrivals

The impact of the Klondike gold rush was felt all over Canada. It led to an expansion of cities such as Vancouver and Edmonton, and the establishment of the Yukon territory. A period of optimism was ushered in by the new Liberal government, elected in 1896 under the first French-Canadian premier, Wilfred Laurier, who firmly believed that "the 20th century will belong to Canada."

The new central Canadian provinces provided a home for European immigrants eager to farm large tracts of prairie land. By 1913, this wave of immigration had peaked at 400,000. Finally Canada began to profit from a prosperous world economy and establish itself as an industrial and agricultural power.

1914 poster promoting immigration to Canada

Supporting the Allies

The first overseas test of Canada's military forces came in 1899, when the Boer War broke out in South Africa; the second in 1914, when Europe entered World War I. Initially,

Laurier was cautious in his approach to the South African crisis, but pressure from the English-speaking population led to the dispatch of 1,000 soldiers to Cape Town in 1899. Before the Boer War ended in 1902, some 6,000 men had made the journey to serve with the British on the South African battlefields. They returned with a stronger sense of national identity than many of their compatriots at home had expected. But, while the experience of war infused some with a new sense of national unity, it also laid bare divisions. There were fights between French- and English-speaking university students, as well as disputes among Ontario conservatives and French-speaking Quebec politicians.

Before matters could come to a head, another crisis loomed. Joining the Allies in Flanders, the Canadians found renewed glory during World War I. Canadian pilot, Billy Bishop, was the Allies' greatest air ace, and another Canadian, Roy Brown, was the pilot credited with downing the Red Baron. Canadian troops were the heroes of two major battles, Ypres (1915) and Vimy Ridge (1917). When peace was declared on November 11, 1918, there were 175,000 Canadian wounded, and 60,000 had died for their country.

Independent Status

Canada had played so significant a role during World War I that it gained recognition as an independent country, winning representation

Canadians advance at Paardeberg in the Boer War, 1900

1899 The first Canadians are sent to fight in the Boer War	**1911** Robert Borden and the Conservatives win federal election, defeating Liberal party leader Wilfred Laurier on the issue of the Naval Bill	**1917** Munitions ship explodes in Halifax harbor wiping out 5 sq km (2 sq miles) of the town, killing 2,000, and injuring 9,000	**1918** Canadians break through the German trenches at Amiens beginning "Canada's Hundred Days"
1900	**1905**	**1910**	**1915**	**1920**
1903 Canada loses the Alaska boundary dispute when a British tribunal sides with the US	**1914** Britain declares war on Germany, automatically drawing Canada into the conflict in Europe. The War Measures Act orders German and Austro-Hungarian Canadians to carry identity cards		**1922** Canadians Charles Best, Frederick Banting, and John MacLeod win the Nobel Prize for the discovery of insulin

Dr. Frederick Banting

in the League of Nations. This independence was confirmed in 1931 with the passing of the Statute of Westminster, which gave Canada political independence from Britain and created a commonwealth of sovereign nations under a single crown.

Soup kitchen during the Great Depression

However, national optimism was curtailed by the Great Depression that originated with the Wall Street Crash in 1929. Drought laid waste the farms of Alberta, Saskatchewan, and Manitoba. One in four workers was unemployed, and the sight of men riding boxcars in a fruitless search for work became common.

World War II

The need to supply the Allied armies during World War II boosted Canada out of the Depression. Canada's navy played a crucial role in winning the Battle of the Atlantic (1940–43), and thousands of Allied airmen were trained in Canada. Canadian regiments soon gained a reputation for bravery – for example, many died in the 1942 raid on Dieppe. Thousands battled in Italy, while others stormed ashore at Normandy. In the bitter fighting that followed, the Second and Third Canadian Divisions took more casualties holding the beachheads than any unit under British command. It was also the Canadians who liberated much of Holland.

The Canadian prime minister of the day was the Liberal Mackenzie King (1935–48). He ordered a plebiscite to have conscripts sent overseas to meet an infantry shortage in the last months of the war, monitored the building of the Alaska Highway (see pp266–7), and directed a massive war effort.

An International Voice

When peace finally came in September 1945, Canada had the third-largest navy in the world, the fourth-largest air force, and a standing army of 730,000 men. Although the price Canada had paid during World War II was high – 43,000 people died in action and the national debt quadrupled – the nation found itself in a strong position. A larger population was better able to cope with

German prisoners captured by Canadian Infantry on D-Day, June 6, 1944

1925	1930	1935	1940	1945
1926 The Balfour Report defines British dominions as autonomous and equal in status	*Air Canada logo*	**1937** Trans-Canada Air Lines, now Air Canada, begins regular flights	**1942** Around 22,000 Japanese Canadians are stripped of non-portable possessions and interned	**1944** Canadian troops push farther inland than any other allied units on D-Day
1929 The Great Depression begins	**1931** The Statute of Westminster grants Canada full legislative authority		**1941** Hong Kong falls to the Japanese, and Canadians are taken as POWs	**1945** World War II ends. Canada joins the UN. Canada's first nuclear reactor goes on line in Chalk River, Ontario

Large Canadian grain carrier approaches the St. Lawrence Seaway in 1959 – its inaugural year

its losses and much of the debt had been spent on doubling the gross national product, creating durable industries that would power the postwar economy. Since World War II, Canada's economy has continued to expand. This growth, combined with government social programs such as old-age security, unemployment insurance, and medicare, means Canadians have one of the world's highest standards of living and a quality of life which draws immigrants from around the world. Since 1945, those immigrants have been made up largely of southern Europeans, Asians, South Americans, and Caribbean islanders, all of whom have enriched the country's multicultural status.

Internationally, the nation's reputation and influence have grown. Canada has participated in the United Nations since its inception in 1945 and is the only nation to have taken part in almost all of the UN's major peacekeeping operations. Perhaps it is only fitting that it was a future Canadian prime minister, Lester Pearson, who fostered the peacekeeping process when he won the Nobel Peace Prize in 1957 for helping resolve the Suez Crisis. Canada is also a respected member of the British Commonwealth, la Francophonie, the Group of Eight industrialized nations, the OAS (Organization of American States), and NATO (North Atlantic Treaty Organization).

The French–English Divide

Given all these accomplishments, it seems ironic that the last quarter of a century has also seen Canadians deal with fundamental questions of national identity and unity. The driving force of this debate continues to be the historic English–French rivalry. The best-known players of these late 20th-century events are Prime Minister Pierre Trudeau (1968–84) and Quebec Premier René Lévesque (1976–85).

When Jean Lesage was elected as Quebec Premier in 1960, he instituted the "Quiet Revolution" – a series of reforms that increased provincial power. However, this was not enough to prevent the rise of revolutionary

Quebec Premier René Levesque and Canadian Prime Minister Pierre Trudeau during the 1980 referendum

1950 The Canadian Army Special Force joins UN soldiers in the Korean War

1957 Lester Pearson wins the Nobel Peace Prize for helping resolve the Suez Crisis

Lester Pearson

1980 Quebec votes against separation in the 1980 Quebec Referendum

1950	1955	1960	1965	1970	1975	1980

1949 New-foundland joins the Confederation. Canada joins NATO

1965 Canada's new flag is inaugurated after a bitter political debate

1976 The Olympic games are held in Montreal under tight security. René Lévesque and the separatist *Parti Québecois* win a provincial election

Marc Garneau

1990 demonstration for Quebec independence in Montreal

nationalists. In October 1970, British Trade Commissioner James Cross and Quebec Labor Minister Pierre Laporte were kidnapped by the French-Canadian terrorist organization, the Front du Libération de Québec (FLQ). Cross was rescued by police but Laporte was later found murdered. Trudeau invoked the War Measures Act, sent troops into Montreal, and banned the FLQ. His actions eventually led to nearly 500 arrests.

Trudeau devoted his political life to federalism, fighting separatism, and giving Canada its own constitution. In contrast, Quebec Premier René Lévesque campaigned for a 1980 referendum in Quebec on whether that province should become independent. A majority voted against, but the results were far from decisive, and separatism continued to dominate the country's political agenda. However, in 1982, the Constitution Act fulfilled Trudeau's dream, entrenching federal civil rights and liberties such as female equality.

A Move Toward Conservatism

In 1984 the leader of the Progressive Conservatives, Brian Mulroney, won the

general election with the largest majority in Canadian history. Dismissive of Trudeau's policies, Mulroney's emphasis was on closer links with Europe and, in particular, the US. In the years that followed, two major efforts were made to reform the constitutional system. The 1987 Meech Lake Accord aimed to recognize Quebec's claims to special status on the basis of its French culture, but Mulroney failed to implement the amendment since it did not obtain the consent of all provinces. The Charlottetown Accord of 1992, which raised the issue of aboriginal self-government, was triggered by Quebec sovereignty issues. The Accord was rejected in a national referendum held in 1992.

Today, many of these reforms are finally in place and hopefully aiding Canadian unity. Quebec's French heritage has official recognition, and the Inuit rule their own territory of Nunavut.

Independence for Nunavut

On April 1, 1999, Canada gained its newest territory, the Inuit homeland of Nunavut. The campaign for an Inuit state began in the 1960s when the Inuit desire for a political identity of their own was added to aboriginal land

Signing ceremony in Iqaluit, April 1, 1999

claims. Nunavut's first Premier was 34-year-old Paul Okalik, leader of the first-ever Inuit majority government over an 85 percent Inuit population. English is being replaced as the official language by the native Inuktitut, and traditional Inuit fishing and hunting skills are being reintroduced. By 2012, the federal government had invested over Can$1 billion in public services for Nunavut.

1985	1990	1995	2000	2005	2010	2015

1988 Calgary hosts the XV Winter Olympics

1999 The Inuit territory of Nunavut established

Canadian & Nunavut flags

2010 Vancouver & Whistler host the XXI Winter Olympics

1984 Aboard the US shuttle *Challenger*, Marc Garneau becomes the first Canadian in space

1989 The Canada–US Free Trade agreement goes into effect

1997 A 13-km (8-mile) bridge connecting Prince Edward Island to the mainland is opened

2006 Conservative government under Stephen Harper wins minority government. This achievement is repeated in 2008

2012 Canada celebrates Queen Elizabeth II's Diamond Jubilee

ATLANTIC CANADA

Introducing Atlantic Canada

Atlantic Canada is renowned for rocky coastlines, picturesque fishing villages, sun-warmed beaches, cozy country inns, and friendly people. Each province has a distinctive flavor. In northeastern New Brunswick, French-speaking Acadian culture flourishes, while the south coast offers the pristine, tide-carved beauty of the Bay of Fundy. Nova Scotia, famous for the stunning natural scenery of the Cabot Trail, is also home to historic towns like seafaring Lunenburg and Annapolis Royal, the only town in Canada designated a National Historic Site. Prince Edward Island is known for its emerald-green farmland, sandy beaches, and rich lobster catches. In Newfoundland, the mountains of Gros Morne National Park rise 800 m (2,625 ft) above sparkling blue fjords. Labrador offers an imposing and stunning coastal landscape, often with a backdrop of glittering icebergs.

The fresh maritime scenery of Two Islands beach, known as "The Brothers" for its twin offshore islands, in Parrsboro, Nova Scotia

Contemporary Acadian homesteads flourish after 400 years of a unique culture in northeastern New Brunswick

◀ Nova Scotia lighthouse

Key

≡ Expressway
≡ Divided highway
▬ Highway
═ Other road
╍ Main railway
▬ Minor railway
▬ Regional border
△ Summit

Nain

Hopedale
Makkovik
Cape Harrison
Kanairiktok
Rigolet
Lake Melville
Labrador   Cartwright
Happy Valley-Goose Bay

NEWFOUNDLAND & LABRADOR

Mary's Harbour
Belle Isle
Cape Bauld
Blanc-Sablon
St. Anthony
St. Barbe
Roddickton
La Tabatière   Port Saunders
Harrington Harbour

Gulf of St. Lawrence

Baie Verte
Gros Morne 808m
Deer Lake
Grand Falls
Gander
Corner Brook
Bonavista
Newfoundland
Clarenville
Carbonear
Table Mountain 587m
St. John's
Îles de la Madeleine
Channel-Port aux Basques
Marystown
Argentia
Grand Bank
St-Pierre & Miquelon (FRANCE)

Cabot Strait

ris

Sydney

OTIA

et our

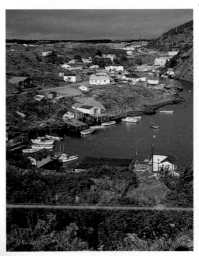

Perched on the Atlantic Coast, Quidi Vidi village, one of the oldest in Newfoundland

0 km   250
0 miles   250

Getting Around

Air Canada and West Jet offer regular flights throughout the region. The Confederation Bridge connects Borden, Prince Edward Island, to Cape Tormentine in New Brunswick. A ferry travels between Wood Island, Prince Edward Island, and Pictou, Nova Scotia, and another links Digby, Nova Scotia, and Saint John, New Brunswick. VIA Rail also operates between Nova Scotia and New Brunswick. Newfoundland must be accessed by air or by ferry from Sydney, Nova Scotia, to either Port aux Basques or Argentia. A high-speed ferry travels between Yarmouth, Nova Scotia, and Bar Harbor and Portland, both in Maine. Bus services cross the provinces, but many areas are remote, so check availability.

For additional map symbols *see back flap*

Maritime Wildlife of Atlantic Canada

The provinces of Atlantic Canada – Nova Scotia, New Brunswick, and Prince Edward Island – along with Newfoundland and Labrador, the Quebec north shore of the St. Lawrence River, and the Gaspé Peninsula, constitute a rich and diverse maritime habitat for wildlife. The climate is dominated by the ocean, being influenced by the moderating Gulf Stream that flows north from the Caribbean and by the southward flow of icy waters, often bearing icebergs, from the Canadian Arctic. The terrain of the eastern Canadian coastline varies from rocky headlands to soft, sandy beaches. Both sea and land mammals inhabit this coast, as do hundreds of species of seabird.

The piping plover is a small, endangered shore bird that lives and breeds along the Atlantic coast of Canada.

Shoreline Habitat

The maritime shoreline encompasses rocky cliffs, sandy beaches, and salt-flat marshes. Moving a little inland, the landscape shifts to bog, forest, and meadow. It is an inviting habitat for many smaller mammals such as raccoons and beavers, and also provides a home for a diversity of bird life. Where the shoreline meets the water, fertile intertidal zones are a habitat for mollusks, algae, and invertebrae.

The river otter lives in "families," frequenting rivers, lakes, and ocean bays, in its search for fish.

The common puffin is a shoreline bird, which lives on cliff edges and is characterized by a brightly colored bill and its curious, friendly nature.

The raccoon, with its ringed tail and black-masked face, preys upon fish, crayfish, birds and their eggs.

The beaver, symbol of Canada, lives in marshy woodland near streams and rivers. It gnaws down trees, using them to build dams and its lodge.

Ocean Habitat

The sea around Atlantic Canada is influenced by the cold Labrador Current flowing from the north, the Gulf Stream from the south, and the large outflow of fresh water at the mouth of the St. Lawrence River. The region is home to myriad ocean creatures, and the highest tides in the world at the nutrient-rich Bay of Fundy. Off Newfoundland lie the Grand Banks, once one of the Earth's richest fishing grounds. Over-fishing has endangered fish stocks, and quotas are now limited.

Lobster, a favorite seafood of the area, is caught in traps set near the shore. Rigid conservation rules have been put in force to protect its numbers.

The adult blue whale is the world's largest mammal, reaching up to 30 m (100 ft) long. Today, whale-watching is a growing eco-tourism enterprise, particularly in Digby, where this and other species congregate.

The Atlantic salmon, unlike its Pacific cousins, returns to its home stream to spawn several times during its lifetime. Atlantic salmon are renowned sport fish (see p29).

Bottle-nosed dolphins, characterized by their long beaks and "smiles," live off the east coast, in both New Brunswick and Nova Scotia.

Seabirds of the Atlantic Coast

The maritime coast of eastern Canada is a perfect environment for seabirds. Rocky cliffs and headlands provide ideal rookeries. The rich coastal waters and intertidal zones ensure a generous larder for many species, including the cormorant and storm petrel. Some Atlantic Coast seabirds are at risk due to environmental changes, but puffins and razorbills, in particular, continue to thrive.

The double-crested cormorant or "sea crow," as it is sometimes known, is a diving fishing bird, capable of capturing food as deep as 10 m (30 ft) under water.

Leach's storm-petrel is part of the Tubenose family of birds, whose acute sense of smell helps them navigate while out at sea.

The Acadians

Few stories surrounding the settlement of the New World evoke as many feelings of tragedy and triumph as the tale of the Acadians. Colonizing Nova Scotia's fertile Annapolis Valley in the 1600s, 500 French settlers adopted the name Acadie, hoping to establish an ideal pastoral land. They prospered and, by 1750, numbered 14,000, becoming the dominant culture. The threat of this enclave proved too much for a town run by the British, and in 1755 the Acadians were expelled overseas, many to the US. When England and France made peace in 1763, the Acadians slowly returned. Today their French-speaking culture still thrives in some areas.

Acadian women play a part in summer festivals, displaying local woolcraft and linen textiles.

Ile Sainte-Croix was the earliest Acadian settlement, established by the French in New Brunswick in 1604. The neat, spacious layout of the village is typical.

Acadian Farming

As hardworking farmers, Acadians cleared the land of the Annapolis Valley, built villages, and developed an extensive system of dikes to reclaim the rich farmland from tidal waters. Summer crops were carefully harvested for the winter; potatoes and vegetables were put in cellars, and hay stored to feed cattle and goats. By the 19th century, Acadian farmers had expanded their crop range to include tobacco and flax.

An important crop, hay was raked into *"chafauds,"* spiked haystacks that dried in the fields for use as winter animal feed.

The Expulsion of the Acadians took place in August 1755. British troops brutally rounded up the Acadians for enforced deportation. More than 6,000 Acadians were put on boats, some bound for the US, where they became the Cajuns of today. Some returned in later years, and today their descendants live in villages throughout Atlantic Canada.

The Acadian people maintained a traditional farming and fishing lifestyle for centuries, re-created today at the Village Historique Acadien *(see p83)*.

The Church of Saint Anne in Sainte-Anne-du-Ruisseau represents Acadian style in its fresh simplicity and elegance. Catholicism was very important to the Acadians, who turned to their priests for succour during the 1755 diaspora.

Acadian musicians have reflected their culture since the 17th century. Playing lively violin and guitar folk music, they are known for their upbeat tunes and ballads of unrequited love and social dispossession.

Acadian life revolved around the farmsteads in each community. Men tilled the fields and fished while women helped with the annual harvest.

Henry Wadsworth Longfellow

One of the most popular poets of the 19th century, both in the US and Europe, the American Henry Longfellow (1807–82) is best known for his long, bittersweet narrative poems. Based on the trials and injustices of the Acadian civilization, *Evangeline*, published in 1847, traces the paths of a young Acadian couple. The poem, now regarded as a classic, stirringly records Evangeline's tragic loss in this land intended as an idyll when their love was destroyed through the upheavals and expulsion of the 18th century: "Loud from its rocky caverns, the deep-faced neighbouring ocean [sings], List to the mournful tradition sung by the pines of the Forest, … List to a Tale of Love in Acadie, home of the happy."

NEWFOUNDLAND AND LABRADOR

With towering peaks, vast landscapes, and 17,000 km (10,500 miles) of rugged coastline, Newfoundland and Labrador displays wild, open spaces and grand spectacles of nature. In this captivating land, massive icebergs drift lazily along the coast, whales swim in sparkling bays, and moose graze placidly in flat open marshes.

Newfoundland's west coast offers some of the most dramatic landscapes east of the Rockies. The granite mountains of Gros Morne National Park shelter deep fjords, while the eastern part of the island has a more rounded terrain, featuring the bays and inlets of Terra Nova National Park. Part of the area's appeal is retracing the history of past cultures that have settled here, including Maritime Archaic Indians at Port au Choix, Vikings at L'Anse-Aux-Meadows, and Basque whalers at Red Bay in the Labrador Straits.

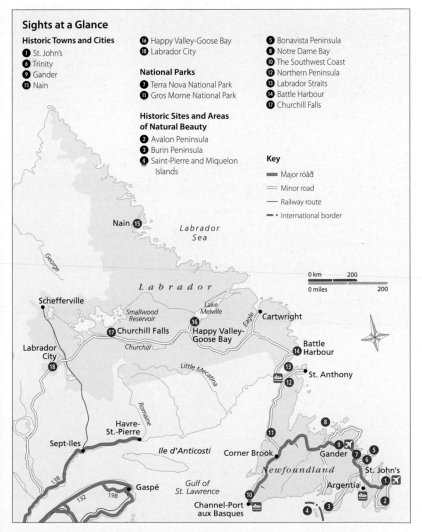

Sights at a Glance

Historic Towns and Cities
- ❶ St. John's
- ❻ Trinity
- ❾ Gander
- ❶❺ Nain

- ❶❻ Happy Valley-Goose Bay
- ❶❽ Labrador City

National Parks
- ❼ Terra Nova National Park
- ❶❶ Gros Morne National Park

Historic Sites and Areas of Natural Beauty
- ❷ Avalon Peninsula
- ❸ Burin Peninsula
- ❹ Saint-Pierre and Miquelon Islands

- ❺ Bonavista Peninsula
- ❽ Notre Dame Bay
- ❶⓿ The Southwest Coast
- ❶❷ Northern Peninsula
- ❶❸ Labrador Straits
- ❶❹ Battle Harbour
- ❶❼ Churchill Falls

Key
- ▬▬ Major road
- ═══ Minor road
- ─── Railway route
- ▬·▬ International border

Nain ❶❺

Labrador Sea

George

Labrador

Schefferville

Smallwood Reservoir

Lake Melville

Cartwright

Eagle

❶❼ Churchill Falls

❶❻ Happy Valley-Goose Bay

Churchill

Battle ❶❹ Harbour

Labrador City ❶❽

Little Mecatina

❶❸

❶❷ St. Anthony

Romaine

Havre-St.-Pierre

Sept-Iles

138

Ile d'Anticosti

Corner Brook

❶❶

❽

❾ ✈ ❼ ❺

Gander ❻

Newfoundland

St. John's

❶ ✈

Argentia

❷

Gaspé

132   198

Gulf of St. Lawrence

❶⓿

Channel-Port aux Basques

❹   ❸

◀ Cape St. Mary's Ecological Reserve, Avalon Peninsula, Newfoundland, Canada

For map symbols *see back flap*

① St. John's

Italian explorer Giovanni Caboto (John Cabot) *(see p48)* aroused great interest in Newfoundland (after his 1497 voyage on behalf of Henry VII of England) when he described "a sea so full of fish that a basket thrown overboard is hauled back brimming with cod." Cabot started a rush to the New World that made St. John's a center of the fishing industry, and one of North America's oldest settlements. Today, St. John's still bustles with the commerce of the sea: fishing, oil exploration, and the ships of a hundred nations waiting to be serviced. The people of St. John's are known for their friendliness, a delightful counterpoint to the harsh, rugged beauty that surrounds this historic town.

Downtown St. John's, seen from the approach by sea

Exploring St. John's

The capital of Newfoundland is easily explored on foot. Most of the sights are within a short distance of each other moving east along Water Street. Approaching by sea offers the best view of the harbor, in particular the steep cliff-lined passage on the east side where pastel-colored old houses cling to the rocks.

🏛 Murray Premises

cnr Water St. & Beck's Cove.
Open 8am–10:30pm daily. ♿
At the west end of Water Street stands Murray Premises. Built in 1846, these rambling brick and timberframe buildings are the last remaining examples of the large mercantile and fish-processing premises that were common on the St. John's waterfront. Murray Premises once bustled with the work of shipping cod to world markets.

It narrowly escaped destruction in a huge fire that engulfed the city in 1892, and the buildings mark the western boundary of the fire's devastation. Now a Provincial Historic Site, the restored buildings are home to a boutique hotel and offices.

🏛 The Rooms

9 Bonaventure Ave. **Tel** (709) 757 8000.
Open 10am–5pm Mon–Sat (to 9pm Wed; Museum & Art Gallery also open noon–5pm Sun). **Closed** Jan 1, Mon mid-Oct–May; Dec 25.
Ⓦ **therooms.ca**

A major landmark, The Rooms is a modern facility housing three provincial institutions: the Provincial Archives; the Museum of Newfoundland, which charts the province's history over the past 9,000 years; and the Art Gallery of Newfoundland and Labrador, which showcases the work of local, national, and international artists.

🏛 The Waterfront

Water St. **Tel** (709) 576 8106. ♿
Tracing the edge of St. John's waterfront, Water Street is the oldest public thoroughfare in North America, dating to the late 1500s when trading first started. Once a brawling wharfside lane of gin mills and brothels, Water Street and Duckworth Street now offer gift shops, art galleries, and some of Newfoundland's top restaurants. Harbour Drive, along the waterfront, is a great place to stroll, while George Street is the hub of the city's nightlife.

🏛 Commissariat House

King's Bridge Rd. ℹ (709) 576 8106.
Commissariat House, now a historical site, was built in 1836 and was once the home of 19th-century British officials. The Georgian building now contains a multi-media experience of early 19th century St. John's. Nearby Government House, built during the 1820s, is the official residence of the province's Lieutenant Governor.

🏛 The Battery

Battery Rd. ℹ (709) 576 8106.
The colorful houses clinging to sheer cliffs at the entrance to the Harbour are known as the Battery. With the look and feel of a 19th-century fishing village, this is one of St. John's most photographed sites. The community is named for the military fortifications built here over centuries to defend the harbor. Local residents used the battery's guns in 1763 to fight off Dutch pirate ships.

🎖 Signal Hill Historic Site of Canada

Signal Hill Rd. **Tel** (709) 772 5367.
Open Visitor Centre: Jun–Sep: 8:30am–8pm; Sep–Oct: 8:30am–4:30pm; Oct–May: 8:30am–4:30pm Mon–Fri.
Closed Jan 1 Dec 25, 26. ♿ ♿

This lofty rise of land presents spectacular views of the open Atlantic, the harbor entrance, and the historic splendor of the city of St. John's.

🏛 Cabot Tower

Signal Hill Rd. **Tel** (709) 772 5367.
Open Visitor Centre: May 23–Jun 12: 10am–6pm Wed–Sun; Jun 13–Sep 9: 10am–8pm Tue–Sat, 10am–6pm Sun & Mon; Sep 6–Oct 14: 10am–6pm Sat–Wed; Oct 15–mid-May: by appt. ♿

View of Signal Hill from St. John's picturesque fishing harbor

The Cabot Tower as it rises above Signal Hill over the harbor

The building of Cabot Tower at the top of Signal Hill began in 1897 to celebrate the 400th anniversary of Cabot's arrival. On summer weekends, soldiers in period dress perform 19th-century marching drills, with firing muskets and cannon. It was here that another Italian, Guglielmo Marconi, received the first transatlantic wireless signal in 1901.

🚉 Quidi Vidi Village
Quidi Vidi Village Rd. **Tel** (709) 729 2977. **Open** daily. Brewery open 10am–5:30pm Mon–Sat. 🕐 for brewery tour.

On the other side of Signal Hill, the weathered buildings of ancient Quidi Vidi Village nestle around a small harbor. Above the village, the Quidi Vidi Battery was a fortified gun emplacement built in 1762 to defend the harbor entrance. The province's most popular microbrewery, Quidi Vidi Brewery, is also located on the harbor and offers tasting tours in summer.

🚉 Pippy Park
Nagles Place. **Tel** (709) 737 3655. **Open** daily. 🕐

Visitors are sometimes startled to see moose roaming free in St. John's, but it happens often in this 1,400-ha (3,460-acre) nature park, 4 km (2 miles) from the town center. The park is also home to the ponds and gardens of the local Botanical Gardens. The only Fluvarium in North America is based here too, featuring nine underwater windows that look onto the natural activity of a rushing freshwater trout stream.

🚉 Cape Spear Lighthouse Historic Site of Canada
Tel (709) 772 5367. **Open** May 23–Jun 12: 10am–6pm Wed–Sat; Jun 13–Oct 14: 10am–6pm daily; grounds open all year. 🕐 🕐

Ten km (6 miles) southeast of town, Cape Spear marks the most easterly point in North America. Set atop seaside cliffs, the majestic Cape Spear Lighthouse has long been a symbol of Newfoundland's independence. Two lighthouses sit here. The original, built in 1836 and the oldest in Newfoundland, stands beside a graceful, modern, automated lighthouse, added in 1955.

🚉 East End
King's Bridge Rd. 🛈 (709) 739-8899. East End is one of St. John's most architecturally rich neighborhoods, with narrow, cobblestone streets and elegant homes.

St. John's City Center

① Murray Premises
② The Rooms
③ The Waterfront
④ Commissariat House
⑤ The Battery
⑥ Signal Hill
⑦ Cabot Tower

Whale- and bird-watching boats tour the Avalon Peninsula frequently

❷ Avalon Peninsula

🚌 St. John's. 🚢 Argentia. 🛈 Dept. of Tourism, Confederation Building, St. John's (709) 576 8106.

The picturesque community of Ferryland on the Avalon Peninsula is the site of a large-scale archeological excavation of the Colony of Avalon, a settlement founded by English explorer Lord Baltimore and 11 settlers in 1621. This was Baltimore's first New World venture, intended to be a self-sufficient colony engaged in fishing, agriculture, and trade, with firm principles of religious tolerance.

Boat-tour sign in Witless Bay

By the end of the following year there were 32 settlers. The population continued to grow, and for many years it was the only successful colony in the area. Although excavations to date have unearthed only five percent of the colony, it has proved to be one of the richest sources of artifacts from any early European settlement in North America. Over half a million pieces have been recovered, such as pottery, clay pipes, household implements, and structural parts of many buildings, including defensive works, a smithy, and a waterfront commercial complex. An interpretive center tells the story of the colony and a guided tour includes the chance to watch archeologists working on site and in the laboratory.

At the southern end of the peninsula, **Cape St. Mary's Ecological Reserve** is the only nesting seabird colony in the province that can be approached on foot. A short trail leads along spectacular seacliffs to a site where over 8,000 northern gannets nest on a rock just a few yards over the cliff.

On the southwest side of the peninsula, overlooking the entrance to the historic French town of Placentia, visitors can stroll through **Castle Hill National Historic Site**. These French fortifications dating back to 1662 protected the town, and the site of the remains offers fine coastal views.

🐦 Cape St. Mary's Ecological Reserve

off Route 100. **Tel** (709) 277 1666. **Open** year round. Interpretive Centre: **Open** May–Oct: daily. 🏞 ♿

🏛 Castle Hill National Historic Site of Canada

Jerseyside, Placentia Bay. **Tel** (709) 227 2401. **Open** late Jun–Aug: 8:30am– 8pm; Sep–mid-Jun: 8:30am–4:30pm. 🏞 ♿ 🅿

❸ Burin Peninsula

🚌 St. John's. 🚢 Argentia. 🛈 Columbia Drive, Marystown Jun–Nov: (709) 279 1211; Dec–May: (709) 279 1887.

The Burin Peninsula presents some of the most dramatic and impressive scenery in Newfoundland. Short, craggy peaks rise above a patchwork green carpet of heather, dotted by scores of glittering lakes. In the fishing town of Grand Bank, **The Provincial Seamen's Museum** is a memorial to Newfoundland seamen who perished at sea. The nearby town of Fortune offers a ferry to the French-ruled islands of Saint-Pierre and Miquelon.

🏛 The Provincial Seamen's Museum

Marine Drive. **Tel** (709) 832 1484. **Open** May–Oct: daily. ♿ limited. 🅿

❹ Saint-Pierre and Miquelon Islands

🏔 6,400. ✈ 🚤 🚢 🛈 PO Box 4274, Place de Géneral de Gaulle (508) 41 02 00. 🌐 st-pierre-et-miquelon.com

These two small islands are not Canadian but French, and have been under French rule since the 17th century. Saint-Pierre, the only town on the island of the same name, is a charming French seaside village. The **Saint-Pierre Museum** details the islands' history, including their lively role as a bootlegger's haven during Prohibition in the 1920s when over three million cases of liquor passed through this tiny port annually. Many of the harborfront warehouses originally built for this trade are still standing.

Le Cabestan ferry takes visitors to Saint-Pierre and Miquelon

Cape Bonavista Lighthouse, built on the spot believed to be John Cabot's first landing place in the New World

Miquelon Island is made up of two smaller islands, Langlade and Grand Miquelon, joined by a narrow, 12-km (7-mile) long strand. The road across this sandy isthmus crosses grassy dunes where wild horses graze and surf pounds sandy beaches. A ferry leaves Saint-Pierre for the smaller village of Miquelon three times a week, usually on Tuesday, Wednesday, and Sunday. Another ferry goes to Langlade every day except Tuesday.

🏛 Saint-Pierre Museum
Rue du 11 Novembre. **Tel** (508) 410 435. **Open** Jun–Oct: Tue–Sun. 🅿 ♿

❺ Bonavista Peninsula
🚌 St. John's. 🚢 Argentia.
ℹ Discovery Trail Tourism Association (709) 466 3845.
🌐 **thediscoverytrail.org**

Bonavista Peninsula juts out into the Atlantic ocean, a rugged coastal landscape of seacliffs, harbor inlets, and enchanting small villages such as Birchy Cove and Trouty.

The town of Bonavista is believed to be where Italian explorer John Cabot *(see p48)* first stepped ashore in the New World. His monument stands on a high, rocky promontory, near the Cape Bonavista Lighthouse, built in 1843.

Along the Bonavista waterfront, the huge 19th-century buildings of Ryan Premises, once a busy fish merchants' processing facility, are now restored as a National Historic Site. Ryan Premises include three large buildings where fish were dried, stored, and packed for shipping, and displays on the history of the fisheries in North America. The waterfront salt house offers local music.

❻ Trinity
🏛 300. ℹ Trinity Visitor Centre, West St. (709) 464 2042.

The charming village of Trinity, with its colorful 19th-century buildings overlooking the blue waters of Trinity Bay, is easily one of the most beautiful Newfoundland communities. Best explored on foot, Trinity has a range of craft shops and restaurants. The **Trinity Museum** contains over 2,000 artifacts, illustrating the town's past.

Also here is Hiscock House, a turn-of-the-century home, restored to the style of 1910, where merchant Emma Hiscock ran the village store, forge, and post office while raising her six children.

🏛 Trinity Museum
Church Rd. **Tel** (709) 464 3599.
Open mid-Jun–mid-Oct: 10am–5:30pm daily. 🅿 🎫

❼ Terra Nova National Park
Trans-Canada Hwy. 🚌 from St. John's.
Open May–mid-Oct: daily. 🅿 ♿
🚻 limited. ℹ Glovertown (709) 533 2801. 🌐 **pc.gc.ca**

The gently rolling forested hills and deep fjords of northeastern Newfoundland are the setting for Terra Nova National Park. The park's Marine Interpretation Centre offers excellent displays on the local marine flora and fauna, including a fascinating underwater video monitor that broadcasts the busy life of the bay's seafloor. Whale-watching tours are also available.

A lookout over the forested hills of Terra Nova National Park

❽ Notre Dame Bay

🚌 Gander. ⛴ Port-aux-Basques;
Argentia (seasonal). ℹ️ Notre Dame
Junction, Rte 1. 🆆 kittiwakecoast.ca

On the east side of Notre Dame
Bay, traditional Newfoundland
outports maintain a way of life
that echoes their history. The
Twillingate Museum, located in
an elegant Edwardian rectory in
Twillingate, has several rooms
furnished with period antiques.
Also on display are aboriginal
artifacts collected from nearby
sites, and marine memorabilia
recounting the region's
fascinating shipping history.
  Boat tours take passengers
out into the bay for a close-up
look at the huge icebergs that
float by in spring and summer,
and to see the many whales
that roam about offshore.
Nearby Wild Cove and Durrell
are romantic villages.

The elegant Edwardian rectory that houses
the Twillingate Museum

❾ Gander

🏙️ 10,000. ✈️ ➡️ ℹ️ 109 Trans-
Canada Hwy (709) 256 7110.

Best known for its illustrious
aviation history, Gander is a small
town and a useful tourist center
for fuel and food. In Grand Falls-
Windsor, 100 km (57 miles) west
of Gander, the Mary March

A display of tools at the Mary March Provincial Museum

Provincial Museum, named after
the last survivor of the now extinct
Beothuk people, traces the span
of central Newfoundland's history
from the Aboriginal cultures of
9,000 years ago to the industrial
development of the 20th
century. Behind the museum,
visitors can take a guided tour
through the historic village.

❿ The Southwest Coast

🚌 Ferry dock terminal. ⛴ Port-aux-
Basques. ℹ️ Port-aux-Basques (709)
695 3688.

In southern Newfoundland the
45-km (28-mile) Granite Coastal
Drive along Route 470 from
Channel Port-aux-Basques to
Rose Blanche leads through a
landscape of ancient, jagged,
green mountains and along a
rocky, surf-carved shoreline.
Near Rose Blanche, a 500-m
(545-yd) boardwalk trail winds
through bright wildflower-
strewn heath to the impressive
Barachois Falls. There is a
charming picnic spot at the foot
of the 55 m (180 ft) falls. The
area is noted for its many

shipwrecks, and so the Rose
Blanche Lighthouse, built in
1873, stands in defiant splendor
atop the harbor headland.

⓫ Gros Morne National Park

Tel (709) 458 2417. 🚌 Corner Brook.
⛴ St. Barbe. **Open** daily. 🅿️ ♿ 📷
🆆 pc.gc.ca

A UNESCO World Heritage Site,
Gros Morne is Newfoundland's
most scenic landscape masterpiece. Here the Long Range
Mountains rise 700 m (2,000 ft)
above the blue fjord that cuts
into the coastal range. Some
of the world's oldest mountains,
these are pre-Cambrian and
several million years older than
the Rockies.
  The best way to see the North
Side of the park is on a boat
tour along Western Brook Pond,
a narrow fjord cradled between
soaring cliffs where waterfalls
vaporize as they tumble from
great heights. Wildlife,
including moose,
caribou, and eagles,
is frequently
seen and
heard.

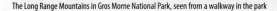

The Long Range Mountains in Gros Morne National Park, seen from a walkway in the park

For hotels and restaurants in this region see pp350–59 and pp364–83

⑫ Northern Peninsula Tour

A land of legends and mystery, the Northern Peninsula of Newfoundland offers adventurous travelers the chance to experience over 40 centuries of human history, from early aboriginal people through colonization to today's modern fishing life. The road north travels along a harsh and rocky coast. Along the way, important historic sites, such as L'Anse-aux-Meadows, tell the story of the earlier cultures who chose this wild land as their home.

Tips for Drivers

Tour length: 430 km (267 miles) along Hwy 430. **Starting point:** Deer Lake, at junction of Hwy 1. **Stopping off points:** Gros Morne's Wiltondale Visitors' Centre and Tablelands; Port au Choix National Historic Site; Grenfell Museum in St. Anthony.

⑤ Port au Choix
This historic site is dedicated to exhibitions of Maritime Archaic Indians and Dorset Eskimos who lived here in 2000 BC and AD 500.

Cook's Harbour

⑥ **L'Anse-aux-Meadows**

St. Anthony

Main Brook

④ Hawke's Bay
A whaling station early in the 20th century, Hawke's Bay boasts excellent salmon fishing waters.

③ The Arches
This lovely spot is named for three limestone arches that are probably 400 million years old.

430

⑤

④

Englee

③

430

② Gros Morne National Park
This fine place has a reputation as one of the most beautiful parks in the whole of Canada.

②

⑥ L'Anse-aux-Meadows National Historic Site
The reconstructions of three Norse buildings are the focal points of this UNESCO World Heritage Site, which is the earliest known European settlement in the New World.

①

Deer Lake

① Deer Lake
A good fuel and refreshment center for those starting on the tour, Deer Lake and its surrounding area is remarkable for its jagged landscape, salmon river (the Humber), forests, lakes, and farms.

Key

■ Tour route

= Other roads

0 kilometres 25

0 yards   25

Fishermen's huts in the village of Red Bay on the coast of Labrador

⓭ Labrador Straits

🚢 Blanc Sablon. 🚹 Forteau (709) 931 2013. 🅆 **labradorcoastaldrive. com**

Hauntingly beautiful coastal landscapes explain why the Labrador Straits is a popular place to visit in this province. A summer ferry service crosses the straits from St. Barbe, Newfoundland to Blanc Sablon, Quebec, just a few kilometers from the Labrador border. From there, an 85-km (53-mile) road leads east along the Labrador Coastal Drive through a wild countryside of high, barren hills, thinly carpeted by heath and wind-twisted spruce. The route takes in small outport fishing villages, where fishing is still the economic mainstay for some. Atlantic Canada's tallest lighthouse was built here in 1854, near L'Anse-Amour. Known as the Point Amour Lighthouse, it stands at 30-m (109-ft) and is now a Provincial Historic Site. Another significant spot to stop is the Maritime Archaic Burial Mound National Historic Site, North America's oldest Burial mound, where a Maritime Archaic Indian child was leaid to rest 7,500 years ago.

The highway passes through the town of Red Bay, home to the **Bay National Historic Site**, where visitors can learn about the Basque mariners' presence during the 16th century, view the Right Whale Exhibit Museum, and visit the Interpretation Centre. Visitors can also take a short boat ride to Saddle Island, where a tour leads past the foundations of the shanties, shipworks, and cooper shops where as many as 1,500 men worked each season, rendering whale oil for lamps in Europe.

🏠 **Red Bay National Historic Site** Route 510. **Tel** (709) 920 2142. **Open** Jun–early Oct: daily. 🐾 ♿

⓮ Battle Harbour

🚢 Mary's Harbour 🚹 Mary's Harbour, Newfoundland (709) 921 6325. 🅆 **battleharbour.com**

Once considered the unofficial capital of Labrador (from the 1870s to the 1930s), Battle Harbour, a small settlement on an island just off the southern coast of Labrador, was once a thriving fishing community. In 1965, the dwindling population was relocated to St. Mary's on the mainland, but

Inuit children in Nain

all of the town's buildings, many of which date back 200 years, were left standing, and in the 1990s the town was restored. Today, visitors can tour the island and get a taste of the way life once was in remote Labrador.

⓯ Nain

⛰ 1,150. 🔁 🚢 🚹 Town Council, Nain (709) 922 2842.
🅆 **tourismnunatsiavut.com**

Nain is Newfoundland and Labrador's most northern community. A large part of the small population is Inuit, and the town is rich with traditional art, much of which cacn be bought at Torngat Arts & Crafts in the center of town. Nain is also home to world-famous carvers such as John Terriak and Gilbert Hay.

The best way to explore Nain and the Nunatsiavut region is by taking the Northern Ranger ferry from Happy Valley-Goose Bay and visting the small fishing communities along the way. These include Rigolet, the most southern Inuit community in the world; Makkovik, a good place to buy traditional Labrador art; and Postville, which was once a trading post for Inuit families. Nearby Hopedale boasts some of Canada's oldest wooden-framed constructions, including

Battle Harbour Island with icebergs on the horizon

A snowy street in Nain during the long winter

the **Hopedale Mission National Historic Site**, where stories and artifacts are displayed.

Hopedale Mission National Historic Site
Agvituk Historical Society, Hopedale.
Tel (709) 933 3881. **Open** daily.

The Moravian Church in Happy Valley-Goose Bay

⓰ Happy Valley-Goose Bay

8,000. ✈ ⛴ ℹ Labrador (709) 896 3489. 🎫 book ahead.

The largest town in the wilderness of Central Labrador, Happy Valley-Goose Bay was a strategically important stopover for transatlantic flights during World War II. German, Italian, and British pilots now train at the NATO base here.

The nearby community of North West River is home to the Labrador Heritage Museum, where exhibitions depict its fascinating history. It pays particular attention to the life of trappers, with displays that include animal furs, trapper's tools, and a traditional tilt (wilderness shelter).

⓱ Churchill Falls

ℹ Churchill Falls Development Corporation (709) 925 3335. 🎫 obligatory, book ahead.

The town of Churchill Falls is ideally placed for visitors to stock up on supplies, fill up with gas, and check tyres as there are no service stations between Happy Valley-Goose Bay and Labrador City. Churchill Falls is famous as the site of one of the largest hydroelectric power stations in the world. Built in the early 1970s, the plant is an extraordinary feat of engineering, diverting the Churchill River (it is Labrador's largest) and its incredible volume of water to power the underground turbines that produce 5,225 megawatts of power – enough to supply the needs of a small country. Guided tours are available of this impressive complex.

⓲ Labrador City

7,700. ✈ ⛴ ℹ Labrador West Tourism Development Corporation (709) 944 7631.

In the midst of ancient tundra, Labrador City is a mining town that shows the modern, industrial face of Canada. The town is home to the largest open-pit iron mine in the world and the community has largely grown up around it since the late 1950s.

The vast open wilderness surrounding Labrador City, with its myriad pristine lakes and rivers, is renowned as a sportsman's paradise that attracts hunters and anglers from around the world. The western Labrador wilderness is also home to the 700,000 caribou of the George River herd. The herd moves freely through the area for most of the year, grazing the tundra in small bands. Professional outfitters take groups of visitors out to track the herd through the region. Many tourists make the trip to admire the animals.

The Gateway Labrador visitor center at L'Anse au Clair has an exhibit of artifacts representing the best of Labrador West and its history, culture, and people. It also covers the fur trading and mining history of Labrador. The on-site craft shop features local handcrafted products, and visitors have an opportunity to talk to locals about further exploring the region.

The Northern Ranger Ferry

The Northern Ranger Ferry is an overnight passenger ferry and the primary mode of transportation for many communities along the coast. It departs from Happy Valley Goose-Bay and Cartwright, and explores the historic region of Nunatsiavut. Stops along the way include Rigolet, Makkovik, Postville, Hopedale and Natuashish, where the ferry docks for one to three hours. Nain is the final destination on the journey. Icebergs are a common sight.

NEW BRUNSWICK, NOVA SCOTIA, AND PRINCE EDWARD ISLAND

The beauty and lure of the sea is always close at hand here. Stunning coastal scenery, picturesque centuries-old villages, world-class historic sites, and a wealth of family attractions have turned these three Maritime Provinces into one of Canada's top vacation destinations. New Brunswick's ruggedly beautiful Bay of Fundy is matched by the gently rolling landscape of Acadian villages tucked into quiet coves and long sandy beaches. With its sparkling bays and ancient weathered fishing towns, Nova Scotia embodies the romance of the sea. Elegant country inns and historic sites bring the past to life. Canada's smallest province, Prince Edward Island, is known for its vibrant green farmlands, red bluffs, deep blue waters, and golf courses, and is enjoyed by cyclists, anglers, and hikers.

Sights at a Glance

Historic Towns and Cities
- ❷ Saint John
- ❹ Fredericton
- ❺ Grand Falls
- ❽ Bouctouche
- ⓫ Amherst
- ⓬ Truro
- ⓭ Parrsboro
- ⓮ Windsor
- ⓯ Wolfville
- ⓰ Annapolis Royal
- ⓱ Digby
- ⓲ Shelburne

- ⓳ Lunenburg
- ⓴ Mahone Bay
- ㉑ Peggy's Cove
- ㉒ Halifax

National Parks
- ❶ Fundy National Park
- ❼ Kouchibouguac National Park

Historic Sites and Areas of Natural Beauty
- ❸ Passamaquoddy Bay
- ❻ Acadian Peninsula

- ❾ Village Historique Acadien
- ❿ Prince Edward Island
- ㉓ Eastern Shore
- ㉔ Cape Breton Island

Key
- ═══ Highway
- ▬▬ Major road
- ═══ Minor road
- ── Railway route
- ▬•▬ International border

For map symbols see back flap

Humpback whales at play in the Bay of Fundy

❶ Fundy National Park

Tel (506) 887 6000. 🚉 Moncton.
🚌 Sussex. ⛴ Saint John. **Open** daily.
🌄 May–Oct. ♿ 📷 🅆 **pc.gc.ca**

Along New Brunswick's
southern shore, the tremendous
tides of the Bay of Fundy are a
powerful feature of everyday
life. Twice a day, over 100 billion
tons of water swirl
into and out of the
bay, creating a tidal
shift of up to 15 m
(48 ft) and carving
out a stunning wild
and rocky shoreline.

One of the best
places to experience
these world-famous
tidal wonders is at
Fundy National Park,
which is filled with wildlife and
hiking trails. Here at low tide,
visitors can walk out for over a
kilometer. The Bay is a favorite
with naturalists, who study the
fascinating creatures that live
half their lives under water and
the other half above.

Moose in Fundy
National Park

❷ Saint John

🏙 70,000. ✈ 🚌 ⛴ 🚉 **𝒊** City Hall,
King St. (506) 658 2990.
🅆 **discoversaintjohn.com**

New Brunswick's second city,
Saint John, still retains the charm
of a small town. In 1785, 14,000
loyalists escaping the turmoil of
the American Revolution built
Saint John in under a year.

More recently, restoration
has made Saint John's historic
center a delightful place to

explore. The Saint John City
Market is the oldest continuing
farmers' market in Canada, with
colorful produce stacked high,
fresh seafood vendors, cafés,
and an excellent traditional
fish restaurant.

In nearby Market Square, an
airy atrium links buildings that
were once the city's center of
commerce. Here visitors will
find upscale restaurants and
stores. Market Square
is also the home of
the lively **New
Brunswick Museum**.
Three floors offer
clever and enter-
taining exhibits on
New Brunswick's
geological, cultural,
and natural history.
Children particularly
enjoy the Hall of
Whales and the three-level Tidal
Tower in which water rises and
falls in real-time,
re-creating the height
of the tides roaring
away just outside.

Nearby, the Loyalist
House Museum is
located in an impressive
Georgian house built
by Loyalist David Merritt
in around 1810. Inside,
the house has been
renovated to reflect the
lifestyle of a wealthy
family of that time, with
authentic period
furnishings.

**🏛 New Brunswick
Museum**
Market Square. **Tel** (506) 643
2300. **Open** daily **Closed**
Nov– mid-May: Mon. 📷 ♿

❸ Passamaquoddy Bay

🚌 St. Stephen. ⛴ Black's Harbour &
Letete. **𝒊** St. Andrew's Tourism
Bureau (506) 529 3556.

There is a genteel historic charm
to the villages surrounding the
island-filled waters of Passamaquoddy Bay, and none is more
charming or intriguing than the
lovely resort town of St. Andrews-
by-the-Sea. The beautifully
renovated Marriott Algonquin
Resort, with its elegant grounds
and 18-hole golf course, recalls
early 20th-century days when
St. Andrews was renowned as
an exclusive getaway of the rich
and powerful.

In town, Water Street is lined
with intriguing boutiques, craft
shops, and fine restaurants
housed in century-old buildings.
At the town dock, tour
companies offer sailing, whale-
watching, and kayaking trips.
Nearby, the elegant Georgian
home built for Loyalist Harris
Hatch in 1824 is now the location
of the **Ross Memorial Museum**
which contains an extensive
collection of antiques and art.

Ferries depart from Blacks
Harbour in the St. George area
several times daily for Grand
Manan Island, 30 km (18 miles)
south of St. Andrews. For Campobello Island, 20 km (12 miles)
south of St. Andrews, a ferry
departs from Letete to Deer
Island, from where another ferry

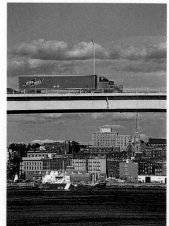
View of Saint John from the St. John River

The charming Victorian vista of Fredericton seen from across the St. John River

goes to Campobello. The Roosevelt Campobello International Park is a 11-sq-km (4-sq-mile) preserve on Campobello Island built around the elegant summer home of US President Franklin D. Roosevelt. The 34-room Roosevelt Cottage has been restored, and includes artifacts belonging to Roosevelt and his family.

Renowned for its rugged coastal beauty, Grand Manan Island has high rocky cliffs, picturesque fishing villages, brightly painted boats, and weathered piers. It is popular with birdwatchers as it attracts large flocks of seabirds annually.

The Ross Memorial Museum
188 Montague St. **Tel** (506) 529 5124. **Open** late May–early Oct: Mon–Sat.

❹ Fredericton

48,000. ✈ 🚌 ℹ Carlton Tourism Division (506) 460 2041.
w tourismfredericton.ca

Straddling the St. John River, Fredericton is New Brunswick's provincial capital. Its Victorian homes and waterfront church make it one of the prettiest small cities in Atlantic Canada. Several historic buildings reflect the town's early role as a British military post. The **Beaverbrook Art Gallery** contains an impressive collection of 19th- and 20th- century paintings, including Salvador Dali's masterpiece *Santiago el Grande* (1957). **King's Landing Historical Settlement**, 37 km

(22 miles) west of Fredericton is a living history museum that re-creates daily life in a rural New Brunswick village of the 19th-century. Over a hundred costumed workers bring villagers' homes, church, and school to life.

Beaverbrook Art Gallery
703 Queen St. **Tel** (506) 458 8545. **Open** daily. 🚻 ♿ 🛍
w beaverbrookartgallery.org

King's Landing Historical Settlement
Rte 2, W of Fredericton. **Tel** (506) 363 4999. **Open** Jun–early Oct: 10am–5pm daily. 🚻 ♿ partial.

❺ Grand Falls

5,900. 🚌 ℹ Malabeam Reception Centre. 🚻

From Fredericton to Edmundston, the St. John River flows through a pastoral valley of rolling hills, woods, and farmland. The town of Grand Falls consists of one

well-appointed main street, Boulevard Broadway, which is a useful refreshment stop. The town was named Grand Falls for the mighty cataract the St. John's River creates as it tumbles through Grand Falls Gorge. Framed by parkland, the surge of water drops more than 25 m (40 ft). Over time it has carved a gorge 1.5 km (1 mile) long, with steep sides as high as 70 m (200 ft) in places.

Upriver and north through the valley, the town of Edmundston offers the **New Brunswick Botanical Garden**. Paths lead through eight themed gardens and two arboretums that provide dazzling input for the senses. Bright colors, delicate scents, and even soft classical music delight visitors.

New Brunswick Botanical Garden
Saint-Jacques, Edmundston. **Tel** (506) 737 4444. **Open** May–Oct: 9am–dusk daily. 🚻 **w** umce.ca/jardin

The deep waterfall valley of Grand Falls Gorge

Endless sandy beaches stretch to the horizon at Kouchibouguac National Park

❻ The Acadian Peninsula

🚊 Bathurst. 🚌 Bathurst.
🚢 Dalhousie. 🛈 Jun–Sep: Water St.,
Campbellton (506) 789 2367; Oct–May:
Campbellton Chamber of Commerce
(506) 759 7856.

The quiet coastal villages, beaches, and gentle surf of the Acadian peninsula have made it a favorite vacation destination. Established here since the 1600s, the Acadians have long enjoyed a reputation for prosperous farming, pretty villages and a strong folk music tradition (*see pp66–7*).

In Shippagan, the small fishing town at the tip of the mainland, the **Marine Centre and Aquarium** holds tanks with over 3,000 specimens of Atlantic sealife and displays on local fishing industries.

Nearby, the Lamèque and Miscou islands are connected by causeways to the mainland. On Miscou Island, a 1-km (0.5-mile) boardwalk leads through a peat bog with signs about this unique ecosystem. The 35-m (85-ft) high Miscou Lighthouse is the oldest operating wooden lighthouse in Canada.

Home to many Acadian artists, Caraquet is the busy cultural center of the peninsula. On the waterfront, adventure centers offer guided kayak trips on the Baie des Chaleurs. For those wanting an introduction to the story of the Acadians, the **Acadian Wax Museum** features a self-guided audio tour past 23 tableaus from Acadian history. The scenes begin with the founding of the "Order of the Good Times" at Annapolis Royal in 1604 and focus on the expulsion of 1755.

🐟 **Marine Centre and Aquarium**
100 Aquarium Street, Shippagan.
Tel (506) 336 3013. **Open** mid-May–
mid-Oct: 10am–6pm daily. 🐾 ♿

🏛 **Acadian Wax Museum**
Rte 11, Caraquet. **Tel** (506) 284 2591.
Open Jun–Sep: daily. 🐾 ♿

❼ Kouchibouguac National Park

Tel (506) 876 2443. 🚊 Miramichi. 🚌
Miramichi. 🚢 Miramichi. **Open** daily.
🌐 parkscanada.gc.ca/
kouchibouguac

The name of this park comes from the native Mi'kmaq word for "River of Long Tides." The park's 238 sq km (92 sq miles) encompass a salt-spray world of wind-sculpted dunes, salt marshes packed with wild life, and 25 km (16 miles) of fine sand beaches, as well as excellent terrain for cyclists. A popular activity is the Voyageur Canoe Adventure, a three-hour canoe paddle to offshore sandbanks where hundreds of gray seals relax in the sun.

❽ Bouctouche

🏘 2,400. 🚌 🛈 Jun–Sep: 14 Acadia
St. (506) 743 8811; Oct–May:
Bouctouche Chamber of Commerce
(506) 759 7856. 🌐 bouctouche.org

A seaside town with a strong Acadian heritage, Bouctouche is home to **Le Pays de la Sagouine**. This theme village is named for La Sagouine, the wise washerwoman created by Acadian authoress Antonine Maillet (b. 1929). Theatrical shows here act out her tales.

Nearby, the Irving Eco-Centre studies and protects the beautiful 12-km (8-mile) network of dunes, saltmarshes, and beach that extend along the entrance to Bouctouche Harbour.

🎭 **Le Pays de la Sagouine**
57 Acadia St. **Tel** 1 800 561 9188.
Open mid-Jun–Sep: 10am–6pm daily.

The raised boardwalk at the Irving Eco-Centre, La Dune de Bouctouche

⑨ Village Historique Acadien

After the tragic deportation of 1755–63 *(see p66–7)*, Acadians slowly returned to the Maritimes, clearing new farmlands and rebuilding their way of life. The Village Historique Acadien portrays a rural Acadian community between 1770 and 1949. The village's 60 restored historic buildings, including several working farms, cover 364 ha (900 acres). Throughout the village, period-costumed bilingual guides re-create the daily activities of the 19th century. Visitors can ride in a horse-drawn wagon, watch the work of the blacksmith, print shop, or gristmill, and also tour working farms and homes where women are busy spinning, weaving, and cooking.

VISITORS' CHECKLIST

Practical Information
Route 11, 10 km (6 miles) W of Caraquet. **Tel** (506) 726 2600.
Open Jun–Sep: 10am–6pm daily.

Transport
🚌 from Bathurst.

School and Chapel
Through centuries of turmoil, Catholicism was a vital mainstay of the Acadian people. Priests were also schoolteachers; education was highly prized by the community.

Cooper's Shop Tinsmith
Lobster Pound

The Chapel was built by pioneer Acadians and dates from 1831.

Men in horse-drawn cart
Traditional methods are used on the farms; tilled by local people arriving each day, the harvest is moved in carts to barns for winter.

Doucet Farm was first built in 1840 and has been fully restored to its original appearance.

Mazerolle Farm sells fresh bread and rolls, which are baked daily in a large oven in the farmhouse.

Poirier
Tavern

Savoie House
Education Centre

Robin
shed

Godin
House

Forge
In many ways the center of the community, the blacksmith was a feature of every Acadian village, repairing farm equipment and shoeing horses for the people of the area.

0 meters 100
0 yards 100

The Visitors' Reception Centre offers an audiovisual presentation, and typical Acadian food in its restaurant.

⑩ Prince Edward Island

Beautiful and pastoral, Prince Edward Island is famous for its lush landscapes. Wherever you look, the island's rich colors, emerald green farmlands, red-clay roads, and sapphire sea, seem to combine and recombine in endless patterns to please the eye. The island is also a popular destination for golfers who come to tee off on some of Canada's best courses, as well as a haven for sun worshipers who revel in the sandy beaches that ring the island. Prince Edward Island seems made for exploring at a leisurely pace. Meandering coastal roads present an ever-changing panorama of sea, sand, and sky. Small historic towns are home to elegant country inns and art galleries. In the evenings, the island's famous lobster suppers await, caught fresh daily from the surrounding waters.

Green Gables House
Set amid leafy green paths, this 19th-century home was the setting for the popular *Anne of Green Gables* tales.

Malpeque Bay
Cabot Beach Provincial Park covers part of the bay. Ten million of the world-famous Malpeque oysters are caught here each year.

North Cape

Mill River

Portage

Egmont Bay

Malpeque

Cavendish

Kensington

Hunter River

Victoria

Key

▬ Major road
▭ Minor road
═ Rivers
— National Park boundaries

KEY

① **Cedar Dunes Provincial Park**, features a restored 1875 lighthouse, sandy beaches, and a large coastal campground.

② **Confederation Bridge**, opened in 1997 at a total cost of Can$840m, runs for 13 km (8 miles) to the mainland.

③ **Brudenell River Provincial Park**, is surrounded by rocky coastlines and fine sea views.

④ **Panmure Island**

Main street, Summerside
This quiet city with its attractive tree-lined streets is known for its Lobster Carnival each July.

★ Prince Edward Island National Park
Characterized by 40 km (25 miles) of coastline leading onto red cliffs, pink and white sand beaches, and mild seas, this park offers unbeatable sport and vacationing facilities and has an educational Visitors' Centre for those interested in its marine wildlife.

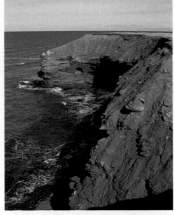

★ Charlottetown
Elegant 19th-century row houses characterize the streets of this sleepy town, the smallest of Canada's provincial capitals; in 1867 the Confederation of Canada was formed here.

VISITORS' CHECKLIST

Practical Information
ℹ️ Water St., Charlottetown (902) 368 4444 or 1 800 463 4734.
🌐 peiplay.com

Transport
✈ Charlottetown. 🚌 & 🚢 to Wood Islands, Borden-Carleton, and boat to Souris.

East Point Lighthouse
The island's easternmost point is home to a 19th-century lighthouse with a restored radio room. Now unmanned and fully automatic, it is open to visitors.

Red Point Beach
Characteristic red rocks lead down to wide beaches; the sand here mysteriously squeaks underfoot, much to the delight of vacationing children.

St. Peter's

Souris

To Magdalen Islands

Hillsborough River

Georgetown

Orwell

Valleyfield River

Northumberland Strait

To Nova Scotia

0 km   100
0 miles   100

For additional map symbols see back flap

Exploring Prince Edward Island

The smallest province in Canada, Prince Edward Island's concentration of activity means every corner of the island is accessible. Charlottetown, known as the birthplace of Canada, is centrally located, and its tree-lined streets make a gentle start to exploring the outlying country. Red clay roads guide the visitor through farms and fishing villages to tiny provincial parks scattered throughout the island. Traveling the north coast takes in the splendid rolling green scenery of PEI National Park, with its famous beaches, while southward, warm swimming spots abound.

Fishing huts overlooking French River near Cavendish

Cavendish

This is such a busy little town that it can be hard to see the gentle, pastoral home of the *Anne of Green Gables* novels. The best place to get in touch with its charm is at the site of **Lucy Maud Montgomery's Cavendish Home**, where the author lived for many years, a simple and authentic site. The town is also the location of **Green Gables Heritage Place**, the novels' fictional 19th-century home.

🏛 **Lucy Maud Montgomery's Cavendish Home**
Route 6. **Tel** (902) 963 2231. **Open** mid-May–mid-Oct: 10am–5pm. 🅿 ♿

🏛 **Green Gables Heritage Place**
Route 6. **Tel** (902) 963 7874.
Open May 21–Oct 31. ♿

Cavendish
Routes 6 & 13. 🛈 (902) 963 7830.

Prince Edward Island National Park

Green Gables is part of Prince Edward Island National Park, whose western entrance is in Cavendish. This is the park's busier side. The soft sand and gentle surf of Cavendish Beach make it one of the most popular beaches in the province. The park's coastal road leads to North Rustico Beach, which is a favorite with sightseers. At the park's western end, the Homestead Trail leads for 8 km (5 miles) through rustic green woodlands and meadows.

The park's quieter eastern side features a long stretch of pristine beach and dunes, and a scenic coastal road. The Reeds and Rushes Trail is a lovely short boardwalk track leading to a freshwater marsh pond where local species of geese and duck nest and feed.

🌿 **Prince Edward Island National Park**
🚌 Charlottetown. ⛴ Wood Islands.
🛈 (902) 672 6350. **Open** daily. 🅿 ♿
🌐 **pc.gc.ca**

The South Coast

Enchanting vistas are found along the roads of the south shore, between Confederation Bridge and Charlottetown. Visitors will also find Victoria-by-the-Sea, a small village that is home to some of the island's most interesting craftshops.

En route to Charlottetown, visitors can make a short detour to **Fort Amherst-Port-la-Joye National Historic Site**. It was here, in 1720, that the French built the island's first permanent settlement. The British captured it in 1758, and built Fort Amherst to protect the entrance to Charlottetown Harbour. While the fort is long gone, the earthworks can still be seen in the park-like surroundings.

🏛 **Fort Amherst-Port-la-Joye National Historic Site of Canada**
Rocky Point. **Tel** (902) 566 7626.
Open Jul–Sep 2: daily. 🅿 ♿

The red bluffs of Cavendish Beach, one of the most favored spots in Prince Edward Island National Park

For hotels and restaurants in this region see pp350–59 and pp364–83. For transport information see p413

View of 19th-century church at Orwell Corner Historic Village

Panmure Island

The natural beauty of the island's eastern area is easy to experience on Panmure Island, south of Georgetown. Level roads make it popular with cyclists. In summer, the octagonal wooden **Panmure Island Lighthouse** is open, and the view from the top takes in a long vista of the island's beaches, saltmarshes, and woodlands. The lighthouse still guides ships into port as it did when it was first built in 1853.

▦ Panmure Island Lighthouse
Panmure Island. **Tel** (902) 838 3568.
Open Jul–Aug: 9am–7pm daily. ▨

Orwell Corner Historic Village

Just outside of the small hamlet of Orwell, Orwell Corner Historic Village re-creates the day-to-day life of a small 19th-century crossroads community. Orwell Corner was thriving until well into the 20th century, when changes in transportation and commerce lessened the importance of the settlement. This charming villlage was restored and opened in 1973. Among the buildings are a blacksmith's, church, schoolhouse, and Clarke's store, the social center of the village. At Orwell Corner is the PEI Agricultural museum, which tells the story of PEI from the mid 1700s to the 1950s.

Just 1 km (0.5 mile) away is the **Sir Andrew Macphail Homestead**. This Victorian house and its surroundings were the much-loved home of Macphail, a local doctor,

journalist, teacher, and soldier who counted among his friends prime ministers and acclaimed writers such as Kipling. The house features many exhibits dealing with Macphail's life. Outside, trails wind through deep woodlands.

▦ Orwell Corner Historic Village
Orwell. **Tel** (902) 651 8513.
Open May–Oct: daily ▨ ▨ ▨

▦ Sir Andrew Macphail Homestead
Off Rte 1, Orwell. **Tel** (902) 651 2789.
Open Jun–Nov: 10am–6pm daily.
▨ ▨

Charlottetown

The birthplace of Canada is a charming coastal city. Voted a Cultural Capital of Canada, the small city has an abundance of performing arts, local shopping, and world class cuisine. The national **Confederation Centre of the Arts** hosts an array of live entertainment including the popular musical *Anne of Green Gables*. **Province House National**

Historic Site is where the 1864 Charlottetown Conference was held, which led to the formation of Canada as a nation. Much of the building has been meticulously restored.
Peake's Quay provides the perfect setting for a stroll, waterfront shopping, coastal excursions, live music, dining or a taste of the ever popular Cow's ice cream, which is made to a recipe said to date back to the time of *Anne of Green Gables*.

▥ Confederation Centre of the Arts
145 Richmond St. **Tel** (902) 628 1864.
Open daily. ▨

▥ Province House National Historic Site of Canada
165 Richmond St. **Tel** (902) 566 7626.
Open daily; call ahead for hours. ▨

Charlottetown
▯ Water St. 800 955 1864.
▥ discovercharlottetown.com

Historic properties on Great George Street, Charlottetown

Lucy Maud Montgomery

The island's most famous author, Lucy Maud Montgomery, was born in Cavendish in 1874. Nearby Green Gables House became the setting of her internationally best-selling novel, *Anne of Green Gables* (1908), set in the late 19th century. The manuscript was accepted only on the sixth attempt. To date, millions of copies of *Anne* have been published, in 16 languages. In 1911, Lucy married and moved to Ontario, where she raised two sons. She continued to write, producing 17 more books, ten of which feature Anne, with all but one set on Prince Edward Island. She died in 1942 and was buried overlooking the farms and fields of her beloved native Cavendish, the Avonlea of which she wrote so often.

Author Lucy Maud Montgomery

⓫ Amherst

 9,500. 🚌 *i* Rte 104, exit 1
(902) 667 8429.

A busy commercial and
agricultural town, Amherst
overlooks the world's largest
marsh, the Tantramar. Along its
edge, hayfields grow on land
reclaimed by Acadian-built dikes
in the 1600s. **The Cumberland
County Museum** is located in
the family home of Senator R.B.
Dickey, one of the Fathers of
Confederation. It focuses on the
area's industrial development, as
well as local and natural history.
   Nearby are **Fort Beauséjour**
and its museum, and the
archaeological digs at the
Acadian village of Beaubassin.

🏛 **Cumberland County Museum**
150 Church St. **Tel** (902) 667 2561.
Open Tue–Sat. 🅿 ⛔

🏚 **Fort Beauséjour**
Trans-Canada Hwy 2, Exit 513A.
Open Jun–mid-Oct: daily. 🅿 ⛔ 📷

⓬ Truro

 11,700. 🚉 🚌 *i* Victoria Square
(902) 893 2922.

Located at the hub of Nova
Scotia's main transportation
routes, Truro is the site of
a unique geographical
phenomenon, the tidal bore.
As the great Fundy tides return
landward, sweeping into the
Minas Basin, they generate a
wave, or "bore," that is driven for
several kilometers up the rivers
that empty into the back of the
basin. An information display
next to the Salmon River
explains each process and posts

Façade of Haliburton House in Windsor, home of the famous humorist

the tidal times. On the nearby
Shubenacadie River, visitors can
ride the bore in rafts. The waves
generated can reach 2 m (7 ft)
in height, creating a churn of
whitewater that the rafts race
through as they follow it for
miles upstream.

⓭ Parrsboro

 1,500. *i* Main St. (902) 254 3266.

Located on the north shore
of the Minas Basin, Parrsboro
is famous as the home of the
world's highest tides, which
reach over 15 m (50 ft) in
height. Rockhounds are
drawn to the Minas Basin
whose beaches
are scattered
with semiprecious
gems and fossils.
The displays at
**Fundy
Geological
Museum** in
Parrsboro feature superb
examples of local amethysts.
There are also dinosaur
footprints and bones.

Prosauropod dinosaur skull from
Fundy Geological Museum

🏛 **The Fundy
Geological Museum**
162 Two Islands Rd. **Tel** (902) 254
3814. **Open** Jun–mid-Oct: daily; late
Oct–May: Tue–Sun. 🅿 ⛔

⓮ Windsor

 3,800. 🚌 *i* Hwy 101, exit 6
(902) 798 2275.

A quiet town whose elegant
Victorian homes overlook the
Avon River, Windsor was the
home of Judge Thomas Chandler
Haliburton, lawyer, historian,
and the author of the Canadian
"Sam Slick" stories, which achieved
enormous popularity in the
mid-1800s. Haliburton was one
of the first widely recognized
humorists in North America. His
clever, fast-talking character Sam
Slick was a Yankee clock peddler
who coined idiomatic terms such
as "the early bird gets the worm,"
and "raining cats and
dogs." His elegant
home is now the
**Haliburton House
Provincial Museum**.
Surrounded by
gardens that Haliburton
tended and loved, the
house is furnished in Victorian
period antiques and contains
many of his personal possessions,
including his writing desk.

🏛 **Haliburton House
Provincial Museum**
414 Clifton Ave. **Tel** (902) 798 2915.
Open Jun–mid-Oct: daily.
🅿 ⛔ limited.

Two Island Beach in Parrsboro, famous for the two large rock outcrops known as the "Brothers Parrsboro"

For hotels and restaurants in this region see pp350–59 and pp364–83

⓯ Wolfville

🏘 3,700. ℹ️ Willow Park (902) 542 7000.

The home of the acclaimed Acadia University, Wolfville and the surrounding countryside radiate a truly gracious charm. Here the green and fertile Annapolis Valley meets the shore of the Minas Basin, and keen visitors can follow country roads past lush farmlands, sun-warmed orchards and gentle tidal flats.

Much of the valley's rich farmland was created by dikes built by the Acadians in the 1600s. After the Great Expulsion of 1755, the British offered the land to struggling New England villagers on the condition that the entire village would relocate. These hardworking settlers, known as Planters, proved so successful that the towns of the Annapolis Valley flourished.

Wolfville is a pretty town of tree-lined streets and inviting shops and restaurants. Nearby, the town's Visitor Information Center marks the start of a 5-km (3-mile) trail along the Acadian dikes to the graceful church at the **Grand Pré National Historic Site**. When the British marched into the Acadian village of Grand Pré in August 1755, it marked the beginning of the Great Uprooting, *Le Grand Dérangement*, which eventually forced thousands of Acadians from Nova Scotia (*see pp66–7*). In 1921 a stone church modeled after French country churches was built on the site of the old village of Grand Pré as a memorial to this tragedy. The French Cross marks the spot where the Acadians boarded the ships. Visitors can also stroll around the garden grounds, where a statue of Evangeline, the heroine of Longfellow's epic poem about the Acadians, stands waiting for her lover, Gabriel. The site's information center features exhibits on the Acadians and their history. After the Great

Longfellow's Evangeline

Uprooting, many families hid locally, while some returned in later years.

🏛 **Grand Pré National Historic Site**
Hwy 101, exit 10. **Tel** (902) 542 3631.
Open May–Oct: daily. ♿ ♿

⓰ Annapolis Royal

🏘 550. 🚌 ℹ️ Prince Albert Rd. (902) 532 2562.

Toward the eastern end of the Annapolis Valley is the historic town of Annapolis Royal, the first capital of the colony of Nova Scotia. The British-built **Fort Anne National Historic Site** witnessed many battles between the English and the French for control of the area.

Kejimkujik Park entrance sign

The nearby fur-trading post of Port Royal (*see p49*), the first European settlement in the New World north of Florida, was built in 1605 by Samuel de Champlain. The **Port Royal National Historic Site** is an exact replica of the original colony, based on French farms of the period, from plans drawn by Champlain.

An hour's drive inland from Annapolis Royal lies **Kejimkujik National Park**, which covers 381 square km (148 sq miles) of inland wilderness laced with lakes and rivers. The park has many paddling routes and 15 hiking trails, ranging from short walks to a 60-km (37-mile) perimeter wilderness and wildlife trail.

🏛 **Fort Anne National Historic Site**
St. George St. **Tel** (902) 532 2397.
Open daily (Oct 16–May 14: by appt; call (902) 532 2321). ♿ ♿

🏛 **Port Royal National Historic Site**
15 km W. of Annapolis Royal. **Tel** (902) 532 2898. **Open** May–Oct: 9am–5:30pm (to 6pm Jul & Aug). ♿ ♿

🌲 **Kejimkujik National Park**
Hwy 8. **Tel** (902) 682 2772. **Open** daily. ♿ mid-May–Oct. ♿

⓱ Digby

🏘 2,100. ✈ 🚌 ⛴ ℹ️ Shore Rd (902) 245 5714.

This fishing town is synonymous with the plump scallops that are the prime quarry of its fishing fleet. The area around Digby also offers splendid scenery and is the starting place for a scenic trip along Digby Neck to the rocky coastal landscape of beautiful Long and Brier Islands.

The waters off Long and Brier Islands brim with finback, minke, and humpback whales, and whale-watching tours are one of the region's favorite pastimes. Some visitors may even glimpse the rare right whale, as about 200 of the 350 left in the world spend their summers in the Bay of Fundy.

Children having fun in a canoeing lake at Kejimkujik National Park

Common room and dining room at Port Royal National Historic Site, Annapolis Royal ▶

The Dory Shop Museum in Shelburne, center of local boat-building

❽ Shelburne

🏠 2,000. 🚌 ℹ️ Dock St. (902) 875 4547.

A quiet historic town nestled on the shore of a deep harbor, Shelburne was founded by 3,000 United Empire Loyalists fleeing persecution after the American Revolution in 1775. More loyalists followed over the next few years, and Shelburne's population swelled to 16,000, making it at the time the third-largest town in British North America. Over time, many of those settlers relocated to Halifax or returned to England, leaving behind the fine 18th-century homes they had built.

A walk along Water Street leads past some of the town's most attractive historic homes to the **Dory Shop Museum**. This two-storey structure has been a commercial dory (flat-bottomed) boat-building shop since its founding in 1880. During the days of the Grand Banks schooner fleet, Shelburne dories were famous for their strength and seaworthiness. The museum's first floor features displays on the industry and the salt-cod fishery. Upstairs, skilled shipwrights demonstrate the techniques of dory building.

The 1995 film *The Scarlet Letter* was shot in Shelburne, with the whole main street becoming a movie set. The town is also home to the only active cooperage in Canada.

🏛 Dory Shop Museum
Dock St. **Tel** (902) 875 3219.
Open Jun–Sep: daily. 🅿️ 🚻 limited.

❾ Lunenburg

🏠 2,600. 🚌 ℹ️ May–Sep: (902) 634 8100; Oct–Apr: (902) 634 3170.
🌐 **explorelunenburg.ca**

No town captures the seafaring romance of Nova Scotia as much as Lunenburg. In the mid-1700s the British, eager for another loyal settlement, laid out a town plan for Lunenburg. They then offered the land to Protestant settlers from Switzerland, Germany, and France. Although these were mainly farmers, they soon turned to shipbuilding and the town became a major center for the trade. In 1996 the town was declared a UNESCO World Heritage Site, one of the best-preserved planned settlements in the New World. Lunenburg is also the home port of *Bluenose II*, a replica of Canada's most famous schooner.

The Fisheries Museum of the Atlantic fills several buildings along the waterfront. Its docks are home to the *Theresa E. Conner*, the last of the Grand Banks Schooners, and the side-trawler, *Cape Sable*.

🏛 Fisheries Museum of the Atlantic
Bluenose Dr. **Tel** (902) 634 4794.
Open mid-May–mid-Oct: daily; late Oct–May: Mon–Fri. 🅿️ 🚻 limited.

One of Mahone Bay's three waterfront churches

❿ Mahone Bay

🏠 990. 🚌 ℹ️ Destination Southwest Nova Association (902) 624 6151. 🌐 **mahonebay.com**

The small seaside town of Mahone Bay has been called the "prettiest town in Canada." Tucked into the shores of the bay that shares its name, the waterfront is lined with historic homes dating to the 1700s, and

View of the Lunenberg Fisheries Museum of the Atlantic along the town's romantic waterfront

at the back of the harbor three stately churches cast their reflection into the still waters.

The town has attracted some of Canada's finest artists and craftspeople, whose colorful shops line the main street. The small **Settlers Museum** offers exhibits and artifacts relating the town's settlement by foreign Protestants in 1754, and its prominence as a boat-building center. There is also a collection of 18th- and 19th-century ceramics and antiques.

🏛 **Settlers Museum**
578 Main St. **Tel** (902) 624 6263.
Open Jun–Sep: Tue–Sun.

㉑ Peggy's Cove

🗺 60. ℹ Sou'wester Restaurant (902) 823 2561.
🅦 peggyscoveregion.com

Peggy's Point Lighthouse stands atop wave-worn granite rocks in Peggy's Cove and is one of the most photographed sights in Canada, a symbol of Nova Scotia's enduring bond with the sea. The village, with its colorful houses clinging to the rocks, and small harbor lined with weathered piers and fish sheds, has certainly earned its reputation as one of the province's most picturesque fishing villages. This is a delightful place to stroll through, with early morning and late afternoon being the most peaceful times. Just outside the village, at the Whaleback promontory, is a memorial to the victims of the tragic Swissair 111 crash of 1998.

The village was also the home of well-known marine artist and sculptor, William E. deGarthe (1907–83). Just above the harbor, the deGarthe Gallery has a permanent exhibition of 65 of his best-known paintings and sculptures.

Right outside the gallery, the Fishermen's Monument is a 30-m (90-ft) sculpture created by deGarthe as his memorial to Nova Scotian fishermen. Carved into an outcropping of native granite rock, the sculpture depicts 32 fishermen, and their

The best-known symbol of Atlantic Canada, Peggy's Point Lighthouse

wives and children. According to local legend, the large angel in the sculpture is the original Peggy, sole survivor of a terrible 19th-century shipwreck, for whom the village was named.

㉒ Halifax

See pp90–91.

㉓ The Eastern Shore

🚉 Halifax. 🚌 Antigonish. 🚌 Pictou.
ℹ Canso (902) 366 2170.

A tour along the Eastern Shore is a trip through old-world Nova Scotia, through towns and villages where life has changed little since the turn of the 20th century. The tiny house and farm that comprise the Fisherman's Life Museum in Jeddore, Oyster Ponds (60 km/ 37 miles east of Halifax) was the home of an inshore fisherman, his wife, and their 13 daughters

around 1900. Today, the homestead is a living-history museum where guides in period costume (many of them wives of local fishermen) reenact the simple daily life of an inshore fishing family, still the heart of Nova Scotia culture. Visitors who arrive at midday may be invited to share lunch cooked over a woodburning stove. There are also daily demonstrations that include rug-hooking, quilting, and knitting, and visitors can tour the fishing stage where salted fish were stored.

Sherbrooke Village is the largest living-history museum in Nova Scotia. Between 1860 and 1890, this was a gold and lumber boomtown. As the gold ran out, Sherbrooke once again became a sleepy rural village. In the early 1970s, 25 of Sherbrooke's most historic buildings were restored. Within the village, scores of costumed guides bring 19th-century Nova Scotia to life. A ride on a horse-drawn wagon offers an overview of the town; the drivers share bits of local history as the horses trot along the village roads. At the Apothecary, visitors can watch the careful mixing of patent medicines, and those interested in the Ambrotype Studio can dress in period costumes, sitting very still while the vintage camera records their image on glass. Just outside town a massive waterwheel turns, powering the Lumber Mill.

🏛 **Sherbrooke Village**
off Hwy 7. **Tel** (902) 522 2400.
Open Jun–Oct: daily. 🪧

The Apothecary at the living-history museum Sherbooke Village

㉒ Halifax

With its bustling waterfront, pretty parks, and unique blend of modern and historic architecture, Halifax is a fascinating city. Its cultured flavor belies its 250-year history as a brawling military town. Founded in 1749 by General George Cornwallis, Halifax was planned as Britain's military center north of Boston. The city has a long history of adventure, being the town where legalized pirates, or privateers, brought captured ships to be shared with the crown. On December 6, 1917, the city was devastated by an explosion caused by the collision of a Norwegian ship with a French munitions ship in the harbor. Today, Halifax is one of Canada's foremost centers of higher learning and has many colleges and five universities.

Exploring Halifax

This is an easy town to explore on foot, as many of the better museums, historic sites, shops, and restaurants are located within the fairly contained historic core.

Downtown, leading west from Brunswick Street, is hilly and green, ideal for a leisurely walk to appreciate the old-style architecture. Citadel Hill offers excellent views of the city, the harbor, and Dartmouth.

🏛 Historic Properties

1869 Upper Water St. **Tel** (902) 422-3077. **Open** daily. ♿

The Historic Properties are a wharfside collection of very old stone and timber-frame structures, which were originally built in the 19th century to hold the booty captured by privateers. Today, they house an intriguing collection of specialty and gift shops, pubs, and fine restaurants. This is one of the city's favorite gathering spots on warm summer nights, with crowds of strollers enjoying the lights of the harbor and music drifting from nearby pubs.

🏛 Maritime Museum of the Atlantic

1675 Lower Water St. **Tel** (902) 424 7490. **Open** May–Oct: daily; Nov–Apr: Tue–Sun. 📷 ♿ 📷 on request.

This harborfront museum offers extensive displays on Nova Scotia's seafaring history, including small craft, a restored chandlery, and, at the dock outside, the elegantly refitted 1913 research vessel *Acadia*. The museum's most popular exhibit is the *Titanic* display, which offers artifacts recovered from the ship. There are fragments of the ship's grand staircase, as well as a mural-sized photo showing the staircase in its original state. After the 1912 catastrophe, many of the bodies that were recovered were brought to Halifax, and 150 are buried at Fairview Lawn Cemetery.

🏛 Harbourfront

ℹ (902) 490 5946.

The Halifax Harbourwalk features interesting gift shops, cafés, and restaurants in historic settings along the boardwalk. This delightful promenade leads to the Halifax–Dartmouth Ferry Terminal, North America's oldest town ferry. A trip across the harbor is an inexpensive way to enjoy a panorama of Halifax.

🏛 Government House

1451 Barrington St. **Tel** (902) 424 7001. **Open** Jul–Aug: Mon, Fri–Sun. 📷 compulsory.

The current home of Nova Scotia's Lieutenant Governor this beautiful building's Georgian façade lends an urban grandeur. Completed in 1807, it cost over £30,000 (Can$72,000), a huge amount for a humble fishing village. Tours last 30 minutes and take in several rooms.

The bandstand of Halifax Public Gardens, framed in flowers

🏛 Pier 21

1055 Marginal Road **Tel** (902) 425 7770. **Open** May–Nov: daily; Nov–Apr: variable. 📷 ♿ 🌐 **pier21.ca**

Canada's entry point for more than a million immigrants and refugees, Pier 21 is now a National Historic Site. It offers powerful and emotional displays and fascinating images.

🌿 Halifax Public Gardens

Spring Garden Rd. **Open** mid-Apr–late Nov: 8am–dusk daily. ♿

Created in 1836, the Public Gardens are a beautiful 7-ha (17-acre) oasis of Victorian greenery and color in a bustling city. A peaceful place to stroll, the gardens' paths wind past

The waterfront of Halifax, seen from the town ferry

duck ponds, fountains, and a seemingly endless array of vivid flower beds. In the center of the gardens, an ornate bandstand is the site of Sunday concerts. On weekends (daily in summer), craftspeople gather outside the park's cast-iron fence to display their varied and colorful wares.

Halifax Citadel National Historic Site

5425 Sackville St/Citadel Hill. **Tel** (902) 426 5080. **Open** May–Oct: daily. Grounds: all year. 🌐 summer. 🚻 ☕

Overlooking the city, this huge star-shaped fortress has a commanding view of the world's second-largest natural harbor. Built between 1828 and 1856, the citadel and its outlying fortifications provided a formidable defense. Visitors can stroll the parade grounds where the kilted regiment of the 78th Highlanders perform with twice-daily musket drills. A cannon is fired daily at noon.

Halifax's famous town clock, built in 1803 as a gift from British royalty

Old Town Clock

Citadel Hill.

At the base of Citadel Hill stands the city's most recognized landmark, the Old Town Clock. The clock was a gift in 1803 from Edward, the British Duke of Kent and then military commander, who had a passion for punctuality. He designed the clock with four faces so that both soldiers and citizens would arrive at their appointed destinations on time.

Province House

1726 Hollis St. **Tel** (902) 424 4661. 🗓 Jul–Aug: 9am–5pm Wed–Fri; Sep–Jun: 9am–4pm Mon–Fri. ♿

Built between 1811 and 1819, Province House is the oldest seat of government in Canada. In 1864 the Fathers of Confederation held two days of meetings here on the formation of Canada (see p52). Visitors can tour the rooms where these plans were laid.

Halifax City Center

① Historic Properties
② Maritime Museum of the Atlantic
③ Harbourfront
④ Government House
⑤ Pier 21
⑥ Halifax Public Gardens
⑦ Halifax Citadel National Historic Site
⑧ Old Town Clock
⑨ Province House

㉔ Cape Breton Island

Magnificent natural beauty is the attraction on Cape Breton. Every year thousands of people travel the famous Cabot Trail through the craggy splendor of Cape Breton Highlands National Park *(see p98–9)*. But Cape Breton's beauty is not limited to these two renowned sights; it can be found along inviting country roads and in the less explored corners of this green, fertile island. Particularly stunning are the Mabou Highlands, which cradle the gentle waters of Lake Ainslee, Bras d'Or Lake where eagles soar over scenic shores, and romantic coastal villages such as windswept Gabarus. The reconstructed 18th-century French garrison and village, Fortress Louisbourg, is also highly popular.

St. Pierre Church at Cheticamp
Built in 1883, the silver spire of this church is typical of Catholic style. The church is in the center of the town of Cheticamp, which offers whale-watching opportunities and is the focus of the 3,000-strong local Acadian community.

Glenora Distillery
Located on the scenic Ceilidh Trail, Glenora was Canada's first single-malt distillery and is renowned for its Glen Breton Rare, a 10-year-old whisky. Visitors can also enjoy a pub, an inn, and a gift shop.

Lake Ainslee
This tranquil lake, encircled by scenic roads, attracts many bird species, such as ospreys and loons, which feed on its shores.

KEY

① **The Alexander Graham Bell Museum**, sits on the shores of Bras d'Or Lake, Bell's summer home for 30 years. Plans, copies, and prototypes of many of his most famous inventions can be seen here.

② **Bird Islands**

③ **Sydney Mines coastal town**, dates back to the 1700s, with mining shafts that reach 5 km (3 miles) out to sea.

Margaree Harbour

Mabou

105

Port Hastings

St.

104

Isle Madame

Key

━━ Major road
━━ Minor road
━━ Scenic route
── River
── National Park boundary

Bay St. Lawrence

Cape Breton Highlands National Park

Ingonish Beach

Cabot Trail Highway
This sublime 300-km (186-mile) drive around the island's northwest and its national park attracts more visitors each year.

St. Ann's

105

Baddeck

St. Andrew's Channel

223

Iona

4

Big Pond

327

ras d'Or Lake

125

Gabarus

Glace Bay

4

Sydney
The third-largest town in Nova Scotia, Sydney is a comparatively small town with a long history as a mining center. The main draw today is its heritage housing.

0 kilometers   15
0 miles   15

Pioneer cottages
hese 19th-century settlers' ottages in Iona's Highland Village are fully restored.

Fortress Louisbourg
The reconstructed fort and village is ideal for a walk and tour through the 1744 past of French Canada. Attractive hiking trails surround the site (see pp100–101).

For additional map symbols see back flap

Exploring Cape Breton Island

The largest island in Nova Scotia, Cape Breton has a wild beauty and grandeur that makes for some of the most impressive scenery in Canada. From the rolling highlands, sprinkled with sparkling streams, to fine sandy beaches, the island's 300-km (200-mile) Cabot Trail provides one of the most memorable tours in Canada. Other inviting country roads lead to the stunning Mabou Hills, surrounding Lake Ainslee, and to romantic little towns including Baddeck, with its connection to Alexander Graham Bell, and the Acadian settlement of Cheticamp near the green Margaree Valley.

Lobster fishing boats in the Main à Dieu harbor on Cape Breton Island

Cape Breton Highlands National Park

In 1936 the Canadian Government set aside the 950 sq km (366 sq miles) of magnificent highlands in the northern tip of Cape Breton Island to form Cape Breton Highlands National Park. The park contains some of Canada's most famous scenery, with its mountains, green wilderness, and windswept coastal beauty. The best-known feature of the park is the spectacular 106-km (66-mile) section of the Cabot Trail highway, which traces much of the park's boundary in a loop from Cheticamp to Ingonish.

The Cabot Trail is the only route through the park, and most attractions are found along it. Entering the park from the west, the trail ascends along the flanks of the coastal mountains. The 24 look-out points along the trail present far-reaching views of the highlands rising from the sea. Continuing inland, the trail travels across the highland plateau. Just past French Lake, the short Bog Walk is a board-walk trail through a highland fen,

with educational panels that describe this unique bog ecosystem, which is home to rare orchids. Visitors may even catch a glimpse of the park's many moose grazing here in a wetland marsh.

Crossing the French and Mackenzie Mountains, the trail descends dramatically to the charming old community of Pleasant Bay. It then reenters the highlands, crossing North Mountain, which, at 457-m (1,500-ft), is the highest point in the park. The trail descends into the Aspy River Valley, where

Picturesque Ingonish Beach on Cape Breton Island

a gravel road leads to the base of the 30-m (100-ft) high Beulach Ban Falls.

At Cape North, another side road leads to the scenic whale-watching destination of Bay St. Lawrence just outside the park. Farther on, the Scenic Loop breaks away from the Cabot Trail and follows the coast, offering awesome views as it descends to White Point. This road rejoins the Cabot Trail to the east, where it reaches the resort town of Ingonish. The Highland Links Golf Course here is ranked among the top public golf courses in Canada.

🌿 Cape Breton Highlands National Park
ℹ️ Cheticamp. **Tel** (902) 224 2306. **Open** mid-May–mid-Oct; Cabot Trail open daily throughout year. 🚻 ♿ limited. 🔤 **pc.gc.ca**

Baddeck

Across the lake from the estate of Alexander Graham Bell, who loved the little town, Baddeck lies in rich farmland and is very much the island's premier resort destination. Set on the northwest side of Bras d'Or Lake, Baddeck is still the small, friendly town that charmed visitors in the 19th century. All amenities are within walking distance. The town's main street follows the waterfront and is lined with shops, cafés, and restaurants. Boat cruises around the lake are available from several places on Water Street by the shore.

The town's top attraction is the **Alexander Graham Bell National Historic Site**. The museum here contains the world's largest collection of photographs, artifacts, and documents about the life of this famous humanitarian and inventor. There are early telephones and several of his later inventions, including a copy of his HD-4 Hydrofoil.

Baddeck
ℹ️ 454 Chebucto St (902) 295 1911.

🏛 Alexander Graham Bell National Historic Site
559 Chebucto St (Hwy 205). **Tel** (902) 295 2069. **Open** May–Oct: daily; Nov–Apr: by appt. 🚻 ♿

A fly-fisher tries his hand in the salmon- and trout-filled waters of the Margaree River

Margaree River Valley

Small and emerald green, the Margaree River Valley is a favorite with hikers, antique-hunters, and sightseers. The river has attracted salmon and trout anglers in large numbers since the mid-19th century.

In the little town of North East Margaree, the tiny but elegant **Margaree Salmon Museum** will fascinate even non-anglers with its beautiful historic rods and reels.

Paved and gravel roads follow the Margaree River upstream to the scenic spot of Big Intervale, where the headwaters come tumbling out of the highlands. For a taste of Gaelic culture, follow the Ceilidh Trail all the way to the **Glenora Distillery**, Canada's first single-malt distillery.

Margaree Valley
i Margaree Fork (902) 248 2803.

Margaree Salmon Museum
60 E. Big Interval Rd. **Tel** (902) 248 2848. **Open** mid-Jun–mid-Oct: 9am–5pm daily. ♿ limited.

Glenora Distillery
Route 19/Ceilidh Trail. **Tel** (902) 258 2662. **Open** daily May–Oct. ♿

Cheticamp

This vibrant town is the largest Acadian community in Nova Scotia. Its beautiful Saint Pierre Church is visible from miles out at sea. The Acadians of Cape Breton are skilled craftspeople, and the town's seven cooperatives produce pottery and hooked rugs. Cheticamp's best-known rug hooker was Elizabeth Le- Fort, whose large and intricate works depicting prominent moments in history have hung in the Vatican and in the White House. Several of her finest rugs are on display at the **Dr. Elizabeth LeFort Museum** at Les Trois Pignons.

Cheticamp is also a popular whale-watching destination; tours are available for seeing many varieties of whale.

Dr. Elizabeth LeFort Museum
15584 Main St. **Tel** (902) 224 2642. **Open** May–Oct: daily. ♿

Sydney

The only city on Cape Breton Island, Sydney is the second-largest town in Nova Scotia. Once the location of the biggest steel plant in North America, the town's main industries are now customer support centers and tourism. Sydney has a small, attractive historic district around the Esplanade, with several restored buildings, such as Cossit House and Jost House, both dating from the 1870s. Downtown, boutiques, stores, and restaurants can be found along the town's main drag, Charlotte Street.

Sydney
i Sydney (902) 539 9876.

Alexander Graham Bell

Alexander Graham Bell

Alexander Graham Bell was born in 1847 in Scotland. Bell's mother was deaf, and, as a child, he became fascinated by speech and communication. In 1870, Bell and his family moved to Ontario *(see p222)*. His work involved transmitting the voice electronically, and he began experimenting with variations of the technology used by the telegraph. In 1876 he transmitted the world's first telephone message, "Watson, come here, I want you." With the patenting of his invention, Bell secured his role as one of the men who changed the world. In 1877, Bell married Mabel Hubbard, one of his deaf students. In 1885, the couple visited Cape Breton, where Bell later built his beautiful estate, Beinn Bhreagh, by Bras d'Or Lake. There he lived and worked each summer until he died in 1922. In Baddeck, the Alexander Graham Bell Museum focuses on his life and varied work.

Fortress of Louisbourg

Built between 1713 and 1758, the magnificent Fortress of Louisbourg was France's bastion of military strength in the New World. Today, it is the largest military reconstruction in North America. Inside, scores of historically costumed guides bring the excitement of an 18th-century French trading town to life. The streets and buildings are peopled with merchants, soldiers, fishmongers, and washerwomen, all going about the daily business of the 1700s. From the lowliest fisherman's cottage to the elegant home of the Chief Military Engineer, attention to detail throughout is superb. The costumed interpreters offer information about the fortress, its history, and the lives of people they portray.

Overview of the Fortress
A seat of government and a well-garrisoned military stronghold for New France, the Fortress of Louisbourg was home to a town of thousands.

0 meters 50

0 yards 50

The Quay and Fredcric Gate
The Quay was the center of commercial activity in the town. It is still central to the fort, as many activities now take place at the Gate's imposing yellow arch.

KEY

① Officers' rooms

② **The Icehouse**, was used to store fresh food for the Governor's table.

③ **The Guardhouse**, held the vital human line of defense; guards were stationed here while on duty.

★ **The Engineer's Residence**
Responsible for all public construction projects at the fortress, the engineer was one of the most important and powerful men in the community.

★ **King's Bastion**

The largest building in the Citadel, the King's Bastion Barracks was home to the 500 French soldiers who lived, ate, and slept here.

King's Bakery

Visitors can buy warm bread from this working bakery that produced the soldiers' daily rations.

The Forge

Traditional skills are in evidence here, with costumed workers demonstrating exactly the carefully learned craft of the 18th century.

The Dauphin Gate

Soldiers in historic uniforms at the gate challenge visitors, just as they would have in the 18th century. The gate's artistic details are based on archeological relics from the original gate recovered in the 1960s and drawings found in French archives.

Village and St. Lawrence River, Bas-Saint-Laurent, Quebec ▶

QUEBEC

Introducing Quebec

Quebec is the largest of Canada's provinces and the biggest French-speaking territory in the world, with many of its seven million citizens holding firm to the language and culture inherited from their French ancestors. Landscapes range from pastoral valleys and villages along the American border, to vast expanses of tundra on the shores of Hudson Bay. At Quebec's heart is the St. Lawrence River. Its north shore begins with the scenic Charlevoix region edging a wilderness of lakes, forest, and tundra that stretches to the Hudson Strait, past one of the world's largest power projects at James Bay. To the south lies the mountainous Gaspé Peninsula. There are two major cities; multiethnic Montreal, and Quebec City, the provincial capital and North America's only walled city.

The picturesque lakeside resort of St- Jovite in the Laurentian Mountains set amid a backdrop of magnificent fall colors

Quebec's largest city, Montreal, has a vibrant downtown area that comes to life after dark

For additional map symbols *see back flap*

Key

- ═══ Expressway
- ▬▬▬ Divided highway
- ▬▬▬ Highway
- ═══ Other road
- ▬▬ Main railway
- ▬▬ Minor railway
- ▬▬ International border
- ▬▬ Regional border
- △ Summit

Kangiqsujuaq

Quaqtaq

Akpatok Island

Kangirsuk

U n g a v a

Lac aux Feuilles

Gyrfalcon Islands

Rivière aux Feuilles

Tasiujaq

Big Island

Kangiqsualujjuaq

Kuujjuaq

Koksoak

Riviere aux Mélèzes

Lac le Moyne

Rivière à la Baleine

George

Caniapiscau

Lac Champdoré

Lac d'Iberville

Schefferville

Réservoir de Caniapiscau

Grande Rivière

Q U E B E C

Lac Manouane

Mont Wright
899m

Rivière-St-Paul

St-Augustin

La Tabatière

Mont Yapeitso
1135m

Monts Otish

Gagnon

Monts Groulx

L a u r e n t i a n M o u n t a i n s

Natashquan

Harrington Harbour

Lac Plétipi

Réservoir Manicouagan

Albanel

Manicouagan

Sept-Îles

Moisie

Magpie

Havre-St-Pierre

Natashquan

Lac Manouane

Port-Cartier

Port-Menier

Île d'Anticosti

Peribonca

Réservoir Pipmuacan

Baie-Trinité

Grande-Vallée

Hauterive

Cap-Chat

Murdochville

Lac St-Jean

Forestville

St. Lawrence

Matane

Mont-Joli

New-Richmond

Alma

Chicoutimi

Rimouski

Campbellton

-licien

Tadoussac

Trois-Pistoles

Kedgwick

Rivière-du-Loup

Edmundston

Baie-St-Paul

St-Pascal

St.Léonard

Québec City

Trois-Rivières

St-Georges

Drummondville

Lac-Mégantic

Sherbrooke

-ean

Magog

0 kilometers   200

0 miles   200

Infantrymen parade in La Citadelle *(see pp140–41)* overlooked by Fairmont Le Château Frontenac

SOUTHERN AND NORTHERN QUEBEC

QUEBEC CITY AND THE ST. LAWRENCE RIVER

MONTREAL

Getting Around

Airports serve every major city. Bus services tour the whole province and include Voyageur Lines, Orléans Express, and smaller regional services. Greyhound buses, based in the US, travel to Montreal and across Quebec. Limocar bus travel covers the Laurentian Mountains and Autobus Viens serves the Eastern Townships. Rail services are limited to the southern part of Quebec. The region also has a comprehensive network of high standard highways for exploring by car.

For hotels and restaurants in this region see pp350–59 and pp364–83

Maple Forests

Long the pride of Quebec and Ontario, there is more to Canada's ancient maple forests than their annual display of beauty. Every fall, turning leaves splash crimson and orange across the south, but it is in springtime that the trees give up their most famous product: maple syrup. Extracting techniques which were developed by native peoples were passed to Europeans in the 17th century. Traditional methods changed little until the 1940s, when part of the process was mechanized. Many age-old methods remain, however, including the final hand-stirring of the syrup.

Maple trees, either red maple *(Acer rubrum)* or sugar maple *(Acer saccharum)*, grow to heights of well over 30 m (100 ft), with thick trunks a meter (3 ft) in diameter. While their main product is the syrup, the hard wood is used for furniture and, of course, the leaf itself is the national symbol of Canada, officially established on the flag in 1965.

Collecting sap from trees by tapping maple trunks is the first step. Cuts are made low in the wood in spring as sap rises.

Transporting the sap in large barrels on a horse-drawn sleigh through the snowy forests is traditional. In the 1970s this was largely replaced by a network of plastic tubing that take the sap directly from tree trunks to the sugar shacks.

Sugar shacks are built in the forest in the center of the sugar bush, the cluster of maple trees that are producing sap. Men and women alike work long hours at slowly evaporating the sap, reducing it to syrup. Quebecois have their own rite of spring: when the first syrup is ready, it is poured onto the crisp snow outside the shacks to make a tasty frozen taffy.

Maple Syrup Products

Although 80 percent of Canada's annual maple harvest eventually becomes maple syrup, there is more to the industry than simply a sweet sauce. Boiled for longer, the syrup hardens into a pale golden sugar that can be used to sweeten coffee or eaten like candy. Maple butter, which is whipped with sugar, is also popular. Savory products benefit too; ham and bacon can be cured in syrup, which is delicious. The sweet-toothed people of Quebec use the syrup to make sugar pie, a tart with a sweet, fudge filling. Syrup is graded according to quality; clear golden fluid, produced at the start of the season, is the most prized, and is generally bottled. Later, darker syrup is used in cooking, and the final, even darker, batch makes a base for synthetic flavors or syrups. Over Can$100 million is spent annually on maple products.

Maple products are used in a variety of foods, both sweet and savory

The Story of Maple Syrup

The first maple-sugar farmers were native Canadians. Long before European settlers arrived in the 16th century, tribes all over Northeast America sweetened savory dishes with syrup. An Iroquois legend tells the story of a chief in ancient times who, hurling an ax at a tree, found it stuck in the trunk at the end of the next day, dripping sweet fluid. That night the chief's wife boiled the day's hunt in the sap, and the syrup was born. Folk tales apart, it is certain that native people discovered the sap and techniques for refining it, few of which have changed, and passed their knowledge to Europeans freely.

Boiling maple sap involves 40 liters (88 pts) of sap to create one liter (2.2 pts) of syrup. The gold color and maple flavor develop as distillation takes place. The paler first syrup of the season is the most valuable.

Transforming sap into maple syrup takes place very slowly. The sap bubbles over a wood fire (maple wood is prefered) until about 98 percent of its water content evaporates. Modern processes use mechanized evaporators to boil the sap and draw off the steam, but even hi-tech methods still require a final hand-stirred simmering.

The St. Lawrence Seaway

Extending from the Gulf of St. Lawrence on the Atlantic coast to Duluth at the western end of Lake Superior in Minnesota, the St. Lawrence Seaway and Great Lakes System flows across North America for over 3,700 km (2,300 miles). The St. Lawrence Seaway itself stretches 553 km (344 miles) from Montreal to Lake Erie and covers 245,750 square km (95,000 sq miles) of navigable water. Open from March to December, it is the world's longest deep-draft inland waterway. Ships carry a huge quantity of domestic traffic, but over 60 per cent of the total freight travels to and from overseas ports, mainly from Europe, the Middle East, and Africa. Traffic varies: cargoes of grain travel in superships alongside pleasure boats.

Locator Map
■ The St. Lawrence Seaway

The History of the Seaway

The Seaway has ancient beginnings: in 1680, French monk Dollier de Casson started a campaign to build a mile-long canal linking Lac St. Louis and Montreal, which was finally opened in 1824 as the Lachine Canal. In 1833, the first Welland Canal (from Lake Ontario to Lake Erie) opened. The fourth Welland Canal was the first modern part of the Seaway to be built in 1932. 1951 brought US and Canadian cooperation to bear on a new seaway, which began in Canada in 1954. On April 25, 1959, the Seaway opened, linking the Great Lakes to the world.

Pleasure boats cruise the Seaway near the Thousand Islands by Kingston, Ontario. Each summer, small craft take advantage of the excellent sailing and waterskiing available in this section of the Seaway.

The *D'Iberville*, first ship to cross the Seaway

Ottawa

Ontario

Kingston •

Toronto •

Lake Ontario

↑ *Lake Huron*

United States

Lake Erie

0 kilometers   100
0 miles   100

Montreal is the historic beginning of the Seaway. It was here that the first link was built to the lakes during the 18th century, opening up pathways to the center of North America. The Seaway is open nine months each year, despite much freezing weather.

Gulf of St. Lawrence

Cargo ships carry iron ore, grain, coal, and other bulk commodities through the waterway: more than 2 billion tons of cargo have been shipped since 1959. Canada's heavy industry could not continue without the Seaway.

Quebec

Quebec City

St. Lambert Lock bypasses the Lachine Rapids west of Montreal. The Seaway is a watery staircase to America's heartland. The process involves raising and lowering the ships the height of a 60-story building.

• Montreal

Construction of the Seaway

In 1895, the US and Canadian governments appointed a Deep Waterways Commission to study the feasibility of what was to become today's St. Lawrence Seaway; it reported in favor of the project two years later. After 50 years of intercountry wrangling, the jointly financed project was begun on August 10, 1954 – in the words of Canadian Prime Minister Louis St. Laurent "a bond rather than a barrier between Americans and Canadians." The massive undertaking was beset with problems not previously encountered, especially the discovery of ancient rock formations so hard that new machinery had to be created to dig through them. All work, including relocating villages and dredging the existing canals, had to be carried out with minimum disruption to the daily boat, rail, and car traffic of major cities. Nonetheless, the four-year construction was completed almost to the day.

The Seaway in profile with locks and rising water levels

MONTREAL

Montreal is the second largest city in Canada. The pious 17th-century French founders of this vibrant island metropolis might be a little surprised to have produced a place that revels so much in its reputation for joie de vivre, but at least their edifices remain; the spires of some of Canada's finest churches still rise above the skyline.

Montreal's location at the convergence of the St. Lawrence and Ottawa rivers made it Canada's first great trading center. It was founded in 1642 by a group of French Catholics as a Christian community and port. Much of its economic power has now moved west to Toronto, and what makes Montreal interesting today is a cultural, rather than a geographical, confluence. About 70 percent of its 3 million residents are of French descent, another 15 percent have British origins, and the rest represent nearly every major ethnic group. Many speak three or more languages. The communities form a kind of mosaic, with the anglophones in the west, the francophones in the east, and other ethnic communities in pockets all over the island. There is nothing rigid about these divisions: Anglophones eat and drink in the restaurants and bistros of the historic French district, and francophones visit the traditionally English area. The most interesting neighborhoods sprawl along the southern slopes of Mont-Royal – the 234-m (767-ft) hill from which the city derives its name. Vieux-Montréal's network of narrow, cobblestone streets huddles near the waterfront, while the main shopping area is farther north along Rue Sainte-Catherine. It extends below the city's surface in the maze of tunnels that connect the Underground City, the complex of homes, stores, and leisure venues that spreads out beneath the bustling city. Other modern attractions include the Olympic Park stadium and the Musée d'Art Contemporain, built in the 1990s to complement Montreal's fine historic museums.

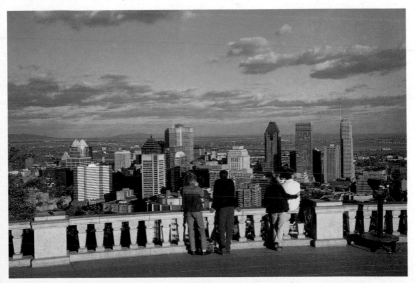

Visitors admiring the skyline of Montreal

◀ Basilique Notre-Dame

Exploring Montreal

Montreal occupies a 50-kilometer (30-mile) long island at the confluence of the St. Lawrence and the Ottawa River. The city core, where many sights are found, is fairly compact and lies to the south and east of Montreal's main landmark, Plateau Mont-Royal. Vieux Montréal, the old city, is nestled on the shore of the St. Lawrence, while the modern downtown lies between it and Plateau Mont-Royal. Streets follow a fairly consistent grid pattern making the city easy to navigate.

The skyscrapers of downtown Montreal at dusk

Key

═══ Highway

═══ Major road

Pedestrian walkway

═══ Railway

Major sight

Sight

Sights at a Glance

Historic Buildings and Areas

① Vieux Port
③ Château Ramezay
④ Sir George-Etienne Cartier National Historic Site
⑦ Chinatown
⑧ Plateau Mont-Royal
⑨ Place des Arts
⑬ McGill University
⑮ Underground City
⑯ Square Dorchester and Place du Canada
⑲ Rue Sherbrooke
㉖ Lachine

Parks and Gardens

㉑ Parc du Mont-Royal
㉒ Olympic Park pp128–9
㉓ Jardin botanique de Montréal

Islands

㉔ Parc Jean-Drapeau

Churches and Cathedrals

② Basilique Notre-Dame-de-Montréal pp116–17
⑪ Christ Church Cathedral
⑰ Cathédrale Marie-Reine-du-Monde
⑳ Oratoire St-Joseph

Museums and Galleries

⑤ Centre des sciences de Montréal
⑥ Centre d'Histoire de Montréal
⑩ Musée d'art contemporain de Montréal pp120–21
⑫ McCord Museum of Canadian History
⑭ Musée des Beaux-Arts pp122–23
⑱ Centre Canadien d'Architecture
㉕ Maison Saint-Gabriel

For map symbols see back flap

Getting Around

A tunnel and 15 bridges link Montreal island to the mainland, and the Ville-Marie Expressway carries road traffic right into its heart. The most convenient way to get around within the city is on the métro and bus system, which service most sites of interest.

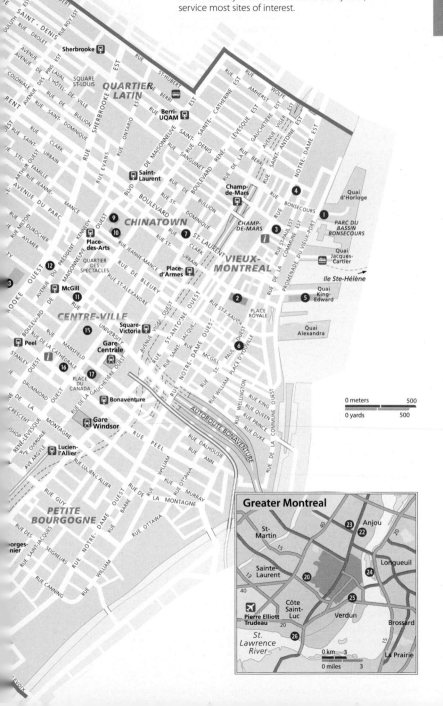

Street-by-Street: Vieux-Montréal

Montreal's founders, led by Paul Chomédy de Maisonneuve, built the Catholic village of Ville Marie, that was to become Montréal, on the Saint Lawrence river in 1642. Missionary efforts failed to flourish, but the settlement blossomed into a prosperous fur-trading town with fine homes and a stone stockade. As Montreal expanded in the mid-20th century, the old city, Vieux-Montréal, fell into decline. In 1980, however, the district underwent a renaissance. The remaining 18th-century buildings were transformed into the restaurants, bistros, and boutiques that are so fashionable today, especially those of rue Notre-Dame and rue St-Paul.

View from the river
This clutch of historic streets leading down to the great St. Lawrence River is a district of romance and charm in the midst of this modern city.

❷ ★ Basilique Notre-Dame
One of the most splendid churches in North America, the city's 1829 Catholic showpiece has a richly decorated and colorful interior.

Pointe-à-Callière
Archeological Museum
An underground tour here leads visitors past excavated ruins and early water systems dating from the 17th century.

For hotels and restaurants in this region see pp350–59 and pp364–83; for transport information see p410

Hôtel de Ville
The city hall was created in French Second Empire style in 1872–78, and restored to its glory in 1922. The marble hall features a statue of the first mayor.

Locator Map
See Montreal Map pp112–113

RUE BONSECOURS

RUE NOTRE-DAME

RUE SAINT-CLAUDE

PLACE JACQUES CARTIER

RUE SAINT-VINCENT

RUE SAINT-PAUL

RUE DE LA COMMUNE

PROMENADE DES ARTISTES

Chapelle Notre Dame-de-Bonsecours
Long the spiritual home of Quebec's sailors, this church has fine views of the river from its tower.

Marché Bonsecours
The neo-Renaissance façade of this elegant building conceals its lively history, from its early 19th-century days as Canada's Parliament to a thriving time as a vegetable market.

3 ★ Château Ramezay
Once the home of Montreal's governing city council, this 18th-century building pays tribute to the settling of Quebec with its fine museum of early tools and artifacts.

| 0 metres | 100 |
| 0 yards | 100 |

Key

— Suggested route

❶ Vieux-Port

333 Rue de la Commune. **Tel** (514) 496 7678. 🚇 Central Station. 🚌 55, 515, Terminus Voyager. 🚇 Square Victoria. 🌐 oldportofmontreal.com

In its glory days of the 19th century, the Vieux-Port of Montreal was one of the most important inland harbors in North America, but it declined in the early 20th century. By the late 1980s, the Canadian government had begun to transform it into one of the most popular parks in Montreal. Its waterside walkways and open grassy fields blend almost seamlessly into the lovely streets of Vieux-Montréal, giving the old city a wide window onto the river.

Cyclists enjoying the waterfront promenade, Vieux-Port

The port has a bustling, recreational atmosphere. On summer afternoons, visitors and Montrealers alike stroll, cycle, or in-line skate along the Promenade du Vieux-Port.

❸ Château Ramezay

280 Rue Notre Dame E. **Tel** (514) 861 3708. 🚇 VIA Rail. 🚌 14, 55, 515, Terminus Voyager. 🚇 Champ-de-Mars. **Open** Jun–Sep: 10am–6pm daily; Oct–May: 10am–4:30pm Tue–Sun. **Closed** Jan 1, Dec 25. 🎦 🐾 🛍️ 🌐 chateauramezay.qc.ca

When Montreal's 11th governor, Claude de Ramezay, arrived in the city in 1702, he was homesick for Normandy and decided to build a residence that was reminiscent of the châteaux back home, with stone walls, dormer windows, and copper roof. The squat round towers, added in the 19th century, reinforce the effect.

❷ Basilique Notre-Dame-de-Montréal

In the center of Place d'Armes sits the Basilica, Montreal's grandest Catholic church. Originally built in the 17th century, a new building was completed in 1829. American architect James O'Donnell excelled himself by building a vast vaulted cavern that was Canada's first Neo-Gothic church, and provides 3,000 seats in the nave and two tiers of balconies. Splendidly redecorated in the 1870s, the intricate woodcarving is the work of Canadian craftsman Victor Bourgeau.

The main altar is surrounded by delicate pine and walnut woodcarving.

The nave is illuminated by a rose window under an azure ceiling.

★ Reredos
The focus of the nave is backed by azure, beneath a golden starry sky.

★ Pulpit
This ornate construction was sculpted by Philippe Hébert. The prophets Ezekiel and Jeremiah stand at its base.

Many of de Ramezay's governor successors lived here and the building also housed the West India Company. This is one of the most impressive remnants of the French regime open to the public in Montreal.

The château has been restored to its original style. Of particular interest is the Nantes Salon, with its 18th-century carved paneling by the French architect Germain Boffrand.

Uniforms, documents, and furniture on the main floor reflect the life of New France's ruling classes, while the cellars depict the doings of humbler colonists. The scarlet automobile, made for the city's first motorist, is an interesting sight.

❹ Sir George-Etienne Cartier National Historic Site

458 Rue Notre Dame E. **Tel** (514) 283 2282. 🚇 Central Station. 🚌 Terminus Voyager. 🚇 Champ-de-Mars. **Open** May 18–Jun 23 & Sep 3–Oct 14: 10am–5pm Fri–Sun & public hols; Jun 24–Sep 2: 10am–5pm daily. **Closed** Jan–Mar. 🎧 ♿ 📷 🎫

George-Etienne Cartier (1814–73) was a Father of Confederation (*see p52*) and one of the most important French-Canadian politicians of his day. This national historic site comprises two adjoining graystone

Ormolu clock at the Etienne Cartier

houses owned by the Cartiers on the eastern edge of the old town. One is dedicated to Cartier's career as a lawyer, politician, and railroad-builder. In this house, you can sit at a round table and listen in either French or English to a very good summary of the political founding of modern Canada.

The second house focuses on the Cartiers' domestic life and the functioning of a Victorian upper middle-class family. Visitors can wander through formal rooms full of rich furniture and listen to snatches of taped conversation from "servants" talking about their lives.

The twin towers rise 69 m (226 ft) above the basilica and are visible across the old city.

The Vieux Séminaire dates from 1685 and still belongs to the Sulpician Fathers, the priests who also run the basilica. It is the oldest building in Montreal.

VISITORS' CHECKLIST

Practical Information
110 Rue Notre Dame W.
Tel (514) 842 2925.
Open 8am–4:30pm Mon–Fri (4pm Sat). 🎧 ♿ 📷 🎫 daily.
W notredamebasilica.ca

Transport
🚇 Place d'Armes.

Pipe Organ
The renowned maker Casavant built the organ above the north door in 1891. Recitals are still held frequently.

Stained-glass windows
The basilica's beautiful windows were imported from Limoges in 1930. Each tells a story of Montreal's past; this shows New World pioneer Maisonneuve climbing Mont Royal in 1643.

Children playing outside the Centre des sciences de Montréal

❺ Centre des sciences de Montréal

King Edward Pier. **Tel** (514) 496 4724. 🚇 Central Station. 🚌 Terminus Voyager. 🚇 Champs-de-Mars. **Open** variable; check website. 🌐 montrealsciencecentre.com

Dominating the Vieux-Port's King Edward Pier, this huge, airy building is home to a number of permanent and temporary exhibitions that focus on technology, engineering, and science, as well as other subjects. Among the permanent exhibitions, "Cargo" shows visitors how cargo transits through a large port like Montreal. The experience includes games, films and cutaway containers. The exhibits were produced in collaboration with Quebec's Ministry of Education and are designed to appeal to children.

Attached to the Centre des sciences de Montréal is the IMAX Telux theater that shows educational documentaries in 3-D on its immense screen.

❻ Centre d'Histoire de Montréal

335 Place d'Youville. **Tel** (514) 872 3207. 🚌 61. 🚇 Square Victoria. **Open** Tue–Sun. **Closed** mid-Dec–mid-Jan. 📷

The exhibits in this museum trace the history of Montreal from the first Indian settlements to the modern age, with the focus on everyday life. The museum is housed in a handsome, red-brick fire station with a gracefully gabled roof built in 1903. There are three floors of exhibits. On the first floor, "Montreal, 5 Times", the museum's permanent exhibition, traces five passages in Montreal's history, beginning in 1535 with the meeting of First Nations peoples and European explorers and ending with the cultural boom of the 1960s. The museum's second and third floors are devoted to year-round temporary exhibitions, all of which showcase the city's advancements, its people, and their experiences, while a third-floor observation deck offers a scenic view of the Old Port and Old Montreal.

Centre d'Histoire de Montréal

❼ Chinatown

🚇 Champ-de-Mars; Place des Arts.

The name has become a little anachronistic, as many of the restaurants and shops in this 18-block district just northeast of the Old City are now owned by Vietnamese and Thai immigrants. Most arrived in Montreal in the wake of 20th-century upheavals in Southeast Asia. The Chinese, however, were here first. They began arriving in large numbers after 1880, along with many European immigrants. The Chinese community stuck together in this corner of the city in an attempt to avoid discrimination from some of the town's residents. As they grew more prosperous, many of the descendants of the first immigrants moved to the wealthier areas of Montreal, leaving Chinatown to the elderly and to the newly arrived. Many thousands of them now return during the weekends, making the narrow streets busy and full of people shopping for silk, souvenirs, vegetables, records, and barbecued meat.

Restaurants specialize in a range of delicious cuisines, serving Szechuan, Cantonese, Thai, Vietnamese, and Korean food, fragrantly filling the air with the smell of hot barbecued pork and aromatic noodles.

For those seeking respite from the bustle of the streets and their vibrant market stalls, there is a lovely little garden dedicated to the charismatic Chinese leader Sun Yat-sen on Clarke Street. Other features of the area include two large, Chinese-style arches, which span de la Gauchetière Street, and, strangely enough, a pair of authentic pagodas on the roof of the modern Holiday Inn hotel.

A brightly colored market stall in vibrant Chinatown

Parc Lafontaine, a popular spot with a leisurely atmosphere in Plateau Mont-Royal

❽ Plateau Mont-Royal

Tel Tourisme Montreal: (514) 844 5400. Sherbrooke; Mont-Royal.

No neighborhood captures the essence of Montreal more fully than the Plateau. Its main thoroughfares are lined with bistros, bookstores, boutiques, and sidewalk cafés. Nightclubs veer from the eccentric to the classic, and eateries from snack bars and sandwich shops to some of the best dining locations in the city. Jazz bars, too, are popular in this area.

The area's residents are a mix of students, working-class French-speakers, trendy young professionals, and ethnic families with roots in Europe and Latin America. They gather either in Parc Lafontaine, a neighborly expanse of green with an outdoor theater, or in "Balconville," a distinctly Montrealer institution linked to the duplexes and triplexes that many residents live in. To save interior space, these stacks of single-floor flats are studded with balconies linked to the street by fanciful, wrought-iron stairways. In summer they become centers for parties, family gatherings, and picnics.

The large working-class families for whom these homes were built in the early part of the century lived very modestly, but they managed to amass enough money to build large, beautiful parish churches, notably the Eglise Saint-Jean-Baptiste. The Catholic bourgeoisie lived a little farther south, in gracious Second-Empire homes on Rue Saint-Denis or Carré Saint-Louis.

Mile End, an area that stretches roughly northeast from Mont Royal to St. Laurent Boulevard, is one of the city's trendiest districts. The ambiance is relaxed, with plenty of cafés, art galleries, and boutiques. Be sure to try the famous Montreal bagels at one of the St. Viateur bagel shops.

❾ Place des Arts

260 Blvd. de Maisonneuve W. **Tel** (514) 842 2112. Place des Arts.
w pdarts.com

This complex of halls and theaters sits at the heart of the Quartier des Spectacles entertainment district and is Montreal's prime center for the performing arts. Both the Opéra de Montréal (Montreal Opera) and the Orchèstre Symphonique de Montréal (Montreal Symphony Orchestra) make their home here. The buildings of Place des Arts share a spacious central plaza with the outstanding Musée d'Art Contemporain (*see pp120–21*).

Place des Arts, Montreal's top entertainment venue

⓾ Musée d'art contemporain de Montréal

Opened in 1964, the Montreal Museum of Contemporary Art is the only institution in Canada dedicated exclusively to modern art. Located in downtown Montreal, more than 60 percent of the approximately 7,600 paintings, drawings, photographs, videos, and installations in the permanent collection are by Quebec artists. Works date from 1939, but the emphasis is on the contemporary. There are also works by innovative international talents, such as the controversial Bill Viola, Louise Bourgeois, and Andrès Serrano. The exhibits are in wide, well-lit galleries whose elegance helped to earn the Musée a Grand Prix from Montreal Council.

Casier pour objet du désir (2000)
Francine Savard's sculpture is a magnified 3D grid constructed with linden wood.

First Floor

★ **Sans titre** (1988)
Quebec-born artist Richard Mill's colorful abstract painting is part of the museum's "A Matter of Abstraction" exhibition. Covering the period from the early 1940s to 2010, the 104 works by 46 significant artists focus on the museum's collection of Quebec art.

Street Level

Key

- ☐ Permanent exhibition space
- ☐ Temporary exhibition space
- ☐ Pierre Granche sculpture
- ☐ Movie theater
- ☐ Video gallery
- ☐ Multimedia gallery
- ☐ Theater/Seminar hall
- ☐ Art workshops
- ☐ Nonexhibition space

Entrance Hall
The museum uses this airy modern space, hung in places with pieces from its collection, for special events and receptions. A pleasant first-floor restaurant overlooks the hall.

Museum Guide

Only a small proportion of the exhibits in the museum are on permanent display. They occupy the upper floor space along with rotating and visiting items. There is also a sculpture garden, accessible from the main museum building, that has rotating exhibits and is a good spot to rest during a tour of the galleries.

★ **Comme si le temps …
de la rue** (1991–2)
Pierre Granche's permanent installation within the Place des Arts complex is based on Egyptian mythological figures whose shapes symbolize Montreal. Created to contrast with its urban milieu, the work exudes humor and poetry.

Museum façade
Built in the 1990s, the MAC building shows 320 artworks, taken from their much larger rotating collection.

⓫ Christ Church Cathedral

1444 Union Ave. **Tel** (514) 843 6577.
🚇 Central Station. 🚌 15. 🚇 McGill.
Open 8am–5:30pm daily. ♿

Architect Frank Wills completed Christ Church in 1859 as the seat of the Anglican bishop of Montreal. This graceful Gothic limestone building, with a triple portal and a tall slender spire, has exterior walls decorated with gargoyles. The church was too heavy for the land, and the stone spire was replaced in 1940 with a treated aluminum steeple. Many local workers find respite at noon concerts in the cathedral's cool, dim interior with its pointed arched nave and magnificent stained-glass windows, some from the William Morris studio in London.

Inuit slippers at the McCord Museum

Christ Church Cathedral, based on a 14th-century English design

⓬ McCord Museum

690 Sherbrooke St. W. **Tel** (514) 398 7100. 🚇 Central Station. 🚌 24. 🚇 McGill. **Open** 10am–6pm Tue, Thu & Fri; 10am–9pm Wed, 10am–5pm Sat & Sun. **Closed** Mon (except Jun 24–Sep 3). ♿ 🇼 mccord-museum.qc.ca

Lawyer David Ross McCord (1844–1930) was an avid collector of virtually everything that had to do with life in Canada, including books, photographs, jewelry, furniture, clothing, documents, papers, paintings, toys, and porcelain.

In 1919, he gave his considerable acquisitions to McGill University with a view to establishing a museum of Canadian social history. That collection, now more than 140,000 artifacts, is housed in a stately limestone building that was once a social center for McGill students. The museum has a good section of early history, as well as exceptional folk art. A particularly fine collection of Indian and Inuit items features clothing, weapons, jewelry, furs, and pottery. A separate room is devoted to the social history of Montreal. The museum's most celebrated possession is a vast collection of photographs that chronicle every detail of daily life in 19th-century Montreal.

⓭ McGill University

845 Rue Sherbrooke W. **Tel** (514) 398 4455. 🚇 Central Station. 🚌 24. 🚇 McGill. **Open** 9am–6pm Mon–Fri. 🎧 book in advance. ♿ 🇼 mcgill.ca

When it was founded in 1821, Canada's best-known university was set on land left for the purpose by fur trader and land speculator James McGill (1744–1813). The university's main entrance is guarded by the Classical Roddick Gates. Behind them an avenue leads to the domed Neoclassical Arts Building, which is the oldest structure on campus.

The rest of the 70 or so buildings range from the ornately Victorian to the starkly concrete. One of the loveliest is the **Redpath Museum of Natural History**, which holds one of the city's most eclectic and eccentric collections. A huge number of fossils, including a dinosaur skeleton, sit alongside African art, Roman coins, and a shrunken head.

🏛️ **Redpath Museum of Natural History**
859 Rue Sherbrooke W. **Tel** (514) 398 4086. **Open** 9am–5pm Mon–Fri; 1pm–5pm Sun. **Closed** Sat. ♿

⑭ Musée des Beaux Arts

The oldest and largest art collection in Quebec contains almost 36,000 objects, including paintings, sculptures, prints, drawings, photographs, and decorative objects, housed in four pavilions. The Michal and Renata Hornstein Pavilion focuses on world cultures, with theme-based areas that include pre-Columbian, African, Asian, and Islamic arts. The galleries in the Jean-Noël Desmarais Pavilion focus on European art from the Middle Ages to the 20th century, especially the Renaissance. In the Claire and Marc Bourgie Pavilion works include Inuit art and paintings from the colonial period to the 1960s. Devoted to the decorative arts and design, the Liliane and David M. Stewart Pavilion features pieces by Gallé, Lalique, and Frank Lloyd Wright.

Façade of Jean-Noël Desmarais Pavilion
This pavilion holds a collection of about 26,000 pieces, from Old Masters to international contemporary art.

★ **Portrait of a Young Woman** (c.1665)
This famous work originated in Rembrandt's native Holland. Painted in characteristically realist style, the sitter's pensive concentration is thrown into sharper relief by the deep black background.

Michal and Renata Hornstein Pavilion

Connected to the Desmarais Pavilion by an underground tunnel that contains an exhibition on ancient cultures, this gallery is dedicated to pre-1960 America and includes Meso-American, Inuit, and Amerindian art, as well as early European-style furniture, domestic silver, and decorative art. Later galleries follow the history of Canadian painting, from church sacred art to early native studies by wandering artist Paul Kane and the impressionism of James Wilson Morrice. The Group of Seven and Paul-Emile Borduas are among those representing the 20th century.

18th-century silver teapot

Level 3

Access to the Michal and Renata Hornstein Pavilion

Level S2

VISITORS' CHECKLIST

Practical Information
1379–1380 Rue Sherbrooke W.
Tel (514) 285 2000.
Open 11am–5pm Tue, Thu–Sun;
11am–9pm Wed. **Closed** Mon.
🏛 for special exhibitions. ♿ ✏
Ⓦ mbam.qc.ca

Transport
🚉 Central Station. 🚌 24.
🚇 Guy Concordia.

A street-level entrance to the labyrinthine Underground City

Level 4

★ **Man of the House of Leiva** (1590)
El Greco's haunting portrayals of the Spanish aristocracy are a Renaissance highlight.

⓯ Underground City

🚉 Central Station. 🚌 Terminus Voyager. 🚇 Peel, McGill, Bonaventure.

When Montreal opened its first métro (or subway) lines in 1966, it inadvertently created a whole new layer of urban life – the Underground City. It is theoretically possible to lead a rich life in Montreal without once stepping outside.
The first métro stations had underground links to just the two main train stations, a few hotels, and the shopping mall under the Place Ville-Marie office tower. This has turned into a vast network of over 30 km (19 miles) of well-lit, boutique-lined passages that includes more than 1,600 shops, 200 restaurants, hotels, film theaters, and concert halls.

⓰ Square Dorchester and Place du Canada

ℹ 1001 Rue Square Dorchester.
Tel (514) 873 2015. 🚉 Central Station. 🚌 Terminus Voyager. 🚇 Peel, Bonaventure, Lucien-L'Allier.

These two open squares create a green oasis in downtown Montreal. On the north side of Boulevard René-Lévesque, statues including Canada's first French-Canadian prime minister, Sir Wilfrid Laurier, share Square Dorchester with a war memorial. On Place du Canada a statue of the country's first prime minister, Sir John A. Macdonald, looks out over the stately Boulevard René-Lévesque.
The buildings surrounding the park are eclectic. The mix includes a Gothic church, a shiny, black bank tower and the Sun Life Building (1933), a huge stone fortress that housed the British Crown Jewels during World War II.

Gallery Guide

The exceptional painting collections are contained on levels 3 and 4 of the Desmarais Pavilion. Level 2 offers a fine café. The museum shop and main entrance are on level 1. Lower level S2 has contemporary art galleries and tunnel access to the Michal and Renata Hornstein Pavilion.

Key

▫ Contemporary art
▫ Art of ancient cultures
▫ 19th-century European art
▫ African art
▫ Old Masters
▫ Temporary exhibitions
▫ Nonexhibition space

Varied architecture, from historic to post-modern, in Square Dorchester

Place du Canada, Square Dorchester, and the Cathédrale Marie-Reine-du-Monde ▶

Marie-Reine-du-Monde façade with statues of Montreal's patron saints

⑰ Cathédrale Marie-Reine-du-Monde

1085 Rue Cathédrale. **Tel** (514) 866 1661. 🚇 Central Station. 🚌 Terminus Voyager. 🚇 Bonaventure. **Open** 7am–6:15pm Mon–Fri, 7:30am–6:15pm Sat, Sun. ♿

When Montreal's first Catholic cathedral burned down in 1852, Bishop Ignace Bourget decided to demonstrate the importance of the Catholic Church in Canada by building a new one in a district dominated at the time by the English Protestant commercial elite. To show his flock's loyalty to the Pope, he modeled his new church on St. Peter's Basilica in Rome.

The cathedral, which was completed in 1894, has dimensions that are a quarter of those of St. Peter's. The statues on the roof represent the patron saints of all the parishes that constituted the Montreal diocese in 1890. The magnificent altar canopy, a replica of the one Bernini made for St. Peter's, was cast in copper and gold leaf. Another reminder of Bourget's loyalty to Rome can be found on the pillar in the northeast corner of the church. Here lies a marble plaque listing the names of all the Montrealers who served in the Papal armies during the Italian war of independence in the 1850s.

The altar canopy in the cathedral

⑱ Centre Canadien d'Architecture

1920 Rue Baille. **Tel** (514) 939 7000. 🚇 Central. 🚌 Terminus Voyager. 🚇 Guy Concordia. **Open** 11am–6pm Wed–Sun, 11am–9pm Thu. **Closed** Mon & Tue. 🅿 ♿ 📷 book ahead. 🌐 cca.qc.ca

Visitors enter this museum and international research center through an unobtrusive glass door in an almost windowless façade of gray limestone that fronts this large U-shaped building. Well-lit exhibition rooms house a series of regular exhibits in rotation. The primary exhibits focus on architecture, design, and landscape architecture. The two arms of the modern building embrace the ornate Shaughnessy House, which faces Boulevard René-Lévesque Ouest. Now part of the Centre, the house was built in 1874 for the president of the Canadian Pacific Railway, Sir Thomas Shaughnessy, and has an art-nouveau conservatory with an intricately decorated ceiling.

The Centre is also a major scholarly institution. Its extensive collection of architectural plans, drawings, models, and photographs is the most important of its kind anywhere. The library alone has in excess of 215,000 volumes on the world's most significant buildings.

⑲ Rue Sherbrooke

🚇 Central Station. 🚌 Terminus Voyager. 🚇 Sherbrooke.

In the latter half of the 19th century, Montreal was one of the most important cities in the British Empire. Its traders and industrialists controlled about 70 percent of Canada's wealth, and many built themselves fine homes on the slopes of Mont Royal in an area that became known as the Golden, or Square, Mile. Rue Sherbrooke between Guy and University was their Main Street, and its shops, hotels, and churches were the most elegant in the country.

Some of that elegance survived the modernizing bulldozers of the 1960s. Holt Renfrew, Montreal's upscale department store, and the stately Ritz-Carlton Hotel still stand. So do two exquisite churches, the Presbyterian St. Andrew and St. Paul, and the Erskine American United at the corner of avenue du Musée, which boasts stained-glass windows by Tiffany. Boutiques, bookstores, and galleries fill many of the rows of graystone townhouses. Millionaires not quite wealthy enough to make it into the Square Mile built graceful row homes on rues de la Montagne, Crescent, and Bishop nearby. Many of these now house trendy shops and bistros.

Farther west is the Grande Seminaire, where Montreal's Roman Catholic archdiocese still trains its priests.

Historic home on Rue Sherbrooke, the "Golden Square Mile"

Montreal's largest shrine, Oratoire Saint-Joseph, showing the steps climbed annually by pilgrims

⑳ Oratoire Saint-Joseph

3800 Chemin Queen Mary. **Tel** (514) 733 8211. 🚇 Central Station. 🚌 Terminus Voyager. 🚇 Côte-des-Neiges. **Open** daily. ♿

Every year, two million pilgrims climb the 283 steps (99 of which can be climbed in prayer on the knees) to the entrance of this vast church. Their devotion would no doubt please Brother André (1845–1937), the truly remarkable man responsible for building this shrine to the husband of the Virgin Mary. It began when he built a hillside chapel to St. Joseph in his spare time. Montreal's sick and disabled joined him at his prayers, and soon there were reports of miraculous cures. Brother André began to draw pilgrims, and the present oratory was built to receive them. Pilgrims can pray on his tomb. He was beatified in 1982 and canonized in 2010.

The church's octagonal copper dome is one of the biggest in the world – 44.5 m (146 ft) high and 38 m (125 ft) wide. The interior is starkly modern; the elongated wooden statues of the apostles in the transepts are the work of Henri Charlier, who was also responsible for the main altar and the huge crucifix. The striking stained-glass windows were made by Marius Plamondon. The main building houses a museum depicting André's life. Beside the crypt church, a votive chapel is ablaze with flickering candles that have been lit by hopeful pilgrims.

㉑ Parc du Mont-Royal

Tel (514) 843 8240. 🚇 Central Station. 🚌 11. 🚇 Mont-Royal. **Open** 6am–midnight daily. ♿

The steep green bump that rises above the city center is only 234 m (767 ft) high, but Montrealers call it simply "the mountain" or "la montagne." Jacques Cartier gave the peak its name when he visited in 1535 and it, in turn, gave its name to the city. The hill became a park in 1876 when the city bought the land and hired Frederick Law Olmsted, the man responsible for designing New York's Central Park, to landscape it. Olmsted tried to keep it natural, building a few lookouts linked by foot-paths. Succeeding generations have added Beaver Lake, a 30-m high (98-ft) cross made of steel girders, and the Voie Camilien Houde, a thoroughfare that cuts through the park from east to west.

The mountain's 101 ha (250 acres) of meadows and hardwood forests still offer Montrealers a precious escape from urban life, as well as spectacular views of the city. The wide terrace in front of the Chalet du Mont-Royal pavilion looks out over the skyscrapers of the down-town core. The northern boundary of the park abuts two huge cemeteries, the Catholic Notre-Dame-Des-Neiges and the old and stately non-denominational Mount Royal Cemetery, where many of Canada's finest rest.

A view of Montreal from the lofty Parc du Mont-Royal

㉒ Olympic Park

Designed for the 1976 Olympic Games, Montreal's Olympic Park showpieces a number of stunning modern buildings. Paris architect Roger Taillibert created the Stadium, now known to many Montrealers as "The Big O," a reference to its round shape. The stadium, seating 56,000, is used today for concerts by international stars, as well as for big exhibitions, and as a modern attraction in a historic city. Arching up the side of the stadium is the Montreal Tower, with its fine views. Nearby, the Biodôme environmental museum replicates four world climates, while the Esplanade Financière Sun Life offers free outdoor activities for all the family on weekends.

View of Olympic Park
An exceptional tourist attraction, the park can be toured fully during the day. Another popular way to visit is for a concert or sporting event.

★ Biodôme
Here are stunning re-creations of climate zones: a steamy rainforest, the freezing Polar World, the fertile forests of the Laurentian Mountains, and the fish-filled St. Lawrence ecosystem.

KEY

① **The Rio Tinto Alcan Planetarium** offers a fresh approach to astronomy with two shows – one scientific, the other more whimsical.

② **The Biodôme** was first used as a velodrome for the 1976 Olympics – hence the unusual cycling hat design of its roof.

③ **A cable car** shoots up the side of the tower at speed; tickets can be combined with a guided tour of the Stadium or Biodôme.

④ **The stadium roof** was originally intended to be retractable. However, due to structural problems, it was replaced in 1998 by a detached, permanently closed roof.

⑤ **The Esplanade Financière Sun Life** presents a program of free outdoor activities for all, from mini-tennis to skateboarding events.

★ Montreal Tower
At 175 m (575 ft) this is the world's tallest inclined tower, arching over the stadium in a graceful sweep. A cable car takes visitors up the side of the tower to its large viewing deck in less than two minutes.

VISITORS' CHECKLIST

Practical Information
3200 Viau St. **Tel** (514) 252 4737.
Open Jun–Sep: 1–10pm Mon,
9am–10pm Tue–Sun; Oct–May:
1–6pm Mon, 9am–6pm Tue–Sun.
🚻 🛗 🏠 🖥 📷
w parcolympique.qc.ca

Transport
🚇 Viau and Pie-IX.

★ Olympic Stadium
The first event to take place in this cavernous space was the spectacular opening ceremonies of the 1976 Summer Olympic Games.

Viewing Deck
This glass platform provides some stunning views of the city. Signs point out sights of interest that can be as far as 80 km (50 miles) away.

Sports Centre
This fully equipped center offers unbeatable facilities, including a 15-m (50-ft) deep scuba diving pool. The center is closed to the public for renovation work until at least fall 2014, so check before visiting.

Plan of the Olympic Park Area

1. Saputo Stadium
2. Pierre-Charbonneau Centre
3. Maurice-Richard Arena
4. Biodôme
5. Olympic Stadium
6. Sports Centre/Montreal Tower
7. Botanical Gardens
8. Esplanade Financière Sun Life
9. Rio Tinto Alcan Planetarium

0 meters   50
0 yards   50

The Jardin botanique is an oasis of calm away from the rush of the city

㉓ Jardin botanique de Montréal

4101 Rue Sherbrooke E. **Tel** (514) 872 1400. 🚇 Pie-IX. **Open** times vary throughout the year so check website before visiting. ♿ 🅿 ♿
w espacepourlavie.ca

Montreal's botanical garden is among the largest in the world, a fine accomplishment for this northern city with a brutal climate. Its 75-ha (182-acre) enclose 30 outdoor gardens, 10 green-houses, a "courtyard of the senses" in which blind interpreters help visitors discover the touch and smell of exotic flowers, and a bug-shaped Insectarium full of creepy-crawlies, both preserved and living. Its most peaceful havens are the 2.5-ha (6-acre) Chinese Garden, a delightful replica of a 14th-century Ming garden, and the exquisite Japanese Garden.

Bonsai tree at the Jardin botanique

㉔ Parc Jean-Drapeau

20 Chemin Tour de Lille. **Tel** (514) 872 6120. 🚇 Jean Drapeau. 🚌 Vieux-Port. **Open** 6am–midnight daily. ♿

Encompassing both Ile-Sainte-Hélène and Ile-Notre-Dame, Parc Jean-Drapeau is a popular visitor's attraction and a hub for major events, such as Piknic Electronik which is held every Sunday throughout the summer.

The small forested Ile-Sainte-Hélène, sitting in the middle of the St. Lawrence River, has played a major role in Montreal's emergence as a modern city. Originally named after Samuel de Champlain's wife *(see p49)*, it was the site of Expo '67, the world fair that brought millions of visitors to the city in the summer of 1967.

Several reminders of those days remain – most notably La Ronde, the fair's amusement park, and the dome that served as the United States Pavilion. This is now the Biosphere, an interpretive center that examines the Great Lakes and St. Lawrence River system. Between the dome and the roller coasters is the Fort de l'Ile-Sainte-Hélène, built in 1825 to protect Montreal from a potential American attack. Its red stone walls enclose a grassy parade square that is used today by members of the Olde 78th Fraser Highlanders and the Compagnie Franche de la Marine, re-creations of two 18th-century regimental military formations that fought each other over the future of New France until 1759. The fort also houses the **Musée David M. Stewart**, a small and excellent museum of social and military history with educational activities for schools and younger visitors.

The Ile-Notre-Dame, a 116-ha (286-acre) wedge of land encircled by the St. Lawrence Seaway, did not exist until 1967, when it was created with rock excavated for the Montreal métro system. It shared Expo '67 with Ile-Sainte-Hélène, and today the two islands constitute the Parc Jean-Drapeau. Ile-Notre-Dame's most popular attraction by far is the monumental Casino de Montréal, a province-owned gambling hall housed in the old French and Quebec pavilions. Every day, thousands line up at its tables and slot machines. The casino never closes. There are more refined entertain-ments – a rowing basin, excavated for the 1976 Olympics, superb floral gardens, and a carefully filtered body of water, which is the site of the city's only swimming beach. Ile-Notre-Dame's Circuit Gilles-Villeneuve, named for the Canadian champion, plays host to Formula 1 races.

Built for Expo '67, the Biosphere has displays on Canadian river systems

The province-owned Casino on Ile-Notre-Dame is open to the hopeful 24 hours a day

Ⅲ Musée David M. Stewart
20 Chemin Tour de Lille. **Tel** (514) 861 6701. **Open** 10am–5pm Wed–Mon. **Closed** Jan 1, Dec 25.

㉕ Maison Saint-Gabriel

2146 Place de Dublin. **Tel** (514) 935 8136. 🚇 Charlevoix. 🚌 57. **Open** late Jun–Sep: Mon–Sat; Sep–Jun: Tue–Sun. obligatory.

This isolated fragment of New France at first appears lost among the apartment buildings of working-class Pointe-Saint-Charles. It was a farm when the formidable Marguerite Bourgeoys, Montreal's first schoolteacher and now a canonized saint, bought it in 1668 as a residence for the religious order she had founded in 1655.

The house, rebuilt in 1698 after a fire, is a fine example of 17th-century architecture, with thick stone walls and a steeply pitched roof built on an intricate frame of original heavy wooden timbers.

Marguerite Bourgeoys and her tireless sisters worked the farm and ran a school on the property for native and colonial children. They also housed and trained the *filles du roy* (the "king's daughters"), orphaned young girls sent abroad to be the women of his new colony. The house's chapel, kitchen, dormitory, and drawing rooms are full of artifacts dating from the 17th century. These include a writing desk the saint used herself and a magnificent vestment and cope, embroidered in silk, silver, and gold by a wealthy hermit who lived in a hut on the property.

㉖ Lachine

Blvd. St. Joseph. **Tel** (514) 873 2015. 🚇 Lionel Groulx. 🚌 191.

Lachine comprises a suburb of southwest Montreal and includes a small island of the same name west of the Lachine Rapids, where the St. Lawrence River widens to form Lac-Saint-Louis. Lachine is now part of Montreal, but has a long history of its own. The old town along Blvd. Saint-Joseph is charming. Many of its fine old homes have become restaurants and bistros with outdoor terraces that overlook Parc René-Lévesque and the lake. One of the oldest houses, built by merchants in 1670, is now the **Musée de Lachine**, a historical museum and art gallery. The **Fur Trade at Lachine National Historic Site** is a building dedicated to the fur trade, which for years was Montreal's main support.

The Lachine Canal, built in the 19th century to bypass the rapids, links the town directly to the Vieux-Port. The canal itself is now blocked to shipping, but the land along its banks has been turned into parkland with a bicycle trail.

Ⅲ Musée de Lachine
1 Chemin du Musée. **Tel** (514) 634 3478. **Open** Apr–Nov: 11:30am–4:30pm Wed–Sun. reserve.

Ⅲ Fur Trade at Lachine National Historic Site
1255 Blvd. St. Joseph. **Tel** (514) 637 7433. **Open** Apr–mid-Oct: daily; rest of year: by reservation only.

A view of the historical Musée de Lachine from the reclaimed canal

QUEBEC CITY AND THE ST. LAWRENCE RIVER

The heart and soul of French Canada, Quebec City sits overlooking the St. Lawrence River on the cliffs of Cap Diamant. As provincial capital, the city is the seat of regional government, and nowadays is the heart of French-Canadian nationalism. Parisian in atmosphere, with every tiny street worth visiting, Quebec City is almost entirely French-speaking. The European ambiance, architecture, and the city's crucial historical importance all contributed to it being named as a United Nations World Heritage Site in 1985. One of the world's great waterways, the St. Lawrence River is home to rare marine wildlife. Right and minke whales swim as far upstream as Tadoussac and feed at the mouth of the Saguenay River. The Laurentian Mountains rise up above the St. Lawrence on the north shore, a year-round natural playground. Nearer Quebec City, the rich scenery of the Charlevoix region is among the most beautiful in the country, contrasting with the soaring cliffs and wilderness of the Gaspé Peninsula. Offshore, Ile d'Anticosti is a stunning nature preserve.

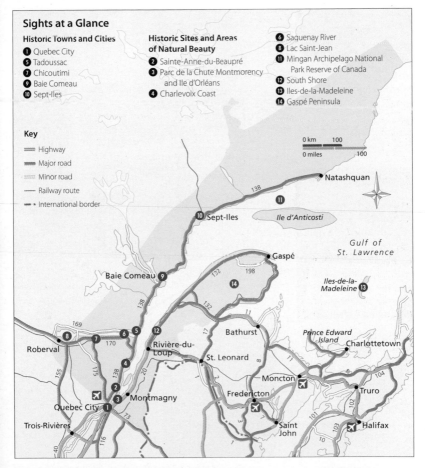

Sights at a Glance

Historic Towns and Cities
1. Quebec City
5. Tadoussac
7. Chicoutimi
9. Baie Comeau
10. Sept-Iles

Historic Sites and Areas of Natural Beauty
2. Sainte-Anne-du-Beaupré
3. Parc de la Chute Montmorency and Ile d'Orléans
4. Charlevoix Coast

6. Saguenay River
8. Lac Saint-Jean
11. Mingan Archipelago National Park Reserve of Canada
12. South Shore
13. Iles-de-la-Madeleine
14. Gaspé Peninsula

Key
- ═══ Highway
- ▬▬ Major road
- ═ ═ Minor road
- ── Railway route
- ▬ • International border

0 km 100
0 miles 100

Natashquan
138
11
10 Sept-Iles   Ile d'Anticosti

Gulf of St. Lawrence

Gaspé
Baie Comeau 9   132   198
14   Iles-de-la-Madeleine 13

169
8   7   170   6   5   12
Roberval   Rivière-du-Loup   132   11
138   Bathurst   Prince Edward Island   Charlottetown
155   175   138   4   St. Leonard
20   Moncton   104
3   2   Fredericton   Truro
Quebec City 1   Montmagny   102
Trois-Rivières   73   101   103
116   Saint John   10   Halifax
40

◄ Fairmont Le Château Frontenac rising behind buildings in Old Quebec   **For map symbols** *see back flap*

❶ Street-by-Street: Quebec City

One of the oldest communities on the American continent, Quebec City was discovered as an Iroquois village by the French explorer Jacques Cartier and founded as a city in 1608 by explorer Samuel de Champlain *(see p49)*. The British gained dominance over the city and the rest of the province at the Plains of Abraham battle just outside the city walls in 1759. Today the town is renowned as the heart of French Canada. The oldest part of the city is Basse-Ville, or Lower Town, which was renovated in the 1970s. With its winding staircases and cafés, it is a charming destination.

Musée du Fort
Military history is brought to life here in sound-and-light shows reenacting six Quebec sieges and battles, and numerous war relics.

★ **Basilique Notre-Dame-de-Québec**
This 1647 cathedral provides a rich setting for relics from early French rule in Quebec, and Old Master paintings.

Holy Trinity Anglican Cathedral
An elegant 1804 stone Neo-Classical façade conceals an English oak interior.

Fairmont Le Château Frontenac
Quebec City's best-known landmark has risen over the city since 1893, and has 618 luxurious guest rooms.

Key
— Suggested route

Musée de la civilisation
Human history through the ages is explored in this airy modern building linked to historic houses in the rest of the town, including Maison historique Chevalier.

★ **Place Royale**
A virtual microcosm of Canadian history, Place Royale has experienced a renaissance, and the surrounding streets, with their 18th-and 19th-century architecture, have been sandblasted back to their original glory.

The funicular travels from Terrasse Dufferin to Lower Town, providing excellent aerial views of the historic city center.

Maison historique Chevalier
Linked with the Musée de la civilisation, this home built for an 18th-century merchant showcases the decorative arts. Quebec furniture and the famous Quebec silverware feature in every room, as well as exhibits showing how well-to-do families lived in the 18th and 19th centuries.

0 meters   100
0 yards   100

Quebec City

Containing the only walled city north of the Rio Grande, Quebec City has narrow cobblestone streets and 18th-century buildings that lend a European air to this small provincial capital, just 55 square km (21 square miles). Most of the sights are packed into one accessible corner, above and below the Cap Diamant cliffs, with the Citadel rising up protectively at the top of the cliff. As Quebec's capital, the city is home to the provincial parliament, the Assemblée Nationale, which conducts its debates almost entirely in French in splendid chambers behind the ornate 19th-century façade of the grandiose Hôtel du Parlement.

Fairmont Le Château Frontenac dominates the skyline of Quebec City

Exploring Quebec City

Most of the main sights are easily reached on foot. The city can conveniently be divided into three parts. Basse-Ville, or Lower Town, is the oldest part, and rambles along the St. Lawrence River at the foot of Cap Diamant. Above lies the walled city, Haute-Ville, or Upper Town. This area is full of shops and restaurants, similar to the Basse-Ville, but both Catholic and Protestant cathedrals are here, as is the imposing Fairmont Le Château Frontenac. Beyond the walls stretches Grande Allée, with the Hôtel du Parlement where the provincial parliament of Quebec sits.

🏛 Terrasse Dufferin

Sweeping along the top of Cap Diamant from Fairmont Le Château Frontenac to the edge of the Citadel, this boardwalk is well equiped with benches and kiosks, and offers unmatched views of the St. Lawrence River, the Laurentian Mountains, and Ile

d'Orleans. During the freezing winter, Les Glissades de la Terrasse, an ice slide for toboggans is installed on the terrace.

🏛 Parc des Champs-de-Bataille

835 Ave. Wilfrid Laurier. **Tel** (418) 649 6157. **Open** daily. 🏛

Once a battlefield where the future of Canada was decided, the Battlefields Park is now a delightful grassy recreation ground, with grand monuments and a dedicated fountain –the only clues to the area's bloody and dramatic history. On September 13, 1759, British regulars under General James Wolfe defeated the French army on this clifftop field, the Plains of Abraham, just outside the walls of Quebec *(see pp50–51)*, establishing permanent British rule in Canada. In 1908, the 103-ha (254-acre) battlefield was turned into one of the largest urban parks in North America.

Joan of Arc at Parc des Champs-de-Bataille

🏛 Assemblée Nationale

Ave. Honoré-Mercier & Grande Allée E. **Tel** (418) 643 7239. 🏛 🏛 daily.

The Assemblée Nationale, Quebec's provincial parliament, meets just outside the walls of the Old City in this graceful Second-Empire building, completed in 1886 as a showcase of provincial history. Niches along the imposing façade and up the sides of the tall central tower display 22 bronze figures, each representing a person who played a vital role in Quebec's development. The first inhabitants of the territory are honored in a bronze rendition of a First Nations family by the main door. Inside, the blue chamber is the hub of Quebec's political activity.

🏛 Fortifications de Québec

Tel (418) 648 7016. **Open** May–Oct: daily. 🏛 🏛 🏛 **parkscanada.gc.ca/fortifications**

After a century of peace, the French-built fortifications that had secured Quebec since 1759 were transformed in the 1870s from a grim military necessity into this popular attraction. On the city's northern and eastern edges, low and high ramparts studded with cannons defend the clifftop and the plains, with the walls on the western side reaching 9 m (30 ft) at some points. Three elegant gates, the Saint-Jean, the Kent, and the Saint-Louis, pierce the western stretch. A fourth gate, Prescott

Quebec's 18th-century fortifications in the Parc d'Artillerie

Abundant produce stalls draw crowds at the market in Vieux Port

Gate, sits on the city's eastern side. Visitors can walk along the top of the walls for almost 5 km (3 miles).

🏛 Vieux Port
ℹ 100 Rue Quai Saint-Andre. **Tel** (418) 648 3300. ♿

This delightful area has its focus around the old harbor northeast of the walled city. In contrast to the crammed heritage of much of the Lower Town, Vieux Port is an airy riverside walking site, full of new and restored modern attractions. Boat cruises downriver to the Chute Montmorency waterfalls (*see p143*) are available. Waterfront walks pass chic boutiques, apartment blocks, the city's open-air theatre, and shops in trendy warehouse settings.

🏛 Musée de la civilisation
85 Rue Dalhousie. **Tel** (418) 643 2158. **Open** late Jun–early Sep: daily; late Sep–early Jun: Tue–Sun. 🅿 📷 ♿ 🆆 mcq.org

Top contemporary Canadian architect Moshe Safdie designed this modern limestone and glass building in Basse-Ville to house Quebec's museum of history and culture. Although highly up-to-date in feel, the construction has won several prizes for blending in well with its historic surroundings. Three heritage buildings are part of the museum's structure including Maison d'Estebe, an 18th-century merchant's house. The museum also uses another nearby 18th-century house, Maison historique Chevalier, for displaying Quebec architecture and furniture in period setting.

Museum exhibits include "This is Our Story," which reflects on the city's First Nation and Inuit history, and the remains of a 250-year-old French flat-bottomed boat. Many exhibits are hands-on, and, during workshops for families, participants are encouraged to try on costumes from different eras.

Antique and modern architecture of the Musée de la civilisation

Quebec City

Key

■ Street-by-Street map: see *pp134–5*

Place Royale

Rue Saint Pierre. **Tel** (418) 646 3167.

Of all the squares in Canada, Place Royale has undoubtedly the most history. Samuel de Champlain, the founder of Quebec, planted his garden on this site, and the French colonial governor Frontenac turned it into a market in 1673. A bust of Louis XIV was installed in 1686, and the square was named Place Royale.

Today it remains much as it did in the 18th century, exuding an air of elegance and delicate grandeur. A cobblestone court in the center of Basse-Ville, Place Royale is surrounded by steep-roofed early 18th-century buildings with pastel-colored shutters that were once the homes of wealthy traders. The square declined in the 19th century but is now fully restored and a favorite for street performers.

Rue du Petit-Champlain bustling with shoppers

Rue du Petit-Champlain

below Dufferin Terrace in Old City. **Tel** (418) 692 2613. ♿ partial.

W quartierpetitchamplain.com

The aptly named Escalier Casse-Cou, or Breakneck Stairs, descends from Haute-Ville past several levels of gift shops to end on this narrow little walkway In the oldest part of the town. French artisans built homes here as early as the 1680s, and Irish dockworkers moved to the area in the 19th century. Much of the historic architecture remained, but the area fell into decline early in the 20th century. The workers' homes have been transformed into 50 art and speciality shops and restaurants, and the short pedestrian walkway has become one of the liveliest spots in old Quebec City. While often crowded, some inter- esting boutiques can be found.

A familiar landmark of the city, the 618-room Fairmont Le Château Frontenac hotel

Place d'Armes

French colonial soldiers once used this attractive, grassy square just north of Château Frontenac as a parade ground, but its uses today are more congenial. Open horse-drawn carriages wait here to offer visitors a journey that reveals the square in all its charm. In the center, the Monument de la Foi commemorates the 300th anniversary of the 1615 arrival of Catholic Recollet missionaries. On the southwest corner next to the fine Anglican cathedral, lies the grand early 19th-century former Palais de Justice. The Musée du Fort opposite contains a large scale model of Quebec City in the 19th century.

Fairmont Le Château Frontenac

1 Rue des Carrières. **Tel** (418) 692 3861. ♿ (see p352)

The steep, copper-roofed landmark that dominates the skyline of Old Quebec is a luxury hotel, built by the Canadian Pacific Railway on the heights overlooking the St. Lawrence River. In the 19th century, US architect Bruce Price designed the hotel as a French-style château on a huge scale, with dozens of turrets, towers, and a high copper roof studded with rows of dormer windows. Building continued for almost a century after the first section of the hotel was opened in 1893, with a final part completed in 1993. Made from brick and stone, the hotel now has 618 guest rooms and three gourmet restaurants. The public areas are sumptuous and elegant.

Basilique-cathédrale Notre-Dame de Québec

Place de l'Hôtel de Ville. **Tel** (418) 694 0665. **Open** 8:30am–4pm daily. ♿

This magnificent cathedral is the principal seat of the Roman Catholic archbishop of Quebec, whose diocese once stretched from here to Mexico. Fire destroyed the first two churches on the site before 1640, and the first cathedral built here was torn down by the British in 1759. A fourth version burned down in 1922. The present cathedral replaced it in the style of the 1647 original. Some modern materials, including concrete, steel, and plaster, have been used to re-create the light feel; glowing stained-glass windows, richly gilded decoration, and the graceful baldachin over the main altar add to the effect.

Imposing façade of the Basilique-cathédrale Notre-Dame de Québec

🖼 Rue du Trésor

off Place d'Armes.

This tiny alley just across rue de Buade from Holy Trinity cathedral is something of a Quebecois institution. Closed to cars, the little street is packed in summer with visitors eager to have their portraits drawn, painted, or caricatured by the dozens of street artists who gather here. Browsing for sketches and watercolors of Quebec scenes can be fun.

🏛 Holy Trinity Anglican Cathedral

31 Rue des Jardins.
Tel (418) 692 2193.
Open daily. ♿

After worshiping for nearly a century in the city's Catholic churches, in 1804 the Anglicans of Quebec finally had their own cathedral built at state expense. Their new mother church was the first Anglican cathedral outside Britain and is modeled on London's huge Neo-Classical St. Martin's in the Fields. To this day, gifts from England remain, including the prayer book and Bible donated by the British King George III. Cut from the King's Windsor Forest in England, the pews are of oak, and the eight-bell peal is the oldest in Canada. In the summer artists and artisans fill the verdant church grounds.

Reliquary from the Ursuline Convent

🏛 Monastère des Ursulines

Rue Donnacona. **Tel** (418) 694 0694.
Open daily. ♿

In 1639, Mère Marie de l'Incarnation brought the Ursuline order of nuns to Quebec and oversaw the construction in 1641 of the nunnery, which later burned down. Today, visitors can see the Saint-Augustin and Sainte-Famille wings, which date from a period of rebuilding between 1686 and 1721. Surrounded by fruit orchards, the charming complex has gradually evolved over the past four centuries. One of the buildings is North America's oldest girls' school (boys have been admitted since 2010).

The Hôtel de Ville seen from the small park in its grounds

Nearly a hundred nuns still live and work here, so access is limited. The beautifully decorated chapel and French antiques, including Louis XIII furniture, scientific instruments, paintings, and embroideries, are displayed in the Musée des Ursulines within the monastery. The museum also tells the story of the nuns' educational and missionary achievements. Mère Marie completed the first Huron, Algonquin, and Iroquois dictionaries. Copies are on display, along with embroidery and liturgical clothes from the 17th to 19th centuries.

🖼 Hôtel de Ville

2 Rue des Jardins. **Tel** (418) 641 6010.
Open 8:30am–4:30pm daily. ♿

This imposing building stands at the western end of the rue de Buade, a popular gathering place for Quebec artists offering their wares. Built in 1833, and still the town hall to the city, it is the grounds that are the focus

for the city's people. The small park here holds theater performances in the summertime and is a meeting place for festival-goers.

🖼 Séminaire de Québec

2 Côte de la Fabrique. **Tel** (418) 692 2843. **Open** summer. 🎟 obligatory. 🚻 ♿

In 1663, the first bishop of Quebec, Francois de Laval, built a seminary next to his cathedral to train Catholic priests for his huge diocese. Over the centuries it has been added to and now forms a graceful complex of 17th-, 18th-, and 19th-century buildings centered on a peaceful courtyard.

Within the seminary, visitors can admire the excellent 18th-century paneling that covers the walls of the chapel. The Musée de l'Amérique francophone is part of the complex and has a wonderfully eclectic collection, including a converted chapel decorated with fascinating wooden *trompe l'oeils*.

The 19th-century interior of the chapel at the Séminaire de Québec

La Citadelle

Both the French and British armies contributed to the building of this magnificent fort. The French started construction in 1693, with work completed in 1831 by the British. The purpose of the fort was to defend Quebec against an American attack that never came. Today the fortifications are a pleasant walkway that provides a tour around the star-shaped fortress. The Citadelle is home to the famous Royal 22e Régiment, a French-Canadian regiment also known as the Vandoos. Because the Citadelle is still a working military barracks, visitors can see the regiment perform their daily tasks as well as their parade drill.

The Fortifications
From the mid-19th century, the Citadelle served as the eastern flank of Quebec City's defenses.

Governor-General's residence
This splendid mansion with its double central staircase and marble hall has been the official home of Canada's governors-general since the 19th century.

Cape Diamond Redoubt
The oldest building in the Citadelle, the Redoubt dates back to 1693 when it was built under the leadership of the French Count Frontenac as a first citadel for Quebec. The Redoubt offers fine views of the St. Lawrence River.

KEY

① **Cap Diamant** is the highest point of the Cape Diamond cliffs, from which the Lower Town descends.

② **Old Military Prison**

③ **Trenches** around the Citadelle have always been key defensive structures.

④ **The Vimy Cross** was erected in memory of the Canadians who fell at the WWI battle of Vimy Ridge in 1917.

⑤ **The Prince of Wales Bastion** is the highest natural point in old Quebec. Nearby is a now disused French powder magazine.

Chapel
A key part of the fortress, this private chapel used to be a British powder magazine and is now used for ceremonial purposes.

For hotels and restaurants in this region see pp350–59 and pp364–83. For transport information see p410

★ **Changing of the Guard, Parade Square**
Every day from June 24 to Labour Day, the Changing of the Guard
takes place. The ceremonial dress of the Vandoos, scarlet tunic
and blue trousers, is of British design.

VISITORS' CHECKLIST

Practical Information
1 Cote de la Citadelle.
Tel (418) 694 2815. **Open** daily.
🅿️ ♿ 🚻 in museum. 🎥 📷
📷 obligatory.
W **lacitadelle.qc.ca**

The Barracks
As a fully operational military site,
the barracks is home to Canada's
most dashing regiment, the Vandoos,
who fought with bravery in both
world wars.

Plains of
Abraham

Entrance to the Citadelle

Ticket booth

| 0 meters | 25 |
| 0 yards | 25 |

★ **Dalhousie Gate**
One of the original structures remaining from the 19th century,
Dalhousie Gate is surrounded by portholes and gun fittings. These
helped the four-pointed fortress to cover its north, south, and west
flanks with defensive fire.

❷ Sainte-Anne-de-Beaupré

One of Canada's most sacred places, the shrine to the mother of the Virgin Mary was originally built in the 17th century. In 1650 a group of sailors who landed here after surviving a shipwreck vowed to build a chapel in honor of Saint Anne, the patron saint of those in shipwrecks. Over 800,000 visitors now visit every year, including an annual pilgrimage on Saint Anne's Feastday on July 26. This Neo-Romanesque-style basilica was built in the 1920s, and was the fifth church to be built on this site. In the entrance stand two columns of crutches, testimony to the faith of generations of Roman Catholics. The dome-vaulted ceiling is decorated with gold mosaics portraying the life of Saint Anne. She is represented in a large gilt statue in the transept, cradling the Virgin Mary.

Statue of Saint Anne
The focus of the upper floor, the richly decorated statue sits in front of the relic of Saint Anne, presented to the shrine by Pope John XXIII in 1960.

Plan of the Shrine

1. Basilica
2. Monastery
3. Church store
4. Museum
5. Blessing Office

The Basilica

In 1876, Saint Anne was proclaimed patron saint of Quebec, and in 1887 the existing church was granted basilica status. The Redemptorist order became the guardians of the shrine in 1878.

Entrance to Basilica's upper floor

KEY

① **Stained-glass windows**, show the progress of pilgrims through the shrine, with the rose window as centerpiece.

② **Bright mosaic floor tiles echo ceiling patterns**

★ **The Basilica**
There has been a church on this site since 1658. In 1922, the previous basilica burned down. Today's version was built in 1923 and consecrated in 1976.

★ **Pietà**
A faithful copy of Michelangelo's original in St. Peter's, Rome sits at the ambulatory's north end.

Basilica interior
Lit by sun streaming through the stained-glass windows, the cream and gold interior is decorated in every corner.

Montmorency Falls at Ile d'Orléans, Quebec's most dramatic waterfall

❸ Parc de la Chute Montmorency and Ile d'Orléans

Montmorency Falls (418) 663 3330.
Open Jan: 10am–4pm Sat & Sun; Feb–mid-Apr: 10am–4pm Thu–Sun; mid-Apr–mid-Jun, Sep & Oct: 9am–6pm daily; mid-Jun–Aug: 8:30am–7:30pm daily. **Closed** Nov–Christmas.
mid Apr–Oct. Ile d'Orléans Tourist Centre, 490 Cote du Pont, St. Pierre (418) 828 9411.

Located 7 km (4.5 miles) east of Quebec City, Montmorency Falls is Quebec's most celebrated waterfall. Higher than Niagara Falls, the cascade is created as the Montmorency River empties out into the St. Lawrence River – a total of 30 m (100 ft) higher than the 56-m (175-ft) plunge of Niagara Falls from the Niagara River to Lake Ontario. The park surrounding the Falls offers a suspension bridge, an aerial tram, and a series of trails that climb the surrounding cliffs.

A bridge nearby crosses the river to the Ile d'Orléans, which is covered with flowers, strawberry fields, and farmland. The villages give a fascinating look at rural life in Quebec.

❹ Charlevoix Coast

495 Blvd. de Comporte, La Malbaie (418) 665 4454.
tourisme-charlevoix.com

The Charlevoix Coast runs 200 km (130 miles) along the north shore of the St. Lawrence River, from Sainte-Anne-de-Beaupré in the west to the mouth of the Saguenay Fjord. A UNESCO Biosphere Reserve because of its fine examples of boreal forest, the area is a slim band of flowery rural beauty on the southern edge of tundra that stretches northward. Gentle valleys protect old towns reaching to the river, with coastal villages sheltering beneath tall cliffs. Lying in a fertile valley is the exceptionally pretty Baie-Saint-Paul, its streets lined with historic houses and inns.

Just 35 km (21 miles) north of Baie-Saint-Paul lies the **Parc des Grands Jardins**, a vast expanse of lakes and black-spruce taiga forest with a herd of caribou. Small mountains offer walking and hiking. Farther downstream is the tiny and tranquil island Isle-aux-Coudres. The lush, green farmland here is sprinkled with historic farms and a windmill.

Parc des Grands Jardins
Rte. 381. **Tel** (418) 439 1227.
Open May– Oct: daily; Nov–Apr: Sat & Sun.

Moulin de L'Isle-aux-Coudres, in the Charlevoix region

The town of Tadoussac at the confluence of the St. Lawrence and Saguenay rivers

❺ Tadoussac

🏔 850. 🚌 🛥 𝒊 197 Rue des Pionniers (418) 235 4744.

Lined with boutiques, the old streets of this little town make a gentle start to exploring the local stretch of the St. Lawrence River. In 1600, French traders picked this site to establish the first fur-trading post in Canada, noticing that for generations native Indians had held meetings here to trade and parley. In the 19th century, the first Hôtel Tadoussac was built and steam-ships began to transport well-heeled tourists to the village for a taste of its wilderness beauty.

Justifying two centuries of tourism, the scenery here is magnificent. Backed by rocky cliffs and towering sand dunes, the waterfront faces over the estuary at the confluence of the St. Lawrence and Saguenay rivers. In the town, the re-creation of the 17th-century fur-trading post and the oldest wooden church in Canada, the Petite Chapelle built in 1747, are popular.

However, the main attraction in Tadoussac lies offshore. Whale-watching tours offer trips into the estuary to see many species in their natural environment. The thriving natural conditions in the estuary support a permanent colony of white beluga whales, which are joined in summer by minke, humpback, fin, and blue whales.

❻ Saguenay River

🚆 Jonquière. 🚌 Chicoutimi.
𝒊 412 Blvd. Saguenay Est 100, Chicoutimi (418) 543 9778.
Ⓦ **saguenaylacsaintjean.ca**

The Saguenay River flows through North America's southern-most natural fjord. This was formed from a retreating glacier splitting a deep crack in the Earth's crust during the last Ice Age, 10,000 years ago. Inky waters, 300m (985-ft) deep in places, run for 155 km (95 miles) beneath cliffs that average 300 m (985 ft) in height. Due to the exceptional depth, ocean liners can travel up to La Baie, a borough of Saguenay.

Running from Lac St. Jean to the St. Lawrence estuary, the Saguenay is best known for its lush borderlands and the wildlife that thrives in its lower reaches. Much of the pretty Bas Saguenay, the southern half of the river, is a federal marine park. A colony of a thousand whales lives here.

Beautiful views of the length of the fjord are available on the western shore at Cap Trinité, a cliff that rises 320 m (1,050 ft) over the channel, with a well-known 10-m (33-ft) statue of the Virgin Mary surveying the scenery from the lowest ledge.

❼ Chicoutimi

Saguenay. 🏔 64,600. 🚆 Jonquière. 🚌 Chicoutimi. 𝒊 412 Blvd. Saguenay Est 100 (418) 543 9778.

Snug in the crook of mountains on the western shore of the Saguenay, Chicoutimi is one of northern Quebec's most expansive towns, despite its modest population. The cultural and economic center of the Saguenay region, Chicoutimi's waterfront district has now been restored. A stroll along the riverside offers good views of the surrounding mountains and the confluence of the Chicoutimi, Du-Moulin, and Saguenay rivers.

Once a center for the paper trade, Chicoutimi still features a large pulp mill, the **Pulperie de Chicoutimi**. Although no longer operational, the plant can be toured, and an adjacent museum shows visitors the intricacies of this long-standing Quebecois industry, which once supplied most of North America's paper needs.

🏛 **Pulperie de Chicoutimi**
300 Dubuc. **Tel** (418) 698 3100. **Open** late Jun–Sep: 9am–6pm daily. ♿

Waterside view of a section of the deep Saguenay fjord

❾ A Tour of Lac-Saint-Jean

In the midst of the rocky, spruce-covered wilderness that characterizes central Quebec, Lac-Saint-Jean is an oasis of tranquillity. Dairy farms, charming villages such as Chambord, and warm sandy beaches border the lake itself, which covers 1,000 sq km (386 sq miles). The lake and its rolling green landscape fill a crater-sized basin left by advancing glaciers at the end of the last Ice Age. Large rivers flow to the lake and tumble dramatically down the basin's steep walls into the blue waters, to be reborn as the source of the Saguenay River.

Tips for Drivers

Starting point: Chambord.
Length: 230 km (144 miles).
Getting around: This is a long, though relaxed drive, and the road is well maintained. Inns and restaurants offer rest on the way in most towns and villages, including Mashteuiatsh. Small side roads make peaceful diversions.

⑥ **Parc National de la Pointe-Taillon**
Stretching into a peninsula, this park is excellent for cycling and hiking, but is best known for its fine, long beaches.

0 kilometers 10
0 miles 10

Chicoutimi

Key

▬ Tour route
═ Other roads

① **Chambord**
Sailing and swimming are top activities here, especially for children and families.

⑤ **Dolbeau**
Most visitors to Dolbeau arrive in July for the ten-day Western Festival, which features rodeos and cowboys in Stetsons.

④ **Mashteuiatsh, Pointe-Bleu**
This Montagnais Indian village is open to visitors who can see at first hand age-old methods of carving, hunting, weaving, and cooking.

③ **Roberval**
This town has a charming waterfront, from which spectators can see the finish of the swimming contest to cross the lake, which has taken place each July since 1946.

② **Village Historique de Val-Jalbert**
This outdoor museum is dominated by the 70-m (200-ft) Ouiatchouan waterfall, which once acted as power for a pulp mill here in the 1920s.

Daniel Johnson Hydroelectric Dam, north of Baie-Comeau

❾ Baie-Comeau

🏠 26,700. ✈ 🚌 🚢 ℹ 337 La Salle (418) 294 2876.

This small town owes its entire existence to the US newspaper, the *Chicago Tribune*, which in 1936 built a mill near the mouth of the Manicougan River to supply its newspaper presses with paper. Declared a historic district in 1985, Baie-Comeau's oldest area is the Quartier Amélie, with rows of fine homes and an impressive hotel dating from the 1930s.

Paper production remains a vital industry in this area, but Baie-Comeau is most important today as a gateway to the enormous Manic-Outardes hydroelectric power complex, situated along Hwy 389, from 22 km (14 miles) to 200 km (130 miles) north of town. The most spectacular example is Manic-5, 212 km (132 miles) from Baie-Comeau. Its gracefully arched Daniel Johnson Dam holds back a vast reservoir that fills a crater geophysicists believe might have been created by a meteorite several millennia ago.

❿ Sept-Iles

🏠 26,000. 🚆 🚌 🚢 ℹ 1401 Boulevard Laure (418) 962 1238.

Until the 1950s, Sept-Iles led a quiet existence as a historic, sleepy fishing village. However, after World War II, the little settlement, set on the shores of a large, circular bay, drew the attention of large companies to

use as a base for expanding the iron mining industry in northern Quebec. Now the largest town along the north shore of the Gulf of St. Lawrence, Sept-Iles has turned into Canada's second largest port as part of the St. Lawrence Seaway. A boardwalk along the waterfront offers visitors the chance to see the large ships in action, and to observe close-up the workings of a busy modern dock.

Although boasting the best of modern marine technology, the town also offers a reminder of its long-standing history. Vieux Poste near the center of the town is a fine reconstruction of a native trading post, where the original inhabitants of the area met to barter furs with French merchants. A small museum with aboriginal art and artifacts sells native crafts.

Despite its industrial importance, Sept-Iles is an area of considerable natural beauty.

Sept-Iles from the air, showing the bustling dock in action

Miles of sandy beaches rim the nearby coastline, and the salmon-rich Moisie River flows into the Gulf of St. Lawrence just 20 km (12 miles) east of the town. The seven rocky islands that gave the city its name make up the Sept-Iles Archipelago Park.

Ideal for campers and hikers with its beaches and nature trails, one of the seven islands, Ile Grand-Basque, is a popular local camping spot. Another small island, Ile du Corossol, has been turned into a bird sanctuary that teems with gulls, terns, and puffins, and can be toured with a guide. Cruises are available for guided trips between islands.

⓫ Mingan Archipelago National Park Reserve of Canada

🚌 Sept-Iles. 🚢 Sept-Iles. ℹ 1401 Boulevard l'Aure (418) 962 1238.

Located along the north shore of the Gulf of St. Lawrence, the Mingan Archipelago National Park Reserve of Canada protects more than 1,000 islands and islets. Barely visited until recently, this unspoiled and unsettled area is fast gaining in popularity for its harsh landscape, rich wildlife, and untouched ecosystems. Puffins, terns, and several gull species find refuge here. Gray, harbor, and harp seals all cluster along the tiny coves and bays, and fin whales are occasional visitors. As well as the abundant wildlife, the islands are home to the largest concentration of monoliths in Canada. Eroded over many centuries by the sea, these limestone carvings have surreal shapes. The best-known rocks look like flowerpots, with grasses sprouting from their peaks. Visitors can book a trip to admire the monoliths by boat.

Until 1974, the Ile d'Anticosti, east of the archipelago, was private property – all 8,000 sq km (3,090 sq miles) of it. The past owner, French chocolate tycoon Henri Menier, bought the island in 1895 and stocked it with a

"Flowerpot" limestone monoliths at Mingan Archipelago National Park Reserve of Canada

herd of white-tailed deer for his friends to hunt. Now numbering 120,000, the deer herd is firmly ensconced but can still be hunted. Wildlife abounds; over 150 species of bird live in the relatively unspoiled forest and on the beaches. The village of Port Menier has 300 residents and acts as the local ferry terminus and lodging center. The island is separate from the Mingan Archipelago National Park so there is no admittance fee.

Seal at Ile d'Anticosti

⑫ South Shore

🚉 Rivière-du-Loup. 🚌 Rivière-du-Loup. 🚢 Rivière-du-Loup. ℹ️ Rivière-du-Loup (418) 867 3015, 1 888 825 1981. 🌐 bassaintlaurent.ca

Communities here can trace their roots back to the old 18th-century settlers of New France. Dotted along the flat, fertile farmland of the south shore of the St. Lawrence River west of Gaspé and inland toward Montreal, the villages cover the area between the region's largest towns of Montmagny and Rimouski. Rivière-du-Loup, a seemingly unremarkable town in this stretch, provides for many people a taste of true Quebec. Featuring an ancient stone church that rears above the skyline, the old town rambles along hilly streets, and its 18th-century cottages have a French atmosphere. From the peak of the old town, views across the river valley are lovely. Other villages in this area feature unusual attractions. Farther along the main Route 132, Trois-Pistoles boasts a history that goes back to 1580, when Basque whalers arrived. The offshore Ile-aux-Basques was a whaling station in the 16th century, and today can be visited to tour the nature preserve in its place. Toward the region's commercial center, Rimouski, lies the Parc National du Bic, a small preserve of 33 square km (13 square miles) dedicated to the two forest zones, deciduous and boreal, it encloses, and its varied coastal wildlife.

⑬ Iles-de-la-Madeleine

ℹ️ 128 Chemin Principal, Cap-aux-Meules (418) 986 2245, 1 877 624 4437. 🌐 tourismeilesdela madeleine.com

The few fishing families who make their homes on this remote archipelago in the middle of the huge gulf of St. Lawrence have taken to painting their cottages in an assortment of mauves, yellows, and reds. The river gives striking views of the little communities on their low-lying, windswept islands, but the islands themselves have more to offer the visitor who makes the boat trip to see them. As well as the charming ancient villages, they are home to what are reputed to be some of the most relaxing beaches in Canada, celebrated for their fine sand and sheltered position.

Painted fisherman's cottage on L'Ile-du-Havre-Aubert, Iles-de-la-Madeleine

⓮ Gaspé Peninsula Tour

Popularly known as La Gaspésie, the Gaspé Peninsula stretches out north of New Brunswick to offer Quebec's wildest and most appealing scenery. As the peninsula spreads east, clumps of trees become dense pine forests, and the landscape becomes rough and rocky; cliffs along the northern coast reach 500 m (1,500 ft). The Chic-Choc mountains reach heights of 1,300 m (4,000 ft) and provide some of the province's best hiking. Shielded by the mountains, the southern coast harbors 18th-century fishing villages, inland fruit farms, exotic gardens, and wilderness national parks.

③ Parc National de la Gaspésie
Over 800 sq km (300 sq miles) of rough terrain mark a change from boreal to subalpine forest.

② Cap Chat
Named for a nearby cat-shaped rock, Cap Chat boasts the tallest windmill in the world at 110 m (330 ft).

① Grand Métis
This small town is home to one of Canada's most beautiful gardens, an exotic haven of 3,000 species, cultivars, and varieties of plants.

Quebec City ← • **Sainte-Flavie**

Matane

Reserve Faunique De Matane

Amqui

132

Causapscal

Routhierville

⑨

0 kilometres 20
0 miles 20

⑨ Vallée de la Matapédia
Starting at the confluence of two excellent salmon-fishing rivers, the picturesque Matapédia Valley is crisscrossed by covered bridges. Concealing long-established fruit farms, the valley's elm and maple trees show stunning fall colors.

⑧ Carleton-sur-Mer
Founded in 1756 by Acadians fleeing the Great Expulsion in Nova Scotia (*see pp66–7*), Carleton-sur-Mer today is a pleasant, relaxed resort town. Quality hotels and restaurants line the airy streets, and many visitors enjoy the mild coastal climate.

④ **Sainte-Anne-des-Monts**
The entrance to the Parc National de la Gaspésie and the wildlife reserves of the Chic-Chocs, this 19th-century village has fine restaurants, and good salmon fishing nearby.

Tips for Drivers

The main road on this tour is Hwy 132, which follows the coastline from Grand Métis along the peninsula in a round trip. While too long to complete in a day, the journey can be broken in many of the local villages. Trips into the interior on the secondary road 299 are ideal for seeing the rocky wilderness.

Mont-Louis
⑤

Grande-Vallé

132

Murdochville

⑥

Reserve Faunique Des Chic-Chocs

198

Gaspé

99

⑦

Grand Rivière

⑤ **Mont Saint-Pierre**
The gateway for visits to the Chic-Choc mountains, this village is also a beach center for hang gliding.

Maria

New Richmond

132

New Carlisle

⑥ **Parc National du Canada Forillon**
The park contains the tail end of the Appalachian Mountains, now cliffs worn into rugged formations by the sea.

⑦ **Rocher Percé**
Situated out to sea south of the small town of Percé, this famous pierced landmark is the result of tidal erosion. In the 1930s, Percé became a popular spot for Canadian artists and still contains many galleries.

Key

▬▬ Tour route

▬▬ Other roads

For additional map symbols see back flap

SOUTHERN AND NORTHERN QUEBEC

The vast area of land that stretches across Quebec from the Ontario boundary to historic Quebec City is rewarding in its diversity. In the south, the rich hilly farmland of the Appalachians and scarlet forests of maple trees attract many visitors each year, while the stark beauty of Nunavik's icy northern coniferous forests bursts into a profusion of wildflowers in spring, alongside the largest hydroelectric projects in the world. The center of the region is Quebec's natural playground, the Laurentian Mountains, a pristine lake-filled landscape offering fine skiing on ancient mountains. Populated by native people until Europeans arrived in the 16th century, the area was fought over by the French and British until the British gained power in 1759. Today French-speakers dominate.

Sights at a Glance

National Parks
- **5** Parc National de la Mauricie

Historic Towns and Cities
- **2** Sherbrooke
- **3** Sainte-Croix
- **6** Trois Rivières
- **7** Joliette
- **8** Terrebonne
- **9** Oka

- **12** Gatineau
- **14** Val d'Or
- **15** Rouyn-Noranda

Historic Sites and Areas of Natural Beauty
- **1** Lac Memphrémagog
- **4** Richelieu Valley
- **10** Sucrerie de la Montagne

- **11** Laurentian Mountains
- **13** Reserve Faunique La Vérendrye
- **16** James Bay
- **17** Nunavik (not shown on map)

Key

- ═══ Highway
- ▬▬ Major road
- ── Minor road
- ── Railway route
- ─ ∙ International border

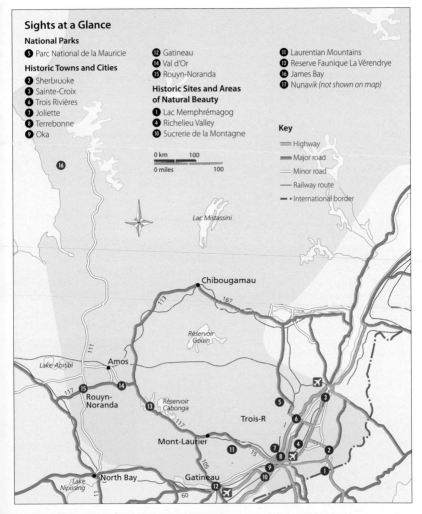

◄ Fall colors reflecting in Lac Sauvage, the Laurentian Mountains, Quebec

For map symbols *see back flap*

Church by Lac Memphrémagog

❶ Lac Memphrémagog

🚌 Magog. 🚢 Magog. ℹ️ 2911 Milletta (hwy 10, exit 115), Magog (800) 267 2744. 🌐 **tourisme-memphremagog.com**

This area belongs to the Eastern Townships, or the "Garden of Quebec" that stretches from the Richelieu River valley to the Maine, New Hampshire and Vermont borders in the US. Set among rolling hills, farmland, woods, and lakes in a landscape that is part of the Appalachians, the Townships are among Canada's top maple syrup producers (see pp106–7).

Lac Memphrémagog itself is long, narrow, and surrounded by mountains. It even boasts its own monster, a creature named Memphré, first spotted in 1798. The lake's southern quarter dips into the state of Vermont, so it is no surprise that the British Loyalists fleeing the American Revolution were this region's first settlers. Their influence can be seen in the late 19th-century redbrick and wood-frame homes of lakeside villages such as Georgeville and North Hatley, and in the resort city of Magog at the northern end of the lake.

Benedictine monks from France bought one of the lake's most beautiful sites in 1912 and established the Abbaye Saint-Benoît-du-Lac. Today the monks produce cider and a celebrated blue cheese called l'Ermite. They are also renowned for Gregorian chant, and visitors can hear them sing mass in the abbey church.

❷ Sherbrooke

🗺️ 155,000. 🚂 🚌 🚢 ℹ️ 785 King St. W. 1 (800) 561 8331, (819) 821 1919. 🌐 **destinationsherbrooke.com**

The self-styled "Queen of the Eastern Townships," Sherbrooke is indeed this region's industrial, commercial, and cultural center. The city lies in a steep-sided valley, with the historic quarter delightfully situated among the rolling farmlands of the Saint-François and Magog Rivers. The first settlers were British Loyalists from the New England states. Although their heritage survives in the fine old homes and gardens of Sherbrooke's North Ward and in street names, today the city is overwhelmingly French speaking. From the town center runs the Promenade du Lac-des-Nations, a lovely waterfront park with 20 km (12 miles) of attractive cycling and walking trails along the banks of the Magog River.

❸ Sainte-Croix

🗺️ 2,600. ℹ️ 6375 rue Garneau (418) 926 2620.

A charming, wooden manor house with bold sweeping front steps, pillars, and carved curlicues is the centerpiece of **Domaine Joly-De-Lotbinière**. This stunning estate was built in 1851 by the local squire (seigneur) according to the Picturesque style. The house is surrounded by banks of geraniums and terraces of walnut trees stretching down to the river. Rare plant finds include 20 red oaks estimated to be more than 250 years old. The gardens were formerly known for cultivating blue potatoes.

🏛️ **Domaine Joly-De-Lotbinière**
Rte. de Pointe-Platon. **Tel** (418) 926 2462. **Open** mid-May–mid-Oct: 10am–5pm daily. 🐾 ♿ partial.

❹ Richelieu Valley

ℹ️ 1080 Chemin des Patriotes Nord, Mont Saint-Hilaire (450) 536 0395, 1 888 736 0395. 🌐 **vallee-du-richelieu.ca**

This fertile valley follows the 171-km (106-mile) Richelieu River from Lake Champlain to the confluence with the St. Lawrence river. **Fort Chambly**, also known as Fort St. Louis, in the industrial town of Chambly along the valley on the Montreal Plain, is the best preserved of a series of ancient buildings that the French erected to defend this vital waterway from Dutch and British attack. Built from solid stone in 1711 to replace the original wooden fortifications set up in 1675, the fort is well preserved. A museum in Saint-Denis-sur–Richelieu commem-orates Quebecois patriots who fought in the failed 1837 rebellion against British rule.

A sign to Fort Chambly in the Richelieu Valley

Today the river flows past attractive villages surrounded by orchards and vineyards; Mont Saint-Hilaire affords fine views of Montreal, and is famed for its apple plantations. Its 19th-century church was declared a historic site in 1965 and features paintings by Canadian Ozias Leduc (see p36).

🏛️ **Fort Chambly**
2 De Richelieu St., Chambly. **Tel** 1 (888) 773 8888 or (450) 658 1585. **Open** May 18–Jun 23 & Sep 3–Oct 14: 10am–5pm Wed–Sun & public hols; Jun 24–Sep 2: 10am–6pm daily. 🐾

The 19th-century church at Mont Saint-Hilaire, Richelieu Valley

Canoeists on Lac Wapizagonke in Parc National de la Mauricie

❺ Parc National de la Mauricie

off Hwy 55 N. Shawinigan. **Tel** (819) 538 3232. 🚌 Shawinigan. **Open** daily. 🅿 ♿ partial. 🎫 for a fee. 🌐 **pc.gc.ca**

Campers, hikers, canoeists, and cross-country skiers love this 536-sq km (207-sq mile) stretch of forest, lakes, and pink Precambrian granite. The park includes part of the Laurentian Mountains *(see p155)*, which are part of the Canadian Shield, and were formed between 950 and 1,400 million years ago. La Mauricie's rugged beauty is also accessible to motorists, who can take the winding 63-km (40-mile) road between Saint-Mathieu and Saint-Jean-de-Piles.

Another great drive starts at Saint-Jean-de-Piles and has good views of the narrow Lac Wapizagonke Valley. With trout and pike in the lake, the area is an angler's delight. Moose and bear roam wild in the park.

❻ Trois-Rivières

🏙 132,000. 🚆 🚌 🚐 ⛴ *i* 1457 Rue Notre Dame (819) 375 1122, 1 800 313 1123. 🌐 **tourismetroisrivieres.com**

Quebec is one of the major paper producers in North America, and Trois-Rivières, a pulp and paper town, is a main center of that industry in the province. This fact often hides the rich historical interest that Trois-Rivières has to offer. The first colonists arrived here from France well before the city was founded in 1634. Although not many of the colonial dwellings remain, the city's charming old section has a number of 18th- and 19th-century houses and shops, many of which have been converted into cafés and bars.

Ursuline nuns have been working in the city since 1697, and the core of the old city is the **Monastère des Ursulines**, a rambling complex with a central dome, a chapel, and a little garden that is now a public park. Rue des Ursulines features several little old houses with varying architectural

The church of the Monastère des Ursulines in Trois-Rivières

styles. Also here is an 18th-century manor house, the 1730 Manoir Boucher-de-Niverville, which is a cultural and historical site that rotates displays on the rich history of the Mauricie region.

🏛 **Monastère des Ursulines**
734 Ursulines. **Tel** (819) 375 7922. **Open** Mar & Apr: Wed–Sun; May–Nov: Tue–Sun; Nov–Feb: call ahead. 🎫

❼ Joliette

🏙 31,100. 🚌 *i* 500 rue Dollard (450) 759 5013.

Two Catholic priests are responsible for turning the industrial town of Joliette on L'Assomption River into a cultural center. In the 1920s, Father Wilfrid Corbeil founded the Musée d'Art de Joliette, whose permanent collection ranges from medieval religious art to modern works. In 1978, Father Fernand Lindsay started the Festival International de Lanaudière, a series of summer concerts by some of the world's best-known musicians.

The nearby town of Rawdon, 18 km (11 miles) west, has a deserved reputation as a place of great natural beauty. Trails wind away from the small town alongside the Ouareau River, leading to the picturesque, rushing Dorwin Falls.

❽ Terrebonne

🏛 36,680. 🚌 🚤 🚍 ℹ 3645 Queen Street (1 800 363 2788).

Just northwest of the outer fringe of Montreal's suburbs, this historic little town on the Mille-Iles River was founded in 1673, but a fire in 1922 engulfed many of its original buildings. However, some graceful 19th-century homes remain, on rue Saint-François-Xavier and rue Sainte-Marie, many of them converted into restaurants and bistros. The town's real gem is the **Ile-des-Moulins**, a pre-industrial complex of living history in the middle of the Mille-Iles River, with water-powered mills for grinding grain, carding wool, and sawing lumber. One of the biggest buildings on the site is the three-floor factory that was the first large-scale bakery in Canada. It was built by the Northwest Company in 1803 to make the saltless ship's biscuits that sustained the *voyageurs* who paddled west every year to collect furs for the company.

Terrebonne is also the center of Quebec's horseriding culture. Popular with locals, rodeo and ranching events take place regularly.

🏠 **Ile-des-Moulins**
Autoroute 25, exit 22 E. **Tel** (450) 471 0619. **Open** Jun–Sep: 1–9 pm daily.
♿ 🌐 iledesmoulins.com

The Oka ferry as it travels across the Lake of Two Mountains

❾ Oka

🏛 5,110. 🚌 🚤 ℹ 183 rue des Anges (450) 479 8389.

The prettiest way to approach this village north of Montreal is on the small ferry that chugs across the Lake of Two Mountains from Hudson. Framed by mountains and orchards, from the water the small Neo-Romanesque 1878 church is visible through the trees. Oka's **Abbaye Cistercienne** was founded by a group of monks who moved to Canada from France in 1881. The decor of the abbey church is somewhat stark, in the Cistercian tradition, but the Neo-Romanesque architecture is gracefully simple and the gardens peaceful. The abbey closed in 2009, but the abbey shop still operates, selling the soft Oka cheese that the monks have developed. Nearby, the Parc d'Oka covers about 20 sq km (7 sq miles) of ponds and forests. It features the best beach and campground in the Montreal area, attracting sports lovers and visitors year-round.

🏠 **Abbaye Cistercienne**
1600 Chemin d'Oka. **Tel** (450) 479 8389. **Open** 8am–8pm Mon–Sat (store open daily). **Closed** lunchtimes.
🌐 abbayeoka.com

❿ Sucrerie de la Montagne

10 km South of Rigaud. 🚗 **Tel** (450) 451 0831. **Open** year round but call ahead. ♿ 🌐 obligatory.
🌐 **sucreriedelamontagne.com**

This typically Canadian treat is set in a 50-ha (120-acre) maple forest on top of Rigaud Mountain near Rang Saint-Georges, Rigaud. It is entirely devoted to the many delights of Quebec's most famous commodity, the maple tree and its produce (*see pp102–3*). The site features a reconstructed 19th-century sugar shack, where collected maple sap is distilled and boiled in large kettles to produce the internationally renowned syrup. Over 20 rustic buildings house a fine bakery, a general store, and comfortable cabins for overnight guests. The heart of the complex is a huge 500-seat restaurant that serves traditional banquets of ham, pea soup, baked beans, pork rinds (called *oreilles du Christ*, or Christ's ears), and pickles, and dozens of maple-based products, including syrup, sugar, candies, taffy, muffins, and bread. Folk music accompanies the nightly feast. The tour includes a thorough explanation of the maple syrup-making process, which is generally thought to have originated with the native people. They later imparted their secrets to European settlers, whose traditional methods are still in use today.

Quebecois Maple Syrup

Rue-St-Louis Church in Terrebonne

⑪ Laurentian Mountains Tour

This whole region, from the lively resort of Saint-Sauveur-des-Monts in the south to north of Sainte-Jovite (also known as Tremblant), is nature's own amusement park, full of lakes, rivers, hiking and cycling trails, and ski runs visited all through the year. The mountains are part of the ancient Laurentian Shield and are a billion years old. Dotted with pretty, old French-style towns, this is a superb area to relax in or indulge in some vigorous sports in the national parks.

Tips for Drivers

Although the 175-km round tour of the Laurentian Mountains can be made from Montreal in a day on Hwy 15, the region is best seen and enjoyed by taking advantage of the slower, but more scenic, Hwy 117. There may be traffic congestion at the peak times of July through August and from December to March.

④ Sainte-Jovite
Full of historic architecture, this village lies in a wooded valley.

⑤ La Conception
Plenty of tiny hotels and street cafés add to the charm of this old village.

⑥ Mont Tremblant
The tallest of the Laurentian range with a vertical rise of about 615 m (2,454 ft), this is a popular international four-season resort.

③ Saint-Faustin-Lac-Carré
Saint-Faustin–Lac-Carré has an important role as the starting-off point for trips around the area. Local woods contain an interpretive center with flora and fauna trails.

② Sainte-Agathe-des-Monts
The largest town in the Laurentians provides busy café society all year round. Lac des Sables in town offers beaches and lake cruises.

① Val-Morin
This enchanting village is a charming introduction to the area, with traditional French homes and churches.

Key

▬ Tour route

═ Other roads

0 kilometers 3

0 miles 3

⑫ Gatineau

Gatineau (known as Hull until 1992), is based just across the river from Ottawa in the province of Quebec, and, as a result, many federal bureaucracies have their headquarters here. For years, Gatineau has been a more relaxed and fun-loving counterpart to the capital, an attitude that reveals itself even in its officialdom – City Hall, for instance, boasts a meditation center. From Hull's establishment in 1800, the city's liquor laws were far more lenient than Ottawa's, and so this was where Ottawa politicians came to party (the city still has a lower drinking age). Gatineau contains Canada's most visited museum, the Canadian Museum of Civilization, which provides a fascinating tour of Canada's history over the past 1,000 years.

VISITORS' CHECKLIST

Practical Information
🗺 263,990. ℹ La Maison du tourisme, 103 Rue Laurier (819) 778 2222, 1 800 265 7822. 🎭 Fall Rhapsody (Sep/ Oct).
🌐 **outaouaistourism.com**

Transport
✈ Ottawa International 12 km (8 miles) south of the city. 🚌 200 Tremblay Rd, Ottawa.

🌳 Gatineau Park
Hwy 5. **Tel** (819) 827 2020, 1 800 465 1867. **Open** daily.
This 360 sq km (140 sq miles) oasis of lakes and rolling hills between the Gatineau and Ottawa Rivers is a weekend playground for city residents. The park contains fragments of Gothic buildings, collected by the former Prime Minister, William Lyon MacKenzie-King.

Casino du Lac-Leamy
1 Casino Blvd. **Tel** (819) 772 2100, 1 800 665 2274. **Open** 24 hours daily. 🅿
Four million visitors a year are lured to this glittering Casino, which is equipped with 1,800 slot machines and 64 gaming

Gaming room in the Casino du Lac-Leamy

tables. Owned by the Quebec Government, the Casino opened in 1996 and is set in a park full of flowers and fountains.

🏛 Alexandra Bridge
Built in 1900, this handsome steel-framed bridge spans the Ottawa River and links Ontario to Quebec. From footpaths, drivers' lanes, and cycle routes, the bridge offers fine views of the

river, the Canadian Museum of Civilization, and the Parliament Buildings in Ottawa.

🏛 Maison du Citoyen
25 Laurier St. **Tel** (819) 243 2345. **Open** 8:30am–4:30pm Mon–Fri. **Closed** public holidays. 🅿
The heart of this complex is a vast atrium, the Agora, meant to serve as an all-weather gathering place for Gatineau's citizens, as well as an airy meditation center for the city's workers. Opening from it are City Hall, a library, a theater, and an art gallery.

🏛 Promenade du Portage
Linked with the city bridges, this main route downtown is full of lively cafés, restaurants, and a microbrewery. After dark the area and nearby Place Aubry become the focus of the city's excellent nightlife.

Gatineau City Center
① Alexandra Bridge
② Canadian Museum of Civilization
③ Maison du Citoyen
④ Promenade du Portage

Canadian Museum of Civilization

This museum was built in the 1980s to be the storehouse of Canada's human history. The architect, Douglas Cardinal, wanted the undulating façades of both buildings to reflect the Canadian landscape. The more curved hall is the Canadian Shield Wing, home to the museum's offices. The Glacier Wing displays the exhibits. Its entry is stunning; the dramatic interior of the Grand Hall contains the world's largest collection of totem poles. The Children's Museum is delightfully diverting, while the IMAX Theatre offers the ultimate cinema experience. The fourth level holds an archive, which is open to the public.

VISITORS' CHECKLIST

Practical Information
100 Laurier St. **Tel** (819) 776 7000,
1 800 555 5621. **Open** 9am–5pm
daily (check website for longer
summer hours). 🅿️ ♿ 📷 🎫
🏠 🍴 🖥️ civilization.ca

The museum façade echoes the rolling Canadian landscape

Canada Hall is a remarkable mazelike journey through 1,000 years of Canada's social history.

Level Three

David M. Stewart Salon

Level Two

The Children's Museum
This extremely popular space contains a "world tour" of interactive exhibits, a busy international market, and this brightly decorated Pakistani trolleybus.

Main Entrance

Group Entrance

Level One

Library

★ **The Grand Hall**
The museum is home to the world's largest and finest collection of totem poles, many of which are displayed in the Grand Hall.

Key to Floor Plan

- Canada Hall
- Children's Museum
- First Peoples Hall
- First Peoples of the Northwest Coast Exhibition
- W.E. Taylor Salon
- Grand Hall
- IMAX Theater
- Special exhibitions
- Non exhibition space

The wildlife preserve of La Vérendrye, seen from the air

⑬ Reserve Faunique La Vérendrye

Tel (819) 736 7431. 🚌 Maniwaki.
Open summer. ♿ partial.

This wildlife preserve is situated approximately 471 km (292 miles) to the northwest of Montreal on Hwy 117. It is celebrated for long, meandering waterways and streams and, with thousands of kilometers of canoe trails, is a legend among canoeists. Its rivers are usually gentle, and the 13,000 sq km (5,000 sq miles) of wilderness are home to large numbers of moose, bear, deer, and beaver. The land is practically untouched, but there are several campgrounds here for those who seek a truly peaceful break. In season, anglers can try for walleye, pike, lake trout, and bass. Hwy 117 traverses the park, providing access to many of its lakes and rivers, and is the starting point of hiking trails.

⑭ Val d'Or

🏙 42,000. 🚌 ℹ️ 1070 3rd Ave. E. (819) 824 9646, 1 877 582 5367.

Val d'Or is principally a mining town and is a major center in the northwestern part of Quebec. The town sights here are not architectural but vivid living history attractions of mines and historic villages from the area's heritage of lumber trade and mining. Miners have been digging gold, silver, and copper out of the ground around Val d'Or since the 1920s. A climb to the top of the 18-m (60-ft) Tour Rotary on the edge of town shows many still-active mineheads.

La Cité de l'Or is a popular attraction, built around the abandoned Lamaque Goldmine, formerly one of the richest sources of gold in the area. In its heyday of the early 20th century, the mine had its very own small town site with a hospital, a boarding house for all single workers, and neat streets lined with little log cabins for married men and their families. The mine managers had more elaborate homes nearby, and there was a sumptuous guesthouse for visiting executives. Much of the Village Minier de Bourlamaque remains intact and was declared a historic site in 1979. Visitors can tour the village, the old analysis office and laboratories, and the minehead. For an extra fee, fascinating tours in coveralls and helmets are available down the 90 m (300 ft) mine shaft.

A moose at La Vérendrye

🏛 **La Cité de l'Or**
90 Ave. Perrault. **Tel** (819) 825 1274, 1 855 825 1274. **Open** Jun–Sep: 9am–6pm daily. 🚫 ♿ partial.

⑮ Rouyn-Noranda

🏙 41,475. 🚌 ℹ️ 1675 Lariviere Av. (819) 797 3195, 1 888 797 3195.

As with all developed areas in the north of Quebec, towns here are based on heavy industry. Rouyn and Noranda sprang up virtually overnight in the 1920s when prospectors found copper in the region. They merged into one city covering 6,600 square km (2,548 square miles) in 1986. Noranda on the north shore of Lake Osisko is a carefully planned company town with its own churches and schools, built to house the employees of the now-defunct Noranda copper mine. The lawns and tree-lined streets have an almost English air. Some residents are still employed in surrounding mines. The Horne Smelter, one of the biggest and most efficient in the world, is based just outside the center of town and can be visited by arrangement.

Rouyn, on the south shore of the lake, is less structured and more commercial. It is also where Noranda residents used to go for recreation, and it is useful as a refreshment and fuel center for those traveling to the northern wilderness. The **Maison Dumulon**, a reconstruction of Rouyn's first post office and general store, celebrates its pioneer spirit with displays on the first settlers.

🏛 **Maison Dumulon**
191 Ave. du Lac. **Tel** (819) 797 7125. **Open** Jun–Sep: daily; Oct–Jun: Wed–Sun. **Closed** Jan 1, Dec 25. 🚫 ♿

Copper being smelted into huge nuggets for export, Noranda

Herds of caribou roam the tundra on the Ungava Peninsula that is Nunavik

⓰ James Bay

ℹ️ Tourisme Quebec (877) 266 5687.

The thinly populated municipality of James Bay is roughly the size of Germany, which makes it much larger than most other municipalities in the region – about 350,000 square km (135,000 square miles). Its landscape, lakes, scrubby trees, and early pre-Cambrian rock is hardly urban, changing from forest to taiga to tundra and becoming gradually more inaccessible in the frozen northern parts. However, what the region lacks in infrastructure it makes up for amply in power capacity. Its six major rivers, which all flow into the Bay, can produce enough electricity to light up the whole of North America. So far, the Quebec government has spent over Can$20 billion in building a third of the number of dams for what is already one of the biggest hydroelectric projects in the world. Five power plants produce nearly 16,000 megawatts of electricity to power much of Quebec and parts of the northeastern US. Le Grand 2 (known as LG 2) is the biggest dam and underground generating station in the world.

The main town in the area is the small settlement of Radisson. A functional but useful tourist center, Radisson also offers good views of the surrounding country. Not all of the Bay's 215 dams and dikes can be seen, but the massive dams and series of reservoirs, especially LG 2, which is just east of town, are visible from above.

One of the vast power stations at James Bay

⓱ Nunavik

ℹ️ Nunavik Tourism Association (819) 964 2876, 1 855 Nunavik.
🌐 **nunavik-tourism.com**

In the far north of Quebec, the pristine Nunavik territory covers an area slightly larger than continental Spain. Its inhabitants number about 12,000, nearly all of them Inuit, who live in 14 communities along the shores of Hudson Bay, the Hudson Strait, and Ungava Bay. Nunavik is Quebec's last frontier, a wild and beautiful land that is virtually inaccessible except by airplane. Caribou herds, polar bears, and musk oxen roam the taiga coniferous forest and frozen Arctic tundra that covers this region. Seals and beluga whales can be found swimming in its icy waters.

Kuujjuaq, near Ungava Bay, is Nunavik's largest district, with a population of just over 1,400. This is a good jumping-off point for expeditions to the valley of Kangiqsujuaq near Wakeham Bay and the rugged mountains around Salluit.

Visitors come to Nunavik and Kuujjuaq to appreciate the many varieties of wildlife which roam freely in their natural setting. Summer is the best time for a trip; temperatures rise, but the ground remains frozen all year round. The region has no railroads (and hardly any roads) and should be explored only in the company of a seasoned and reliable guide. Many Inuit groups and communities offer guide services and the opportunity to experience life on the land with Inuit families. Visitors should be prepared for a very warm welcome and the chance to sample traditional Inuit foods and hospitality.

ONTARIO

Introducing Ontario

The sheer size of Ontario is daunting. It is Canada's second-largest province, covering over one million square miles and stretching all the way from the Great Lakes on the US border to the frozen shores of Hudson Bay. Northern Ontario is relatively inaccessible, but this wild and stunningly beautiful region of turbulent rivers, deep forests, and Arctic tundra can be reached by air, and by the occasional scenic road and railroad. Much of the north is also sparsely populated, in striking contrast to the fertile lands farther south, and bordering Lake Ontario, which have attracted many thousands of immigrants. Both Toronto, Canada's biggest city, and Niagara Falls, the country's leading tourist destination, are here.

The tallest free-standing structure in the western hemisphere, Toronto's CN Tower, at night

0 kilometers 200

0 miles 200

A tour boat approaches the spectacular Horseshoe Falls at Niagara

For additional map symbols *see back flap*

Getting Around

Among several highways skirting the northern shore of Lake Ontario, the main ones are Hwy 401, from Toronto to Montreal in the east and Windsor in the west, and the Queen Elizabeth Way (QEW), from Toronto south to Niagara Falls. Niagara Falls, Toronto, and Ottawa are linked by bus and rail. Hwy 400 runs north from Toronto to Parry Sound, where it becomes Hwy 69 up to the Trans-Canada Highway. Buses cover northerly routes.

THE GREAT LAKES

OTTAWA
AND EASTERN
ONTARIO

TORONTO

Peawanuck

*Cape
Lookout*

*Cape
Henrietta
Maria*

Kinushseo

*Hudson
Bay*

Ekwan   *Swan*

*North Twin
Island*

Attawapiskat

*Akimiski
Island*

*South
Twin
Island*

Kapiskau

Fort Albany

*Charlton
Island*

Albany

River

R I O

Moosonee

Moose Factory

Moose

Mattagami

*Kesagami
Lake*

Hearst

Fraserdale

Kapuskasing

Smooth Rock Falls

Hornepayne

Cochrane

11

Timmins

101

Mountain

Foleyet

Kirkland Lake

Wawa

101

Englehart

icoten Chapleau   Gogama

Cobalt

Lake Temagami

Sault
Marie

17

Sudbury

Sturgeon
Falls

North Bay

Blind
River

17

Mattawa

Thessalon

Espanola

*Lake
Nipissing*

Pembroke

Renfrew

Gatineau

Little Current

69

Barry's Bay

60

417

*Manitoulin
Island*

11

Huntsville

Ottawa

Tobermory

Parry Sound

Bancroft

41

Perth

416

401

*Lake
Huron*

400

11

28

Brockville

Midland

Peterborough

Lansdowne

Owen Sound

Barrie

Kincardine

10

Kingston

21

400

115

Cobourg

6

401

Toronto

Oshawa

*Lake
Ontario*

Kitchener

Sarnia

London

Hamilton

St. Catharines

402

3

Niagara Falls

401

Simcoe

Nanticoke

Windsor

Chatham

Lake Erie

*Lake
St. Clair*

Essex   Leamington

The Neo-Gothic splendor of Ottawa's Parliament Buildings
seen from the top of Nepean Point

Key

  Expressway

  Divided highway

  Highway

  Other road

  Main railway

  Minor railway

  International border

  Regional border

△   Summit

The Hudson's Bay Company

The Hudson's Bay Company was incorporated by King Charles II of England on May 2, 1670. His decision was prompted by the successful voyage of the British ship *Nonsuch*, which returned from the recently discovered Hudson's Bay crammed with precious beaver furs. The king granted the new company wide powers, including a monopoly of trading rights to a huge block of territory bordering the Bay, then known as Rupert's Land. The Company was ordered to develop links with the native Americans of Rupert's Land, and trade took off swiftly. Here fashion played a part: the ladies and gentlemen of 18th-century Europe were gripped by a passion for the beaver hat, and the demand for beaver pelts became almost insatiable.

European fur couriers rapidly built up a roaring trade with native fur trappers, which came to follow a seasonal pattern.

Lands and Trading Posts

From 1670 onward, trading goods were dispatched from England to the Company's main trading sites around Hudson Bay, modest stockaded settlements with safe stores for the merchandise. Larger outposts gradually became self-sufficient, catering to newer, smaller posts as the Company moved ever westward. By 1750, HBC camps were established at the mouths of all the major rivers flowing into Hudson Bay. James Bay's Fort Albany had a jail, a hospital, a smithy, a cooperage, a canoe-building jetty, and sheep and cattle barns, while gallant efforts were made to grow crops. Main trading posts serviced a network of smaller seasonal outposts. They continued their expansion west until the transfer of land rights to the new country of Canada in 1870.

Fort Yukon
1846–1869

Fort Good
Hope 1821

Fort Simpson
1821

Fort St. James
1821

Edmonton
1795

Cumberland
House 1774

Fort Victoria
1843

Key

🦫 Trading post

– – Trading route

〰️ 1670 boundary of Rupert's Land

The Seven Oaks Massacre of June 1816 in Manitoba occurred when HBC workers clashed with the rival North West Company, and 20 men were killed. The two companies agreed in 1821 to join territories and increased in power.

English traders assembled a variety of goods to trade with local tribes in return for the winter's supply of pelts. Transported by ship in spring, the merchandise ranged from trinkets to more substantial items including blankets, knives, and guns.

The Changing Fortunes of HBC

HBC reigned supreme in Canada until the 1840s, but civil disobedience led the British to relinquish claims to Washington State and Oregon in 1846, establishing the US border. No longer able to enforce its monopoly, HBC sold its land to Canada in 1870, retaining only areas around the trading posts. They were in key locations, which boosted HBC's expansion into real estate and retail in the 20th century. Today HBC is one of Canada's top companies, but it is majority-owned by a US firm.

The Bay in Vancouver, one of HBC's modern department stores

The beaver's coat is at its thickest and most valuable in winter, when the natives ventured out into the ice and snow to trap the animal. In spring Indian trappers delivered bundles of soft pelts to the Company's trading posts, in exchange for goods.

Company sailboats first carried materials to trade with native peoples. As the Company grew, it transported building materials, food, and seeds to set up what became sizeable settlements. Ships returned with up to 16,000 beaver pelts.

The Group of Seven

Formed in 1920, the Group of Seven revolutionized Canadian art. Mostly commercial artists working in an Ontario art firm, this small band of painters was inspired by a colleague, Tom Thomson. An avid outdoorsman, Thomson started making trips in 1912 into the wilderness of northern Ontario to produce dozens of brightly colored, impressionistic sketches. His friends realized that he was taking Canadian art in a new direction – these landscapes of their country were largely free of the rigid European focus that had characterized painting until then and a nationalist movement had begun. After World War I and the death of Thomson in 1917, these same friends started the Group and held their first exhibition in Toronto in 1920. Many of the paintings shown depicted Nova Scotian, Ontarian and Quebec wildernesses; a new art was born that forged a sense of national pride between the people and their land in this young country.

The Red Maple is A.Y. Jackson's vibrant landmark of 1914. Inspired by a fall visit to Algonquin Park, it embodied the Group aim of creating a national consciousness.

Edge of the Forest (1919) by Frank Johnston is just one of the Group's works that illustrates their statement: "Art must grow and flower in the land before the country will be a real home for its people." Using the impressive surroundings of their homeland, the Group painters developed a spontaneous technique.

Above Lake Superior was painted by Lawren Harris in 1922. Known for his simple, heroic images, Harris captures the harsh, exhilarating climate of the Great Lakes region in winter, known as "the mystic north." Harris believed that spiritual fulfillment could best be obtained by studying landscape. The Group also held the ethos that truly meaningful expression was accomplished only when the the subject of the work was one the viewer shared with the artist, in this case local landscape.

Falls, Montreal River (1920) was painted by J. E. H. MacDonald, who chose Algoma as his work base. Each of the Group had a preferred individual region in which they found most inspiration, mostly in Ontario. Sketching trips regularly took place in summer, with painters showing each other favorite areas.

The Group of Seven

Based in a converted railway boxcar, the members hiked and boated to favorite places in Algonquin Park, Georgian Bay, Algoma, and Lake Superior to produce new art for their country. Following the 1920 exhibition, entitled The Group of Seven, their striking paintings immediately became popular and the Group went on to exhibit together almost every year. Native inspiration was vital to the Group's subject and technique. The apparently raw and coarse methods were a rejection of the heavy, realist oils produced in Europe at the time. Luminous colors and visible brushstrokes led one critic to remark that the Group had "thrown [their] paint pots in the face of the public." The Group held their final show in 1931 and disbanded the following year to make way for a wider group of painters from across Canada, the Canadian Group of Painters. Founders of a distinctive Canadian art movement based on a love of their country's natural beauty, the Group of Seven painters remain particularly celebrated in Canada and are still given prominence in top galleries across Ontario and the rest of the country today.

The photograph below, taken at Toronto's Arts & Letters Club in 1920, shows, from left to right: Varley, Jackson, Harris, Barker Fairley (a friend and writer), Johnston, Lismer and MacDonald. Carmichael was not present.

Autumn, Algoma (1920)

This richly decorated canvas shows the extraordinary evening colors of the fall in Ontario. Algoma was J.E.H. MacDonald's chosen region, a Canadian Eden in northern Ontario that acted as his inspiration and where he regularly made sketching trips. MacDonald records uniquely Canadian subjects in this painting; the blazing foliage and looming pines serve to record and thus establish a Canadian identity. Influenced by the stark landscapes produced in Scandinavia from around 1900, MacDonald focuses on the chill drama in this scene to add a grandeur to his beloved landscape.

The Group of Seven in 1920

TORONTO

Toronto has shed its prim, colonial image to become one of North America's most dynamic cities, a cosmopolitan mix of almost six million inhabitants drawn from more than 200 ethnic groups. Reveling in its position as the financial and commercial center of Canada, Toronto also boasts fine art museums, suave café-bars, and luxury stores.

Located on the north shore of Lake Ontario, Toronto was originally a native Indian settlement dating from the 17th century, and, after 1720, a French fur-trading post. Fought over by the US and Britain in the War of 1812 *(see p51)*, Toronto has since been a peaceful city, growing dramatically after World War II, with the arrival of over 500,000 immigrants, especially Italians and, more recently, Asians.

The first place to start a visit is the CN Tower, formerly the world's tallest tower and the city's most famous tourist attraction. From the top, it is easy to pick out the sights of the city, and from the bottom, a short stroll leads to the harbourfront or the banking district. To the north of downtown is the boisterous street-life of Chinatown and the superb paintings of the Art Gallery of Ontario. Nearby sits the University of Toronto, on whose perimeters lies the fine Royal Ontario Museum and two delightful specialty collections, the Gardiner Museum of Ceramic Art and the Bata Shoe Museum. A quick subway ride takes the visitor north to Casa Loma, an eccentric Edwardian mansion, and Spadina House, the elegant Victorian villa nearby. Many more attractions are scattered around the periphery, including Toronto Zoo and the Ontario Science Centre. The McMichael Canadian Art Collection, in nearby Kleinburg, contains an outstanding collection of paintings by the Group of Seven, among many others, in a pastoral setting.

Toronto's café society doing what it does best in the downtown area

◀ Toronto financial district city scape at dusk

Exploring Toronto

Toronto is a large, sprawling city that covers over 640 sq km (398 sq miles) on the north side of Lake Ontario. The center offers a pleasant mix of office blocks, leafy residential streets, and shopping areas, while the suburbs, such as North York and Scarborough, are more residential and spread out. The downtown core, encompassing the business district and Chinatown, is bordered by College and Front on the north and south, and Jarvis and Spadina on the east and west.

Sights at a Glance

Historic Areas and Buildings
④ Royal York Hotel
⑧ Mirvish Theatres
⑩ First Post Office
⑬ Toronto City Hall
⑭ Chinatown
⑯ University of Toronto
⑰ Ontario Parliament Buildings
㉓ Spadina House
㉔ Casa Loma
㉕ Fort York
㉖ Little Italy
㉘ Distillery District

Parks and Gardens
⑱ Queen's Park
㉙ The Toronto Islands
㉚ The Beaches and Scarborough Bluffs
㉛ Toronto Zoo

Modern Architecture
① CN Tower p176
③ Rogers Centre

Museums, Galleries, and Concert Halls
② Ripley's Aquarium of Canada
⑤ Hockey Hall of Fame
⑥ Four Seasons Centre for the Performing Arts
⑦ Toronto Dominion Gallery of Inuit Art
⑨ Roy Thomson Hall
⑫ Art Gallery of Ontario pp182–3
⑲ George R. Gardiner Museum of Ceramic Art
⑳ Royal Ontario Museum pp188–9
㉑ Bata Shoe Museum
㉜ Aga Khan Museum and Ismaili Centre
㉝ Ontario Science Centre
㉞ Black Creek Pioneer Village
㉟ McMichael Canadian Art Collection

Shopping Areas
⑪ Queen Street West
⑮ Kensington Market
㉒ Yorkville
㉗ St. Lawrence Market

Toronto and Environs

Toronto's CN Tower dominates the city skyline

Getting Around

Toronto's public transportation is excellent. The subway lines follow the main arteries: Bloor/Danforth (east–west) and Yonge/University (north–south). Buses and streetcars serve the areas around each subway station. Starting in spring 2015, the UPExpress will run every 15 minutes between Pearson International Airport and Union Station.

Key

■ Major sight
■ Other sight
═══ Highway
━━━ Major roads
═══ Minor roads
═══ Pedestrian walkway
═══ Railway

0 meters   500
0 yards   500

For additional map symbols see back flap

Street-by-Street: Harbourfront

Toronto's harbourfront has had a varied history. Lake Ontario once lapped against Front Street, but the Victorians reclaimed 3 km (1.5 miles) of land to accommodate their railroad yards and warehouses. Ontario's exports and imports were funneled through this industrial strip until the 1960s, when trade declined. In the 1980s the harbourfront had a new lease on life, when planners orchestrated the redevelopment of what has now become 10 sq km (4 sq miles) of reclaimed land. It now boasts grassy parks, walkways, smart apartments, many of the city's best hotels, and a cluster of tourist sights in and around the Harbourfront Centre.

❶ ★ View from the CN Tower
Once the world's tallest building, the CN Tower offers views of up to 160 km (100 miles) over Ontario, and a glass floor for those with iron nerves.

Metro Toronto Convention Centre
Split into north and south arenas, the center is used for large-scale business shows as well as trade and consumer exhibitions for the public.

❷ ★ Rogers Centre
Using enough electricity to light the province of Prince Edward Island, a performance at the vast Rogers Centre stadium is an unforgettable experience.

Charter boats
Sailing out into Lake Ontario and around the three Toronto Islands provides fine views of the city. Small sailboats, motorboats, and tours are available.

Ripley's Aquarium of Canada houses more than 15,000 sea creatures in a state-of-the-art building (see p177).

Toronto Harbourfront
The harbourfront is a pleasing and relaxing area of the city. Its many attractions offer something for everyone, from water-related activities to skating, craft studios, dining, and shopping.

Locator Map
See pp172–3

WestJet Theatre
This popular open-air concert venue seats over 1,500 people, with standing room for 3,000 more. A program of film screenings, and music and dance performances runs through the summer evenings.

Steam Whistle Brewing at the Roundhouse is a working brewery in a historic former steam train repair facility. Tasting tours are available.

The Gardiner Expressway divides the city center from the waterfront and leads west to Niagara Falls *(see pp216–19).*

The Power Plant
Contemporary Art Gallery hosts changing exhibitions of major international artists.

SIMCOE STREET

D:

LVD. W.

GARDINER EXPRESSWAY

QUEEN'S QUAY

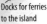

Docks for ferries to the island

| 0 meters | 150 |
| 0 yards | 150 |

Key

— Suggested route

Queen's Quay
The focus of activity on the harborfront, Queen's Quay is a lively area for visitors. Lined with cafés and restaurants, the walkway offers lakeside views as well as street performers and gift shops.

❶ CN Tower

At 553 m (1,815 ft) high, Canada's National Tower was the tallest free-standing structure in world for over three decades, and remains the tallest tower in the western hemisphere. The CN Tower was not originally designed as the world's tallest spire, but it so overwhelmed the city's visitors that it soon became one of Canada's prime tourist attractions. The tower houses the largest revolving restaurant in the world, which rotates fully every 72 minutes. Open seasonally, EdgeWalk at the CN Tower offers the world's highest hands-free walk on a building at 356 m (1,168 ft).

The SkyPod is reached by its own elevator and is the highest accessible point on the tower at 447 m (1,465 ft).

360 The Restaurant at the CN Tower
Spectacular views combine with award-winning cuisine and wines from the world's highest cellar.

The Lookout Level offers visitors the chance to observe the city in comfort, away from the wind; signs identify main Toronto landmarks.

The Outdoor SkyTerrace is protected by steel grilles and illustrates how exposed the tower is, especially in windy weather.

The CN Tower from the Lake
The tower offers fantastic views of Toronto and Lake Ontario. On a clear day it is possible to see as far south as Niagara Falls (see pp216–19).

Glass Floor
The ground is 342 m (1,122 ft) beneath this thick layer of reinforced glass, and even the courageous may feel a little daunted.

The outside elevators, featuring glass fronts and floors, take visitors shooting up the outside of the Tower to the upper levels. Speeds take your breath away and make your ears pop; the elevators can reach the top in under a minute.

The inside staircase has 1,776 steps. Climbing the steps as part of a charity event is a popular fund-raising activity in Toronto.

View of the City from the Lookout Level
At 346 m (1,136 ft) above the city, the LookOut Level provides panoramas of Toronto from interior galleries. Horizons offers upscale bistro dining on this level.

❷ Ripley's Aquarium of Canada

288 Bremner Blvd. **Tel** 647 351 3474.
🚇 Union, St. Andrew. **Open** daily;
check website for details. 🅿️ ♿ 📷
w ripleysaquariumofcanada.com

Opened in fall 2013, this state-of-the-art aquarium houses over 15,000 sea creatures. The building, at the base of the CN Tower, is designed to evoke an angular wave and is handsomely clad in white and grey aluminium.

Inside, visitors gaze at the largest jelly fish tank in the world, and walk through Atlantic and Pacific habitats, along with a unique Great Lakes exhibition. Deep below the Dangerous Lagoon, a travelator ferries visitors through a tunnel where large tooth sawfish and sand tiger sharks swim overhead. To get even closer, head to the touch tanks filled with bamboo sharks, horseshoe crabs, and stingrays.

❸ Rogers Centre

1 Blue Jay Way. **Tel** 416 341 3000.
🚇 Union. **Open** daily. 🅿️ ♿ 📷
w rogerscentre.com

Opened in 1989, the Rogers Centre was the first sports stadium in the world to have a fully retractable roof. In good weather, the stadium is open to the elements, but in poor conditions the roof moves into position, protecting players and crowd alike. Four gigantic roof

Lavish interior lobby of the Royal York

panels are mounted on rails and take just 20 minutes to cover the playing area. The end result looks sort of like a giant hazelnut. However, the building's looks are partially redeemed by a pair of giant-sized cartoon-sculptures on the outside wall, the creation of a popular contemporary artist, Michael Snow.

The Rogers Centre is home to two major sports teams, the Toronto Argonauts from the Canadian Football League, and the Toronto Blue Jays of Major League Baseball. The Rogers Centre is also used for special events and concerts.

❹ Royal York

100 Front St. W. **Tel** 416 368 2511.
🚇 Union. ♿

Dating from 1929, the Royal York has long been Toronto's preeminent hotel, its plush luxury easily outshining its rivals. It was built opposite the city's main train station for the convenience of visiting dignitaries, but for thousands of immigrants, the hotel was the first thing they saw of their new city. The Royal York was designed by the Montreal architects Ross and Macdonald in contemporary Beaux Arts style. Inside, the public areas are lavish and ornate, with slender galleries providing extra grace and charm. The Royal York has been revamped over the years and remains a favorite with high powered visitors, which have included visiting royalty.

Union Station, across the street from the Royal York, was also designed by Ross and Macdonald and shares a similar Beaux Arts style. Inside, the cavernous main hall has a grand coffered ceiling supported by 22 sturdy marble pillars.

The retractable roof of the Rogers Centre rears above the playing field, site of many football and baseball games

For hotels and restaurants in this region see pp350–59 and pp364–83; for transport information see pp410–11

Modern exterior of the Four Seasons Centre for the Performing Arts

❹ Hockey Hall of Fame

Brookfield Place, 30 Yonge St. **Tel** 416 360 7765. 🚇 Union Station, King Station. **Open** Jul, Aug & Mar break: 9:30am–6pm Mon–Sat, 10am–6pm Sun; Sep–Jun: 10am– 5pm Mon–Fri, 9:30am–6pm Sat, 10:30am–5pm Sun. **Closed** Jan 1, Dec 25. 🎦 ♿ 🌐 **hhof.com**

The Hockey Hall of Fame is a lavish tribute to Canada's national sport, ice hockey *(see p40.* Hockey, both ice and grass, originated in Canada; from its simple winter beginnings on frozen lakes and ponds, the game now ignites Canadian passions like no other. The Hall of Fame's ultra-modern exhibition area is inventive and resourceful, with different sections devoted to particular aspects of the game. There are displays on everything from the jerseys of the great players, including

The Stanley Cup at the Hockey Hall of Fame

Wayne Gretzky and Mario Lemieux, to a replica of the Montréal Canadiens' locker room in the old Forum.

Another section traces the development of the goalie's mask from its beginnings to the elaborately painted versions of today. Interactive displays abound, and visitors can stop pucks fired by virtual players. A 3D film that mixes archival footage with computer animation plays every 30 minutes. Another area displays a collection of trophies, including the Stanley Cup, hockey's premier award.

❺ Four Seasons Centre for the Performing Arts

145 Queen St. W. **Tel** 416 363 8231; 416 345 9595 (National Ballet of Canada). 🚇 Osgoode. ♿ 🌐 **coc.ca; national.ballet.ca**

The Four Seasons Centre for the Performing Arts is Canada's first purpose-built opera and ballet house. Completed in 2006, it is home to both the Canadian Opera Company and the National Ballet of Canada. With the world's longest freespan glass staircase and a horseshoe-shaped auditorium featuring phenomenal advancements in modern engineering and accoustical design, it stages a full range of operatic repertoires, from chamber pieces by Mozart and Handel, to some of the monumental 19th- and 20th-century works, such as Wagner's *Ring Cycle*, which require an orchestra of over 100 musicians.

The world-class Canadian Opera Company, under the directorship of Alexander Neef, is the largest producer of opera in Canada. The National Ballet of Canada, with Karen Kain as Artistic Director, is the country's premiere dance company, with more than 60 dancers.

❻ Toronto Dominion Gallery of Inuit Art

79 Wellington St. West. **Tel** 416 982 8473. 🚇 Union Station. **Open** 8am–6pm daily (10am–4pm Sat, Sun). ♿

The Toronto Dominion Centre consists of five jet-black sky-scrapers, a modern tribute to the Toronto Dominion Bank by design consultant Mies Van der Rohe. The southern tower displays a strong collection of Inuit Art on two levels of its foyer. The exhibits were assembled as a centennial project in the 1960s. They bought over 100 pieces in a variety of materials, including caribou antler and walrus tusk, but the kernel of the collection is the stone carving. Soapstone sculptures show mythological beasts and spirits as well as scenes from everyday life. Some of the finest were carved by Johnny Inukpuk (b.1911), whose *Mother Feeding Child* (1962) and *Tattooed Woman* (1958) have a raw, elemental force.

❼ Mirvish Theatres

260 and 300 King St. W. **Tel** 416 872 1212; 1 800 461 3333. 🚇 St. Andrew. ♿ 🌐 **mirvish.com**

In the 1960s, the Royal Alexandra Theatre was about to be flattened by bulldozers when the flamboyant "Honest Ed" Mirvish, the king of the bargain store, came to the rescue. Mirvish saved a fine Edwardian theater, whose luxurious interior of red velvet, green marble, and

The Royal Alexandra, one of the Mirvish Theatres

The patio at the Black Bull on Queen Street West – one of the sunniest spots for a beer in the city

flowing scrollwork once made it the most fashionable place in Toronto. Nowadays, the Royal Alex stages well-known plays and big-hit Broadway musicals. Evening performances are extremely popular, and booking ahead is required. Early arrivals can enjoy the original Edwardian features in the bar before the show. Next door is the Princess of Wales Theatre, which is used for Broadway-style musicals.

❽ Roy Thomson Hall

60 Simcoe St. **Tel** 416 872 4255. 🚇 St. Andrew. **Open** for performances. ♿ 🌐 **roythomson.com**

This Arthur Erickson-designed concert hall is home to the Toronto Symphony Orchestra, but jazz, pop, rock, and world music artists have also graced its stage. The Roy Thomson Hall is also used as a screening venue for the Toronto International Film Festival.

❾ First Post Office

260 Adelaide St. E. **Tel** 416 865 1833. 🚇 King, Queen. 🚋 501, 504. **Open** 9am–5:30pm Mon–Sat, 11am–4pm Sun. ♿ 📷 by appt.

In 1829, the British House of Commons founded their colonial postal service and five years later

established a post office in a far-flung outpost of the newly created town of Toronto. Remarkably, Toronto's First Post Office has survived, weathering many attempts by the city to have it demolished. The only remaining example in the world of a post office dating from the British North American postal era still in operation, the First Post Office functions fully. Visitors make the trip to write a letter with a quill pen and seal it themselves with hot wax. Today's mail, however, is processed by the national service, Canada Post. After a devastating fire in 1978, the building was refurbished to its former carved and decorated appearance using historical city archive records.

Young visitors on Queen Street West

❿ Queen Street West

🚇 Osgoode. 🚋 Queen 501.

Through the day and into the small hours of the morning, Queen Street West buzzes. Students and trendsetters reinvigorated this old warehouse area in the 1980s, but nowadays the street between University and Spadina is more varied, with chic designer stores and stylish restaurants mixed in with more mainstream chain stores. Between Spadina and Bathurst, boutiques, downbeat bars, and a few second-hand stores and fabric shops remain while most stores go progressively upmarket.

Worker at Toronto's First Post Office stamping mail by hand

Street-by-Street: Downtown

Throughout the 19th century, Yonge Street was the commercial focus of Toronto, lined with scores of shops and suppliers. It also separated the city ethnically. In 1964, with the building of the new City Hall and Nathan Phillips Square just across from Old City Hall, Toronto's center of gravity shifted to Queen Street. South of Queen Street lies the Financial District. Gleaming concrete-and-glass tower blocks started replacing Victorian buildings in the 1960s, and today the area is packed with modern skyscrapers – from Mies Van de Rohe's classic black Toronto Dominion Centre to the 65-story Trump Tower, which was built in 2012 and is the country's tallest mixed use skyscraper.

Textile Museum of Canada
This international collection features over 12,000 examples of fabrics, embroidery, and clothing through the ages.

Campbell House Museum
This 19th-century home is a period piece from the days of the Victorian bourgeoisie.

Key

— Suggested route

MCCAUL STREET

ST. PATRICK STREET

SIMCOE STREET

UNIVERSITY AVENUE

QUEEN STREET WE

⓫ ★ **Art Gallery of Ontario**
With exhibits ranging from the 14th to the 21st centuries, the AGO is also home to a number of works by Edgar Degas.

0 meters		100
0 yards		100

Toronto Eaton Centre
Running a full block from Queen to Dundas, the Eaton Centre is downtown's largest mall. Outside its northern end, lively Yonge-Dundas Square sometimes hosts free concerts.

Locator Map
See Toronto Map pp172–3

Yonge Street is the main north–south thoroughfare of the city.

DUNDAS STREET WEST

BAY STREET

Church of the Holy Trinity
This charming Anglican church was built in the 19th century and features an elegant interior.

Nathan Phillips Square is a lively gathering place for concerts, festivals, and civic celebrations.

⑫ ★ Toronto City Hall
Open since 1965, this controversial development has slowly become popular with locals, who use the plaza as a skating rink in winter.

Old City Hall
In sharp contrast to its ultra-modern replacement across the street, the elegant 19th-century Old City Hall now operates as a provincial courthouse.

⓫ Art Gallery of Ontario

Founded in 1900 as the Art Museum of Toronto, the Art Gallery of Ontario holds one of Canada's most extensive collections of fine art and modern sculpture. This modern structure houses European works by Rembrandt, Gainsborough, van Gogh, and Picasso; a superb collection of Canadian art, including the Group of Seven work *(see pp168–9)*; Inuit art; and the world's largest public collection of works by British sculptor Henry Moore. In 2008 the gallery reopened after a major expansion, designed by architect Frank Gehry, to accommodate an unprecedented gift of art and funding from art collector Ken Thomson.

★ African Art Collection
This late-18th-/early-19th-century reliquary figure from Gabon is just one of many exhibits in the African Collection that aims to show the relationships between art and culture in Africa.

★ Henry Moore Sculpture
The museum houses the world's largest public collection of works by Henry Moore, including *Draped Reclining Figure* (1952–3).

Massacre of the Innocents (c.1609–11)
Peter Paul Rubens's early 17th-century masterpiece, discovered in 2001, is a highlight of the European Art collections.

Dundas Street

Key

- ☐ Contemporary art
- ☐ European art
- ☐ Temporary exhibitions
- ☐ Canadian art
- ☐ African art
- ☐ Prints, drawings, and photographs
- ☐ Nonexhibition space

Gallery Guide

The second floor houses collections of Canadian painting, with works by the "Group of Seven" (see pp168–9), and Inuit art. It also houses a significant collection of African and Oceanic art and the Henry Moore Sculpture Centre, which is home to Moore's sculptures, bronzes, and plaster casts. European art and photography are found mainly on the first floor. The Thomson Collection of Ship Models can be found on the Concourse level.

Fourth floor

Third floor

Second floor

Fifth floor

First floor/street level

Main entrance

Concourse

Revamped Façade
The modern extension of the
Art Gallery of Ontario was
designed by Toronto-born
architect Frank Gehry. It is his
first building in Canada.

★ **The West Wind** (1916–17)
Tom Thomson's painting inspired a
distinctive Canadian style exemplified
by the "Group of Seven."

Scene in the Northwest (c.1845)
This painting by Canadian artist Paul
Kane shows British surveyor Captain
John Henry Lefroy. It is part of the
Thomson Collection of Canadian Art
from the middle of the 19th century.

Built in the 1960s, the ultra-modern design of Toronto City Hall is internationally renowned

⑫ Toronto City Hall

100 Queen St. W. & Bay St. 🚇 Queen, Osgoode. 🚋 Queen 501. **Open** 8:30am–4:30pm Mon–Fri. ♿ 📷 self-guided. 🌐 **toronto.ca/city_hall_tour**

Completed in 1964, Toronto's City Hall was designed by the award-winning Finnish architect Viljo Revell. At the official opening, the Prime Minister Lester Pearson announced, "It is an edifice as modern as tomorrow," but for many cityfolk tomorrow had come too soon and there were howls of protests from several quarters. Even now, after nearly 40 years, the building appears uncompromisingly modern. It is the epitome of 1960s urban planning, with two curved concrete and glass towers framing a central circular building where the Toronto councils meet. Nearby, the Old City Hall is a grand 19th-century neo-Romanesque edifice whose towers and columns are carved with intricate curling patterns.

⑬ Chinatown

🚋 Queen 501, Dundas 505, College 506, Spadina 510.

The Chinese community in Toronto numbers around 283,000, over ten percent of the city's total population. There have been several waves of Chinese migration to Canada, the first to British Columbia in the late 1850s during the Gold Rush. The first Chinese to arrive in Toronto came at the end of the 19th century as workers on the Canadian Pacific Railway, settling in towns along the rail route. The Chinese found work in the Toronto laundries, factories, and on the railways. The last immigration wave saw prosperous Hong Kong Chinese come to live in Toronto in the 1990s.

Chinese Canadians inhabit every part of the city but are concentrated in four Chinatowns, the largest and liveliest of which is focused on Spadina Avenue, between Queen and College streets, and along Dundas Street, west of the Art Gallery of Ontario. These few city blocks are immediately different from their surroundings. The sights, sounds, and smells of the neighborhood are reminiscent not of Toronto but of Hong Kong. Stores and stalls spill over the sidewalks, offering a bewildering variety of Chinese delicacies, and at night bright neon signs advertise dozens of delicious restaurants.

Vivid restaurant signs in Chinatown

⑭ Kensington Market

Baldwin St. & Augusta Ave. 🚋 Dundas 505, College 506, Spadina 510.

Kensington Market is one of Toronto's most distinctive and ethnically diverse residential areas. It was founded at the turn of the 20th century by East European immigrants, who crowded into the patchwork of modest houses near the junction of Spadina Avenue and Dundas Street, and then spilled out into the narrow streets to sell their wares. The bazaar they established in their small 1930s houses has been the main feature of the area ever since.

Today, Jewish, Polish, and Russian stall owners and shopkeepers rub shoulders with Portuguese, Jamaican, East Indian, Chinese, and Vietnamese traders in a vibrant street scene that always excites the senses. The focal point of this open-air market is Kensington Avenue, whose lower half, just off Dundas Street, is crammed with thrift shops selling all manner of trendy retro bargains, from original punk gear to flares. Kensington Avenue's upper half is packed with fresh food stores filled with produce from every corner of the globe, ranging from iced fish to stacks of cheeses and exotic fruits.

A Torontonian samples exotic nuts in the bazaar of Kensington Market

Façade of the Ontario Parliament Building, home of the provincial legislature since 1893

⑮ University of Toronto

25 King's College Circle. **Tel** 416 978 5000. 🚇 St. George, Queen's Park. 🚋 College 506. ♿ 📷 11am & 2pm Mon–Fri, 11am Sat. 🌐 **utoronto.ca**

The University of Toronto grew out of a Royal Charter granted in 1827 by King George IV to Toronto's King's College. Seen by the church as challenging its control of education, the new institution weathered accusations of godlessness and proceeded to swallow its rivals, becoming in the process one of Canada's most prestigious universities.

This unusual history explains the rambling layout of the present campus, a leafy area sprinkled with colleges. The best-looking university buildings are near the west end of Wellesley Street. Here, on Hart House Circle, lie the delightful quadrangles and ivy-clad walls of Hart House (1919), built in imitation of some of the colleges of Oxford and Cambridge universities in Britain, and the Soldiers' Tower, a neo-Gothic memorial to those students who died in both world wars. Nearby, King's College Circle contains University College, an imposing neo-Romanesque edifice dating from 1859, Knox College with its rough gray sandstone masonry, and the fine rotunda of the university's Convocation Hall. A visit to the campus can be peacefully rounded off by a short stroll along Philosophers' Walk, where the manicured lawns lead to Bloor Street West.

Reminiscent of old British universities, the University of Toronto

⑯ Ontario Parliament Building

Queen's Park. **Tel** 416 325 7500. 🚇 Queen's Park. 🚋 College 506. **Open** mid-may–Aug: daily; Sep–mid-May: Mon–Fri. ♿ 📷 8:30am–4:30pm.

There is nothing modest about the Ontario Parliament Building, a vast pink sandstone edifice opened in 1893 that dominates the end of University Avenue.

Ontario's elected representatives had a point to make. The province was a small but exceedingly loyal part of the British Empire and clamored to make its mark and had the money to do so. Consequently, the Members of Provincial Parliament (MPPs) commissioned this immensely expensive structure in the Romanesque Revival style. Finished in 1892, its main façade is a panoply of towers, arches, and rose windows decorated with relief carvings and set beneath a series of high-pitched roofs.

The interior is of matching grandeur. Gilded classical columns frame the main staircase and enormous stained-glass windows illuminate long and richly timbered galleries. The chamber is a lavish affair, with a wealth of fine wooden carving that carries epithets urging good behavior, such as "Boldly and Rightly," and "By Courage, not by Craft."

In 1909, a fire razed the west wing, which was rebuilt in Italian marble. The stone was very expensive, so the MPPs were annoyed to find that a large amount of the marble was blemished by dinosaur fossils, which can still be seen today in the west hallway. Visitors can sometimes watch the parliament in session.

The Parliament Buildings, viewed from inner-city Queen's Park

⑰ Queen's Park

College St. & University Ave.
Tel 416 325 7500. 🚋 College 506.
🚇 Queen's Park. ♿

Despite being ringed by a road that links two of downtown's busiest streets, Queen's Park is a peaceful and pleasant grassy space, perfect for catching your breath when visiting the closely packed sights in the surrounding area. The park is fringed to the west by the 19th-century buildings of the University, while the Royal Ontario Museum and the George R. Gardiner Museum of Ceramic Art lie to the north. Since the Legislative Buildings lie right in the middle of the park, its tranquility is occasionally broken by political protesters and special interest groups loudly proclaiming their displeasure with the provincial government.

⑱ Gardiner Museum of Ceramic Art

111 Queen's Park. **Tel** 416 586 8080.
🏛 Museum. **Open** 10am–6pm Mon–Thu; 10am–9pm Fri, 10am–5pm Sat & Sun. **Closed** Jan 1, Dec 25. 📷 ♿
🌐 **gardinermuseum.com**

Opened in 1984, the Gardiner Museum of Ceramic Art is the only showcase of its kind in North America dedicated solely to pottery and porcelain. Skillfully displayed, the collection traces the history of ceramics, with a detailed focus on its principal developmental stages. These start with Pre-Columbian pottery, and the museum has fascinating displays of ancient pieces from Peru and Mexico that incorporate several grimacing fertility gods.

The Greeting Harlequin
Meissen ceramic figure

Examples of brightly colored *maiolica* (glazed, porous pottery), includes painted pots made in Italy from the 15th and 16th centuries. Cheerfully decorated everyday wares are complemented by later Renaissance pieces relating classical myths and history. English delftware (tin-glazed earthenware) is also well represented in the collection. The 18th-century pieces gathered from France, Austria, Germany, and England are superb – particularly the collection of *commedia dell'arte*

figures. These are derived from the Italian theatrical tradition of comic improvisation with a set of stock characters, notably the joker Harlequin. Intricately decorated in rainbow colors, these figurines were placed on dinner tables by the aristocracy to delight, impress, or even to woo their special guests.

Porcelain here is stunning, with many examples of exquisite Meissen from the 18th century. Packed in its own specially made leather carrying case to accompany a fine lady owner on her travels, a special feature is the embellished tea and chocolate service dating from the mid-18th century. Each tiny cup has individual, intricate scenes of a harbor or of merchants and travelers surrounded in gold. The porcelain collection also contains over 100 finely decorated scent bottles from all over Europe.

⑲ Royal Ontario Museum

See pp188–9.

⑳ Bata Shoe Museum

327 Bloor St. W. **Tel** 416 979 7799.
🚇 St. George. **Open** 10am–5pm Mon–Wed, Fri & Sat, 10am–8pm Thu, noon–5pm Sun. **Closed** Good Friday, Dec 25. 📷 ♿
🌐 **batashoemuseum.ca**

The Bata Shoe Museum was opened in 1995 to display the extraordinary range of footwear collected by Sonja Bata, a member of the eponymous shoe manufacturing family, a worldwide concern that sells footwear in 60 countries. To be sure her collection was seen to best effect, Sonja had the prestigious contemporary Canadian architect Raymond Moriyama design the building – an angular modern affair

The modern exterior of the Bata Shoe Museum

complete with unlikely nooks and crannies created to look like a chic shoebox.

The collection is spread over several small floors and features three changing exhibitions developing a particular theme, as well as regularly rotated items selected from the museum's substantial permanent collection. More than a temple to fashion, the museum treats shoes as important ethnological pieces, illustrating not only changes in technology, but also shifting values and attitudes. Entire ways of life can be gleaned from the design of these beautiful objects, from climate and profession to gender and religion.

One fixed feature in the museum is the exhibition entitled "All About Shoes," which provides the visitor with an overview of the functions and evolution of footwear. It begins with a plaster cast of the earliest-known footprint, discovered four million years after it was made in Tanzania, and has an interesting section on medieval pointed shoes. A second permanent feature is the section on celebrity footwear. This rotating display could include Marilyn Monroe's red stiletto heels, a pair of Elton John's platforms, or Michael Johnson's gold lamé sprinting shoes. A fashion section, called Fashion Afoot, includes *haute couture* shoes by Roger Vivier and Christian Louboutin. There is also a display of unusual and improbable footwear including unique French chestnut-crushing

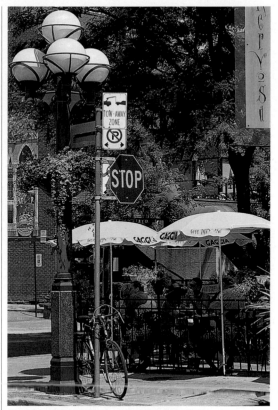

A lazy Sunday afternoon at Café Nervosa in upscale Yorkville

Traditional Indian *Paduka* footwear, the Bata Shoe Museum

boots and a pair of US army boots made for use in the Vietnam War, whose sole is shaped to imitate the footprint of an enemy Vietcong irregular.

㉑ Yorkville

🚇 Bay.

In the 1960s, tiny Yorkville, in the center of the city, was the favorite haunt of Toronto's hippies. With regular appearances by counter-cultural figures such as Joni Mitchell, it was similar to New York's Greenwich Village. The hippies have now moved on, and Yorkville's modest brick and timber terrace houses have either been colonized by upscale shops and fashionable restaurants, or converted into bijou townhouses. Luxury hotels, designer boutiques, private art galleries, fine

jewelers, and quality shoe stores all jam into the neighborhood, attracting shoppers in droves. The area is a lovely place to sit at an outdoor café, nursing a cappuccino and watching the crowds. Yorkville and Cumberland Avenues are the center of all this big spending, as are the elegant and discreet shopping complexes that lead off them, especially the deluxe Hazelton Lanes, at the corner of Yorkville Avenue, which houses trendy upscale brands. The dropout philosophy has been thoroughly replaced by very chic stores – some of the most exclusive retail outlets in the country are found here. Although the recession in the 1990s affected trade somewhat, the area is still prosperous and thriving. Café society really takes off at night, but Yorkville can be an expensive place to have fun.

⑲ Royal Ontario Museum

Founded in 1912, the Royal Ontario Museum (ROM) holds a vast and extraordinarily wide-ranging collection drawn from the fields of fine and applied art, the natural sciences, and archaeology. Special highlights include the dinosaur gallery, and an Asian Arts gallery featuring Chinese sculpture and architecture and Japanese art and culture. The ROM has undergone a major transformation over the years, and many galleries have been restored. The Michael Lee-Chin Crystal addition is a bold chrystalline formation designed by architect Daniel Libeskind, which contains a main museum entrance and cutting-edge galleries.

Key

- Samuel Hall Currelly Gallery
- Asian and Middle Eastern Arts
- Natural History
- Textiles, costume and glass
- Canada Galleries
- World Cultures
- Michael Lee-Chin Crystal spaces
- Non-exhibition space

The futuristic-looking Royal Ontario Museum

Gallery Guide

The museum has an exceptional array of themed galleries, spanning both World Cultures and Natural History. With six million objects in the ROM's collections, there is something new to discover around every corner. The Canada Galleries are located on the first floor.

The Green Room
This elegant English parlour dates from the 1750s. One of several room settings featured in the European galleries, it boasts the original green paneled walls popular among the gentry of the time.

Learning Centre & Library

Canada Gallery: First Peoples
This spacious gallery celebrates Canadian culture, with a dynamic approach to the country's aboriginal traditions. Many of the unique and vibrant aboriginal artifacts are displayed for the first time.

Level B1

Theater

Garfield Weston Exhibition Hall

For hotels and restaurants in this region see pp350–59 and pp364–83; for transport information see pp410–11

Fifth floor
Restaurant
Lounge

Fourth
floor

Institute for
Contemporary
Culture

Curatorial
Centre

Third
floor

Second floor

Stuffed Albatross
This huge bird has a
wingspan of 3 m (9 ft). It
is a main feature of the
bird gallery, which offers
interactive exhibits.

Museum Store

First floor
(street level)

Main entrance

★ **Galleries of Africa: Egypt**
With a large collection of
mummies, burial masks, and
domestic artifacts, the Egyptian
collection contains the remains of
a buried court musician, in a
painted golden coffin so intricate
that scholars dare not open it.

Bat Cave
Painstakingly reconstructed
from a 4-km (2-mile) long
Jamaican bat cave, some 3,000
wax and vinyl bats fly to greet
the visitor in this eerie
darkened cavern.

★ **Dinosaur Gallery**
The most popular gallery in the ROM is
now on the second floor of the Michael
Lee-Chin Crystal, with dinosaur skeletons
set in simulations of the Jurassic Age and
animation techniques as used in the 1990s
blockbuster *Jurassic Park*.

㉓ Spadina Museum, Historic House & Gardens

285 Spadina Rd. **Tel** 416 392 6910. 🚇 Dupont. **Open** Jan–Mar: noon–5pm, Sat & Sun; Apr–Aug: noon–5pm, Tue–Sun; Sep–Dec: noon–4pm, Tue–Fri; noon–5pm, Sat & Sun. **Closed** Mon; Good Fri, Dec 25, 26, Jan 1. 🖼 ♿ 📷 obligatory.

James Austin, first president of the Toronto Dominion Bank, had this elegant Victorian family home built on the bluff overlooking Spadina Avenue in 1866. The last of the Austins, moved out in 1982 and the building, its contents, and gardens were left to the Historical Board of Toronto. Spadina Museum has been restored to accurately reflect how the Austin family lived during the 1920s and '30s. The general ambience appeals, but there are several enjoyable features, notably the Art Nouveau frieze in the Billiard Room and a trap door in the Palmroom that allowed gardeners to tend to the plants unseen by the family.

The front door of Spadina House with garlanded Victorian columns

㉕ Fort York

250 Fort York Blvd. **Tel** 416 392 6907. 🚌 511, 509. **Open** daily. **Closed** Good Fri, Dec 25–26, Jan 1. 🖼 ♿ 📷

The British built Fort York in 1793 to reinforce their control of Lake Ontario and, from this, Toronto grew. The weaknesses of the fort were exposed when the Americans overran it after a long battle in the War of 1812 *(see p51)*. After the war, the British strengthened the fort, and its garrison gave a boost to the local economy. The military compound has been painstakingly restored, and its barracks, old powder magazine, and officers' quarters make for a pleasant visit. It is the largest collection of original War of 1812 buildings in Canada.

㉔ Casa Loma

This unusual Gothic revival house was designed by E.J. Lennox, the man responsible for Toronto's Old City Hall. With its combination of architectural elements, the house is a remarkable tribute to Sir Henry Pellatt (1859–1939), one of the most influential industrialists of early 20th century Canada. He made a fortune in hydroelectric power during the early 1900s, harnessing the strength of Niagara Falls for electricity. In 1906, Pellatt decided to build himself a castle. Three years and Can$3.5 million later, construction was halted due to the outbreak of World War I.

The Study hid secret doors in its wooden panels, one leading to Sir Henry's wine cellar.

The Terrace looks over delightful formal gardens and a fountain against a backdrop of hills and rhododendron forest.

★ **The Great Hall**
Oak beams support a ceiling 18-m (60-ft) high, in a hall featuring a 12-m (40-ft) tall bay window.

The Bathroom was designed for Sir Henry's personal use. It contains a free-standing shower with six heads and features lavish decoration.

Fresh vegetables on sale in Little Italy

㉖ Little Italy

College St. W. 512. 207 Queen's Quay W. 416 203 2500.

There are half a million people of Italian descent resident in Toronto. The first major wave of Italian migrants arrived between 1885 and 1924. Italians have been in Toronto since 1830, and their sense of community, together with the instability of Italy after World War II, led to another large influx in the 1940s and 1950s. Italians now live and work in every corner of the city.

Italian touches appear in the proliferation of espresso bars and cinemas showing Italian films, while the food offered by the sidewalk cafés is terrific.

㉗ St. Lawrence Market

91 Front St. E. King. **Open** daily. North market building: Farmers' Market 5am–3pm Sat, Antiques Market dawn–5pm Sun.
stlawrencemarket.com

Arrive with an appetite and join the crowds queuing for peameal bacon sandwiches, wood-oven baked bagels, and the most succulent Portuguese *churrasco* chicken rolls in the city. With over 100 vendors, the market is the city's come-to spot for fresh seafood, fine meats, exotic cheeses, and top-quality fruit and vegetables. There's crafts and more downstairs.

㉘ Distillery District

Mill St, between Parliament & Cherry sts. **Tel** 416 364 1177. 505. **Open** daily. thedistillerydistrict.com

This successful redevelopment of the Victorian Gooderham and Worts whiskey distillery boasts some of the best shopping in the city with fashion, crafts, and artisanal food makers occupying the industrial buildings. There are also plenty of restaurants, bars, and cafés with large patios. A Christmas market is held in the first two weeks of December.

Façade of house and formal gardens
Five acres (2 ha) of garden add to the charm of the estate with perennial borders, roses, lawns, and woodland.

★ **Conservatory**
White walls offset the Victorian stained-glass dome. The marble flower-beds conceal steam pipes for the rare plants.

Children learning to canoe and exploring the lagoons of the Toronto Islands

㉙ The Toronto Islands

🚋 Spadina 510 from Union, then ⛴ Queen's Quay. ℹ️ 416 392 8193.
🌐 **toronto.ca/parks/island**

In Lake Ontario, just offshore from the city, the three low-lying Toronto Islands, connected by footbridges, shelter Toronto's harbor and provide easy-going recreation in a car-free environment. Here, amid the cool lake breezes, visitors can escape the extremes of the summer heat, which can reach up to 35°C (95°F). Whatever the weather, there are views of the CN Tower *(see p176)*.

It takes about an hour to walk from one end of the islands to the other. In the east is Ward's Island, a sleepy residential area; Centre Island, home to the Centreville Amusement Park for children, is in the middle, and to the west lies Hanlan's Point which has one of the country's few public clothing-optional beaches.

㉚ The Beaches and Scarborough Bluffs

Beaches: 🚋 Queen 501. Bluffers Park: 🚇 Victoria Park, then 🚌 Kingston Rd 12 eastbound to Brimley, then 10-minute walk south down Brimley

The Beaches is one of Toronto's most beguiling neighborhoods, its leafy streets running up from the lakeshore. The area lies to the east of downtown, between Woodbine Avenue and Victoria Park Avenue. Queen Street East, the main thoroughfare, is liberally sprinkled with excellent cafés and designer clothes shops. The Beaches was a restrained and quiet neighborhood, but its long, sandy beach and boardwalk have made it extremely desirable. Roller-blading and cycling are popular here – a 3-km (2-mile) boardwalk runs along the beach and is very busy in summer, as is the large public swimming pool. The waters of Lake Ontario have improved greatly, and many of Toronto's beaches have been awarded blue flags; call 416 392 7161 for water-quality reports.

At its eastern end, the Beaches borders Scarborough, the large suburb whose principal attraction is also along the rocky lakeshore. Here, the striking Scarborough Bluffs, outcrops of rock made from ancient sands and clay, track along Lake Ontario for 16 km (10 miles). A series of parks provides access: Scarborough Bluffs and the Cathedral Bluffs parks offer great views of jagged cliffs, and Bluffers Park is ideal for picnics.

㉛ Toronto Zoo

361A Old Finch Ave., Scarborough. **Tel** 416 392 5900. 🚇 Kennedy, then 🚌 86A (weekdays all year plus weekends in summer). **Open** May–Sep: 9am–7pm daily; check website for rest of year. **Closed** Dec 25. ♿ ♿ 📷 🌐 **torontozoo.com**

Toronto has one of the world's best zoos, occupying a large slice of the Rouge River Valley.

The animals are grouped according to their natural habitats, both outside, amid the mixed forest and flatlands of the river valley, and inside large, climate-controlled pavilions.

Visitors can tour the zoo by choosing one of the marked trails, or hop aboard the Zoo-mobile, a 30-minute ride with commentary that gives an excellent overview. It takes about four hours to see a good selection of animals, including such Canadian species as moose, caribou, and grizzly bear. There is also a pair of giant pandas and a polar bear enclosure. Splash Island provides a spot for young visitors to cool off in the water, amid walrus and beaver sculptures.

㉜ Aga Khan Museum and Ismaili Centre

77 Wynford Dr. 🚇 Eglinton, then 🚌 Eglinton 34 east to Wynford Dr. **Open** 10am–8pm Tue–Sun.
🌐 **akdn.org/museum**

Opening in summer 2014, the Aga Khan Museum is the first major museum to be devoted solely to Islamic art and heritage in North America. It is dedicated to fostering knowledge and understanding among people of all cultures through its displays of art, objects, and artefacts of historical significance from the Muslim world.

The design of the rectilinear, white stone museum mirrors the geometric patterns that define Islamic art. The contemporary building sits in

A mother and baby orangutan at Toronto Zoo

A hands-on exhibit at Ontario Science Center

formal landscaped gardens with five reflecting pools.

The Aga Khan is the 49th hereditary Imam of the Shia Imami Ismaili Muslims, and the museum's permanent exhibit consists of over 200 pieces from his family's private collections. Major temporary exhibits are also staged, along with performances of traditional music from the Islamic World.

Adjacent to the museum, the Ismaili Centre offers spaces for prayer, intellectual engagements, and social gatherings.

❸ Ontario Science Centre

770 Don Mills Rd. **Tel** 416 696 3177. Eglinton or Pape, then Eglinton 100 or Don Mills 25. **Open** 10am–4pm Mon–Fri, 10am–5pm Sat & Sun. **Closed** Dec 25. **ontariosciencecentre.ca**

One of Toronto's most popular sights, the Ontario Science Centre attracts children in droves. They come for the center's interactive displays and hands-on exhibits exploring and investigating all manner of phenomena, from the Solar System to the human brain. At KidSpark children can make music, experiment with tracks, balls, and cogs, and join a construction team to build a house, while the Science Arcade is all about fun with physics.

❸ Black Creek Pioneer Village

Cnr Steeles Ave. W. & Jane St. **Tel** 416 736 1733. Finch, then 60. **Open** May & Jun: 9:30am–4:30pm Mon–Fri, 10am–5pm Sat & Sun; Jul–Sep: 10am–5pm daily; Sep–Dec 23: 9:30–4pm Mon–Fri, 10am–4:30pm Sat & Sun. **Closed** Jan–Apr.

Over the years, some 40 19th-century buildings have been moved to historic Black Creek Pioneer Village in the northwest of the city from other parts of Ontario. Inevitably, the end result is not entirely realistic – no Ontario village ever looked quite like this – but this living history showpiece is still great fun. Staff in period costume demonstrate traditional skills such as candlemaking, baking, and printing. Among the more interesting buildings are the Doctor's House from 1860, and the Laskay Emporium general store, which shows the array of goods that could be bought. The Tinsmith Shop is manned by skilled craftsmen, and there is a Masonic Lodge meeting room.

Five buildings are credited to Daniel Stong, a 19th-century pioneer; his pig house, smoke house, grain barn, and two contrasting homes – the first and earlier dwelling is a crude log shack, the second a civilized house with a brick fireplace, outside of which is a garden planted with herbs.

❸ McMichael Canadian Art Collection

10365 Islington Ave., Vaughan. **Tel** (905) 893 1121. **Open** May–Oct: 10am–5pm daily; Nov–Apr: 10am–4pm daily. **Closed** Dec 25. **mcmichael.com**

On the edge of Kleinburg, about 30 minutes' drive north of downtown Toronto, Robert and Signe McMichael built themselves a fine log-and-stone dwelling overlooking Humber River Valley. The McMichaels were also avid collectors of Canadian art, and in 1965 they donated their house and paintings to the government. The art collection has greatly increased and, with approximately 6,000 pieces, is now one of the most extensive in the province.

The focus of the McMichael is the work of the Group of Seven (*see pp168–9*), with the permanent galleries dedicated to displaying a selection of their works. The keynote paintings are characteristically raw and forceful landscapes illustrating the wonders of the Canadian wilderness. Both Tom Thomson (a famous precursor of the Group) and Lawren Harris are well represented. There are also ongoing exhibitions devoted to contemporary Inuit and First Nations art.

The log and stone façade of the McMichael Art Collection building

OTTAWA AND EASTERN ONTARIO

Eastern Ontario is justly famous for its history and natural beauty. The myriad lakes and waterways that dominate the landscape here once served as trade highways through the wilderness for native people and explorers. Today they form a beautiful natural playground, with spectacular opportunities for outdoor activities such as boating, fishing, hiking, and skiing. The St. Lawrence is one of the world's great waterways and begins near the small, historic city of Kingston. North of Lake Ontario lies the Canadian Shield, with the ancient lakes, rocks, and forest that epitomize Canada. A favorite with many Canadian vacationers, Algonquin Provincial Park is one of the country's most famous wilderness areas. Also popular is the picturesque Kawartha Lakes region. Rising majestically over the Ottawa River, Canada's capital is a storehouse of national history and stately architecture that attracts over 7.7 million visitors each year.

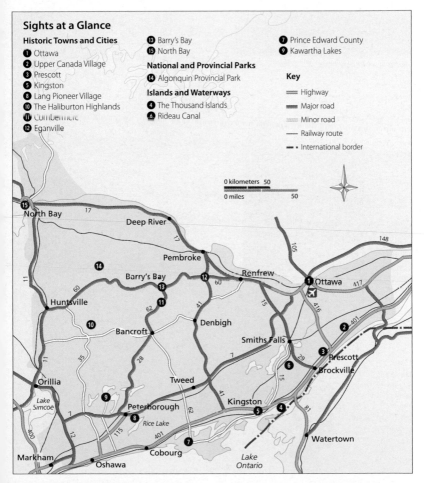

Sights at a Glance

Historic Towns and Cities
- ❶ Ottawa
- ❷ Upper Canada Village
- ❸ Prescott
- ❺ Kingston
- ❽ Lang Pioneer Village
- ❿ The Haliburton Highlands
- ⓫ Combermere
- ⓬ Eganville

- ⓭ Barry's Bay
- ⓯ North Bay

National and Provincial Parks
- ⓮ Algonquin Provincial Park

Islands and Waterways
- ❹ The Thousand Islands
- ❻ Rideau Canal

- ❼ Prince Edward County
- ❾ Kawartha Lakes

Key
- ══ Highway
- ▬ Major road
- ═ Minor road
- ── Railway route
- ▬▪ International border

0 kilometers 50
0 miles 50

● Street-by-Street: Ottawa

Ottawa was a compromise choice for Canada's capital, picked in part because of the rivalry between the English and French and the cities that grew into today's urban giants, Toronto and Montreal. This compromise has from its foundation in 1826, grown into a city with an identity all its own. Named capital of the Dominion of Canada in 1857, Ottawa has a fine setting on the banks of the Ottawa and Rideau rivers. Far more than just the political capital, the city has grown into a mix of English and French residents and historic and modern buildings with plenty of attractions to keep its six million annual visitors busy.

A member of the RCMP leading his horse by the Parliament buildings

Centennial Flame was first lit in 1967 to commemorate a century of Confederation. It burns continually.

★ Parliament Buildings
The Changing the Guard takes place outside daily from late June to late August. The spectacular ceremony adds to the grandeur of this seat of government.

Rideau Canal
Built in the mid-19th century, the Canal is now a playground for visitors, its banks lined with grassy cycling and walking paths.

WELLINGTON STREET

National War Memorial
Annually, on November 11, a memorial service takes place here to honor Canada's war veterans.

Fairmont Château Laurier is a luxury hotel, and arguably Canada's most famous. It has offered sumptuous accommodation to Canada's great and good since it was built in 1912.

Major's Hill Park
This peaceful, open-air space in the heart of the busy capital is marked by a statue of an Anishinabe scout, in honor of the First Nations' role in the development of Canada.

Nepean Point is a spot from which the whole of central Ottawa can be seen.

| 0 meters | | 100 |
| 0 yards | | 100 |

Key

— Suggested route

MACKENZIE AVENUE

SUSSEX DRIVE

Royal Canadian Mint
This Can$20 Olympic skiing coin was created by the Mint as a souvenir for the 1988 Winter Olympic Games in Calgary. The mint produces only special edition and investment pieces.

★ National Gallery
Featuring more than 25,000 artworks, this is the country's premier collection of the fine arts, housed in this outstanding granite and glass building.

Exploring Ottawa

The core of the capital is relatively contained, and many of the top sights can be easily accessed on foot. Traveling south through the city, the Rideau Canal is Ottawa's recreation ground year round, from boating and strolling during summer to skating across its icy surface in the freezing Canadian winter. The National Arts Centre is a focus for theater, music, and dance; history and art buffs can spend days visiting museums and galleries, both large and small. Ottawa is a city of festivals too; notably Winterlude, a three-weekend February celebration, while in spring the Canadian Tulip Festival transforms the city into a sea of flowers. Canada Day celebrations, on July 1, also attract thousands of visitors.

Away from downtown, it may seem that the suburban National Capital Region is overflowing with museums for every enthusiast. Attractions include the Central Experimental Farm and the Canada Aviation Museum.

Cash register from a 19th-century shop at the Bytown Museum

Ottawa's majestic Neo-Gothic Parliament Buildings

🏛 Parliament Buildings

Parliament Hill, 111 Wellington St. **Tel** (613) 992 4793. **Open** daily. **Closed** Jan 1, Jul 1, Dec 25. **W** **parl.gc.ca**

Dominating the skyline, the country's government buildings overlook downtown Ottawa in a stately manner. Undaunted by the tall buildings that have crept up around them in the 150 years since they became Ottawa's center of power, the East and West Blocks glow green above the city because of their copper roofing. The Gothic Revival sandstone buildings were completed in 1860. Located on a 50-m (165-ft) hill, the Parliament offers a view of the Ottawa River. The Parliament Buildings are distinctly reminiscent of London's Westminster, both in their Victorian Neo-Gothic style and in their position. Largely destroyed in a fire in 1916, all the buildings are now restored to their former grandeur.

The Parliament Buildings can be toured year round, including when the House of Commons and Senate are in session. Hand-carved sandstone and limestone characterize the interior of the government chambers. In the summertime, Mounties patrol the neat, grassy grounds outside the Parliament, where visitors mingle and spot politicians. On July 1, which is Canada Day, Parliament Hill is the site of a large outdoor concert and celebration. Thousands flock to the area to listen to music and watch the fireworks.

🏛 Bytown Museum

Ottawa Locks. **Tel** (613) 234 4570. **Open** mid-May–mid-Oct: 10am–5pm daily (to 8pm Thu; to 7pm mid-Jun–Aug); mid-Oct–mid-May: 11am–4pm daily. 🅿 **W** **bytownmuseum.ca**

Housed in Ottawa's oldest stone building (1827), the Bytown Museum traces the history of Ottawa's early years from the construction of the Rideau Canal through the rough and

Key to Symbols *see back flap*

Map labels

Canada Aviation Museum

MacDonald-Cartier Bridge

GATINEAU

SUSSEX DRIVE

Ottawa River

BOTELER

BOLTON

CATH

Royal Canadian Mint ⑤

Notre Dame Cath

Champlain Statue

National Gallery of Canada ④

Alexandra Bridge

Major's Hill Park

Bytown Museum ②

Fairmont Château Laurier Ho

Centre Block

Parliament Buildings ①

East Block

West Block

Supreme Court of Canada 🅿

STREET

SPARKS ST

O'CONNOR ST

i

National Archives & National Library

WELLINGTON

BANK

AVENUE

Canadian War Museum

QUEEN STREET

ALBERT STREET

KENT STREET

GLOUCE

SLATER STREET

LAURIER

STREET

NEPE

BAY STREET

LYON ST

Bus Station 2 km (1.

Ottawa International Airport 15 km (9 miles)

0 meters		500
0 yards		500

Key

▪ Street-by-Street map: *see pp196–7*

tumble days of Bytown, to the city's emergence as Canada's capital and beyond. The British Royal Engineer in charge of building the Rideau Canal, Lt. Colonel John By, set up his headquarters on this location in 1826. While work was underway, the building was used as a storehouse for military supplies, gun powder, and silver coins. The museum hosts exhibitions, guided tours, and family events.

The elegant Wilfrid's Restaurant at the Château Laurier

🏨 Fairmont Château Laurier

1 Rideau St. **Tel** (613) 241 1414. ♿
W fairmont.com/laurier-ottawa

This wonderful stone replica of a French château is a fine example of the establishments built by railroad companies in the early 1900s. It has attracted both the great and the good since it opened as a hotel in 1912. Centrally located at the foot of Parliament Hill, its interior features large rooms with high ceilings, decorated with Louis XV-style reproductions. The hotel attracts an upscale clientele, including celebrities and government mandarins. Zoé's Lounge, a restaurant with soaring columns, chandeliers, and palms, lit by an atrium, is a wonderful place for lunch, as is the hotel's larger restaurant, Wilfrid's.

Demob sign at the War Museum

🏛 Canadian War Museum

1 Vimy Pl. **Tel** (819) 776 7000, 1 800 555 5621. **Open** mid-May–mid-Oct: 9:30am–6pm daily (to 8pm Thu); mid-Oct–mid-May: 9:30am–5pm Tue–Sun (to 8pm Thu). 🎟 free Jul 1. ♿
W warmuseum.ca

Canadians may have a reputation as a peaceful people but they have seen their share of the world's battlefields. This museum, housed in a stunning modern building close to Parliament Hill, looks at the country's military history and at how this history has shaped the nation and its people. Exhibits range from the earliest wars fought on Canadian soil between the French and the British to the present day. The LeBreton Gallery houses an extensive collection of military technology including vehicles, artillery, and other artifacts. The Beaverbrook Collection of War Art contains 13,000 works and is one of the largest collections of military art in the world. The Memorial Hall offers a space for quiet reflection. Its concrete walls are reminiscent of the rows of gravestones in Allied war cemeteries. The hall's sole artifact is the headstone from the grave of Canada's Unknown Soldier. The museum's Regeneration Hall, with its view of the Peace Tower on Parliament Hill, represents hope for a better future.

Sights at a Glance

Map labels: Bordeleau Park, ROSE STREET, ST. PATRICK ST, KING EDWARD AVENUE, MURRAY STREET, CLARENCE STREET, YORK, GEORGE STREET, RIDEAU STREET, NELSON STREET, CHAPEL STREET, FRIEL STREET, BESSERER STREET, STEWART STREET, WILBROD STREET, CUMBERLAND STREET, WALLER ST, NICHOLAS STREET, LAURIER AVENUE EAST, OSGOODE STREET, ⑦ ByWard Market, Conference Centre, ⑨ QUEEN, Rideau Canal, COLONEL BY DRIVE, ELIZABETH DR, ⑩ Canada Agriculture & Food Museum, ⑧ Laurier House, Canada Science & Technology Museum, Train Station 3 km (1.8 miles)

⬛ Royal Canadian Mint

320 Sussex Dr. **Tel** 1 800 276 7714.
Open daily. 🅿️ ♿ 🎥 obligatory.
W mint.ca

Founded in 1908 as a branch of the British Royal Mint, this no longer produces regular Canadian cash currency. Instead, it strikes many special-edition coins and Maple Leaf bullion investment coins. The mint also processes about 70 percent of the country's gold in its refinery, which is among the largest in North America.

Tours take place throughout the day; book to ensure you see the process that turns sheets of metal into bags of shiny gold coins. Weekend tours may be less interesting as the production lines are unlikely to be running.

The façade of Ottawa's imposing Cathédrale Notre Dame

⬛ Notre-Dame Cathédrale

Cnr Sussex Dr. & St. Patrick St. **Tel** (613) 241 7496. **Open** daily. ♿

Built between 1841 and 1865, Notre Dame, with its twin spires, is Ottawa's best-known Catholic church. It is situated in the ByWard Market area and features a spectacular Gothic-style ceiling. The windows, carvings, and the huge pipe organ are also well worth seeing. Philippe Parizeau (1852–1938) carved the woodwork in mahogany. In niches around the sanctuary, there are wooden etchings of prophets and apostles, crafted by Louis-Philippe Hebert (1850–1917), now painted to look like stone. Joseph Eugene Guigues, the first bishop of Ottawa, oversaw the completion of Notre Dame, and his statue is outside the basilica.

ByWard Market is known as a lively area of Ottawa

⬛ ByWard Market

Bounded by Cumberland, Sussex, George, and St. Patrick. **Tel** (613) 562 3325. **W** byward-market.com

This neighborhood bustles all year round; outdoors in the summer, inside in winter. The area is located just east of Parliament Hill, across the Rideau Canal, and offers a colorful collection of craft shops, cafés, boutiques, bistros, nightclubs, and farmers' market stalls. Special attractions include the food market in the ByWard Market Building on George Street, and the cobblestoned Sussex Courtyards. The cafés are among Ottawa's most popular places to lunch.

⬛ Laurier House

335 Laurier Ave. E. **Tel** (613) 992 8142.
Open mid-May–Jun & Sep–mid-Oct: 10am–5pm Thu–Mon; July & Aug: 10am–5pm daily. 🅿️

A national historic site, Laurier House, a Victorian town house built in 1878, served as the chief residence of two notable Canadian prime ministers, Sir Wilfrid Laurier and William Lyon Mackenzie King. Beautifully furnished throughout, it houses memorabilia, papers, and personal possessions of both former national leaders.

Rideau Canal

W pc.gc.ca/rideaucanal

Built in the mid-19th century, the Rideau Canal, a UNESCO World Heritage Site, travels through lakes and canals from Ottawa to the city of Kingston (*see p204*). The canal flows through the capital, providing an attractive pastoral sight, with its walking and cycling paths bordering the water. Once used for shipping, the canal is now a recreational area. In summer, visitors stroll along its banks, while through Ottawa's freezing winter the canal, at 7.8 km (5 miles) long, turns into the world's longest skating rink. It is popular with locals during the winter festival, and also as a means of commuting to work.

⬛ Canada Agriculture and Food Museum

Experimental Farm Dr, cnr Prince of Wales and Carling Ave. **Tel** (613) 991 3044. **Open** 9am–5pm daily. **Closed** Dec 25. 🅿️ ♿ 🎥
W agriculture.technomuses.ca

This museum at the Central Experimental Farm, a crop research station and National Historic Site, allows visitors to explore the sights and sounds of farm life through animals, exhibitions, treasures from the collection, hands-on demonstrations, and delicious foods. The farm's livestock barns and show cattle herds are especially

Children can get close to animals at the Canada Agriculture and Food Museum

The waterside restaurant at the National Arts Centre, seen from the Rideau Canal

popular with children, and everybody loves the tours of the site in wagons drawn by huge Clydesdale horses.

National Arts Centre

53 Elgin St. **Tel** (613) 947 7000. **Open** daily. nac-cna.ca

Completed in 1969, the National Arts Centre (NAC) has four stages, an elegant canal-side restaurant, and a summer terrace. The building, designed by noted Canadian architect Fred Lebensold, comprises three interlocking hexagons. Many exponents of Canadian and international dance, theater, and musical forms, including the National Arts Centre Orchestra, perform here regularly. NAC's Southern Hall auditorium seats 2,300; the Theatre, with its innovative apron stage, seats 897; the Studio, a marvelous venue for experimental productions, comfortably seats 300; and the cabaret-style Fourth Stage seats 150. Reserving tickets well in advance is recommended.

Canadian Museum of Nature

240 McLeod St. **Tel** (613) 566 4700, 1 800 263 4433. **Open** May–Aug: 9am–6pm Fri–Tue, 9am–8pm Wed & Thu; Sep–Apr: 9am–6pm Tue–Sun (to 8pm Thu). nature.ca

Canada's national natural history museum entertains with its well thought-out galleries highlighting birds, fossils and dinosaurs, and mammals. The Vale Earth Gallery has beautiful geological specimens, and kids will enjoy the Arctic marine exhibits where they can captain a research vessel. In the Animalium, visitors get a close up look at giant snails, tarantulas, and scorpions.

Canada Science and Technology Museum

1867 St. Laurent Blvd. **Tel** (613) 991 3044. **Open** 9am–5pm daily (early Sep–Apr: closed Mon). sciencetech.technomuses.ca

Discover a whole new world at this interactive museum, whose exhibits include a wide range of fascinating displays exploring Canada's space history, transport-ation through the ages, and modern and industrial technology. A vintage steam locomotive can be boarded (for a 10-minute ride, Jul–Sep only) and the more modern-minded may enter a mini-control room and pull levers to launch a make-believe rocket. Visitors can also join a mission to save a colony on Mars.

Canada Aviation and Space Museum

Aviation & Rockcliffe Parkways. **Tel** (613) 993 2010. **Open** May–early Sep: daily; early Sep–Apr: Wed–Mon. aviation.technomuses.ca

This huge building near Rockcliffe Airport houses over 130 aircraft, which have flown both in war and peace. A replica of the famous 1909 *Silver Dart*, the first aircraft to fly in Canada, is here, as is the nose cone from the *Avro Arrow*, the supersonic superfighter that created a political crisis in Canada when the government halted its development in the 1950s. The *Spitfire*, valiant friend of the Allies in World War II, features alongside historic bush planes such as the *Beaver* and early passenger carrier jets. Displays detail the exploits of Canadian war heroes, plus era aircraft, while the interactives along the Walkway of Time trace the history of world aviation.

Model of a rocket at the Canada Science and Technology Museum

National Gallery of Canada

Opened in 1988, the National Gallery of Canada provides a spectacular home for the country's impressive collections of art. Located near the heart of the capital, architect Moshe Safdie's memorable pink granite and glass edifice is architecture as art in its own right. The National Gallery is one of the three largest museums in the country, and is Canada's top art gallery, with excellent collections of both national and international exhibits. The museum is a short stroll from the Rideau Canal and Major's Hill Park.

Library

Level 2

No.29 (1950)
A vivid example of Jackson Pollock's idiosyncratic drip technique, this was part of an enormous canvas carefully cut into sections, hence its title, *No. 29*.

★ Rideau Street Chapel
Set in a peaceful inner courtyard, this 1888 chapel was saved from bulldozers nearby and moved here for safety.

Key

- Special exhibition space
- Canadian gallery
- Contemporary art
- European and American galleries
- Prints, drawings, and photographs
- Inuit art
- Non-exhibition space

Inuit sculpture
This is represented in ancient and modern forms; *Aurora Borealis decapitating a young man* dates from 1965.

Gallery Guide

On its first level the gallery houses the world's largest collection of Canadian art. It also features international displays and major traveling exhibitions. The second level contains the European and American Galleries and the gallery of prints, drawings, and photographs. Visitors can relax in the two courtyards or in the fine café.

National Gallery Plaza
Measuring 9 m (30 ft) high, the giant spider "Maman"
by sculptor Louise Bourgeois (1911–2010) towers over
the plaza. Designed in 1999 and cast in 2003, the bronze
sculpture features a pouch of 26 white marble eggs.

VISITORS' CHECKLIST

Practical Information
380 Sussex Dr. **Tel** (613) 990 1985.
Open May–Sep: 10am–5pm daily
(to 8pm Thu); Oct–Apr: 10am–
5pm Tue–Sun (to 8pm Thu).
Closed Jan 1, Good Friday, Dec
25. 🎟 for special exhibitions.
🎧 11am & 2pm. 🎦 💻 📷
🆆 gallery.ca

Transport
🚌 1, 3, 9.

★ The Jack Pine (1916)
In many ways the father of
Canada's nationalist art
movement of the early
20th century, Tom Thomson
of the Group of Seven first
attracted notice with his vivid,
sketchy, impressionist paintings
of the Ontario landscape, here
shown with a brightly colored
oil of a provincial tree framed
in wilderness.

Level 1

**Virgin and Child with an
Angel** (c.1535–1539)
Francesco Salviati (1510–1563)
was taught by painter Andrea
del Sarto in Florence. The
placement of the divine group
in a grotto, with a landscape
in the distance, recalls
Sarto's work.

Ground
level

Auditorium

Water Court
This delightful airy space is a sharp
contemporary contrast to the treasures of
yesteryear that abound in the rest of the
gallery. Water Court is used as a contemplative
gallery for sculpture.

Lecture
hall

Main
entrance

❷ Upper Canada Village

13740 County Road 2, Morrisburg. Exit 758 off Hwy 401, then drive south to County Road 2. **Tel** (613) 543 4328. **Open** mid-May–Aug: 9:30am–5pm daily; Sep: 9:30am–5pm Wed–Sun. 🎨 🚻 🌐 uppercanadavillage.com

This recreated 19th-century town is made up of 40 authentic pre-Confederation (1867) buildings, relocated from the surrounding area to save them from flooding during construction of the St. Lawrence Seaway in the 1950s. Today, it is preserved as a tourist attraction and is a colorful reminder of the province's social history. Costumed villagers work in the blacksmith's forge and the sawmill while tinsmiths and cabinetmakers employ the tools and skills of the 1860s. A bakery, cheese factory, and general store are in operation. Special events throughout the year include themed weekends and battle re-enactments. Adjacent to Upper Canada Village, the **Battle of Crysler's Farm Memorial** commemorates those who died in the War of 1812.

❸ Prescott

🗺 4,100. 🚌 𝒊 360 Dibble St W. (613) 925 2812. 🌐 **prescott.ca**

The major attractions in this 19th-century town are its architecture and access to the St. Lawrence River. Prescott's refurbished waterfront area and its busy marina make for a pleasant waterside stroll. Some

The 1838 lighthouse overlooks the pleasure boats of Prescott's marina

visitors come for the excellent scuba diving. There are 22 wrecks that sank between the late 19th- and mid-20th-centuries within an hour's drive.

Fort Wellington National Historic Site, east from the center of town, attracts many visitors. Originally built during the War of 1812 and rebuilt in 1838, four walls and some buildings remain. These include a stone blockhouse which is now a military museum, incorporating refurbished officers' quarters.

🏛 **Fort Wellington**
Prescott. **Tel** (613) 925 2896. **Open** mid-May–Jun & Sep–mid-Oct: 10am–5pm Thu–Mon; Jul & Aug: 10am–5pm daily. 🚻 🌐 pc.gc.ca/fortwellington

❹ The Thousand Islands

𝒊 10 King St. East, Gananoque (613) 382 3250. 🌐 **1000islandstourism.com**

The St. Lawrence River, one of the world's great waterways, is a gateway for ocean-going vessels traveling through the Great Lakes. Few stretches of the trip compare in charm or beauty to the Thousand Islands, an area that contains a scattering of over a thousand tiny islands, stretching from just below Kingston downriver to the waterside towns and cities of Gananoque, Brockville, Ivy Lea, and Rockport. Cruising opportunities abound from the Kingston boarding site.

River sights include the curious Boldt's Castle, a folly built on one of the islands by millionaire hotelier Boldt and abandoned in grief when his wife died in 1904. It was Oscar, Boldt's head chef at the Waldorf Astoria who, entertaining summer guests at the castle, concocted Thousand Island salad dressing.

A sailboat travels the Thousand Islands

Landlubbers will enjoy the scenery from the Thousand Islands Parkway, which runs from pretty Gananoque to Mallorytown Landing.

❺ Kingston

🗺 120,000. ✈ 🚉 🚌 ⛴ 𝒊 209 Ontario St. (613) 548 4415. 🌐 tourism.kingstoncanada.com

Once a center for ship building and the fur trade, Kingston was briefly (1841–44) the capital of the United Province of Canada *(see p53)*. Constructed by generations of shipbuilders, the city's handsome limestone buildings reflect a dignified lineage. Kingston is still one of the freshwater sailing capitals of North America and the embarkation point for many local cruises. It is also home to more museums than any other town in Ontario. The restored British bastion **Fort Henry National Historic Site of Canada** is a living military museum brought to life by guards in bright scarlet period uniforms who are trained in drills, artillery exercises, and traditional fife and drum music of the 1860s. Canada's top army training university, the Royal Military College of Canada, is also based in the city and The

Guard at Fort Henry

RMC Museum, housed in an 1846 Martello Tower, tells the story of today's cadets and their forebears (open in summer only).

West of the downtown area lies the **Marine Museum of the Great Lakes**. There are displays on the history of the Great Lakes and the ships that sailed on them, including the first ship built for the Lakes here in 1678. The museum also contains a 3,000-ton icebreaker, a fine example of shipbuilding in the last century. Boats are lifted 4 m (13 ft) at Kingston Mills lock station. Located about 7 km (4 miles) north of downtown Kingston, it is a great spot for walking, boat watching and picnicing.

🔲 **Fort Henry**
Kingston. **Tel** (613) 542 7388. **Open** mid-May–Aug: 9:30am–5pm daily. 🎟 ♿ 🌐 forthenry.com

🏛 **Marine Museum of the Great Lakes**
55 Ontario St. **Tel** (613) 542 2261. **Open** Mar–mid-May & Sep–Nov: 10am–4pm Mon–Fri; mid-May–Aug: 10am–4pm daily. 🎟 ♿
🌐 marmuseum.ca

❻ Rideau Canal

🌐 pc.gc.ca/rideaucanal

The Rideau Canal, originally a defensive barrier protecting Canada against the Americans and finished in 1832, stretches for 200 km (125 miles). The best way to enjoy this sparkling necklace of scenic waterway is by boat. A great feat of 19th-century engineering, which includes 47 locks and

A view of the Rideau Canal passing through Westport village

Historic house along the main street of Picton in peaceful Quinte's Isle

24 dams, the system allows boaters to float through tranquil woods and farmland, scenic lakes, and to stop in quaint villages, as well as visit the Rideau **Canal Museum** at Smith's Falls. The canal north of Kingston also contains a number of provincial parks which offer canoe routes. Also popular is the 400-km (250-mile) Rideau Trail, a hiking system linking Kingston and Canada's capital city, Ottawa.

🏛 **Rideau Canal Museum**
34 Beckwith St. S., Smiths Falls. **Tel** (613) 284 0505. **Open** mid-May–Sep daily. 🎟 ♿

❼ Prince Edward County

ℹ 116 Main St., Picton. **Tel** (613) 476 2421. 🌐 pec.on.ca

Charming and known for its relaxed pace and old-fashioned hospitality, Prince Edward County is surrounded by Lake Ontario and the Bay of Quinte, and is sometimes referred to as Quinte's Isle. The island is renowned for its two camping and sunbathing beaches in Sandbanks Provincial Park. There, mountains of fine sand reach 25 m (82 ft) and are considered one of the most significant fresh-water dune systems in the world.

United Empire Loyalists *(see p50)* settled in the County following the American Revolution (1775), founding engaging small towns and a strong farming industry. Visitors can absorb the local historic architecture by traveling along the country roads and the Loyalist Parkway, either cycling or by car, pausing to appreciate the island's charming views.

❽ Lang Pioneer Village

104 Lang Rd., Keene (10 km/6 miles east of Peterborough). **Tel** (705) 295 6694. **Open** mid-May–mid-Jun: 10am–3pm Mon–Fri; mid-Jun–Aug: 10am–4pm daily. 🎟 ♿
🌐 langpioneervillage.ca

Located on the tiny Indian River 4 km (2 miles) north of Keene, Lang Pioneer Village is a traditional representation of Canada's past, featuring 20 restored 19th-century buildings, heritage gardens, and farmyard animals. Visitors can watch an ancient restored grist mill in action, and workers in period costumes display ancient skills while telling stories of what life was once like. Blacksmiths and tinsmiths ply their trade in an authentic smithy and will give lessons. Villagers also demonstrate traditional methods of keeping the home clean, mending clothing, and cooking meals over open fires. Throughout the summer season, visitors can enjoy traditional afternoon teas at the Keene Hotel (1–3pm, for an additonal cost). Special events across the year focus on how the pioneers celebrated the various harvests and Christmas. There are also regular music workshops.

Lush bullrushes surround a pond in Petroglyphs Provincial Park

9 Kawartha Lakes

🛈 Peterborough (705) 742 2201.
🚂 Peterborough.
🆆 thekawarthas.net

The Kawartha Lakes are part of the 386-km (240-mile) Trent–Severn Waterway that runs from Lake Ontario to Georgian Bay and was originally built in the 19th century. Today the area is a playground for vacationers, with water-based activities including cruises and superb fishing. Renting a houseboat from one of the coastal villages is a popular way of exploring the locality. At the center of the region lies the friendly city of Peterborough, notable for its university, pleasing waterfront parks, and the world's largest hydraulic liftlock. Thirty-four km (21 miles) north lies the Curve Lake Indian Reserve's Whetung Ojibwa Centre, one of the best places locally for native arts and crafts.

Petroglyphs Provincial Park, 55 km (34 miles) to the north of Peterborough, is better known to locals as the "teaching rocks" for the 900-plus aboriginal rock carvings cut into the park's white marble outcrops. Rediscovered in 1954, these wonderfully preserved symbols and figures of animals, boats, spirits, and people were made by spiritual leaders to record their dreams and visions. Today the stones are housed in a huge glass building, built around them in 1984 to protect them from frost. The stones remain respectfully regarded to this day as a sacred site by native peoples.

📷 **Petroglyphs Provincial Park**
2249 Northey's Bay Rd, Woodview, off Hwy 28. **Tel** (705) 877 2552. **Open** mid-May–mid-Jun & Sep–mid-Oct: Wed–Sun; mid-Jun–Sep: daily. ♿ 🅿

10 The Haliburton Highlands

🛈 Haliburton (705) 286 1777.
🆆 experiencehaliburton.ca

The Haliburton Highlands are one of Ontario's year-round outdoor destinations, renowned for their forests, lakes, and spectacular scenery. In the summer, thousands of visitors enjoy boating, fishing, and swimming in this region. In fall, busloads of tourists travel to appreciate the celebrated seasonal colors; others come for the deer hunting. Winter brings skiers and snowboarders.

The village of Haliburton is found along scenic Highway 35, which winds its way through exceptional scenery from Minden north to the considerable charms of Dorset. The fire tower atop a rock cliff overlooking the village gives spectacular views of the Lake of Bays and the surrounding area. This spot is a fantastic viewing point for the myriad colors of Ontario's fall trees with their lovely bright red and orange shades.

The Madonna at Pioneer Museum

11 Combermere

🗺 250. 🛈 Ottawa Valley Tourist Association, 9 International Dr., Pembroke (613) 732 4364.
🆆 ottawavalley.org

The village of Combermere is a central point for people heading to a number of provincial parks in Eastern Ontario, including Algonquin (see pp208–9), Carson Lake, and Opeongo River. Along with Wilno and Barry's Bay, Combermere is one of three Madawaska Valley townships, and is a good tourist center for fuel and refreshments. A few kilometers (2 miles) south of Combermere lies the **Madonna House Pioneer Museum**. Founded by Catherine Doherty, this Catholic lay community has grown to have mission outposts around the world. It is managed by volunteers, who live on its cooperative farm. Since 1963, a recycling program has been raising money for the world's poor.

🏛 **Madonna House Pioneer Museum**
Hwy 517. **Tel** (613) 756 3713. **Open** mid-May–mid-Oct: 10am–5pm Tue–Sat.

Golfers taking a break between games to enjoy the Haliburton scenery

Cottages outside Barry's Bay, a popular spot for vacationers

⑫ Eganville

🗺 1,300. 🛈 Ottawa Valley Tourist Association, 9 International Dr., Pembroke (613) 732 4364.

This highway 60 village with its little restaurants and gas station provides a handy tourist center for visitors to this picturesque region. Local attractions include the **Bonnechere Caves**, 8 km (5 miles) away. The caves were at the bottom of a tropical sea 500 million years ago. Gradually raised over millennia from the ocean bed, they are covered with fossils of primitive life forms. The privately owned site is open for tours in summer.

🐾 **Bonnechere Caves**
Tel (613) 628 2283. **Open** mid-May–mid-Oct: daily. ♿ 🖼

⑬ Barry's Bay

🗺 1,250. 🛈 Ottawa Valley Tourist Association, 9 International Dr., Pembroke (613) 732 4364.

An attractive little town, Barry's Bay has a sizeable Polish population, as does its neighbor Wilno, site of the first Polish settlement in Canada. The area is home to many craftspeople and artisans, who sell their wares in the local villages. Barry's Bay is also popular for stores selling outdoor gear and watersport equipment. Year-round sports facilities can be found at nearby Kamaniskeg Lake and Redcliffe Point, both of which are popular places for renting cottages.

Perched high on a hill, nearby Wilno overlooks scenic river valleys and boasts the fine church and grotto of St. Mary's.

⑭ Algonquin Provincial Park

See pp208–209.

⑮ North Bay

🗺 54,000. ✈ 🚉 🚌 🛈 1375 Seymour St. (705) 472 8480.

Billing itself as the Gateway to the Near North, North Bay sits at the eastern end of Lake Nippissing, 350 km (217 miles) north of Toronto. The region's most famous natives are undoubtedly the Dionne quintuplets. Born in 1934, the Quints' original modest family homestead has been relocated and now forms the town's popular **Dionne Quints Museum**.

Lake Nippissing nearby is famous for its fishing and wilderness scenery. Boat cruises across the lake follow the old French explorers route. North Bay makes a good starting-point for trips to the area's many vacation spots.

🏛 **Dionne Quints Museum**
17 Seymour St. **Tel** (705) 472 8480. **Open** mid May–mid-Oct: daily. ♿ 🖼

The Dionne Quints

The hamlet of Corbeil experienced a natural miracle on May 28, 1934: the birth of the Dionne quintuplets; Annette, Emilie, Yvonne, Cecile, and Marie, the five identical girls born to Oliva and Elzire Dionne. The Quints' combined weight at birth was only 6.1 kg (13 lbs 5 oz), and the babies' lungs were so tiny that small doses of rum were required daily to help them breathe. Experts put the chances of giving birth to identical quintuplets at 1 in 57 million. The girls became international stars, attracting countless visitors to North Bay during the 1930s. A Quint industry sprang up with curiosity-seekers flocking to watch the young girls at play. The Dionne homestead was moved to North Bay in 1985, and visitors can travel back over 60 years to marvel anew at the birth of the Quints in this small farmhouse.

⑭ Algonquin Provincial Park

To many Canadians, Algonquin, with its lush maple and pine woods, sparkling lakes, and plentiful wildlife, is as familiar a symbol of Canada as is Niagara Falls.

Founded in 1893, this is the oldest and most famous park in Ontario, stretching across 7,630 sq km (2,946 sq miles) of wilderness. Wildlife abounds; visitors have a chance to see beavers, moose, and bears in their natural habitats, and the park echoes with the hauntingly beautiful call of the loon, heard often in northern Ontario. Every August, on Thursday evenings, "wolf howls" are organized, whereby park staff attempt to elicit answers from these native animals by imitating their cries. Opportunities for outdoor activities are plentiful; most visitors like to try one of the 2,000 km (1,243 miles) of canoe routes through the forested interior.

Killarney Lodge
This is one of the park's rental lodges, rustic buildings that are popular during the spring, summer, and fall.

Canoe Lake
Two thousand kilometers (1,243 miles) of canoe trails surround the park. They range from beginner and family routes, some as short as 6 km (4 miles), to 70-km (50- mile) treks for the experienced. Routes are well planned and marked.

Kiosk

Three Mile Lake

North Tea Lake

Cedar Lake

Br

Cat Lak

H Uc

Big Trout Lake

Tim River

River

Petawawa

60

Smoke Lake

KEY

① **The Algonquin Art Centre**, exhibits international art displays, with a focus on nature and wildlife. Painters featured have included Tom Thomson, precursor of the famous Group of Seven *(see pp168–9)*.

② **The Algonquin Logging Museum**, tells the story of this traditional local trade, illustrated by a river dam and log-moving "alligator."

Moose near Highway 60
Visitors can usually spot a few moose each day, especially near lakes and salty puddles by roadsides, which these huge animals seem to love.

Lake Opeongo
With over 2,400 lakes, Algonquin is justly celebrated for its matchless fishing opportunities. Lake Opeongo, one of the largest in the park, is famous for its abundance of lake trout and smallmouth bass.

Park Visitor Centre
Opened in 1993 to celebrate Algonquin's centenary, the Centre contains a museum with displays on the park's wildlife and natural history.

0 km   10
0 miles   10

Brewer Lake
This scenic fishing lake is situated on the Highway 60 corridor. A 56-km (35-mile) journey through the park, this beautiful route is popular with daytrippers and those wishing to catch the major sights in limited time.

Key

━━ Major road
═══ Minor road
─── Provincial Park boundary

For additional map symbols *see back flap*

THE GREAT LAKES

The varied charms of the Canadian Great Lakes region, from the sleepy little farming towns bordering Lake Erie to the island-studded bays of Lake Huron and the wilderness encircling Lake Superior, tend to be obscured by the fame of Niagara Falls. One of the world's most famous sights, the falls occur where the Niagara River tumbles 50 meters (164 ft) between Lakes Erie and Ontario. Native tribes once lived on the fertile land around the area's lakes and rivers, and fur traders used the lakes as a vital waterway. The War of 1812 resulted in British Canada securing trade rights to the northern lakeshores. Between 1820 and 1850 settlers established farms, and mining and forestry flourished in Canada's then richest province. Today, the Trans-Canada Highway follows the untamed northern shores of Lakes Huron and Superior for over 1,000 km (620 miles), eventually reaching the bustling port of Thunder Bay. The Agawa Valley Tour Train, which leaves from Sault Ste. Marie, offers popular day-long rail tours into the wilderness.

Sights at a Glance

National and Provincial Parks
- **6** Point Pelee National Park
- **14** Georgian Bay Island National Park
- **22** Killarney Provincial Park

Historic Towns and Cities
- **1** Hamilton
- **2** Niagara-on-the-Lake
- **7** Windsor
- **8** London
- **9** Stratford
- **10** Kitchener-Waterloo
- **11** Brantford

- **12** Orillia
- **16** Sainte-Marie among the Hurons
- **17** Goderich
- **23** Temagami
- **24** Sault Ste. Marie
- **26** Thunder Bay

Areas of Natural Beauty
- **3** Niagara Falls
- **4** Welland and the Welland Canal
- **5** Lake Erie
- **13** Muskoka
- **15** Nottawasaga Bay
- **18** Sauble Beach

- **19** Lake Huron
- **20** Bruce Peninsula
- **21** Manitoulin Island
- **25** Lake Superior

Key
- ═══ Highway
- ▬▬▬ Major road
- ═══ Minor road
- ─── Railway route
- ━ ∙ International border

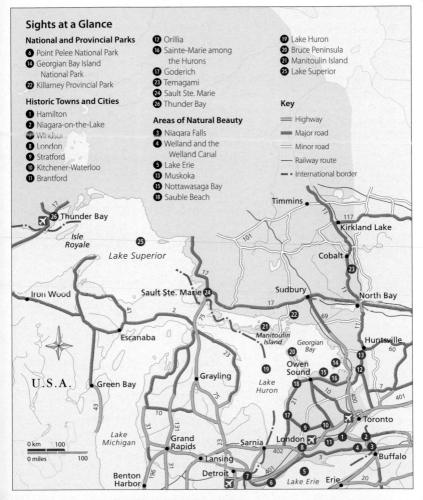

◀ Morning light shining on the rocky shoreline of the Bruce Peninsula, Ontario

For map symbols *see back flap*

The imposing façade of Dundurn Castle in Hamilton

❶ Hamilton

🗺 520,000. ✈ ✈ 🚗 🚌 ℹ 28 James St. S. (905) 546 2666. 🌐 **tourismhamilton.com**

The city of Hamilton sits at the extreme western end of Lake Ontario, some 70 km (44 miles) from Toronto. It was known as a steel town, and the city's mills used to churn out around 60 percent of Canada's total production. Despite the town's industrial roots, is a likeable place. **Dundurn Castle** is a Regency-style villa dating from the 1830s, whose interior holds a fine collection of period furnishings. It was built for the MacNabs, one of the most influential families in Ontario, who included in their number Sir Allan Napier MacNab, a Premier of Canada from 1854–6.

Another sight is the **Royal Botanical Gardens**, comprising forests, marshes, and small lakes over some 1,093 ha (2,700 acres) on the north side of Hamilton harbor. Among the notable gardens here are a fine Rose Garden; the Laking Garden with its peonies and irises; and the heavily perfumed Lilac Arboretum. The Rock Garden, built in 1935, contains an ampitheater, conifers, tulips, and cherry trees.

Also in town, the Canadian Warplane Heritage Museum has a display of more than 40 operational aircraft dating from World War II to the jet age.

🏛 **Dundurn Castle**
610 York Blvd. **Tel** (905) 546 2872.
Open mid-May–early Sep: 10am–4pm daily; early Sep–mid-May: noon–4pm Tue–Sun. 🔲 ♿ partial.

🌿 **Royal Botanical Gardens**
680 Plains Rd. West. **Tel** (905) 527 1158. **Open** daily. 🔲 ♿

❷ Niagara-on-the-Lake

🗺 15,000. 🚌 ℹ 26 Queen St. (905) 468 4263. 🌐 **niagaraonthelake.com**

Niagara-on-the-Lake is a charming little town of elegant clapboard mansions and leafy streets set where the mouth of the Niagara River empties into Lake Ontario. The town was originally known as Newark and under this name it became the capital of Upper Canada (as Ontario was then known) in 1792. Just four years later, the British decided to move the capital farther away from the US border, and chose York (now Toronto) instead. It was a wise decision. In 1813, the Americans crossed the Niagara River and destroyed Newark in the War of 1812 *(see pp50–51)*. The British returned after the war to rebuild their homes, and the Georgian town they constructed has survived pretty much intact.

Today, visitors take pleasure in exploring the town's lovely streets, but there is one major attraction, **Fort George**, a carefully restored British stockade built in

Rose in the Royal Botanical Gardens

the 1790s just southeast of town. The earth and timber palisade encircles ten replica buildings including three blockhouses, the barracks, a guard house, and the officers' quarters. There is also a powder magazine store, where all the fittings were wood or brass, and the men donned special shoes without buckles to reduce the chance of an unwanted explosion. Guides in old-style British military uniforms describe life in the fort in the 19th century.

Niagara-on-the-Lake is also home to the annual Shaw Festival, a prestigious theatrical season featuring the plays of George Bernard Shaw and other playwrights, which runs from April to October.

🏛 **Fort George**
Queen's Parade, Niagara Pkwy.
Tel (905) 468 6614. **Open** May–Oct: 10am–5pm daily (weekends only Apr & Nov). 🔲 ♿

Gardens in front of an early 19th-century inn at Niagara-on-the-Lake

❸ Niagara Falls

See pp216–17.

❹ Welland and The Welland Canal

🗺 50,000. ✈ 🚌 ℹ
60 East Main St. (905) 735 8696.
🌐 **wellandcanal.com**

An important steel town, Welland is bisected by the famous Welland Canal, which was built to solve the problem of Niagara Falls. The Falls

Aerial view of the small village of Long Point on the shore of Lake Erie

presented an obstacle that made it impossible for boats to pass between lakes Ontario and Erie. Goods had to be unloaded on one side of the Falls and then carted to the other, a time-consuming and expensive process. To solve the problem, local entrepreneurs dug a canal across the 45-km (28-mile) isthmus separating the lakes early in the 19th century, choosing a route to the west of the Niagara River.

The first **Welland Canal** was a crude affair, but subsequent improvements have created today's version, which has eight giant locks adjusting the water level by no less than 99 m (324 feet). A remarkable feat of engineering, the canal is capable of accommodating the largest of ships. You can drive alongside the northerly half of

the canal, on Government Road from Lake Ontario to Thorold, where seven of the eight locks are situated. The viewing platform at Lock No. 3 provides a great vantage point and has an information center detailing the canal's history.

Welland boasts another eyecatching attraction: 28 giant murals decorate some of the city's downtown buildings.

❺ Lake Erie

ℹ 660 Garrison Rd., Fort Erie (905) 871 1332. 🔳 **forteriecanada.com**

Lake Erie is named after the native people who once lived along its shores. The Erie were renowned for their skills as fishermen. Some 400 km (249 miles) long and an average of 60 km (37 miles) wide, Lake Erie

is the shallowest of the Great Lakes and separates Canada from the US. Its northern shore is one of the most peaceful parts of Ontario, with a string of quiet country towns and small ports set in rolling countryside. Three peninsulas reach out from the Canadian shoreline, one of which has been conserved as the Point Pelee National Park, home to a virgin forest and, during spring and summer, thousands of migrating birds (see p214).

About 30 km (19 miles) south of Niagara Falls, the small town of Fort Erie lies where the Niagara River meets Lake Erie, facing its sprawling US neighbor, Buffalo. The massive Peace Bridge links the two, and most people cross the border without giving Fort Erie a second look. They miss one of the more impressive of the reconstructed British forts that dot the Canada-US border. Old **Fort Erie** is a replica of the stronghold, destroyed by the Americans in the War of 1812. Entry is across a drawbridge, and the interior holds barracks, a powder magazine, and officers' quarters. The fort's battlefield is the site of one of the War of 1812's bloodiest battles, fought here during the siege of the fort in 1814.

🏛 **Fort Erie**
350 Lakeshore Rd. **Tel** (905) 871 0540. **Open** mid-May–Oct: daily. 🈁 ♿ partial.

A merchant ship on the Welland Canal near the town of Welland

⑥ Point Pelee National Park

Tel (519) 322 2365. 🚊 Windsor.
🚌 Windsor. **Open** daily. 🅿 ♿ 🎫
w pc.gc.ca /pointpelee

A long, fingerlike isthmus, Point Pelee National Park sticks out into Lake Erie for 20 km (12 miles) and forms the southernmost tip of Canada's mainland. The park has a wide variety of habitats including marshlands, open fields, and ancient deciduous forest. These woods are a rarity, as they are one of the few places in North America's Carolinian Life Zone where many of the trees have never been logged. The profusion of species creates a junglelike atmosphere, with red cedar, black walnut, white sassafras, hickory, sycamore, and sumac, all struggling to reach the light. This varied vegetation attracts thousands of birds, which visit on their spring and fall migrations. Over 370 species have been sighted here, and they can be observed from lookout points and forest trails. Every fall, hosts of orange-and-black monarch butterflies can also be seen here. A marshland boardwalk trail winds through Point Pelee and has good observation spots along the way. Bikes and canoes can be rented at the start of the boardwalk, and there is a concession stand here. Farther into the park, the visitor center features displays of local flora and fauna.

Water cascades at the main entrance of Windsor's Casino

⑦ Windsor

🏙 211,000. ✈ 🚆 🚊 🚌 🛈 333 Riverside Drive W. (519) 255 6530.
w visitwindsoressex.com

A car manufacturing town, just like its American neighbor Detroit, Windsor and its factories produce hundreds of US-badged vehicles every day. Windsor has clean, tree-lined streets and a riverside walkway, but its most noted attraction is a riverside Casino that draws thousands of visitors. The city has many lively bars and cafés, the best of which are

Contemporary painting at Windsor Art Gallery

along the first three blocks of the main street, Ouellette. Also of interest, the nearby **Art Gallery of Windsor**, also on the riverside, is noted for its excellent visiting exhibitions.

During Prohibition millions of bottles of alcohol were smuggled from Windsor into

the US across the Detroit River. Visitors can tour the Italiante Canadian Club Brand Center which includes whisky tasting.

From Windsor, it is an easy 20-km (12-mile) drive south along the Detroit River to the British-built Fort Malden at Amherstburg. Not much is left of the fort, but there is a neatly restored barracks dating from 1819, and the old laundry now holds an interpretation center. This relates the fort's role in the War of 1812 *(see pp50–51)*, where the English plotted with the Shawnee to invade the US.

🏛 **Art Gallery of Windsor**
401 Riverside Dr. W. **Tel** (519) 9770 013.
Open Wed–Sun. ♿
w artgalleryofwindsor.com

⑧ London

🏙 370,000. ✈ 🚆 🚊 🚌 🛈 267 Dundas St. (519) 661 5000, 1 800 265 2602. **w** londontourism.ca

Likeable London sits in the middle of one of the most fertile parts of Ontario and is the area's most important town. It is home to the respected University of Western Ontario, which has a striking modern art gallery and a campus with dozens of Victorian mansions. In addition, the few blocks that make up the town center are notably refined and well tended. The finest buildings in the center are the two 19th-century cathedrals, St. Paul's, a red-brick Gothic Revival edifice built for the Anglicans in 1846, and the more ornate, St. Peter's Catholic Cathedral erected a few

Kayakers alongside the boardwalk at Point Pelee National Park

years later. In the northwest of the city, the Museum of Ontario Archaeology focuses on the 1,100-year history of the settlement of the area. The Lawson Iroquoian Village here is a reconstruction of a 500-year-old village, once occupied by the Neutral Indians, with elm longhouses and cedarwood palisades.

Reconstruction of a 500-year-old longhouse at Lawson Indian Village

❾ Stratford

🏙 30,000. 🚌 ❗ 47 Downie St. 1 800 561 7926.
ⓦ **welcome to stratford.com**

In 1830, an innkeeper called William Sargint opened the "Shakespeare Inn" beside one of the rough agricultural tracks that then crisscrossed southern Ontario. The farmers who

The Underground Railroad

Neither underground nor a railroad, the name "Underground Railroad" (UGRR) was founded by abolitionists in the 1820s. The UGRR helped slaves from the southern United States to escape to both Canada and the free northern states. It was a secretive organization, especially in the South where the penalties for helping a slave to escape were severe. Slaves were moved north from safe house to safe house right up to the end of the American Civil War in 1865. Reverend Josiah Henson was one of those who escaped on the UGRR, and later founded a school for ex-slaves. Harriet Beecher Stowe's 1851 abolitionist novel *Uncle Tom's Cabin* was based on his life story.

Reverend Josiah Henson

settled nearby called the local river the "Avon" and named the town that grew up here "Stratford," after William Shakespeare's home town.

In 1952, local journalist Tom Patterson (1920–2005) organized a Shakespeare Festival. This first event was a humble affair held in a tent, but since then the festival has grown into one of Canada's most important theatrical seasons, lasting from May to early November (www.stratfordfestival.ca). The leading plays are still Shakespearean, but other playwrights are showcased too, including modern works.

Stratford is an attractive town with plenty of green lawns, riverside parks, and swans. The town is geared toward visitors, offering countless guesthouses and several good restaurants. The visitor center produces a book with information and photographs of all the town's bed-and-breakfasts. They also organize heritage walks through the town, which pass its many historic buildings. One of the town's architectural highlights is the Victorian town hall, with its turrets. Stratford has a plethora of art galleries, as well as craft boutiques and other stores.

Stratford's River Avon and Huron Street bridge, overlooked by the distinctive Victorian courthouse

❸ Niagara Falls

Although the majestic rumble of the falls can be heard from miles away, there is no preparation for the sight itself, a great arc of hissing, frothing water crashing over a 57-m (188-ft) cliff amid dense clouds of drifting spray. There are actually two cataracts to gaze at as the speeding river is divided into twin channels by Goat Island, a tiny spray-soaked parcel of land. On one side of Goat Island is the Canadian Horseshoe Falls, and on the far side, across the border, is the smaller American Falls. Stunning close-up views of the falls are available from the vantage point of the Maid of the Mist boat trips. Even better is the walk down through a series of rocky tunnels that lead behind Horseshoe Falls, where the noise from the crashing waters is deafening.

American Falls
The Niagara River tumbles over the 260-m (850-ft) wide American Falls.

Rainbow Bridge
From the elegant span of the Rainbow Bridge there are panoramic views over the falls. The bridge itself crosses the gorge between Canada and the US. Here, on sunny days, rainbows rise through the spray.

KEY

① **Customs**

② **Bird Kingdom**, is Canada's only indoor aviary and features over 400 exotic birds.

③ **The Minolta Tower**, like the Skylon Tower, offers panoramic views of the whole area. Three observation decks look out over the falls.

Clifton Hill
This street boasts a range of attractions. Ripley's Believe it or Not Museum features a dog with human teeth as just one of its offerings.

VISITORS' CHECKLIST

Practical Information
130 km (84 miles) SW of Toronto.
ℹ Niagara Falls Tourism, 5515
Stanley Ave., Niagara Falls (905)
356 6061 or 1 (800) 563 2557.
🅦 **niagaraparks.com**

Transport
🚆 from Toronto. 🚌 from Toronto.

★ Horseshoe Falls
Shaped like a horseshoe, this is the
larger set of falls at Niagara, being
some 670 m (2,200 ft) wide and
57 m (188 ft) high.

0 meters	250
0 yards	250

Journey Behind the Falls
An elevator from the Horseshoe Falls
leads to the Journey Behind the Falls,
where a series of rocky tunnels take
visitors behind a wall of water so
thick it blocks out daylight.

★ Maid of the Mist boat trip
These intrepid vessels gets very close to
the foot of the falls. Raincoats are supplied
as passengers can expect to get wet on
this thrilling trip.

Skylon Tower
The tower has an observation deck,
which gives a bird's-eye view of the
falls. It is also open at night so
visitors can see the floodlit waters.

Exploring Niagara Falls

Niagara Falls is a welcoming little town that stretches along the Niagara River for about 3 km (2 miles). Renowned as a honeymoon destination, the town is well equipped to satisfy the needs of the 14 million people who visit the falls each year. It is divided into three main sections: to the south are the falls themselves, and these are flanked by a thin strip of parkland that stretches out along the river bank as far as Clifton Hill, the glitziest street in Ontario, lined with garish amusement park attractions. To the west is the main motel strip, Lundy's Lane. To the north, on Bridge Street, lies the business district and the train and bus stations.

and head upriver to the crashing waters under the falls. Raincoats are provided on this invigorating and wet trip.

A wax museum and an array of other attractions at Clifton Hill

Horseshoe Falls

Named for their shape, the 675-m- (2,200-ft-) wide and 52-m- (170-ft)- high Horseshoe Falls are formed by the turbulent waters of the Niagara River roaring over a semi-circular cliff to plunge into the bubbling cauldron below. By these means the Niagara River adjusts to the differential between the water levels of lakes Erie and Ontario, which it connects. The falls remain an awe-inspiring sight, despite the fact that the flow of the river is regulated by hydroelectric companies, which siphon off a substantial part of the river to drive their turbines. One result has been a change in the rate of erosion. By the 1900s, the falls were eroding the cliff beneath them at a rate of 1 m (3 ft) a year. Today, the rate is down to 30 cm (1 ft) a year.

The Maid of the Mist pleasure trip

Maid of The Mist

5920 River Rd. **Tel** (905) 358 5781.
Open Apr–Oct: daily. 🚻 ♿
W maidofthemist.com

The best way to appreciate the full force of the falls is to experience the Maid of the Mist boat trip. Boats depart from the jetty at the bottom of Clifton Hill

Clifton Hill

This short, steep street runs up from the edge of the Niagara River gorge and is lined with a string of fast food restaurants and tourist attractions. The flashing lights and giant advertising billboards point the way to such sights as the Guinness Book of World Records, House of Frankenstein, That's Incredible Museum, Houdini's Museum and Ripley's Believe it or Not! Museum, where visitors can speak to a genie in a crystal bottle and see oddities such as a man with a greater-than-usual number of pupils in his eyes.

White Water Walk

4330 Niagara Pkwy. **Tel** (905) 374 1221. **Open** mid-Apr–mid-Nov: daily.
🚻 ♿

The great force of the Niagara River's torrent is best admired from down at the bottom of the canyon. The Great Gorge

The dramatic arc of thundering waters at Horseshoe Falls

For hotels and restaurants in this region see pp350–59 and pp364–83

Wooden boardwalk along the Niagara River at the Great Gorge Adventure

Adventure provides this close-up view by means of a tunnel and an elevator, which lead from the top of the gorge to a riverside boardwalk. The whirlpools and rapids here are some of the most spectacular, yet treacherous, in the world.

The Old Scow

Just above the falls, stranded on the rocks in the middle of the river, is the Old Scow, a flat-bottomed steel barge that was shipwrecked in August 1918. It was being towed across the Niagara River by a tugboat when the lines snapped. The scow hurtled towards the falls, getting within 767 m (2,460 ft), of the brink, and the two-man crew appeared to be doomed. Luckily the boat grounded itself on this rocky ledge just in time. The crew's ordeal was, however, far from over: they had to wait another 29 hours before being finally winched to safety. The Old Scow has been rusting away on the rocks ever since.

⊠ Niagara Glen Nature Reserve

3050 River Road. **Open** daily.
The small Niagara Glen Nature Reserve lies 7 km (4 miles) downriver from the falls. This segment of the gorge has been preserved in pristine condition, with bushes and low trees tumbling down the rocky cliffside. This is how it may have looked before the coming of the Europeans. Seven different

hiking trails lead past boulders, caves, and wild flowers. The walks are easy on the way down but a steep climb on the way up.

Whirlpool Aerocar

3850 Niagara Pkwy. **Tel** (905) 354 5711. **Open** daily, weather permitting.

The Niagara River makes a dramatically sharp turn about 4.5 km (3 miles) downstream from the falls, generating a vicious, raging whirlpool, one of the most lethal stretches of water in the whole of North America.

Butterfly at the Botanic Gardens and Conservatory

The effect is created when the river pushes against the northwest side of the canyon, only to be forced to turn around in the opposite direction. The most stunning view of the whirlpool rapids is from the Aerocar, a

specially designed cable car that crosses the gorge, high above the river. A different perspective of the falls can be seen from here.

⊠ Niagara Parks Botanical Gardens and Butterfly Conservatory

2565 Niagara Pkwy. **Tel** (905) 358 0025. **Open** daily. 🦋 for conservatory.

The Niagara Parks Botanical Gardens are located 9 km (6 miles) downstream from the falls and comprise over 40 ha (99 acres) of beautifully maintained gardens divided into several different zones. One of the prettiest areas in summer is the rose garden, which displays over 2,400 different varieties. The extensive annual garden, which houses many rare species imported from all parts of the globe, puts on a year-round show. The gardens also include an arboretum that has examples of many different types of trees from beech and mulberry to magnolia and yew.

The butterfly conservatory is even more popular. At the beginning of a visit, a video is shown in the theater. The film explains the life cycle of a butterfly, from egg and larvae through to the emergence of the adult. Over 2,000 butterflies are housed in a huge heated dome where they fly free – one of the largest collections in the world. A series of pathways pass through the dome, leading past the lush tropical flora on which the butterflies make their homes.

The Whirlpool Rapids are best seen from the Spanish Aero Car

A boat trip takes visitors up close to spectacular Horseshoe Falls ▶

Alexander Graham Bell's library at the Bell Homestead in Brantford

⑩ Kitchener-Waterloo

🗺 350,000. 🚇 🚌 ℹ️ 79 St. Joseph St. (519) 585 7517, 1 800 265 6959. 🌐 **explorewaterlooregion.com**

Originally called Berlin by the German immigrants who settled here in the 1820s, the town was renamed Kitchener (after the British Empire's leading general) during World War I. Today, the town is a supply center for the surrounding farming communities, including religious groups such as the Mennonites *(see box)*. Visitors can see the fascinating sight of traditionally dressed Mennonites in their horse-drawn buggies around town. Every year, the town hosts the nine-day **Oktoberfest**, a celebration of German culture, with everything from sausages and sauerkraut to lederhosen and lager, and over 40 family events.

⑪ Brantford

🗺 100,000. 🚇 🚌 ℹ️ 399 Wayne Gretzky Pkwy (519) 751 9900.

Brantford is an unassuming manufacturing town that takes its name from Joseph Brant (1742–1807), the leader of a confederacy of tribes called the Six Nations. An Iroquois chief himself, Brant settled here in 1784. He soon decided that the interests of his people lay with the British, and his braves fought alongside the Redcoats during the American War of Independence (1775–83). Sadly, he had chosen the losing side and, after the war, his band was forced to move north to Canada, where the British ceded the natives a piece of land at Brantford. The Iroquois (Six Nations) still live in this area, and host the Grand River Pow Wow, featuring traditional dances and crafts, and held here every July or August. Brantford is also known for its association with the telephone. In 1876, the first ever long-distance call was made from Brantford to the neighboring village of Paris by Alexander Graham Bell (1847–1922), who had emigrated from Scotland to Ontario in 1870. Bell's old home, conserved as the **Bell Homestead National Historic Site**, is located on the outskirts of town. The site has two buildings: Bell's homestead is furnished with many original family pieces, re-creating the setting in which the telephone was invented; the other, housing Canada's first telephone business office, was moved here from downtown Brantford in 1969.

Brantford is also the birthplace of native poet and author E. Pauline Johnson.

Fruit seller in Brantford

🏠 Bell Homestead National Historic Site

94 Tutela Heights Rd. **Tel** (519) 756 6220. **Open** 9:30am–4:30pm Tue–Sun. **Closed** Dec 24–Jan 1. 🅿️ ♿ 📷

⑫ Orillia

🗺 32,000. 🚌 ℹ️ 50 Andrew St. S. (705) 325 1311.

Orillia is a pleasant country town that was the home of the novelist and humorist Stephen Leacock (1869–1944). Leacock's tremendously popular *Sunshine Sketches of a Little Town* poked fun at the vanities of provincial Ontario life in the fictional town of Mariposa. His old lakeshore home has been conserved as the **Stephen Leacock Museum**, containing original furnishings as well as details of his life.

Orillia lies along a narrow strip of water linking Lake Couchiching to Lake Simcoe and is a good base from which to cruise both lakes. On the shore, Orillia's Centennial Park has a marina and a long boardwalk that stretches all the way to Couchiching beach.

🏛 Stephen Leacock Museum

50 Museum Drive, Old Brewery Bay. **Tel** (705) 329 1908. **Open** daily; renovations during 2014 so call ahead. 🅿️ ♿ 🌐 **leacockmuseum.com**

Bethune Memorial House in the town of Gravenhurst, Muskoka

⑬ Muskoka

🚇 Gravenhurst. 🚌 Gravenhurst, Huntsville. ℹ️ 1342 Hwy 11 North RR #2, Kilworthy (705) 689 0660.

Muskoka comprises an area north of Orillia between the towns of Huntsville and Graven-hurst. The center of this lake country is Gravenhurst, a resort at the south end of Lake Muskoka. Here, a national historic site is devoted to the life

THE GREAT LAKES | 223

and work of Doctor Norman Bethune (1890–1939), who pioneered mobile blood transfusion units during the Spanish Civil War. **Bethune Memorial House**, his birthplace, has been restored in late 19th-century style.

🏛 **Bethune Memorial House**
235 John St. N. **Tel** (705) 687 4261. **Open** seasonal; call ahead. 🖼

Windsurfing off Turgean Bay Island in Georgian Bay

⑭ Georgian Bay Islands National Park

Tel (705) 526 9804. 🚌 to Honey Harbour, then 🚢. **Open** daily. 🖼 summer. 📷
W pc.gc.ca/georgianbay

The waters of Georgian Bay are dotted with thousands of little islands, often no more than a chunk of rock guarded by a windblown pine. The bay is large, beautiful, and flows into Lake Huron. Sixty of its islands have been incorporated into the Georgian Bay Islands National

The Mennonite Religious Community

The Mennonite Christian sect was founded in Europe in the early 16th century. The Mennonites were persecuted because they refused to swear any oath of loyalty to the state or take any part in war. In the 17th century, a group split off to form its own, even stricter, sect. These Ammanites (or Amish) emigrated to the US and then to Ontario in 1799. The old-order Amish own property communally and shun modern machinery and clothes, traveling around the highways in distinctive horse-drawn buggies and dressed in traditional clothes.

Amish couple driving a buggy

Park. The park's center is Beausoleil Island, the hub of the area's wide range of facilities.

Beausoleil is also crossed by scenic hiking trails, but it is important to come properly equipped since it is a remote spot. The only way to reach the island is by water taxi from the hamlet of Honey Harbour. The journey takes about 40 minutes. Day trips around the islands are available from the "DayTripper's Ferry," which runs daily from mid-May to mid-October.

In Penetanguishene, east of Nottawasaga Bay, Discovery Harbour is a superb reconstruction of the British naval base that was established here in 1814. There are replicas of the barracks, blacksmith's shop, houses, and the original Officers' Quarters. The harbor holds a pair of replica ships, the *Tecumseth* and the *Bee*. The below-decks area of the former is furnished as per the ship's 1815 log. The remains of its original hull are also on display.

⑮ Nottawasaga Bay

🚉 Wasaga Beach, Collingwood.
ℹ 45 St. Paul St., Collingwood (705) 445 7722, 1 888 227 8667.
W visitsouthgeorgianbay.ca

Part of scenic Georgian Bay, Nottawasaga Bay is one of the region's most popular vacation destinations. Wasaga Beach has miles of golden, sandy beach and many chalets and cottages. As well as swimming and sunbathing, there is the curious Nancy Island Historic Site, behind Beach Area 2. The site has a museum which houses the preserved HMS *Nancy:* one of few British boats to survive the War of 1812 *(see pp50–51)*.

Located on the southern shores of Georgian Bay, Collingwood and the Blue Mountains make an excellent location for hiking, cycling, and paddling in summer. In winter, Blue Mountain is one of Ontario's top destinations for skiing, snowboarding, and snowshoeing.

Discovery Harbour, Penetanguishene's restored British naval base

⑯ Sainte-Marie-among-the-Hurons

Sainte-Marie-among-the-Hurons is one of Ontario's most compelling attractions. Located 5 km (3 miles) east of the town of Midland, the site is a reconstruction of the settlement founded here among the Huron natives by Jesuit priests in 1639. The village is divided into two main sections, one for Europeans (complete with a chapel and workshops), the other for Hurons, with a pair of bark-covered longhouses. Marking the boundary between the two is the small church of Saint Joseph, a simple wooden building where the Jesuits set about trying to convert the Hurons. Their efforts met with a variety of reactions, and the complex relationship between the two cultures is explored here in detail.

Exterior of Longhouse
The exterior of the longhouse had bark-covered walls built over a cedar pole frame that was bent to form an arch.

★ **Fireside Gathering**
Inside the longhouse, fish, skins, and tobacco were hung from the ceiling to dry. An open fire burned through the winter. The smoke caused health problems to the Huron.

Church of Saint Joseph
This is the grave site of two Jesuit priests, Jean de Brébeuf and Gabriel Lalement, who were captured, bound to the stake, then tortured to death by the Iroquois.

KEY

① **In the hospital** the Jesuits used French medicines with limited success. The Huron had no resistance to European diseases such as influenza and measles.

② **The blacksmith's shop** was important as Sainte-Marie needed essential items such as hinges and nails, often made by using recycled iron.

③ **The carpenter's shop** had an abundant supply of local wood, and craftsmen from France were employed by the priests to build the mission.

④ **Bastions** helped defend the mission from attack. Built of local stone to ward off arrows and musket balls, they also served as observation towers.

Ojibway Wigwam by the Palisades
This wigwam is built to Ojibway design and lies next to the wooden palisade which encloses the mission. It is believed that the Jesuits built these to make visiting Ojibway feel at home.

★ Traditional Crafts
The costumed guides here have been trained in the traditional crafts employed by both the Huron and the French, including 17th-century cooking and blacksmith's work.

VISITORS' CHECKLIST

Practical Information
Hwy 12
(5 km, 3 miles east of Midland).
Tel (705) 526 7838.
Open May–Oct: 10am–5pm daily.
w hhp.on.ca

Interior of Chapel
The old chapel has been carefully re-created and, with the light filtering in through its timbers, it is easy to imagine what it was like for the priests as they gathered to say mass each day before dawn.

Entrance

0 meters 25
0 yards 25

The Cookhouse Garden
At Sainte-Marie, care is taken to grow crops the Huron way, with corn, beans, and squash planted in rotation. This system provided a year-round food supply, which was supplemented with meat and fish.

⓱ Goderich

🏠 7,600. ✈ 🛈 cnr Hamilton St. & Hwy 21. **Tel** (519) 524 6600, 1 800 280 7637.

Goderich is a charming town overlooking Lake Huron at the mouth of the Maitland River. It was founded in 1825 by the British-owned Canada Company, which had persuaded the Ontario government to part with 1 million ha (2.5 million acres) of fertile land in their province for just 12 cents an acre, a bargain of such proportions that there was talk of corruption. Eager to attract settlers, the company built the Huron Road from Cambridge, in the east, to Goderich. The town was laid out with the main streets radiating out from the striking, octagon-shaped center.

Goderich possesses two excellent museums. The first, the **Huron County Museum**, houses a large collection of antique farm implements, as well as a military gallery and a reconstruction of a 19th-century town street. There is also a huge, steam-driven thresher. The **Huron Historic Gaol National Historic Site**, built between 1839 and 1842, is a preserved Victorian prison. Fascinating tours are available of its dank cells, the jailers' rooms, and the Governor's 19th-century house. The town is also renowned for its sunsets, particularly as viewed from the shore of Lake Huron.

🏛 **Huron Historic Gaol National Historic Site**
181 Victoria St. N. **Tel** (519) 524 2686. **Open** May–Aug: 10am–4:30pm

The golden sands of Sauble Beach on the shore of Lake Huron

Mon–Sat, 1–4:30pm Sun; Sep & Oct: 1–4pm Mon–Fri, 10am–4:30 pm Sat, 1–4:30pm Sun. ♿

🏛 **Huron County Museum**
110 North St. **Tel** (519) 524 2686. **Open** Jan–Apr: 10am–4:30pm Mon–Fri, 1–4:30pm Sat; May–Dec: 10am–4:30pm Mon–Sat, 1–4:30pm Sun. ♿ ♿

⓲ Sauble Beach

🚌 Owen Sound. 🛈 RR1, Sauble Beach (519) 422 1262.
🌐 **saublebeach.com**

One of the finest sandy beaches in Ontario, Sauble Beach stretches for 11 km (7 miles) along the shores of Lake Huron. Running behind this beach is a long, narrow band of campsites, cabins, and cottages. The center of the resort is at the pocket-sized village of Sauble Beach, which has a population of only five hundred. The quiet back streets of the village also offer

friendly guesthouses and B&Bs. The most attractive and tranquil camping is found at Sauble Falls Provincial Park, north of the beach.

⓳ Lake Huron

🛈 Sarnia, Southern shore (519) 336 3232. 🛈 Barrie, Georgian Bay (705) 725 7280 🛈 Sault Ste. Marie, North shore (705) 945 6941.
🌐 **ontariotravel.net**

Of all the Great Lakes, it is Lake Huron which has the most varied landscapes along its shoreline. To the south, the lake narrows to funnel past the largely industrial towns of Sarnia and Windsor on its way to Lake Erie while its southeast shore is bounded by a gentle bluff, marking the limit of one of Ontario's most productive agricultural regions. Farther north, the long, thin isthmus of Bruce Peninsula stretches out into Lake Huron, signaling a dramatic change in the character of the lakeshore. This is where the southern flatlands are left behind for the more rugged, glacier-scraped country of the Canadian Shield. This transition can be seen clearly in the area of Georgian Bay. This is an impressive shoreline of lakes, forests, beaches, and villages that attracts large numbers of visitors. The lake's island-sprinkled waters are a popular area for water sports. Outdoor activities here include swimming, hiking, and fishing.

Historic storefront in the charming town of Goderich

THE GREAT LAKES | 227

⑳ Bruce Peninsula Tour

The 100-km (62-mile) Bruce Peninsula divides the main body of Lake Huron from Georgian Bay and also contains some of the area's most scenic terrain. Bruce Peninsula National Park lies along the eastern shore and boasts craggy headlands and limestone cliffs with several hiking paths. Beyond the port of Tobermory, at the peninsula's tip, Fathom Five Marine National Park, comprises 19 uninhabited islands. The park is popular with divers because of its clear waters and amazing rock formations.

Tips for Drivers

Tour Route: The route follows Route 9 and Hwy 6. It can be reached from Owen Sound in the south, or Tobermory in the north.
Length: 100 km (62 miles).
Stopping-off points: Diving trips and tours to Flowerpot Island leave from Tobermory, which also has good accommodation.

① Stokes Bay
The hamlet of Stokes Bay, with its sandy beaches and good fishing, is typical of the villages here. It is close to the the peninsula's main sights.

② Cabot Head
The Cabot Head Lighthouse and keeper's house can be reached via the scenic coast road from the village of Dyer's Bay.

③ Bruce Peninsula National Park
The park's rugged cliffs are part of the Niagara Escarpment, a limestone ridge that stretches across southern Ontario and along the peninsula.

⑥ Fathom Five Marine Park
Off the northern tip of the peninsula, the park's boundaries enclose an area around 19 islands. Divers are drawn here by the clear, calm waters and shipwrecks.

④ Tobermory
At the northern tip of the peninsula, this small fishing village is a hub for tourist acitivities in the area. Ferries to Flowerpot Island leave from here.

⑤ Flowerpot Island
The only island in Fathom Five Marine Park with basic facilities, it is noted for the rock columns that dot the coastline.

Dyer's Bay
Miller Lake
Ferndale
Barrow Bay
Hope Bay
Pike Bay
Wiarton

| 0 meters | 500 | |
| 0 yards | | 500 |

Key
▬ Tour route
▭ Other roads

㉑ Manitoulin Island

🏠 12,600. ℹ️ 70 Meredith St, Little Current (705) 368 3021.

Hugging the northern shores of Lake Huron, Manitoulin Island is, at 2,800 sq km (1,100 square miles), the world's largest freshwater island. A quiet place of small villages, farmland, woodland, and lakes, its edges are fringed by deserted beaches. The lake's North Channel separates Manitoulin from the mainland, its waters attracting summer sailors, while hikers come to explore the island's trails.

The Ojibway people first occupied the island more than 10,000 years ago, naming it after the Great Spirit – Manitou. First Nations peoples still constitute over a quarter of the island's population. Every August, on Civic Holiday weekend, they celebrate their culture in one of Canada's largest powwows, the Wikwemikong Cultural Festival (Bay of the Beaver).

On the north shore, Gore Bay houses five tiny museums that focus on the island's early settlers. Nearby, the island's largest settlement is Little Current, a quiet town with a handful of motels and restaurants. From May to September the Chi Cheemaun car ferry connects Tobermory on the Bruce Peninsula to Manitoulin Island.

Gore Bay on Manitoulin Island

Reflections in George Lake, Killarney Provincial Park

㉒ Killarney Provincial Park

Tel (705) 287 2900. 🚌 Sudbury. **Open** daily. 🎟️ for some facilities.

Killarney Provincial Park is a beautiful tract of wilderness with crystal-blue lakes, pine and hardwood forests, boggy lowlands, and the spectacular La Cloche Mountains, which are known for their striking white quartzite ridges. This magnificent scenery has inspired many artists, particularly members of the Group of Seven *(see pp168–9)*, one of whom, Franklin Carmichael, saw the park as Ontario's most "challenging and gratifying landscape." The park's 100-km (62-mile) La Cloche Silhouette Trail takes between a week and ten days to complete and attracts numbers of serious hikers to its stunning views of the mountains and of Georgian Bay. Canoeists can paddle on the park's many lakes and rivers by following a network of well-marked canoe routes.

㉓ Temagami

🏠 900. 🚌 ℹ️ Chamber of Commerce, Lakeshore Rd. (705) 569 3344.

The tiny resort of Temagami and its wild surroundings have long attracted fur traders and trappers, painters, and writers, most famously Grey Owl *(see p254)*, the remarkable Englishman who posed as a Native Canadian and achieved celebrity status as a naturalist and conservationist in the 1930s. The resort sits on the distinctively shaped Lake Temagami, a deep lake with long fjords and bays as well as 1,400 islands, which are

One of Lake Temagami's numerous canoe routes

crisscrossed by numerous scenic canoe routes, hiking and mountain bike trails.

Even more remote is the Lady Evelyn Smoothwater Wilderness Park, farther to the west. The only way in is by canoe or float plane from Temagami, but the reward is some of Ontario's most stunning scenery. Much more accessible is the 30-m (98-ft) high Temagami Fire Tower lookout point, which provides panoramic views of the surrounding pine forests, and the charming Finlayson Provincial Park, a popular place to picnic and camp; both are located on Temagami's outskirts.

❷ Sault Ste. Marie

🏙 75,000. ✈ 🚌 ℹ️ 99 Foster Dr. (705) 759 5442.

Where the rapids of St. Mary's River link Lake Superior to Lake Huron sits the attractive town of Sault Ste. Marie, one of Ontario's oldest European communities. The town was founded as a Jesuit mission and fur trading post by the French in 1688. Called the "Sault" (pronounced "Soo") after the French word for "rapids," the trading station prospered after 1798 when the rapids were bypassed by a canal. Since then, the canal has been upgraded time and again, and today transports the largest of container ships to the interior, thereby maintaining a thriving local economy.

Although there are regular boat trips along the canal, visitors are drawn to Sault Ste. Marie's main tourist attraction, the **Agawa Canyon Tour Train**, which offers day-long rail tours from the city into the wilderness. The train weaves north through dense forest, past secluded lakes and over yawning ravines to reach the spectacular scenery of Agawa Canyon where there is a 90-minute break for lunch.

In town, the Roberta Bondar Pavilion is a huge tentlike structure decorated with murals depicting Sault's history. Named after Canada's first female astronaut, who was on the

Canal locks at Sault Ste. Marie

Discovery mission in 1992, the pavilion is also the venue for concerts, exhibitions, and a summer farmers' market.

🚆 Agawa Canyon Tour Train
129 Bay St. **Tel** (705) 946 7300. **Open** Jul–mid-Oct: once daily. 🅿 ♿

❷ Lake Superior

ℹ️ Ontario Travel Information Centre, Sault Ste. Marie (705) 945 6941.

The least polluted and most westerly of the Great Lakes, Lake Superior is the world's largest body of freshwater, with a surface area of 82,000 sq km (31,700 sq miles). It is known for sudden violent storms, long a source of dread to local sailors. The lake's northern coast is a vast weather-swept stretch of untamed wilderness dominated by dramatic granite outcrops and seemingly limitless forest. This challenging area is best experienced in Pukaskwa National Park and Lake Superior Provincial Park, both reached via the Trans-Canada Highway (Hwy 17) as it cuts a dramatic route along the lake's north shore.

❷ Thunder Bay

🏙 109,000. ✈ 🚆 🚌 ℹ️ Terry Fox Information Centre, Hwy 11/17 E. (807) 983 2041, 1 800 667 8386.

On the northern shore of Lake Superior, Thunder Bay is Canada's third-largest freshwater port, its massive grain elevators dominating the city's waterfront. Grain is brought to Thunder Bay from the prairies farther west before being shipped to the rest of the world via the Great Lakes.

The town was originally established as a French trading post in 1679. These early days are celebrated at Old Fort William, a replica of the old fur trading post, with costumed traders, French explorers, and natives. Fort William was amalgamated with the adjacent town of Port Arthur to form Thunder Bay in 1970.

🏛 Old Fort William
Off Broadway Ave. **Tel** (807) 473 2333. **Open** mid-May–mid-Oct: 10am–5pm daily. 🅿 ♿ 🌐 fwhp.ca

Lake Superior, the world's largest freshwater lake

An abandoned farm in a durum wheat field near Assiniboia, Saskatchewan ▶

CENTRAL CANADA

Introducing Central Canada

Central Canada covers the provinces of Manitoba, Saskatchewan, and eastern Alberta and encompasses the most productive agricultural and energy-rich part of the country. The region is dominated by prairie, (often associated with borderless fields that stretch to the horizon) and covers a vast area of the western interior, which is the size of Mexico. The region is not all prairie, but has a variety of landscapes, from the forested aspen parkland to the west and north of the plains to the tundra of northern Manitoba and the rocky desert of the badlands in the southwest.

The Broadway Bridge and central Saskatoon overlooking the South Saskatchewan River

Grain elevators and wheat cars punctuate the vast fields of the Canadian prairies

For additional map symbols *see back flap*

Getting Around

Winnipeg, Edmonton, Regina, and Saskatoon, the four main cities of the region, are well served by public transportation, with regular air, train, and bus connections from British Columbia and other provinces. All four cities also have international airports. From Winnipeg, the Trans-Canada Highway follows the route established in the 19th century by the Canadian Pacific Railway, going 1,333 km (828 miles) west to Calgary. The more scenic Yellowhead Highway starts at the Forks in Winnipeg and runs through Yorkton and Saskatoon, reaching Edmonton at 1,301 km (808 miles), continuing on through Jasper National Park and British Columbia.

Key

- ▬ Expressway
- ▬ Divided highway
- ▬ Highway
- ═ Other road
- ➤ Main railway
- ─ Minor railway
- ▬ International border
- ▬ Regional border
- △ Summit

The prairies of Manitoba, one of Canada's richest agricultural areas

Dinosaurs and Prehistoric Canada

It is easier to imagine gunslingers and coyotes in the desert-like badlands of the Red Deer River Valley in Alberta than it is to envisage the dinosaurs who once lived in this region. Over 75 million years ago the area was a tropical swamp, similar to the Florida Everglades, and the favored habitat of these huge reptiles, which dominated the Earth for some 160 million years. All the dinosaur specimens found here originate from the Cretaceous period (144–65 million years ago). Dramatic changes in the region's weather patterns, from wet and tropical to dry desert, helped to preserve an incredible number of dinosaur remains in the area. Today, the Dinosaur Provincial Park is a UNESCO World Heritage Site.

Locator Map

This Triceratops skull shows the dinosaur's flaring bony frill, which was used primarily for courtship and display. Its two horns were an awesome 1 m (3 ft) long. More types of horned dinosaurs have been found here in Alberta than anywhere else.

Trained staff carefully dig out a groove around the bone while it is still in the ground. Once removed it will be carefully matched to its adjoining bone.

The Magnolia is thought to be one of Earth's first flowering plants, or angiosperms, and became widespread during the Cretaceous period.

Joseph Burr Tyrrell found the first important dinosaur skeleton sections in the Red Deer River Valley, Alberta, in 1884. A geologist, Tyrrell stumbled across the skull of a 71.5 million-year-old Albertosaurus while surveying coal deposits. Subsequently, palaeontologists rushed here to search for fossils. Drumheller's Royal Tyrrell Museum of Palaeontology is named after him *(see p252)*.

An artist's re-creation of the Cretaceous landscape depicts the types of flora living at the time. Tree ferns dominated the country, and grew in large forests to heights of 18 m (60 ft). Similar species still grow in the tropics.

Horseshoe Canyon lies along the Red Deer River, its high, worn hills visibly layered with ancient sediments. Ice Age glaciers eroded the layers of mud and sand that buried the remains of dinosaurs and plants. Erosion continues to form this barren, lunar landscape, exposing more bones, petrified wood, and other fossils.

This dinosaur nest on display at the Royal Tyrrell Museum was discovered at Devil's Coulee, Alberta, in 1987, and contains several embryos and eggs of the plant-eating Hadrosaur.

The Royal Tyrrell Field Station in the Dinosaur Provincial Park opened in 1987. It offers visitors interpretive displays explaining the history of the area's dinosaurs.

Simulated Dinosaur Dig

The Royal Tyrrell Museum offers the chance to experience the thrill of excavation on a realistic dinosaur dig in Midland Provincial Park. Two digging programs are designed for ages 7–12, and 12 and older. Using the real tools and techniques of palaeontology, and with Museum educators as guides, visitors can uncover casts of dinosaur bones, map the quarry, make a field jacket, and learn how to read fossils. There is also a 90-minute hike through the Badlands where visitors can investigate real dinosaur remains.

The leg bone of a duck-billed dinosaur is revealed to be complete. Beneath it another piece of bone has been covered with strips of plaster of Paris to protect it during transportation to a laboratory.

The reconstructed skeleton of a Gorgosaurus towers over the Dinosaur Hall at the Royal Tyrrell Museum. The first dinosaur discovered in the area, Gorgosaurus was a fierce meat eating predator. Despite being eight meters (26 ft) long and weighing some two tons (2,032 kg), this dinosaur was capable of reaching speeds of 20 km/h (12 mph).

Canadian Mounties

The Royal Canadian Mounted Police are a symbol of national pride. Canada's first Prime Minister, Sir John A. Macdonald, founded the North West Mounted Police in 1873 in Ontario after violence in the west of the country (between illicit liquor dealers and local natives) reached a climax with the Cypress Hills Massacre *(see p251)*. Marching west, the Mounties reached the Oldman River, Alberta, 70 km (43 miles) west of the Cypress Hills, where they built Fort Macleod in 1874. The principal aims of the Mounties were to establish good relations with the aboriginal peoples of the Prairies and to maintain order over new settlers in the late 1800s. The Mounties won respect for their diplomacy, policing the Canadian Pacific Railway workers and the Klondike Gold Rush in the Yukon during the 1890s. In recognition of their service they gained the Royal prefix in 1904.

The lush Cypress Hills were the site of a gruesome massacre which led to the founding of the North West Mounted Police.

The march west covered 3,135 km (1,949 miles) from Fort Dufferin, Manitoba to southern Alberta. A force of 275 men, 310 horses, and cattle, was sent to catch the illicit whiskey traders operating in the west. Battling with extreme temperatures, plagues of insects, and lack of supplies, the Mounties arrived at the Oldman River in 1874.

The Long March

Inspector James M. Walsh sealed the Mounties' reputation for bravery when he took only six men on a parley with Sioux Chief Sitting Bull. The Sioux had retreated to the area after their defeat of US General Custer at the Battle of the Little Big Horn in 1876. Although the Sioux were the traditional enemies of the local Blackfoot and Cree Indians, there was no fighting after the arrival of the Mounties. Walsh's force succeeded in enforcing law and order across mid-west Canada, winning respect for their diplomacy. Blackfoot native chief Crowfoot praised their fairness saying, "They have protected us as the feathers of a bird protect it from winter."

Sioux Chief Sitting Bull

James M. Walsh

The adventures of the pioneering Mounties have long been a source of inspiration to countless authors and filmmakers. Square-jawed and scarlet clad, the Mountie was the perfect hero. Perhaps the best-known "Mountie" film was the 1936 "Rose Marie" starring crooner Nelson Eddy and Jeanette MacDonald.

The skilled horsemen of the Musical Ride are selected after two years on the force. The officers then begin seven months of intensive training.

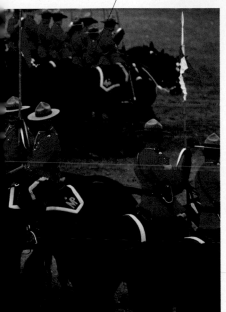

The Musical Ride

The Musical Ride is a thrilling spectacle of 32 riders and horses performing a series of traditional cavalry drills set to music. The drills have not changed since their original use in the British army over a century ago. Staying in tight formation, the horses do the trot, the canter, the rally, and the charge. Every summer the Ride is performed in different venues across Canada and the US.

As an enduring symbol of Canada the image of the Mounties has adorned everything from postage stamps and currency to this 1940s promotional tourist poster for Lake Louise in Banff National Park.

32 specially bred horses take part in the Musical Ride. A mixture of thoroughbred stallion crossed with black Hanoverian mare, the horses train for two years.

Today's Mounties are a 28,000-strong police force responsible for the enforcement of federal law across Canada. Their duties range from counting migratory birds to exposing foreign espionage. Jets, helicopters, and cars are all used by modern Mounties.

CENTRAL CANADA

Central Canada covers a vast region of boreal forest and fertile grasslands, often known as the Prairies, which traverses Manitoba, Saskatchewan, and part of Alberta. Originally, First Nations peoples lived here, and depended on the herds of buffalo that provided them with food, shelter, and tools. By the end of the 19th century the buffalo were hunted almost to extinction. European settlers built towns and farms, some taking native wives and forming a new cultural grouping, the Métis. By the 20th century the area's economy came to rely on gas, oil, and grain. Today the Prairies, punctuated by striking, tall grain elevators, are known for the flatness of their landscape and the intriguing history of their towns.

Sights at a Glance

Historic Towns and Cities
1 Winnipeg
2 Steinbach
3 Selkirk
5 Gimli
6 Portage La Prairie
8 Dauphin
9 Yorkton
10 Fort Qu'appelle
11 Regina
12 Moose Jaw
13 Saskatoon
16 Maple Creek
17 Medicine Hat
18 Lethbridge

21 Red Deer
23 Edmonton
24 Vegreville
27 North Battleford and Battleford
28 Batoche National Historic Site
29 Duck Lake
30 The Pas
31 Flin Flon
32 Churchill

Rivers and Lakes
4 Lake Winnipeg

National and Provincial Parks
7 Riding Mountain National Park
14 Grasslands National Park

15 Cypress Hills Interprovincial Park
20 Dinosaur Provincial Park
22 Elk Island National Park
25 Wood Buffalo National Park
26 Prince Albert National Park

Museums
19 Royal Tyrrell Museum

Key
= Highway
= Major road
= Minor road
= Railway route
- International border

◀ Prairie and farmlands below the foothills of southern Alberta   **For map symbols** *see back flap*

❶ Winnipeg

Winnipeg is a cosmopolitan city located at the geographic heart of Canada. Over half of Manitoba's population live here, mostly in suburbs that reflect the city's broad mix of cultures. Winnipeg's position, at the confluence of the Red and Assiniboine rivers, made it an important trading center for First Nations people going back some 6,000 years. From the 1600s Europeans settled here to trade fur. During the 1880s grain became the principal industry of the west, aided by a railroad network routed through Winnipeg. Today, this attractive city, with its museums, historic buildings, and excellent restaurants, makes for an enjoyable stay.

Exploring Winnipeg

Most of Winnipeg's sights are within easy walking distance of the downtown area. The excellent Manitoba Museum of Man and Nature and the Ukrainian Cultural Centre lie east of the Exchange District.

At the junction of the Red and Assiniboine rivers lies The Forks, a family entertainment center devoted to the city's history. At the junction of Portage and Main streets, lie the city's financial and shopping districts with their banks and malls.

🏛 St. Boniface

Riel Tourism, 219 Provencher Blvd. **Tel** 1(866) 808 8338. **Open** Mon–Fri (daily in summer). ♿ 📷

Canada's second-largest French-speaking community outside of Quebec lives in the historic district of St. Boniface. This quiet suburb faces The Forks across the Red River and was founded by priests in 1818 to care for the Métis *(see p53)* and the French living here. In 1844 the Grey Nuns built a hospital that now houses

the St. Boniface Museum. Priests built the Basilica of St. Boniface in 1818. Although the building was destroyed by fire in 1968, its elegant white façade is one of the city's best-loved landmarks. Métis leader Louis Riel was buried here after his execution following the rebellion at Batoche in 1881.

🏛 Manitoba Children's Museum

45 Forks Market Rd. **Tel** (204) 924 4000. **Open** daily. 📷 ♿
W childrensmuseum.com

Located within The Forks complex, this refurbished museum provides a series of enticing hands-on exhibits aimed at children from the ages of 3 to 11. In the Engine House children can play at being train drivers on a reconstructed 1952 diesel engine while learning the history of Canada's railroad. They can also browse the internet or produce a TV show in a studio.

🏛 The Forks National Historic Site

Forks Market Rd. **Tel** (204) 957 7618, (204) 983 6757. **Open** daily. 📷 some attractions and special events. ♿
W theforks.com

The historic riverside parkland of The Forks stretches along the west shore of the Red River from the Esplanade Riel Pedestrian Bridge to the confluence with the Assiniboine River. The riverside walkway offers fine views of the city center and St. Boniface cathedral, and you can access the French Quarter via the pedestrian bridge.

For more great views, head to the observation Tower at The Forks Market and Johnston Terminal. This once bustling railroad terminus is now filled with shoppers searching out crafts, folk art, and specialty food. Kids will enjoy

The brightly colored building housing the Manitoba Children's Museum

Cruise boats and canoes can be hired from The Forks harbor

the Variety Heritage Adventure Park, a playground with a pretend train, tipi, and fort, just north of the Children's Museum.

🏠 Dalnavert

61 Carlton St. **Tel** (204) 943 2835.
Open Wed–Sat. 🚫 ♿ 📷
Built in 1895, this beautifully restored Victorian house is an excellent example of Queen Anne Revival architecture. Its elegant red brick exterior is complemented by a long wooden veranda. The house once belonged to Sir Hugh John Macdonald, the former premier of Manitoba, and the only surviving son of Canada's first prime minister, John A. Macdonald. The interior's rich furnishings reflect the lifestyle of an affluent home in the late 19th century.

The Golden Boy statue adorns the dome of the Legislative Building

🏛 Legislative Building

Cnr Broadway & Osborne. **Tel** (204) 945 5813. **Open** daily. ♿ 📷 Jul–Sep.
The Legislative Building is built of a rare and valuable limestone complete with the remains of fossils threaded through its façade. The building is set in 12 ha (30 acres) of beautifully kept gardens dotted with statues of poets such as Robert Burns of Scotland, and Ukrainian Taras Ahcvchenko, which celebrate the province's ethnic diversity.

🖼 Winnipeg Art Gallery

300 Memorial Blvd. **Tel** (204) 786 6641.
Open Tue–Sun. 🚫
This gallery boasts the largest collection of contemporary Inuit art in the world, with over 10,000 carvings, prints, drawings, and textiles. Especially striking is the large four-panel fabric collage wall-hanging, "Four Seasons of the Tundra" by Inuit artist Ruth Qaulluaryuk. The Gallery also contains Gothic and Renaissance altar paintings and tapestries donated by Irish peer Viscount Gore.

Winnipeg Town Center

① St. Boniface suburb
② Manitoba Children's Museum
③ The Forks National Historic Site
④ Dalnavert
⑤ Legislative Building
⑥ Winnipeg Art Gallery
⑦ Exchange District and Old Market Square
⑧ Manitoba Museum of Man and Nature *(see p243)*
⑨ Canadian Museum of Human Rights

⊞ Exchange District and Market Square

133 Albert St. **Tel** (204) 942 6716. 📅 call to book. 🅆 **exchangedistrict.org**

When the Canadian Pacific Railway decided to build its transcontinental line through Winnipeg in 1881, the city experienced a boom that led to the setting up of several commodity exchanges. Named after the Winnipeg Grain Exchange, this district was soon populated with a solid array of handsome terracotta and cut stone hotels, banks, warehouses, and theaters. The Exchange District is now a National Historic Site and has been restored to its former glory. It now houses boutiques, craft stores, furniture and antique stores, galleries, artists' studios, and residential lofts.

The center of the district is Old Market Square, a popular site for staging local festivals and outdoor concerts.

🏛 Canadian Museum for Human Rights

85 Waterfront Dr. **Tel** (204) 289 2000. **Open** due to open in 2014, check website for opening times. 🅴 🅆 **humanrightsmuseum.ca**

Located in an iconic building designed by Antoine Predock, the Canadian Museum for Human Rights sits at the forks of the Red and Assiniboine rivers, a historic meeting place for over 5,000 years, and has transformed the Winnipeg skyline.

The museum's goal is to increase awareness of human rights in Canada and around the world, and to open up a forum for dialogue on the subject through interactive exhibitions, learning programs, and tours.

Original 19th-century walls enclose the buildings at Lower Fort Garry National Historic Site

⊞ Lower Fort Garry National Historic Site

5981 Hwy 9. **Tel** (204) 785 6050. **Open** mid-May–Jun: 9am–5pm Mon–Fri; July & Aug: 9am–5pm Wed–Mon. 🅴 🅆 **pc.gc.ca/garry**

Located 32 km (20 miles) north of Winnipeg on the banks of the Red River, Lower Fort Garry National Historic Site is North America's only restored stone fort from the fur-trading era. Walls and buildings that have stood on the bank of the Red River for over 180 years tell inspiring tales of innovation, discovery, and struggle.

Costumed interpreters bring to life the history of the setting to the sounds of metal being hammered and aromas from the campfire.

Sculpture in the Leo Mol garden, Assiniboine park

🏛 Royal Canadian Mint

520 Lagimodière Blvd. **Tel** (204) 983 6429. **Open** 9am–5pm daily (post-Labour Day–24 May: Tue–Sat). **Closed** Jan 1, Dec 25. 🅴 🅴 🅴 🅴 🅆 **mint.ca**

The Royal Canadian Mint is housed in a striking building of rose-colored glass. The mint produces more than four billion coins annually for Canadian circulation, as well as for 60 other countries including Thailand and India.

🛝 Assiniboine Park

2355 Corydon Ave. **Tel** (204) 927 6000. **Open** daily. 🅴

Stretching for 153 ha (378 acres) along the south side of the Assiniboine River, Assiniboine Park is one of the largest urban parks in central Canada.

One of the park's best-loved attractions is the Leo Mol Sculpture Garden, which has some 50 bronze sculptures by the celebrated local artist. The park's Conservatory offers a tropical palm house which has seasonal displays of a wide range of flowers and shrubs. The park also features an English garden, a miniature railroad, and a fine example of a French formal garden. The Pavilion Gallery showcases artists from the province and also has a permanent exhibition on Winnie the Pooh. In summer, the Lyric Theatre hosts live music.

The Assiniboine Park Zoo contains over 250 different species, specializing in cold-hardy animals from the northern latitudes and mountain ranges such as polar bears, cougars, elk, and bald eagles. A large statue of Winnie the Bear is thought to be modeled on the Winnie the Pooh of the A.A. Milne books.

The park's numerous cycling and walking trails are popular in summer, as is cross-country skiing, skating, and tobogganing in winter.

A pink glass pyramid houses Canada's Royal Mint

The Manitoba Museum

Outstanding displays of the region's geography and people are imaginatively presented at this excellent museum, which opened in 1970. The visitor proceeds through chronologically organized galleries with displays that range from pre-history to the present day. Each geographical area also has its own gallery: from the Earth History Gallery, which contains fossils up to 500 million years old, to the re-creation of Winnipeg in the 1920s, including a cinema, and a dentist's office. One of the museum's biggest draws is a full-size replica of the Nonsuch, a 17th-century ketch.

Key

- Orientation Gallery
- Earth History Gallery
- Arctic/Sub-Arctic Gallery
- Boreal Forest Gallery
- Grasslands Gallery
- Discovery Room
- Urban Gallery
- Nonsuch Gallery
- Hudson's Bay Company Gallery
- Parklands/Mixed Woods Gallery
- Temporary exhibits
- Non-exhibition space

Moose Diorama
A moose and her calf among the conifers of the boreal forest are part of a display that includes a group of Cree people rock painting and gathering food before the harsh winter sets in.

Boreal Mezzanine

Earth History Mezzanine

Nonsuch Gallery
This two-masted ketch, built in England in 1968, is a replica of the Nonsuch that arrived in Hudson Bay in 1688 in search of furs.

Main entrance

Gallery Guide

The galleries are arranged on two levels, with steps connecting to mezzanines in the Earth History and Boreal Forest galleries. Part of a three-story addition houses the museum's Hudson's Bay Company collection.

Buffalo Hunt
A Métis hunter chasing buffalo symbolizes the museum's focus on man's relationship with his environment.

Big horn steer at the Mennonite Heritage Village, Steinbach, Manitoba ▶

Ploughing with horses at the Mennonite Heritage Village, Steinbach

❷ Steinbach

🏔 13,000. 🚌 ℹ️ (204) 326 9566.

About an hour's drive south-east of Winnipeg, Steinbach is a closely knit community with impressive businesses in trucking, printing, manufacturing, and especially car dealerships. These are run largely by the Mennonites, members of a Protestant religious sect who are noted for their fair dealing.

Steam Engine at the Mennonite Heritage Village

The Mennonites arrived in Steinbach on ox-drawn carts in 1874, having fled from religious persecution in Russia. Despite not having a rail link, the town thrived, as the Mennonites were good farmers and, later, car dealers. The nearby **Mennonite Heritage Village** re-creates a 19th-century Mennonite settlement, with some buildings dating from the 1870s, and a church and school furnished to the period. Its restaurant serves home-made meals such as borscht, a soup made with red cabbage and cream. The store offers locally crafted items. In early August, the village hosts the four-day Pioneer Days event.

🏛 **Mennonite Heritage Village**
Hwy 12 North. **Tel** (204) 326 9661.
Open May, Jun & Sep: 10am–5pm Mon–Sat, noon–5pm Sun; Jul & Aug: 10am–6pm Mon–Sat, noon–6pm Sun; Oct–Apr: 10–4pm Mon–Fri. 🅿 ♿
W **mennoniteheritagevillage.com**

❸ Selkirk

🏔 9,600. 🚌 ℹ️ Red River North Tourism, 18 Main St. (204) 482 2020.
W **redrivernorthtourism.com**

Named after the fifth Earl of Selkirk, Thomas Douglas, whose family had an interest in the Hudson's Bay Company, Selkirk was established in 1882 when settlers arrived along the shores of the Red River. Today, on Main Street, a 7.5-m (25-ft) high statue of a catfish proclaims Selkirk as the "Catfish capital of North America." Sport fishing is a year-round activity, attracting enthusiasts from across North America.

The city's Marine Museum on Eveline St. displays six restored historic ships, including the 1897 S.S. *Keenora*, Manitoba's oldest steamship.

❹ Lake Winnipeg

🚉 Winnipeg. ✈ Winnipeg. ℹ️ Travel Manitoba (204) 927 7800, 1 800 665 0040. W **travelmanitoba.com**

Lake Winnipeg is a huge stretch of water some 350 km (217 miles) long that dominates the province of Manitoba, connecting the south of the province to the north at Hudson Bay via the Nelson River. Today, the resorts that line the lake are popular with locals and visitors alike.

Numerous beaches line the southeastern coast of the lake, including Winnipeg Beach, with one of the best windsurfing bays on the lake. A wood carving of an Indian head by native artist Peter "Wolf" Toth stands in the local park. Called *Whispering Giant*, the sculpture honors the Ojibwa, Cree, and Assiniboine First Nations people of Manitoba.

Grand Beach in the **Grand Beach Provincial Park** has long powdery-white sand beaches and huge grass-topped dunes over 12 m (39 ft) high. Stretching back from the beach, the marsh, which is also known as the lagoon, is one of the park's treasures, and supports many species of birds, such as the rare and endangered Piping Plover.

Moving west from the lake, **Oak Hammock Marsh** provides an important habitat for over 300 species of birds and animals. The marsh's tall grass prairie, meadows, and aspen-oak bluffs house birds such

Historic ships outside the Marine Museum of Manitoba in Selkirk

For hotels and restaurants in this region see pp350–59 and pp364–83

Carved cedar sculpture in the park at Winnipeg Beach

as the ruff (a shorebird), the garganey (a duck), and the sharp-tailed sparrow.

Farther north, **Hecla/ Grindstone Provincial Park** occupies a number of islands in the lake. A causeway links the mainland to Hecla Island, which was originally inhabited by the Anishinabe (Ojibwa) people. The first European settlers here were Icelanders who arrived in 1875. Today, the lakeside village of Hecla is a pretty open-air museum featuring several restored 19th-century buildings. From Hecla there are many hiking and biking trails that lead to viewpoints for sightings of waterfowl such as great blue herons and the rare western grebe.

🌳 **Grand Beach Provincial Park**
Hwy 12, nr Grand Marais. **Tel** (204) 754 5040. **Open** daily. 🅿️ ♿ partial.

🌳 **Hecla/Grindstone Provincial Park**
Hwy 8, nr Riverton. **Tel** (204) 378 2261. **Open** daily.

❺ Gimli

🏔️ 2,000. 🚌 ℹ️ Centre St. (204) 642 7974.

Located on the western shores of Lake Winnipeg, Gimli is the largest Icelandic community outside Iceland. The settlers arrived, having gained the rights to land, at nearby Willow Creek in 1875. They soon proclaimed an independent state, which lasted until 1897 when the government insisted that other immigrants be allowed to settle in Gimli. Today, the **New Iceland Heritage Museum** tells the story of the town's unusual history.

Gimli has a distinctly nautical atmosphere, with cobbled sidewalks leading down to a picturesque harbor and a wooden pier. At the Icelandic Festival of Manitoba, held every August, visitors can play at being Vikings, listen to folk music, and eat Icelandic specialties.

About 25 km (15 miles) west of Gimli, the Narcisse Wildlife Management Area has been set up to preserve the

Statue of a Viking in the village of Gimli

habitat of thousands of red-sided garter snakes that can be seen here during early spring and early fall, on a specially designated short trail.

🏛️ **New Iceland Heritage Museum**
The Waterfront Centre, Unit 108, 94 First Ave. **Tel** (204) 642 4001. **Open** May–Aug: 9am–4pm daily; Sep–Apr: 1–4pm Sat & Sun. 🅿️ ♿

❻ Portage la Prairie

🏔️ 13,000. 🚌 🚍 ℹ️ 97 Sask Ave. E. (204) 239 8334.

Portage la Prairie lies at the center of a rich agricultural area growing wheat, barley, canola, and vegetables. The town is named after the French term for an overland detour, as Portage la Prairie lies between Lake Manitoba and the Assiniboine River, which formed a popular waterway for early travelers. Today, this thriving farming community contains the Fort La Reine Museum and Pioneer Village, on the site of the original fort built by the French explorer, La Vérendrye, in 1738. The museum offers exhibits of tools and photographs detailing 19th-century prairie life. The popular railroad display features a caboose, a watchman's shack, and the cigar-stained business car of Sir William Van Horne, founder of the Canadian Pacific Railroad. Pioneer Village successfully re-creates a 19th-century settlement with authentic stores and a church.

Pioneer Village, part of the Fort La Reine complex at Portage la Prairie

❼ Riding Mountain National Park

Hwys 10 & 19. **Tel** (204) 878 7275. **Open** daily. 🚶 🅦 **pc.gc.ca/riding**

One of western Manitoba's most popular attractions, Riding Mountain National Park is a vast 3,000-sq-km (1,158-sq-miles) wilderness. The best hiking trails and some of Manitoba's most beautiful scenery are to be found in the center of the park, where a highland plateau is covered by forests and lakes. To the east, a ridge of evergreen forest including spruce, pine, and fir trees houses moose and elk. A small herd of bison can also be found in the park near Lake Audy. Bison were reintroduced here in the 1930s after they had been hunted out at the end of the 19th century. The most developed area here is around the small settlement of Wasagaming where information on the park's network of trails for cycling, hiking, and horseback riding is available. Canoes can also be hired for exploring Clear Lake.

For a unique camping experience, yurts and oTENTiks (a cross between a tent

One of a small herd of bison at Riding Mountain National Park

and a cabin) at Wasagaming Campground can be booked through Parks Canada.

❽ Dauphin

🏙 8,000. ✈ 🚌 🚆 🚍 ⓘ 100 Main St. S. (204) 622 3140.

A pleasant tree-lined town, Dauphin was named after the King of France's eldest son by the French explorer La Vérendrye. Located north of Riding Mountain National Park, Dauphin is a distribution-and-supply center for the farms of the fertile Vermilion River valley. The **Fort Dauphin Museum** in town is a replica of an 18th-century trading post. Exhibits include a trapper's birchbark canoe and several early pioneer

buildings, including a school, church, and blacksmith's store.

Today, the town's distinctive onion-shaped dome of the Church of the Resurrection is a tribute to Dauphin's Ukrainian immigrants who began to arrive in 1891.

🏛 Fort Dauphin Museum

4th Ave. SW & Jackson St. **Tel** (204) 638 6630. **Open** May–Sep. 🚶

❾ Yorkton

🏙 19,500. 🚌 ⓘ Jct Hwy 9 & Hwy 16 (306) 783 8707.
🅦 **tourismyorkton.com**

Founded as a farming community in 1882, Yorkton is located in central Saskatchewan. The striking architecture of its churches, especially St. Mary's Church, reflects the town's Ukrainian heritage. The church was built in 1914. Its 21-m (68-ft) high dome, icons and paintings are stunning. The Yorkton branch of the **Western Development Museum** (one of four in the province) tells the story of immigrants to the region.

🏛 Western Development Museum

Hwy 16A. **Tel** (306) 783 8361. **Open** 9am–5pm Mon–Fri; noon–5pm Sat, Sun, daily in summer. 🚶 ♿

The magnificent dome at St. Mary's Church, Yorkton

The elegant façade of Motherwell Homestead

❿ Fort Qu'Appelle

🏙 2,000. ⓘ 160 Company Ave. (306) 332 5266. 🅦 **fortquappelle.com**

Named after an 1864 Hudson's Bay Company fur trading post, the picturesque town of Fort Qu'Appelle is located between Regina and Yorkton on Highway 10. The **Fort Qu'Appelle Museum** is built on the site of the old fort and incorporates a small out-building that was part of the original structure. The museum houses native artifacts such as antique beadwork and a collection of pioneer photographs.

The 430-km (267-mile) long Qu'Appelle River stretches across two-thirds of southern Saskatchewan. At Fort Qu'Appelle the river widens into a string of eight lakes bordered by several provincial parks. Scenic drives through the countryside are just one of the attractions of the valley.

About 30 km (19 miles) east of Fort Qu'Appelle is the **Motherwell Homestead National Historic Site**. This gracious house with ornamental gardens was built by politician William R. Motherwell. Motherwell introduced many agricultural improvements to the area and was so successful that he rose to become Saskatchewan's agriculture minister from 1905 to 1918.

🏛 Fort Qu'Appelle Museum

cnr Bay Ave. & Third St. **Open** Jun–Aug: 1–5pm daily. 🚶 ♿ limited.

🏠 Motherwell Homestead

Off Hwy 22. **Tel** (306) 333 2116. **Open** mid-May–Jun: Wed, Thu, Fri; Jul & Aug: daily. 🚶 ♿ limited.

⓫ Regina

🗺 193,000. ✈ 🚆 🚌 ℹ Hwy 1 E
(306) 789 5099, 1 800 661 5099.
🌐 **tourismregina.com**

Regina is a friendly, bustling city and the capital of Saskatchewan. The city was named for Queen Victoria by her daughter, Princess Louise, who was married to the Governor General of Canada. Regina was established in 1882 after starting life as a tent settlement called Pile O'Bones. This is a derivation of "oskana" (a Cree word meaning buffalo bones), from the piles of bones left behind after hunting.

Today, Regina is a thriving modern city whose highrise skyline contrasts with the 350,000 trees of the man-made Wascana Centre, a 9-sq-km (3.5-mile) urban park containing a vast man-made lake. The lake's Willow Island is a popular site for picnics and can be reached by ferry. The park is also a haven for some 60 species of waterfowl, including Canada geese. The **Royal Saskatchewan Museum** borders beautiful Wascana Park. Its Earth Sciences Gallery depicts 3.5 billion years of geological history of Saskatchewan, while the First Nations Gallery traces 10,000 years of aboriginal culture in the province. The Life Sciences Gallery shows Saskatchewan's eco-regions and the impact of the "human factor." The original

Canadian goose in Wascana Centre Park

One of several murals on downtown buildings in Moose Jaw

headquarters for the North West Mounted Police lies west of the city center.

Today, the Royal Canadian Mounted Police Depot Division trains all Canada's Mounties and is also the site of the **RCMP Heritage Centre**. Here, the story of the Mounties is told from their beginnings following the Cyprus Hills Massacre in 1873 *(see p251)*. Among the highlights are the ceremonies and drills that are regularly performed by special trained groups of Mounties, including the Sergeant Major's Parade and Sunset Retreat Ceremonies.

🏛 **Royal Saskatchewan Museum**
2445 Albert St. **Tel** (306) 787 2815.
Open daily. **Closed** Dec 25. ♿
🌐 **royalsaskmuseum.ca**

🏛 **RCMP Heritage Centre**
5907 Dewdney Ave. W. **Tel** 1 866 567 7267. **Open** daily. 🅿 🎁 ♿
🌐 **rcmp heritagecentre.com**

⓬ Moose Jaw

🗺 34,300. 🚆 🚌 ℹ 540 Diefenbaker Dr. (306) 693 8097, 1 866 693 8097.

The quiet town of Moose Jaw was established as a railway terminus by the Canadian Pacific Railroad in 1882. A terminus for the American Soo Line from Minneapolis, Minnesota soon followed. Today, 46 murals celebrate the lives of the early railroad pioneers and home-steaders, decorating buildings around 1st Avenue. Nearby, River Street has 1920s hotels and warehouses that reflect Moose Jaw's time as "sin city" during the 1920s – when Prohibition in the United States meant that illegally produced liquor was smuggled from Canada to Chicago, by gangsters such as the infamous Al Capone.

The Moose Jaw branch of the Western Development Museum focuses on transportation and has a gallery on the Snow Birds, Canada's top aerobatic team.

Cadets of the Royal Canadian Mounted Police Academy in Regina are put through their paces

Traditional powwow dancer in Wanuskewin Park, Saskatoon

⓭ Saskatoon

🏔 224,000. ✈ 🚉 🚌 🚏
ℹ 101–202 Fourth Ave. N. (306) 242 1206, 1 800 567 2444.
W tourismsaskatoon.com

Founded in 1882 by Ontario Methodist John Lake as a temperance colony, Saskatoon is located in the middle of prairie country. Today, the city is an agricultural and commercial hub, and a busy regional center for cattle ranchers and wheat farmers from surrounding communities. The region's history is told just south of the center in Saskatoon's branch of the Western Development Museum, which focuses on the town's boom years in the 1900s, re-creating the bustling main street of a typical prairie town, including its railroad station and a hotel. The town center houses The Ukrainian Museum of Canada with its brightly colored traditional textiles, and the Mendel Art Gallery, with a permanent art collection and changing exhibitions of international, national, and regional artwork.

The South Saskatchewan River meanders through the city and is bounded by many lush parks, including the outstanding 307-ha (760-acre) **Wanuskewin Heritage Park**. The park is devoted to Northern Plains First Nations history, with archaeological sites that confirm the existence of hunter-gatherer communities some 6,000 years ago. Some of the digs are open to the public in summer. The park's wooded hills and marshy creeks are still held to be sacred lands by the Northern Plains peoples who act as interpretive guides. Easy-to-follow trails lead the visitor past tipi rings, an ancient medicine wheel, buffalo trails, and a buffalo jump *(see p300)*.

🦬 **Wanuskewin Heritage Park**
Off Hwy 11. **Tel** (306) 931 6767.
Open daily. **Closed** Christmas period.
♿ 🅿 limited. **W wanuskewin.com**

⓮ Grasslands National Park

Jct Hwys 4 & 18. ℹ Val Marie (306) 298 2257. **Open** daily; check website for opening hours of visitor centers.
W pc.gc.ca/grasslands

Situated in the southwest corner of Saskatchewan, Grasslands National Park was set up in 1988 to preserve one of the last original prairie grasslands in North America. The park is an area of climatic extremes where summer temperatures can be as high as 40 °C (104 °F), and winter ones as low as -40 °C (-48 °F). This environment supports a range of rare wildlife, including short-horned lizards and ferruginous hawks. The rugged landscape along the Frenchman River valley is the only remaining

Black-tailed prairie dog

habitat of the black-tailed prairie dog in Canada. Visitors may hike and camp in the park, but facilities are basic.

East of the park is the striking, glacially formed landscape of the **Big Muddy Badlands**. In the early 1900s, caves of eroded sandstone and deep ravines provided hideouts for cattle thieves such as Butch Cassidy.

📷 **Big Muddy Badlands**
Off Hwy 34. **Tel** (306) 267 3312. Tours in summer from Coronach. 🎫

Buttes (isolated flat-topped hills) in the Big Muddy Badlands seen from Grasslands National Park

⓫ Cypress Hills Interprovincial Park

Hwy 41. **i** (403) 893 3833. **Open** daily. **w** cypresshills.com

Crossing the border between Saskatchewan and Alberta, the Cypress Hills Interprovincial Park offers fine views of the plains from its 1,400-m (4,593-ft) high peaks. The park's landscape is similar to the foothills of the Rocky Mountains, with its lodgepole pine forests and abundant wild flowers. Walking trails through the park offer the visitor the chance to see moose, elk, and white-tailed deer, as well as the 220 or more species of bird that stop here during migration, such as the rare trumpeter swan and mountain chickadee.

In the eastern section of the park, in Saskatchewan, **Fort Walsh National Historic Site** houses a reconstruction of Fort Walsh, which was built in 1875 by the Mounties to keep out the illicit whiskey traders who were causing trouble among the natives. Costumed guides relate the history of the North West Mounted Police.

Fort Walsh National Historic Site

Cypress Hills Interprovincial Park. **Tel** (306) 662 2645. **Open** mid-May–Jun: 9:30am–5:30pm Tue–Sat; Jul & Aug: 9:30am–5:30pm daily. **w** pc.gc.ca/fortwalsh

⓰ Maple Creek

2,300. **i** Hwy 1 West (306) 662 4005.

Located on the eastern edge of the Cypress Hills and affectionately known as "Old Cow Town," Maple Creek was established as a ranching center in 1882. The town still has a look of the Old West with trucks and Stetson-wearing ranchers filling the downtown streets. Maple Creek's many original 19th-century storefronts include the elegantly refurbished Commercial Hotel with its marble-floored lobby.

High Level Bridge over the Oldman River, Lethbridge

⓱ Medicine Hat

61,000. **i** 8 Gehring Rd. SW. (403) 527 6422, 1 800 481 2822. **w** tourismmedicinehat.com

The south Saskatchewan River Valley is the picturesque setting for the town of Medicine Hat, the center of Alberta's gas industry. Founded in 1883, Medicine Hat also became a center for the manufacture of clay products, such as pottery, due to the natural abundance of clay along the banks of the South Saskatchewan River. Today, the **Medalta Potteries National Historic Site** in the 150-acre (60-ha) Historic Clay District is a living, working museum dedicated to telling the stories of the industry and the people who worked there.

Medalta Potteries National Historic Site

713 Medalta Ave. SE. **Tel** (403) 529 1070. **Open** mid-May–Aug: Tue–Sat. **w** medalta.org

⓲ Lethbridge

86,700. **i** 2805 Scenic Dr. S. (403) 329 6777, 1800 661 1222. **w** exploresouthwestalberta.com

Coal, oil, and gas are the basis of Lethbridge's success. Alberta's third-largest city was named after mine-owner William Lethbridge in 1885, but First Nations peoples such as the Blackfoot Indians have inhabited the area since prehistoric times.

Lying on the banks of the Oldman River, Lethbridge is home to the notorious Fort Whoop-up, established in 1869 by whiskey traders John Healy and Alfred Hamilton for the sole purpose of profiting from the sale of illicit, and often deadly, whiskey. Many Indians, drawn by the lure of the drink, were poisoned or even killed by the brew, which was made with substances such as tobacco and red ink. Today, a reconstruction of Fort Whoop up and three galleries conjure up life at the fort in the 1870s.

Cypress Hills Massacre

On June 1, 1873 a group of whiskey traders attacked an Assiniboine camp, killing several women, children, and braves in retaliation for the alleged theft of their horses by natives. Many native people had already died from drinking the traders' liquor, which was doctored with substances such as ink and strychnine. The massacre led to the formation of the North West Mounted Police. Their first post at Fort Macleod in 1874, and another at Fort Walsh in 1875, marked the end of the whiskey trade and earned the Mounties the natives' trust.

Two Assiniboine Indians from an engraving made in 1844

⑲ Royal Tyrrell Museum

The outstanding Royal Tyrrell Museum was opened in 1985 and is the only museum in Canada devoted to 4.5 billion years of the Earth's history. The layout of the exhibits enables visitors to follow the course of evolution through displays of dinosaurs and fossils from different ages. The museum uses interactive computers, videos, and three-dimensional dioramas to re-create distinct prehistoric landscapes, bringing the age of the dinosaurs and the study of palaeontology to life.

VISITORS' CHECKLIST

Practical Information
Hwy 838, 6 km NW of Drumheller.
Tel (403) 823 7707, 1 888 440
4240. **Open** May–Sep: daily;
Oct–Apr: Tue–Sun. 🅿 ♿
Ⓦ tyrrellmuseum.com

Transport
🚌 Calgary.

Key

☐ Cretaceous Alberta Gallery
☐ Preparation Lab
☐ Lords of the Land
☐ Burgess Shale
☐ Devonian Reef
☐ Dinosaur Hall
☐ Bearpaw Sea
☐ Mammal Hall
☐ Cretaceous Garden
☐ Permian
☐ Palynology Playroom
☐ Ice Ages Gallery
☐ Non-exhibition space

Dinosaur Hall
In Dinosaur Hall, a T-rex towers over a display of some 35 complete dinosaur skeletons.

The Ice Ages Gallery displays skeletons and fossils of the giant woolly mammoths, mastodons, bison, and sabre-toothed tigers that inhabited North America.

Gallery Guide

The collection is housed on several levels reached by a series of ramps. Each area contains a display on an era of geological time. Introductory exhibits on fossils and dinosaurs are followed by displays on prehistoric mammals and the Ice Ages. The largest and most popular part of the museum is the Dinosaur Hall.

Organized Treks

Visitors on a trek through the Badlands

The Royal Tyrrell Museum has a Field Centre within Dinosaur Provincial Park *(see opposite)*. As well as interesting displays on the park's history, the Field Centre is the starting point for guided tours run by the park (by bus or on foot). These allow participants to learn more about the creatures that populated ancient Alberta. There is also a self-guided walking tour.

Auditorium

Black Beauty Skull
This T-rex was found in the Crowsnest Pass area of south-western Alberta. The black discoloration was the result of a chemical reaction as the skeleton fossilized.

Elk Island National Park's largest lake, Astotin Lake, is skirted by a popular hiking trail

⑳ Dinosaur Provincial Park

Rte 544. **Tel** (403) 378 4342. **Open** daily. 🚻 🕸 **albertaparks.ca/dinosaur**

Two hours' drive southeast of the town of Drumheller, the UNESCO World Heritage Site of Dinosaur Provincial Park, established in 1955, contains one of the world's richest fossil beds. Located along the Red Deer River Valley, the park includes dinosaur skeletons mostly from the late Cretaceous Period, about 75 million years ago (*see pp234–5*). More than 300 mostly intact skeletons have been made here and more than 30 institutions worldwide have specimens from this valley on display.

From Drumheller it is possible to drive the 48-km (30-mile) loop **Dinosaur Trail** through the "Valley of the Dinosaurs." The trail passes the Royal Tyrrell Museum, takes in stunning views of the badlands landscape from highpoints such as Horseshoe Canyon, and leads to intriguing rock hoodoos.

🚻 **Dinosaur Trail**
🛈 Drumheller (403) 823 1331.
🕸 **traveldrumheller.com**

㉑ Red Deer

🏠 92,000. 🚌 🛈 101–4200 Hwy 2 (403) 346 0180.
🕸 **tourismreddeer.net**

Located midway between Calgary and Edmonton, this bustling city was founded in 1882 by Scottish settlers as a stopover point for travelers. A modern city with good cultural and recreational facilities, Red Deer is the hub of central Alberta's rolling parkland district. The city has some interesting buildings, such as the award-winning St. Mary's Church, and the landmark Water Tower, known as the "Green Onion." The city's beautiful reserve of Waskasoo Park is located along the Red River.

㉒ Elk Island National Park

Hwy 16. **Tel** (780) 922 5790. **Open** daily. 🚻 🕸 **pc.gc.ca/elkisland**

Established in 1906 as Canada's first animal sanctuary, Elk Island became a national park in 1913. It offers a wilderness retreat only half-an-hour's drive from Edmonton. This 194 sq km (75 sq miles) park provides a habitat for large mammals such as elk, the plains bison, the rarer, threatened wood bison, and moose. The park's landscape of transitional aspen parkland (an area of rolling meadows, woodlands, and wetlands) is, according to the World Wildlife Fund for Nature, one of the most threatened habitats in North America.

Aspen trees grow mostly on dry ridges, while balsam, poplar, and white birch grow near wet areas. Plants such as sedges and willows also thrive in the wetlands alongside a host of birds such as the swamp sparrow and yellow warbler.

Elk Island is a popular day trip from Edmonton as well as being a picturesque weekend picnic spot for locals. There are 13 hiking trails of varying difficulties and lengths. During the summer a wide range of activities is available in the park including swimming, canoeing, and camping. Cross-country skiing is the most popular winter activity.

Hoodoos, towers of rock sculpted by erosion, near Drumheller

Ice Palace at West Edmonton Mall

㉓ Edmonton

🏙 1 million. ✈ 🚁 🚉 🚌 ℹ 990 Jasper Ave. (780) 496 8400, 1 800 463 4667. 🆆 edmonton.com/tourism

Edmonton spans the valley of the North Saskatchewan River and sits in the center of Alberta province, of which it is the capital. Established as a series of Hudson's Bay Company trading posts in the 1790s, this city is now the focus of Canada's thriving oil industry.

Edmonton's downtown area is centered on Jasper Avenue and Sir Winston Churchill Square, where modern highrises sit among shops and restaurants. The gigantic **West Edmonton Mall** contains over 800 stores, an amusement and water park, over 100 restaurants, a bowling center, an ice rink,

and 27 movie theaters. In contrast is one of Alberta's oldest buildings, the delightful Alberta Legislature, opened in 1913. Overlooking the river, on the site of the old Fort Edmonton, the building has beautiful landscaped grounds.

Southwest of downtown, Fort Edmonton Park re-creates the original Hudson's Bay Company fort with reconstructions of street areas in 1885 and 1920. Here visitors can experience past times, wandering around original shops and businesses, as well as taking rides on a horse-drawn wagon, steam train, or street car.

West of downtown is the Royal Alberta Museum with natural history displays; to the northwest is the Telus World of Science, which boasts an IMAX theatre, Observatory, and Star Theatre.

🏬 **West Edmonton Mall**
170th St. & 87th Ave. **Tel** (780) 444 5200. **Open** daily. ♿

㉔ Vegreville

🏙 5,300. 🚌 ℹ at giant Pysanka (780) 632 2606.

Along the Yellowhead Hwy, heading eastward from Edmonton, lies the predominantly Ukrainian town of Vegreville. Its community is famous for producing

traditionally Ukrainian, highly decorated Easter eggs (or pysanki). Visible from the road is a giant pysanka covered with intricate bronze, gold, and silver designs that tell the story of the region's Ukrainian settlers, and celebrates their religious faith, bountiful harvests, and the protection they received from the RCMP. The egg is 7 m (23 ft) high, and is made of over 3,500 pieces of aluminum.

A giant decorated Easter egg celebrates Vegreville's heritage

㉕ Wood Buffalo National Park

Main access: Fort Smith, NWT.
Tel (867) 872 7900. **Open** daily. 🅿
🆆 pc.gc.ca/woodbuffalo

The largest national park in Canada, Wood Buffalo is about the size of Denmark, covering an area of 44,807 sq km (17,474 sq miles). The park was made a UNESCO World Heritage Site in 1983 because of the range of habitat it offers for such rare species of animal as the wood bison or buffalo.

There are three different environments here: fire-scarred forest uplands; a large, poorly drained plateau filled with streams and bogs; and the Peace-Athabasca Delta, full of sedge meadows, marshes, and shallow lakes. Sightings of bald eagles and peregrine falcons are common, and the park is the only remaining natural nesting site of the rare whooping crane in the world.

The Grey Owl Story

Long before conservation became popular, the renowned naturalist by the name of Grey Owl, took up the cause. Inspired by his Mohawk wife, Anahareo, he wrote the first of several best-selling books, *Men of the Last Frontier*, in 1931, the same year he became the official naturalist of Prince Albert National Park. He built a cabin on the peaceful shores of Lake Ajawaan from where he ran a beaver protection program. When Grey Owl died of pneumonia in 1938, there was uproar when a newspaper discovered that he was really an Englishman. Born in Hastings in 1888, Archibald Stansfield Belaney took on the identity of Grey Owl when he returned to Canada after World War I. He wore buckskins and wore his hair in Apache-style braids. A generation later Grey Owl's legacy remains the protection of Canada's wildlife.

Grey Owl feeding a beaver

㉖ Prince Albert National Park

Established in 1927, Prince Albert National Park covers 3,875 sq km (1,500 sq miles) of wilderness, from the gently rolling terrain of aspen parkland in the south to the spruce and fir trees of the northern boreal forest. These distinct environments house different wildlife populations, with moose, wolf, and caribou in the forests, and elk, bison, and badger in the parkland. The center of the park, and the most accessible areas for visitors, are the hiking and canoeing trails around the Kingsmere and Waskesiu Lakes. The townsite of Waskesiu is the best place from which to begin exploring the park.

VISITORS' CHECKLIST

Practical Information
Off Hwy 2. **Tel** (306) 663 4522.
🖼 Nature center.
Open May–Aug: 8am–8pm daily.
Closed Dec 25 & 26.
W pc.gc.ca/princealbert
W waskesiuwildernessregion.com

Key

━━ Major road
━ Minor road
▪ ▪ Hiking route
━ Rivers

Grey Owl's cabin by Ajawaan Lake
A 20-km (12-mile) trail leads to Grey Owl's log cabin, "Beaver Lodge."

Beach resort at Waskesiu Lake
The village of Waskesiu offers visitors a wide range of facilities, including stores, hotels, and a sandy lakeside beach.

Kingsmere Lake

Crean Lake

The Hanging Heart Lakes form a waterway that leads to Lake Crean – one of the popular canoe trips in the park.

The Nature Centre explains the park's ecology.

0 km   3
0 miles   3

Waskesiu Lake

• **Waskesiu**

↪ Prince Albert

View over Waskesiu Lake
Fall foliage across the boreal forest seen around the lake from Kingsmere Road.

Mud Creek Trail is a 2-km (1-mile) loop that skirts the lake then follows Mud Creek. In spring, spawning fish attract bears.

For map symbols *see back flap*

Gun with carriage at Fort Battleford National Historic Site

❷ North Battleford and Battleford

🏔 16,500. ✈ 🚂 ℹ Visitors' center, jct Hwys 16 & 40 (306) 445 2000, 1 800 243 0394. 🆆 **tourismbattlefords.com**

North Battleford and Battleford, together known as The Battlefords, face each other across the North Saskatchewan River Valley. Named after a ford in the Battle River, the area was the site of age-old conflicts between the Blackfoot and Cree. An important early settlement in the West, it was chosen as the seat of the North-West Territories government from 1876 to 1882. Today, the communities are thriving industrial centers, although the North Battleford branch of the Western Development Museum focuses on rural life.

The **Allen Sapp Gallery** displays works by Allen Sapp, one of Canada's best-loved contemporary artists. His simple, delicately colored paintings and drawings celebrate the traditions of the Northern Plains Cree community.

Between the Saskatchewan and Battle rivers is the **Fort Battleford National Historic Site** containing a well-restored North-West Mounted Police post. The stockade has original buildings, including the look-out point in the commander's residence, officers' quarters, and restored barracks now housing a museum. Costumed guides tell the story of when 500 settlers took refuge in the stockade during the North-West Rebellion.

🏛 Allen Sapp Gallery
1 Railway Ave. **Tel** (306) 445 1760. **Open** Jun–Sep: 11am–5pm daily; Oct–May: noon–4pm Wed–Sun. ♿

🏛 Fort Battleford National Historic Site
Off Hwy 4. **Tel** (306) 937 2621. **Open** mid-May–Jun: 10am–4pm Wed, Thu, Fri; Jul–Aug: 10am–4pm daily. 🅿 ♿ 🆆 **pc.gc.ca/battleford**

❷ Batoche National Historic Site

Rte 225 off Hwy 312. **Tel** (306) 423 6227. **Open** mid-May–Jun: Mon–Fri; Jul & Aug: daily; Sep–mid-Oct: Thu–Sat. 🅿 ♿ 🆆 **pc.gc.ca/batoche**

The original village of Batoche was the site of the Métis's last stand against the Canadian Militia, led by Louis Riel and Gabriel Dumont in 1885 *(see p53)*.

From the 17th century, white fur traders in the west had married Indian wives and adopted tribal languages and customs. The resulting mixed raced peoples, the Métis, had originally rebeled in 1869 in the Winnipeg area in defense of their land rights. When history began to repeat itself in 1885, Métis rebels recalled Riel from exile in Montana to declare a provisional government at Batoche. Violence erupted on May 9, 1885 into what was to become known as the North-West Rebellion. Riel surrendered, was tried for treason, and hanged in Regina.

Today, the Batoche National Historic Site of Canada occupies the site of the village and battle-field. The 6-sq-km (2.5-sq-miles) park houses the bullet-ridden St. Antoine de Padou Church and Rectory as well as the cemetery where the Métis leaders are buried. An interpretive center features an audio-visual presentation telling the history of Batoche and the rebellion through the eyes of the Métis.

St. Antoine de Padou Church and Rectory at Batoche National Historic Site

Polar Bears

Known as the "Lord of the Arctic," the magnificent polar bear can weigh as much as 650 kg (1,433 lb). In the fall the bears begin to congregate along the bay east of Churchill waiting for ice to form in order to hunt seals. Their acute sense of smell can detect a scent up to 32 km (20 miles) away and pick up the presence of seals under 1 m (3 ft) of snow and ice.

Between 900 and 1,000 bears pass by and through Churchill during the season. The best way to view them is in a tundra buggy, a large buslike vehicle that is warm, safe, and elevated over 2 m (6.5 ft) from the ground.

The majestic polar bear

for centuries, used by both natives and, later, European explorers and fur traders to travel from the northern forests to the prairies. Today, visitors may follow the historic route on guided canoe tours as well as fishing for northern pike, lake trout, walleye, and perch.

❷ Churchill

🗺 800. ✈ 🚉 ℹ 211 Kelsey Blvd. (204) 675 2022.

Located at the mouth of the Churchill River on Hudson Bay, the town retains the look of a basic pioneer town, with no luxury hotels, few paved roads, and few trees. This vast Arctic landscape is snow-free only from June through to the end of September. Churchill has no road access and can be reached only by plane or train from Winnipeg, Thompson, and The Pas. Despite its remote situation, Churchill was an important point of entry into Canada for early European explorers and fur traders arriving by boat in the 18th century. The Hudson's Bay Company established an outpost for fur-trading here in 1717.

Today, visitors come to see the polar bears, beluga whales, and the splendid tundra flora in this region. In the spring and fall the tundra's covering of moss, lichens, and tiny flowers bursts into an array of colors. In the summer beluga whales move upriver and can be seen from boat trips or on scuba dives. Churchill is also one of the best places to see the Northern Lights.

❷ Duck Lake

🗺 670. 🚉 ℹ 301 Front St. (306) 467 2057. 🌐 **trailsof1885.com**

A little to the west of the small farming village of Duck Lake lies a plaque commemorating the first shots fired in the North-West Rebellion. On March 26, 1885, a police interpreter and a Cree emissary scuffled during a parley, and the officer was killed. During the ensuing battle, 12 NWMP officers and six Métis died. The Battle of Duck Lake is depicted in a series of murals at the town's interpretive center.

❸ The Pas

🗺 15,000. ✈ 🚉 🚍 ℹ 324 Ross Ave. (204) 623 7256.

Once a key fur-trading post dating back some 300 years, The Pas is now a major industrial distribution and transportation center for Manitoba's northwest. Nearby Clearwater Lake Provincial Park is named for the lake itself, which is said to be so clear that it is possible to see the bottom at 11 m (35 ft). The park also offers a walking trail through "the caves," a geological phenomenon where rock masses split away from cliffs to create huge crevices that provide shelter for a number of animals, including black bears, moose, wolves, and foxes.

❸ Flin Flon

🗺 5,600. ✈ 🚍 ℹ Hwy 10A (204) 687 4518.

Steep hilly streets reflect the fact that Flin Flon lies on Precambrian rock (as old as the formation of the Earth's crust itself, roughly 3.8 billion years ago), and the area is famous for its distinctive greenstone. The town bears the name of a fictional character of a popular novel, *The Sunless City* by J.E.P. Murdock. The book was read by a prospector at the time he staked his claim here in 1915. Copper and gold are still mined in Flin Flon, but visitors mostly come to experience the vast wilderness of the nearby Grass River Provincial Park.

The distinctive Grass River, where strings of islands dot the countless lakes of the river system, has been a trade route

Polar bear warning sign near Churchill

Winter sunset, Mount Seymour Provincial Park, British Columbia ▶

BRITISH COLUMBIA AND THE ROCKIES

Introducing British Columbia and the Rockies

The dramatic beauty of British Columbia and the Rockies' mountain ranges, forests, and lakes make it a much visited area. There is a wide variety of landscapes available here, from the northern Rockies with their bare peaks, to the south's Okanagan Valley with its orchards and vineyards. The region's temperate climate means that BC has more species of plants and animals than anywhere else in the country.

Millions of visitors come here every year, drawn by a wide range of outdoor activities. To the west, Vancouver Island offers ancient rainforest and the impressive coastal scenery of the Pacific Rim National Park Reserve. Lying between the Pacific Ocean and the Coast Mountains, Vancouver is a stunningly attractive city, with good transportation links to the rest of the region, including Calgary in the east.

Rainforest in Gwaii Haanas National Park Reserve and Haida Heritage Site on Haida Gwaii

Illuminated by over 3,500 lights, Victoria's Parliament Buildings are reflected in the waters of Inner Harbour on Vancouver Island

For additional map symbols *see back flap*

Key

— Expressway
— Divided highway
— Highway
⋯ Other road
— Main railway
— Minor railway
— International border
— Regional border
△ Summit

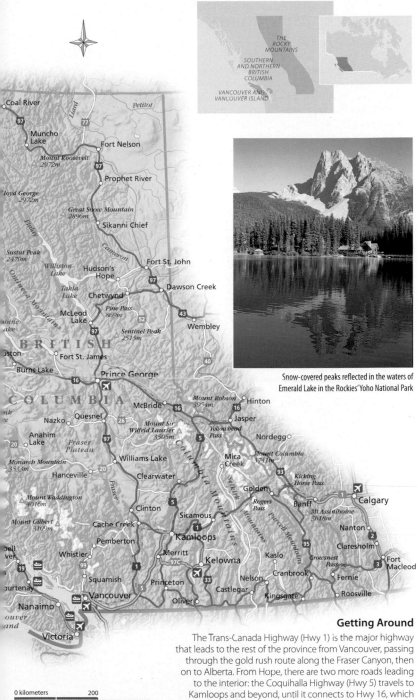

Snow-covered peaks reflected in the waters of
Emerald Lake in the Rockies' Yoho National Park

0 kilometers   200

0 miles   200

Getting Around

The Trans-Canada Highway (Hwy 1) is the major highway
that leads to the rest of the province from Vancouver, passing
through the gold rush route along the Fraser Canyon, then
on to Alberta. From Hope, there are two more roads leading
to the interior: the Coquihalla Highway (Hwy 5) travels to
Kamloops and beyond, until it connects to Hwy 16, which
cuts through Jasper National Park; and Hwy 3 runs east and
west through BC. VIA Rail runs a scenic route from Vancouver
to Jasper. Bus routes cover most destinations.

The Rocky Mountains

The Canadian Rocky Mountains are a younger section of the Western Cordillera, a wide band of mountain ranges that stretch from Mexico to Canada. Formed between 120 and 20 million years ago, they include some of Canada's highest peaks, the 325-sq-km (125-sq-mile) Columbia Icefield, and glacial lakes. In summer wild flowers carpet the alpine meadows; in winter both visitors and locals take advantage of the snow-covered slopes to indulge in winter sports. The flora and fauna of the Canadian Rockies are protected within several National Parks; the most noted being Banff, Jasper, and Yoho *(see pp304–315)*, which houses the renowned Burgess Shale fossil beds.

Locator Map
 The Canadian Rockies

Watson Lake

Fort Nelson

The Liard River Hot Springs, are located along the famous Alaska Highway *(see pp266–7)*. They are the result of surface water trickling down through cracks and fissures to the superheated rocks of the Earth's crust, which reach temperatures of 1,000 °C (1,832 °F). Steam is then released and rises to the surface where it condenses as water.

Fort St. John

Dawson Creek

Grande Prairie

Jas

Prince George

Hoodoos are mushroom-shaped pedestals of rock, sculpted by wind and sand. These are found among the bare peaks of Muncho Lake Provincial Park, at the northern end of the Canadian Rockies.

Kamloo

From the Icefields Parkway (Hwy 93), a scenic route that runs from Lake Louise in Banff National Park to Jasper, it is possible to view the saw-toothed appearance of the youngest peaks in the range. These were formed during the last episode of uplift, about 20 to 15 million years ago. Older ranges such as the Appalachians *(see p27)* have rounded tops formed by long-term erosion.

Maligne Canyon is a 50-m deep (164-ft), limestone gorge in Jasper National Park. The canyon was formed by the meltwaters of a glacier that once covered the valley. Today, the Maligne River rushes through this narrow channel, which also drains a series of underground caves.

The Lewis Overthrust in Waterton Lakes National Park is a geological phenomenon. When rocks were moving east during the formation of the Rockies, a single mass composed of the lowest sedimentary layer of the Rockies – known as the Lewis Thrust – came to rest on top of the prairies.

0 km   100
0 miles   100

Field   • Banff   Calgary

nt
on

Columbia
Icefields

elowna

The Burgess Shale fossil beds in Yoho National Park are a UN World Heritage Site and contain fossils dating from the Cambrian to the Permian ages some 570–290 million years ago. There are two main fossil beds; Walcott's Quarry, and Mt. Stephen, known for its wealth of trilobite (Cambrian marine animal) fossils.

The Formation of the Rocky Mountains

There are three main forces responsible for the formation of the Rocky Mountains. First, large areas of the Earth's crust (known as tectonic plates), constantly moving together and apart, created uplift. Second, the North American plate was subducted by the Pacific plate, which caused a chain of volcanoes to form from the molten rock of the oceanic crust. Third, erosion caused by the Ice Ages, as well as rivers and wind, deposited sedimentary rocks on the North American plate, which was then folded by more plate movement between 50 and 25 million years ago. The Rockies' jagged peaks reflect their recent formation.

Volcanoes   North America Plate
Pacific Plate

1 Some 150 million years ago, the Pacific plate moved east, adding to the molten rock from great depths of the North American Plate. This then rose up to form the Western Cordillera Mountains.

Pacific Plate   Sediments

2 The Cordillera was eroded over millions of years and during various Ice Ages. This led to sediments being deposited in the sagging, wedge-shaped crust east of the mountain range.

Cordillera Mountains   Rockies

3 Around 50 million years ago, the Pacific plate continued to push east, forcing the Cordillera range eastward, compressing sedimentary rocks, folding and uplifting them to form the Rockies.

Forestry and Wildlife of Coastal British Columbia

From its southern border with the United States to the northern tip of Haida Gwaii, the coastal region of British Columbia ranks as the richest ecological region in Canada. The warm waters of the north Pacific Ocean moderate the climate, creating a temperate rainforest teeming with life such as the black tail deer, black bear, and cougar. Dense forest still covers many islands, bays, and inlets along the coast, and is home to a large number of plant and animal species, including some of the tallest trees in Canada. Douglas Fir and Sitka Spruce can grow as high as 91 m (300 ft).

Trumpeter swans are so-called for their distinctive brassy call. They are found on marshes, lakes, and rivers.

Temperate Rainforest Habitat

High rainfall and a mild climate have created these lush forests of cedar, spruce, and pine, with their towering Douglas Firs and Sitka Spruces. Housed beneath the dripping forest canopy is a huge variety of ferns, mosses, and wild flowers, including orchids. Today, environmentalists campaign to protect these ancient forests from the threat of logging.

Bald eagles, with their distinctive white heads, can be seen in large numbers diving for fish in the ocean near Haida Gwaii. The area is noted for having one of the largest bald-eagle populations in BC.

The white black bear, also known as the kermode or "spirit bear," is unique to coastal British Columbia. It is related to the black bear, and is an agile salmon catcher.

Harlequin ducks are small and shy, and the males have striking markings. A good swimmer, the harlequin enjoys fast-flowing rivers and the strong surf of the Pacific.

Black tail deer are found only on the north Pacific coast. They are the smallest member of the mule deer family and are preyed on by cougars in the area.

Salmon

BC's coastal waters are home to five Pacific salmon species: pink, coho, chinook, sockeye, and chum. Together they support one of the main commercial food fisheries in the world, though numbers are declining in some parts of BC. Pacific salmon spawn in freshwater streams only once in their life, then die.

Their offspring migrate downstream and out to sea, where they grow to adults ranging in size from 7 kg (15 lb) to over 45 kg (100 lb). At maturity they swim long distances upstream in order to return to the waters of their birth.

Chinook Salmon leaping while swimming upstream to spawn.

Sockeye Salmon are highly prized in BC's fishing industry for their firm, tasty flesh.

Coastline Habitat

The warm waters of the north Pacific Ocean provide a habitat for more species of wildlife than any other temperate coastline. This distinctive region is characterized by having thousands of islands and inlets, which provide a home for a range of animals. Mammals such as gray, humpback, and orca whales can be seen here, as can sea otters, seals, and sea lions.

Northern sea lions live in colonies along the rocky BC coast. Large, lumbering animals, they have short "forearms" that enable them to move on land.

The glaucous gull is a large, gray-backed sea gull, which nests along coastal cliffs, and on the numerous small islands here.

Killer whales (or orcas) are found off the sheltered eastern coast of Vancouver Island and up BC's mainland coast. They are known as "killer" because they feed on other mammals.

Sea otters were hunted, almost to extinction, for their thick fur coats. Today, these playful creatures are numerous off the coast of mainland BC and Vancouver Island.

The Alaska Highway

The building of the Alaska Highway was an extraordinary achievement. Winding through 2,451 km (1,523 miles) of wilderness, mountains, muskeg (mosscovered bog), and forest, the first road was completed in 1942, only eight months and twelve days after construction began. Linking the United States to Alaska through British Columbia, it was built after the Japanese attacked Pearl Harbor in 1941, as a military supply route and to defend the northwest coast of Alaska.

Locator Map
■ *Map area*

Today, the original gravel road has been replaced by a two-lane, mostly asphalt highway. The highway's many curves are gradually being straightened, shortening its total length, and the present road now covers 2,394 km (1,488 miles).

Kluane National Park and Reserve contains some of the most dramatic scenery to be seen along the highway. The Kluane Mountains are among the highest in Canada, and icefields cover around half of the park's area.

Whitehorse is the capital of the Yukon and the center of the province's forestry and mining industries. The town, at mile 910 of the highway, retains a frontier atmosphere, and it is still possible to hear coyotes at night.

Historical Mile 836 marks the site of the Canol Project. This oil pipeline was built alongside the highway, to aid the military effort. The pipe ran an incredible 965 km (600 miles) to an oil refinery in Whitehorse.

Teslin Lake derives its name from the Tlingit language, meaning "long and narrow waters." The highway follows the 130-km long (80-mile) stretch of water, lined by snow-capped peaks. Today, the area attracts anglers eager to catch the plentiful trout, grayling, and pike, and hunters looking for game.

The Alaska Highway in winter is often covered in snow and affected by frost heave. Since it was opened to the public in 1949, teams of maintenance workers have ensured that the road is open year round.

Construction of the Highway

The Alaska Highway was built in under nine months by US army engineers and Canadian construction workers. The recruiting poster for workers warned: "This is no picnic… Men will have to fight swamps, rivers, ice, and cold. Mosquitoes, flies, and gnats will not only be annoying but will cause bodily harm. If you are not prepared to work under these… conditions, DO NOT APPLY."

The workers shared mobile army camps that were moved along the route as construction progressed. If a company got stuck in one of many dismal swamps, they employed such techniques as laying corduroy – where whole trees were laid side by side, then spread with gravel. In some places en route as many as five layers were required.

Bogged-down truck waits for corduroy to be laid

Watson Lake

Fort Nelson

Muncho Lake Provincial Park

BRITISH COLUMBIA

Kwadacha Wilderness Provincial Park

Spatsizi Plateau Wilderness Provincial Park

t. Edziza ovincial Park

Fort St. John

Dawson Creek

Peace River

The Peace River Valley section of the highway winds through fertile farmland, between Dawson Creek and Fort St. John. Before the Peace River suspension bridge was built in 1943, travelers crossed the river by ferry.

Historic Mile 588 or "Contact Creek" is the point where two teams of builders, from the north and south, met in 1942.

0 km   100
0 miles   100

The Sign Post Forest at Watson Lake has over 65,000 signs. The first was erected in 1942 by a GI missing his hometown of Danville, Illinois.

Key

▬ Alaska Hwy
═ Other roads
▢ National and Provincial Parks
-- Provincial boundaries

VANCOUVER AND VANCOUVER ISLAND

Looking out toward the waters of the Georgia Strait, Vancouver occupies one of the most beautiful settings of any world city. The coastal mountains form a majestic backdrop for the glass towers and copper-topped skyscrapers of the city. It was Captain James Cook who claimed the area for the British when he stepped ashore at Nootka Sound, Vancouver Island, in 1778. Until then the area had been inhabited for more than 10,000 years by the First Nations peoples, whose cultural heritage is celebrated in two of Canada's best museums: the UBC Museum of Anthropology in Vancouver and Victoria's Royal BC Museum. Established as a city after a fire destroyed the fledgling town of Granville in 1886, Vancouver offers historic districts, lush gardens, and wilderness parks within its environs. A short ferry ride away, Vancouver Island's world-famous Pacific Rim National Park is a major whale-watching center.

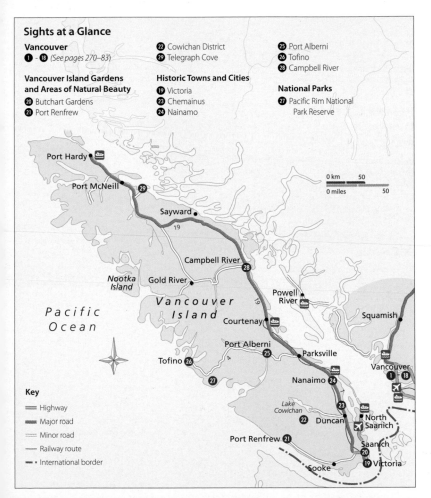

Sights at a Glance

Vancouver
- ❶ - ❽ (See pages 270–83)

Vancouver Island Gardens and Areas of Natural Beauty
- ⓴ Butchart Gardens
- ㉑ Port Renfrew

- ㉒ Cowichan District
- ㉙ Telegraph Cove

Historic Towns and Cities
- ⓳ Victoria
- ㉓ Chemainus
- ㉔ Nainamo

- ㉕ Port Alberni
- ㉖ Tofino
- ㉘ Campbell River

National Parks
- ㉗ Pacific Rim National Park Reserve

Key
- ═══ Highway
- ▬▬ Major road
- ═══ Minor road
- ─── Railway route
- ─ • ─ International border

◀ Partial view of Ga'akstalas and Sky chief totem poles in Stanley Park, Vancouver   For map symbols *see back flap*

Exploring Vancouver

The heart of Vancouver is its downtown area, a finger of land
bounded by the waters of English Bay. The city center radiates
from Robson Square. The 405-ha (1,000-acre) Stanley Park
occupies the tip of the peninsula, next to the West End.
The historic Chinatown and Gastown districts are
close to Main Street, the city's south to north axis.

Sights at a Glance

Historic Streets and Buildings

2 Chinatown
12 Old Hastings Mill Store Museum

Parks and Gardens

1 Dr. Sun Yat-Sen Classical
    Chinese Garden
9 Queen Elizabeth Park and
    Bloedel Conservatory
10 VanDusen Botanical Garden
13 Stanley Park
15 Lynn Canyon Park and
    Ecology Centre
16 Grouse Mountain
17 Capilano Suspension Bridge
18 Lighthouse Park

Modern Architecture

4 BC Place Stadium

Museums and Galleries

3 Science World
5 Vancouver Art Gallery
6 Vancouver Maritime Museum
7 Museum of Vancouver and
    H.R. MacMillan Space Centre
11 *University of British Columbia
    Museum of Anthropology pp280–81*

Shopping Areas

8 Granville Island
14 Lonsdale Quay Market

Key

- Sight
- Highway
- Major road
- Minor road
- Pedestrian walkway
- Railway
- Skytrain

For additional map symbols *see back flap*

Getting Around

Vancouver's transportation system includes the SeaBus, bus, and SkyTrain, one of the longest automated light rapid transit systems in the world. The Canada Line is a tunnel connecting the waterfront to Richmond and the airport. The SeaBus runs between Lonsdale Quay in North Vancouver and Waterfront Station downtown, where it is possible to connect with the bus and SkyTrain system. Many Vancouverites commute by car, and rush hour traffic is to be avoided because access to downtown is limited to a few bridges, including the hectic Lions Gate Bridge.

Vancouver's stunning harbor with mountains as a backdrop

Street-by-Street: Waterfront and Gastown

One of Vancouver's oldest areas, Gastown faces the waters of Burrard Inlet and lies between Columbia Street in the east and Burrard Street in the west. The district grew up around a saloon, opened in 1867 by John "Gassy Jack" Deighton whose statue can be seen on Maple Tree Square. Today, Gastown is a charming mix of cobblestone streets, restored 19th-century buildings, and storefronts. Chic boutiques and galleries line Powell, Carrall, and Cordova streets. Restaurants and cafés fill the mews, courtyards, and passages. Two eateries open onto Blood Alley, named for the city's first slaughterhouses. On the corner of Water and Cambie streets, visitors can hear the musical chimes of the steam clock every 15 minutes, and be entertained by street performers.

★ Canada Place
Canada Place is a waterside architectural marvel of white sails and glass that houses a hotel, a cruise ship terminal, and FlyOver Canada, which is a breathtaking flight simulator attraction.

The SeaBus
Stunning views of the harbor can be seen from the SeaBus, a catamaran that ferries passengers across Burrard Inlet between the central Waterfront Station and Lonsdale Quay in North Vancouver.

The Waterfront Station occupies the imposing 19th-century Canadian Pacific Railroad building.

★ Harbour Centre Tower
The Harbour Centre is a modern high-rise building best known for its tower. Rising 177 m (581 ft) above the city, on a clear day it is possible to see as far as Victoria on Vancouver Island.

For hotels and restaurants in this region see pp350–59 and pp364–83; for transport information see p411

Water Street
Much of the quaint charm of Gastown can be seen here. Water Street boasts gas lamps and cobblestones, as well as shops, cafés, and the famous steam clock.

Locator Map
See map pp270–71

Steam Clock
The world's first steam clock is still maintained by the man who built it in the 1970s. It toots every 15 minutes on the corner of Water and Cambie streets.

"Gassy" Jack Statue
Gastown is named after John "Gassy Jack" Deighton, an English sailor noted both for his endless chatter and for the saloon he opened here for the local sawmill workers in 1867.

The Inuit Gallery on Cambie Street offers a variety of original Inuit art such as jewelry and paintings.

WATERFRONT ROAD EAST

0 meters 100
0 yards 100

WATER STREET

OVA STREET WEST

CAMBIE STREET

ABBOTT STREET

CARRALL STREET

WEST

Shopping on Cordova St West is a delightful experience with its range of small galleries and trendy boutiques.

Triangular Building
Reminiscent of New York's Flatiron Building, this striking structure was built in 1908–9 as a hotel and forms the corner of Alexander and Powell streets. It is now an apartment building.

Key

— Suggested route

Peaceful pavilion in the Dr. Sun Yat-Sen Classical Chinese Garden

❶ Dr. Sun Yat-Sen Classical Chinese Garden

578 Carrall St. **Tel** (604) 662 3207. 🚇 & 🚌 Central Station, 19, 22. 🚢 Downtown terminal. **Open** variable hours so check website before visiting. **Closed** Jan 1, Dec 25. 🅿 📷 ♿ Ⓦ **vancouverchinesegarden.com**

Opened in 1986, the first full-sized Ming Dynasty-style classical Chinese garden built outside of China offers a refuge from Vancouver's bustling city center. The garden owes its tranquillity to ancient Taoist principles, which aimed to create a healthy balance between the contrasting forces of man and nature.

Over 50 skilled craftsmen came from Suzhou, China's Garden City, to construct the garden, using traditional tools and techniques. Pavilions and walkways were all built with materials from China. Many of the plants and trees symbolize different virtues. Willow is a symbol of feminine grace, and the plum and bamboo represent masculine strength. Complimentary Chinese tea rounds out the soothing atmosphere.

❷ Chinatown

Pender St. 🚌 East Hastings & East Pender Sts routes. Ⓦ **vancouver-chinatown.com**

Vancouver's Chinatown is older than the city itself. In 1858 the first wave of Chinese immigrants was drawn to Canada by the promise of gold. The Canadian Pacific Railroad attracted even more Chinese workers in the 1880s with jobs to build the new railroad. Today Chinatown stretches from Carrall to Gore Streets and still provides a warm welcome for more recent Asian immigrants.

Declared an historic area in 1970, Chinatown has restored many of its notable houses with their elaborately decorated roofs and covered balconies. The main drag, Pender Street, is the best place to view the architectural details that decorate the upperstories of the buildings, such as highly painted wooden balconies. Street signs with colorful Chinese characters add to the authentic atmosphere.

Bilingual sign in Chinatown

Whether buying mouthwatering duck, or watching the spicy dumplings known as won tons being made at top speed, or settling down to taste the myriad dishes available in numerous fine restaurants, the main attraction for the visitor is food. There is also a fascinating range of stores, from bakeries selling a selection of savory and sweet buns to traditional herbalists, and jewelers specializing in jade. In contrast to the bustling markets there are also several relaxing tearooms, as well as the nearby Dr. Sun Yat-Sen Chinese Garden, which also offers tea and cakes and has weekly evening concerts of Chinese music under the soft light of lanterns throughout the summer.

❸ Science World

1455 Quebec St. **Tel** (604) 443 7440. 🚇 Central Station. 🚌 Central Station. **Open** 10am–5pm Mon–Fri, 10am–6pm Sat & Sun. **Closed** Dec 25. 📷 ♿ Ⓦ **scienceworld.ca**

Overlooking the waters of False Creek, near the Main Street Railway Station, stands the 47-m- (155-ft-) high steel geodesic dome that now houses Vancouver's science museum, Science World. The dome was

The striking geodesic dome housing Vancouver's interactive Science World

For hotels and restaurants in this region see pp350–59 and pp364–83; for transport information see p411

designed for Expo '86 and inspired by American inventor R. Buckminster Fuller. It is now one of the city's most striking landmarks and home to the highly interactive science museum.

In the Eureka! Gallery, visitors can design their own inventions. The Sara Stern Search Gallery lets visitors touch the furs and bones of animals, while the Puzzles and Illusions Gallery boggles the mind with its optical tricks and displays. For 2- to 6-year-olds, the Kidspace Gallery provides a safe and colorful environment for learning and play. The outdoor Ken Spencer Science Park features interactive environmental exhibits.

The museum is renowned for its OMNIMAX® Theatre, where a huge screen shows films of flights through such epic landscapes as Mount Everest and the Grand Canyon, as well as Kelly Slater surfing in Tahiti.

❹ BC Place Stadium

777 Pacific Blvd. **Tel** (604) 669 2300. 🚇 Stadium. **Open** varies, depending on scheduled events. 🐾 🎦 May–Oct: Tue–Fri. ♿ **w** bcplacestadium.com

Standing out from the city's skyline, the state-of-the-art, retractable roof of the BC Place Stadium was unveiled in 2011. When the arena opened in 1983, it had a white fabric roof and was the first covered stadium in Canada and the largest air-supported dome in the world. The versatile stadium is able to convert in a matter of hours from a football field seating 60,000 people to a more intimate concert bowl seating up to 30,000.

Among the famous guests who have visited the dome are Queen Elizabeth II and Pope John Paul II. Visitors hoping to catch a glimpse of a celebrity or two can take behind-the-scenes tours to the locker rooms, playing fields, and media lounges. The stadium also houses the **BC Sports Hall of Fame and Museum**, which chronicles the history of the region's sporting heroes.

The state-of-the-art BC Place Stadium

🏛 **BC Sports Hall of Fame and Museum**
BC Place Stadium. **Tel** (604) 687 5520. **Open** 10am–5pm daily. 🐾 ♿ **w** bcsportshalloffame.com

❺ Vancouver Art Gallery

750 Hornby St. **Tel** (604) 662 4719. 🚇 Central Station. 🚌 Central Station. 🚌 3. **Open** 10am–5pm daily (to 9pm Tue; admission by donation). 🐾 ♿ **w** vanartgallery.bc.ca

What was once British Columbia's imposing provincial courthouse now houses the Vancouver Art Gallery. The building was designed in 1906 by Francis Rattenbury, an architect known for the Gothic style of Victoria's Parliament building and the Empress Hotel (see p284). The interior was modernized in 1983 by Arthur Erickson, another noted architect,

Decorative Victorian features on the Vancouver Art Gallery façade

who designed the UBC Museum of Anthropology (see pp280–81).

The Vancouver Art Gallery presents a full range of national and international art by groundbreaking contemporary artists and major historical figures, including the most significant body of work by British Columbian artist Emily Carr. The gallery also houses a permanent collection of 10,000 works of art. Visitors can take part in talks and tours, or visit interpretive sites and learning centers, as well as the Gallery Café and the Gallery Store.

❻ Vancouver Maritime Museum

1905 Ogden Ave. **Tel** (604) 257 8300. 🚇 & 🚌 Central Station. **Open** 10am–5pm Tue–Sat & holiday Mondays, noon–5pm Sun. **Closed** Dec 25. 🐾 (entry by donation 5–8pm Thu). ♿ **w** vancouvermaritime museum.com

Celebrating Vancouver's history as a port and trading center, this museum's star feature is the schooner, *St. Roch*. Built as a supply ship for the Mounties in 1928, in 1940–42 it was the first ship to navigate the Northwest Passage in both directions.

Other displays include *Map the Coast,* which tells the story of British Captain George Vancouver and the crews of the *Chatham* and the *Discovery*, who charted the inlets of the coast of BC in 1792. The Children's Maritime Discovery Centre has a powerful telescope through which the busy port can be viewed.

Steel sculpture in front of the Museum of Vancouver's distinctive façade

There are very few chain stores on the island, and the smaller stores are known for their variety, originality, and quality, displaying a range of local arts and crafts such as rugs, jewelry, and textiles.

The island is also a center for the performing arts and boasts several music, dance, and theater companies.

A daily public market offers a cornucopia of foods that reflect Vancouver's ethnic diversity. Waterside cafés and restaurants occupy the False Creek Shore where there was once a string of sawmills.

❼ Museum of Vancouver and H.R. MacMillan Space Centre

1100 Chestnut St., Vanier Park. **Tel** (604) 736 4431; Space Centre (604) 738 7827. 🚉 Central Station. 🚌 Central Station. 🚌 22. **Open** Museum: 10am– 5pm Mon–Wed, Fri–Sun; until 8pm Thu. Space Centre: 10am–3pm Mon–Fri, 10am–5pm Sat, noon–5pm Sun. 🅿 ♿ 🅆 **museumof vancouver.ca,** 🅆 **spacecentre.ca**

Located in Vanier Park near the Vancouver Maritime Museum (see p275), the Museum of Vancouver is a distinctive addition to the city's skyline. Built in 1967, the museum's curved, white, concrete roof is based on a First Nations hat. Outside, a stunning sculpture, which looks like a giant steel crab, sits in a fountain on the museum's south side.

Displays here include the Orientation Gallery, which re-creates British Columbia's rocky coastline and mountainous interior. Vancouver's history is explored from the culture of the First Nations of the area to the city's pioneering days. The museum is also noted for its depiction of everyday life, with exhibits such as an 1880s Canadian Pacific Railroad car, and the 1950s gallery, with a vintage Ford Thunderbird and a working jukebox.

At the same location, the H.R. MacMillan Space Centre is popular with both children and adults, who can explore the universe in the Planetarium and in the GroundStation Canada Theatre.

❽ Granville Island

1661 Duranleau St. **Tel** (604) 666 5784. 🚉 Central Station. 🚌 Central Station. 🚌 50. **Open** Market: 9am– 7pm daily; other stores: 10am–7pm daily. ♿ 🅆 **granvilleisland.com**

Today, this once down trodden industrial district has a glorious array of stores, galleries, and artists' studios in its brightly painted warehouses and tin sheds. The fire of 1886 destroyed almost all of fledgling Vancouver and drove people south across the water to Granville Island and beyond. Many of the early buildings were constructed on land reclaimed in 1915 to cope with the burgeoning lumber and iron industries.

Granville Island Brewing Company sign

❾ Queen Elizabeth Park and Bloedel Conservatory

4600 Cambie St. **Tel** Conservatory: (604) 257 8584. 🚌 15. **Open** Conservatory: 10am–5pm daily (May– mid-Sep: 9am–8pm Mon–Fri, 10am–8pm Sat & Sun). 🅿 for Conservatory. ♿

Queen Elizabeth Park is located on Little Mountain, Vancouver's highest hill (152-m/499-ft), and has fine views of the city. Despite being built on the site of two former stone quarries, the park's gardens are continually in bloom from early spring.

The plastic-domed Bloedel Conservatory is perched on top of the hill, and grows plants from many climactic zones in the world, from rainforest plants and trees to desert cacti. There are also free-flying colorful tropical birds and fishponds filled with Japanese carp.

The plastic dome of the Bloedel Conservatory in Queen Elizabeth Park

A dazzling fall display of reds and oranges, one of many attractions in Stanley Park

⑩ VanDusen Botanical Garden

5251 Oak St. **Tel** (604) 257 8463.
🚉 Central Station. 🚌 Central Station, 17. **Open** 10am–dusk daily. **Closed** Dec 25. 🅿️ ♿
🌐 **vandusengarden.org**

This 22-ha (55-acre) garden was opened in 1975. In 1960 the land was under threat from its original owners, the Canadian Pacific Railroad, who wanted to build high-rise apartments. It took a campaign by local people and a donation from Mr W.J. VanDusen, a wealthy local businessman, to save the site.

Today, visitors enjoy a spectacular display of over 7,500 families of plants from six continents, set among lakes and marble sculptures. The Perennial Garden is filled with roses in summer, while September heralds the blazing reds and oranges of fall. The Visitor Center is leading the Garden's green initiatives: the roof uses solar panels and collects rainwater to be used throughout the gardens.

Marble statue in Botanical Gardens

⑪ University of British Columbia Museum of Anthropology

See pp280–81.

⑫ Old Hastings Mill Store Museum

1575 Alma Rd. **Tel** (604) 734 1212. 🚌 4th Ave. route. **Open** Jun 15–Sep 15: 1–4pm Tue–Sun; Sep 16–Dec 1 & Feb 15–Jun 14: 1–4pm Sat & Sun. **Closed** Dec & Jan. Donation. ♿
🌐 **hastings-mill-museum.ca**

The Old Hastings Mill Store Museum was Vancouver's first general store and post office and one of the few wooden buildings to survive the Great Fire of 1886. Built in 1865, it was moved from its original site at Gastown in 1930 to the shores of Jericho Beach and then to its present home on Alma Street, at the corner of Point Grey Road. Starting in the 1940s, local people contributed a variety of historic artifacts, and today it is an interesting small museum. Behind the pretty clapboard exterior, the museum's exhibits include a range of Victorian artifacts such as a horse-drawn cab, antique sewing machines, and an

The Old Hastings Mill Store Museum, one of Vancouver's oldest buildings

extensive collection of native artifacts including impressive hand-woven baskets.

⑬ Stanley Park

2099 Beach Ave. **Tel** (604) 257 8400.
🚉 Central Station. 🚌 Central Station, 123, 135. ⛴ Horseshoe Bay. **Open** daily. ♿

This is a magnificent 404-ha (1,000-acre) park of tamed wilderness, just a few blocks from downtown, that was originally home to the Musqueam and Squamish native Canadians. Named after Lord Stanley, Governor General of Canada, the land was made a park by the local council in 1886. It offers visitors the opportunity to experience a range of typical Vancouver attractions. There are beaches, hiking trails, and fir and cedar woods as well as wonderful views of the harbor, English Bay, and the coastal mountains. Bicycles can be rented for the popular ride around the 10-km (6.5-mile) perimeter seawall. The park is also home to the **Vancouver Aquarium** where visitors can watch dolphins and beluga whales through the glass of enormous tanks. The African penguins at Penguin Point are a popular exhibit.

🐟 **Vancouver Aquarium**
Stanley Park. **Tel** (604) 659 3474. **Open** Jul & Aug: 9:30am–6pm daily; Sep–Jun: 10am–5pm daily. 🅿️ 🎦 ♿
🌐 **vanaqua.org**

⑪ University of British Columbia Museum of Anthropology

Founded in 1947, this outstanding museum houses one of the world's finest collections of Northwest coast native peoples' art. Designed by Canadian architect Arthur Erickson in 1976, the museum is housed in a stunning building over-looking mountains and sea. The tall posts and huge windows of the Great Hall were inspired by the post-and-beam architecture of Haida houses and are a fitting home for a display of full-size totem poles, canoes, and feast dishes. Through the windows of the Great Hall, the visitor can see the magnificent outdoor sculpture complex, which includes two houses designed by contemporary Haida artist Bill Reid.

★ **The Great Hall**
The imposing glass and concrete structure of the Great Hall is the perfect setting for totem poles, canoes, and sculptures.

Outdoor Haida Houses and Totem Poles

Set overlooking the water, these two Haida houses and collection of totem poles are faithful to the artistic tradition of the Haida and other tribes of the Pacific northwest, such as the Salish, Tsimshan, and Kwakiutl. Animals and mythic creatures representing various clans are carved in cedar on these poles and houses, made between 1959 and 1963 by Vancouver's favorite contemporary Haida artist Bill Reid and Namgis artist Doug Cranmer.

Carved red cedar totem poles

Climbing figures
These climbing figures are thought to have decorated the interior of First Nations family houses. Carved from cedar planks, the spare style is typical of Coast Salish sculpture.

Ceramic jug
This beautifully decorated jug was made in Central Europe in 1674 by members of the Anabaptist religious sect. The foliage motifs are in contrast to the freely sketched animals that run around the base.

★ **The Raven and
the First Men** (1980)
Carved in laminated yellow
cedar by Bill Reid, this modern
interpretation of a Haida creation
myth depicts the raven, a wise
and wily trickster, trying to
coax mankind out into
the world from a
giant clamshell.

VISITORS' CHECKLIST

Practical Information
6393 NW Marine Drive.
Tel (604) 822 5087.
Open Apr–Sep: 10am–5pm daily
(to 9pm Tue); Oct–May: 10am–
5pm Wed–Sun (to 9pm Tue).
Closed Dec 25 & 26.
🚫 ♿ ✏ 📷 🌐 **moa.ubc.ca**

Transport
🚌 4 UBC, 10 UBC.

Gallery Guide

*The museum's collections are arranged on
one level. The Ramp gallery leads to the Great
Hall, featuring the cultures of Northwest
coast First Nations peoples. The Multiversity
Galleries contain artifacts from other
cultures, and a range of 15th- to
19th-century European ceramics
is housed in the Koerner
European Ceramics Gallery.*

Wooden Frontlet
Decorated with abalone shell, this
wooden frontlet was a ceremonial
head-dress worn only on important
occasions such as births
and marriages.

**Red cedar carved
front doors**
This detail comes from the
set of stunning carved red
cedar doors that guard the
entrance to the museum.
Created in 1976 by a group
of First Nations artists from
the 'Ksan cultural center
near Hazelton, the doors
show the history of the first
people of the Skeena River
region in British Columbia.

Key

☐ The Great Hall

☐ Bill Reid Rotunda

☐ Multiversity Galleries

☐ Koerner European
Ceramics Gallery

☐ Temporary exhibition space

☐ Michael M. Ames Theatre

☐ Non-exhibition space

⑭ Lonsdale Quay Market

123 Carrie Cates Ct., North Vancouver.
Tel (604) 985 6261. 🚋 Lonsdale.
Open 9am–7pm daily. ♿
Ⓦ lonsdalequay.com

The striking concrete-and-glass building housing the Lonsdale Quay Market forms part of the North Shore SeaBus terminal. The market has a floor devoted to food – everything from fresh-baked bread to blueberries – as well as an array of cafés and restaurants that serve a variety of ethnic cuisines. On the second floor, visitors will find specialty shops offering a wide choice of hand-crafted products and gift items from local designers, as well as Kid's Alley, a row of child-oriented shops. The complex includes a hotel and spa, a pub, and a nightclub.

The modern fountain at Lonsdale Quay

⑮ Lynn Canyon Park and Ecology Centre

3663 Park Rd. **Tel** (604) 990 3755.
🚋 Hastings. 🚋 Lonsdale Quay, then bus 228 or 229. **Open** daily. Ecology Centre Jun–Sep: 10am–5pm daily; Oct–May: 10am–5pm Mon–Fri, noon–4pm Sat & Sun. **Closed** Jan 1, Dec 25 & 26. 🐾 donation. 📷 💻
Ⓦ dnv.org/ecology

Located between Mount Seymour and Grouse Mountain, Lynn Canyon Park is a popular hiking destination noted for its lush second-growth temperate

rain forest. The original 90-meter (295-ft) trees were logged in the early 20th century and a few of the huge stumps with circum-ferences of up to 11 meters (36 ft) can still be seen lying on the forest floor. Some of the stumps have springboard notches left by lumberjacks of the time.

Several marked trails, some of them steep and rugged, lead through the canyon, with longer hikes heading into surrounding park land. Many of the trails, however, are gentle strolls through Douglas fir, western hemlock, and western red cedar. If you venture far enough into the forest it is possible to see black bears, cougars, and blacktail deer, but most visitors keep to the main trails where they are more likely to see squirrels, jays, woodpeckers, and banana slugs, which can grow to lengths of 26 cm (10 inches). There are wonderful views from the 50-m (164-ft) high suspension bridge that crosses the canyon. From here, it's a short walk to 30 Foot Pool, a popular summer spot for sunbathing and swimming. A 40-minute walk takes hikers to the beautiful Twin Falls.

The nearby Ecology Centre offers guided walks, shows natural history films, and features interesting displays on the flora, fauna, and ecology of the area. Global environ-mental concerns are also covered.

Panoramic view of Vancouver's skyline from Grouse Mountain

⑯ Grouse Mountain

6400 Nancy Greene Way. **Tel** (604) 980 9311. 🚋 Lonsdale Quay. 🚌 236.
Open 9am–10pm daily. 🍽 ♿ 🚻
💻 Ⓦ grousemountain.com

From the summit of Grouse Mountain visitors experience the grandeur of BC's dramatic landscape and stunning views of Vancouver. On a clear day it is possible to see as far as Vancouver Island in the west, the Coastal Mountains to the north and toward the Columbia Mountains in the east.

A tough 3-km (2-mile) trail goes to the top of the 1,127-m (3,700-ft) mountain, but most visitors choose to take the Skyride cable car. In the summer there are many activities including mountain bike tours, nature walks, and hang-gliding competitions, not to mention logger sports such as chain-saw sculpture shows. In the winter, the summit has all the amenities of a ski resort, including ski schools, 26 ski runs, equipment rental, snowboarding, and 13 illuminated slopes for night skiing.

At the Refuge for Endangered Wildlife, an enclosed natural habitat that is home to two orphaned grizzly bears and three gray wolves, wildlife rangers give daily talks. The Theatre in the Sky presents a video that takes viewers on an aerial tour of BC; another video tells the tale of the orphaned bears.

The Skyride cable car, Grouse Mountain

⑰ Capilano Suspension Bridge

3735 Capilano Rd., North Vancouver.
Tel (604) 985 7474. 🚌 Highlands 236.
Open daily (hours vary according to season). **Closed** Dec 25. 🏷 🎫 May–Oct. ✏ 📷 **W** capbridge.com

The Capilano Suspension Bridge has been a popular tourist attraction since it was built in 1889. Pioneering Scotsman George Grant Mackay, drawn by the wild beauty of the place, had already built a small cabin overlooking the Capilano Canyon. Access to the river below was almost impossible from the cabin, and it is said that Mackay built the bridge so that his son, who loved fishing, could easily reach the Capilano River.

The present bridge, which dates from 1956 and is the fourth to be constructed here, hangs 70 m (230 ft) above the canyon and spans 137 m (450 ft), making it one of the longest such bridges in the world. Nature lovers are drawn by the views and the chance to wander through old-growth woods (old trees that have never been felled) past trout ponds and a 61-m (200-ft) waterfall. The Treetops Adventure attraction includes seven suspension bridges through evergreens, taking participants up 30 m (100 ft) above the forest floor.

Atkinson Lighthouse

⑱ Lighthouse Park

Off Beacon Lane, West Vancouver.
Open 6am–10pm daily.
W lighthousepark.ca

Named after the hexagonal lighthouse built at the mouth of Burrard Inlet in 1910 to guide ships through the foggy channel, Lighthouse Park is an unspoiled area with 75 ha (185 acres) of old growth forest and wild, rocky coast. The trees here have never been logged and some of the majestic Douglas firs are over 500 years old.

There is a variety of hiking trails in the park, some leading to a viewpoint near the 18-m (60-ft) Point Atkinson Lighthouse. On a clear day one can see stunning vistas across the Strait of Georgia all the way to Vancouver Island. A 2-hour hike leads through about 5 km (3 miles) of old-growth forest, taking walkers through the fairly rugged terrain of moss-covered gullies and steep rocky outcrops with breathtaking views of the sea and surrounding area. Wear good walking shoes or boots, stay on the trails and be prepared for inclement weather.

The drive to the park itself is spectacular. Scenic **Marine Drive** winds along the West Vancouver coastline edging past beaches, clinging to rocky shoreline and passing some of Canada's priciest real estate. On the way, there are a couple of towns that are worth a stop. **Ambleside** has a long beach, which is a favorite with families and dogs but packed on sunny summer weekends. From here there are great views of Stanley Park and the Lions Gate Bridge. A seawall walkway leads to Dundarave Pier, with panoramic views sweeping from Vancouver right around to the Strait of Georgia. **Dundarave** itself is a small village with a pleasing cluster of shops, cafés, and restaurants, as well as a beach that is not so busy as the beach at Ambleside.

The Capilano Suspension Bridge crossing the dramatic and tree-covered Capilano Canyon

⑲ Victoria

A quiet, attractive city, Victoria's reputation for having an old-fashioned, seaside-town atmosphere is enhanced in the summer by the abundance of flowers in hanging baskets and window boxes that decorate every lampost, balcony, and storefront. Established as a Hudson's Bay Company fur-trading post in 1843 by James Douglas, Victoria had its risqué moments during its gold rush years (1858–63), when thousands of prospectors drank in 60 or more saloons on Market Square. Victoria was established as the provincial capital of British Columbia in 1871 but was soon outgrown by Vancouver, now BC's largest city. Today, Victoria is still the province's political center as well as one of its most popular attractions for visitors.

Fishing boats and pleasure craft moored in Victoria's Inner Harbour

Octagonal main dome in the Parliament Buildings

Exploring Victoria

A stroll along Victoria's Inner Harbour takes in many of the city's main attractions, such as the Royal British Columbia Museum with its dramatic depictions of the geology and native cultures of the region. Dominating the area are two late 19th-century buildings: the Fairmont Empress Hotel and the Parliament Buildings, designed by noted architect, and Victoria's adopted son, Francis Rattenbury. Between Fort Street and View Street is the four-story shopping mall, the Bay Centre. Bastion Square, with its restaurants and boutiques, lies to the south of Market Square and its restored 1850s buildings.

🏛 Parliament Buildings
501 Belleville St. **Tel** (250) 387 3046. **Open** 9am–5pm Mon–Fri. **Closed** Jan 1, Dec 25. ♿ 📷 Mon–Fri (summer: 6pm Mon–Fri, weekends). 🌐 leg.bc.ca

Victoria's many-domed Parliament Buildings are an impressive sight, particularly at night when the façades are illuminated by thousands of lights. Designed by Francis Rattenbury, the buildings were completed in 1897. Rattenbury, a 25-year-old British architect who had arrived in British Columbia only the year before, won a provincial competition to design the new Parliament Buildings. He went on to design several of the province's structures, including the nearby Fairmont Empress Hotel.

The history of British Columbia is depicted throughout the Parliament Buildings. A statue of explorer Captain George Vancouver is perched on top of the main dome. Inside, large murals show scenes from the past.

The Parliament Buildings illuminate the waters of the Inner Harbour

For hotels and restaurants in this region see pp350–59 and pp364–83; for transport information see p411

Sights at a Glance

① Market Square
② Bastion Square
③ Maritime Museum
 of British Columbia
④ The Bay Centre
⑤ Fairmont Empress Hotel
⑥ Parliament Buildings

⑦ Royal BC Museum
 See pp288–9
⑧ Thunderbird Park
⑨ Helmcken House
⑩ Beacon Hill Park
⑪ Emily Carr House

↑ ✈ **Victoria Airport**
 25 km (15 miles)

0 meters 250
0 yards 250

Bastion Square is a popular lunch spot
for locals and visitors

🏨 Fairmont Empress Hotel

721 Government St. **Tel**
(250) 384 8111. **Open** daily.
🚻 🌐 fairmont.com/
empress-victoria

Completed in 1908 to
a Francis Rattenbury
design, the Empress is
one of Victoria's best-
loved sights. Close to
the Parliament Buildings,
the hotel overlooks the
Inner Harbour and
dominates the skyline
with its ivy-covered
Edwardian splendor.
Visitors can sample the
luxurious decor of the
hotel's public bars and
lounges, such as the
Empress Room, and the
Palm Court with its lovely
Tiffany-glass dome.

🏛 Bastion Square

Government St. **Tel** (250) 885 1387.
Open daily. 🚻 🌐 bastionsquare.ca
This beautifully restored square
faces Victoria's picturesque
harbor and contains some of
the city's oldest 19th-century
buildings. What were once
luxury hotels and offices, built
during the boom era of the late
1800s, now house several
eclectic restaurants. Restoration
began in 1963 when it was
discovered that the Hudson's
Bay Company's fur-trading post
Fort Victoria, established in 1843,
once stood on this site. Today,
this pedestrian square includes
the MacDonald Block building,
built in 1863 in Italianate style,

with elegant cast-iron columns
and arched windows. The old
courthouse, built in 1889,
houses the Maritime Museum
of British Columbia. In summer,
both visitors and workers lunch
in the courtyard cafés.

🏛 Market Square

560 Johnson St. **Tel** (250) 386 2441.
Open 10am–5pm Mon–Fri,
11am–4pm Sun & public hols.
Closed Jan 1, Dec 25. 🚻 limited.
🌐 marketsquare.ca

Two blocks north of Bastion
Square on the corner of
Johnson Street, Market Square
has some of the finest Victorian
saloon, hotel, and store façades
in Victoria. Most of the buildings
were built in the 1880s and
1890s, during the boom period
of the Klondike Gold Rush. After
decades of neglect, the area
received a face-lift in 1975.
The square is now a shoppers'
paradise, with a variety of stores
selling everything from books and
jewelry to musical instruments
and other arts and crafts.

Key to Symbols *see back flap*

One of the giant totem poles on display at Thunderbird Park

❂ Thunderbird Park

Cnr Belleville & Douglas Streets.

This compact park lies at the entrance to the Royal British Columbia Museum *(see pp288–9)* and is home to an imposing collection of plain and painted giant totem poles. During the summer months it is possible to watch native artists in the Thunderbird Park Carving Studio producing these handsome carved totems. The poles show and preserve the legends of many different tribes from the aboriginal peoples of the Northwest Coast.

🏛 Helmcken House

10 Elliot St. Square. **Tel** (250) 356 7226.
Open 10am–5pm Mon–Sat (to 9pm Thu), 1–5pm Sun. **Closed** Mon Sep–May. 🅿 🚻 🎫

Located in Elliot Square in the Inner Harbour area, the home of Hudson's Bay Company employee Dr. John Sebastian Helmcken was built in 1852 and is thought to be one of the oldest houses in British Columbia. The young doctor built his house with Douglas fir trees felled in the surrounding forest. This simple but elegantly designed clapboard dwelling contains many of the original furnishings, including the piano, which visitors are permitted to play. Among other exhibits are a collection of antique dolls and the family's personal belongings, such as clothes, shoes, and toiletries.

🏛 Maritime Museum of British Columbia

28 Bastion Square. **Tel** (250) 385 4222.
Open 10am–5pm daily. 🚻
🌐 **mmbc.bc.ca**

At this fascinating three-story museum of coastal history, exhibits tell the stories of the giant canoes of the Coast Salish First Nations Peoples. Other displays include the tall ships of the first European explorers, pirate ships, and whalers. Tumultuous tales of coastal shipwrecks are gruesomely captivating. On the top floor is the former courtroom of the notorious Sir Matthew Baillie Begbie, also known as the "Hanging Judge." The 19th-century courtroom is preserved in all its glory.

🏬 The Bay Centre

1150 Douglas St. **Tel** (250) 952 5690.
Open 10am–6pm Mon–Wed & Sat, 10am–9pm Thu–Fri, 11am–6pm Sun. ♿ 🌐 **thebaycentre.ca**

The Bay Centre is a shopping mall within walking distance of the Inner Harbour and was intially built behind the façades of several historic buildings on Government Street. The Driard Hotel, designed in 1892 by John Wright, was saved from demolition by a public campaign, as were the fronts of the 1910 Times Building and the fine, 19th-century Lettice and Sears Building. Behind these elegant façades, there are three floors of stores selling everything from fashion and gifts to handmade chocolates and gourmet food.

🏠 Emily Carr House

207 Government St. **Tel** (250) 383 5843. **Open** May–Oct: 11am–4pm Tue–Sat. 🚻 ♿ 🎫 🌐 **emilycarr.com**

Emily Carr, one of Canada's best-known artists *(see pp36–7)*, was born in 1871 in this charming, yellow clapboard house. It was built in 1864 by prominent architects Wright and Saunders, under instruction from Emily's father, Richard Carr. Located just a few minutes walk from Inner Harbour, both the house and its English-style garden are open to visitors. All the rooms are appropriately furnished in late 19th-century period style, with some original family pieces. Visitors can see the dining room where Emily taught her first art classes to local children. Emily's drawing of her father still sits upon the mantel in the sitting room where, as an eight-year-old, she made her first sketches.

❂ Beacon Hill Park

Douglas St. **Tel** (250) 361 0600.
Open daily. ♿

In the late 19th century this delightful park was used for stabling horses, but in 1888

Emily Carr House where renowned painter Emily Carr was born

John Blair, a Scottish landscape gardener, redesigned the park to include two lakes and initiated extensive tree planting. Once a favorite haunt of artist Emily Carr, this peaceful 74.5-ha (184-acre) park is now renowned for its lofty old trees (including the rare Garry oaks, some of which are over 400 years old), picturesque duck ponds, and a 100-year-old cricket pitch.

🏛 Art Gallery of Greater Victoria

1040 Moss St. **Tel** (250) 384 4171. **Open** 10am–5pm Tue–Sat; 10am–9pm Thu, noon–5pm Sun. 🅿 🆆 **aggv.ca**

This popular gallery's contemporary facilities are located in the heritage neighborhood of Rockland, a few blocks west of Craigdarroch Castle. Inside, visitors will find a diverse presentation of exhibitions, including contemporary, Canadian, heritage, and national touring exhibitions. On permanent exhibition is the work of British Columbia's premier artist, Emily Carr, featuring her paintings of the British Columbian coastal forests and depictions of the lives of native peoples, as well as excerpts from her writings and archival photographs.

Shinto shrine detail at the Art Gallery

In its quaint courtyard garden, the gallery also houses the only original Japanese Shinto shrine in North America.

🏰 Craigdarroch Castle

1050 Joan Cres. **Tel** (250) 592 5323. **Open** Jun–Sep: 9am–7pm daily; Oct–May: 10am–4:30pm daily. **Closed** Jan 1, Dec 25, 26. 🅿 🆆 **thecastle.ca**

Completed in 1890, Craigdarroch Castle was the pet project of respected local coal millionaire Robert Dunsmuir. Although not a real castle, the design of this manor home was based on that of his ancestral home in Scotland and mixes several architectural styles such as Roman and French Gothic.

When the castle was threatened with demolition in 1959, a group of local citizens formed a society that successfully battled for its preservation. Today, the restored interior of the castle is a museum that offers an insight into the lifestyle of a wealthy Canadian entrepreneur.

The castle is noted for having one of the finest collections of Art Nouveau lead-glass windows in North America, and many of the rooms and hallways retain their patterned wood parquet floors and intricately carved paneling in white oak, cedar, and mahogany. Every room is filled with opulent Victorian furnishings from the late 19th century and decorated in original colors such as deep greens, pinks, and rusts. Several layers of the paint have been painstakingly removed from the drawing room ceiling to reveal the original hand-painted and stencilled decorations beneath, including wonderfully detailed butterflies and lions.

A tower at Craigdarroch Castle in the French Gothic style of a château

🏛 Government House

1401 Rockland Ave. **Tel** (250) 387 2080. **Open** daily (gardens only). ♿ 🆆 **ltgov.bc.ca**

The present Government House building was completed in 1959 after fire destroyed the 1903 building, which was designed by renowned architect Francis Rattenbury.

As the official residence of the Lieutenant-Governor of British Columbia, the Queen's representative to the province, the house is not open to the public, but visitors can view 5.6 ha (14 acres) of stunning public gardens with beautiful lawns, ponds, an English country garden, and a Victorian rose garden. From Pearke's Peak, a mount formed from the rocky outcrops that surround the property, there are marvelous views of the grounds.

The 1959 Government House, built with blue and pink granite

The Royal British Columbia Museum

The Royal British Columbia Museum tells the story of this region through its natural and human history. The museum is regarded as one of the best in Canada for the striking way it presents its exhibits. A series of imaginative dioramas re-create the sights, sounds, and even smells of areas such as the seashore, the ocean, and the coast forest, all of which occupy the second floor Natural History Gallery.

The region's history is presented on the third floor, including a reconstruction of an early 20th-century town. Visitors can experience the street life of the time in a cinema showing silent films and a saloon. The collection of native art and culture in the First Peoples Gallery includes a ceremonial Big House.

Third Floor

19th-century Chinatown
As part of an 1875 street scene, this Chinese herbalist's store displays a variety of herbs used in traditional Chinese medicine.

★ First Peoples Gallery
Made of cedar bark and spruce root in around 1897, this hat bears the mountain goat crest of the raven clan.

First Nations' Ceremonial Masks
The mouse, raccoon, and kingfisher are carved on these masks belonging to the Martin family, who wore them to dance on ceremonial occasions.

Key to Floor Plan

- ☐ First Peoples Gallery
- ☐ Modern History Gallery
- ☐ Feature exhibits
- ☐ Natural History Gallery
- ☐ National Geographic IMAX theater
- ☐ Non-exhibition space

Exterior of the museum
The museum's main exhibits building was opened in 1968 after years of having to occupy several sites in and around the Legislative Buildings. The museum also houses provincial archives and a cultural precinct.

For hotels and restaurants in this region see pp350–59 and pp364–83; for transport information see p411

Modern History Gallery
A variety of streets, stores and public buildings, from the 1700s to 1990s, are re-created in this gallery. Here, the Grand Hotel occupies an authentic wooden sidewalk.

VISITORS' CHECKLIST

Practical Information
675 Belleville St.
Tel 1 888 447 7977
or (250) 356 7226.
Open 10am–5pm daily. **Closed**
Jan 1, Dec 25. 🌐 royalbcmuseum.bc.ca

Transport
🚌 5, 28, 30.

Second
Floor

★ Natural History Gallery
A full-size prehistoric tusked mammoth guards the entrance to the Natural History Gallery which includes several lifelike dioramas that re-create British Columbia's coastal forests and ocean life since the last Ice Age.

★ Seashore Diorama
This diorama uses sound, film, lighting, and realistic animals such as this northern sea lion.

First
Floor

Gallery Guide
The main exhibits of the museum are housed on the second and third floors. The Natural History Gallery, on the second floor, reconstructs a range of environments from the Coast Seashore to the Old Growth Forest displays. The third floor has the First Peoples and Modern History galleries.

Main Entrance

The lily pond in the formal Italian garden at Butchart Gardens

⑳ Butchart Gardens

800 Benvenuto Ave., Brentwood Bay. **Tel** (250) 652 4422, 1 866 652 4422. 🚊 Victoria. 🚌 Victoria. **Open** 9am daily; closing times vary by season. 🅿 ♿ 🔳 butchartgardens.com

These beautiful gardens were begun in 1904 by Mrs. Jennie Butchart, the wife of a cement manufacturer. When her husband moved west to quarry limestone near Victoria, Mrs. Butchart began to design a new garden, which would stretch down to the water at Tod Inlet. When the limestone deposits ran out, Mrs. Butchart decided to add to her burgeoning garden by landscaping the quarry site into a sunken garden which now boasts a lake overhung by willow and other trees laden with blossom in spring. A huge rock left in the quarry was turned into a towering rock garden. Today visitors can climb stone steps to see stunning views from the top. As their popularity grew, so the gardens were filled with thousands of rare plants collected from around the world by Mrs. Butchart.

Today, the gardens are arranged into distinct areas. There is a formal Italian garden with a lily pond that features a fountain bought in Italy by the Butcharts in 1924. The rose garden is filled with the scent of hundreds of different blooms in summer. During the summer the gardens are illuminated and play host to evening musical performances.

㉑ Port Renfrew

🗺 200. 🛈 2070 Phillips Rd., Sooke (250) 642 6351.

Port Renfrew is a small, friendly fishing village and ex-logging town. A popular daytrip from Victoria, the town offers visitors access to Botanical Beach where a unique sandstone shelf leaves rock pools filled with marine life such as starfish at low tide.

Port Renfrew is famed for its hiking along old logging roads: the Sandbar Trail goes through a Douglas fir plantation to a large river sandbar where it is possible to swim at low tide. A more serious hike is the 47-km (29-mile) Juan de Fuca Marine Trail from Port Renfrew to China Beach. This trail offers a range of hikes, from treks lasting several days to short beach walks. The town is one of two starting points for the West Coast Trail in Pacific Rim National Park Reserve (see pp292–3).

㉒ Cowichan District

🚌 & 🚌 from Duncan. 🛈 381A Trans-Canada Hwy, Duncan (250) 746 4636, 1 888 303 3337. 🔳 cvrd.bc.ca

Located on the south central coast of Vancouver Island, about 60 km (37 miles) north of Victoria, the Cowichan District incorporates both the Chemainus and Cowichan Valleys. Cowichan means "warm land" in the language of the Cowichan peoples, one of British Columbia's largest First Nations groups; the area's mild climate means the waters of Cowichan Lake are warm enough to swim in during the summer months. The largest

freshwater lake on the island, Lake Cowichan offers excellent fishing, canoeing, and hiking.

Between the town of Duncan and the lake lies the Valley Demonstration Forest, which has scenic lookouts and signs explaining forest management. Duncan is known as the City of Totems as it displays several poles in the downtown area. The Quw'utsun' Cultural and Conference Centre shows films on the history of the Cowichan Tribe. The gift shop sells traditional artifacts including Cowichan sweaters. You can also visit a First Nations carver in his studio at the Maritime Centre in Cowichan Bay.

Stunning vista over Lake Cowichan in the Cowichan Valley

㉓ Chemainus

🗺 4,100. 🚌 🚌 🚢 🛈 9796 Willow St. (250) 246 3944. 🔳 chemainus.bc.ca

When the local sawmill closed in the late 1970s, picturesque Chemainus transformed itself into a major attraction with the painting of giant murals around the town that depict the history of the region. Local artists continued the project and today there are more than 40 murals on the outside walls of local buildings, based on real events in the town's past.

First Nations' faces looking down from a Chemainus town mural

Pleasure craft and fishing boats moored in Nanaimo harbor

Larger-than-life images of Cowichan natives, pioneers, and loggers have revitalized the town. Visitors enjoy browsing in the town's various antique stores and relaxing in the many pleasant sidewalk cafés.

Environs

Some 70 km (45 miles) south of Chemainus, Swartz Bay is the departure point on Vancouver Island for ferries to the Southern Gulf Islands and the mainland. Visitors are drawn to the 200 mostly uninhabited islands by their tranquility and natural beauty. It is possible to stroll along empty beaches where sightings of eagles and turkey vultures are common. There are fishing charters for visitors who enjoy catching salmon and cod, and kayaking tours offering stops on isolated shores to view otters, seals, and marine birds.

Salt Spring is the most populated Gulf island, with about 10,500 inhabitants. In the summer, visitors come to wander around the pretty village of Ganges, where a busy marina surrounds the wooden pier. The village offers stores, cafés, galleries, and colorful markets.

㉔ Nanaimo

🗺 78,800. ✈ 🚌 🚆 ⛴ ℹ 2450 Northfield Rd. (250) 751 1556, 1 800 663 7337. 🌐 tourismnanaimo.com

Originally the site of five Coast Salish native villages, Nanaimo was established as a coal-mining town in the 1850s. As the second-largest city on Vancouver Island, Nanaimo has plenty of malls and businesses along the Island Highway, but it is the Old City Quarter on the waterfront in the heart of downtown Nanaimo that visitors enjoy most.

The Old City Quarter has many 19th-century buildings, including the Nanaimo Court House, designed by Francis Rattenbury in 1895. The **Vancouver Island Conference Centre** includes a re-creation of an old schoolroom, a First Nations exhibit, and a Sports Hall of Fame. Other exhibits include native artifacts displayed in a village diorama.

🏛 **Vancouver Island Conference Centre**
101 Gordon St. **Tel** (250) 244 4050. **Open** 10am–5pm daily. 🅿 ♿ 📷 book in advance.

㉕ Port Alberni

🗺 25,000. ✈ 🚌 ⛴ ℹ 2533 Port Alberni Hwy (250) 724 6535.

Port Alberni sits at the head of Alberni Inlet, which stretches 48 km (30 miles) from the interior of Vancouver Island to the Pacific Ocean in the west. The town now depends upon hikers, kayakers, and wildlife watchers, and it is a popular haunt for salmon fishers. Every year the Salmon Derby and Festival offers thousands of Canadian dollars for the biggest fish caught during the last weekend in August. The town's other attractions include a 1929 locomotive offering train rides along the waterfront during the summer from the 1912 Port Alberni Railway Station to the steam operated MacLean Sawmill. Many visitors come to cruise on the freighter M.V. *Frances Barkley*. The ships deliver mail down the inlet, as well as offering trips to Ucluelet, Bamfield, and other waypoints near the Pacific Rim National Park. It also carries kayaks and canoes for those hoping to sail around the Broken Group Islands *(see p292)*.

Just east of Port Alberni, it is possible to hike among awe-inspiring old growth Douglas firs and red cedars in the outstanding Cathedral Grove, located in the MacMillan Provincial Park.

A carved eagle soars over Port Alberni Pier

A 1929 steam locomotive offering rides along Port Alberni's waterfront

㉖ Tofino

🏠 1,700. 🛈 1426 Pacific Rim Hwy.
1 888 720 3414. 🌐 **tourismtofino.com**

Once a timber town, Tofino is now a busy tourist center for the Pacific Rim National Park Reserve *(see below)*. Its sandy beaches and woodland trails attract visitors all year round; in the summer, surfing, hiking, kayaking, and whale-watching also draw the crowds. The Pacific Rim National Park Reserve begins just past the junction of Tofino/Ucluelet.

In Tofino, the **Eagle Aerie Gallery** displays works by First Nations artist Roy Vickers, while The **Whale Centre Maritime Museum**

Sunset at Chesterman Beach, Tofino

showcases artifacts from local shipwrecks and First Nations history. It also organizes whale-watching excursions.

Just north of Tofino, the UNESCO Biosphere Reserve of Clayoquot Sound features a diverse range of ecosystems, including islands, mountains, and temperate rainforests. Boating and paddling day trips can be arranged through

several tour operators in Tofino, and hiking trails are easily accessible on a few islands.

🏛 **Eagle Aerie Gallery**
350 Campbell St. **Tel** (250) 725 3235.
Open 10am–5pm daily.

🏛 **The Whale Centre Maritime Museum**
411 Campbell St. **Tel** (250) 725 2132.
Open 9am–8pm daily.
🌐 **tofinowhalecentre.com**

㉘ Campbell River

🏠 32,000. 🛈 1235 Shoppers Row (250) 830 0411.
🌐 **campbellrivertourism.com**

Located on the northeast shore of Vancouver Island, Campbell River is renowned as a center for salmon fishing. The waters of

㉗ Pacific Rim National Park Reserve

The Pacific Rim National Park Reserve is composed of three distinct areas: Long Beach, the West Coast Trail, and the Broken Group Islands, all of which occupy a 130-km (80-mile) strip of Vancouver Island's west coast. The park is a world famous area for whale-watching, and the Wickaninnish Interpretive Centre off Hwy 4 has the latest information on their movements. Long Beach offers a range of hiking trails, with parking at all trail heads and beach accesses. The most challenging hike is the 75-km (47-miles) West Coast Trail, between Port Renfrew and Bamfield. The Broken Group Islands are popular with kayakers.

The Broken Group Islands
This is an archipelago of some 100 islets popular with kayakers and scuba divers.

The Schooner Cove Trail is one of nine scenic and easy-to-follow trails along the sands of Long Beach.

The Wickaninnish Interpretive Centre has viewing platforms for whale-watching.

Tofino

Long Beach

Port Albion

Ucluelet

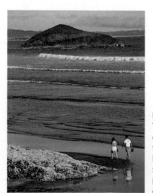

Long Beach
The rugged, windswept sands of Long Beach are renowned for their wild beauty, with crashing Pacific rollers, unbeatable surfing opportunities, rock pools filled with marine life, and scattered driftwood.

DODD ISLAND

TURRET ISLAND

EFFINGHAM ISLAND

For hotels and restaurants in this region see pp350–59 and pp364–83; for transport information see p411

The crashing waters of Elk Falls along the Campbell River

river. Visitors can rent a fishing boat or try their luck catching fish from the 183-m (600-ft) Discovery Pier in the town.

Just 3 km (1.8 miles) north-west of Campbell River, Elk Falls Provincial Park houses large Douglas Fir forests and several waterfalls, including the impressive Elk Falls.

㉙ Telegraph Cove

🚍 Port McNeill. 🛈 1594 Beach Drive, Port McNeill (250) 956 3131.

Located on the northern end of Vancouver Island, Telegraph Cove is a small, picturesque boardwalk village, with distinctive high wooden houses built on stilts that look over the waters of Johnstone Strait. In

summer, the Northern resident killer whales, drawn to the area by the migrating salmon, come to cavort on the gravel beds in the shallow waters of Robson Bight, an ecological reserve established in 1982. Visitors may view the antics of the whales from tour boats or from Port McNeill.

Killer whales in the waters of Johnstone Strait, Vancouver Island

Discovery Passage are on the migration route for five major species of salmon, including the giant Chinook. There are boat tours, which follow the fish up

---

Migrating gray whales

Whale Watching

More than 20 species of whale are found in British Columbia's coastal waters. Around 22,000 gray whales migrate annually from their feeding grounds in the Arctic Ocean to breed off the coast of Mexico. The whales tend to stay near to the coast and often move close enough to Vancouver Island's west shore to be sighted from land. From March to August there are daily whale-watching trips from Tofino and Ucluelet.

West Coast Trail
This trail passes stunning scenery, including moss-draped rainforest and deep, rocky gullies.

Key

▬ Major road

═ Minor road

▪▪ West Coast Trail

— National Park boundary

▬ Rivers

Bamfield

0 meters   10
0 yards   10

At the Nitinat Narrows hikers on the West Coast Trail must take a short ferry ride across this pretty waterway. The trail is open from May to September.

Port Renfrew

THE ROCKY MOUNTAINS

The Canadian Rockies occupy a band of the provinces of British Columbia and Alberta nearly 805 km (500 miles) wide, and are part of the range that extends from Mexico through the US into Canada. Between 65 and 100 million years ago, a slow but massive upheaval of the Earth's crust caused the rise of the Rocky Mountains and the dramatic, jagged appearance of their peaks, 50 of which are over 3,048 m (10,000 ft) high. A region of spectacular beauty, the landscape of the Rockies is dominated by snow-topped peaks, luminous glaciers, and iridescent glacial lakes, now protected in a series of national parks. The discovery of natural hot springs at Banff in 1883 prompted the federal government to create Canada's first national park. Since 1984 Banff, Jasper, Yoho, and Kootenay parks have become UNESCO World Heritage sites.

Sights at a Glance

Historic Towns and Cities

1 Calgary
2 Fort Macleod
5 Fernie
7 Cranbrook
10 Radium Hot Springs
16 Prince George
17 Grande Prairie
18 Fort St. John
19 Fort Nelson

National and Provincial Parks

3 Waterton Lakes National Park
9 Glacier National Park
11 Kootenay National Park
13 Banff National Park
14 Yoho National Park
15 Jasper National Park
20 Muncho Lake Provincial Park

Historical Sites and Places of Natural Beauty

4 Crowsnest Pass
6 Fort Steele Heritage Town
8 The Purcell Mountains
12 Kananaskis Country

Key

— Highway
— Major road
--- Minor road
— Railway route
-·- International border

0 km   150
0 miles   150

◄ Mount Edith Cavell's Angel Glacier and meltwater lake, Jasper National Park, Alberta   **For map symbols** see back flap

● Calgary

Established in 1875, Calgary is famous for hosting the Winter Olympics of 1988, and for its Stampede. Calgary covers the largest area of any city in Alberta, and lies between the eastern foothills of the Rockies and the Prairies. It is a sophisticated place, with skyscrapers, galleries, and theaters, but it retains the air of a frontier town where pick-up trucks and cowboy boots are not out of place. The city's western atmosphere belies the fact that its modern skyline has grown since the oil boom of the 1960s. Noted for its proximity to Banff National Park, Calgary's center, with its offices and stores, is 128 km (79 miles) east of Banff Townsite *(see p307)*.

Some of the shops and exhibition spaces inside Art Central

Calgary Tower
101 9th Ave. SW. **Tel** (403) 266 7171. **Open** daily. 🅿 &
W calgarytower.com
The Calgary Tower is one of the city's tallest structures, with two elevators that hurtle to the top in 62 seconds, and two emergency staircases composed of 802 steps apiece. From street level to the top, Calgary Tower measures 191 m (627 ft). At the top there is a restaurant and a glass-floored observation deck, both of which offer incredible views across to the Rockies and eastward over the vast plains of the Prairies.

Art Central
100 7th Ave. SW. **Tel** (403) 543 9600. **Open** daily. & **W** artcentral.ca
A former bowling alley and pool hall at the corner of Centre Street and 7th Avenue, in downtown Calgary, this building underwent a complete overhaul in 2004 and reinvented itself as a visual arts complex. Spread out over three levels, Art Central accommodates 57 individual spaces for studios, galleries, eclectic boutiques, and artist exhibitions and demonstrations. The complex also houses a restaurant and café.

Eau Claire Market
200 Barclay Parade SW. **Tel** (403) 264 6450. **Open** daily. &
Housed in a brightly colored warehouse, this market provides a welcome contrast to the surrounding office blocks downtown. Located on the Bow River, opposite Prince's Island Park, it offers specialty stores selling a fine variety of gourmet foods, contemporary arts, craft markets, cinemas, cafés, and restaurants. Walkways connect to a footbridge that leads to Prince's Island Park.

🔄 Prince's Island Park
The pretty Prince's Island Park lies close to the city center on the banks of the Bow River. This tiny island is connected to the city via several bridges, including a pedestrian bridge at the end of 4th Street SW.

Calgary Tower surrounded by the skyscrapers of the city's skyline

Sights at a Glance

① St. George's Island
② Fort Calgary
③ Glenbow Museum
④ EPCOR Centre for the Performing Arts
⑤ Calgary Tower
⑥ Art Central
⑦ Calgary Chinese Cultural Centre
⑧ Eau Claire Market
⑨ Prince's Island Park

For hotels and restaurants in this region see pp350–59 and pp364–83; for transport information see p412

During hot summers, visitors and locals picnic under the cool shade of the park's many trees, as well as using its walking and biking trails.

🏛 Calgary Chinese Cultural Centre

197 1st St. SW. **Tel** (403) 262 5071. **Open** daily. 🎫 for museum. ♿ 🌐 culturalcentre.ca

Located in downtown Calgary, the Chinese Cultural Centre was completed in 1992. It is modeled on the 1420 Temple of Heaven in Beijing, which was used exclusively by emperors. The center was built by artisans from China using traditional skills. The Dr. Henry Fok Cultural Hall is the highlight of the building with its 21-m-high (70-ft) ceiling and an impressive dome adorned with dragons and phoenixes.

Blue tiles inside the dome of the Calgary Chinese Cultural Centre

Each of the dome's four supporting columns is decorated with lavish gold designs, which represent the four seasons.

🏛 Glenbow Museum

130 9th Ave. SE. **Tel** (403) 268 4100. **Open** daily. 🎫 ♿ 🌐 glenbow.org

Located in the heart of downtown Calgary, the Glenbow Museum is one of western Canada's largest museums, hosting three major temporary exhibitions annually, in addition to having over 20 permanent galleries. The museum houses an excellent collection of Canadian and contemporary art, as well as a wide range of objects that chronicle the history of the Canadian West through First Nations and pioneer artifacts. An extensive military collection includes medieval armor and Samurai swords. Glenbow's gallery, Niitsitapiisinni, traces the story of the Blackfoot people of the northwestern plains of Alberta and Montana.

🎭 EPCOR Centre for the Performing Arts

205 8th Ave. SE. **Tel** (403) 294 9494. **Open** daily. 🎫 🌐 epcorcentre.org

Opened in 1985, this large complex houses four theaters and a concert hall, as well as having five rental boardrooms. Located in the heart of the city on Olympic Plaza, the center has staged events as diverse as k.d. lang concerts and the High Performance Rodeo.

The lobby of the EPCOR Centre for the Performing Arts

For keys to Symbols see back flap

Mountie's cabin in the Interpretive Centre at Fort Calgary Historic Park

🏠 Hunt House and Deane House

806 9th Ave. SE. **Tel** (403) 269 7747. **Open** Deane House: daily. 🅿️

The Hunt House lies across the Elbow River from the Fort Calgary Interpretive Centre. This small log house is one of the few buildings left from the original settlement of Calgary in the early 1880s.

Nearby Deane House was built for the Superintendent of Fort Calgary, Captain Richard Burton Deane, in 1906. Today, the house is a restaurant where visitors can enjoy a meal in a delightful period setting.

🏠 Fort Calgary Historic Park

750 9th Ave. SE. **Tel** (403) 290 1875. **Open** daily. 🅿️ 🚻

Fort Calgary was built by the North West Mounted Police in 1875 at the confluence of the Bow and Elbow Rivers. The Grand Trunk Pacific Railway (later amalgamated with the CPR), arrived in 1883, and the tiny fort town grew to over 400 residents in a year. In 1887, a fire destroyed several of the settlement's key buildings and a new town was built out of the more fire-resistant sandstone. In 1914 the land was bought by the Grand Trunk Pacific Railway and the fort was leveled. Pieces of the fort were discovered during an archeological dig in 1970, and the well-restored site was opened to the public in 1978.

Today, the reconstructed fort offers an interpretive center, which tells of Calgary's colorful past through exhibits such as a re-created quartermaster's store and carpenter's workshop. There are also delightful walks along the river.

⬛ St. George's Island

St. George's Island sits on the edge of the Bow River, near downtown Calgary. The island houses part of the magnificent Calgary Zoo, including the Canadian Wilds, Botanical Gardens, Penguin Plunge, and Prehistoric Park.

The zoo prides itself on the exciting presentation of its animals, which can be seen in their appropriate habitats. Canadian Wilds is a series of environments that highlights the diversity of the Canadian landscape and its wildlife. There are aspen woodlands where it is possible to see the endangered woodland caribou, and visitors can wander the boreal forest environment, maybe spotting the rare whooping crane in the shallow wetlands area. Penguin Plunge features over 40 birds housed in a shoreline landscape.

The zoo is surrounded by the Botanical Gardens, which has a vast greenhouse displaying plants from around the world.

The Prehistoric Park offers a reconstructed Mesozoic landscape, where visitors can picnic among 29 life-size dinosaurs.

The stately whooping crane at Calgary Zoo, St. George's Island

⬛ Stampede Park

1410 Olympic Way SE. **Tel** (403) 261 0101. **Open** daily. 🅿️ some events. 🚻 🌐 calgarystampede.com

Famous as the site of the Calgary Stampede, the park offers year-round leisure and conference facilities. There is a permanent horse racetrack, as well as two ice-hockey stadiums, one of which is housed inside the

Calgary Stampede

An exuberant ten-day festival of all things western, the Calgary Stampede is held every July in Stampede Park. Originally established as an agricultural fair in 1886, the Stampede of 1912 attracted 14,000 people. In the 1920s one of its still-popular highlights, the risky but exciting covered wagon races, became part of the show.

Today's festival has an array of spectacular entertainments that dramatize scenes from western history. They can be seen both on site and in Calgary itself. The fair starts with a dazzling parade through the city, and then features bull riding, tie-down roping, and steer wrestling. The main events are *Showdown Sunday – Rodeo's Richest Afternoon*, and chuckwagon racing which have combined prize money of over Can$2 million.

Heritage Park Historical Village houses some 70 historic buildings

Canada Olympic Park was the site of the 1988 XV Olympic Winter Games. Today, both locals and visitors can enjoy the facilities all year round, including riding on the bobsleds and luge tracks, mountain biking, and zip-lining. The views toward the Rockies and over Calgary from the 90-m (295-ft) high Olympic Ski Jump Tower are truly stunning. Canada's Sports Hall of Fame has 12 galleries featuring 520 legends from 60 sports.

striking Saddledome, named for its saddle-shaped roof. Trade shows, such as antiques and home improvements, and concerts are also held here.

🡒 Fish Creek Provincial Park

Bow Bottom Trail SE. **Tel** (403) 297 5293. **Open** daily. ♿ partial.

Established in 1975, Fish Creek Provincial Park is one of North America's largest urban parks, covering 13 sq km (5 sq miles) of forest along the Fish Creek valley. Park guides hold slide shows on both the ecology and history of the region, detailing the park's many archeological sites, such as buffalo jumps dated between 750 BC and 1800 AD.

The park's forest is a mix of white spruce, aspen, and balsam poplar. In winter, many of the hiking trails become cross-country ski trails, popular with locals and visitors alike. The Canada goose, the great blue heron, and the bald eagle are among a variety of birds that visit the park during both summer and winter.

🡒 Heritage Park Historical Village

1900 Heritage Drive SW. **Tel** (403) 268 8500. **Open** Village open May–Oct; museum and café open all year. **Closed** Nov–Apr. ♿ ♿
W **heritagepark.ca**

Heritage Park Historical Village sits on the shore of Glenmore Reservoir, and contains over 70 historic buildings, from outhouses to a 2-story hotel, which have been brought here from sites all over western Canada. The buildings have been organized into time periods, which range from an 1880s fur-trading post to the shops and homes of a small town

between 1900 and 1914. Most of the 45,000 artifacts that furnish and decorate the village have been donated by residents of Calgary and the surrounding towns, and vary from teacups to steam trains.

Among the most thrilling of the exhibits, a working 19th-century amusement park has several rides, and three original, operating steam locomotives. A replica of the SS *Moyie*, a charming sternwheeler paddle boat, takes visitors on 30-minute cruises around the Glenmore Reservoir. You can also ride one of two vintage electric streetcars to the park's front gates and walk down a 1930s–40s urban streetscape. The sense of stepping back in time is enhanced by the clip-clopping of horsedrawn carriages, and by the smells and sounds of shops such as the working bakery and the blacksmith's, which are all staffed by costumed guides.

Victorian drink container at Heritage Park

🡒 Canada Olympic Park

88 Canada Olympic Rd. SW. **Tel** (403) 247 5452. **Open** 10am–9pm Mon–Fri, 9am–5pm Sat & Sun. ♿ ♿

🏛 Telus Spark

220 St. George's Drive NE. **Tel** (403) 817 6800. **Open** daily; hours vary so check website before visiting. ♿ ♿
W **sparkscience.ca**

Relocated and redesigned in 2011, the Telus Spark is a popular interactive museum. It offers such exhibits as Being Human, Earth & Sky, and the Creative Kids Museum. Live theater programs and science demonstrations take place in the Presentation Theatre. The latest technology allows for a memorable experience of the center for both kids and adults alike. There is also an interactive outdoor park.

🏛 The Military Museums

4520 Crowchild Trail SW. **Tel** (403) 974 2850. **Open** 9am–5pm Mon–Fri, 9:30am–4pm Sat & Sun. ♿ ♿
W **themilitarymuseums.ca**

The Military Museums include naval, air force, and army museums under one roof. The focus is on the history of the Canadian Forces, from the Northwest Rebellion in 1885 to today.

Sherman tank on display outside the Military Museums

The mountain-ringed Waterton Lake in Waterton Lakes National Park

❷ Fort Macleod

🏛 3,100. 🚌 ℹ The Fort – Museum of the North West Mounted Police, 219 Jerry Potts Blvd. (403) 553 4703. 🖥 fortmacleod.com

Alberta's oldest settlement, Fort Macleod was established in 1874 as the first North West Mounted Police outpost in the west. Sent to control lawless whiskey traders at the Fort Whoop-up trading post, the Mounties set up Fort Macleod nearby (see p236).

Today's town retains many of its historic buildings, and the reconstructed fort palisades house the fort's museum, which tells the story of the Mounties' journey.

The world's oldest and best-preserved buffalo jump lies just 16 km (10 miles) northwest of Fort Macleod. **Head-Smashed-In Buffalo Jump** is a UNESCO World Heritage site. This way of hunting buffalo, in which aboriginal people wearing buffalo skins stampede herds of the animals to their deaths over a cliff, was perfected by the Blackfoot tribe. The site takes its name from the brave whose head was smashed in when watching the kill from under the cliff.

🏛 Head-Smashed-In Buffalo Jump
Hwy 785, off Hwy 2. **Tel** (403) 553 2731. **Open** daily. 🅿 ♿

❸ Waterton Lakes National Park

🚗 Calgary. ℹ Park Info Centre, open mid-May–Oct (403) 859 5133. **Open** daily. 🅿 ♿ partial. 🖥 pc.gc.ca

Scenery as amazing as any of that found in the Rockies' other national parks characterizes the less-known Waterton Lakes National Park. Located in the southwest corner of Alberta along the US border, the park is an International Peace Park and manages a shared ecosystem with Glacier National Park in the US.

The park owes its unique beauty to the geological phenomenon of the Lewis Overthrust, which was forged over a billion years ago (before the formation of the Rockies) when ancient rock was pushed over newer deposits. Thus, the peaks of the mountains rise up sharply out of the flat prairies.

Waterton's mix of lowland and alpine habitats means it has the widest variety of wildlife of any of Canada's parks, from bears to bighorn sheep, and from waterfowl to nesting species such as sapsuckers.

❹ Crowsnest Pass

ℹ Frank Slide Interpretive Centre (403) 562 7388. **Open** daily. **Closed** public holidays. 🅿 🖥 history.alberta.ca

Crowsnest Pass is located 1.5 km (1 mile) off Highway 3, in Alberta close to the border with BC. Like

Visitors on an underground tour of Bellevue Mine at Crowsnest Pass

most Rocky Mountain passes, it is enclosed by snowcapped mountains. In the early 1900s this area was dominated by the coal-mining industry and was the site of Canada's worst mine disaster. In 1903, a huge mass of rock slid off Turtle Mountain into the valley below, hitting the town of Frank and killing 70 people. The Frank Slide Interpretive Centre offers two award-winning audio/visual presentations about this tragic event. A trail through the valley is marked with numbered stops and leads hikers to the debris left by the disaster. Visitors can learn more about the history of local mining communities at the Bellevue Mine, which offers tours through the same narrow tunnels that working miners took daily between 1903 and 1961. Tours are available of Leitch Collieries, a fascinating early mining complex. Sleepovers are also available.

The Rocky Mountains tower over houses in the town of Fernie

❺ Fernie

🏠 4,800. 🚌 ℹ️ 102 Commerce Rd, off Hwy 3. (250) 423 6868.
🌐 tourismfernie.com

Fernie is an attractive, tree-lined town set amid a circle of pointed peaks on the British Columbia side of Crowsnest Pass. The town owes its handsome appearance to a fire that burned it to the ground in 1904 and again in 1908, since when all buildings have been constructed from brick and stone. Among several historic buildings, the 1911 courthouse stands out as

the only château-style courthouse in BC. Fernie is known for its winter sports, and boasts the best powder snow in the Rockies. The skiing season runs from November to April. The nearby Fernie Alpine Resort is huge and capable of taking over 13,000 skiers and riders up the mountain every hour. During the summer, the Mount Fernie Provincial Park offers a broad range of hiking trails through its magnificent mountain scenery. Boat trips on the many nearby lakes and rivers are popular, as is the fishing.

Helicopter trips take visitors close to the mountains to see the formations and granite cliffs particular to this region of the Rockies.

❻ Fort Steele Heritage Town

9851 Hwy 95. **Tel** (250) 417 6000.
Open daily. 🏠 ♿ 🌐 fortsteele.ca

A re-creation of a 19th-century pioneering supply town, this settlement was established in 1864, when gold was discovered at Wild Horse River. Thousands of prospectors and entrepreneurs arrived by the Dewdney Trail, which linked Hope to the gold fields. The town was named after the North West Mounted Police Superintendent, Samuel Steele,

19th-century barber's shop at Fort Steele Heritage Town

who arrived in 1887 to restore peace between warring groups of Ktunaxa native peoples and European settlers. The town underwent a brief boom with the discovery of lead and silver, but the mainline railroad was routed through Cranbrook instead, and by the early 1900s Fort Steele was a ghost town.

Today, there are over 60 reconstructed or restored buildings, staffed by guides in period costume, including the general store, livery stable, and Mountie officers' quarters, where personal items such as family photographs, swords, and uniforms create the illusion of recent occupation. Demonstrations of traditional crafts such as quilt- and ice cream-making are also held here. Tours at the nearby Wild Horse River Historic Site include the chance to pan for gold.

The Buffalo

The large, shaggy-headed type of cattle known as buffalo are really North American bison. These apparently cumbersome beasts (a mature bull can weigh as much as 900 kg/1,980 lbs) are agile, fast, and unpredictable.

Before European settlers began moving west to the plains, in the 18th and 19th centuries, the buffalo lived in immense herds of hundreds of thousands. It is estimated that as many as 60,000,000 roamed here. Initially hunted only by the Plains Indians, who respected the beasts as a source of food, shelter, and tools, the buffalo were subsequently hunted almost to extinction by Europeans. By 1900 less than 1,000 animals remained. In 1874 a rancher called Walking Coyote bred a small herd of just 716 plains bison whose descendants now roam several Canadian national parks.

A North American plains bison

The luxurious dining car on a restored train at Cranbrook's rail museum

❼ Cranbrook

🚠 19,000. ✈ 🚌 ℹ 2279
Cranbrook St. N. (250) 426 5914.

Cranbrook is the largest town in southeast BC and lies between the Purcell and the Rocky Mountain ranges. A major transportation hub for the Rocky Mountain region, Cranbrook is within easy reach of a variety of scenic delights, including alpine forest and the lush, green valleys of the mountain foothills. A range of wildlife such as elk, wolves, cougar, and the highest density of grizzlies in the Rockies, may be spotted on one of many hikes available here.

The town's main attraction is the **Canadian Museum of Rail Travel**, which includes a collection of deluxe "hotels on wheels" dating from between the 1880s and the 1950s that can be used for touring the facilities.

🏛 The Canadian Museum of Rail Travel
57 Van Horne St. S. **Tel** (250) 489 3918.
Open Apr–mid-Oct: daily; late Oct–Apr: Tue–Sat. 🅿 ♿

❽ The Purcell Mountains

🚉 Kamloops. ℹ 500 10th Ave. N./ Hwy 95, Golden (250) 344 7125.

The rugged and beautiful Purcell Mountains face the Rockies across the broad Columbia River Valley. The region is one of the most remote in the Rockies and attracts hunters and skiers from across the globe. A high range

of granite spires, called the Bugaboos, also draws mountain climbers. In the north of the Purcell range, and in one of its few accessible areas, the Purcell Wilderness Conservancy, covers a vast 21 sq km (8 sq miles). Carefully regulated hunting expeditions for bear, mountain goats, and elk are permitted here.

From the nearby pretty town of Invermere, it is possible to access one of the most difficult trails in Canada; the Earl Grey Pass Trail extends some 56 km (35 miles) over the Purcell Mountains. It is named after Earl Grey, Canada's Governor General from 1904 to 1911, who chose the Purcell range as the place to build a vacation cabin for his family in 1909. The trail he traveled followed an established native route used by the Kinbasket natives of the Shuswap First Nations. Today the trail is notoriously dangerous; bears, avalanches, and fallen trees are often hazards along the way. Hiking along it requires skill and experience and should not be attempted by a novice.

❾ Glacier National Park

🚌 Revelstoke/Golden. ℹ Revelstoke (250) 837 7500. **Open** daily. 🅿 ♿
🌐 pc.gc.ca

Glacier National Park covers 1,350 sq km (520 sq miles) of wilderness in the Selkirk Range of the Columbia Mountains. The park was established in 1886, and its growth was linked to the growth of the railroad, which was

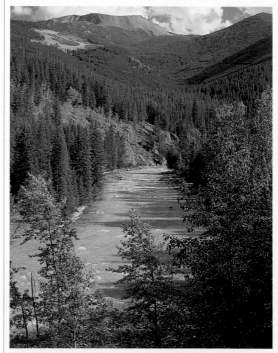

The Purcell Mountains are noted for remote rivers, forests, and mountains

The Illecillewaet Glacier is one of 420 glaciers in Glacier National Park

routed through Roger's Pass in 1885. Today, many of the park's most accessible walking trails follow abandoned railroad lines. Other trails offer visitors stunning views of the park's 420 glaciers, including the Great Glacier, now known as the Illecillewaet Glacier.

The park is known for its very wet weather in summer and almost daily snowfalls in winter, when as much as 23 m (75 ft) of snow may fall in one season. The threat of avalanche is serious here, and visitors should stop at the Roger's Pass Center for up-to-date information.

The Roger's Pass line was abandoned by the CPR due to avalanches, and a tunnel was built underneath it instead. The Trans-Canada Highway (Hwy 1) follows the route of the pass as it bisects the park, en route to the lovely town of Revelstoke. From here visitors may access the forests and jagged peaks of Mount Revelstoke National Park.

⑩ Radium Hot Springs

🏕 1,000. 🛈 Chamber of Commerce, 7556 Main St. E. (250) 347 9331, 888 347 9331. 🆆 radiumhotsprings.com

This small town is famous for its mineral springs and is a good base for exploring the nearby Kootenay National Park. In the summer, flower-filled pots decorate the storefronts of the many coffee shops and pubs along the main street, and the town has more motel rooms than residents. Many of the 1.2 million annual visitors come to bathe in the healing waters of the springs. There are two pools, a hot soaking pool for relaxing in, and a cooler swimming pool. Locker rooms, swimsuits, showers, and towels can all be rented, and massages are readily available. Visitors can explore the nearby Columbia Valley Wetlands too. Fed by glacial waters from the Purcell and Rocky mountains, the Columbia River meanders through these extensive marsh lands, which provide an important habitat for over 250 migratory waterfowl such as Canada geese and tundra swans.

Taking the waters at Radium Hot Springs

⑪ Kootenay National Park

🚌 Banff. 🛈 Park Info Centre, open May–Sep (250) 347 9615. **Open** daily. 🅿 ♿ 🆇 🆆 pc.gc.ca

Kootenay National Park covers 1,406 sq km (543 sq miles) and is known for its ecology, climate, and diversity of landscape. The 94-km (58-mile) Kootenay Parkway (Hwy 93S) bisects the park from north to south. It winds through the narrow gorge of Sinclair Canyon, past the world famous Radium Hot Springs Pools, along the deep red cliffs of the Redwall Fault, and up over the Sinclair Pass. The road continues into the Kootenay River Valley, past Hector Gorge, and into the Vermilion Valley. Short nature trails introduce you to magical Paint Pots, iron-rich mineral springs with rust-colored clay banks. Visitors will see the Marble Canyon, whose 35-m (96-ft) deep dolomite walls are carved by the glacial waters of Tokumm Creek. The Fireweed Trail at Vermilion Pass features vibrant regenerating forests growing along the Continental Divide, in the wake of old forest fires.

The ochre-colored Paint Pot pools in Kootenay National Park

⑫ Kananaskis Country

🚌 Canmore. 🛈 907 7th Ave., Canmore. (403) 678 1295. 🆆 albertaparks.ca

Kananaskis Country is a verdant region of the Rocky Mountain foothills, with mountain peaks, lakes, rivers, and alpine meadows. Located southwest of Calgary on the boundary of Banff National Park, this 4,000 sq km (1,544 sq miles) of wilderness is popular for hiking and viewing wildlife such as eagles, wolves, and bears. The town of Canmore serves as the center of this large recreational area, and has plenty of accommodations, as well as information on outdoor activities such as wildlife tours.

🅴 Banff National Park

The best known of the Rockies' national parks, Banff was also Canada's first. The park was established in 1885, after the discovery of natural hot springs by three Canadian Pacific Railroad workers in 1883. Centuries before the arrival of the railroad, Blackfoot, Stoney, and Kootenay native peoples lived in the valleys around Banff. Today, Banff National Park covers an area of 6,641 sq km (2,564 sq miles) of some of the most sublime scenery in the country. The park encompasses impressive mountain peaks, forests, glacial lakes, and mighty rivers. Some four million visitors a year enjoy a range of activities, from hiking and canoeing in summer, to skiing in winter.

Peyto Lake
One of the most rewarding walks in Banff is a short stroll from the Icefields Parkway, near Bow Summit, which leads to a vista over the ice-blue waters of Peyto Lake.

Parker Ridge

Jasper

Saskatchewan River

93

Mistaya Lake

93

Bow Lake

Bow River

1

View from Icefields Parkway
Renowned for its stunning views of high peaks, forests, lakes, and glaciers, this 230-km (143-mile) road runs between Lake Louise and Jasper.

Saskatchewan River Crossing lies at the junction of three rivers, along the route used by explorer David Thompson, who first came here in the late 1700s and began mapmaking.

Bear Safety

Both grizzly and black bears are found in the Rockies' national parks. Although sightings are rare, visitors should observe *The Mountain Guide*, a Parks Canada publication free to all park visitors that provides wildlife safety tips. The fundamental rules are: don't approach the animals, never feed them, don't run, and stay calm. Bears have an excellent sense of smell, so if you are camping be sure to lock food or trash inside a car or in the bear-proof boxes provided.

Grizzly bear in Banff

Valley of the Ten Peaks
A scenic road from Lake Louise winds to Moraine Lake, which is ringed by ten peaks each over 3,000 m (10,000 ft) high.

For hotels and restaurants in this region see pp350–59 and pp364–83

Johnston Canyon

This spectacular gorge boasts two impressive waterfalls, and is one of the most popular trails in the park. The walk can be reached from the Bow Valley Parkway *(see p306)*, and has walkways close to the falls. Displays along the way explain the canyon's geology.

Key

━━ Highway
━━ Major road
── Rivers

Lake Minnewanka
is Banff's largest lake and is a popular place for picnics and boat trips.

Bankhead

An interpretive hiking trail displaying historic photographs leads visitors around this coal mine and ghost town.

Lake Louise

The turquoise waters of Lake Louise are an abiding symbol of the beauty of the Rockies. It was here that one of the first resorts was established in Banff, with visitors beginning to arrive in 1885.

For additional map symbols *see back flap*

Exploring Banff National Park

It is impossible to travel through Banff National Park and not be filled with awe. There are some 25 peaks that rise over 3,000 m (10,000 ft) in Banff, which are magically reflected in the turquoise waters of the park's many lakes. Banff townsite offers visitors a full range of facilities, including the therapeutic hot springs that inspired the founding of the park, and is an excellent base for exploring the surrounding country. Even the highway is counted an attraction here. The Icefields Parkway (Hwy 93) winds through stunning mountain vistas and connects Banff to Jasper National Park, beginning from the renowned Lake Louise.

Icefields Parkway (Highway 93)

The Icefields Parkway is a 230-km (143-mile) scenic mountain highway that twists and turns through the jagged spines of the Rocky Mountains. The road is a wonder in itself, where every turn offers yet another incredible view as it climbs through high passes from Lake Louise to Jasper.

The road was built during the Depression of the 1930s, as a work creation project. Designed for sightseeing, the highway was extended to its present length in 1960, with plenty of pull-offs to allow visitors to take in the views.

Bow Summit is the highest point on the highway, at 2,068 m (6,785 ft), and has a side road that leads to the **Peyto Lake** viewpoint, which looks over snow-topped peaks mirrored in the brilliant blue of the lake. In summer, Bow Summit's mountain meadows are covered with alpine flowers. From here, it is also possible to see the Crowfoot Glacier, a striking chunk of ice in the shape of a crow's foot, hanging over a cliff-face. Farther north a trail leads down from a parking lot to **Mistaya Canyon** with its vertical walls, potholes, and an impressive natural arch. The highway passes close by the Icefields (which cross the park boundaries into Jasper National Park), and the Athabasca Glacier is clearly visible from the road. Mountain goats and bighorn sheep are drawn to the mineral deposits by the roadside.

The Bow Valley Parkway passing scenic country along the river

The Bow Valley Parkway

The Bow Valley Parkway is a 55-km (35-mile) long scenic alternative to the Trans-Canada Highway, running between Banff and Lake Louise. The road follows the Bow River Valley and offers visitors the chance to explore the gentle country of the valley with many interpretive signs and view-points along the way. From the road it is possible to see the abundant wildlife such as bears, elk, and coyotes.

About 19 km (12 miles) west of Banff, one of the best short walks leads from the roadside to the **Johnston Canyon** trail. A paved path leads to the canyon and two impressive waterfalls. The path to the lower falls is wheelchair accessible, and the upper falls are a slightly longer 2.7-km (1.5-mile) hike. A boardwalk along the rock wall leads to the floor of the canyon, offering valley views close to the railroad crossing through the mountains. One of the most striking natural phenomena in the canyon is the Ink Pots, a series of pools where vivid blue-green water bubbles up from underground springs. Interpretive signs explain how this fascinating canyon took shape, and how the water created its unique rock formations.

Lake Minnewanka Drive

This narrow, winding 14-km (8.5-mile) loop road begins at the Minnewanka interchange on the Trans-Canada Highway. From here it is a pleasant drive to picnic sites, hiking trails, and three lakes. Lake Minnewanka is Banff's biggest lake, almost 28 km (17 miles) long.

A popular short trail leads to **Bankhead**, the site of an abandoned coal mine that was the first settlement in Banff and whose heyday was in the first half of the 19th century. The footpath displays old photographs and notices which depict the life of the miners.

Lake Minnewanka, the largest lake in Banff National Park

Banff Springs Hotel, styled after the baronial castles of Scotland

Banff

The town of Banff grew up around the hot springs that were discovered here in the 1880s. The Canadian Pacific Railroad's manager, William Cornelius Van Horne, realized the springs would attract visitors, so he built the grand Banff Springs Hotel in 1888. The resort was very popular, and the town expanded to accommodate the influx. Located at the foot of Sulphur Mountain, The **Cave and Basin National Historic Site** is the site of the original spring found by the railroad workers in 1883 and is now a museum telling the story of Banff's development. The **Upper Hot Springs Pool**, also at the base of Sulphur Mountain, is a popular resort where visitors can relieve their aches in the mineral-rich, healing waters.

At 2,281 m (7,484 ft) above sea level, Sulphur Mountain provides a spectacular view of the surrounding area. Although there is a 5-km (3-mile) trail to the top, a glass-enclosed gondola (cable car) carries visitors to the summit in eight minutes. Here the viewing platforms offer beautiful vistas of the Rockies.

Banff is busy all year round. In winter, snow sports from skiing to dog-sledding are available, while summer visitors include

hikers, cyclists, and mountaineers. The **Banff Park Museum** was built in 1903 and houses specimens of animals, plants, and mineral samples.

Ⅲ Banff Park Museum
91 Banff Ave. **Tel** (403) 762 1558.
Open daily. **Closed** Jan 1, Dec 25.
🚭 🚶

Gondolas or cable cars taking visitors up Sulphur Mountain

Lake Louise
ℹ️ by Samson Mall (403) 522 3833.
One of Banff National Park's major draws, the beauty of Lake Louise is an enduring image of the Rockies. Famed for the blueness of its water and the snow-capped peaks that surround it, Lake Louise also boasts the Victoria Glacier, which stretches almost to the water's

edge. Trails around the lake offer exhibits that explain the lake's formation some 10,000 years ago, at the end of the last Ice Age. The amazing color of the water of this and other lakes in the park comes from deposits of glacial silt, known as rock flour, suspended just beneath the surface. Dominating the landscape at one end of the lake is the imposing hotel Château Lake Louise, built in 1894.

During the summer, a gondola carries visitors up to Mount Whitehorn for stunning views of the glacier and the lake. In winter, the area attracts large numbers of skiers, ice-climbers, and snowboarders.

In Lake Louise village visitors can stock up on supplies, such as food, clothes, and gas.

Moraine Lake
Less well known than Lake Louise, Moraine Lake is every bit as beautiful, with its shimmering turquoise color. The lake has a pretty waterside lodge that offers accommodations, meals, and canoe rentals. There are several trails that all start at the lake: one lakeside path follows the north shore for 1.5 km (1 mile), while the climb, which leads up Larch Valley-Sentinel Pass trail, offers more stunning vistas, ending at one of the park's highest passes.

⑭ Yoho National Park

Inspired by the beauty of the park's mountains, lakes, waterfalls, and distinctive rock formations, this area was named Yoho, for the Cree word meaning "awe and wonder." Yoho National Park lies on the western side of the Rockies range in BC, next to Banff and Kootenay National Parks.

The Park offers a wide range of activities, from climbing and hiking to boating or skiing. The park also houses the Burgess Shale fossil beds, an extraordinary find of perfectly preserved marine creatures from the prehistoric Cambrian period, over 500 million years ago. Access to the fossil beds is by guided hike and is limited to a maximum of 12 people each trip.

WAPTA ICEFIELD

Emerald Lake
The rustic Emerald Lake Lodge *(see p367)* provides facilities at this quiet, secluded place in the middle of the park. The lake, which is named for the intense color of its waters, is a popular spot for canoeing, walking, and riding horses.

Natural Bridge
Found in the center of the park, over the waters of the Kicking Horse River, Natural Bridge is a rock bridge formed by centuries of erosion, which have worn a channel through solid rock.

0 km		3
0 miles		3

Vancouver, Glacier National Park

Key

— Highway

— Major road

— Rivers

Hoodoo Creek
These fabulous, mushroom-like towers of rock have been created by erosion and can be accessed from a short, but very steep, trail.

The Yoho Valley is
noted for its stunning
scenery, including
the Takakkaw Falls.

VISITORS' CHECKLIST

Practical Information
Hwy 1.
ℹ Park Info. Centre, Field
(250) 343 6783. **Open** daily.
🚴 🚻 📷 ⛺
🅦 pc.gc.ca

Takakkaw Falls
Takakkaw means "it is wonderful"
in the language of the local natives,
and these are among the most
impressive falls in Canada, having a
drop of 254 m (833 ft). The falls can
be accessed along the Yoho Valley
Road, which is open seasonally.

Burgess Shale is
a UNESCO World
Heritage Site set
up to protect two
fossil beds. Day-long
guided hikes here are
by reservation only.

*Calgary,
Banff
National
Park*

Kicking Horse River
This wild river rushes through Yoho alongside
the original 1880s railroad. Today the tracks
carry freight and the "Rocky Mountaineer"
tourist train *(see p415)*.

Lake O'Hara
Shadowed by the majestic peaks of Mounts Victoria and Lefroy, Lake
O'Hara is astonishingly beautiful. However, guests wishing to use the
area's excellent hiking trails must book in advance as access is limited
to protect this fragile environment.

Lake O'Hara nestled amongst the peaks of Yoho National Park ▶

⓯ Jasper National Park

The most northerly of the four Rocky Mountain national parks, Jasper is also the most rugged and the largest, covering an area of 10,878 sq km (4,199 sq miles) of high peaks and valleys dotted with glacial lakes. The Columbia Icefield *(see p313)*, a vast area of 400-year-old ice that is 365 m (1,197 ft) thick in places, is part of the national park. From the icefield, fingers of ice reach down through many of Jasper's valleys.

Some of the most accessible hiking trails in the park start from the Maligne Lake and Canyon, and the town of Jasper. The town is located roughly in the park's center and is the starting point for many of the most popular walks and sights here.

Pyramid Lake
Ringed by jagged peaks, both Pyramid and nearby Patricia Lake lie close to Jasper town.

The Jasper Tramway
Only a few kilometers out of Jasper town is the popular Jasper Tramway, which takes visitors to a viewing platform near the summit of The Whistlers at 2,277 m (7,472 ft). Panoramic vistas take in the park's mountains, forests, and lakes.

Snake Indian River

Jasper Lake

Victoria Cross Range

Prince George

16

93a

0 km   20
0 miles   20

Mount Edith Cavell
It is possible to drive up this mountain as far as Cavell Lake from where the trail leads to Angel Glacier and to the flower-strewn Cavell Meadows.

Key

━━ Major road

═══ Minor road

── Rivers

Maligne Canyon
One of the most beautiful canyons in the Rockies, its sheer limestone walls and several impressive waterfalls can be seen from the many footbridges that are built both along and across its walls.

Miette Hot Springs
Visitors here enjoy relaxing in the warmest spring waters in the Rockies. The springs are said to have healing effects because of their high mineral content.

Edmonton

Medicine Lake
Renowned for its varying water levels, Medicine Lake is drained by a series of underground tunnels and caves. It is also one of Jasper's prettiest lakes.

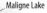

Maligne Lake

Miette Range

Rocky River

Malgine Range

Athabasca River

93

Banff National Park
Yoho National Park
Calgary

Columbia Icefield

Sunwapta River offers white-water rafters a choice of conditions, from calm to turbulent.

Athabasca Falls
The dramatic, rushing waters of these falls are the result of the Athabasca River being forced through a narrow gorge.

For additional map symbols *see back flap*

Exploring Jasper

Established in 1907, Jasper National Park is as staggeringly beautiful as anywhere in the Rockies, but it is distinguished by having more remote wilderness than the other national parks. These areas can be reached only on foot, horseback, or by canoe, and backpackers need passes from the Park Trail Office for hikes that last more than one day. Jasper also has a reputation for more sightings of wildlife such as bear, moose, and elk than any of the other Rockies' parks.

Although most of the park services are closed between October and Easter, visitors who brave the winter season have an opportunity to cross-country ski on breathtaking trails that skirt frozen lakes. In addition, they can go ice fishing, downhill skiing, or on guided walking tours on frozen rivers. In the summertime there are a range of daytrips which are easily accessible from the park's main town of Jasper.

Downhill skiing is just one of the outdoor activities around Jasper

Columbia Icefield and Icefield Centre

Icefields Parkway. **Tel** (780) 852 6288. **Open** May–Oct: daily. & W pc.gc.ca

The Columbia Icefield straddles both Banff and Jasper national parks and forms the largest area of ice south of Alaska. The Icefield, which covers 325 sq km (125 sq miles) and can be as thick as 365 m (1,197 ft), was created during the last Ice Age.

Around 10,000 years ago, ice filled the region, sculpting out wide valleys, sheer mountain faces, and sharp ridges. Although the glaciers have retreated over the last few hundred years, during the early years of the 20th century ice covered the area where the Icefields Parkway now passes. An interpretive center explains the Ice Age and the impact of the glaciers on the landscape of the Rockies. Tours of the Athabasca Glacier, in 4-wheel drive Sno-coaches, are available from the center, which also has information on local trails.

Athabasca Falls

Located at the junction of highways 93 and 93A, where the Athabasca River plunges 23 m (75 ft) to the river bed below, these are among the most dramatic waterfalls in the park. Despite being a short drop compared with other falls in the Rockies, the force of the waters of the Athabasca River being pushed through a narrow, quartz-rich gorge transforms these waters into a powerful, foaming torrent.

Jasper

The town of Jasper was established in 1911 as a settlement for Grand Trunk Pacific Railroad workers, who were laying track along the Athabasca River Valley. As with Banff, the coming of the railroad and the growth of the parks as resorts went hand-in-hand, and the town expanded to include hotels, restaurants, and a visitor center. Today, many of the park's main attractions are close to the town, which is located at the center of the park, on both Highway 16 and Icefields Parkway (Hwy 93).

Just 7 km (4.5 miles) out of town is the Jasper Tramway station, from where visitors may take a brisk, 7-minute ride up **The Whistlers**. The trip whisks visitors up to the upper terminal at 2,277 m (7,472 ft), where there is a clearly marked trail

The wild waters of Athabasca River make it a popular venue for white-water rafting

For hotels and restaurants in this region see pp350–59 and pp364–83

leading to the summit at 2,470 m (8,100 ft). On a clear day the view is incomparable. For those who would rather walk than ride the tram, there is a 2.8-km (1.7-mile) trail to the top of the mountain. The trail winds upward, offering panoramic views of both the Miette and Athabasca valleys, and, in July, the lush meadows are blanketed with colorful wild flowers.

Patricia and Pyramid Lakes

North of Jasper townsite, the attractive Patricia and Pyramid lakes nestle beneath the 2,763-m (9,065-ft) high Pyramid Mountain. A popular daytrip from the town, the lakes are noted for windsurfing and sailing. Equipment rental is available from two lakeside lodges.

The deep blue waters of Pyramid Lake beneath Pyramid Mountain

Maligne Lake Drive

Maligne Lake Drive begins 5 km (3 miles) east of Jasper townsite and leads off Hwy 16, following the valley floor between the Maligne and the Queen Elizabeth ranges. This scenic road travels past many magnificent sights, with viewpoints along the way offering panoramas of Maligne Valley. Among the route's most spectacular sights is the Maligne Canyon, reached by a 4-km (2.5-mile) interpretive hiking trail that explains the special geological features behind the gorge's formation. One of the most beautiful in the Rockies, Maligne Canyon has sheer limestone walls as high as 50 m (150 ft) and many waterfalls, which can be seen from several foot bridges. The road ends at

A boat cruise on Maligne Lake, the largest natural lake in the Rockies

Maligne Lake. The largest natural lake in the Rockies, Maligne is 22 km (14 miles) long and surrounded by snow-capped mountains. There are several scenic trails around it, one of which leads to the Opal Hills and amazing views of the area. Guided walks around here can be organized from Jasper, and it is possible to rent fishing tackle and canoes and kayaks to go out on the lake.

Medicine Lake

Medicine Lake is also reached from a side road off Maligne Lake Drive. The lake is noted for its widely varying water levels. In autumn the lake is reduced to a trickle, but in springtime the waters rise, fed by the fast-flowing Maligne River. A vast network of underground caves and channels are responsible for this event.

Miette Hotsprings

Tel (780) 866 3939, 1 800 767 1611. **Open** May–Oct: daily. 🅿️ ♿

Located 61 km (38 miles) north of Jasper along the attractive Miette Springs Road, these springs are

the hottest in the Rockies, reaching temperatures as high as 53.9°C (129°F). However, the thermal baths are cooled to a more reasonable 39°C (102°F) for bathers. The waters are held to be both relaxing and healthy – they are rich in minerals, such as calcium, sulfates, and small amounts of hydrogen sulfide (which smells like rotten eggs).

The resort of Miette Springs houses two pools, including one suitable for children. The springs are part of a leisure complex that offers both restaurants and hotels.

Mount Edith Cavell

Named after a World War I heroine nurse, this mountain is located 30 km (18.5 miles) south of Jasper townsite. The scenic road that climbs it is paved but has some rough sections and narrow switchbacks. The road ends at Cavell Lake by the north face of the mountain. From here, a guided trail leads to a small lake beneath the Angel Glacier. A three-hour walk across the flower strewn Cavell meadows has views of the glacier's icy tongue.

A peninsula of ice from Angel Glacier seen from Mount Edith Cavell

Typical kitchen of the late 1900s at Grande Prairie Museum

⑯ Prince George

🏔 72,000. ✈ 🚉 🚌 ℹ 101–1300 First Ave. (250) 562 3700.
🌐 **tourismpg.com**

The largest town in Northern British Columbia, Prince George is a bustling supply-and-transportation center for the region. Two major highways pass through here, the Yellowhead (Hwy 16) and Highway 97, which becomes the Alaska Highway at Dawson Creek. Established in 1807 as Fort George, a fur-trading post at the confluence of the Nechako and Fraser rivers, the town is well placed for exploring the province.

Today, Prince George has all the facilities of a larger city, including a university specializing in First Nations history and culture, as well as its own symphony orchestra and several art galleries. **The Exploration Place Museum and Science Centre** lies on the site of the original Fort, within the 26-ha (65-acre) Fort George Park, and has a collection of artifacts from native cultures, European pioneers, and early settlers.

Over 1,600 lakes and rivers are within an hour's drive of the community, making Prince George an ideal location for angling enthusiasts.

🏛 **The Exploration Place Museum and Science Centre**
333 Becott Place. **Tel** (250) 562 1612. **Open** 9am–5pm daily. **Closed** Jan 1, Dec 25 & 26. 🅿 ♿
🌐 **theexplorationplace.com**

⑰ Grande Prairie

🏔 55,000. ✈ 🚌 ℹ 11330 106th St. (780) 539 7688. 🌐 **gptourism.ca**

Grande Prairie is a large, modern city in the northwest corner of Alberta. Surrounded by fertile farming country, the city is a popular stop for travelers heading north toward Dawson Creek and the Alaska Highway *(see pp266–7)*. The city is the hub of the Peace River region; it offers extensive opportunities for shopping in its giant malls and many downtown specialty stores, with the added draw of having no provincial sales tax *(see p384)*.

Running through the city center is the attractive wilderness of Muskoseepi Park. Covering 405 ha (1,000 acres), the park offers a variety of outdoor activities including walking and biking trails, and cross-country skiing.

The **Grande Prairie Museum** is also housed in the park and has 10 buildings containing over 16,000 historical artifacts. There are several reconstructions, including a 1911 schoolhouse, a rural post office, and a church. A renowned display of dinosaur bones recovered from the Peace River Valley are also on display at the museum.

Bear Creek, which runs through Muskoseepi Park, has become a magnet for bird watchers as sightings of eagles are common. The Grand River wetlands, particularly those at Crystal Lake, located in the north-east corner of the city, contain one of the few breeding grounds for the rare trumpeter swan.

🏛 **Grande Prairie Museum**
Cnr 102nd St. & 102nd Ave. **Tel** (780) 532 5482. **Open** daily. **Closed** Jan 1, Dec 25. 🅿 ♿

⑱ Fort St. John

🏔 21,000. ✈ 🚌 ℹ 9523 100th St. (250) 785 3033. 🌐 **fortstjohn.ca**

Fort St. John is located at Mile 47 of the Alaska Highway among the rolling hills of the Peace River Valley. During the construction of the Highway in 1942, the tiny town dramatically expanded from a population of about 800 to 6,000. When completed, the highway turned Fort St. John into a busy supply center that caters to visitors exploring the area, as well as supporting the growth of agriculture in the surrounding countryside. However, the town boomed when oil was found

Lush farmland along the Peace River in northern British Columbia

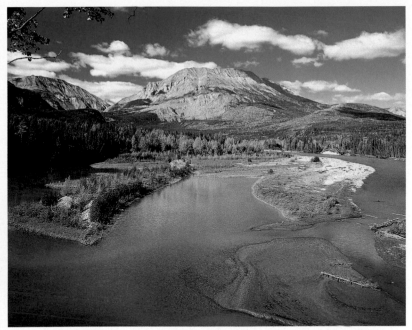

The green waters of Muncho Lake framed by mountains in Muncho Lake Provincial Park

here in the 1950s, in what proved to be the largest oil field in the province. Today, Fort St. John's pride in its industrial and pioneering heritage is reflected in the local museum, which has a 41-m (136-ft) high oil derrick at its entrance and a range of exhibits that tell the story of the local oil industry.

⓳ Fort Nelson

🅰 6,000. 🛪 🚌 𝑖 5319 50th Ave. S. (250) 774 2541.
🆆 **northernrockies.ca**

Despite the growth of the oil, gas, and lumber industries in the 1960s and 70s, Fort Nelson retains the atmosphere of a northern frontier town. Before the building of the Alaska Highway in the 1940s, Fort Nelson was an important stop on route for the Yukon and Alaska, and until the 1950s was without running water or electricity. Fur trading was the main activity until the energy boom; even today both native and white trappers hunt wolf, beaver, and lynx, for both their fur and their meat.

Today, the town has an air and bus service, a hospital, and good visitor facilities such as motels, restaurants, and gas stations. Local people are famous for their friendliness, and during the busy summer months run a program of free talks describing life in the north to visitors. A small museum displays photographs and artifacts that tell the story of the building of the 2,451-km (1,523-mile) Alaska Highway.

Lynx near Fort Nelson

⓴ Muncho Lake Provincial Park

Off Hwy 97. **Tel** (250) 776 7000.
Open daily.

One of three provincial parks (including Stone Mountain and Liard River Hot Springs) that were established after the building of the Alaska Highway in 1942, Muncho Lake occupies the most scenic section of the road. The park encompasses the

bare peaks of the northern Rockies, whose stark limestone slopes incorporate the faults, alluvial fans, and hoodoos that are a testament to thousands of years of glacial erosion. The Highway skirts the eastern shoreline of the 12-km (7.5-mile) long Muncho Lake before crossing the Liard River where the Mackenzie Mountain range begins. In early summer, passing motorists are likely to see moose grazing among meadows filled with colorful wildflowers. The park's bogs are popular with botanists eager to see the rare yellow Lady's Slipper orchid. The roadside also attracts goats, sheep, and caribou, drawn by delicious deposits of sodium, known as mineral licks.

Visitors may stay in the park at one of the campgrounds or lodges in order to explore its 861 sq km (332 sq miles) of wilderness. The deep waters of Muncho Lake house a good supply of trout for anglers.

SOUTHERN AND NORTHERN BRITISH COLUMBIA

Southern British Columbia covers the region south of Prince George, down to the US border. There is a vast variety of natural beauty here, including the forests and waterfalls of Wells Gray Provincial Park, and the lush valleys, wineries, and lake resorts of the Okanagan Valley. One of the most stunning wildernesses in North America, northern British Columbia spreads north of Prince Rupert, between the Coast Mountains in the west, the Rockies in the east, and the Yukon. Its dramatic landscape ranges from the volcanic terrain around Mount Edziza, with its lava flows and cinder cones, to the frozen forests of Atlin Provincial Park. Haida Gwaii can be accessed by ferry, and much of the trip is across open ocean. For 10,000 years the archipelago has been home to the Haida people, who are famous for their totem-carving.

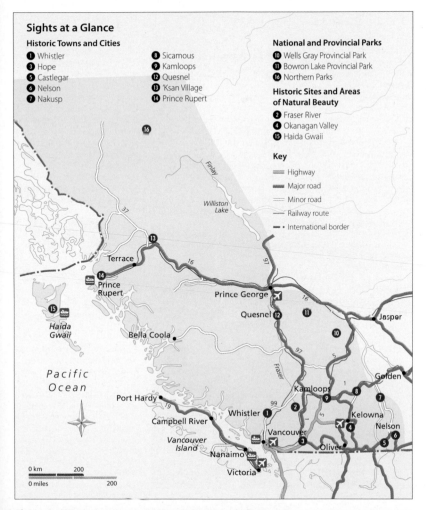

Sights at a Glance

Historic Towns and Cities

1 Whistler
3 Hope
5 Castlegar
6 Nelson
7 Nakusp
8 Sicamous
9 Kamloops
12 Quesnel
13 'Ksan Village
14 Prince Rupert

National and Provincial Parks

10 Wells Gray Provincial Park
11 Bowron Lake Provincial Park
16 Northern Parks

Historic Sites and Areas of Natural Beauty

2 Fraser River
4 Okanagan Valley
15 Haida Gwaii

Key

▬▬ Highway
▬▬ Major road
═══ Minor road
─── Railway route
─ • International border

0 km 200
0 miles 200

◄ Grapevines of Blue Mountain Vineyard and Cellars overlooking Vaseux Lake, Okanagan Valley   **For map symbols** see back flap

The Trans-Canada Highway overlooking the Fraser Canyon along the Fraser River

❶ Whistler

🏔 10,000. 🚌 ℹ️ 4230 Gateway Drive (604) 935 3357. 🌐 whistler.com

Whistler is the largest ski resort in Canada. Set among the Coast Mountains, 125 km (78 miles) north of Vancouver, the resort is divided into four distinct areas: Whistler Village, Village North, Upper Village, and Creekside. Whistler and Blackcomb mountains have the greatest vertical rises of any ski runs in North America. The skiing and snowboarding here can be among the best in the world, with mild Pacific weather and reliable winter snow. In summer, there is snowboarding and skiing on Blackcomb's Horstman Glacier, and mountain biking.

Whistler Village offers visitors a full range of facilities, from comfortable bed-and-breakfasts to luxurious five-star hotels. Café-lined cobbled squares and cozy bars and restaurants cater to all tastes, while a range of stores sells everything from ski-wear to native arts

and crafts. Whistler was the 2010 Winter Olympics venue for most snow sports, from downhill skiing to luge.

❷ Fraser River

ℹ️ Vancouver 1 800 667 3306.

The majestic Fraser River travels 1,375 km (854 miles) through some of BC's most stunning scenery. The river flows from its source in the Yellowhead Lake, near Jasper, to the Strait of Georgia, near Vancouver. Along the way, it heads north through the Rocky Mountain trench before turning south near the town of Prince George. It continues by the Coast Mountains, then west to the town of Hope through the steep walls of the Fraser Canyon, and on toward Yale.

It was Fraser Canyon that legendary explorer Simon Fraser found the most daunting when he followed the river's course in 1808.

However, when gold was discovered near the town of Yale 50 years later, thousands of prospectors swarmed up the valley. Today, Yale is a small town with a population of 200 and the delightful **Yale Museum**, where exhibits focus on the history of the gold rush, as well as telling the epic story of the building of the Canadian Pacific Railroad through the canyon. This section of river is also a popular white-water rafting area, and trips can be arranged from the small town of Boston Bar. At Hell's Gate the river thunders through the Canyon's narrow walls, which are only 34 m (112 ft) apart.

🏛 **Yale Museum**
31187 Douglas St. **Tel** (604) 863 2324. **Open** May–Sep: daily. 🦽 ♿
🌐 **historicyale.ca**

❸ Hope

🏔 6,100. 🚌 ℹ️ 919 Water Ave. (604) 869 2021. 🌐 hope.ca

Located at the southern end of the Fraser Canyon, Hope is crossed by several highways, including Hwy 1 (the Trans-Canada) and Hwy 3. Hope is an excellent base for exploring the Fraser Canyon and southern BC, as well as being within easy reach of several pro-vincial parks. The beautiful country of Manning Provincial Park, with its lakes, mountains, and rivers, is noted for its outdoor activities – swimming, hiking, fishing, and sailing in summer, and downhill and cross-country skiing in winter.

The ski resort at alpine Whistler Village in British Columbia

For hotels and restaurants in this region see pp350–59 and pp364–83

❹ Okanagan Valley Tour

The Okanagan Valley is actually a series of valleys, linked by a string of lakes, that stretches for 250 km (155 miles) from Osoyoos in the south, to Sicamous in the north. The main towns here are connected by Highway 97, which passes through the desert landscape near Osoyoos, and on to the lush green orchards and vineyards for which the valley is most noted. Mild winters and hot summers have made the Okanagan one of Canada's favorite vacation destinations.

Tips for Drivers

Starting point: On Highway 97 from Vernon in the north; Osoyoos in the south.
Length: 175 km (109 miles).
Highlights: Blossom and fruit festivals are held in spring and summer, when roadside stalls offer a cornucopia of fruit, and wine tours are available year-round.

④ **Kelowna** The biggest city in the Okanagan, Kelowna lies on the shores of Lake Okanagan between Penticton and Vernon, and is the center of the wine- and fruit-growing industries.

⑤ **Vernon**
Surrounded by farms and orchards, Vernon owes its lush look to the growth of irrigation in 1908. Several small resorts are set around the nearby lakes.

③ **Summerland** This small but charming lakeside resort boasts several 19th-century buildings and stunning views from the top of Giant's Head Mountain.

② **Penticton** This sunny lakeside town is known for the long Okanagan Lake Beach, windsurfing, and local winery tours, as well as for its Peach Festival, held every August.

⑥ **Historic O'Keefe Ranch**
Founded by the O'Keefe family in 1867, this historic ranch displays original artifacts belonging to the family who lived here until 1977. The original log cabin remains, as does the church and store.

| 0 km | 25 |
| 0 miles | 25 |

① **Osoyoos**
Visitors are drawn here by hot summers, the warm waters and sandy beaches of Lake Osoyoos, and the nearby pocket desert.

Key

▬ Tour route
═ Other roads

Impressive historic stone buildings in the attractive town of Nelson

❺ Castlegar

🏚 8,000. ✈ 🚌 ℹ️ 1995 6th Ave. (250) 365 6313.

Located in southeastern BC, Castlegar is a busy transportation hub. The town is crossed by two major highways, Hwy 3 and Hwy 22, and lies at the junction of the important Kootenay and Columbia rivers.

In the early 1900s, a steady influx of Doukhobors (Russian religious dissenters fleeing persecution) began arriving here. The **Doukhobor Discovery Centre** reflects the group's heritage and houses a variety of traditional clothes and tools, and antique farm machinery.

Traditional Doukhobor tunic

🏛 **Doukhobor Discovery Centre** 112 Heritage Way. **Tel** (250) 365 5327. **Open** May–Sep: daily. ♿ ♿

❻ Nelson

🏚 10,500. 🚌 ℹ️ 225 Hall St. (250) 352 3433. 🌐 discovernelson.com

One of the most attractive towns in southern British Columbia, Nelson overlooks Kootenay Lake. Established in the 1880s as a mining town, with the coming of the railroad in the 1890s, Nelson flourished as a center for transporting ore and timber. The town owes its good looks to its location on the shores of the lake and to the large number of public buildings and houses that were constructed between 1895 and 1920. British Columbia's best-known architect, Francis Rattenbury (see p285), played a part in the design of some of the town's most prestigious and beautiful structures, such as the elegant Burns building which was built in 1899 for millionaire cattle rancher and meat packer, Patrick Burns. Rattenbury also designed the Nelson Court House in 1908, a stately stone building with towers and gables.

Today, the town has a thriving cultural scene, with an art walk during the summer, as well as numerous cafés, book, and craft shops. Visitors also enjoy the short ride on Car 23, a 1906 streetcar that operated in the town between 1924 and 1949 (it was restored in 1992), and which today travels along Nelson's delightful waterfront. The infocenter provides visitors with a map and guide for the heritage walking tour of the town's historic buildings.

❼ Nakusp

🏚 1,800. ℹ️ 92 6th Ave. NW. (250) 265 4234.

With the snow-topped Selkirk Mountains as a backdrop, and overlooking the waters of Upper Arrow Lake, Nakusp is a charming town. Originally developed as a mining settlement, the town is now known for its mineral hot springs. There are two resorts close to town; the Nakusp and Halcyon Hot Springs, both of which provide therapeutic bathing in hot waters, rich in sulfates, calcium, and hydrogen sulfide, said to be good for everyday aches, as well as arthritis and rheumatism. Roughly 40 km (25 miles) to the

The town of Nakusp overlooking picturesque Upper Arrow Lake

south of Nakusp, in the Slocan Valley, are two fascinating abandoned silver mining towns, New Denver and Sandon. Sandon had 5,000 inhabitants at the height of the mining boom in 1892. It also had 29 hotels, 28 saloons, and several brothels and gambling halls. A fire in 1900, poor metal prices, and dwindling ore reserves crippled the mines, and Sandon became a ghost town. Today, the town has been declared an historic site, and its homes and businesses are being carefully restored. The nearby town of New Denver suffered a fate similar to Sandon's, but is also noted as the site of an internment camp for the Japanese during World War II. The Nikkei Internment Memorial Centre on Josephine Street is the only center in Canada devoted to telling the story of the internment of over 20,000 Japanese Canadians. The center is surrounded by a formal Japanese garden.

⑧ Sicamous

🏔 3,200. 🚌 ℹ️ 446 Main St. (250) 836 3313.

Sicamous is an appealing waterfront village known for its 3,000 houseboats, as well as its charming cobblestone streets hung with flower-filled planters. Located between Mara and Shuswap lakes, at the junction of the Trans-Canada Highway and Highway 97A, the town is ideally placed for touring the lakes, and the town of Salmon Arm, at the northern end of the Okanagan Valley (see p321). Over 250 houseboats are available for renting in the summer, and there are 12 marinas and a houseboat store. From the boats it is possible to view the inlets and forested landscape of Lake Shuswap where wildlife such as black bear, deer, moose, coyote, and bobcat have been spotted along the shore. In summer, visitors and locals enjoy both the

Houseboats moored along the waterfront at Sicamous

good public beach on the lake, as well as the pleasant walk along a marked waterfront trail.

⑨ Kamloops

🏔 90,000. 🚆 🚉 🚌 ℹ️ 1290 West Trans-Canada Hwy (250) 372 8000. 🌐 **tourismkamloops.com**

Kamloops means "where the rivers meet" in the language of the Secwepemc First Nations. The largest town by area in BC's southern interior, it lies at the crossroads of the north and south Thompson rivers. Three major highways also meet here; the Trans-Canada, Hwy 5, and Hwy 97 to the Okanagan Valley, as do the Canadian Pacific and Canadian National railroad. European settlement began in 1812, when fur traders started doing business with local natives. The **Secwepemc Museum and Heritage Park** focuses on the cultural history of the Secwepemc First Nations and has a wide variety of artifacts, including a birch-bark canoe, hunting equipment, traditional clothing and cooking utensils. Outside, in the Heritage Park, short trails lead visitors through the archeological remains of a 2,000-year-old Shuswap winter village site, which includes four authentically reconstructed winter pit houses and a summer camp. The village has a hunting shack, a fish-drying rack, and a smoke house.

A horse's snow shoe on display at Kamloops

The museum store sells pine-needle and birch-bark baskets, moccasins, and a wide variety of beaded and silver jewelry.

In the town center, the Art Gallery has a small but striking collection that features landscape sketches by A.Y. Jackson, one of the renowned Group of Seven painters (see pp168–9).

🏛 Secwepemc Museum and Heritage Park
355 Yellowhead Hwy. **Tel** (250) 828 9749. **Open** Jun–Sep: daily; Sep–May: 8:30am–4:30pm Mon–Fri. 🚫 ♿

⑩ Wells Gray Provincial Park

Tel (250) 674 3334. 🚉 Clearwater. 🚌 Clearwater. **Open** daily. 🌐 **wellsgray.ca**

Wells Gray Provincial Park is one of the most beautiful wildernesses in British Columbia, and offers wonders comparable to the Rockies in the east. The park was opened in 1939 and is distinguished by alpine meadows, thundering waterfalls, and glacier-topped peaks that rise as high as 2,575 m (8,450 ft). The Canadian National Railroad and Hwy 5 follow the Thompson River along the park's western edge, offering stunning views.

From the Clearwater Valley Road, off Hwy 5, there are several trails, from easy walks to arduous overnight hikes in remote country. A selection of small trails, just a few minutes from the road, lead to the spectacular sight of Dawson Falls.

⓫ Bowron Lake Provincial Park

Tel (778) 373 6107. 🚗 Quesnel. 🚌 Quesnel. **Open** May–Sep. 🛶 (canoe trip) ♿ partial.

Bowron Lake Provincial Park is located about 120 km (75 miles) east of Quesnel on Highway 26 in the Cariboo Mountains. The park is renowned for having a 112-km (70-mile) rectangular waterway composed of nine lakes, three rivers, streams, small lakes, and many portages (trails linking the waterways). There is a week-long canoe trip here, but it is limited to 50 canoeists at a time, and passes must be obtained from the visitor center. It is a special trip that allows visitors to come quietly upon wildlife such as moose or beaver. In late summer, bears come to feed on the spawning sockeye salmon in the Bowron River.

A grizzly bear rearing up

⓬ Quesnel

🏔 9,500. ✈ 🚗 🚌 ℹ️ 703 Carson Ave. (250) 992 8716.

Quesnel is a busy logging town that started life as a gold rush settlement between 1858 and 1861. The town was the last along the Gold Rush Trail, or Cariboo Road (now Hwy 97), which was lined with mining towns between here and

A 19th-century horse and carriage in the streets of Barkerville

Kamloops. Quesnel occupies an attractive position in a triangle formed by the Fraser and Quesnel rivers. The town's sights include the Riverfront Trail System, a tree-lined 12-km (7-mile) path that runs along the banks of both rivers. Just outside the town's limits, Pinnacles Provincial Park features the geological wonder of hoodoos, rocky columns formed 12 million years ago when the volcanic surface was eroded by Ice Age meltwaters. From Quesnel, 87 km (54 miles) east on Hwy 26, lies the historic mining town of **Barkerville**. The town was born when Englishman Billy Barker dug up a handful of gold nuggets in 1862. Today, it is a good example of a perfectly preserved 19th-century mining town, with over 120 restored or reconstructed buildings and costumed guides. Visitors can see a blacksmith at work in his forge, watch showgirls put on the kind of display the miners would have seen at the theater, or take a ride on a stagecoach.

🏛 **Barkerville Historic Town**
87 km E. of Quesnel, Hwy 26. **Tel** (250) 994 3332. **Open** daily. 🛶 ♿

⓭ 'Ksan Village

Tel (250) 842 5544, 1 877 842 5518. **Open** grounds: year round; houses: Apr–Sep: daily. 🛶 ♿ 🌐 **ksan.org**

Some 290 km (180 miles) east of Prince Rupert, 'Ksan Village is a re-creation of an 1870 native settlement, established in the 1950s to preserve the culture of the Gitxsan First Nations. Gitxsan natives have lived in the area for thousands of years, particularly along the beautiful Skeena River valley. Their way of life was under threat by an influx of white settlers who arrived in the 1850s at Prince Rupert to work their way up river to mine or farm.

Noted for their skill in carving and painting masks, totems, and

Gitxsan carved cedarwood totem pole in 'Ksan Village

canoes, Gitxsan elders are now schooling new generations in these skills at 'Ksan Village. Within the complex are seven traditional long houses containing a carving school, museum, and gift shop.

⓮ Prince Rupert

🏔 13,000. ✈ 🚗 🚌 ⛴ ℹ️ 100 1st Ave. W. (250) 624 5637, 1 800 667 1994. 🌐 **visitprincerupert.com**

Prince Rupert is a vibrant port city, and the second-largest on BC's coast. Located on Kaien Island, at the mouth of the Skeena River, the city is circled by forests and mountains, and overlooks the beautiful fjord-studded coastline. The busy harbor is the main access point for Haida Gwaii and Alaska.

Like many of BC's major towns, Prince Rupert's development is linked to the growth of the railroad. Housed in the 1914 Grand Trunk Railroad Station, the Kwinitsa Railway Museum tells the story of businessman Charles Hay's big plans for the town, which were largely unfulfilled: he went down with the *Titanic* in 1912.

Tsimshian First Nations were the first occupants of the area, and as recently as 150 years ago the harbor was lined with their large cedar houses and carved totems. The **Museum of Northern British Columbia** focuses on northwest coast First Nations culture and history. Tsimshian dance, song, and drama are performed in a traditional long house and there are Archaeological tours.

ⅢⅢ **Museum of Northern British Columbia**
100 1st Ave. W. **Tel** (250) 624 3207. **Open** Jun–Sep: daily; Oct–May: Tue–Sat. **Closed** Dec 25, 26. 🅿️ ♿ 📷
ⓦ museumofnorthernbc.com

⓯ Haida Gwaii

🚉 & 🚌 Prince Rupert. ⅈ 3220 Wharf St., Queen Charlotte. (250) 559 8316 (open all year).
ⓦ gohaidagwaii.ca

Shaped like a bent ice-cream cone, the Haida Gwaii (previously called Queen Charlotte Islands) are an archipelago of about 150 islands across from the city of Prince Rupert.

The islands were left untouched by the last Ice Age, and have an eco-system unique to Canada. The forests house distinctive species of mammal such as the dusky shrew and short-tailed weasel. There is also a large population of bald eagles, and the spring brings hundreds of migrating gray whales past the shores.

The islands have been the home of the Haida people for thousands of years. Today, the Haida are recognized for their artistic talents, particularly their carvings and sculptures from cedar wood and argillite (a black slatelike stone found only on these islands).

Atlin Lake in remote Atlin Provincial Park

It was the Haida who led environmental campaigns against logging companies in the 1980s, leading to the founding of the **Gwaii Haanas National Park Reserve and Haida Heritage Site** in 1988. The park has centuries-old rainforest, with 1,000-year-old Sitka spruce, red cedar, and western hemlock.

🌳 **Gwaii Haanas National Park Reserve and Haida Heritage Site**
Tel (250) 559 8818. **Open** daily. 🅿️ (no fee in winter).

⓰ Northern Parks

Mount Edziza, Spatsizi; Hwy 37. Atlin; Hwy 7. ⅈ (250) 771 4591.
ⓦ hellobc.com

The provincial parks of northern British Columbia comprise Mount Edziza Provincial Park, Spatsizi Plateau Wilderness Provincial Park, and, farther north, Atlin Provincial Park. These offer remote landscapes, with high peaks, icefields, and tundra.

Established in 1972, Mount Edziza Provincial Park is distinguished by its volcanic landscape which includes lava rivers, basalt plateaus, and cinder cones. The park can be reached by boat or float plane. There is no vehicle access within the park, and only long, rugged overland trails or chartered float planes take visitors through open meadows, arctic birch woods, and over creeks.

Across the highway lies the even more rugged country of Spatsizi Plateau Wilderness Provincial Park, which includes the snow-capped peaks of the Skeena Mountains. Gladys Lake, a small lake in the center of the park, is an ecological reserve for the study of sheep and mountain goats. Access to the park is again limited to a small road leading from the village of Tatogga along Hwy 37. The village also offers guides and float plane hire.

The spectacular Atlin Provincial Park is only accessible from the Yukon on Hwy 7, off the Alaska Hwy. About one-third of the park is covered by large icefields and glaciers.

Masset, one of three major towns on Graham Island, Haida Gwaii

NORTHERN
CANADA

Introducing Northern Canada

Northern Canada covers the Yukon, Northwest Territories, and Nunavut, and stretches up to within 800 km (500 miles) of the North Pole, and from the Atlantic Ocean west to the Pacific, 37 percent of Canada's total area. The landscape is incredibly harsh: barren, treeless, frozen tundra dominates most of the year, with subarctic forest, mountains, glaciers, and icy lakes and rivers. Nonetheless, an abundance of wildlife flourishes, with musk ox, caribou, polar bears, and seals. At the height of the brief summer the "midnight sun" provides 24-hour days, while the Aurora Borealis *(see p341)* illuminates dark winters with ribbons of colored light. Development in the far north has occurred only where conditions are hospitable, often where the land is most scenic and varied. Populated by First Nations people some 25,000 years ago and the Inuit about 3000 BC, this uniquely dramatic land is enjoyed by 500,000 visitors a year.

Glorious flaming fall colors rise above the evergreens in the north of the Yukon

◀ A caribou herd, Dempster Highway, near Eagle Plains in the Yukon Territories

Getting Around

The watchword when traveling in this region is cost; trips, accommodations, and even food are all far more expensive than in the rest of the country. In the Yukon all major towns are connected by bus, but the most flexible way to travel around is by car. Air is the best means of traveling in Nunavut and the Northwest Territories. There are 600 landing strips and small airports here. Visitors should be aware that accommodations are equally restricted. In many settlements only one hotel is available, but the Yukon towns are well equipped with places to stay.

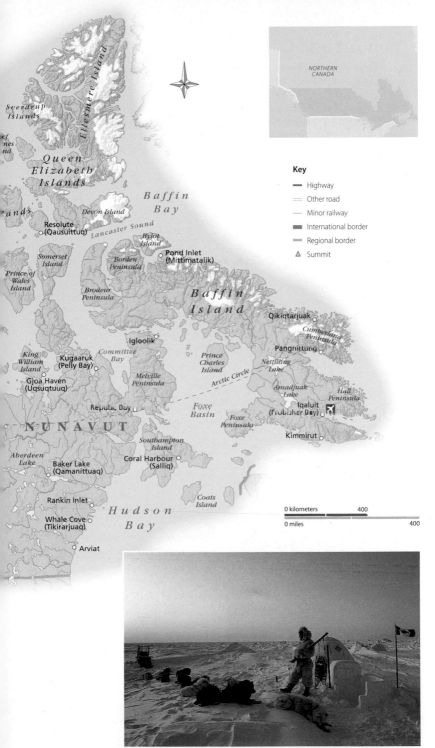

NORTHERN CANADA

Key

— Highway

··· Other road

— Minor railway

▬ International border

▬ Regional border

△ Summit

Sverdrup
Islands

ef
nes
nd

Queen
Elizabeth
Islands

Ellesmere Island

*Baffin
Bay*

ands

Devon Island

Resolute
(Qausuittuq)

Lancaster Sound

Bylot
Island

Pond Inlet
(Mittimatalik)

Somerset
Island

Borden
Peninsula

Prince of
Wales
Island

Brodeur
Peninsula

*Baffin
Island*

Qikiqtarjuak

*Cumberland
Peninsula*

Igloolik

Pangnirtung

King
William
Island

Kugaaruk
(Pelly Bay)

*Committee
Bay*

Prince
Charles
Island

Nettilling
Lake

Gjoa Haven
(Uqsuqtuuq)

*Melville
Peninsula*

Amadjuak
Lake

Arctic Circle

Hall
Peninsula

Repulse Bay

*Foxe
Basin*

Iqaluit
(Frobisher Bay)

N U N A V U T

*Foxe
Peninsula*

Kimmirut

Aberdeen
Lake

*Southampton
Island*

Baker Lake
(Qamanittuaq)

Coral Harbour
(Salliq)

Rankin Inlet

*Coats
Island*

Whale Cove
(Tikirarjuaq)

*H u d s o n
Bay*

Arviat

0 kilometers   400

0 miles   400

Inuit in the Northwest Territories using a dog sledge for transportation

For additional map symbols *see back flap*

Inuit Art and Culture

For centuries, the hunting and trapping lifestyle has created a distinct culture for the Inuit. Their customs have remained largely the same throughout the communities of eastern and central Northern Canada, although regional differences can be seen in the varied artforms. The Inuit have a limited written tradition, and much of 21st-century culture is still oral. It might seem surprising, given the outstandingly harsh environment and limited natural resources, that their communities offer a flourishing artistic output, but it is the hardship of northern life that has promoted artistic achievement. For example, the Inuit use their tool-making skills for sculpture. Inuit culture is closely tied to their lansdcape and environment, which has inspired many artists and mythmakers.

This woodblock print of a girl meeting a polar bear represents an artform developed in the 1950s. Stone cuts and stencils are also used to interpret drawings by older artists.

Warm clothing is both functional and decorative. Often painstakingly handwoven from scraps from the remains of a kill, women dress their families mostly in fur and wool.

Inuit beadwork and jewelry was made in earlier times from bone and ivory; colored stones and beads are now used. Each piece shows birds, animals, or people, and is unique. Western influences include new designs in silver and gold.

This soapstone carving of an Inuk (Inuit person) with a seal reflects the vital role seals have always played in Inuit culture.

Inuit Woman Preparing Char

The outdated, if not offensive, name for the Inuit people is "eskimo," a native Cree word meaning "eaters of raw meat." The Inuit traditionally eat their meat uncooked, as the Arctic has no trees for firewood. Much of the caribou, polar bear, and fish was sundried or mixed with sauces made from summer fruits and berries. The arrival of the stone and modern fuels has changed the menu somewhat, although tradition remains at the heart of the community's eating habits.

These dancing costume ornaments are carved from ivory or whalebone and worn by Inuit dancers to celebrate ceremonial events. As with clothing, Arctic bird feathers are used for decoration.

Inuit father and son in parkas, which are traditionally made by the women of the family. They use caribou, wolf, and polar bear fur. Today, imported Western fabrics are added for decoration.

Inuit fishermen have made the best possible use of their often limited natural resources and still rely largely on small-scale fishing for food.

Inuit homes are no longer the traditional igloo. Most people have moved to camps or community housing.

Inuit Myth

Set on the very fringes of the habitable world, the Inuit guarded against the threat of starvation with a supernatural belief system based on the respect of the animals they hunted,

Carving of Inuk fighting his spirit

being careful to guard against divine retribution. Their myths promote the belief that every living creature has a soul, and that the village shaman could travel between the upper and lower worlds to commune with, and appease, the spirits in control of the hunt and the weather. Since earliest times hunting tools and weapons have been carved with the representations of the appropriate guardian spirit, and singers and musicians are well versed in legends of sea spirits and human heroes.

Traditional hunting and fishing remains at the core of Inuit culture, although in the 1960s the Ottawa government unsuccessfully tried to stop these ancient practices.

Drum dancing is one of the varied forms of traditional music, and plays an important part in most of life's great events: births, weddings, a successful hunt, and honoring a person who has died. Another form of music, throat singing, is usually performed by two women facing one another to recount a legend, life event, or myth.

NORTHERN CANADA

Still one of the most remote destinations on Earth, Northern Canada's Arctic beauty is now accessible to adventurous travelers in search of untouched terrain for superlative, challenging hiking and exploring. Many of the settlements at this brink of the world were established only in the 20th century. Some of the first towns grew up around RCMP outposts, established to monitor trappers, explorers, and whalers in Canadian territory; more recently defense outposts have developed new settlements. Local Inuit communities have gradually given up their nomadic life, and many are now settled around these outposts. These small towns are bases for exploring the stunning surroundings. In the winter the north is cold, descending to -50°C (-58°F), yet in summer warm air sweeps over the cold land, and the tundra bursts into bloom. The thaw acts in defiance of eight long months of winter when everything is draped in a blanket of white. This is a startlingly beautiful land with deserted plains, icy trails, rare wildlife, and gentle people, and is ripe for discovery.

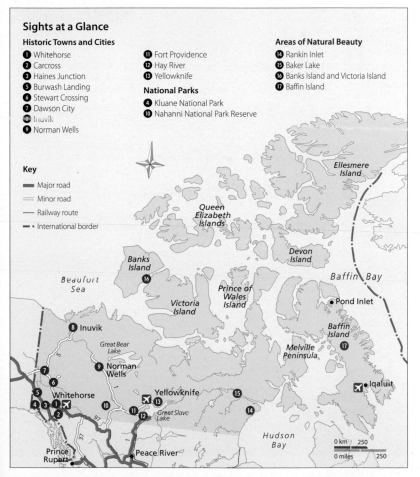

Sights at a Glance

Historic Towns and Cities
1 Whitehorse
2 Carcross
3 Haines Junction
5 Burwash Landing
6 Stewart Crossing
7 Dawson City
8 Inuvik
9 Norman Wells
11 Fort Providence
12 Hay River
13 Yellowknife

National Parks
4 Kluane National Park
10 Nahanni National Park Reserve

Areas of Natural Beauty
14 Rankin Inlet
15 Baker Lake
16 Banks Island and Victoria Island
17 Baffin Island

Key
▬ Major road
═ Minor road
— Railway route
—•— International border

Photographer capturing the Northern Lights (aurora borealis), Northwest Territories   **For map symbols** see back flap

❶ Whitehorse

Whitehorse takes its name from the local rapids on the Yukon River that reminded miners in the gold rush of "the flowing manes of albino Appaloosas." The town evolved when 2,500 stampeders on the hunt for gold braved the arduous Chilkoot and White Pass trails on foot in the winter of 1897–98 and set up camp here by the banks of Lindeman and Bennett Lakes. Boatmen made over 7,000 trips through the rapids during the spring thaw of 1898 before a tramway was built around them. On the spot where gold miners could catch a boat downstream to the mines of the Klondike and the glittering nightlife of Dawson City in the Yukon, a tent town sprang up and Whitehorse was born. This regional capital is the fastest-growing town in the northern territories, but despite all modern amenities, the wilderness is always only a few moments away.

🏛 MacBride Museum of Yukon History

1124 First Ave. **Tel** (867) 667 2709. **Open** mid-May–Sep: daily; Sep–mid-May: Tue–Sat. 🅿 ♿
🆆 macbridemuseum.com

The MacBride Museum is housed in a log cabin along the river. From Gold Rush fever to the birth of Whitehorse, this is the place to learn about the history of the Yukon. Gold to Government – Yukon's Modern History is one of several fascinating galleries. Other galleries cover wildlife, archaeology, and beadwork from the area's First Nations. Among the special features are Engine 51 from the White Pass and Yukon Route railway, and a log cabin depicting fictional character Sam McGee. In the summer there are daily talks and skits.

🏛 Log Skyscrapers

208 & 210 Lambert St.

Two blocks away from the Old Log Church Museum on Elliott Street are the unique log skyscrapers. Now several decades old, these log cabins have two or three floors. Currently used for residential purposes, one was home to a Yukon member of parliament. Worth a detour, the cabins offer a pleasing diversion from the rather functional architecture that characterizes much of the rest of town.

🏛 Old Log Church Museum

303 Elliott St. **Tel** (867) 668 2555 **Open** May–Aug. 🅿 ♿
🆆 oldlogchurchmuseum.ca

In August 1900, Anglican missionary Rev. R. J. Bowen was sent to Whitehorse to build a church. He held services in one tent and lived in a second, as the log building took shape. The church opened on October 17 and the log rectory was built that winter. These buildings are among the few remaining here from the gold rush period. In 1953, the log church became the Diocese of Yukon cathedral and is said to be the only log cathedral in the world. Now, exhibits and interactive programs feature Inuit and First Nations cultures, missionaries, and the development of the Anglican church in the north.

The Old Log Church, constructed entirely from local timber

🏛 S.S. Klondike National Historic Site

End Second Ave. **Tel** (867) 667 3910. **Open** mid-May–mid-Sep: 9:30am–5pm daily. 🅿 ♿
🆆 pc.gc.ca

Originally built in 1929, the S.S. *Klondike* paddle-steamer sank in 1936. Rebuilt from its wreckage, the *Klondike* made 10 supply trips each season to Dawson City. In the early 1950s, bridges along the road to Dawson were built too low, blocking the passage of the sternwheelers, so all journeys stopped. The

The city center of Whitehorse, sheltered in the Yukon River valley

For hotels and restaurants in this region see pp350–59 and pp364–83

S.S. *Klondike* in its permanent home in Whitehorse

Klondike ceased operating in 1955 and was beached forever in White-horse. It is now restored to its heyday in every detail, right down to the 1937 *Life* magazines on the tables and authentic staff uniforms. Although no longer operational, the boat is a National Historic Site, with regular guided tours of the interior on offer.

🎣 Lake Laberge
Klondike Hwy. **Tel** (867) 667 3084. **Open** daily, weather permitting.
Largest of the lakes in the area, Lake Laberge is 62 km (39 miles) from Whitehorse along the Klondike Hwy. Frozen for half of the year, with temperatures dropping below -30°C (-22°F), this popular summer swimming, fishing, and boating destination comes to life during the annual thaw. The lake is famous among locals as the site of the funeral pyre of Yukon poet Robert Service's *Cremation of Sam McGee*, which relates the demise of a fictional local hero. Trout fishing is excellent; fish were barged here by the ton during the Klondike gold rush to feed the hordes of hopeful miners.

Local mountain goat

🐾 Yukon Wildlife Preserve
Takhini Hot Springs Rd. **Tel** (867) 456 7300. **Open** daily. 🅿

This sanctuary was set up in 1965 for research and breeding purposes and lies about 25 km (16 miles) from the town off the Klondike Hwy on the Takhini Hot Springs Road. A beautiful reserve of forest, grassland, meadows, and water areas, it has ten species of northern mammals in large enclosures. Moose, bison, elk, caribou, mountain goats, deer, Dall sheep, as well as musk ox and lynx, can all be seen here protected in the 300-ha (750-acre) parkland of their natural roaming habitat.

Whitehorse City Center

① MacBride Museum of Yukon History
② Log Skyscrapers
③ Old Log Church Museum
④ S.S. *Klondike*

Lake Laberge, Yukon Wildlife Preserve

Airport 5 km (3 miles)

① MacBride Museum

WOOD STREET
STEELE STREET
MAIN STREET
ELLIOTT STREET
FIRST AVENUE

Old Log Church Museum ③
② Log Skyscrapers

SIXTH AVENUE
LAMBERT STREET
HANSON STREET
HAWKINS STREET
FOURTH STREET
SECOND AVENUE
THIRD AVENUE
YUKON River

FIFTH AVENUE
HOGE STREET
LEVES BLVD
④ S.S. Klondike

JECKELL STREET
ROBERT SERVICE WAY

0 meters 250
0 yards 250

Key to Symbols *see back flap*

Male caribou resting near Carcross, as herds migrate across the Yukon

❷ Carcross

🏔 450. 🚌 ℹ️ (867) 821 4431.
Open mid-May–Sep daily.

Carcross is a small village that lies at the picturesque confluence of Bennett and Tagish lakes, an hour's drive south of Yukon's regional capital, Whitehorse. Early miners crossing the arduous Chilkoot Pass on their journey to the bounty of the gold mines in the north named the site "Caribou Crossing" after herds of caribou stormed their way through the pass between Bennett and Nares lakes on their biannual migration. The town was established in 1899 in the height of the gold rush with the arrival of the White Pass and Yukon railroad. "Caribou Crossing" was abbreviated officially to Carcross to avoid duplication of names in Alaska, British Colombia, and a town in the Klondike. Carcross has a strong native tradition, and was once an important caribou hunting ground for the Tagish tribe. Tagish guides worked for US Army surveyors during the building of the Alaska Highway in 1942 *(see pp266–7)*. Just 2 km (1 mile) north is the "smallest desert in the world", Carcross Desert. Blasted by strong winds, the sandy plain is barren, and the only remnant of a glacial lake that dried up after the last Ice Age. The strength of the winds allows little vegetation to grow, but the spot is memorable.

❸ Haines Junction

🏔 589. 🚌 ℹ️ Kluane National Park and Reserve (867) 634 7207.

Haines Junction is a handy fuel and food stop for visitors on the way to the impressive Kluane National Park and Reserve. The town has a post office, restaurant, and hotels. Trips into the park for rafting canoeing, and various hiking excursions can be organized from the town, as the park's administrative headquarters are here. Those wishing to raft should book well ahead. Haines Junction was once a base camp for the US Army engineers who in 1942 built much of the Alcan Highway (now known as the Alaska Highway) that links Fairbanks in Alaska to the south of Canada. The St. Elias Mountains tower above the town, and air trips can be taken from here to admire the views of the frozen scenery, glaciers, and icy peaks of this wilderness.

Kaskawulsh Glacier rising over Kluane National Park and Reserve

❹ Kluane National Park and Reserve

Tel (867) 634 7207. 🚌 Haines Junction. **Open** year round. 🚫 ♿
🎫 🅦 pc.gc.ca

This superb wilderness area is a United Nations World Heritage Site. Covering 21,980 sq km (8,487 sq miles) of the southwest corner of the Yukon, the park shares the St. Elias mountain range, the highest in Canada, with Alaska. The whole park comprises one of the largest nonpolar icefields in the world.

Two-thirds of the park is glacial, filled with valleys and lakes that are frozen year-round, broken up by alpine forests, meadows, and tundra. The landscape is one of the last surviving examples of an Ice Age environment, which disappeared in the rest of the world around 5,000–10,000 BC. Mount Logan, at 5,959 m (19,545 ft), is Canada's tallest peak. Numerous well-marked and established trails make for excellent hiking here, and several conveniently start from

The St. Elias range dominates the small town of Haines Junction

Kluane National Park and Reserve displays radiant foliage in fall, as seen here in the Alsek River area

the main road. There are some less defined routes, which follow the old mining trails. There are trails to suit both the novice and experienced hiker, ranging from a 2-hour stroll to a 10-day guided trek.

Kluane's combination of striking scenery and an abundance of wildlife, including moose, Dall sheep, and grizzly bears, make it the Yukon's most attractive wilderness destination. Trips into the park are organized from nearby Haines Junction. Due to the hazardous weather, untamed wildlife, and isolated conditions, safety measures are mandatory here.

❺ Burwash Landing

🚹 88. **i** Whitehorse (867) 667 3084.

Northwest of Haines Junction by 124 km (77 miles), this little village at the western end of Kluane Lake lies just outside Kluane National Park on the Alaska Hwy. A community was established here in 1905, after a gold strike in a local creek, and Burwash Landing is now a service center. Visitors can also enjoy stunning panoramas of Kluane Lake to the south.

The village is noted for the **Kluane Museum of Natural History**, with many animal-related exhibits, including a mammoth's tooth and

numerous displays on local natural history. Focus is also given to the traditional lifestyle of the region's tribe of Southern Tutchone people.

🏛 Kluane Museum of Natural History
Burwash Landing. **Tel** (867) 841 5561. **Open** mid-May–mid-Sep: daily. 🅿 &

❻ Stewart Crossing

🚹 35. 🚌 **i** Whitehorse (867) 667 3084.

Approximately 180 km (113 miles) east of Dawson City (see p340), Stewart Crossing is a small community at the junction of the Klondike Hwy and the Silver Trail, which leads to the small mining settlements of Mayo, Elsa, and Keno, once famous for their silver trade During the gold rush in the late 19th century, the area was referred to as the "grubstake," because enough gold could be panned from the river sandbars

here during the summer to buy the following year's stake. Stewart Crossing is a modest service center that also operates as the starting-point for canoe trails on the Stewart River. Unusual for this wild terrain, these boat trips are suitable for children and beginners. Trips should be organized in Whitehorse or Dawson City.

About an hour north, at Km 655.1, is the **Tintina Trench Rest Area**. Providing in a glance visible proof of the geological theory of plate tectonics, the trench itself stretches for several hundred kilometers across the Yukon, with layers of millennia-old rock gaping open to the skies. "Tintina" means "chief" in the local native language, and this is one of the largest geological faults in the Yukon system. This area is an ideal place to view the trench, which runs up to here along the route of the Klondike Hwy, from a course parallel with the Yukon River that begins at Fortymile village.

Broad Valley by Stewart Crossing near the Yukon River, Yukon

Winter at Kluane National Park and Reserve, Yukon Territory ▶

The Palace Grand Theatre in Dawson City

⑦ Dawson City

📍 1,350. ✈ 🚌 ℹ cnr Front & King Sts. (867) 993 5575. 🅦 **dawsoncity.ca**

The town of Dawson City came into prominence during the Klondike gold rush of 1898 *(see pp54–5)*, when the population boomed and the city grew from a moose pasture into a bustling metropolis of some 30–40,000 people, all seeking their fortune in the new "Paris of the North." The town continues to mine gold, but tourism is now one of Dawson City's key sources of income.

Dawson City Museum has exhibits on the Klondike, with features on the gold rush and artifacts from that period. A popular attraction is **Diamond Tooth Gertie's**, the gambling hall complete with a honky-tonk piano and can-can girls.

🏛 **Dawson City Museum**
595 5th Ave. **Tel** (867) 993 5291. **Open** mid-May–Sep: 10am–6pm daily; late Sep–May: by appointment. 🖼 🅻 🅦 **dawsonmuseum.ca**

🎰 **Diamond Tooth Gertie's**
Cnr 4th Ave. & Queen St. **Tel** (867) 993 5525. **Open** May–mid-Sep: daily; variable in winter. 🖼 🅻

⑧ Inuvik

📍 3,500. ✈ ℹ 2 Firth St. (867) 777 8600. 🅦 **inuvik.ca**

About 770 km (480 miles) north of Dawson City, Inuvik lies at the tip of the Dempster Hwy, the most northerly road in Canada. Inuvik has only a very recent history. Founded in the 1950s as a supply center for military projects in the NWT, the town prospered in the oil boom of the 1970s. Full of functional contemporary architecture, Inuvik's charm lies more in its location as a good visitors' center for the region – there are a few hotels and several shops, no mean feat for a town that boasts just a single traffic light. It is, nonetheless, the most visited town in the northern Arctic, popular as a craft center for the Inuit and as a starting point for a tour of the far north.

Inuvik welcomes its visitors

Environs
The settlement of Paulatuk lies 400 km (250 miles) east of Inuvik and is one of the smallest communities in the territory. It is well placed for hunting, fishing, and trapping game; these activities remain its staple support after many centuries. Its location is also useful as a stepping-stone to the wilderness. Tourism is becoming popular, and trips into Tuktut Nogait National Park with Inuit guides are available. The unusual Smoking Hills, which are composed of sulfide-rich slate and coal can be seen when flying to and from Paulatuk.

⑨ Norman Wells

📍 800. ✈ ℹ Visitor Information Center and Museum, 23 MacKenzie Drive (867) 587 2415. **Open** daily. 🅦 **normanwells.com**

In 1920 crude oil discoveries were made here near a small Dene settlement. Oil production surged in World War II when the US established a pipeline to supply oil to the Alaska Highway while it was being built, and the town grew.

Today Norman Wells is the starting point for the Canol Heritage Trail, a long-distance path of wilderness trail through to the Canol Road above the Ross River in the Yukon Territory, which links up with the Yukon Highway system. There are few facilities along the trail, making it one of the toughest trekking paths in the world. Despite the difficulties, this is a popular destination with experienced hikers.

⑩ Nahanni National Park Reserve

Tel (867) 695 7750. ✈ Fort Simpson. **Open** year round. 🖼 ℹ Nahanni National Park Reserve, 10002-100 Street, Fort Simpson, NWT. 🅦 **pc.gc.ca**

Nahanni National Park Reserve sits astride the South Nahanni River between the border with the Yukon and the small settlement of Fort Simpson.

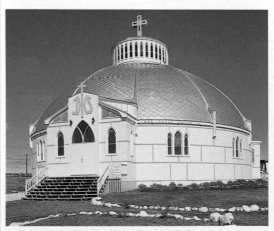
Inuvik's town church and hall, shaped like an igloo against the climate

The vast expanses of Nahanni National Park in summer

In 1978, it was one of the first places in the world to be designated a UNESCO World Heritage Site to protect its geological history. The park is a great wilderness with four vast river canyons, hot springs, and a spectacular undeveloped waterfall, Virginia Falls. The falls, at 90 m (295 ft), are twice the height of Niagara but have less volume, and boast excellent flora and fauna. At least 16 species of fish enjoy the cascades, and more than 180 varieties of bird live overhead. Wolves, grizzly bears, and woodland caribou move freely in the park.

The park's main activities are whitewater rafting and canoeing. In summer, watersports take precedence over walking tours, as the rivers thaw, and the landscape bursts into bloom with wild flowers. The park is usually reached by float plane.

⓫ Fort Providence

⚲ 750. **🚌** **ℹ** Northern Frontier Visitors Association, 4–4807 49th St., Yellowknife (867) 873 4262.

The Dene people call this village "zhahti koe," which means mission house in their native tongue. Fort Providence began life as a Catholic mission and was later enlarged by the Hudson's Bay Company *(see pp166–7)*, which set up an outpost here in the late 19th century. Attracted by this and the prospect of employment, the local Dene First Nations people settled here permanently. Today the town is a Dene handicrafts center.

Just north of the village lies the Mackenzie Bison Sanctuary. The sanctuary is home to the world's largest herd of 2,000 rare pure wood bison. The park stretches for 100 km (60 miles) north along the banks of Great Slave Lake, and bison can be seen along the road.

⓬ Hay River

⚲ 3,700. **✈** **🚌** **ℹ** MacKenzie Hwy (867) 874 3180. **Open** Jun–Sep.

Set on the banks of Great Slave Lake, the small community of Hay River is the major port in the Northwest Territories. A lifeline, the town supplies the High Arctic settlements and the northernmost towns in the country, particularly Inuvik, with essentials. When the river thaws in spring, it supplies freight. The town looks designed for the purpose it serves – the wharves are lined with barges and tugs, as well as the local fishing fleet.

Unusually for this area, Hay River's history stretches back over a millennium. The Dene moved here centuries ago, lured by the town's strategic position on the southern shore of the Great Slave Lake, for its hunting and fishing. Attractions here are based on local industry; as a shipping center, the harbor is a bustling place to spot barges. The original Dene settlement, now a village of 300 people, sits across the river north from the Old Town and welcomes visitors.

The Northern Lights

The Northern Lights, or *aurora borealis*, are believed to be the result of solar winds entering the Earth's ionosphere some 160 km (100 miles) above the surface of the planet. Emanating from the sun, these winds collide with the gases present in the Earth's upper atmosphere, releasing energy that becomes visible in the night sky. The stunning consequences are visible in the Yukon and the NWT, most often from August to October. Some aboriginal groups attach religious significance to the Lights, believing them to be the spirits of dead hunters, while 19th-century gold prospectors mistook them for vapors given off by ore deposits. Whatever one's beliefs, the sparkling ribbons of light are an awesome sight.

⑬ Yellowknife

Originally a native Dene settlement, Yellowknife is named after the yellow-bladed copper hunting knives used by its first residents. The Hudson's Bay Company closed its outpost here in 1823 due to failing profits, but the Old Town thrived again with gold mining in the 1930s and again after 1945. With improved road communications, the city became the regional capital of the Northwest Territories in 1967. Growing bureaucratic needs and four diamond mines 300 km (186 miles) north of Yellowknife have helped it flourish.

Makeshift houseboats on the Great Slave Lake

The Old Town

Just 1 km (0.5 mile) north of downtown, the Old Town is situated on an island and a rocky peninsula on Great Slave Lake. By 1947 Yellowknife had outgrown itself, and the New Town rose from the sandy plain southward. An unusual community thrives here on Yellowknife Bay, many living on makeshift houseboats. Also interesting is the variety of older architecture that can be seen from a stroll around this now residential area. Shops and accomodations are found farther south in the New Town. A good vantage point from which to survey the area is the Bush Pilots Monument at the north end of Franklin Avenue.

Wildcat Café

3904 Wiley Road. **Tel** (867) 873 4004. **Open** Jun–Sep: 11am–9pm daily. ♿ The oldest restaurant in Yellowknife, this institution is open only during the summer. A true frontier stop, and one of Yellowknife's earliest permanent buildings, the log cabin is set under the hill of the Old Town and has been refurbished in

Yellowknife City Center

① The Old Town
② Wildcat Café
③ Prince of Wales Northern Heritage Centre
④ Legislative Assembly

Niven Lake

Airport 4 km (2.5 miles)

Back Bay

Wildcat Café ②

Bush Pilots Monument

① OLD TOWN

④ Legislative Assembly

ℹ️

③ Prince of Wales Northern Heritage Centre

DOWNTOWN

INGRAHAM TRAIL

NIVEN DRIVE

MCAVOY RD

INGRAHAM DRIVE

49TH AVE

45TH ST

44TH ST

46TH AVE

FRANKLIN AVENUE (50TH AVENUE)

SCHOOL DRAW AVENUE

49TH AVENUE

49TH ST

47TH ST AVE

48TH STREET

51ST AVE

52ND AVENUE

47TH STREET

50TH AVENUE

50TH ST

52ND ST

Yellowknife Bay

| 0 meters | 400 |
| 0 yards | 400 |

1930s style. Its atmospheric interior is reminiscent of the pioneer days. Perhaps understandably, this establishment is the most photographed building in Yellowknife. It underwent renovations in 2011, but retains its authenticity.

Prince of Wales Northern Heritage Centre, Yellowknife, Northwest Territories

🏛 Prince of Wales Northern Heritage Centre

4750 48th Street. **Tel** (867) 873 7551. **Open** daily. **Closed** public holidays. 🚻 �W **pwnhc.ca**

This local museum's displays feature typically northern artifacts such as a mooseskin boat, as well as items illustrating the history of flying in the north. Changing exhibits explain life in the subarctic and Beaufort Delta regions.

🏛 Legislative Assembly

Frame Lake. **Tel** (867) 669 2230, 1 800 661 0784. **Open** Mon–Fri. 🚻 📷 �W **assembly.gov.nt.ca**

Built in 1993, this headquarters of local government has a tall domed roof. Signifying equal rights for all ethnic groups, the government chamber is the only round one of its kind in the country, with a large oval table to give all delegates equal responsibility, in the manner practiced by aboriginals. Decorated with paintings and Inuit art, the chamber is graced with a large polar bear rug. The official public government rooms can be toured when the council is not in session.

⑭ Rankin Inlet

🏠 2,600. ℹ Kivalliq Regional Visitor Centre (867) 645 3838. ✈

Founded in 1955 when North Rankin Nickel Mine opened, Rankin Inlet is the largest community in the stony plateau of Kivalliq, which stretches east of the Canadian Shield to Hudson Bay. This small town is the government center for the Kivalliq region, whose population, now 85 percent aboriginal, has settled mainly on the coast.

This region is characterized by its rural way of life and stunning scenery. **Iqalugaarjuup Nunanga Territorial Park**, 10 km (6 miles) from the town center, contains a traditional Thule (ancestor of the Inuit) restored native site with stone tent rings, meat stores, and semi-subterranean winter houses.

🏞 Iqalugaarjuup Nunanga Territorial Park

10 km (6 miles) NW of Rankin Inlet, on the Meliadine River. **Tel** (867) 975 7700. **Open** daily, weather permitting.

⑮ Baker Lake

🏠 1,700. ✈ ℹ (867) 793 2456.

Baker Lake is geographically at the center of Canada and is the country's only inland Inuit community. Located at the source of the Thelon River, the area has always been a traditional summer gathering place for the Inuit. Today it is an important center for Inuit art, especially textiles. Heading

westward, the **Thelon Wildlife Sanctuary** can also be visited. Visitors can see herds of musk ox in their natural habitat and glimpse other indigenous animals and birds.

🏞 Thelon Wildlife Sanctuary

300 km (200 miles) w. of Baker Lake. **Tel** (867) 975 7700. **Open** daily.

⑯ Banks Island and Victoria Island

ℹ (867) 979 4636.

Located in the Arctic Ocean, Banks Island is home to the largest herds of musk ox in the world. They dwell in **Aulavik National Park**, on the remote northern tip of the island. This numbers among the world's most remote wildlife destinations, and is accessible only by plane. Note that the park is best accessed from the Northwest Territories.

Split between the Northwest Territories and Nunavut, Victoria Island has a town in each – Ulukhaktok in NWT and the Inuit Cambridge Bay in Nunavut, where local native people traveled each summer for char fishing and caribou and seal hunting. The town today is a service center for locals and visitors along the Arctic coast. Polar bears, musk ox, wolves, and Arctic birds live nearby.

🏞 Aulavik National Park

Sachs Harbour. **Tel** (867) 690 3904. **Open** daily, weather permitting. 🚻 �W **pc.gc.ca**

An Inuit igloo builder near Baker Lake, practicing this traditional skill

For hotels and restaurants in this region see pp350–59 and pp364–83

⑰ Baffin Island

Part of Nunavut, Baffin Island is one of the most remote places in North America. At 500,000 sq km (193,000 sq miles), the island is the fifth largest on the planet, with more than 60 percent of its landmass lying above the Arctic Circle. Sparsely populated, the island is inhabited by just 11,000 people, 9,000 of whom are Inuit. Most people live in one of eight settlements scattered throughout the island, the chief of which is Iqaluit, capital of the territory of Nunavut.

With its spectacular fjords and knife-edged mountains sparkling with glaciers, Baffin Island offers a chance to experience all the outdoor activities of the Arctic. Canoeing, kayaking, trekking, and thrilling walks are all unbeatable here. Many of the activities often take place in the company of abundant wildlife, including polar bears and whales.

Arctic Bay

Bylot Island

Sirmilik National Park

Brodeur Peninsula

Borden Peninsula

Pond Inlet
Pond Inlet is a jewel in Nunavut's twinkling crown. Blessed with stunning scenery of mountains, glaciers, and icebergs, it is surrounded by abundant Arctic marine life. Snowmobiling and dogsledding to the floe edge are popular.

Prince Charle Island

Auyuittuq National Park

Auyuittuq is the third-largest national park in Canada at 19,089 sq km (7,370 sq miles). It is one of the few national parks with land above the Arctic Circle. A spectacular destination, the park displays a pristine wilderness of mountains, valleys, and fjords. In spring the meadows thaw out from under their snowy coverlets, and wildflowers burst into bloom. Within the park, wildlife abounds, with animals ranging from snow geese and arctic foxes to polar bears sharing the territory. Even in the brief summer, the weather can be tricky, with the risk of snow. Be prepared for cool weather, though temperatures can rise. The nearby town of Pangnirtung is a craft center.

Wildflowers flourish beneath Auyuittuq's frozen peaks

Cape Dorset is of interest archeologically because predecessors of the modern Inuit, the Thule and Dorset peoples, lived in this area. Cape Dorset is also known for its print-making tradition.

Key

— River

— National Park boundary

For hotels and restaurants in this region see pp350–59 and pp364–83

Pangnirtung
This little town of 1,300 residents sits at the southern end of the Pangnirtung Fjord, the 100-km (62-mile) hiking trail which is the most popular on Baffin. Some of the cliff faces here are more than 1,500 m (4,921 ft) high.

ACCESSING CANADA'S NORTH

While tourism to Nunavut increases every year, the only access to these remote settlements is by air, which is very expensive compared to mainline routes. Despite the cost, however, every community has its own airport.

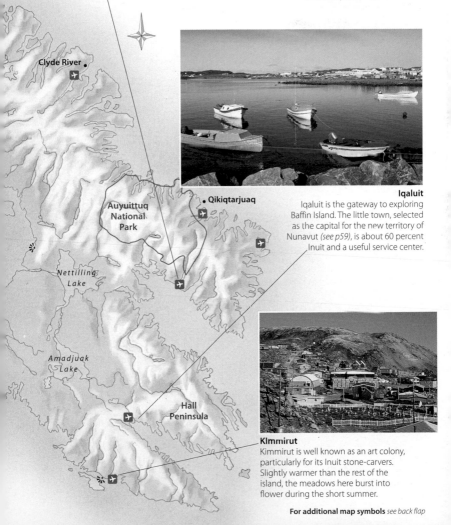

Iqaluit
Iqaluit is the gateway to exploring Baffin Island. The little town, selected as the capital for the new territory of Nunavut *(see p59)*, is about 60 percent Inuit and a useful service center.

Kimmirut
Kimmirut is well known as an art colony, particularly for its Inuit stone-carvers. Slightly warmer than the rest of the island, the meadows here burst into flower during the short summer.

For additional map symbols *see back flap*

TRAVELERS' NEEDS

WHERE TO STAY

As expected in a country of its size, Canada has a wide range of lodgings, from stately, world-famous hotels, such as Quebec City's Fairmont Le Château Frontenac, to family-run, intimate bed-and-breakfasts (B&Bs). There is also a variety of excellent middle-range accommodations, including rural inns, cabins to rent in scenic spots, elegant town apartments, hostels, houseboats, and convenient motels. Whether visitors need a mid-journey bed for the night or a seasonal rental, there is ample choice, and advance booking may not always be necessary. The listings on pages 350–59 describe a selection of venues for every taste and budget.

Contemporary room with a Jacuzzi bath in Château Montebello, Outaouais *(see p353)*

Grading and Facilities

There is no government-sponsored hotel grading system in Canada, but the voluntary "Canada Select", where places are rated by numbers of stars, is usually accurate. Note, however, that a four-star establishment in Canada's far north or in the countryside may not have the same facilities as one with the same rating in a major city.

The Canadian Automobile Association (CAA) also operates an assessment system, mostly for hotels and motels along main highways, and this is widely recognized as consistent and accurate. Look into CAA membership (or affiliated memberships) for discounts.

Air-conditioning is usually standard, except in national park lodges, some motels and B&Bs, as well as cooler coastal and northern regions. Central heating is efficient across the country. Cable TV, radio, irons and ironing boards, and coffee-making facilities are fairly standard. Private bathrooms are usual, but some exceptions exist. Specify if you want a bathtub or shower, and where

relevant, remember to ask for double or twin beds when booking a double room.

Prices

With such a wide range of accommodations, prices vary immensely. In cities, the top hotel's presidential suite may command a daily rate in excess of Can$1,000, while a hiker's hostel provides a dormitory bed for under Can$30. Budget hotels and B&Bs usually charge below Can$70 a night per person – but check because prices tend to rise in high season and fall in low season. Note that high season can also mean winter due to skiing or polar-bear watching, although it generally refers to summer.

Reservations

Advance reservations are recommended in major cities, where festivals, conventions, meetings, and sports and musical events are held year-round *(see pp42–5)*. Provincial tourist offices or airlines *(see p401)* can assist in bookings.

Children

Traveling with children is relatively easy in Canada. Most properties supply cots or junior-sized beds in parents' rooms. Major hotels offer babysitting services, usually for a fee. They may require 24 hours' notice. A minor (child under 18) traveling to Canada with one parent may need written consent (or other documentation) from the second parent under the anti-abduction regulation.

Disabled Travelers

Most new public buildings provide wheelchair facilities with ramps and wide doors. However, some lodgings date from the 19th century and may not have such facilities, so always check in advance.

Façade of the award-winning Le Priori hotel, Quebec City *(see p353)*

Luxury Hotels

Canada's major cities boast some world-class establishments. The railroad age of the late 19th century ushered in château-style hotels, a unique Canadian architectural style. Nowadays,

Rustic Clayoquot Wilderness Resort, surrounded by forested slopes *(see p357)*

The Goods and Services Tax (GST) is a standard national charge of 5 percent throughout the country; this affects most accommodation classes. In Nova Scotia, New Brunswick, Prince Edward Island, Newfoundland and Labrador, Ontario, and British Columbia the GST and PST are combined as Harmonized Sales Tax (HST) of 12 to 15 percent. Smaller hotels may not charge the GST.

Recommended Hotels

Within the listings given in this guidebook, accommodations fall into five categories. "Luxury" describes lodgings of distinction where impeccable service matches discerning design. "Boutique" refers to intimate, usually smaller, non-chain hotels. "Motel/hotel" includes chains or less luxurious establishments. "Cozy" category describes B&Bs (known as *gîtes* in Quebec) or country inns and holiday homes, while "resorts" refers to destination-type lodgings, which offer recreational activities such as swimming, skiing, horseback riding, and canoeing.

Outstanding lodgings have been highlighted as DK Choice entries. These may include a special B&B or funky boutique hotel with excellent service, upscale tents in Canada's wilderness offering a memorable experience, or a remote stay in a lighthouse keeper's home on an island. Whatever their special feature may be, these promise a truly Canadian experience.

most of these château-hotels, including Ottawa's Château Laurier *(see p355)*, are operated by Fairmont Hotels. Luxury chains are well represented: Relais & Châteaux, Four Seasons, Hilton, Radisson, Sheraton, and Westin chains operate in the major cities.

Chain Hotels

Canada has numerous franchise and chain hotels and motels. Reliable and comfortable, if occasionally a little bland, chains vary in style and price from grand resorts to the less expensive but well-known Days Inn, Best Western, Choice Hotels, and Howard Johnson. Popular with families and business travelers, many such properties provide services including fax and Wi-Fi access.

Efficiency Apartments

In addition to traditional cottages for rent, there is a variety of other options available. Motorhomes or RVs (Recreational Vehicles) are popular and can be leased in major cities. Most have air-conditioning, refrigerators, ovens, and bathrooms. Campgrounds are found throughout Canada and most provide laundry facilities, a convenience store, and Wi-Fi. Sports or interpretive nature programs are also often available.

Cottages or cabins are quintessentially Canadian. Ontario is famous for its selection of well-equipped rural vacation homes, which are available

weekly, monthly, or seasonally. National parks also rent lodges and offer campgrounds.

Bed-and-Breakfasts

B&Bs are popular across Canada. Ranging from historic inns to rural farmhouses, each provides personal service and insight into local life. Call the provincial tourist office for a detailed list with tariffs.

Accommodations Taxes

Remember that lodgings of almost every kind are subject to taxes on top of the basic tariff. Provincial Sales Tax (PST) must be paid on accommodations and on goods and other services. It varies from province to province and ranges between 5 and 10 percent. Rules vary slightly between provinces. For example, Alberta has no PST, but levies a 4 percent lodging tax on hotel and motel stays; campsites, B&Bs, and guesthouses are tax-free.

Plush interior of the Fairmont Château Laurier, Ottawa *(see p355)*

Where to Stay

Newfoundland and Labrador

CHANGE ISLANDS: Seven Oakes Island Inn and Cottages $
Historic
NL, A0G 1R0
Tel *(709) 621 3256*
W sevenoakesislandinn.com
A restored 19th-century home with a wraparound deck and sweeping ocean views.

CORNER BROOK: Marble Mountain Resort $$
Resort
Exit #8 TCH, NL, A2H 2N2
Tel *(1 800) 636 2725*
W skimarble.com
Rooms come with well-equipped kitchens and fireplaces.

GRAND-FALLS WINDSOR: Hill Road Manor B&B $$
Historic
1 Hill Rd, NL, A2A 1G9
Tel *(1 866) 489 5451*
W hillroadmanor.com
This 1939 B&B retains its original high ceilings and French doors. Breakfast menu changes daily.

NORRIS POINT: The Tides Inn $$
Motel
263 Main St, NL, A0K 3V0
Tel *(1 877) 350 3310*
W thetidesinn.ca
Spacious rooms at this quiet inn within Gros Morne National Park.

DK Choice

PORTUGAL COVE-ST. PHILIP'S: At the Beach House Atlantica $$
Luxury
38 Beachy Cove Rd, NL, A1M 2G7
Tel *(709) 895 1250*
W atthebeachhouse.ca
All the oceanfront rooms at this charming hotel have a kitchen or refrigerator, a patio or balcony, and a Jacuzzi. The award-winning Atlantica restaurant is on site, and a barbecue is available on request. Step outside to spot whales and icebergs.

QUIRPON: Quirpon Lighthouse Inn $$$
Rooms with a view
NL, A0K 2X0
Tel *(1 877) 254 6586*
W linkumtours.com
Unique accommodation in a restored 1922 lighthouse keeper's home. Located on the edge of Iceberg Alley.

ST. JOHN'S: Blue on Water $$
Boutique
319 Water St, NL, A1C 1B9
Tel *(1 877) 431 2583*
W blueonwater.com
Premier boutique hotel on North America's oldest street. Modern design with great harbor views.

TWILLINGATE: Hillside B&B $
B&B
5 Youngs Ln, NL, A0G 4M0
Tel *(709) 884 1666*
W bbcanada.com
Affordable option in the center of Iceberg Alley. Continental breakfast included. Hiking trails nearby.

New Brunswick, Nova Scotia, and Prince Edward Island

ANTIGONISH: Azelia Farmhouse B&B $
Boutique
309 Connors Rd, RR 2, NS, B2G 2K9
Tel *(902) 863 4262*
W bbcanada.com
Quaint rooms at this B&B. Alpacas graze in surrounding pastures.

BAY FORTUNE: Inn at Bay Fortune $$
Historic
Rte. 310, RR 4, PE, C0A 2B0
Tel *(902) 687 3745*
W innatbayfortune.com
Charming historical inn. Friendly owners and exceptional food.

BOUCTOUCHE: Auberge le Vieux Presbytère $$
Historic
157 Chemin du Couvent, NB, E4S 3B8
Tel *(506) 743 5568*
W vieuxpresbytere.nb.ca
Set in an old Catholic rectory with spacious rooms and beautiful gardens. Superb dining.

CARAQUET: Hotel Paulin $$
Luxury
143 Blvd St-Pierre W, NB, E1W 1B6
Tel *(506) 727 9981*
W hotelpaulin.com

Picturesque Great George Inn, Charlottetown

Price Guide
For a standard double room per night, including breakfast (where served), service charges, and taxes.

$	up to Can$100
$$	Can$100 to 200
$$$	over Can$200

Antique furnishings and excellent fare made with local produce in this historic boutique inn.

CHARLOTTETOWN: The Great George Inn $$$
Luxury
58 Great George St, PE, C1A 4K3
Tel *(902) 892 0606*
W thegreatgeorge.com
Set in a heritage building with luxurious rooms and suites that include Jacuzzis and fireplaces.

DIGBY: The Digby Pines $$
Luxury
103 Shore Rd, NS, B0V 1A0
Tel *(902) 245 2511*
W digbypines.ca
Elegant accommodations with heated outdoor pool, nightly bonfires, and kids' playground.

EDMUNDSTON: Auberge Les Jardins Inn $$
Boutique
60 Rue Principale, NB, E7B 1V7
Tel *(506) 739 5514*
W lesjardinsinn.com
Inn with charming rooms and old-fashioned decor. Cheaper motel rooms available as well.

FREDERICTON: Delta Fredericton $$$
Resort
225 Woodstock Rd, NB, E3B 2H8
Tel *(506) 457 7000*
W deltahotels.com
Family-friendly urban resort with pools and superb dining facilities.

GEORGETOWN: The Georgetown Inn $$
Boutique
62 Richmond St, PE, C0A 1L0
Tel *(902) 652 2511*
W peigeorgetownhistoricinn.com
Quaint rooms, some with ocean views and screened-in decks. Friendly hosts and fabulous dining.

GRAND TRACADIE: Dalvay By The Sea $$$
Rural
Rte. 6, Dalvay Beach, PE, C0A 1P0
Tel *(902) 672 2048*
W dalvaybythesea.com
Designated National Historic Site in a

Contemporary room at Hilton, St. John

charming but remote spot. Ample outdoor activities and a fine restaurant.

HALIFAX: Cambridge Suites $$
Chain hotels
1583 Brunswick St, NS, B3J 3P5
Tel *(902) 420 0555*
[w] cambridgesuiteshalifax.com
Contemporary rooms in the heart of downtown. Wonderful rooftop patio with harbor views.

INGONISH: Keltic Lodge Resort and Spa $$$
Resort
383 Middle Head Peninsula, NS, B0C 1L0
Tel *(902) 285 2880*
[w] kelticlodge.ca
Charming property in a breathtaking setting. Three restaurants with sweeping ocean views.

INVERNESS: Cabot Links Resort $$$
Resort
15933 Central Ave, NS, B0E 1N0
Tel *(902) 258 4653*
[w] cabotlinks.com
Luxurious rooms, all with beautiful views, modern furnishings, and spa-like bathrooms. Fabulous dining and a terrific golf course.

LIVERPOOL: White Point Beach Resort $$
Resort
75 White Point Beach Resort Rd, Hunts Point, NS, B0T 1G0
Tel *(902) 354 2711*
[w] whitepoint.com
Gorgeous family resort with a lodge as well as lakefront cabins. Dining, golf, and spa facilities.

LOUISBOURG: Point of View Suites $$
Rooms with a view
15 Commercial St Ext, NS, B1C 2J4
Tel *(902) 733 2080*
[w] louisbourgpointofview.com
Modern suites with views over Fortress of Louisbourg. Fun, historic dining experience on site.

MONCTON: Amsterdam Inn and Suites $$
Chain hotels
2550 Mountain Rd, NB, E1G 3V7
Tel *(506) 383 5050*
[w] amsterdaminns.com
Great-value hotel with big rooms, friendly staff, and good breakfasts. Close to casino and attractions.

DK Choice

PEGGY'S COVE: Oceanstone Seaside Resort $$$
Resort
8650 Peggy's Cove Rd, Indian Harbour, NS, B3Z 3P4
Tel *(902) 823 2160*
[w] oceanstoneresort.com
Situated right by the ocean, these lavish accommodations come with Jacuzzis, vaulted ceilings, and postcard pretty views. Conveniently located to Halifax and Peggy's Cove, yet in a beautiful remote setting right next to the crashing waves.

RUSTICO: Barachois Inn $$$
Luxury
2193 Church Rd, PE, C0A 1N0
Tel *(902) 963 2194*
[w] barachoisinn.com
Heritage buildings furnished with antiques. Welcoming hosts and great breakfasts.

SHEDIAC: The Tait House $$$
Luxury
293 Main St, NB, E4P 2A8
Tel *(506) 532 4233*
[w] maisontaithouse.com
Historic building featuring exquisite rooms with modern amenities. Excellent restaurant.

ST. ANDREWS: Europa Inn $$
Motel
48 King St, NB, E5B 1Y3
Tel *(506) 529 3818*
[w] europainn.com
Centrally located with comfortable rooms, gourmet breakfasts, and a good restaurant.

ST. JOHN: Hilton St. John $$
Chain hotels
1 Market Square, NB, F2L 4Z6
Tel *(506) 693 8484*
[w] 3.hilton.com
Spacious and modern rooms, some with amazing harbor views. Heated indoor saltwater pool.

ST. PETER'S: The Inn at St. Peter's $$
Rooms with a view
1668 Greenwich Rd, PE, C0A 2A0
Tel *(902) 961 2135*
[w] innatstpeters.com
Ocean-view rooms and cottages set in lovely grounds. Great restaurant and attentive owner.

SUMMERSIDE: Clark's Sunny Isle Motel $
Motel
720 Water St East, PE, C1N 4J1
Tel *(902) 436 5665*
[w] sunnyislemotel.com
Great value for comfortable rooms and landscaped gardens. A walking trail along the waterfront.

WEST POINT: West Point Lighthouse Inn $$
Rooms with a view
364 Cedar Dunes Park Rd, O'Leary, PE, C0B 1V0
Tel *(902) 859 3605*
[w] westpointlighthouse.com
Unique and beautifully appointed accommodations in a historic lighthouse.

Montreal

CHINATOWN: Holiday Inn Select Montréal Center-Ville $$
Motel
99 Ave Viger Ouest, H2Z 1E9
Tel *(514) 878 9888*
[w] holidayinn.com
Reliable chain hotel with an indoor pool, gym, and sauna. Rooftop pagodas and pretty Chinese gardens.

DOWNTOWN: Auberge de Paris $
Budget
907 Rue Sherbrooke Ouest, H2L 1L3
Tel *(514) 522 6124*
[w] aubergemontreal.com
Modern hostel with comfortable rooms and secure lockers. Women's-only dorm with private bathrooms. On-site bistro.

DOWNTOWN: Hôtel Viger $
Budget
1001 Rue Saint-Hubert, H2Y 3Y3
Tel *(514) 845 6058*
[w] hotel-viger.com
Basic, clean accommodations with bathrooms and TV sets.

For more information on types of hotels *see page 349*

DOWNTOWN: Hotel Château Versailles $$
Boutique
1659 Rue Sherbrooke Ouest, H3H 1E3
Tel *(514) 933 3611*
W versailleshotels.com
Luxury hotel with period features and a French restaurant.

DOWNTOWN: Hotel du Fort $$
Boutique
1390 Rue du Fort, H3H 2R7
Tel *(514) 938 8333*
W hoteldufort.com
Well-lit and spacious rooms with kitchenettes. Good for families.

DOWNTOWN: Delta Montréal $$$
Chain hotels
475 Ave du Président Kennedy, H3A 1J7
Tel *(514) 286 1986*
W deltamontreal.com
Great-value hotel with grand rooms, some with views of the sprawling city and Mont-Royal.

DOWNTOWN: Fairmont La Reine Elizabeth $$$
Luxury
900 René-Lévesque Ouest, H3B 4A5
Tel *(514) 861 3511*
W fairmont.com
Distinguished hotel favored by celebrities. Well located for skiing, river rafting, golf, and tennis.

DOWNTOWN: Residence Inn $$$
Chain hotels
2170 Lincoln Ave, H3H 2N5
Tel *(514) 935 9224*
W residencemontreal.com
Rooms have kitchenettes and a dining area. Breakfast buffet.

DOWNTOWN: Ritz-Carlton Montréal $$$
Luxury
1228 Rue Sherbrooke Ouest, H3G 1H6
Tel *(514) 842 4212*
W ritzmontreal.com
Plush rooms, exquisite dining, and magnificent grounds.

PLATEAU MONT-ROYAL: Auberge de la Fontaine $$
Boutique
1301 Rue Rachel Est, H2J 2K1
Tel *(514) 597 0166*
W aubergedelafontaine.com
Two Second-Empire homes converted into a stylish, eccentrically decorated hotel.

PLATEAU MONT-ROYAL: Le Jardin d'Antoine $$
Boutique
2024 Rue St-Denis, H2X 3K7
Tel *(514) 843 4506*
W hotel-jardin-antoine.qc.ca
Located in the trendy Latin Quarter. Airy and deluxe rooms overlook a courtyard garden.

Indoor pool at the luxurious Delta Montréal, downtown Montreal

VIEUX-MONTREAL: Auberge les Passants du Sans Soucy $$
Historic
171 Rue Saint-Paul Ouest, H2Y 1Z5
Tel *(514) 842 2634*
W lesanssoucy.com
A 1723 home furnished with antiques. An art gallery in the lobby and excellent breakfasts.

VIEUX-MONTREAL: Auberge du Vieux-Port $$$
Rooms with a view
97 Rue de la Commune Est, H2Y 1J1
Tel *(514) 876 0081*
W aubergeduvieuxport.com
Roof terrace overlooks park, bike paths, and Vieux Port. Refined rooms and renowned restaurant.

DK Choice

VIEUX-MONTREAL: Hostellerie Pierre du Calvet $$$
Luxury
405 Rue Bonsecours, H2Y 3C3
Tel *(514) 282 1725*
W pierreducalvet.ca
Opulent elegance in a 1725 stone-built house. Rooms evoke history with original fireplaces, oak paneling, and window seats. Breakfast is served in the atrium where several parrots reside. Two superb restaurants feature outstanding service, cuisine, and decor.

VIEUX-MONTREAL: Hotel Gault $$$
Boutique
449 Rue Saint-Hélène, H2Y 2K9
Tel *(514) 904 1616*
W hotelgault.com
Exemplary service and quirky design. Hidden library in the lobby.

VIEUX-MONTREAL: Hotel InterContinental Montréal $$$
Luxury
360 Rue Saint-Antoine Ouest, H2Y 3X4
Tel *(514) 987 9900*
W intercontinental.com
Modern high-rise in city's financial and entertainment district. Lap pool, sauna, and massage services.

VIEUX-MONTREAL: Hotel le Saint James $$$
Luxury
355 St. Jacques St, H2Y 1N9
Tel *(514) 841 3111*
W hotellestjames.com
Plush rooms. Sweeping wrought-iron staircase from balconied mezzanine to the restaurant.

Quebec City and the St. Lawrence River

BAIE SAINT-PAUL: Auberge La Maison Otis $$
Boutique
23 Rue Saint-Jean-Baptiste, QC, G3Z 1M2
Tel *(418) 435 2255*
W maisonotis.com
Charming country inn with a spa, restaurant, and gardens. Salmon fishing, golf, and skiing nearby.

DK Choice

BAIE SAINT-PAUL: Hotel La Ferme $$
Luxury
50 Rue de la Ferme, QC, G3Z 1M2
Tel *(418) 435 2255*
W lemassif.com
In 2012, Cirque-du-Soleil's co-founder Guy Laliberté established this eco-friendly hotel in artsy Baie Saint-Paul. A range of rooms, including dorms, are available. Enjoy locavore dining and shop in the on-site farmers' market during summer.

GASPÉ: La Gite du Mont-Albert $$
Resort
2001 Route du Parc, Sainte-Anne-des-Monts, QC, G4V 2E4
Tel *(418) 763 2288*
W sepaq.com
Stay in the lodge or rent a cabin in serene environs. Ample opportunities to hike and ski.

Cozy interiors of the Auberge du Vieux-Port, Vieux-Montreal

ILES-DE-LA-MADELEINE: Hotel au Vieux Convent $$
Historic
292 Rte 199, Havre-aux-Maisons, QC, G4T 5A4
Tel *(418) 969 2233*
W domaineduvieuxcouvent.com
This refurbished convent is a heritage landmark. Ocean-view rooms plus six apartments.

L'ILE VERT: Les Maisons du Phare de l'Ile Verte $
Budget
2802 Chemin du Phare, QC, G0L 1K0
Tel *(418) 898 2730*
W ileverte.net
Simple accommodations with kitchens in an island lighthouse. Breakfasts served, but other meals are self-catered.

LA MALBAIE: Fairmont Le Manoir Richelieu $$
Luxury
181 Rue Richelieu, QC, G5A 1X7
Tel *(418) 665 3703*
W fairmont.com
Resembles a castle perched on a cliff. Beach, bike and ski pathways, as well as golf course at hand.

LAC-SAINT-JEAN: Hôtel du Jardin $$
Motel
1400 Blvd du Jardin Saint-Félicien, QC, G8K 2N8
Tel *(418) 679 8422*
W hoteldujardin.com
Comfortable modern hotel with spacious rooms. Some have whirlpool baths. Massage center.

PERCÉ: Hôtel La Normandie $$
Rooms with a view
221 Route 132 W, QC, G0C 2L0
Tel *(418) 782 2112*
W normandieperce.com
Clapboard inn overlooking Percé Rock. Beautiful perennial gardens and an excellent seafood restaurant on site.

QUEBEC CITY: Hotel Particulier Belley
Boutique
249 Rue Saint-Paul, QC, G1K 3W5
Tel *(418) 692 1694*
W hotelbelley.com
Former tavern sheltered beneath old fortifications. Uniquely decorated small rooms.

QUEBEC CITY: Fairmont Le Château Frontenac $$$
Luxury
1 Rue des Carrières, G1R 4P5
Tel *(418) 692 3861*
W fairmont.com
Picturesque castle with magnificent river views and personalized amenities. There is a cozy bar on site.

QUEBEC CITY: Hotel Clarendon $$$
Historic
57 Rue Sainte-Anne, QC, G1R 3X4
Tel *(418) 692 2480*
W hotelclarendon.com
Art-Deco hotel offering old-fashioned European luxury. Restaurant and live jazz bar.

QUEBEC CITY: Le Priori $$$
Boutique
15 Rue Sault-au-Matelot, QC, G1K 3Y7
Tel *(418) 692 3992*
W hotelpriori.com
Once architect Jean Baillairgé's home. Stone walls juxtaposed with modern furniture and art.

SEPT-ILES: Hôtel Sept-Iles $$
Budget
451 Arnaud Ave, QC, G4R 3B3
Tel *(418) 962 2581*
W hotelseptiles.com
Balconies overlook the river. Basic rooms and an on-site restaurant.

TROIS-RIVIERES: Delta Trois-Rivieres $$
Chain hotels
1620 Rue Notre-Dame Centre, QC, G9A 6E5
Tel *(418) 376 1991*
W deltahotels.com
Modern high-rise popular with families. Sunday breakfast buffet.

Southern and Northern Quebec

LAURENTIAN MOUNTAINS: Auberge de la Montagne-Coupée $$
Rooms with a view
1000 Ch. de la Montagne Coupée, Saint-Jean-de-Matha, QC, J0K 2S0
Tel *(450) 886 3891*
W montagnecoupee.com
Comfortable inn amid forested hills. Breakfast and dinner included.

LAURENTIAN MOUNTAINS: Hotel La Sapiniére $$
Boutique
1244 Chemin La Sapinière, Val David, QC, J0T 2N0
Tel *(819) 322 2020*
W sapiniere.com
A lakeside getaway renowned for its fine lodging, spa, and dining.

MAGOG: Auberge L'Étoile-sur-le-Lac $$
Rooms with a view
1200 Principal Ouest, QC, J1X 2B8
Tel *(819) 843 6521*
W etoilesurlelac.com

The designer Le Priori hotel, Quebec City

Some balconies overlook Lac Memphremagog. Meals served on terrace in summer. Spa on site.

NORTH HATLEY: Manoir Hovey $$$
Luxury
575 Rue Hovey, QC, J0B 2C0
Tel *(819) 842 2421*
W hoveymanor.com
Romantic inn modeled on George Washington's Virginia home. Some rooms have fireplaces. Award-winning restaurant.

NUNAVIK: Auberge Kuujjuaq Inn $$$
Motel
550 Airport Rd, Kuujjuaq, QC, J0M 1C0
Tel *(819) 964 2903*
W nvkuujjuaq.ca
Basic accommodations amid elemental Tundra wilderness. Lodging in Quebec's north is scarce so book ahead.

DK Choice

OUTAOUAIS: Château Montebello $$$
Luxury
392 Rue Notre-Dame, Montebello, QC, J0V 1L0
Tel *(819) 423 6341 2*
W fairmont.com
This two-in-one property is home to the world's largest log hotel, plus the adjacent Kenauk, a remote seigneury with secluded lakeside cabins. Enjoy drinks around the six-sided fireplace before dining on exquisite local cuisine. A range of outdoor activities is on offer.

RICHELIEU VALLEY: Les Trois Tilleuls $$
Luxury
290 Rue Richelieu, St-Marc-sur-Richelieu, J0L 2E0
Tel *(514) 856 7787*
W lestroistilleuls.com
Historic country inn bordering the Richelieu River. Excellent spa, art gallery, and beautiful gardens and walkways on site.

For more information on types of hotels *see page 349*

**ROUYN-NORANDA: Hotel
Albert** $$
Chain hotels
84 Principal, QC, J9X 4P2
Tel *(819) 762 3545*
�W bestwestern.com
An old-fashioned hotel with
basic, comfortable rooms.

Toronto

AIRPORT: Hotel Indigo $$
Motel
135 Carlingview Drive, M9W 5E7
Tel *(416) 637 7000*
�W hotelindigo.com
Modern hotel near the airport
with easy access to downtown.

**DOWNTOWN: The Primrose
Best Western Hotel** $
Budget
111 Carlton St, M5B 2G3
Tel *(416) 977 8000*
�W torontoprimrosehotel.com
Well-located with comfortable
rooms and a seasonal pool.

**DOWNTOWN: DoubleTree
by Hilton Hotel** $$
Chain hotels
108 Chestnut St, M5G 1R3
Tel *(416) 977 5000*
�W doubletree.com
Elegant rooms with plush bedding.
Indoor water park on site.

DOWNTOWN: Eaton Chelsea $$$
Chain hotels
33 Gerrard St W, M5G 1Z4
Tel *(416) 595 1975*
�W chelsea.eatonhotels.com
Waterslide and in-room spa
service. Four on-site restaurants,
and shops and bars nearby.

**DOWNTOWN: Hilton
Toronto Hotel** $$$
Chain hotels
145 Richmond St W, M5H 2L2
Tel *(416) 869 3456*
�W hilton.com
Luxury in the middle of the city's
shopping and financial district.

DOWNTOWN: Hyatt Regency $$$
Boutique
370 King St W, M5V 1J9
Tel *(416) 343 1234*
�W hyattregencytoronto.com
Urban chic hotel at the heart of
the entertainment district.

**DOWNTOWN: Le Royal Meridien
King Edward** $$$
Luxury
37 King St E, M5C 1E9
Tel *(416) 863 9700*
�W thekingedwardhotel.com
Full amenities at this regal hotel.
Elaborate afternoon tea.

**DOWNTOWN: Radisson Hotel
Admiral Toronto-Waterfront** $$$
Chain hotels
249 Queen's Quay W, M5J 2N5
Tel *(416) 203 3333*
�W radisson.com
Stylish waterfront hotel with
stunning views. Outdoor pool.

**DOWNTOWN: Sheraton Center
Toronto** $$$
Luxury
123 Queen St W, M5H 2M9
Tel *(416) 361 1000*
�W starwoodhotels.com
The 43rd Floor Club Lounge
commands splendid city views.
Business and fitness centers.

**DOWNTOWN: Shangri-La
Hotel** $$$
Luxury
188 University Ave, M5H 0A3
Tel *(647) 788 8888*
�W shangri-la.com/toronto/
Luxurious rooms with Asian-style
decor. Close to entertainment
and shopping.

**DOWNTOWN: The Fairmont
Royal York** $$$
Luxury
100 Front St W, M5J 1E3
Tel *(416) 368 2511*
�W fairmont.com
Iconic hotel with impeccable
service and unmissable spa.

**DOWNTOWN: The Westin
Harbour Castle** $$$
Luxury
1 Harbour Square, M5J 1A6
Tel *(416) 869 1600*
�W starwoodhotels.com/westin
Luxury waterfront hotel with three
restaurants. Free local shuttle.

DK Choice

**DOWNTOWN:
Windsor Arms Hotel** $$$
Luxury
18 St. Thomas St, M5S 3E7
Tel *(416) 971 9666 7*
�W windsorarmshotel.com
This iconic Neo-Gothic
institution boasts a stone-carved
doorway and lobby. Rooms
feature mahogany furnishings,
fireplaces, and bathrooms with
limestone floors. There are
separate dining rooms for fine
and casual dining, as well as
for afternoon tea. Enjoy the
splendid spa and saltwater pool.

**EAST END: Accommodating
the Soul B&B** $$
Boutique
114 Waverley Rd, M4L 3T3
Tel *(416) 686 0619*
�W accommodatingthesoul.com

Relaxed retreat on the beach.
Close to shops, bistros, and
lakeshore boardwalk.

**NORTH: Hilton Toronto/
Markham Suites Conference
Center & Spa** $$
Business
8500 Warden Ave, L6G 1A5
Tel *(905) 470 8500*
�W hilton.com
Full conference center, as well as
three restaurants and spa on site.

WEST END: Drake Hotel $$$
Boutique
1150 Queen St W, M6J 1J3
Tel *(416) 531 5042*
�W thedrakehotel.ca
Bohemian-inspired 1890 heritage
hotel. Grand lobby staircase.

WEST END: Gladstone Hotel $$$
Boutique
1214 Queen St W, M6J 1J6
Tel *(416) 531 4635*
�W gladstonehotel.com
Unique 1889 landmark with
artistic, themed rooms.

Ottawa and Eastern
Ontario

COBURG: King George Inn $$
Boutique
77 Albert St, ON, K9A 2L9
Tel *(905) 373 4610*
�W thekinggeorgeinn.com
Housed in a former provincial
jail with themed and non-
themed rooms Family rooms
with bunk beds are also available.

**FENELON FALLS: Eganridge
Inn & Spa** $$
Resort
26 Country Club Drive, ON, K0M 1N0
Tel *(705) 738 5111*
�W eganridge.com

Opulent furnishings in the lobby at
Fairmont Royal York, downtown Toronto

Inviting room with a four-poster bed, Swiss Hotel, Ottawa

Offers rooms with terraces, private cottages, and a lodge. Private dining room and an excellent spa.

HALIBURTON: Sir Sam's Inn & Waterspa $$$
Resort
1491 Sir Sam's Rd, Eagle Lake, ON, K0M 1N0
Tel *(705) 754 2188*
w sirsamsinn.com
Outdoor pool, indoor sauna, water spa at this lakeside inn. Ample opportunities to water ski, windsurf, sail, or kayak.

HUNTSVILLE: Arowhon Pines Lodge $$$
Resort
Arowhon Rd, Algonquin Park, ON, P1H 2G5
Tel *(866) 633 5661*
w arowhonpines.ca
Lakeside log cabins and luxury suites in Algonquin Park. Outdoor activities on offer. No TV/ Internet.

KINGSTON: Kingston Secret Garden B&B Inn $$
Historic
73 Sydenham St, ON, K7L 3H3
Tel *(613) 531 9884*
w thesecretgardeninn.com
Heritage home with antique furnishings and private baths. Friendly and informative owners.

KINGSTON: Rosemount Inn & Spa $$$
Historic
46 Sydenham St S, ON, K7L 3H1
Tel *(613) 531 8844*
w rosemountinn.com
A mid-19th century property offering afternoon tea and wine-inspired spa treatments.

NORTH BAY: Best Western North Bay $$
Motel
700 Lakeshore Drive, ON, P1A 2G4
Tel *(705) 474 5800*
w bestwesternnorthbay.com
Good location for lake and museums. Modern amenities.

OTTAWA: Swiss Hotel $$
Boutique
89 Daly Ave, ON, K1N 6E6
Tel *(613) 237 0335*
w swisshotel.ca
Family-run hotel in a quiet neighborhood. Some rooms have fireplaces and Jacuzzis.

OTTAWA: Delta Ottawa City Center $$$
Chain hotels
101 Lyon St N, ON, K1R 5T9
Tel *(613) 237 3600*
w deltahotels.com
Choose from bedroom suites or studios with kitchenettes and balconies. Kids' center on site.

DK Choice

OTTAWA: Fairmont Château Laurier $$$
Luxury
1 Rideau St, ON, K1N 8S7
Tel *(613) 241 1414*
w fairmont.com
Ottawa's 1912 landmark fairy-tale castle is a popular meeting place for afternoon tea or dinner. Spend the evening on old-style elegance while spotting celebrities at the piano bar. Over 400 rooms, an indoor Art-Deco pool, and spa services available. Exemplary service.

OTTAWA: Lord Elgin Hotel $$$
Luxury
100 Elgin St, ON, K1P 5K8
Tel *(613) 235 3333*
w lordelginhotel.ca
Historic landmark hotel in downtown Ottawa. Amenities include a lap pool, whirlpool, and sauna.

PICTON: Merrill Hill $$$
Boutique
343 Main St E, ON, K0K 2T0
Tel *(613) 476 7451*
w merrillinn.com
Red brick 1887 mansion boasts elegant, well-appointed rooms and a highly-regarded restaurant.

RICE LAKE: Victoria Inn $$
Historic
5316 Rice Lake Scenic Drive, Gore's Landing, ON, K0K 2E0
Tel *(905) 342 3261*
w thevictoriainn.ca
Century-old inn on the shores of Rice Lake. The turret rooms have wonderful views.

The Great Lakes

COLLINGWOOD: The Westin Trillium House, Blue Mountain $$$
Resort
220 Gord Canning Drive, Blue Mountains, ON, L9Y 0V9
Tel *(705) 443 8080*
w westinbluemountain.com
At Blue Mountain ski resort. Kids' club, aquatic center, and golf courses. Kitchenettes available.

DK Choice

GODERICH: Benmiller Inn & Spa $$
Luxury
81175 Benmiller Line, ON, N/A 3Y1
Tel *(519) 524 2192*
w benmillerinnandspa.com
Set in a forested valley, this eco-friendly inn offers elegant accommodations in many buildings, including a historic mill. An excellent spa with river views awaits, as does a five-star restaurant. Lake Huron's beaches and an extensive trail network are nearby.

HAMILTON: Sheraton Hotel Hamilton $$
Business
116 King St W, ON, L8P 4V3
Tel *(905) 529 5515*
w sheratonhamilton.com
Geared more toward business travelers, but still a good base to explore local sights. Indoor pool.

JORDAN: Inn on the Twenty $$$
Boutique
3845 Main St, ON, L0R 1S0
Tel *(905) 562 5336*
w innonthetwenty.com
Highly rated country inn set on the Wine Route. Features include fireplaces and whirlpools.

NIAGARA FALLS: Old Stone Inn $
Historic
5425 Robinson St, ON, L2G 7L6
Tel *(905) 357 1234*
w oldstoneinn.on.ca
Boutique property housed in century-old flourmill. Easy access to attractions, but quiet location.

NIAGARA FALLS: Sheraton on the Falls $$
Rooms with a view
5875 Falls Ave, ON, L2G 3K7
Tel *(1888) 229 9961*
W sheratononthefalls.com
Book here to sleep mere metres from the falls. Every room offers incomparable views.

NIAGARA-ON-THE-LAKE: Harbour House $$$
Boutique
85 Melville St, ON, L0S 1J0
Tel *(905) 468 4683*
W niagarasfinest.com
Highly rated hotel, perfectly located where the falls meet the lake. Short stroll to local wineries.

PORT STANLEY: Inn on the Harbour $$
Boutique
202 Main St, ON, N5L 1H6
Tel *(519) 782 7623.*
W innontheharbour.ca
Rustic yet elegant inn next to a fishing wharf. Eclectic decor.

SAULT STE. MARIE: Delta Sault Ste. Marie Waterfront Hotel $$
Rooms with a view
208 St. Mary's River Drive, ON, P6A 5V4
Tel *(705) 949 0611*
W deltahotels.com
A harborfront hotel overlooking the marina. Convenient location.

STRATFORD: Foster's Inn $$
Boutique
111 Downie St, ON, N5A 1X2
Tel *(1888) 728 5555*
W fostersinn.com
Centrally located hostel with original maple hardwood floors.

THUNDER BAY: Best Western Nor'Wester Resort $$
Resort
2080 Hwy 61, ON, P7J 1B8
Tel *(807) 473 9123*
W bestwestern.com
Modern hotel with amethyst fireplaces and heated indoor pool. Golfing, fishing, and skiing nearby.

TOBERMORY: Blue Bay Motel $$
Motel
32 Bay St, ON, N0I1 2R0
Tel *(519) 596 2392*
W bluebay-motel.com
Eco-friendly hotel at the harbor. Close to diving, kayaking, and boat tours, plus hiking and skiing trails.

WINDSOR: Hilton Windsor $$
Rooms with a view
277 Riverside Dr, ON, N9A 5K4
Tel *(519) 973 5555*
W hilton.com
Rooms with fantastic views of the Detroit skyline and the river. Short walk to casino.

Central Canada

CHURCHILL: Lazy Bear Lodge $$$
Rural
313 Kelsey Blvd, MB, R0B 0E0
Tel *(866) 687 2327*
W lazybearlodge.com
This wooden lodge is a good base for wildlife viewing. Packages include pick-ups, meals, and tours.

DRUMHELLER: Newcastle Country Inn $$
B&B
1130 Newcastle Trail, AB, T0J 0Y2
Tel *(403) 823 8356*
W newcastlecountryinn.net
Rooms in this comfortable, three-star inn include a continental breakfast and Wi-Fi.

DK Choice

EDMONTON: Mettera Hotel on Whyte $$$
Boutique
10454 82 Ave, AB, T6E 4Z7
Tel *(780) 465 8150*
W metterra.com
A contemporary hotel located in trendy Old Strathcona. Unique "fire and water" suites, three restaurants, 24-hour business and fitness centers, plus a full-service spa. Price includes deluxe breakfasts, Wi-Fi, and evening wine-tasting (Mon–Sat). Close to restaurants, entertainment, and nightlife.

EDMONTON: Union Bank Inn $$$
Boutique
10053 Jasper Ave, AB, T5J 1S5
Tel *(780) 423 3600*
W unionbankinn.com
Housed in the 1911 Union Bank building. Wi-Fi, à la carte breakfast, and nightly wine and cheese trays.

LETHBRIDGE: Lethbridge Lodge Hotel & Conference Center $$
Business
320 Scenic Drive, AB, 11J 4B4
Tel *(403) 328 1123*
W lethbridgelodge.com

Premium business hotel with a tropical courtyard and an indoor pool. Good breakfast buffet.

MOOSE JAW: Temple Gardens Mineral Spa Resort $$$
Resort
24 Fairford St E., SK, S6H 0C7
Tel *(306) 694 8310*
W templegardens.sk.ca
Spa-resort in historic downtown known for its natural geothermal pool and therapeutic treatments.

REGINA: Radisson Plaza Hotel Saskatchewan Regina $$$
Chain hotels
2125 Victoria Ave, SK, S4P 0S3
Tel *(306) 522 7691*
W radisson.com
Historic hotel built in 1927 with park and city views. Spa, fitness center, and convention facilities.

RIDING MOUNTAIN NATIONAL PARK: Elkhorn Resort $$
Resort
#3 Mooswa Drive E., Onanole, MB, R0J 1N0
Tel *(204) 848 2802*
W elkhornresort.mb.ca
Year-round resort surrounded by boreal forest. Spa, horseback riding, golf, and winter sports.

SASKATOON: Delta Bessborough Hotel $$$
Historic
601 Spadina Crescent, SK, S7K 3G8
Tel *(306) 244 5521*
W deltahotels.com
Iconic "railway hotel" with business and fitness centers, indoor pool, full-service spa, and restaurants.

SASKATOON: The James Hotel $$$
Luxury
620 Spadina Crescent E., SK, S7K 3T5
Tel *(306) 244 6446*
W thejameshotel.ca
Modern boutique hotel scenically located at the river's edge. Stylish lounge. Includes a full breakfast.

Sheraton on the Falls, right next to the Niagara Falls

Key to Price Guide *see page 350*

DK Choice

WINNIPEG: Fort Gary Hotel $$
Luxury
222 Broadway Ave, MB, R3C0R3
Tel *(204) 942 8251*
w fortgartyhotel.com
This opulent hotel, built in 1913, is a National Historic Site, noted for its romantic interiors and plush amenities. There is an exceptional spa, fitness center with pool, conference center, and a revolving restaurant. Palm Lounge offers a lavish Sunday brunch and nightly music.

Vancouver and Vancouver Island

BARKLEY SOUND: Eagle Nook Wilderness Resort $$$
Rural
Box 289, Ucluelet, BC, V0R 3A0
Tel *(604) 357 3361*
w eaglenook.com
Idyllic hideaway set in 70 acres (28 ha) of wilderness. Ideal for kayaking, wildlife viewing, and salmon fishing.

SOOKE : Sooke Harbour House $$$
Luxury
1528 Whiffin Spit Rd, BC, V9Z 0T4
Tel *(250) 642 3421*
w sookeharbourhouse.com
Oldest B&B on the island with ocean and mountain views. Biking, kayaking, and hiking nearby.

TOFINO: Middle Beach Lodge $$
Resort
400 Mackenzie Beach Rd, BC, V0R 2Z0
Tel *(250) 725 2900*
w middlebeach.com
Oceanfront, rustic log cabins with fireplaces and hot tubs. One lodge for families; others are adults only.

DK Choice

TOFINO: Clayoquot Wilderness Resort $$$
Resort
380 Main St, BC, V0R 2Z0
Tel *(250) 726 8235*
w wildretreat.com
Unique deluxe outpost with luxury en-suite tenting. Guests can try their hand at swift-water kayaking, surfing, fly fishing, bear watching, rock climbing, and hiking. A spa, yoga classes, and a gym on site too. There is a ranch-style cookhouse with an open kitchen and stone fireplace. Guests are transferred from Tofino in a private seaplane.

Rooms with gorgeous views at Fairmont Waterfront, Vancouver

VANCOUVER: Georgian Court Hotel $$
Boutique
773 Beatty St, BC, V6B 2M4
Tel *(604) 682 5555*
w georgiancourthotel
vancouver.com
Deluxe hotel with a women-only floor, on-site restaurants, and spa service. Jogging, walking, and cycling paths nearby.

VANCOUVER: Greystone B&B $$
Historic
2006 West 14th St, BC, V6J 2K4
Tel *(250) 732 1375*
w greystonebb.com
A 1910 Craftsman house with just two rooms plus a suite with two bedrooms, a full kitchen, and garden access.

VANCOUVER: Quality Hotel Inn at False Creek $$
Motel
1335 Howe St, BC, V6Z 1R7
Tel *(604) 682 0229*
w innatfalsecreek.com
Inexpensive, family-oriented suites, great for extended stays. Free pass to nearby fitness center.

VANCOUVER: Thistle Down House $$
Historic
3910 Capilano Rd, BC, V7R 4J2
Tel *(604) 986 7173*
w thistle-down.com
A 1920 heritage-listed home with bright rooms. Some have fireplaces, balconies, and patios.

VANCOUVER: Fairmont Hotel Vancouver $$$
Historic
900 West Georgia St, BC, V6C 2W6
Tel *(604) 684 3131*
w fairmont.com
Elegant, old-fashioned landmark. Relax at the fabulous spa after hiking or skiing. Disabled-friendly.

VANCOUVER: Fairmont Waterfront $$$
Rooms with a view
900 Canada Place Way, BC, V6C 3L5
Tel *(604) 691 1991*
w fairmont.com

Spectacular glass-and-steel design hotel located beside pretty walkways. Appreciate mountain and ocean views from the pool.

VANCOUVER: Four Seasons $$$
Luxury
791 West Georgia St, BC, V6C 2L4
Tel *(604) 689 9333*
w fourseasons.com
Family-friendly hotel near Stanley Park's bike paths and Sea Walk. An indoor-outdoor pool on site.

VANCOUVER: Metropolitan Hotel Vancouver $$$
Luxury
645 Howe St, BC, V6C 2Y9
Tel *(604) 687 1122*
w metropolitan.com
Popular with business travelers. Intimate rooms, a health center, squash courts, and a golf course.

VANCOUVER: O Canada B&B $$$
Historic
1114 Barclay St, BC, V6E 1H1
Tel *(604) 688 0555*
w ocanadahouse.com
Home-made breakfasts and a guests' pantry at this 1897 home. Yoga and biking gear available. Sherry served in the evenings.

VICTORIA: Days Inn Victoria on the Harbour $$
Chain hotels
427 Belleville St, BC, V8V 1X3
Tel *(250) 386 3451*
w daysinn.com
A good-value hotel within walking distance of downtown. Pool and free parking.

VICTORIA: Inn at Laurel Point $$
Rooms with a view
680 Montréal St, BC, V8V 1Z8
Tel *(250) 386 8721*
w laurelpoint.com
A stunning contemporary waterfront hotel overlooking the Inner Harbour. Glassed balconies allow harbor views from bed. Japanese gardens.

VICTORIA: Fairmont Empress $$$
Luxury
721 Government St, BC, V8W 1W5
Tel *(250) 384 8111*
w fairmont.com
This iconic ivy-clad landmark dating from 1908 offers old-fashioned elegance. The Rose Gardens slip down to Inner Harbour. Excellent service.

For more information on types of hotels *see page 349*

**VICTORIA: Humboldt House
Bed & Breakfast** $$$
Boutique
867 Humboldt St, BC, V8V 2Z6
Tel *(250) 383 0152*
W humboldthouse.com
Old Victorian home in a quiet
neighbourhood. Themed rooms
and in-room champagne break-
fasts. Short walk to downtown.

The Rocky
Mountains

DK Choice

**BANFF:
Fairmont Banff Springs** $$$
Luxury
405 Spray Ave, AB, T1L 1J4
Tel *(403) 762 2211*
W fairmont.com
Iconic "Castle of the Rockies" in
Banff National Park with un-
paralleled views of Bow River
and Mount Rundle. Watch the
sunset while sipping cocktails.
Enjoy the spa, mineral baths,
golf course, and pools.
Horseback rides and naturalist-
guided hikes of the park
available. Impeccable service.

CALGARY: Hotel Arts $$$
Boutique
119 12th Ave SW, AB, T2R 0G8
Tel *(403) 266 4611*
W hotelarts.ca
Some rooms at this hip hotel have
balconies, marble baths, and
two-person Jacuzzis. The hotel
bar's patio overlooks the pool.

**CANMORE: Quality Resort
Château Canmore** $$
Rooms with a view
1718 Bow Valley Trail, AB, T1W 2X3
Tel *(403) 678 6699*
W chateaucanmore.com
Rooms at this all-suite hotel have
fireplaces, kitchenettes, and
mountain views. Kids up to 18
can stay with adults for free.

**CRANBROOK: Elizabeth
Lake Lodge** $$
Rooms with a view
590 Van Horne St S., BC, V1C 4W7
Tel *(250) 426 6114*
W elizabethlakelodge.com
Rooms with views of the Elizabeth
Lake Bird Sanctuary. Some have
kitchenettes. RV sites as well.

FIELD: Emerald Lake Lodge $$$
Rural
PO Box 10, BC, V0A 1G0
Tel *(250) 343 6321*
W crmr.com

Log cabin in mountainous Yoho
National Park with fireplaces,
chessboards, and a billiard table.

**FORT NELSON: Woodlands
Inn & Suites** $$
Motel
3995 50th Ave S., BC, V0C 1R0
Tel *(250) 774 6669*
W woodlandsinn.ca
Full-service hotel with fitness
center, kitchenettes, coin laundry,
and free airport shuttle.

GOLDEN: Vagabond Lodge $$
Resort
1581 Cache Close, BC, V0A 1H0
Tel *(250) 344 2622*
W vagabondlodge.ca
Luxurious boutique-style resort
with splendid mountain views
from some balconies. No
telephones or TVs in rooms.

**LAKE LOUISE: Fairmont
Château Lake Louise** $$$
Resort
111 Lake Louise Drive, AB, T0L 1E0
Tel *(403) 522 3511*
W airmont.com
Overlooks Lake Louise. Enjoy
canoeing, hiking, and horseback
riding. Children and pets welcome.

**PRINCE GEORGE: Norton
Ranch Cottages** $$
Luxury
*6505 Lower Mud River Rd, BC, V2N
5C3*
Tel *(250) 560 5165*
W nortonranch.com
Luxury Western-style cottages on
a ranch. Horse- and pet-friendly.

**RADIUM HOT SPRINGS: The
Radium Resort** $$
Resort
8100 Golf Course Rd, BC, V0A 1M0
Tel *(250) 347 9311*
W radiumresort.com
Golf resort with a variety of suites
and room types. Golf lessons,
skiing, and bird-watching.

Bright lobby of the Prince of Wales
Hotel in Waterton Lakes

**WATERTON LAKES: Prince of
Wales Hotel** $$$
Resort
*Waterton Lakes National Park, AB,
T0K 2M0*
Tel *(403) 859 2231*
W glacierparkinc.com
Quirky summer-only inn on bluff
overlooking lake. Good mountain
views and wildlife watching.

Southern and
Northern British
Columbia

DK Choice

**108 MILE RANCH:
The Hills Health Ranch** $$
Resort
4871 Hwy 97, BC, V0K 2Z0
Tel *(250) 791 5225*
W thehillshealthranch.com
Stay on a working ranch amid
splendid mountain scenery.
Trail riding through forested
mountains, cowboy cookouts,
yoga lessons, and a health and
weight loss center are some of
the facilities on offer. Cabins are
available as well.

**BARKERVILLE: Kelly and King
House B&Bs** $$
Historic
Main St, BC, V0K 2R0
Tel *(866) 994 0004*
W kellyhouse.ca
Stay in a restored Gold Rush
village. Book one of the en suite
rooms or the entire house.

CHASE: Quaaout Lodge & Spa $$
Resort
1663 Little Shuswap Rd, BC, V0E 1M2
Tel *(250) 679 3090*
W quaaoutlodge.com
Resort overlooking Little Shuswap
Lake. Horseback riding, fishing,
canoeing, hiking, and golfing.

**HARRISON HOT SPRINGS:
Harrison Hot Springs** $$
Resort
100 Esplanade Ave, BC, V0M 1K0
Tel *(604) 796 2244*
W harrisonresort.com
Enjoy the five mineral hot spring
pools while gazing at stars and
mountains. Peaceful lake views.

HOPE: Manning Park Resort $$
Resort
*7500 Hwy 3, Manning Provincial
Park, BC, V0X 1R0*
Tel *(250) 840 8822*
W manningpark.com
Wide range of accommodations.
Indoor and outdoor sports as well.

Key to Price Guide *see page 350*

KAMLOOPS: Plaza Hotel $$
Historic
405 Victoria St, BC, VC2 2A9
Tel *(250) 372 8075*
w theplazahotel.com
Boutique heritage hotel located
downtown. Free acccess to
nearby pool and fitness facilities.
Complimantary breakfast.

KELOWNA: Hotel Eldorado $$$
Rooms with a view
500 Cook Rd, BC, V1W 3G9
Tel *(250) 763 7500*
w hoteleldoradokelowna.com
Lakeside 1920s charm with
modern luxuries. Lively bar and
popular Sunday brunch.

**PENTICTON: Penticton
Lakeside Resort** $$$
Resort
21 Lakeshore Dr W, BC, V2A 7M5
Tel *(250) 493 8221*
w pentictonlakesideresort.com
Hotel with a private beach and
pier, a play center, and a casino.
Suites with Jacuzzis and balconies.

**PRINCE RUPERT: Prince Rupert
Crest Hotel** $$
Rooms with a view
222 First Ave W, BC, V8J 1A8
Tel *(250) 624 6771*
w cresthotel.bc.ca
This four-star property is located
on a bluff near Cow Bay. Rooms
offer harbor, city, mountain, and
Kaien Island views. Pet-friendly.

**WHISTLER: Holiday Inn
Whistler Village** $$$
Chain hotels
4295 Blackcomb Way, BC, V0N 1B4
Tel *(604) 938 0878*
w whistlerhi.com
Rooms feature kitchenettes and
fireplaces. Children are welcome.
Short walk to the Blackcomb lift.

**WHISTLER: Fairmont Château
Whistler** $$$
Luxury
4599 Château Blvd, BC, V0N 1B4
Tel *(604) 938 8000*
w fairmont.com
Luxurious castle-like hotel with a
golf course and spa on site, and
hiking trails nearby. Kid-friendly.

Northern Canada

**DAWSON CITY: Downtown
Hotel** $$
Motel
1026 2nd Ave, YT, Y0B 1G0
Tel *(867) 993 5346*
w downtownhotel.ca
Decor reminiscent of the Klondike
Gold Rush era. Free airport
shuttle and Jacuzzi.

Warm and inviting interiors of the Fairmont Château Whistler

DK Choice

**DAWSON CITY: Bombay
Peggy's Inn & Pub** $$$
Historic
2nd Ave & Princess St, YT, Y0B 1G0
Tel *(867) 993 6969*
w bombaypeggys.com
Built in 1900 and restored to its
Victorian elegance, this small
hotel has individually themed
rooms. Some bathrooms have
clawfoot tubs. Serves croissants
in the morning, and chocolate
and port in the afternoon.
Adjoining pub offers a selection
of single-malt scotch, Yukon-
brewed beers, and martinis.

**FORT SIMPSON: Janor
Guest House** $$
Motel
10003 99B Ave, NT, X0E 0N0
Tel *(867) 695 2077*
w janor.ca
Comfortable rooms with free
Internet. Continental breakfasts.

**HAINES JUNCTION: Dalton
Trail Lodge** $$$
Rural
Box 5331, YT, Y0B 1L0
Tel *(867) 634 2099*
w daltontrail.com
Wilderness lodge owned by a
Swiss-German couple. Packages
include fishing and hiking.

HAY RIVER: Ptarmigan Inn $$
Motel
10 J. Gagnier St, NT, X0E 1G1
Tel *(867) 874 6781*
w ptarmiganinn.com
Centrally located with executive
suites and some rooms with kitch-
enettes. Special packages on offer.

INUVIK: Capital Suites $$$
Motel
198 Mackenzie Rd, NT, X0E 0I0
Tel *(867) 678 6300*
w capitalsuites.ca
Studios and one-and two-bed-
room suites. Free Internet and
guest laundry facilities.

IQALUIT: Capital Suites $$$
Motel
807 Aviq St, NU, X0A 0H0
Tel *867 975 4000*
w capitalsuites.ca
Conveniently located hotel with
local Inuit art decorating the
walls. Internet and TV.

IQALUIT: Frobisher Inn $$$
Business
Astro Hill, NU, X0A 0H0
Tel *(867) 979 2222*
w frobisherinn.com
Deluxe rooms feature Jacuzzis
and fireplaces. Three restaurants
and movie theater on site.

**WHITEHORSE: Coast High
Country Inn** $$
Motel
1051 1th Ave, YT, Y1A 1H1
Tel *(867) 667 4471*
w coasthotels.com
Antique furniture and brick
fireplace in lobby. Rooms have
kitchenettes and there are
walking trails nearby.

WHITEHORSE: Skky Hotel $$
Boutique
91622 Alaska Hwy, YT, Y1A 3E4
Tel *(867) 456 2400*
w skkyhotel.com
Refined inn, close to downtown.
Restaurant is open for breakfast
and dinner. Free airport shuttle.

**YELLOWKNIFE: Bayside
Bed & Breakfast** $$
Boutique
3505 McDonald Drive, NT, X1A 2H2
Tel *(867) 445 5003*
w bbcanada.com/4822.html
Located in scenic Old Town with
lovely views of Yellowknife Bay
from the deck. The Dancing Moose
Café serves breakfast and lunch.

YELLOWKNIFE: Explorer Hotel $$
Business
4825 49th Ave, NT, X1A 2R3
Tel *(867) 873 3531*
w explorerhotel.ca
Enjoy cocktails in the Trappers
Lounge and supper at Traders Grill.

For more information on types of hotels *see page 349*

WHERE TO EAT AND DRINK

What makes Canadian cuisine unique is its regional specialties: Alberta beef, Arctic char fish from Canada's north, salmon from BC, Nova Scotia lobster, and Quebec French *tortières* (meat pies) to name a few. While these specialties can be sampled in their place of origin, many of the larger towns offer a choice of Canada's best regional produce, and in some areas this includes Canadian wines and beers *(see p363)*. In fact, the "locavore" and "100-mile diet" movements, where chefs take pride in featuring local produce, have swept the

nation. Traditional game, including rabbit, caribou, and bison, are now gourmet dishes at cosmopolitan restaurants, while French haute cuisine is available in major cities. Since Canada is a nation of immigrants, ethnic restaurants are common everywhere. German, Greek, Chinese, Thai, Indian, Ukrainian, African, and Italian cuisines, along with other international favorites, provide a wide range of options at a price to suit every budget. The listings on pp364–83 describe a selection of restaurants chosen for their variety, service, and good value.

White-linen tables and intimate decor of Vancouver's CinCin Restaurant & Bar *(see p378)*

Types of Restaurants

Eating out in Canada is surprisingly affordable, especially when compared to European prices. Restaurants are extremely varied, with the tearoom, bistro, brasserie, and theater café competing with the more usual family restaurant and fast-food outlet. Many pubs also serve excellent bar food at reasonable prices.

Lobster suppers are a unique Canadian dining experience. Held throughout the summer on Prince Edward Island, these lively gatherings often take place in church grounds on wooden tables, or on beachfronts where fishermen have just brought in the catch. Equally unique, though by no means public, are Inuit dinners. Traveling through the Arctic north might result in an

invitation to join an Inuit family for the evening meal of sundried caribou sweetened with berry sauces or smoked and dried local fish.

Vegetarian

Vegetarian options are on the increase throughout Canada. Expect to see at least one vegetarian or even vegan dish on the menu, and gluten-free items often feature too. "Healthy Eating" is a government initiative promoting heart-healthy eating. The menus of participating restaurants feature the heart symbol to denote low-fat dishes. Anyone on a special or weight-loss diet should ask the chef to leave out certain high-calorie ingredients. Fresh fruit is easily obtained throughout the south of the country, and is

abundant during summer and early autumn in the primary growing areas of Ontario and British Columbia's Okanagan Valley. Some of the best berries and peaches in the world are enjoyed here during summer. However, most food in the Northwest Territories and Nunavut is imported and mostly either canned or frozen. Fresh food in Canada's north is hard to obtain, and very expensive.

Alcohol

The minimum age of public purchase and consumption of alcohol is 19 across most of the country, except in Quebec, Manitoba, and Alberta, where it is 18. Canada produces many award-winning wines *(see p363)*, which are increasingly available everywhere.

Open-air dining in downtown Montreal *(see pp367–9)*

Quaint decor at Marcel's, one of downtown Toronto's best French bistros *(see p373)*

Throughout much of Canada, the distribution of alcohol is controlled by the provincial government. While alcohol is not sold in corner stores and supermarkets, liquor stores sell a range of quality wines and spirits. Separate government-run stores sell only beer.

Eating Hours and Reservations

Lunch tables are usually available from noon to 2pm. Although dinner is usually served between 6pm to 9pm, later seatings, sometimes well into the night, are available in larger cities. Reserving a table in advance is a good idea. Call ahead and cancel if your plans change.

Paying and Tipping

It is possible to eat well in Canada for a bargain price. A snack in a café seldom costs more than Can$10. In a good restaurant, a three-course meal with wine often costs Can$45–$70. Even gourmet dinners can start at Can$45. Luncheon items are generally less expensive, with similar choices to the dinner menu. Restaurant tax includes the 5 percent GST (Goods and Services Tax) and the varying provincial sales tax, applicable everywhere except Alberta. Taxes are included on the final cheque. Service charges are rarely included,

but might be added to the bill for a large group. Tipping is generally expected, and should be about 15 percent of the net cheque. Normally, a tip should increase if you are bringing a larger party to a restaurant and for exceptional service. Tipping is also expected in bars and nightclubs.

Children

Most restaurants offer high chairs or booster seats, and some provide crayons and coloring books to keep kids amused. Note that a children's menu or half-portions might be available for those under eight years old. Parents are expected to keep children seated at the table and to take noisy or upset youngsters outside until they calm down.

Disabled Facilities

Most new restaurants, as well as existing establishments undergoing renovation, have made their sites wheelchair-accessible. However, many older and rural establishments may not have such facilities and should be checked out in advance.

Dress Code

Most restaurants operate a "smart-casual" dress policy, especially at lunchtime, but exceptions to this can include sneakers (trainers), cut-off jeans,

and dirty or ripped clothes. The rule generally runs as follows: the more expensive and exclusive the restaurant, the more formal the attire required. Evening dress is rarely necessary.

Smoking

More than 80 percent of Canadians do not smoke, and local by-laws are restricting areas where the minority of smokers can legally smoke. Smoking is not allowed in any public places, including bars, cafés, restaurants, and several terraces and patios. When picnicking in a park, extinguish your cigarette completely for fear of starting a forest fire.

Recommended Restaurants

Within these listings, eating establishments reflect Canada's widely multicultural society, which extends into the far north, "backcountry" regions, as well as major cities. Hence, restaurant themes describe cuisine types; Chinese, Indian, Hungarian, Greek and so on.

Restaurants which carry the "DK Choice" designation are specially recommended. They may feature a chef's table, exquisitely prepared regional specialties paired with a sommelier-recommended wine or beer, or offer exemplary service. Whatever the selection, it is bound to offer a nuanced understanding of Canadian cuisine.

Café-bars in cities are mostly inexpensive and popular options

The Flavors of Canada

With a rich history of multiculturalism, Canada's culinary heritage is as diverse as it is intriguing. Although there is no national cuisine as such, regional specialties have their own strong identities. Seafood dominates Atlantic Canada and BC menus, while steaks and burgers are best in the ranching areas of Alberta and Saskatchewan. Acadian cuisine, reminiscent of French country food, is found in New Brunswick and Nova Scotia. In Northern Canada, age-old Inuit techniques produce a variety of sundried caribou and fish dishes. But the Canadian specialty that is famous the world over is maple syrup.

Vegetable squash

Pacific salmon, caught in the Khutzeymateen River, BC

Fish and Seafood

Bordered by oceans on three sides, Canada offers great seafood, particularly on its east and west coasts. Produce from here can easily make it from the ocean to the dinner plate within 24 hours. Oysters, clams, and scallops are a main feature of East Coast menus. Prince Edward Island is famous for its lobster; those who don't like crustacea can try Atlantic salmon. Pacific salmon, crab, shellfish, and shrimp (prawns) dominate British Columbian fare, along with a typically northern fish, Arctic char. More unusual dishes, often incorporating historic preserving methods, include Solomon Grundy (Nova Scotia's fine marinated herring), and cod tongues, as well as tasty seal flipper pie from Newfoundland.

Freshwater fish, both the farmed and wild versions, is caught in the two million lakes dotted across Canada, and offers a delicate contrast to seafood. In the west of the country, the tender Winnipeg goldeye, trout, and pickerel, which is often cooked over open fires at informal summer outdoor shore lunches throughout the central region, are a uniquely Canadian treat.

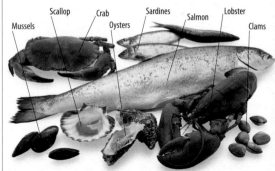

Selection of superb seafood from the clear waters of Canada

Scallop · Crab · Mussels · Oysters · Sardines · Salmon · Lobster · Clams

French-Canadian Dishes and Specialties

The center of French-style gourmet cuisine in Canada is Quebec. Dishes here are reminiscent of the best European food. For some more traditional French-Canadian dishes, cities and towns in the province usually serve specialties. These include *creton*, *tourtière*, and many varieties of pâtisserie. Smoked beef is another popular local delicacy. The Maritime Provinces offer excellent, originally French, Acadian dishes from recipes which are hundreds of years old. As well as meat pies, patés, and stews, rich desserts and cakes feature in their filling menus. Vieux-Montréal's bistros offer many classic delights, such as *escargots à la bourguignonne*. French-Canadians are known for their rich desserts, such as *trempettes* (fried bread soaked in maple syrup) and caramel-soaked *pudding au chomeur*.

Maple sypup

Creton is a coarse, spicy, pork pâté. It is delicious served on hunks of fresh baguette with cornichons (gherkins).

Baskets of rosy apples outside a Nova Scotia farm shop

Fruit and Vegetables

Ontario is the fruitbowl of Canada. In addition to its burgeoning wine industry, the area is famous for its strawberries and cranberries. Peaches and apples are also cultivated here in large quantities, as are blueberries, which also flourish in Nova Scotia and Quebec. Corn, black beans, and vegetable squash (collectively known as the "three sisters") are produced in Ontario along-side zucchini (courgettes), huge tomatoes, and fresh herbs. In New Brunswick, fiddleheads (fern shoots) and dulse (seaweed) are sautéed as a vegetable side dish.

WHAT TO DRINK

Molson "Canadian" and Labatt "Blue" are among the best-selling beers in Canada, but craft beers produced by such microbreweries as Ontario's Creemore Brewery and Quebec's Unibroue are also well respected. Canada produces some excellent wines from hybrid grapes, thanks largely to European wine-makers who have emigrated here. Most wine comes from three areas: a pocket in the southern Okanagan Valley of BC (see p321), Nova Scotia's Annapolis Valley, and a narrow strip along the Niagara Peninsula of southern Ontario. Grape varieties include Riesling, Chardonnay, and Pinot Noir. Rye whisky is distilled in BC; Canadian Club is the most popular brand, but local distilleries produce specialties.

Meat and Game

Alberta's cattle ranches are the source of Canada's finest beef. Most beef in rural areas is served simply, with salad and fries, but one much-loved local dish is Calgary beef hash – corned beef with baked beans and fried potatoes. Lamb and buffalo are also farmed, in smaller numbers. The Yukon, Northwest Territories, and Nunavut supply much of the country's game; caribou, musk ox, and moose are all sent south to be cooked in the European style. Local people, especially the Inuit, smoke meat for the winter months. Their smoked caribou is delicious and very popular. Famous for making the most of a kill, native people use every part of the animal for either clothing or food – even moose fleas are something of a delicacy. Goose, duck, and fish are all smoked or sundried too, providing staples for the very long, harsh winter. Caribou and birds are preserved by being hung out on lines to dry in the Arctic sun.

Fiddlehead fern shoots for sale in a New Brunswick market

Escargots à la bourguignonne are snails cooked in garlic and parsley butter and served in their shells.

Tourtière, a pastry-topped pie filled with meat and vegetables flavored with spices, is country fare.

Pudding au chomeur (literally "unemployed pudding") is an upside-down cake with a rich caramel base.

Where to Eat and Drink

Newfoundland and Labrador

BONAVISTA: Bonavista Social Club $
International
Upper Amherst Cove, NL, A0C 2A0
Tel *(709) 445 5556* **Closed** *Mon–Wed*
Home to the only wood-fired bread oven in the province, this eatery makes everything from multigrain to sourdough bread. The handmade pizzas are particularly noteworthy. Locally sourced ingredients.

CORNER BROOK: Newfound Sushi $
Sushi
117 Broadway, NL, A2H 5B6
Tel *(709) 634 6666* **Closed** *Sun*
One of the few sushi spots on the West Coast. Sushi rolls here named after local landmarks: Humber River Roll or Blow Me Down Roll. Cozy, intimate atmosphere.

CORNER BROOK: Jennifer's The Upper Level Restaurant $$
North American
48–50 Broadway, NL, A2H 4C4
Tel *(709) 632 7979*
Family-run for over two decades, Jennifer's is known for reliable service and some of the best gourmet dining in the area. Try the seafood chowder or the Newfoundland dish *cod au gratin* (flake cod, white sauce, Cheddar cheese, and breadcrumbs).

FERRYLAND: Ferryland Lighthouse Picnics $
North American
Lighthouse Rd, NL, A0A 2H0
Tel *(709) 363 7456* **Closed** *Sep–May; Mon–Tue*
Enjoy a unique picnic experience at this 19th-century lighthouse. After a 40-minute hike, guests are handed a basket filled with goodies and a blanket to spread out in the grass. Great home-made lemonade and cake. Watch for breaching whales in late spring. Reservations mandatory.

GRAND FALLS-WINDSOR: 48 High $$
Fine Dining
48 High St, NL, A2A 1C6
Tel *(709) 489 9299*
Named for the street on which it stands, 48 High offers a gourmet dining experience. Try the zorba penne, the chicken pesto fusilli or the seafood medley platter. Quiet, relaxed ambience.

JOE BATT'S ARM: Nicole's Café $
Contemporary Canadian
159 Main Rd, Fogo Island, NL, A0G 2B0
Tel *(709) 658 3663*
An upscale culinary experience on Fogo Island where traditional Newfoundland dishes are modernized. Be sure to sample the famous Growlers home-made ice cream. Cozy interior with local artwork displayed.

LABRADOR CITY: Mes Amis Dining Room $
North American
Two Seasons Inn, 96 Avalon Dr, NL, A2V 2L3
Tel *(709) 944 2661*
North American dishes with a Newfoundland twist. Try the *cod au gratin*. Space for business lunches as well. Wine list plus a separate bar area.

NORRIS POINT: Sugar Hill Inn's Chanterelles $$
Mediterranean
129 Sexton Ln, NL, A0K 3V0
Tel *(888) 299 2147* **Closed** *Nov–Apr*
Locally sourced ingredients are prepared with authentic olive oils and vinegars for the ultimate Mediterranean flair. The specialty is seafood, including halibut, cod, salmon, shrimp, and scallop. Offers more than 80 varieties of wine.

PORTUGAL COVE: Atlantica $$$
Fine Dining
38 Beachy Cove Rd, NL, A1M 2G7
Tel *(709) 895 1251* **Closed** *Sun*
With Chef Vardy at the helm, this award-winning restaurant has built a menu based on fresh seafood, prime cuts, and local

Price Guide

Prices (in Canadian dollars) are based on a three-course meal for one, including half a bottle of house wine and service.

$	up to Can$45
$$	Can$45 to 70
$$$	over Can$70

produce. The outdoor patio is perfect for summer dining and whale watching.

ROCKY HARBOUR: Java Jack's $
North American
88 Main St N, NL, A0K 4N0
Tel *(709) 458 3004* **Closed** *Oct–mid-May*
Java Jack's started out as a café and is now a trendy restaurant in a heritage home. Fresh fish, wild game, and vegetarian dishes are served with organic greens from the garden.

ST. JOHN'S: Piatto Pizzeria Enoteca $$
Italian
377 Duckworth St, NL, A1C 1H8
Tel *(709) 726 0909*
This pizzeria strictly follows the traditions and processes of Neapolitan pizza making. Calzone and pasta dishes are also served. Some ingredients are grown in the volcanic ash of Mount Vesuvius.

DK Choice

ST. JOHN'S: Raymonds Restaurant $$$
Contemporary Canadian
95 Water St, NL, A1C 1A4
Tel *(709) 579 5800* **Closed** *Sun & Mon*
Housed in a restored classical building overlooking the harbor and the Narrows, Raymonds features an award-winning menu inspired by rustic Atlantic Canadian cuisine. The focus here is on using the province's seafood, wild game, vegetables and berries. For the ultimate dining experience, try the seven-course wine-pairing taste menu.

TWILLINGATE: Canvas Cove Bistro $
Seafood
52 Main St, NL, A0G 4M0
Tel *(709) 884 1888* **Closed** *Oct–Apr*
Sampling the exceptional lobster chowder at this bistro is an absolute must. Large wine menu featuring selections from nearby Auk Island Winery. Try the Newfie Screech banana flambé for dessert.

Beautifully served seafood at St. John's Raymonds Restaurant

Intimate interior of The Blue Door in Fredericton

New Brunswick, Nova Scotia, and Prince Edward Island

ANNAPOLIS ROYAL: German Bakery and Sachsen Café $
German Bakery
358 St. George St, NS, B0S 1A0
Tel *(902) 532 1990*
Friendly, family-owned place with great views over Fort Anne. Sample the authentic *schnitzel*, and *bratwurst* with *sauerkraut*. Fantastic baked goods. Great German beers and wines.

ANTIGONISH: Gabrieau's Bistro ⓘ
Contemporary Canadian
350 Main St, NS B2G 2C5
Tel *(902) 863 1925* **Closed** *Sun*
Gabrieau's has a gorgeous dining room and bar serving delicious fare. Lots of locally sourced ingredients crafted into imaginative dishes. There is also a tapas menu. Good breakfasts, and exceptional desserts.

BADDECK: Herring Choker Deli $
Deli
10158 Hwy 105, Nyanza, NS B0E 1B0
Tel *(902) 295 2275*
Great soups and sandwiches served in huge portions. Try the home-made bread and the cinnamon rolls. Ideal place to pick up a packed lunch.

BRACKLEY: The Dunes Café $$
Contemporary Canadian
3622 Brackley Point Rd, PE, C1E 1Z3
Tel *(902) 672 1883*
Spacious and airy café with beautiful gardens. The menu features a lot of locally sourced seafood used to prepare fresh and inventive dishes. Great wine list and fun cocktails. Fabulous desserts.

CARAQUET: Mitchan Sushi $
Japanese
49 A Blvd St-Pierre W, NB, E1W 1B6
Tel *(506) 726 1103* **Closed** *Mon & Tue*
A local favorite with a friendly atmosphere. The menu features delicious and authentic Japanese food. Sushi and sashimi is made with fresh local fish and seafood.

CHARLOTTETOWN: Lot 30 Restaurant $$
Contemporary Canadian
151 Kent St, PE, C1A 1N5
Tel *(902) 629 3030*
Creative, memorable meals featuring local ingredients. Open and spacious dining room with a large-screen TV showing the chef at work. The tasting menu here is consistently superb. Great service.

CHARLOTTETOWN: Sim's Corner Steakhouse and Oyster Bar $$$
Steakhouse
86 Queen St, PE, C1A 4A7,
Tel *(902) 894 7467*
Choose oysters on display at the oyster bar, then dine on the large patio or in the intimate boudoir-like interior. Excellent food, with good drinks as well.

CHETICAMP: Restaurant Acadien $
Traditional Canadian
15067 Main St, NS, B0E 1H0
Tel *(902) 224 3207*
A cultural experience. Servers in traditional Acadian dress offer dishes such as chicken fricot, blood pudding, and meat pie served with cranberry sauce. Hearty meals and great desserts.

DIGBY: Fundy Restaurant $
Seafood
34 Water St, NS, B0V 1A0
Tel *(902) 245 4950*
Located right on the waterfront, overlooking the Annapolis Basin. Fantastic seafood served in a fun atmosphere. Order the fat Digby

scallops sautéed in garlic butter, or the fried clams. Wash it down with Keith's India Pale Ale.

FREDERICTON: The Schnitzel Parlour $$
German
3136 Woodstock Rd, NB, E3C 1K9
Tel *(506) 450 2520* **Closed** *Sun–Tue*
Friendly owners serve up hearty portions of authentic German food in a welcoming environment. Awesome *schnitzel* as well as home-made chocolates.

FREDERICTON: The Blue Door Restaurant and Bar $$$
Contemporary Canadian
100 Regent St, NB, E3B 3W4
Tel *(506) 455 2583* **Closed** *Sun*
Decadent food served in an intimate atmosphere. Locally sourced ingredients, with fresh takes on old favorites, and great attention to detail. Innovative and consistently delicious dishes.

FREEPORT: Lavena's Catch Café $
Seafood
15 Hwy 217, NS, B0V 1B0
Tel *(902) 839 2517*
Not particularly fancy but considered one of the best seafood restaurants in Nova Scotia. Try the lobster dinner, halibut chowder, or scallops. Live music at weekends.

GEORGETOWN: Clamdiggers Beach House and Restaurant $$
Seafood
7 West St, PE, C0A 1L0
Tel *(902) 652 2466*
Big portions of fresh seafood served up at this beachside eatery. Enjoy a pre-dinner drink on the restaurant deck. Famous for the fried scallops and clams.

The unassuming exterior of Fundy Restaurant, Digby's popular seafood spot

For more information on types of restaurants *see page 361*

HALIFAX: Bistro Le Coq $$
French
1584 Argyle St, NS, B3J 2B3
Tel *(902) 407 4564*
Casual yet elegant spot offering French-style cooking. Enjoy succulent oysters, light crepes, juicy steak *frites*, old-fashioned cocktails, and decadent desserts.

DK Choice

**HALIFAX:
Chives Canadian Bistro** $$$
Contemporary Canadian
1537 Barrington St, NS, B3J 1Z4
Tel *(902) 420 9626*
An unforgettable meal here always starts with a brown paper bag of biscuits served with bowls of warm molasses to dip them in. Sample some of the best local charcuterie, cheeses, seafood, meat, and vegetarian dishes matched with Nova Scotian wines. Chef Craig Finn has also published three best-selling cookbooks.

LA HAVE: LaHave Bakery $
Café
Hwy 331, NS, B0R 1G0
Tel *(902) 688 2908*
Take a quaint cable ferry to this bakery café for great soups and excellent sandwiches. Guests can sit in the antique-furnished interiors, on the sunny front porch, or on the dock at the back.

LUNENBURG: Salt Shaker Deli $$
International
124 Montague St, NS, B0J 2C0
Tel *(902) 640 3434*
Serves award-winning smoked seafood chowder, steaming bowls of local mussels, and fishcakes. Delicious thin-crust pizzas, and Asian inspired dishes (such as Korean BBQ Burrito) as well.

LUNERBERG: Fleur de Sel $$$
French
53 Montague St, NS, B0J 2C0
Tel *(902) 640 2121*
Beautiful and innovative food in a relaxed setting. The changing menu uses local produce with high-end ingredients such as *foie gras*, duck, and lobster. Limited seating, so book ahead.

MABOU: Red Shoe Pub $
Pub
11573 Nova Scotia 19 Trunk, NS, B0E 1X0
Tel *(902) 945 2996*
Lively pub owned by famous Canadian musicians The Rankin Sisters. Delicious pub food served by friendly staff. Live music adds a Cape Breton cultural experience.

MARGATE: Shipwright's Café $$
Contemporary Canadian
11869 Route 6, PE, C0B 1M0
Tel *(902) 836 3403*
A farm-to-table experience in a country home with produce grown on site. Savour delicious food lovingly prepared by the chef, who is also the owner. Save room for the enticing desserts.

MIRIMACHI: The Anglers Reel $$
Seafood
1809 Water St, NB, E1N 1B2
Tel *(506) 773 5651*
Enjoy fresh seafood on a huge sunny deck overlooking scenic Miramachi River. Salmon prepared in 20 different ways, and plenty more seafood and pasta besides.

MONCTON: Pump House Brewery $
Pub
Orange Ln, NB, E1C 4L6
Tel *(506) 855 2337*
This pub serves great food and a range of microbrews. Particularly excellent thin-crust pizzas. A local favorite for weekend evenings.

MONTAGUE: Windows on the Water Café $$
Seafood
106 Sackville St, PE, C0A 1R0
Tel *(902) 838 2080*
Well-prepared hearty meals in a cozy setting. Great views over the water. Delicious seafood dishes served in large portions. Save room for the bread pudding.

NEW GLASGOW: New Glasgow Lobster Suppers $$
Seafood
604 Route 258, Hunter River, PE, C0A 1N0
Tel *(902) 964 2870*
Though a bit of a tourist trap, Lobster Suppers is still worth a visit for an authentic Maritimes lobster experience. The lobster meal comes with unlimited sides, soft-drinks, and desserts. Try the mile high lemon meringue pie.

PEGGY'S COVE: Rhubarb Restaurant $$
Contemporary Canadian
8650 Peggy's Cove Rd, Indian Harbour, NS, B3Z 3P4
Tel *(902) 821 3013*
This gem amongst lots of tourist traps serves excellent fresh, local cuisine. The creative menu has plenty of choice. Great service and beautiful views.

**QUISPAMSIS:
Daughter's Fine Dining** $$
Fine Dining
315 Hampton Rd, NB, E2E 4M9
Tel *(506) 849 3000*   **Closed** *Sun & Mon*
Brilliant service and a varied menu, featuring classic French as well as Asian fusion cuisine. Try the popular whole seared beef tenderloin with Béarnaise sauce.

RUSTICO: The Pearl Café $$$
Contemporary Canadian
7792 Cavendish Rd, PE, C0A 1X0
Tel *(902) 963 2111*
Considered by locals one of Prince Edward Island's best restaurants, Pearl serves delicious food in a quaint setting. Fantastic decor and prompt service. Book ahead.

SHEDIAC: The Tait House $$
Contemporary Canadian
293 Main St, NB, E4P 2A8
Tel *(506) 532 4233*
Fine dining in a restored historic home. Relish well-prepared seafood made with locally sourced ingredients. Extensive wine list, attentive service, and a buzzing atmosphere.

SHELBURNE: The Sea Dog Saloon $$
Seafood
1 Dock St, NS, B0T 1W0
Tel *(902) 875 1131*
Pub and restaurant with a big deck over the water that serves hearty portions of quintessential Nova Scotian food. Be sure to sample the salt cod dinner or the award-winning chowder. All-day breakfast menu.

SOURIS: Sheltered Harbour Café $
Café
2065 Route 2, PE, C0A 2B0
Tel *(902) 687 1997*
Consistently great comfort food with a creative local twist, such as potato skins loaded with

Colourful interior of Halifax's Chives Canadian Bistro

lobster and blueberry bread pudding. Pretty views and impeccable service.

ST. ANDREWS: Rossmount Inn $$$
Contemporary Canadian
4599 Route 127, NB, E5B3S7
Tel *(506) 529 3351*
Located in a grand mansion, Rossmount Inn offers a great fine-dining experience with an emphasis on decadent, locally sourced fresh food, including lobster and suckling pig.

ST. JOHN: Thandi's $$
Indian/International
33 Canterbury St, NB, E2L 2C6
Tel *(506) 648 2377*
Housed in a beautifully renovated heritage building. Primarily serves superb Indian food, but also fantastic steaks and seafood. Popular bar on site.

SUSSEX: Maple Avenue Restobar $$
Contemporary Canadian
Unit 3–60 Maple Ave, NB, E4E 2N5
Tel *(506) 433 3292* **Closed** *Sun & Mon*
An interesting mixed menu of traditionally inspired dishes, as well as pizza, fish and chips, and seafood. Delicious desserts. Live music some evenings.

WOLFVILLE: Privet House Restaurant §§
Contemporary Canadian
406 Main St, NS, B4P 1C9
Tel *(902) 542 7525*
Elegant fine dining in a friendly environment. An innovative menu of regional produce, with everything perfectly executed. Well-curated wine list and lovely desserts.

Montreal

CHINATOWN: Maison Kam Fung $
Chinese
1111 Rue Saint-Urbain, H2Z 1Y6
Tel *(514) 878 2888*
Try delicious Peking Duck and some of the best dim sum in the city. Range of Szechwan and Cantonese dishes to choose from as well. Lavish decor.

DOWNTOWN: Boustan $
Middle Eastern
2020 Rue Crescent, H3G 2B8
Tel *(514) 843 3576*
Inexpensive Lebanese meals with takeout and late-night delivery. Try the tasty shawarma platters, kebabs, and couscous. Range of freshly squeezed juices.

Spacious outdoor seating at Magnan, a restaurant and tavern in Montreal

DOWNTOWN: L'Orchidée de Chine $
Chinese
2017 Rue Peel, H3A 1T6
Tel *(514) 287 1878*
Upscale restaurant serving reasonably priced Hunan, Pekinese, and Szechwan cuisine. Try the crispy duck in pastry or sautéed lamb with spicy sauce.

DOWNTOWN: Restaurant & Taverne Magnan $
Pub
2602 Rue Saint-Patrick, H3K 1B8
Tel *(514) 935 9647*
This legendary Montreal sports bar claims to serve the best roast beef in North America. The food is delicious and there is a good selection of draft beers.

DOWNTOWN: Chez la Mère Michel $$
French
1209 Rue Guy, H3H 2K5
Tel *(514) 934 0473* **Closed** *Mon*
Traditional French restaurant serving fantastic cuisine in a gorgeous Victorian house since 1965. Try their Dover sole *à la meunière* and *coq au vin*. Selection of over 7,000 wines.

DOWNTOWN: Europea $$
French
1227 Rue de la Montagne, H3G 1Z2
Tel *(514) 398 9229*
Run by acclaimed chef Jerome Ferrer. Interesting taster menus and a chef's table with the use of a lot of local produce. Specialties include veal, lobster, bison, *bouillabaisse*, and scallops.

DOWNTOWN: Restaurant Phayathai $$
Thai
1235 Rue Guy, H3H 2K5
Tel *(514) 933 9949*
Come to Phayathai for classic Thai dishes such as *pad thai* noodles and green curry. Try

their fragrant soups featuring ginger, coriander, and lemon. Helpful staff.

DOWNTOWN: Restaurant Julien $$
French
1191 Union, H3B 3C3
Tel *(514) 871 1581* **Closed** *Sun*
Traditional French fare with specialties such as salmon fillet with sorrel cream sauce, duck-breast *tournedos*, and chocolate *marquise*. Spacious summertime canopied terrace. Great wine list.

DOWNTOWN: Le Beaver Club $$$
Fine Dining
900 René-Lévesque Blvd Ouest, H3B 4A5
Tel *(514) 861 3511* **Closed** *Sun–Wed*
The elegant Beaver Club, located at the Fairmont Hôtel le Reine Élizabeth, serves inspired dishes that highlight seasonal and regional fare. Sample the roast beef, grilled salmon, and lamb. Also try what are considered Montreal's best martinis.

DOWNTOWN: Queue de Cheval $$$
Steakhouse
1181 Rue de la Montagne, H3G 1T1
Tel *(514) 390 0091*
This upscale steakhouse is a local favorite with fantastic ambience and service. Try the sirloin, filet mignon, or Kansas cut beef. Outdoor seating in the summer. Reservations are essential.

OUTREMONT: Maïko Sushi $
Japanese
387 Rue Bernard Ouest, H2V 1T6
Tel *(514) 490 1225*
While the service here might be slow, guests get to watch the fantastic chefs at work at the sushi bar. Choose from a range of steaks, *tempura*, and *teriyaki*.

For more information on types of restaurants *see page 361*

Period 1930s ambience at Wilensky's Light Lunch in Saint Urbain

OUTREMONT: Faros $$
Seafood
362 Fairmount Ouest, H2V 2G5
Tel *(514) 270 8437*
This cozy restaurant is a Montreal favorite for fresh seafood dishes. A great place for a romantic meal for two. Try the Faros Feast, which features different pairs of appetizers and mains. Book ahead.

OUTREMONT: Les Deux Singes de Montarvie $$
Bistro
176 Rue Saint-Viateur Ouest, H2T 2L3
Tel *(514) 278 6854* **Closed** *Sun & Mon*
This popular French bistro has a varied menu featuring arctic char, calamari, duck, and more. Intimate ambience. Fantastic French wines.

PLATEAU MONT-ROYAL: Aux Vivres $
Vegetarian
4631 Blvd Saint-Laurent, H2T 1R4
Tel *(514) 842 3479*
What started as a tiny place in 1997 is now one of the city's best vegetarian eateries. Serves vegan and gluten-free fare. No alcohol.

PLATEAU MONT-ROYAL: Café Méliès $
French
3540 Blvd Saint-Laurent, H2X 2V1
Tel *(514) 847 9218*
Bistro-café located in Montreal's indie film center, Ex-Centris. Popular for its generous weekend brunch. Specialties include duck *confit* and quiche.

PLATEAU MONT-ROYAL: Café Santropol $
Contemporary Canadian
3990 Rue Saint-Urbain, H2W 1T7
Tel *(514) 842 3110*
Trendy restaurant in Montreal's Plateau area. Summer dining in a "secret" garden. Serves delicious soups, sandwiches, and desserts.

PLATEAU MONT-ROYAL: L'Anecdote $
North American
801 Rue Rachel Est, H2J 2H7
Tel *(514) 526 7967*
Arguably some of Montréal's best burgers and great home-made mayonnaise. Lovely 1950s decor with movie posters and chrome fittings. Good wine list.

PLATEAU MONT-ROYAL: L'Express $
Bistro
3927 Rue Saint-Denis, H2W 2M4
Tel *(514) 845 5333*
Parisian bistro serving reasonably priced French fare. Specialties include fish soup with Gruyère croutons. Extensive wine cellar.

DK Choice

PLATEAU MONT-ROYAL: Schwartz's Montréal Hebrew Delicatessen $
Deli
3895 Blvd Saint-Laurent, H2W 1L9
Tel *(514) 842 4813*
Romanian-Jewish immigrants made smoked brisket a staple Montreal meal in 1928 when they opened what is now a landmark deli. The food at the Hebrew Delicatessen is consistently good and popular. Choose from lean, medium, or fatty smoked meat. No alcohol. Long lines so expect to wait.

PLATEAU MONT-ROYAL: Thanjai Restaurant $
Indian
4759 Ave Van Horne, H3W 1H8
Tel *(514) 419 9696* **Closed** *Tue*
This popular spot grew from a small takeout place to the full restaurant it is today. Serves a range of flavorful, authentic south Indian dishes such as *dosa*, *idli*, and *pongal*. No alcohol.

PLATEAU MONT-ROYAL: Au Pied de Cochon $$
Bistro
536 Ave Duluth Est, H2L 1A9
Tel *(514) 281 1114* **Closed** *Mon & Tue*
Extremely popular bistro helmed by celebrity chef Martin Picard. Fantastic tender meat and *foie gras*. Try their Duck in a Can.

PLATEAU MONT-ROYAL: Moishe's $$
Steakhouse
3961 Blvd Saint-Laurent, H2W 1Y4
Tel *(514) 845 3509*
A landmark of the boisterous Jewish Quarter, serving juicy steaks, chopped liver, and twice-baked Monte Carlo potatoes.

PLATEAU MONT-ROYAL: Pintxo $$
Basque
256 Rue Roy Est, H2W 1M6
Tel *(514) 844 0222*
Experience a Basque journey of flavor at Pintxo, named after the traditional dish of slices of bread with different toppings: salmon tartar, charcuterie, and cheeses.

PLATEAU MONT-ROYAL: Lawrence Restaurant $$$
French
5201 Blvd St.-Laurent, H2T 1S4
Tel *(514) 503 1070* **Closed** *Mon & Tue*
This bustling restaurant serves great seafood – especially lobster – and tender meats. Mouth-watering home-smoked trout and popular brunches. Attentive, knowledgeable service.

PLATEAU MONT-ROYAL: Van Horne $$
Contemporary Canadian
1268 Ave Van Horne, H2V 1K6
Tel *(514) 508 0828* **Closed** *Sun & Mon*
Renowned Chef Sofiane Ghanmi concocts delicacies such as *foie gras* and oysters at this elegant restaurant. Intimate ambience and artsy decor.

SAINT URBAIN: Wilensky's Light Lunch $
Diner
34 Ave Fairmount Ouest, H2T 2L9
Tel *(514) 271 0247* **Closed** *Sun*
Inexpensive 1930s diner with great period decor. Don't miss the Wilensky's Special: a salami and bologna roll with mustard. Delicious home-made cherry cola.

VIEUX-MONTREAL: Le Cartet $
French
106 Rue McGill, H2Y 2E5
Tel *(514) 871 8887*
Trendy boutique restaurant known for its mimosa-accompanied

breakfasts and brunches. Generous servings and a salad-sandwich bar at front. Try their duck *confit* salad and home-made soups.

VIEUX-MONTREAL: Olive et Gourmando $
Café
351 Rue Saint-Paul Ouest, H2Y 2A7
Tel *(514) 350 1083* **Closed** *Sun & Mon, evenings daily*
Superb little café serving breakfast and lunch. Melt-in-your-mouth croissants and delicious home-made iced tea. Vegan options.

VIEUX-MONTREAL: Stash Café $$
Polish
200 Rue Saint-Paul Ouest, H2Y 1Z9
Tel *(514) 845 6611*
A great introduction to home-style Polish cuisine. Delicious soul food such as hot borscht, *perogies* (dumplings), *nalesniki* (crepes), and an unusual sausage salad.

VIEUX-MONTREAL: Tuck Shop $$
Bistro
4662 Rue Notre-Dame Ouest, H4C 1S7
Tel *(514) 439 7432* **Closed** *Sun & Mon*
Tuck Shop is a dinner-only bistro with a changing seasonal menu. Try the beef tartar, crispy pork belly, or home-made ravioli. Finish with the divine Québec cheese plate.

VIEUX-MONTREAL: Le Club Chasse et Pêche $$$
Canadian
423 Rue Saint-Claude, H2Y 3B6
Tel *(514) 861 1112* **Closed** *Sun & Mon*
Leather-bound menu featuring iconic Canadian fare – exceptional venison, duck, salmon, oysters, and scallops. Affordable wine list.

Freshly made croissants and sandwiches on display at Montreal's Olive et Gourmando

VIEUX-MONTREAL: Toqué! $$$
French
900 Place Jean-Paul-Riopelle, H2Z 2B2
Tel *(514) 499 2084* **Closed** *Sun & Mon*
The innovative chefs at this fine-dining French restaurant offer beautifully presented fusion meals featuring duck, venison, Arctic char, lamb, and salmon. Extensive list of French and other international wines.

Quebec City and the St. Lawrence River

BAIE SAINT-PAUL: Le Saint-Pub $
Pub
2 Rue Racine, Baie-Saint-Paul, QC, G3Z 2P8
Tel *(418) 240 2332*
Popular English-style pub located in the heart of town. Excellent beer-tasting menu with many freshly brewed beers. Great pub food served in generous portions.

BAIE SAINT-PAUL: Le Mouton Noir $$
French
43 Rue Sainte-Anne, QC, G3Z 1N9
Tel *(418) 240 3030* **Closed** *Mon & Tue*
"The Black Sheep" has a gorgeous summer patio overlooking the Gouffre River. Serves award-winning seafood; try the scallops and seared tuna with tomato *ratatouille*. Romantic atmosphere and attentive staff.

BAIE-COMEAU: Restaurant La Cache d'Amélie $$$
French
37 Marquette, Baie-Comeau, QC, G4Z 1K4
Tel *(418) 296 3722*
Upscale restaurant serving what is considered some of the best food on the North Shore. Seasonal menu offering delicious regional fare. Great wine list.

BAS ST. LAURENT, NOTRE-DAME-DU-LAC: Auberge Marie Blanc $$$
Traditional Canadian
2629 Rue Commerciale Sud, Témiscouata-sur-le-Lac, QC, G0L 1X0
Tel *(418) 899 6747* **Closed** *Oct–mid-May*
Located in a quaint summertime inn, the Auberge Marie Blanc restaurant has a beautiful patio overlooking Lake Temiscouta. Superb dishes that focus on locally grown produce – *pour votre santé* (for your health). No alcohol.

Stylish, colorful interior of Montreal's Tuck Shop Bistro

CHARLEVOIX, SAINT-SIMEON: Auberge sur Mer $
Seafood
109 Rue du Quai, QC, G0T 1X0
Tel *(418) 638 2674* **Closed** *Nov–May*
Inn and restaurant with a panoramic view of the river. Basic but delicious meals including salads, sandwiches, and soups. The daily specials may include crab *bisque* and Matane shrimps. There is also a children's menu.

HAVRE-SAINT-PIERRE: Restaurant Chez Julie $
International
1023 Rue Dulcinée, QC, G0G 1P0
Tel *(418) 538 3070*
This unpretentious seafood restaurant is popular with locals. Try the smoked salmon pizza or seafood pizza with *béchamel* sauce. Friendly staff.

ILE D'ORLÉANS, SAINT PIERRE: Le Vieux-Presbytère $$
Traditional Canadian
1247 Rue Msgr. d'Esgly, QC, G0A 4E0
Tel *(418) 828 9723*
Housed in a former presbytery. The cozy dining room in the solarium offers gorgeous views of the St. Lawrence River. Venison, bison, and ostrich, and a range of seafood dishes are part of the daily *table d'hôte* specialties.

ILES-DE-LA-MADELEINE, L'ÉTANG-DU-NORD: La Table des Roy $$
French
1188 Chemin La Vernière, QC, G4T 3E6
Tel *(418) 986 3004* **Closed** *Oct–mid-Jun*
Have a truly gastronomic experience at the former family home of chef Johanne Vigneault. Delicious lobster ravioli, island *bouillabaisse*, and lamb. Locally sourced ingredients, such as smoked herring, where possible. Reservations mandatory.

For more information on types of restaurants *see page 361*

LA MALBAIE: Auberge des Peupliers $$$
Traditional Canadian
381 Rue St.-Raphael, QC, G5A 2N8
Tel *(418) 665 4423*
A fine example of the *Route des Saveurs* (flavor trail) in Quebec's Charlevoix area. The daily local-food specials may include sturgeon and lamb. Fantastic farm-fresh salad.

LAC-SAINT-JEAN, SAINT-GEDEON: Microbrasserie du Lac-St-Jean $
Pub
120 Rue de la Plage, St.-Gédéon, QC, G0W 2P0
Tel *(418) 345 8758* **Closed** *Sep–May; Mon–Wed*
This microbrewery has a great selection of Quebec beers. Delicious regional pub food, including a trout platter, accompanies the drinks.

MATANE: Belle Plage $$
Seafood
1310 Matane-sur-Mer, QC, G4W 3M6
Tel *(418) 562 2323*
Hotel Belle Plage has a great seafood restaurant overlooking the ocean. Features an on-site smokehouse. Don't miss the delectable smoked salmon infused with cognac. Vegetarian and gluten-free options available.

PERCE: La Maison du Pêcheur $
Seafood
155 Place du Quai, QC, G0C 2L0
Tel *(418) 782 5331* **Closed** *mid-Oct–May*
Popular with locals, this Percé restaurant specializes in fresh salmon tartar with seaweed. Other seafood items on the menu include lobster, cod's tongues and cheeks, snow crab, ocean catfish, scallops, and halibut. Great ocean views.

QUEBEC CITY: Le Cochon Dingue Champlain $
Regional
46 Blvd Champlain, QC, G1K 4H5
Tel *(418) 692 2013*
One of four branches in the city, Le Cochon Dingue is a popular Quebec restaurant. Great choice for families, with a children's menu and games. Try the steak *frites*, ribs, and mussel trios. Hearty breakfast menu. French wines.

QUEBEC CITY: Restaurant-Bistro Le Hobbit $
Bistro
700 Rue Saint-Jean, QC, G1R 1R1
Tel *(418) 647 2677* **Closed** *Jan*
Featuring Hobbit-inspired artworks, this local hangout serves affordable, delicious bistro

A range of brews offered on tap at Brasseurs de Temps in Gatineau

fare. Menu changes regularly. Enjoy a refreshing Montreal McAuslan microbrew.

DK Choice

QUEBEC CITY: Aux Anciens Canadiens $$
Traditional Canadian
34 Rue Saint-Louis, QC, G1R 4P3
Tel *(418) 692 1627*
Located in the oldest house in Quebec, dating to 1675, Aux Anciens Canadiens takes guests on a culinary journey back in time. The staff, dressed in period costumes, serve authentic, traditional dishes from the region. Try the indulgent Quebec tasting meat platter for two. Children's menu available as well.

QUEBEC CITY: Café de la Paix $$
French
44 Rue des Jardins, G1R 4L7
Tel *(418) 692 1430*
Several intimate and elegant dining rooms, some private. Go for the *escargots*, Caesar salad, caribou with juniper berries, or beef Wellington. Delicious coffee and dessert. Reserve ahead.

RIMOUSKI: Bistro L'Ardoise $$
Bistro
152 Rue St. Germain Est, QC, G5L 1A8
Tel *(418) 732 3131* **Closed** *Sun*
Trendy bistro serving regional produce. Try the special soups such as *soubise*, and mains such as stuffed rabbit and fresh lamb. Great *foie gras* and *moussaka*.

SAINTE-FLAVIE: Capitaine Homard $$
Seafood
180 Route de la mer, QC, G0J 2L0
Tel *(418) 775 8046* **Closed** *mid-Sep–Apr*
Serving food since 1967, Capitaine Homard offers 1–5 lb (0.5–2.2 kg) fresh Gaspesian lobsters as well as crab, shrimp, and smoked salmon. Try their lobster *bisque*, clam chowder, and other tasty seafood delights.

Southern and Northern Quebec

CHAMBLY: Fourquet-fourchette $$
Regional
1887 Ave Bourgogne, QC, J3L 1Y8
Tel *(450) 447 6370*
Summertime terrace overlooking Fort Chambly. Traditional, native Quebec cuisine, featuring recipes dating to the settlers' period. Food paired with delicious beer from the local brewery, Unibroue.

GATINEAU: Brasseurs de Temps $
Pub
170 Rue Montcalm, QC, J8X 2M2
Tel *(819) 205 4999*
Lively pub and brewery with excellent craft beers and 12 fresh brews on tap. "Museum of Beer" on site. Great upscale pub food, including duck burgers.

Beautiful table setting at Quebec's Aux Anciens Canadiens

GATINEAU: Le Pied de Cochon $
French
248 Rue Montcalm, QC, J8Y 3C1
Tel *(819) 777 5808* **Closed** *Sun & Mon*
A local landmark, Le Pied de Cochon is an upscale, fine-dining restaurant serving traditional French cuisine. The *goût-du-jour* (taste of the day) is a special delight not to be missed.

GATINEAU: Le Twist Café Restaurant Bar $
Bistro French
88 Rue Montcalm, QC, J8X 2L7
Tel *(819) 777 8886*
Popular local hangout for the creatively inclined. All-you-can-eat mussels on Sundays and Mondays. The daily special often features fresh fish. Good range of microbrewery beers.

GATINEAU: Le Tartuffe $$
French
133 Rue de Notre Dame de l'Île, QC, J8X 3T2
Tel *(819) 776 6424* **Closed** *Sun*
Unpretentious French restaurant serving food based on local, seasonal produce. Great venison, Charlevoix veal, lamb, and duck. Extensive wine list.

LAURENTIAN MOUNTAINS: À la Chocolaterie Marie-Claude $
Café
1090 Rue Valiquette, Sainte-Adele, QC, J8B 2M3
Tel *(450) 229 3991* **Closed** *Mon, Wed, Thu*
Choose from more than 30 varieties of delicious handmade chocolates. Great waffles, salads, and croissants. Gelato or chocolate fondue for dessert. Excellent espresso and *café au lait*.

LAURENTIAN MOUNTAINS: Kayak Café $
Canadian
8 Rue du Camping, Labelle, QC, J0T 1H0
Tel *(819) 686 1111* **Closed** *Oct–Apr*
A summertime restaurant that also arranges canoe and kayak excursions. Their versatile menu features soups, mushroom and brie on toast, steaks, mussels, and Queen Elizabeth cake.

LAURENTIAN MOUNTAINS: Restaurant Le Cheval de Jade $$
French
688 Rue de St. Jovite, Mont Tremblant, QC, J8E 3J8
Tel *(819) 425 5233* **Closed** *Sun & Mon*
The chef at this fine dining spot is a *canardier* (duck) master, hence the duck dishes are a must, as is as their specialty, the Mediterranean

Picturesque seating at the popular Outaouais restaurant, Les Fougères

bouillabaisse. Choose from the Discovery and Gastronomic menus. Reservations essential.

LAURENTIAN MOUNTAINS: L'Eau à la Bouche $$$
Regional
3003 Blvd, Sainte-Adele, QC, J8B 2N6
Tel *(450) 229 2991*
Translating as "mouthwatering," L'Eau à la Bouche has a discovery menu that explores different taste sensations. Use of regional organic foods and game where possible. Range of wine pairings.

MONTEREGIE: L'Auberge des Gallants $$
Regional
1171 Chemin Saint-Henri, Sainte-Marthe, QC, J0P 1W0
Tel *(450) 459 4241*
Located inside a wildlife sanctuary, L'Auberge des Gallants is a spa, hotel, restaurant, and sugar shack all in one. Offers upscale dining amid tranquility. There is a generous Sunday brunch.

OUTAOUAIS: L'Orée du Bois $$
French
715 Kingsmere Rd, Chelsea, QC, J9B 1R7
Tel *(819) 827 0332* **Closed** *Mon, Sun (Nov–Apr)*
Housed in a traditional farmhouse with cozy wooden interiors. Serves great seasonal fare: asparagus, mushrooms, raspberries, and regional meats. On-site smokehouse uses maple for flavoring.

OUTAOUAIS: Café 349 $
Contemporary Canadian
349 Rue Main, Shawville, QC, J0X 2Y0
Tel *(819) 647 6424* **Closed** *Sun*
Owner Ruth Smiley-Hahn bakes mouthwatering muffins, and desserts, and serves tasty all-natural country-style meals seasoned with fresh herbs.

OUTAOUAIS: Le Hibou $
Bistro
757 Riverside, Wakefield, QC, J0X 3G0
Tel *(819) 459 8883*
Popular laid-back bistro with live music in the evenings. Delicious home-made pescatarian (fish and vegetarian) food. Sample the beet salad and French onion soup. Friendly service.

DK Choice

OUTAOUAIS: Les Fougères $$$
Fine Dining
783 Route 105, Chelsea, QC, J9B 1P1
Tel *(819) 827 8942*
Experience country elegance in the forested Gatineau Hills. Les Fougères is extremely popular for its fresh regional dishes paired with fine wines selected by the resident sommelier. There is a fantastic 11-course tasting menu. The monthly *table d'hôte* features seasonal, organic local foods. Children's menu available as well.

RIGAUD: Sucrerie de la Montagne $$
Traditional Canadian
300 Rang Saint-Georges, QC, J0P 1P0
Tel *(450) 451 5204*
Traditional sugar shack open year-round. In season, take a tour of the sap-gathering and syrup production facilities. Feast on maple-cured sausages and beans, and pancakes with maple syrup.

ROUYN-NORANDA: Restaurant Brochetterie Grecque $
Greek
152 Ave Principale, QC, J9X 4P5
Tel *(819) 797 0086*
A welcoming atmosphere with Greek music in the background. Home-made locally smoked fish, grilled meats, and *baklava*. Try their specialty *brochettes* (meat on a skewer).

SAINT-DENIS-SUR-RICHELIEU: Les Chanterelles du Richelieu $$
French
611 Chemin des Patriotes, QC, J0H 1K0
Tel *(450) 787 1167* **Closed** *Jan–mid-Mar*
Serves great regional cuisine in a fine dining setting, with dishes featuring Richelieu products wherever possible. Delicious bison *osso-buco*, *foie gras*, and filet mignon. Also has a heritage farmhouse for diners to stay in.

For more information on types of restaurants *see page 361*

SHERBROOKE: Restaurant Le Chou-Bruxelles $
Belgian
1461 Rue Galt Ouest, QC, J1H 2A9
Tel *(819) 564 1848* **Closed** *Mon*
This Belgian joint serves well-prepared rabbit, mussels, salmon, Brome duck, and other regional specialties. Choose from *table d'hôte* and gastronomic menus. Bring your own bottle (BYOB).

SHERBROOKE: L'Arlequin $$
French
875 Belvédère Sud, QC, J1H 4C2
Tel *(819) 573 2818*
Affordable *table d'hôte*. There is an adventurous *gastronomique* menu of smoked venison or lamb with five pepper sauce. Try the regional cheeses. BYOB.

TROIS RIVIERES: Café-Bistro Le Paladar $
Cuban
1260 Rue Notre Dame Centre, QC, G9A 4W9
Tel *(819) 694 9997* **Closed** *Sun & Mon*
Great Havana-inspired food: fried calamari, *potaje cubano* (black bean soup), marinated pork, and other intriguing combinations. Popular with students.

Toronto

DOWNTOWN: Café 668 $
Vegetarian/Asian
885 Dundas St W, M6J 1V9
Tel *(416) 703 0668*
Café 668 offers an extensive menu of Vietnamese, Chinese, and Thai vegetarian cuisine. Try their tempura platters, seaweed tofu soup, or the house special *lor-hon* (vegetable stir-fry). No alcohol.

DOWNTOWN: Ethiopian House $
Ethiopian
4 Irwin Ave, M4Y 1K9
Tel *(416) 923 5438*
Serves authentic Ethiopian food meant to be eaten with one's hands. Scoop up spicy chick peas, chards, or stewed meats with *injera* bread. Generous portions, but service can be slow.

DOWNTOWN: Gandhi's Indian Cuisine $
Indian
554 Queen St W, M5A 1V2
Tel *(416) 504 8155* **Closed** *Sun*
This tiny Indian restaurant has minimal seating, so call ahead. The menu features good appetizers and generous portions of stuffed *roti* (bread). No alcohol. Cash only.

DOWNTOWN: Karine's $
Vegan
109 McCaul, Unit 32, M5T 3K5
Tel *(416) 591 0863*
Home-made vegan food. The all-day breakfast sometimes features meat options. Wide selection of gluten-free desserts. Delicious soy-milk fruit shakes. No alcohol.

DOWNTOWN: Lil' Baci $
Italian
892 Queen St E, M4M 1J2
Tel *(416) 465 4888*
Popular Italian joint dishing up delicious pizzas, pastas, and salads from southern Italy. Economical $10 lunch on weekdays. Ontario craft beers available on tap along with Canadian and Italian wines.

DOWNTOWN: Manpuku Modern Japanese Eatery $
Japanese
105 McCaul St, Unit 29–31, M5T 2X4
Tel *(416) 979 6763* **Closed** *Sun*
Basic but reliable noodle house. Try *takosen* (octopus) and *unatama don* (barbecued eel and rice), both hard to find elsewhere in Toronto, especially at such reasonable prices.

DOWNTOWN: 309 Dhaba $$
Indian
309 King St W, M5V 1J5
Tel *(416) 740 6622*
Unpretentious Indian restaurant serving up scrumptious butter chicken, sizzling *tandoori* dishes, lamb aubergine, and okra chicken. Grand fifty-item luncheon buffet and a six-course tasting menu. Reservations essential.

DOWNTOWN: Biagio $$
Italian
155 King St E, M5C 1G9
Tel *(416) 366 4040* **Closed** *Sun*
Located inside the St. Lawrence Town Hall, Biagio has a formal dining room and a garden patio.

Try the *risotto ai funghi* (risotto with mushrooms) and *sella di'agnello* (rack of lamb).

DOWNTOWN: Biff's Bistro $$
Contemporary Canadian
4 Front St E, M5E 1G4
Tel *(416) 860 0086*
Upscale, modern bistro. Tasty steak *frites*, beef *bourguignon*, and haddock chowder. Oysters available at the bar after 5pm. Exceptional baked-to-order madeleines and profiteroles.

DOWNTOWN: Buca $$
Italian
604 King St W, M5V 1M6
Tel *(416) 865 1600*
Trendy basement *osteria* serving quirky Italian food. Delicious bison *prosciutto* (dry-cured meat served raw) and *nodini* (garlic ball rolls). Rustic decor.

DOWNTOWN: La Palette $$
French
492 Queen St W, M5V 2B2
Tel *(416) 929 4900*
Great spot for a romantic dinner. Features fresh market ingredients. Try the 12-hour-braised venison side ribs. International wines and beers.

DOWNTOWN: Marben $$
Regional
488 Wellington St W, M5V 1C9
Tel *(416) 979 1990* **Closed** *Mon*
Meat-lover's will enjoy the charcuterie board appetizer. Cozy ambience. Features fresh seasonal, regional fare. Good wine list.

DOWNTOWN: N'Awlins Jazz Bar & Grill $$
Cajun-Creole
299 King St W, M5V 0C4
Tel *(416) 595 1958*
N'Awlins is a popular bar and grill featuring live jazz music. House specials here include spicy

Lil' Baci, a well-known Italian restaurant in downtown Toronto seafood, surf 'n' turf, jambalaya, gumbo, blackened catfish, and Cajun-seasoned alligator. Friendly and knowledgeable staff.

DOWNTOWN: Rodney's Oyster House $$
Seafood
469 King St W, M5V 1K4
Tel *(416) 363 8105*
Closed *Sun*
As the name indicates, Rodney's specialty is oysters, both raw and in chowder. Clams, mussels, crab, lobsters, scallops, and shrimp are also on the menu. Good range of salt and freshwater fish.

DOWNTOWN: Segovia $$
Spanish
5 St. Nicholas St, M4Y 1W5
Tel *(416) 960 1010* **Closed** *Sun & Mon*
This casual and colorful Spanish restaurant serves great tapas; try the snails in wine and cream and mussels in saffron. Entrées include paella, scallops, and lamb. Generous portions. Live music and a dance floor.

DOWNTOWN: Sultan's Tent and Café Moroc $$
Moroccan
49 Front St, M5E 1B3
Tel *(416) 961 0601*
Groups can sit down to a traditional *diffa* (lavish banquet) in Sultan's Tent or enjoy a meal at the café. Don't miss the *keskesu* Casablanca and rack of lamb. Evening entertainment includes belly dancing.

DOWNTOWN: Benihana $$$
Japanese
Royal York Hotel, 100 Front St W, M5J 1E3
Tel *(416) 860 5002* **Closed** *Sun & Mon*
Part of the global Japanese restaurant chain known for its *hibachi* steaks and *teppanyaki*. Steak, chicken, seafood, fresh vegetables, and sushi dishes prepared in front of guests.

DOWNTOWN: Big Daddy's Crab Shack & Oyster Bar $$$
Cajun-Creole
212 King St W, M5H 1K5
Tel *(416) 599 5200*
Big Daddy's is a great spot for a casual meal of spicy seafood before the theater. Decor features images of jazz singers and New Orleans streetscapes. Try the fantastic New Orleans Hurricane Cocktail.

Pretty decor at Marcel's Bistro, an authentic French spot in downtown Toronto

DOWNTOWN: Bymark $$$
International
66 Wellington St W, M5K 1J3
Tel *(416) 777 1144* **Closed** *Sun*
Upscale restaurant in the financial heart of the city. Court-yard bar with views of the Mies van der Rohe towers. Great burgers and home-made ices.

DOWNTOWN: Chiado and Senhor Antonio Tapas and Wine Bar $$$
Portuguese
864 College St, M6H 1A3
Tel *(416) 538 1910*
Classy downtown restaurant serving organic food. A reliable favorite. Go for the fresh fish from Portugal, matched with affordable, good Portuguese wine.

DOWNTOWN: Marcel's Bistro $$$
French
315 King St W, M5V 1J5
Tel *(416) 591 8600* **Closed** *Sun*
Located above Saint Tropez restaurant, Marcel's is an authentic southern French bistro. Try the *bouillabaisse*-style fresh fish and seafood stew, mussels, pheasant, snails, venison, and *frites*.

EAST END: Kalyvia $
Greek
420 Danforth Ave, M4K 1P3
Tel *(416) 463 3333*
Home-style Mediterranean food served taverna-style. Patio seating that allows for people-watching in the Greek neighborhood. Fantastic seafood Poikila combos.

EAST END: Lady Marmalade $
International
898 Queen St E, M4M 1J3
Tel *(647) 351 7645*
Quirky breakfast, brunch, and lunch spot in hopping Leslieville. Delicious food with a tinge of Mexico and creative twists on eggs Benedict. Prepare to join the line at weekends. Cash only.

EAST END: Off the Hook $
International
749 Broadview Ave, M4K 2P6
Tel *(416) 465 4356*
Fancy fish n' chips in a casual setting. Choose your fish, batter, and sauce to go with delicious fries and even better coleslaw. Decent local beers on tap.

EAST END: Embrujo Flamenco Tapas Restaurant $$
Spanish
97 Danforth Ave, M4K 1N2
Tel *(416) 778 0007*
A bohemian joint serving seafood, vegetarian tapas, and paella. Good selection of Spanish sherries and wines. Live flamenco shows Wednesday to Sunday.

EAST END: Lolita's Lust $$
Italian
513 Danforth Ave, M4K 1P5
Tel *(416) 465 1751* **Closed** *Sun*
Intimate Italian restaurant. Great mushroom risotto, braised lamb shank, and roast beet salad. Sip one of the delicious martinis.

EAST END: Rodeo Brazilian Steakhouse $$$
Brazilian
95 Danforth Ave, M4K 1N2
Tel *(416) 465 0969* **Closed** *Mon*
Authentic *rodizio* (steakhouse) with an all-you-can-eat Brazilian menu. Choose from fried plantains, fish, roasted pineapple, and *churrascaria*. Live music.

NORTH: Gamberoni Restaurant $
Italian
3238 Yonge St, M4N 2L4
Tel *(416) 482 3063*
Simple Italian fare in generous portions. Reliable favourites include eggplant *parmigiana* and fresh fish. Spaghetti and meatballs for kids.

NORTH: Wildfire Steakhouse & Wine Bar $
Steakhouse
3438 Yonge St, M4N 2N2
Tel *(416) 483 4800*
Upscale steakhouse with a cozy, candlelit atmosphere. House specialties include sterling silver steaks spiced and aged for four weeks. Great *churrasco* (barbecue) ribs, chicken, and lamb.

NORTH: Asian Legend $$
Chinese
418 Dundas St W, M5T 1G7
Tel *(416) 977 3909*
Traditional northern China dim sum and stir fry. Other specialties include crispy pancake, Szechuan smoked duck, and bean curd. Tsingtao and jasmine tea.

For more information on types of restaurants *see page 361*

DK Choice

NORTH: Grano $$
Italian
2035 Yonge St, M4S 2A2
Tel *(416) 440 1986* **Closed** *Sun*
Superb traditional Italian eatery where the owner and staff happily assist with choices and wine pairings. The tasty *antipasto*, soups, and grilled fish dishes are made with sustainable seafood and local produce. Many different dining rooms to choose from, including a terrace. Noisy but amiable atmosphere. Admire works by local artists displayed on the walls.

NORTH: North 44° $$$
Fine Dining
2537 Yonge St, M4P 2H7
Tel *(416) 487 4897*
Elegant Canadian fine dining in a contemporary setting. Popular with celebrities. Gourmet seared duck breast, crisp-skinned chicken, and halibut on the menu.

WEST END: Albert's Real Jamaican $
Jamaican
542 Sainte Clair Ave W, M6C 1A4
Tel *(416) 658 9445*
Modest place serving tasty king fish, excellent beef patties, and chicken *rotis*. Very good spicy ginger beer. No alcohol. Only cash accepted.

WEST END: Fresh $
Vegan
894 Queen St W, M6J 1G3
Tel *(416) 599 4442*
Starting as a tiny juice bar, Fresh has become a Toronto institution with four locations. With an extensive, fully vegan menu, it is a haven for Toronto non-meat-eaters, as well as anyone in search of a healthy meal. All locations get very busy; call ahead and eat your meal in nearby Trinity Bellwoods Park

WEST END: Terroni $
Italian
720 Queen St W., M5C 1K6
Tel *(416) 504 0320*
Lively place popular with families who come to enjoy rustic Italian fare in a shabby-chic setting. Great pizzas and plenty of other dishes to choose from. Second branch on Victoria St. at Adelaide.

WEST END: Piri-Piri Churrasqueira Grillhouse $$
Portuguese
1444 Dupont St, M6P 4H3
Tel *(416) 536 5100*

Intimate seating at Grano, a popular Italian restaurant in Toronto

Authentic Portuguese dishes including fresh grilled fish, seafood, sardines, sausages, and chicken. Try the *piri-piri* (spicy) chicken. Extensive wine list.

WEST END: Universal Grill $$
International
1071 Shaw St, M6G 3N4
Tel *(416) 588 5928* **Closed** *Mon*
Upscale diner with nostalgic decor. Eclectic menu includes *huevos rancheros*, sweet potato fries, grilled steaks, and curries. Popular weekend brunch.

Ottawa and Eastern Ontario

KINGSTON: Chez Piggy $$
Bistro
68-R Princess St, ON, K7L 1A5
Tel *(613) 549 7673*
This popular bistro is in a secluded courtyard within a former stable. Serves tasty fresh fare all day that keeps folks returning to what is locally known as "The Pig."

KINGSTON: Le Chien Noir Bistro $$
Bistro
69 Brock St, ON, K7L 1R8
Tel *(613) 549 5635*
Trendy place with superb farm-to-table comfort food. Range of regional and international wines served by the glass. Attentive service. Good brunch.

KINGSTON: River Mill Restaurant $$
Traditional Canadian
2 Cataraqui St, ON, K7K 1Z7
Tel *(613) 549 5759* **Closed** *Sun*
Located in a heritage wool mill. Elegant, relaxed ambience, with a waterfront location, an

unusual feature in Kingston. Great sampler plate. Extensive wine selection, with vintage and private-order wines.

MINDEN: Wild Orchid Thai Bistro $
Thai
3 North Water St, K0M 2K0
Tel *(705) 286 1532*
This deservedly popular family-run restaurant serves exceptional cuisine at affordable prices. Overlooks Burnt River. No website; call ahead for timings.

OTTAWA: New Mee Fung $
Vietnamese
350 Booth St, ON, K1R 7K1
Tel *(613) 567 8228* **Closed** *Tue*
This busy and noisy joint serves possibly the best Vietnamese in Ottawa. Delectable wraps, satay soup with beef, and barbecued meats. Generous servings and attentive service. Reserve ahead.

OTTAWA: The Table $
Vegetarian
1230 Wellington St, ON, K1Y 3A1
Tel *(613) 729 5973*
Popular vegetarian joint with a constantly changing buffet menu of organic and gluten-free dishes. Dishes are priced by the weight of the plate. No alcohol.

OTTAWA: Yang Sheng $
Chinese
662 Somerset St W, K1R 5K4
Tel *(613) 235 5794*
Popular Cantonese and Schezuan restaurant with specialties such as traditional dim sum, home-made rice and noodle dishes, and barbecued duck and pork. Great soups.

OTTAWA: Light of India $$
Indian
730 Bank St, ON, K1S 3V4
Tel *(613) 563 4411*
An intimate and busy favorite in trendy Glebe serving food from the northern parts of India. Fantastic luncheon buffet that changes daily. Great service.

OTTAWA: The Fish Market $$
Seafood
54 York St, Byward Market, ON, K1N 5T1
Tel *(613) 241 3474*
The Fish Market is popular for its fresh fish dinners, lobster, and oysters. Try the Cajun blackened fish. Extensive, eclectic wine list. The wine bar bistro in the basement plays host to local jazz bands on Sunday, Tuesday, and Wednesday evenings.

OTTAWA: Beckta dining & wine $$$
Contemporary Canadian
226 Nepean St, ON, K2P 0B8
Tel *(613) 238 7063*
Popular experimental restaurant serving consistently delectable regional, seasonal cuisine. Opt for the chef-inspired tasting menu with wine/cheese pairing options. Reserve ahead.

DK Choice

OTTAWA: Domus Café $$$
Fine Dining
87 Murray St, ON, K1N 5M5
Tel *(613) 241 6007* **Closed** *Mon*
With a chic yet unpretentious ambience, Domus Café is a favorite with locals who love renowned chef John Taylor's experimentation with the region's freshest produce. Member of Savour Ottawa, an organization of farmers and chefs that support local produce. Well-informed staff help with wine pairings. Delicious desserts, including home-made sorbets. Superb destination for foodies.

OTTAWA: Wilfrid's $$$
Contemporary Canadian
Fairmont Château Laurier, 1 Rideau St, ON, K1N 8S7
Tel *(613) 241 1414*
Located in the elegant Fairmont Château Laurier, Wilfrid's offers buffet breakfasts and lunches in a room with views of Parliament Hill. Inspired takes on Canadian classic dishes. The pancakes with bananas and maple syrup are a popular breakfast choice, or for lunch try the seafood chowder. Great service.

The Great Lakes

BAYFIELD: Black Dog Village Pub and Bistro $
Pub
5 Main St S, ON, N0M 1G0
Tel *(519) 565 2326*
Black Dog is a pub in a historic building, with 20 drafts on tap and a multitude of scotch to choose from. The pub food on offer is casual, but delicious.

BAYFIELD: Little Inn at Bayfield $$
Fine Dining
26 Main St N, ON, N0M 1G0
Tel *(519) 565 2611*
Located in an erstwhile stage-coach stop, this is an elegant place with lovely street views. Local produce features prominently.

GODERICH: Thyme on 21 $
Fine Dining
80 Hamilton St, ON, N7A 1P9
Tel *(519) 524 4171* **Closed** *Mon*
Though billed as casual cuisine, the award-winning food and Victorian home setting make this place more fine dining than casual. Try the sirloin steak and scallops.

GODERICH: Ivey Dining Room at Benmiller Inn & Spa $$
Fine Dining
81175 Benmiller Rd, ON, N7A 3Y1
Tel *(800) 265 1711*
Ivey Dining Room takes pride in using locally sourced produce to prepare seasonal Canadian cuisine. Gorgeous setting in a lush valley behind a millstream.

HAMILTON: The Landing Restaurant $
International
1479 Baseline Rd, ON, L8E 5G4
Tel *(289) 649 1111*
Excellent rooftop patio restaurant overlooking a marina. The food is casual but good with soups, salads, and sandwiches. Large selection of wines, beers, and cocktails to choose from.

HAMILTON: Wass Ethiopian Restaurant $
Ethiopian
207 James St S, ON, L8P 3A8
Tel *(289) 389 5294*
Sample traditional Ethiopian food with separate meat and vegetarian options. Participate in a coffee ceremony and taste the signature honey wine.

LONDON: Los Comales Latin Food $
Latin American
346 Richmond St, ON, N6A 3C3
Tel *(226) 663 8452* **Closed** *Sun*
International cuisine is not a hallmark of this city, but Los Comales is the exception. Serves delicious authentic Latin American dishes such as *bandeja paisa*, featuring ingredients like yuca.

MISSISSAUGA: Mondello Ristorante $
Italian
127 Queen St S, ON, L5M 1K9
Tel *(905) 819 1727* **Closed** *Mon*
Modest Italian restaurant with delicious home-made pasta. Try the penne à la vodka or wild mushroom risotto. Helpful staff.

MISSISSAUGA: Bistro Narra $$
Austrian/Canadian
3030 Thomas St, A304, ON, L5M 0R4
Tel *(905) 567 8555* **Closed** *Mon*
Well-lit and airy bistro. Delicious crepes – try the pork and apple, or the seafood ones – as well as mushroom salad, pasta, and risotto. Great service.

MUSKOKA: Top of the Cove $$
International
375 South Bay Rd, Honey Harbour, ON, M5H 2G4
Tel *(705) 756 3399* **Closed** *Oct–May*
This summertime waterside restaurant has a great location overlooking the Georgian Bay marina. Delicious food from pasta to burgers and prime steak.

MUSKOKA: Bartlett's Lodge $$$
Fine Dining
PO Box 10004, Algonquin Park, ON, P1H 2G8
Tel *(705) 633 5543* **Closed** *mid-Oct–mid-May*
Picturesque Canadian log resort in the renowned Algonquin Provincial Park. Take a motorized freighter canoe to the lounge and dining room. Locally farmed produce and lake fish are used to create a delicious fine-dining experience. BYOB.

NIAGARA FALLS: Elements on the Falls $
International
6650 Niagara Pkwy, ON, L2G
Tel *(905) 354 3631*
Intriguing interior design and some of the best views of the falls. Try the smoked pork loin chop and bison burgers. Tapas lunch menu.

Wilfrid's, a Canadian restaurant in Ottawa, with great views of Parliament Hill

For more information on types of restaurants *see page 361*

**NIAGARA FALLS: Revolving
Dining Room at Skylon Tower** $
Fine Dining
5200 Robinson St, ON, L2G 2A3
Tel *(905) 356 2651*
Dine more than 700 ft (213 m)
above the falls, with an ever-
changing vista. The menu highlights French cuisine. Children's
menu. Good choice of wines.

DK Choice

**NIAGARA-ON-THE-LAKE:
Olde Angel Inn** $
Pub
224 Regent St, ON, L0S 1J0
Tel *(905) 468 3411*
History abounds at this pub
housed in Ontario's longest-
running inn. Great ambience
with fieldstone fireplaces,
hand-hewn beams, and plank
flooring. Serves traditional
British pub fare, including fish
and chips and bangers and
mash. Range of sweet and
savory pies. Choose from 25
different draft beers.

**NIAGARA-ON-THE-LAKE:
Stone Road Grille** $$
Fine Dining
238 Mary St, ON, L0S 1J0
Tel *(905) 468 4685* **Closed** *Mon*
Though set in an unassuming
mall, once inside, guests are
transported to an elegant dining
experience. Specialties include
charcuterie and smoked salmon.

**PORT DALHOUSIE:
Murphy's Restaurant** $
Seafood
*38 Lakeport Rd, St. Catharine's,
ON, L2N 5B4*
Tel *(905) 934 1913* **Closed** *Mon*
Good location beside the original
Welland Canal. Nautical theme,
with the bar made out of a boat
hull. Best fish and chips on Lake
Ontario. Children's menu.

**SAULT STE. MARIE:
Arturo Ristorante** $
Italian
515 Queen St E, ON, P6A 2A2
Tel *(705) 253 0002* **Closed** *Sun &
Mon*
A family restaurant featuring
Italian decor and wines worthy of
a Tuscan eatery. Superb pasta. Try
the house specials: *gamberoni*
(tiger shrimp) and pepper steak.

**STRATFORD: Pazzo Taverna
and Pizzeria** $
Italian
70 Ontario St, ON, N5A 3H2
Tel *(519) 273 6666* **Closed** *Mon*
Casual but elegant decor.
Gourmet pizzas featuring local
ingredients. Gathering place for
theater-goers. Great lunch spot.

**STRATFORD: The Church
Restaurant** $$
French
70 Brunswick St, ON, N5A 6V6
Tel *(519) 273 3424* **Closed** *Mon*
A local institution housed in an
old church. Great ambience.
Serves fantastic modern French
cuisine. Lavish Sunday brunch.

**THUNDER BAY: The Sovereign
Room** $
Pub
220 Red River Rd, ON, P7B 1A6
Tel *(807) 343 9277* **Closed** *Mon*
Simple decor, but one of the
city's best eateries. Reasonably
priced gourmet food, including
duck *confit* poutine and pork
belly. Generous portions. Good
beer selection.

VAUGHAN: Thai Bamboo $
Thai
2150 Steeles Ave W, ON, L4K 2Y7
Tel *(905) 761 7598* **Closed** *Sun*
Try spicy papaya salad, jungle
chicken, and sweet and sour
deep-fried fish. Sticky rice
dessert. Dine in or take out. Great
spot for lunch.

WINDSOR: Chanoso's $
Asian
225 Ouellette Ave, ON, N9A 4H9
Tel *(519) 254 8530*
Choose from over 100 stir-fry
combos, or build one yourself
at this downtown hot spot.
Shared plates and Asian grill
choices also available.

WINDSOR: Smoke and Spice $
American/Barbecue
7470 Tecumseh Rd E, ON, N8T 1E9
Tel *(519) 252 4999*
Not for the faint of heart or
vegetarians, Smoke and Spice is
where Canada meets the deep
south. Delicious pulled porks and
some of the best ribs in the city.

Central Canada

DK Choice

EDMONTON: Corso 32 $$
Italian
10345 Jasper Ave NW, AB, T5J 1Y7
Tel *(780) 421 4622* **Closed** *Mon*
Minimalist decor in a
transitioning neighborhood
belies the lavish attention
paid to the cuisine at Corso 32.
Chef Daniel Costa's delectable
Italian dishes include handmade
pasta, ravioli in black truffle
sauce, velvety chicken liver
tortellini, fish with anchovy
vinaigrette, and mouthwatering
gelato for dessert. Select wines
and liquors, including Grappa.

**EDMONTON:
Los Tres Carnales** $$
Mexican
10119 100A St, AB, T5J 0R5
Tel *(780) 421 0911* **Closed** *Sun*
Cheerful eatery serving authentic
Mexican food. Choose from fresh
tacos and salsa, tortillas, and spicy
chicken. Beer and sangrias.

EDMONTON: Hardware Grill $$$
Contemporary Canadian
9698 Jasper Ave NW, AB, T5H 3V5
Tel *(780) 423 0969* **Closed** *Sun*
This modern restaurant has
received over 15 Wine Spectator
awards. Savour Canadian delicacies
such as Porcini-crusted sea bass,
Angus steaks, and Alberta lamb.
There is also a tasting menu.

**LETHBRIDGE: Two Guys and
a Pizza Place** $
Pizzeria
316 11 St S, AB, T1J 2N8
Tel *(403) 331 2222*
Serves award-winning pizza
created from an 18th-century

Elegant entrance of the fine dining Church Restaurant in Stratford recipe. The menu also includes great pasta, chicken wings and pork ribs, dessert, beer and wine.

REGINA: Diplomat Steakhouse $$
Steakhouse
2032 S. Broad St, SK, S4P 1Y3
Tel *(306) 359 3366*
A plush interior and intimate booths are the hallmarks of this award-winning steakhouse. Choose from a range of steaks and seafood. Flambé desserts plus wine cellar and rare cognacs.

REGINA: La Bodega Tapas Bar & Grill $$$
Spanish/Latin American
2228 Albert St, SK, S4P 2V2
Tel *(306) 546 3660*
Stylish restaurant serving a creative mix of Spanish and Latin tapas, steaks, and seafood. Start with their lobster guacamole, and also try the *antipasti, foie gras*, and *falafel*. Sunday brunch.

REGINA: Willow on Wascana $$$
Fine Dining
3000 Wascana Dr., SK, S4P 4W7
Tel *(306) 585 3663* **Closed** *Sun*
Savor delicious seasonal Prairie cuisine in a scenic lakeview setting. Innovative dishes on the menu include artisanal produce, roasted duck, bison, and boar.

SASKATOON: Duck Duck Goose Tapas Bar $
Spanish
616 10 St E, SK, S7H 0G9
Tel *(306) 649 3825* **Closed** *Sun*
Popular local hub serving Spanish tapas, continental dishes, and lots of Saskatchewan cider and beer. Specialties include scallop ceviche, ricotta gnocchi, duck poutine, and fried cod.

SASKATOON: Wanuskewin Restaurant $
Traditional Canadian
Hwy 11 N. Corman Park No. 344, SK, S7K
Tel *(306) 931 6767*
This restaurant within the Wanuskewin Heritage Park honors First Nations people by serving authentic cuisine. Try the pulled bison sliders, baked bannock, and rabbit stew.

SASKATOON: Saskatoon Station Place $$
Traditional Canadian
221 Idylwyld Dr. N., SK S7L 6V6
Tel *(306) 244 7777*
Dine in a vintage rail car or in an elegant room amid historic memorabilia. Canadian specialties such as beef and buffalo steaks, lobster, and chicken dishes.

SASKATOON: The Granary $$
Fine Dining
2806 8th St E, SK, S7L 6V6
Tel *(306) 373 6655*
Designed to resemble a grain elevator. The fine dining menu includes filet mignon, lobster, salmon, and Saskatoon berry pie.

SASKATOON: Weczeria Food & Wine $$
French
820 Broadway Ave, SK S7N 1B6
Tel *(306) 933 9600* **Closed** *Sun*
This popular rustic-chic place features innovative dishes cooked in a contemporary French style. Menu changes daily. Local meat dishes include bison and boar.

SASKATOON: Saboroso Brazilian Steakhouse $$$
Brazilian
2600 8 St E #340, SK S7H 0V7
Tel *(306) 249 4454*
Dining is a sensory experience in this traditional Brazilian steakhouse. *Rodizio-* or *goucho-*style carvings at the table include beef, lamb, and pork.

WATERTON PARK: Vimys Lounge and Grill $$
Continental
101 Clematis Ave, AB, T0K 2M0
Tel *(403) 859 2150*
Dine with superb views of Waterton Lakes UNESCO site. Vimys has an eclectic continental menu with specialties such as French onion soup, bison tenderloin, and yak meatballs.

WINNIPEG: Pizzeria Gusto $
Italian
404 Academy Rd, MB, R3N 0B8
Tel *(204) 944 8786* **Closed** *Sun*
Imaginative gourmet pizzas topped with local produce and baked in a wood-burning oven. Other Italian dishes on the menu include *antipasto* and risotto.

WINNIPEG: Carbone $$
International
260 St. Mary Ave, MB, R3C 1M5
Tel *(204) 488 2554*
Family-friendly restaurant that serves delicious coal-fired pizza made with organic flour. Hearty paninis, chicken wings, ribs, and salads, plus gluten-free dishes.

WINNIPEG: Resto Gare $$
French
630 Rue des Meurons, MB, R2H 2P9
Tel *(204) 237 7072* **Closed** *Sun in Jul & Aug*
Set in a former train station in the French Quarter, Resto Gare serves delightful French cuisine. Try the French onion soup or *tourtière* (meat pie). Extensive wine list.

Genoa Bay Café, located right next to the water in the city of Duncan

WINNIPEG: Segovia Tapas Bar and Restaurant $$
Spanish
484 Stradbrook Ave, MB, R3L 0K2
Tel *(204) 477 6500*
Lively restaurant in trendy Osborne/Corydon Village. Tasty Spanish-style dishes include chorizo and apples, ceviche, risotto, and smoked char.

Vancouver and Vancouver Island

CAMPBELL RIVER: Harbour Grill $$$
Fine Dining
112-1334 Island Hwy, BC, V9W 1A7
Tel *(250) 287 4143* **Closed** *Sun*
Overlooking the harbor and marina, Harbour Grill has great views and upscale seafood, steak, and poultry dishes. Try roast duck and fresh halibut. Helpful staff.

DUNCAN: Genoa Bay Café $$
Café
5000 Genoa Bay Rd #9, BC, V9L 5Y8
Tel *(250) 746 7621*
Romantic, casual café located on the water's edge overlooking Genoa Bay. Specialties include clam chowder, calamari, halibut and chips. Delicious desserts, including heirloom carrot cake.

NANAIMO: Asteras Greek Taverna $$
Greek
347 Wesley St, BC, V9R 3A7
Tel *(250) 716 0451*
Excellent prices for authentic Greek food. Varied menu, with dishes such as *Avgolemeno* soup, *spanokopita* (traditional savory pie), *souvlaki* (Greek kebabs), and *ekmek* custard (bread pudding).

For more information on types of restaurants *see page 361*

Beautifully lit and lavishly decorated CinCin Restaurant & Bar, Vancouver

NANAIMO: Mahle House Restaurant $$$
Contemporary Canadian
2104 Hemer Rd, BC, V9X 1L8
Tel *(250) 722 3621* **Closed** *Mon & Tue*
Located in a restored 1904 farmhouse with an English garden. Try the chef's "Adventure Wednesday" five-course dinner. Regular menu changes weekly.

RICHMOND: Fisherman's Terrace Seafood Restaurant $
Chinese
4151 Hazelbridge Way, BC, V6X 4J7
Tel *(604) 303 9739*
Housed in the Aberdeen Centre mall, this extremely popular Chinese joint serves fantastic dim sum complete with chicken feet.

RICHMOND: Pajo's Fish and Chips $
Seafood
12351 3rd Ave, BC, V7E 2Z1
Tel *(604) 272 1588*
On the docks of the Steveston Wharf, this is a fun outdoors restaurant to take kids to. Serves excellent cod, salmon, and hand-cut chips. No alcohol.

SALT SPRING ISLAND: Hastings House $$$
Contemporary Canadian
160 Upper Ganges Rd, BC, V8K 2S2
Tel *(250) 537 2362* **Closed** *Nov–Feb*
Hastings House is a hotel and restaurant set in an English manor overlooking Ganges' harbor. Uses homegrown herbs, fruit, and greens. Menu changes daily. Extensive wine list.

SOOKE: Sooke Harbour House $$$
Seafood
1528 Whiffen Spit Rd, BC, V9Z 0T4
Tel *(250) 642 3421* **Closed** *Tue & Wed*

Savor innovative culinary delights at Sooke Harbour House. Daily set menu with a range of fish and seafood such as sea urchins, and local shellfish. Beautiful gardens provide organic herbs.

TOFINO: SoBo $$
International
311 Neil St, BC, V0R 2Z0
Tel *(250) 725 2341*
Sophisticated Bohemian, or SoBo, has delicious wood stone oven pizzas, barbecued bison, and home-made ice cream and pies. Excellent local and world wines.

DK Choice
TOFINO: The Pointe Restaurant $$$
Fine Dining
The Wickaninnish Inn, 500 Osprey Ln., BC, V0R 2Z0
Tel *(250) 725 3106*
Housed in "The Wick's" cedar lodge, the Pointe has a gorgeous fireplace and stunning views of the Pacific Ocean. Local specialties on offer include fresh seafood, exquisite lamb, and beef. Enjoy sommelier-picked Pacific Northwest wines. The ocean surges over rocks beside diners, making this a great place for storm-watching.

VANCOUVER: Planet Veg $
Indian
1941 Cornwall Ave, BC, V6J 1C8
Tel *(604) 734 1001*
Bustling cafeteria-style vegetarian restaurant. Superb *roti* rolls, rice pots, and some burgers as well. Patient staff helps guests with the menu. Great Indian sweets for dessert. No alcohol.

VANCOUVER: Red Sea Café $
Eritrean/Ethiopian
670 East Broadway, BC, V5T 1X6
Tel *(604) 873 3332*
Pleasant family-run joint serving generous portions for great prices. Delicious *injera* flat bread with all dishes. Order the *keieh tsebhi* (spicy tender chicken stew).

VANCOUVER: Sushi Bella Restaurant $
Sushi
2059 West 4th Ave, BC, V6J 1M7
Tel *(604) 734 4990*
Great spot for traditional sushi and sashimi rolls along with fusion Bella rolls where French is blended with Japanese. Try the ahi tuna poke and fresh ahi sashimi.

VANCOUVER: CinCin Restaurant & Bar $$
Italian
1154 Robson St, BC, V6E 3V5
Tel *(604) 688 7338*
Pronounced chin-chin, this popular Italian restaurant features great tasting menus. Watch the food being prepared on a rotisserie or in a wood-fired oven. Great wine list.

VANCOUVER: East is East $$
Middle Eastern
3243 West Broadway, BC, V6K 2H5
Tel *(604) 734 5881*
Exotic decor with low tables, decorative cushions, and live dancing. Try the Silk Route feast, Eastern Ecstasy dessert, and delicious spicy chai tea.

VANCOUVER: Havana $$
Cuban
1212 Commercial Dr., BC, V5L 3X4
Tel *(604) 253 9119*
Nuevo Latino cuisine with delicious Cuban cocktails. Daily breakfast spread, plus tapas, sandwiches, and entrées. Order the hearty black-eyed pea and chorizo cassoulet when available.

Breathtaking views of the Pacific Ocean at Tofino's The Pointe Restaurant

VANCOUVER: Kirin Restaurant City Centre $$
Chinese
201–555 West 12th Ave, BC, V5Z 3X7
Tel *(604) 879 8038*
One of four Kirins in Vancouver serving delicious home-made dim sum and fresh seafood. Vegetarian options available. Sample the abalone with mushrooms in oyster sauce.

VANCOUVER: Maenam $$
Thai
1938 West 4th Ave, BC, V6J 1M5
Tel *(604) 730 5579* **Closed** *Sun*
Traditional Thai style spot, with some dishes for sharing. Chef's menu available. Great wine pairings. Don't miss the eight-spice fish.

VANCOUVER: Stepho's Souvlaki Greek Taverna $$
Greek
1124 Davie St, BC, V6E 1N1
Tel *(604) 683 2555*
Popular local institution with a noisy but fun atmosphere and simply delicious food in huge portions. Excellent Greek salad.

VANCOUVER: The Foundation $$
Vegetarian
2301 Main St, BC, V5T 3C9
Tel *(604) 708 0881*
Casual and comfortable restaurant. No heating in winter, so dress warmly. Relish the warm broccoli salad and delicious nachos. Great music played all day.

VANCOUVER: Bishop's $$$
Contemporary Canadian
2183 West 4th Ave, BC, V6K 1N7
Tel *(604) 738 2025*
Bishop's has a regional menu that changes weekly. Don't miss the elk *carpaccio* and desserts such as warm date cake. The walls of the restaurant showcase a collection of First Nations' art.

VANCOUVER: C Restaurant $$$
Contemporary Canadian
1600 Howe St, BC, V6Z 2L9
Tel *(604) 681 1164*
Minimalist and trendy restaurant with a waterfront patio, housed in a former warehouse. Lots of fresh seafood and delicious rabbit. Multi-course tasting menus.

VANCOUVER: Chambar $$$
International
562 Beatty St, BC, V6B 2N7
Tel *(604) 879 7119*
Hip fine dining restaurant with an international menu. Specialties include mussels Congolaise with smoked chillies, cilantro, lime, and coconut.

VANCOUVER: Diva at the Met $$$
Fine Dining
645 Howe St, BC, V6C 2Y9
Tel *(604) 602 7788*
The open kitchen at Diva creates a welcoming experience where flavors of regional fare, such as truffled sole or butter toast ice cream, engage the senses. There are various pre-theater, bank holiday and special occasion menus, plus a large selection of artisanal cheeses and decadent desserts.

VANCOUVER: Gotham Steak House & Cocktail Bar $$$
Steakhouse
615 Seymour St, BC, V6B 3K3
Tel *(604) 605 8282*
Most steaks at the Art Deco Gotham are served with the bone still in. Delicious pork and lamb also on offer. Their Seafood Tower features Dungeness crab, Alaska king crab, lobster, and more.

VANCOUVER: Lupo $$$
Italian
869 Hamilton St, BC, V6B 2R7
Tel *(604) 569 2535*
Cozy fine-dining restaurant with an open fireplace. Sample divine dishes such as roasted quail, *risotto nero,* and ling cod.

VANCOUVER: Olive & Anchor Restaurant $$$
International
6418 Bay St, BC, V7W 2H1
Tel *(604) 921 8848*
Overlooking the Horseshoe Bay ferry dock, Olive & Anchor has a solid presentation of multi-cultural favorites. Go for the chicken *tikka masala,* burgers (including tofu), and pasta bowls.

VANCOUVER: The Fish House $$$
Seafood
8901 Stanley Park Dr., BC, V6G 3E2
Tel *(604) 681 7275*
Situated in the green oasis of Stanley Park, this local institution has fine views and delicious seafood. The ouzo-flamed prawns and oyster bar are unmissable. Twenty wines served by the glass.

VANCOUVER: Tojo's Japanese $$$
Japanese
1133 West Broadway, BC, V6H 1G1
Tel *(604) 872 8050*
Tojo's serves some of the city's best sushi, sashimi, and nigiri.

Picturesque terrace seating at The Fish House in Vancouver

Sit at the sushi bar or in one of the romantic niches. Choose from 21 estate sakes.

VANCOUVER: West $$$
Contemporary Canadian
2881 Granville St, BC, V6H 3J4
Tel *(604) 738 8938*
Trendy restaurant where the West Coast takes on traditional Canadian cuisine. A specialty is First Nations' Haida Gwaii Ling cod. Sip on one of their fantastic martinis.

VICTORIA: J & J Wonton Noodle House $
Chinese
1012 Fort St, BC, V8V 3Z9
Tel *(250) 383 0680* **Closed** *Sun & Mon*
Cozy and popular noodle house serving handmade noodles made fresh every day. Go for the delicious wonton soups, green onion cake, and Hunan chicken.

VICTORIA: Red Fish Blue Fish $
Fish & Chips
1006 Wharf St, BC, V8W 1T4
Tel *(250) 298 6877*
Fish and chips shack serving seafood sourced from the Oceanwise sustainability program. Great wild salmon tacones and Fanny Bay oyster sandwiches. Outdoor seating.

VICTORIA: Il Terrazzo $$
Italian
555 Johnson St, BC, V8W 1M2
Tel *(250) 361 0028*
In Old Town, with a lovely courtyard patio, six fireplaces, and a wood-burning oven. Noteworthy *salmone al forno* (almond and black pepper encrusted salmon). Excellent wine list.

For more information on types of restaurants *see page 361*

VICTORIA: Nar Café Bistro $$
Turkish
2540 Windsor Rd, BC, V8S 5H3
Tel *(250) 598 1085*   **Closed** *Sun & Mon*
This small gem of a restaurant is extremely intimate. and serves excellent Turkish food, including kebabs and home-made *mezes*.

VICTORIA: Spinnakers $$
Pub
308 Catherine St, BC, V9A 3S8
Tel *(250) 386 2739*
Superb brewpub with a very knowledgeable staff to help marry beer to food. Sip on their award-winning hand-crafted artisanal ales and specialty beers on tap.

VICTORIA: Fairmont Empress Room $$$
Fine Dining
721 Government St, BC, V8W 1W5
Tel *(250) 389 2727*
Located in the landmark Empress Hotel, delicious regional food and great service are guaranteed. Unforgettable afternoon tea.

The Rocky Mountains

BANFF: Coyote's Southwestern Grill $$
Southwestern
206 Caribou St, AB, T1L 1A2
Tel *(403) 762 3963*
Casual place with delicious home-made food: from the pizzas and salads to the barbecued flank steak and spice-rubbed beef tenderloin. Vegetarian options available.

BANFF: The Banffshire Club $$$
Fine Dining
405 Spray Ave, AB, T1L 1J4
Tel *(403) 762 6860*   **Closed** *Sun & Mon*
Exquisite food in the luxury setting of the Fairmont Banff Springs Hotel, the Banffshire. All ingredients are locally sourced.

BANFF: Le Beaujolais $$$
French
212 Buffalo St, AB, T1L 1B5
Tel *(403) 762 2712*
Excellent French-Canadian specialties, including Arctic char and braised elk. Tasting menu with wine pairings.

BANFF: Sleeping Buffalo Restaurant & Lounge $$$
Traditional Canadian
700 Tunnel Mountain Rd, AB, T1L 1B3
Tel *(403) 760 4484*
Sleeping Buffalo serves delectable game meats such as caribou, bison, and wild boar, all raised at the Canadian Rocky Mountain Resorts' ranch.

BANFF: The Bison Restaurant & Terrace $$$
Traditional Canadian
213, 211 Bear St, AB, T1L 1E4
Tel *(403) 762 5550*
With great mountain views and a seasonal patio, the Bison serves organic, regional cuisine with an emphasis on buffalo and game. No dress code – those in hiking boots welcome.

CALGARY: Pfanntastic Pannenkoek Haus $
Dutch
2439-54th Ave SW, AB, T3E 1M4
Tel *(403) 243 7757*   **Closed** *Mon & Tue*
This pancake house, located in a strip mall, is a great insider's secret. There are over 80 varieties of sweet crepes and savory pancakes to choose from. Alternatively, "build your own *pannenkoek*".

CALGARY: Silver Dragon $$
Chinese
106 3rd Ave SE, AB, T2G 0B6
Tel *(403) 264 5326*
Don't miss this thriving Cantonese and Schezuan place in Chinatown. Come for the trolley-service dim sum brunch. Staff helpful in identifying choices. Make reservations.

CALGARY: River Café $$$
Fine Dining
25 Prince's Island Park, AB, T2P 0R1
Tel *(403) 261 7670*
Located in a tranquil island setting with a gorgeous view of the water from the patio. Sample seasonal organic food, made using regional fish, game, and produce. Great weekend brunches and daily vegetarian options.

CALGARY: Rouge $$$
Fine Dining
1240 8th Ave SE, AB, T2G 0M7
Tel *(403) 531 2767*   **Closed** *Sun*
Rouge is located in a late 19th-century building on the Bow River. Home-grown herbs and local meats are used to prepare delectable regional dishes.

CALGARY: Saltlik Steakhouse $$$
Steakhouse
101 8th Ave SW, AB, T2P 1B4
Tel *(403) 537 1160*
This popular upscale steakhouse has great rancher salads and burgers, but the draw is the delicious Alberta beef steaks and prime ribs. Reserve ahead.

CANMORE: Beamer's Coffee Bar $
Café
120 737-7th Ave, AB, T1W 3H8
Tel *(403) 609 0111*
Canmore favorite offering over 40 types of gourmet, custom-roasted coffee bean, along with teas and delicious home-made sandwiches and cookies.

DK Choice

CANMORE: The Trough $$$
Contemporary Canadian
725B 9 St, AB, T1W 2V7
Tel *(403) 678 2820*   **Closed** *Mon*
The Trough, deservingly popular among foodies, is known for its exquisitely prepared and presented food. Don't miss the delicious Alberta beef tenderloin and scallops. Fantastic wine pairings and mouthwatering desserts, plus a romantic atmosphere. Family-owned, with friendly and helpful staff.

GOLDEN: Eagle's Eye Restaurant $$$
Traditional Canadian
1500 Kicking Horse Trail, BC, V0A 1H0
Tel *(250) 439 5413*   **Closed** *Seasonal*
At 7,900 ft (2,410 m), this is Canada's highest restaurant. Enjoy Alberta lamb and wild boar burgers while taking in fantastic views. Reservations essential. Timings are seasonal; call ahead.

Patio seats with gorgeous mountain views at The Bison Restaurant & Terrace, Banff

Key to Price Guide *see page 364*

Ornate decor of the Emerald Lounge, located in the Jasper National Park

JASPER: Bear's Paw Bakery $
Café
4 Pyramid Lake Rd, Jasper National Park, AB, T0E 1E0
Tel *(780) 852 3233*
This delightful café serves up delicious home-made pastries, sandwiches, and soups. Special coffees and chai on offer. Eat in or takeout options. Great place to go with children.

JASPER: The Emerald Lounge $$$
Traditional Canadian
1 Old Lodge Rd, Jasper National Park, AB, T0E 1E0
Tel *(780) 852 3301*
The patio seating at the Fairmont Jasper Park Lodge commands great views of Whistler's Mountain. Sample from a varied menu that includes a delicious range of grilled meats. Free meals for kids from the children's menu.

KIMBERLY: The Old Bauernhaus $$$
German
280 Norton Ave, AB, V1A 1X9
Tel *(250) 427 5133* **Closed** *Tue & Wed*
Originally a 17th-century Bavarian barn, the Old Bauerhaus was disassembled, shipped, and rebuilt here in 1989. Experience old-world charm while sampling the Bavarian Feast and *schnitzel*. Children's menu available.

LAKE LOUISE: Lake Agnes Tea House $
Café
Access from Fairmont Château Lake Louise, 111 Lake Louise Dr., AB, T0L 1E0
Tel *(403) 763 7242* **Closed** *mid-Oct–May*
Historic refuge that was built as a hikers' shelter. Choose from over 100 varieties of tea plus home-made soups and sandwiches. It's a hot climb up in the summer, so be sure to carry water.

LAKE LOUISE: Elkhorn Dining Room $$$
Traditional Canadian
Mile 22 Bow Lake, Icefield Parkway, Alberta, T0L 1E0
Tel *(403) 522 2167* **Closed** *Seasonal*
Located within the quaint, historic Num-Ti-Jah Lodge, Elkhorn has a phenomenal view of Bow Lake and the surrounding mountains. Beautiful candlelit three-course meals, with lots of game dishes.

LAKE LOUISE: Poppy Brasserie $$$
International
Fairmont Château Lake Louise, 111 Lake Louise Dr., AB, T0L 1E0
Tel *(403) 522 1818*
Hotel-restaurant with stunning views of Lake Louise. Great breakfast/brunch buffet. The menu features a mix of regional Canadian and some international dishes, including Japanese specials. Booking recommended for dinner.

LAKE LOUISE: The Post Hotel Dining Room $$$
Fine Dining
200 Pipestone Rd, AB, T0L 1E0
Tel *(403) 522 3989*
Promises a memorable dining experience. Helpful staff assist in choosing the perfect wine from among 2,200 varieties. Exquisite regional and international cuisine. Try the caribou, beef stroganoff, and lobster salads.

NELSON: The Outer Clove $$
Unique
536 Stanley St, BC, V1L 1N2
Tel *(250) 354 1667* **Closed** *Sun*
This unusual restaurant serves exclusively garlic-themed dishes from appetizers and mains to desserts, including garlic chocolate chip cookies and garlic ice cream. Chefs use 5 lb (2.2 kg) of garlic every day in deliciously inventive ways. A must-try.

REVELSTOKE: 112 Restaurant and Lounge $$$
Fine Dining
112 First St E, BC, V0E 2S0
Tel *(250) 837 2107*
The Regent Hotel's 112 is a refined restaurant with specialties such as rack of lamb, charbroiled steaks, and *cioppino* (fish stew). Sip on the delicious, locally brewed Mt. Begbie draft beer.

Southern and Northern British Columbia

FORT LANGLEY: Beatniks Bistro $
Bistro
9194 Glover Rd, BC, V1M 2S4
Tel *(604) 888 4487*
With a relaxed atmosphere and attentive staff, Beatniks serves everything from burgers to seafood linguine. Great Okanagan microbrewery beers, signature cocktails and wines.

HARRISON HOT SPRINGS: Morgan's Bistro $
Canadian
160 Esplanade Ave, BC, V0M 1K0
Tel *(604) 491 1696* **Closed** *mid-Nov–Apr*
Morgan's has a great summertime patio with a view over Harrison Lake. Sample its diverse menu, with home-made focaccia to accompany salads, tenderloin, braised short ribs, and lamb chops.

KELOWNA: The Yellowhouse Restaurant $$
Canadian
526 Lawrence Ave, BC, V1Y 6L7
Tel *(250) 763 5136*
At this restaurant in a Victorian house everything is home-made: from the stock and soups to the sauces and desserts. Try the steelhead trout, crab cakes, or rack of lamb. Great martinis.

Elkhorn Dining Room, found inside the quaint Num-Ti-Jah Lodge, Lake Louise

DK Choice

KELOWNA:
Waterfront Wines $$
Canadian
1180 Sunset Dr., BC, V1Y 9W6
Tel *(250) 979 1222* **Closed** *Sun &*
holiday Mon
Trendy, award-winning restaurant
with minimal, airy interiors.
Superb sommelier-advised
pairings of fine Okanagan wines
to some of the freshest regional
fare. Delicacies include wild
salmon, pork shoulder, and duck
breast. Sharing plates are
available too. In season, try their
delectable wild mushrooms
including morels. Sip one of the
cocktails, wines, or craft beers on
the summer patio.

OSOYOOS: The Diamond
Steak and Seafood House $$
Mediterranean
8903 Main St, BC, V0H 1V0
Tel *(250) 495 6223* **Closed** *Mon*
Family-run Greek-Italian place
serving great calamari and Greek
salad. Other popular dishes
include steaks, seafood, and
several kinds of pizzas. Try their
specialty prime rib. Good choice
of local wines available. Cozy
fireplace in the winter.

PRINCE GEORGE: Spicy Greens
Restaurant $
Asian
6545 Hart Hwy, BC, V2K 3A4
Tel *(250) 564 3509*
Spicy Greens serves delicious
home-made Asian fare,
specifically South Indian,
Sri Lankan, and Singapore
cuisine. Sample the madras
curries or *mee goreng* (spicy
fried noodles).

PRINCE GEORGE: Shogun
Japanese Steakhouse $$
Japanese
770 Brunswick St, BC, V2L 2C2
Tel *(250) 563 0121*
Reserve seats at the Teppan grill
where chefs create meals in front
of guests. Alternatively choose
the private Shojii room. Generous
portions. Great tempura and
steaks and generous portions.

PRINCE RUPERT: Cow Bay Café $
Café
205 Cow Bay Rd, BC, V8J 1A2
Tel *(250) 627 1212* **Closed** *Sun &*
Mon
Cow Bay is a popular, laid-back
café located on the docks
overlooking the harbor. The
daily whiteboard menu features
vegetarian options and fish of
the day. Dishes are wiped off the
board when they run out, so
arrive early for maximum choice.
Great desserts.

PRINCE RUPERT: Opa Sushi $
Japanese
34 Cow Bay Rd, BC, V8J 1A5
Tel *(250) 627 4560*
This unusual sushi joint is one
of the last fishing net lofts on
the coast. Intimate ambience.
Traditional and innovative West-
Coast inspired sushi at this
intimate eatery.

TERRACE: Don Diego's $
TexMex
3212 Kalum St, BC, V8G 2M9
Tel *(250) 635 2307* **Closed** *Sun*
With a daily changing menu of
inexpensive TexMex food and
a cozy ambience, Don Diego's
is a rightly popular spot.
Delicious *enchiladas*, generous
helpings and lots of gluten-
free options.

WHISTLER: Blacks Pub &
Restaurant $$
Traditional Canadian
4270 Mountain Square, BC, V0N 1B4
Tel *(604) 932 6945*
Located at the base of Blackcomb
and Whistler's Mountain, Blacks is
one of Whistler's oldest
establishments. The sports pub
upstairs features a large selection
of beers on tap.

WHISTLER: Bearfoot Bistro $$$
French
4121 Village Green, BC, V0N 1B4
Tel *(604) 932 3433*
Innovative restaurant where
tasting menus of regional food
are paired with a range of local
and international wines.

Northern Canada

DAWSON CITY: Drunken
Goat Taverna $$
Greek
950 2nd Ave, YT, Y0B 1G0
Tel *(867) 993 5868* **Closed** *Sun &*
Mon
Run by a Greek owner, Drunken
Goat is a picturesque restaurant
serving Greek fare in generous
portions. Get the sharing platters
to sample the varied menu.

DAWSON CITY: Klondike
Kate's $$$
Canadian
1102, 3rd Ave, YT, Y0B 1G0
Tel *(867) 993 6527* **Closed** *Oct–Mar*
This is a family restaurant with a
friendly atmosphere located in
a Gold Rush-era building, dating
from 1904. Great daily specials,
all-day breakfasts, and weekend
brunch. Also serves espressos,
lattes, and fruit smoothies.

The swanky entrance to Barefoot Bistro, a French restaurant in Whistler

FORT PROVIDENCE: Snowshoe Inn Café $
Diner
#1 Mackenzie Dr., NT, X0E 0L0
Tel *(867) 699 3511*
Snowshoe is a family-run inn serving typical diner fare, such as burgers, fish and chips, chicken wings, and shrimp. All-day breakfasts and a full dessert menu.

HAY RIVER: Back Eddy Cocktail Lounge & Restaurant $$
Contemporary Canadian
6 Courtoreille St, NT, X0E 0R0
Tel *(867) 874 6680*
One of Hay River's most popular eateries, this is a combination of restaurant, lounge, and sports bar. Menu includes steak, seafood, and local fish, such as Great Slave Lake fish. Relaxed atmosphere.

INUVIK: Tominoes Restaurant and Shivers Lounge $$
International
185 Mackenzie Rd, NT, X0E 0T0
Tel *(867) 777 2861*
Located in the Mackenzie Hotel, Tominoes is a great setting with both a fireplace and a waterfall. It serves steak, burgers, and pasta, delicious prime rib on Friday nights and popular Sunday brunch. Wind down after dinner with a drink in Shivers Lounge.

IQALUIT: The Gallery $$$
Fine Dining
Astro Hill Complex, NU, X0A 0H0
Tel *(867) 979 2222*
Housed in the Frobisher Inn, the Gallery displays lovely prints from the Pangnirtung Print Collection. Local artists wander in to sell their wares in what amounts to a dinner and art show. Regional fare on offer, including wild muskox and Arctic char. Popular Sunday brunch menu.

IQALUIT: The Granite Room $$$
Fine Dining
1056 Mivvik, NU, X0A 0H0
Tel *(867) 979 4433*
The Granite Room at the Discovery Lodge hotel serves fine cuisine in elegant surroundings. A soup and salad bar, daily *table d'hôte*, and Sunday brunch. Try the caribou steak and Pangnirtung halibut. Worth booking ahead for groups of more than four.

NORMAN WELLS: Yamouri Inn $$
International
1 Town Square, NT, X0E 0V0
Tel *(867) 587 2744*
Yamouri Inn's dining room has a relaxed, cozy atmosphere. The menu is extensive and varied, and a further takout option is available.

Entrance to SKKY Hotel's fantastic international restaurant Volare, in Whitehorse

WHITEHORSE: Antoinette's Food Cache $$
International
4121 4th Ave, YT, Y1A 1H7
Tel *(867) 668 3505* **Closed** *Sun*
Antoinette's has a laid-back atmosphere and warm Caribbean feel, with bright tablecloths and red walls. Food is well-presented and the menu includes curries, bison burgers, Trinidadian halibut, and vegetarian options. Desserts choices include rose petal-infused crème brulée and apple pie.

WHITEHORSE: Burnt Toast Café $$
Contemporary Canadian
2112 2nd Ave, YT, Y1A 1B9
Tel *(867) 393 2605* **Closed** *Sun evenings*
Burnt Toast is a hip restaurant featuring contemporary decor. Dinner menu includes tapas and locally made elk and blueberry sausage. Good Sunday brunch with a variety of egg dishes, home-made granola, and mimosas.

WHITEHORSE: Cellar Steakhouse & Wine Bar $$$
Fine Dining
101 Main St, YT, Y1A 2A7
Tel *(867) 667 2562* **Closed** *Mon–Tue*
Located in the Edgewater Hotel, the Cellar serves steak, seafood, and fish in an elegant, upscale atmosphere. The wine bar offers several international wines.

WHITEHORSE: Volare $$$
International
91622 Alaska Hwy, YT, Y1A 3E4
Tel *(867) 456 2400*
Skky Hotel's tastefully decorated restaurant serves delectable international fare. The menu features ribs, seafood, fish, and poultry. Ask for the chef's featured dessert of the day. Open for breakfast and dinner.

YELLOWKNIFE: Bullocks Bistro $$$
Traditional Canadian
3534 Weaver Dr., NT, X1A 2S9
Tel *(867) 873 3474*
This small place oozes frontier character. Sit at the bar and chat with the cook as he prepares muskox, caribou, bison, and fresh fish from Great Slave Lake.

YELLOWKNIFE: Fuego $$$
International
4915 50th St, NT, X1A 1S1
Tel *(867) 873 3750* **Closed** *Sun*
Great atmosphere with dark oak floors and warm lighting. Wild game and fresh fish feature prominently on the menu. Great spot for a romantic dinner.

DK Choice

YELLOWKNIFE: Thornton's Wine & Tapas Room $$$
Tapas
5125 52nd Ave, NT, X1A 1S8
Tel *867 669 9463* **Closed** *Mon*
The plain exterior and location beside a bowling alley conceal an elegant and classy restaurant. Thornton's has a modern interior with high ceilings, an upscale ambience, and excellent service. Choose from a selection of tapas and main courses. Good wine list and a delicious Sunday brunch. Reserve ahead.

YELLOWKNIFE: Wildcat Café $$$
Traditional Canadian
Wiley Rd, NT, X1A 2S9
Tel *(867) 873 4004* **Closed** *Oct–Mar*
Head to Wildcat Café for a slice of northern history, with the renovated log cabin having played a vital role during the Gold Rush. Serves tasty local fare in a friendly atmosphere during the summer. Delicious desserts and a modest wine list.

For more information on types of restaurants *see page 361*

SHOPPING IN CANADA

Shopping in Canada offers more than the usual tourist fare of Mountie dolls and maple leaf T-shirts. Visitors can choose from a wide range of products, and buy everything from electronic equipment to clothes and jewelry. There is also a variety of goods unique to the country – maple syrup from Quebec, smoked salmon from British Columbia, and cowboy boots from Alberta, to name a few. Native art inspired by centuries-old tradition, includes carvings by west-coast peoples and Inuit paintings and tapestries. In each major city there are covered malls, chainstores, specialty shops, and galleries, as well as street markets to explore. In country areas, beautifully-made crafts by local people can be found. Be aware that sales taxes are added to the price of many items.

Shopping Hours

Store hours vary, but in larger cities most stores are open by 9am and close between 5pm and 9pm. However, some grocery and variety stores are open 24 hours a day, and in major towns several pharmacies are also open for 24 hours. In most towns, stores have late closing until 9pm on Friday evening. However, in smaller towns and villages you should not expect any store, including the gas station, to be open after 6pm. Sunday openings are increasing: usually hours run from noon to 5pm but vary from province to province. Check first, as many may be closed in rural areas. The opening of stores on public holidays also varies from province to province.

How to Pay

Most Canadian stores accept all major credit cards, with VISA and MasterCard being the most popular. Some stores require a minimum purchase in order to use the card. They may limit the use of cards during summer and winter sales. Direct payment, or "switch" transactions, are also widely used, with point-of-sale terminals for bank cards available in most supermarkets and department stores. Travelers' checks are readily accepted with proper identification; a valid passport or driver's license are the usually accepted forms.

US dollars are the only non-Canadian currency accepted in department stores. Bear in mind that the exchange rate is usually lower, sometimes as much as 15 percent, than a bank will give. Large stores may offer money-changing facilities within the store.

Sales Taxes

In Canada there are three types of sales taxes: Provincial Sales Taxes (PST), the federal Goods and Services Tax (GST), and the Harmonized Sales Tax (HST). HST is a combination of PST and GST, and varies between 13 and 15 percent. Ontario, Prince Edward Island, Nova Scotia, New Brunswick, and Newfoundland and Labrador all charge HST. The remaining provinces and territories charge 5 percent GST plus PST of between 7 and 10 percent. Alberta, Northwest Territories, Nunavut and the Yukon do not charge PST.

Canadians love to curse the GST, which currently runs at 5 percent. It is added to most retail transactions; the major exception is basic food items. Since the beginning of April 2007 the GST rebate program for non-residents of Canada has been eliminated.

Consumer Rights and Services

Smart shoppers always check a store's refund policy before buying an item. Policies vary, some stores will refund money on unwanted items, others offer store vouchers, and many will not exchange or refund sale merchandise. Reputable stores will take back defective merchandise within 28 days as long as it is accompanied by the original bill.

Local art and craft work on display in a store, British Columbia

Completely Canadian

Products made in Canada offer shoppers a wide variety of choice. Although most specialty items are on sale across the country, many goods are less expensive in their province of origin. Hand-knitted sweaters and pottery are particularly good value in Atlantic Canada, as is the much-praised Seagull pewter made in Nova Scotia. The Prairie provinces and Alberta specialize in cowboy attire; tooled belts, vests, cowboy hats, and boots. Farther west, British Columbian artisans produce elaborate carvings, including totem poles. Jade jewelry, from locally mined

The vast Eaton Centre on bustling Yonge Street, downtown Toronto

stone, is also reasonable here. Local specialties from Quebec and Ontario include maple syrup and sugar-related products. Quebec artisans make beautiful wood carvings too. In Ontario, native basketwork is good as a lasting souvenir. For those who need an extra suitcase to carry their finds home, the renowned Tilley travel cases and products are made and sold locally throughout Ontario.

Native carvings can be found across Canada, especially in the far north. Genuine Inuit carvings are inspected and stamped by the federal government. A sticker featuring an igloo marks a true piece; it will also be signed by the artist. Since the 1950s, the Inuit have been producing prints of traditional scenes, which are popular, as is native jewelry. Beautifully handmade parka jackets, embroidered panels, and soft deer hide moccasins make excellent gifts.

Contemporary Canadian art features highly in gift shops and galleries countrywide. Photographs and prints are recommended for the budget-conscious shopper. Recordings of Canadian music are freely available in both small independent record stores and larger national chain stores.

Modern sportswear and outerwear is both durable and beautifully designed. Camping, hiking, and boating equipment

Pottery jar, Nova Scotia

are fine buys, as is fishing tackle. With such a strong tradition of outdoor life, a wide range of products is usually available at well below European prices.

Department Stores

The Bay is the major middle-range department store chain across the country. Canadian department stores have suffered financially during the last years of the 20th century. They are changing to meet the competition of US chains, such as Wal-Mart and discount stores, and membership stores including Costco and Price Club. Chains such as Sears and Zeller's occupy the middle to lower end of the market place. Canadian Tire sells everything from auto parts to sporting goods and has become a national institution.

Malls and Shopping Centers

Suburbia may not offer the most culture in Canada, but some of the malls are fine destinations in themselves. The renowned modernist Eaton Centre, however, is in the heart of downtown Toronto and is enclosed by a glass and steel arched roof, with a wonderful sculpted flock of geese soaring over shoppers. Over 42 million visitors annually enjoy this showcase of modern architecture, though it has been derided as "brutalism" by conservative Torontonians. The West Edmonton Mall in Edmonton, Alberta. Over 800 stores, more than 100 restaurants, 34 movie theaters, a huge water park, an amusement park, a theme hotel, a mini-golf course, an ice rink, and a zoo with dolphins are just some of the sights that draw Canadians and visitors alike to this retail paradise.

Exclusive stores are largely found in the country's retail capital, Toronto. Bloor Street and Yorkville Avenue are lined with status brands known the world over, such as Tiffany, Holt Renfrew, Ralph Lauren, and Gucci. Both Vancouver and Montreal have their own selection of world-class luxury stores. Montreal is notable as the fur capital of the country; good department stores will stock a selection of winter and summer furs at very reasonable prices. For those unable to travel to the north, Inuit art features highly in craft shops here.

The Underground City, with hundreds of boutiques, in Montreal

Shopping in Montreal, Toronto, and Vancouver

Canada's three largest cities offer shopping experiences with one thing in common: international fare! Montreal's cosmopolitan edge complements its wide-ranging stores, from chic boutiques to antique shops to an underground network of stores and services. Toronto's shop-'til-you-drop attitude includes the Bay/Bloor neighborhood and Yorkville as well as dozens of ethnic communities selling wares from their home countries. Vancouver shows off with about ten great shopping areas, as befits a spreading coastal city, with *haute couture* alongside art, furniture, and much more.

Eaton Centre in Toronto, containing hundreds of stores

Department Stores and Malls

Canada's most well-known department store is **The Bay/ La Baie**, a modern moniker for the Hudson's Bay Company, which started here in the 17th century as a trading post between the early settlers and the aboriginal peoples. The Bay is found in all three cities, and its distinctive brand of rainbow-striped blankets, sweaters, and coats have always been a hit with visitors. In downtown Toronto, the mammoth **Eaton Centre** shopping complex is anchored at its north end at Yonge and Dundas by the department store Sears and stretches south to Queen, where The Bay is located. In between, shoppers will find a rich choice of chains, from the Apple Store and Indigo Books to Swedish retailer H&M, Roots, and AX Armani Exchange. Montreal's **Place Montréal Trust** is home to 70 boutiques, including several major retailers. A good rendezvous point is the mall's soaring 30-ft fountain. In

Vancouver, the **Pacific Centre** is arguably the city's premiere shopping mall downtown, but in nearby Richmond, the **Aberdeen Centre** plays host to a bevy of Asian stores, restaurants, and services.

Markets

Vancouver's milder climate allows for longer seasons of the outdoor markets, but Canada's two other large cities do not shy away from this popular shopping experience. Montreal's **Jean-Talon Market**, with over 100 vendors, is mainly outdoors from May until October, although it is open year round and contains 20 indoor stores over the underground parking lot. In Toronto, the **St. Lawrence Market**, with 60 vendors, is much loved by locals for its excellent range of fresh produce and meats. Vancouver's **Granville Island** boasts an authentic farmer's market along with several galleries, boutiques, and artisans' stores.

Antiques and Crafts

Toronto's vintage shops are scattered across the city. Try the long stretch of Queen Street East for mid-century modern furniture and quirky shops. The large **Sunday Antique Market** sets up from dawn until 5pm across from the St. Lawrence Market *(see p191)*. **Antiques on King's** showroom is bursting with higher-end pieces. **The Guild Shop** in Yorkville features beautiful items from the Ontario Crafts Council. The shop in the **Textile Museum** is packed with bags, scarves, and all manner of handmade materials. In Montreal, **L'Art des Artisans du Québec** is a perfect store for original gifts made of wood, pewter, and glass, designed by talented Quebec artists. Local crafts are also on sale in the 15 boutiques of **Marché Bonsecours**. In Vancouver, antique shops are spread along Main Street, from Hastings to Marine Drive. The city's **Antique Warehouse** is an attractive stop for aficionados.

Designer Fashion and Jewelry

In Montreal, women's fashion by exclusively Quebec designers can be found at **Anne de Shalla**, while there is a wide variety of designer menswear at **L'Uomo Montréal**. **La Maison Ogilvy**, a respected fashion retailer in Montreal since 1866, stocks high-end items.

In Toronto, most designer stores, including **Tiffany & Co.**, **Royal de Versailles**, and **Gucci**, are centered in the Bloor-Yorkville area, including the

The market on Granville Island in Vancouver

flagship store for **Holt Renfrew**, a Canadian retailer known for its fine products, especially in cosmetics, fashion, and jewelry. Vancouver's Robson Street contains high fashion stores, such as Armani and Canada's own **Roots**. Gastown offers high-end independent boutiques along Water Street and West Cordova.

Art, Books, Music, and Giftware

The largest bookstore chain in the country is Chapters/Indigo, and the large outlets in major centers have excellent music

offerings as well (and cafés). The **Canadian Guild of Crafts** in Montreal not only displays fine giftware in wood, ceramic, blown glass, metal, and handmade jewelry, but also has a permanent collection of Inuit art worth perusing. In Vancouver, rare books or early titles on western Canadiana can be found at **MacLeod's Books**.

Specialty Stores

Canadian Maple Delights in Montreal is the quintessential homage to maple syrup: here there's everything from gelati,

pastries, mustards, vinaigrettes, and jams to 100 other maple treats. In Toronto and Montreal, **La Casa del Habano** is the best place to enjoy a fine Havana cigar with a Cuban cocktail or coffee. And for those so inclined, **Héritage** is a furrier as well as an art gallery in the heart of Vieux-Montréal. Vancouver's **Mountain Equipment Co-op** was started by climbers in the 1970s. It is now one of Canada's best outdoor outfitters and is found in all major cities. A Can$5 lifetime membership fee is payable before any purchases can be made there.

DIRECTORY

Department Stores and Malls

Aberdeen Centre
4151 Hazelbridge Way, Richmond, Vancouver.
Tel (604) 270 1234.
w aberdeencentre.com

The Bay/La Baie
585 Rue Ste-Catherine Ouest, Montreal; 176 Yonge St., Toronto; 674 Granville St., Vancouver.
w thebay.com

Eaton Centre
220 Yonge St., Toronto.
Tel (416) 598 8560.
w torontoeatoncentre.com

Pacific Centre
700 W. Georgia St., Vancouver.
Tel (604) 688 7235.
w pacificcentre.com

Place Montréal Trust
1500 McGill College Ave., Montreal.
Tel (514) 843 8000.
w placemontrealtrust.com

Markets

Granville Island
South shore under the Granville Street Bridge, Vancouver.
w granvilleisland.com

Jean-Talon Market
7075 Ave. Casgrain, Montreal.
w marchepublics-mtl.com

St. Lawrence Market
92 Front St. E., Toronto.
Tel (416) 392 7219.
w stlawrencemarket.com

Antiques and Crafts

Antique Warehouse
226 S.W. Marine Dr., Vancouver.
Tel (604) 324 3661.
w antiquewarehouse.net

Antiques on King
284 King St. W. at John St., Toronto.
Tel (416) 345 9941.

L'Art des Artisans du Québec
Complexe Desjardins, 150 Rue Ste-Catherine Ouest, Montreal.
Tel (514) 288 5379.
w artdesartisans duquebec.com

The Guild Shop
118 Cumberland St., Toronto.
Tel (416) 921 1721.
w theguildshop.ca

Marché Bonsecours
350 Rue St-Paul Est, Montreal.
Tel (514) 872 7730.
w marchebonsecours.qc.ca

Sunday Antique Market
St. Lawrence North Market, Toronto.
Tel (416) 410 1310.
w sundayantique market.com

Textile Museum Shop
55 Centre Avenue, Toronto.
Tel (416) 599 5321.
w textilemuseum.ca

Designer Fashion and Jewelry

Anne de Shalla
Marché Bonsecours, 350 Rue St-Paul Est, Montreal.
Tel (514) 398 0761.
w annedeshalla.com

Gucci
130 Bloor St. W., Toronto.
Tel (416) 963 5127.

Holt Renfrew
1300 Rue Sherbrooke Ouest, Montreal; 50 Bloor St. W., Toronto; Pacific Centre, 727 Dunsmuir St., Vancouver.
w holtrenfrew.com

La Maison Ogilvy
1307 Rue Ste-Catherine Ouest, Montreal.
Tel (514) 842 7711.
w ogilvycanada.com

Roots
1001 Robson St., Vancouver.
Tel (604) 683 4305

1025 Rue Ste-Catherine Ouest, Montreal.
Tel- (514) 845 7995

100 Bloor St. W., Toronto.
Tel (416) 323 3289.
w roots.com

Royal de Versailles
101 Bloor St. W., Toronto.
Tel (416) 967 7201.

Tiffany & Co.
85 Bloor St. W., Toronto.
w tiffany.ca

L'Uomo Montréal
1452 Rue Peel, Montreal.
Tel (514) 844 1008.

Art, Books, Music, and Giftware

Canadian Guild of Crafts
1460 Rue Sherbrooke Ouest, Suite B, Montreal.
Tel (514) 849 6091.
w canadianguild.com

MacLeod's Books
455 West Pender St., Vancouver.
Tel (604) 681 7654.

Specialty Stores

Canadian Maple Delights
84 Rue St-Paul Est, Montreal.
Tel (514) 765 3456.

La Casa del Habano
1434 Rue Sherbrooke Ouest, Montreal.
Tel (514) 849 0037

114 Yorkville Ave., Toronto.
Tel 416 926 9066

Héritage
30 Rue St-Paul Est, Montreal.
Tel (514) 392 9272.

Mountain Equipment Co-op
130 W. Broadway, Vancouver.
Tel (604) 872 7858

400 King St. W., Toronto.
Tel (416) 340 266.
w mec.ca

ENTERTAINMENT IN CANADA

Entertainment in Canada boasts all the sophistication tourists have come to expect from a major North American country, coupled with delightful rural entertainments in relaxing local venues. Covering mainstream world-class productions in Ottawa and the larger cities, Canada also offers the latest in alternative acts and traditional artforms, particularly in its exceptional folk music heritage. Music of the highest quality, both classical and modern, is offered throughout the country, and major cities provide first-rate theater, dance, and film, not to mention many musical shows and film festivals.

Information

Provincial daily newspapers are the most reliable sources of information about forthcoming events; the *Vancouver Sun*, *Montreal Gazette*, *Ottawa Citizen*, and *Toronto Star* are the most popular. Listings are usually published at least once a week. The *Globe & Mail* and *National Post* are produced in Toronto but are sold countrywide and have excellent arts sections. For more detailed local listings, pick up a free weekly, such as *Now* in Toronto and the *Georgia Straight* in Vancouver. Tourist offices *(see p401)* are helpful; some operators may assist in booking tickets. Visitor centers and hotel lobbies have weekly entertainment guides, such as *Where*, a magazine with editions for locations across Canada. In Quebec, French-language entertainment is chronicled by *La Presse* and *Le Devoir*. *Macleans* is a national weekly magazine with arts coverage.

Booking

Ticketmaster outlets are found in many shopping malls and represent major halls across the country. Tickets to venues in Quebec are available from Admission Network. Different offices cater to different sports and artistic events in each city. Most venues, however, can be contacted directly for tickets.

Disabled Visitors

Major Canadian venues are well equipped to deal with wheelchair users. All interior halls contain ramps and restroom access. Parking lots will have designated disabled spaces nearby. A hearing loop system is available at Ottawa's National Arts Centre *(see p201)*, and at most other major venues. Call ahead to check their availability. Outside ramps and elevators are provided to reach concerts halls and theaters at most large centers.

Theater

Toronto, Ottawa, Vancouver, Montreal, Stratford, and Niagara-on-the-Lake are the top theater centers in Canada (most of their productions are in English). Homegrown talent mixes here with shows imported from Europe and the US. Musicals and classical theater are always popular, as is Shakespeare, but there is a wide spectrum of shows – for example, Toronto's Princess of Wales and Royal Alexandra Theatres mount Broadway productions, as well as world premieres, such as *Lord of the Rings*. The main theaters have a principal season from November to May, but summer attractions are on the increase. Musicals and historical reconstructions provide family entertainment; the best-known is the musical *Anne of Green Gables*, performed year-round in Charlottetown.

Film

Hollywood block-busters have no better chance of success than in Canada, where premieres are often parallel with the US, so visitors may well see films in advance of a showing in their own country. Huge IMAX™ and OMNIMAX™ movie theaters can be found in the center of major cities, particularly in Ottawa and Hull.

Canada has a fine history of filmmaking: the documentary genre was invented here, and more recently its art films have attracted a wider audience. The main centers to see the new trends are Montreal, Vancouver, and Toronto. Robert LePage, Canada's own theater and movie impresario, has an international following among the cognoscenti. The surrealist David Cronenberg, director of *Spider* (2002) and *A History of Violence* (2005), is also Canadian.

Façade of The Royal George Theatre, Niagara-on-the-Lake, Ontario

Toronto International Film Festival, a must for avid moviegoers

Quebec's Denys Arcand is admired for his intensely human dramas, such as *Jesus of Montreal* (1989), *Love and Human Remains* (1993) and *The Barbarian Invasions* (2003). The National Film Board selects and releases a work by native talent each year, comprising feature films, animations, and documentaries. Ideal for spotting new talent, every year the Toronto International Film Festival provides a lively magnet to moviegoers, as do parallel festivals held in Montreal and Vancouver.

Classical Music, Ballet, and Opera

Classical music and opera draw large audiences in Canada, and this is reflected by the high quality of performers and venues. The Canadian Opera Company is based at the Four Seasons Centre for the Performing Arts (see p178) in Toronto, with a repertoire ranging from Mozart to cutting-edge pieces sung in English. The National Ballet of Canada is also based here, rival to the Royal Winnipeg Ballet; both companies feature period pieces and experimental work in their seasonal run. Fringe theater takes off in Toronto each summer with 400 shows selected by lottery. Well over 100,000 people annually visit the state-of-the-art Jack Singer Concert Hall in the EPCOR Centre for the Performing Arts to hear the celebrated Calgary

Philharmonic Orchestra. The Vancouver Symphony Orchestra plays at the Orpheum Theatre in Vancouver.

Rock, Folk, and Pop Music

During the 1990s, Canadian pop music acquired a credibility even its kindest supporters would admit had previously been lacking. Quebec's Celine Dion is a superstar and Shania Twain, Bryan Adams, and k.d. lang are international stars. Alanis Morissette and Sarah McLachlan are worthy successors to their country's heritage of folk rock. Young pop icons Avril Lavigne, Nelly Furtado, and Leslie Feist have been wooing teenagers worldwide with their youthful anthems.

Canada is perhaps most famous for its folk music, with such stars as Leonard Cohen, Neil Young, and Joni Mitchell being the best-known faces

Celine Dion, one of Canada's best-selling international artists

from a centuries-old tradition. The product of an intensely musical rural people, the nature of Canadian song changes across the country, moving from the lonesome Celtic melodies on the east coast to the yodeling cowboys in the west. Atlantic Canada has numerous tiny, informal venues, where an excellent standard of music can be found. Quebec's French folksters include singer Gilles Vigneault (see p32) who is also admired in Europe. The Yukon's memories of the gold rush surface in 19th-century vaudeville, reenacted by dancing girls and a honky-tonk piano in Whitehorse.

DIRECTORY

Ticket Agencies

Admission Network
Tel 1 855 790 1245.
W admission.com

Ticketmaster
Tel 1 855 985 5000.
W ticketmaster.ca

Major Venues

Bell Centre Montreal
Tel (514) 932 2582.

Calgary Philharmonic Orchestra
Tel (403) 571 0270.

EPCOR Centre for the Performing Arts Calgary
Tel (403) 294 7455.

Four Seasons Centre for the Performing Arts Toronto
Tel (416) 363 8231.

The National Ballet of Canada
Tel (416) 345 9595 Toronto.

The Newfoundland Symphony Orchestra
Tel (709) 722 4441.

Orpheum Theatre
Tel (604) 665 3050.

Roy Thomson Hall
W roythompson.com

Royal Winnipeg Ballet
Tel (204) 956 2792.

Vancouver Symphony Orchestra
Tel (604) 876 3434.

Entertainment in Montreal, Toronto, and Vancouver

A visit to the three largest cities in the country will not disappoint when it comes to great entertainment. Each is rich in theatre, film, and music venues. Montreal has spawned both French and English musical artists, and annual festivals abound, such as the Festival International de Jazz de Montréal. The renowned Toronto International Film Festival attracts the cream of Hollywood celebrities every September, and Vancouver is no slouch with its vibrant live music scene, dance clubs, and Irish pubs in numerous neighborhoods.

Giant banner in the parade at the annual Toronto Pride Festival

Festivals

Festival fever hits Canada's three largest cities in the summer, but late spring and early fall can offer unique events too. Montreal's own **Cirque du Soleil** often premieres its new productions in its home city, and the **Festival International de Jazz de Montréal** is known for its 350 free concerts. Toronto's **Contact Photography Festival** enables new artists to exhibit alongside internationally famous photographers. The **Toronto Pride Festival** has grown tremendously to include thousands of people of all orientations and gender identities. The city also hosts the **Caribana Festival** on the first weekend in August. The **Vancouver International Film Festival** is fast becoming as popular as the **Toronto International Film Festival**. In July, Vancouver's **Dancing on the Edge Festival** showcases contemporary dance.

Theater

Montreal has an important theater for the Anglophone enthusiast. **The Centaur** is housed in the former Montreal Stock Exchange building and stages high-quality English-language productions by both emerging and established playwrights. Both Canadian and international plays are performed regularly. Toronto's live theater community, the **Mirvish Theatres**, is considered to be the third largest in North America, and the city often showcases the continental premiere of large-scale productions, such as *Lord of*

the Rings. Vancouver's nonprofit **Arts Club Theatre Company** has had over 40 seasons of producing professional live theater. The city also hosts the **Bard on the Beach** – western Canada's largest professional Shakespeare Festival, performed in Vancouver's Vanier Park.

Rock, Folk, and Pop Music

The premier location for rock and pop concerts in Montreal is the **Bell Centre**, while folk music and up-and-coming artists can be found in the Quartier Latin (Latin Quarter) at any of the trendy bistros and bars along Saint-Denis and Ontario Streets. Toronto's largest pop/rock concerts can be enjoyed at the **Rogers Centre** or the **Air Canada Centre**. There is also the **Sony Centre for the Performing Arts** for major shows. During the summer months, rock groups play at the **Molson Amphitheatre** and at **Echo Beach**, right on the waterfront. In Vancouver, **Rogers Arena** usually hosts the biggest rock and pop concerts, while the more intimate **Orpheum Theatre** hosts single or smaller groups of musicians.

Classical Music, Ballet, and Opera

The **Opéra de Montréal**, founded in 1980, is the largest francophone opera company in North America. For dance lovers, **Les Grands Ballets Canadiens de Montréal** has a wide repertoire and invites prestigious international ballet companies each year to Place des Arts. Toronto is home to the **Toronto Symphony Orchestra**, who play at Roy Thomson Hall, and to the **Canadian Opera Company** and

The setting for Bard on the Beach – Vancouver's Shakespeare Festival

Performance by the Opéra de Montréal at the city's Place des Arts

the **Queen Elizabeth Theatre** plays host to both the **Vancouver Opera** and **Ballet British Columbia**.

the **National Ballet of Canada**, which are showcased at the **Four Seasons Centre for the Performing Arts**. In Vancouver,

Bars and Clubs

Montreal has two main clubbing areas: Rue Crescent, a two-block area packed with patios and pubs between Rue de Maisonneuve and Rue Ste-Catherine, and Rue St-Laurent, a predominantly French-speaking neighborhood with more upscale locations

and most of the dance clubs. Toronto's Queen Street and King Street West neighborhoods (from University to Spadina Avenues) are where big, brash dance clubs and comedy venues are located. The city's gay village and its nightclubs are in the Church-Wellesley Streets area. Vancouver's bars and clubs are spread all over: from Robson Street downtown, to the East Side/Main Street where the artsy community owns galleries that double as bars. Kitsilano is the city's homage to California life, with pretty people and beachside bars and clubs.

DIRECTORY

Festivals

Caribana Festival
Toronto. August.
Tel (416) 391 5608.
W caribanatoronto.com

Cirque du Soleil
Frequent premieres in Montreal.
Tel (514) 790 1245.
W cirquedusoleil.com

Contact Photography Festival
May. **Tel** (416) 539 9595.
W contactphoto.com

Dancing on the Edge Festival
Vancouver. July.
W dancingontheedge.org

Festival International de Jazz de Montréal
Late June–early July.
Tel (514) 871 1881.
W montrealjazzfest.com

Toronto International Film Festival
Early September.
W tiff.net

Toronto Pride Festival
June. **Tel** (416) 927 7433.
W pridetoronto.com

Vancouver International Film Festival
Late September–early October.
Tel (604) 683 3456.
W viff.org

Theater

Arts Club Theatre Company
1585 Johnston St., Vancouver.
Tel (604) 687 1644.
W artsclub.com

Bard on the Beach
Vanier Park, Kits Point at the Foot of Whyte Ave., Vancouver.
Tel (604) 739 0559.
W bardonthebeach.org

The Centaur
453 Rue Saint-François-Xavier, Montreal.
Tel (514) 288 3161.
W centaurtheatre.com

Mirvish Theatres
Princess of Wales Theatre, 300 King St. W.
Royal Alexandra Theatre, 260 King St. W.
Ed Mirvish Theatre, 244 Victoria St.
Panasonic Theatre, Toronto.
Tel (416) 872 1212.
W mirvish.com

Theatre Passe Muraille
16 Ryerson Ave., Toronto.
Tel (416) 504 7529.
W passmuraille.on.ca

Rock, Folk, and Pop Music

Air Canada Centre
40 Bay St., Toronto.
Tel 1 855 985 5000.
W theaircanadacentre.com

Bell Centre
1260 Rue de La Gauchetière Ouest, Montreal.
Tel (514) 932 2582.
W centrebell.ca

Echo Beach
909 Lakeshore Boulevard W., Toronto.
Tel (416) 269 5700.
W echobeach.ca

Molson Amphitheatre
909 Lakeshore Boulevard W., Toronto.
Tel (416) 260 5600.
W livenation.ca

Orpheum Theatre
884 Granville St., Vancouver. **Tel** (604) 665 3050. W vancouver.ca/theatres

Rogers Arena
800 Griffiths Way, Vancouver.
Tel 1 855 985 5000.
W rogersarena.ca

Rogers Centre
Next to the CN Tower, Toronto.
Tel 1 855 985 5000.
W rogerscentre.com

Sony Centre for the Performing Arts
1 Front Street E., Toronto.
Tel 1 855 872 7669.
W sonycentre.ca

Classical Music, Ballet, and Opera

Ballet British Columbia
Vancouver.
Tel (604) 732 5003.
W balletbc.com

Canadian Opera Company
Toronto.
Tel (416) 363 8231.
W coc.ca

Four Seasons Centre for the Performing Arts
145 Queen Street W., Toronto.
Tel (416) 363 8231.
W fourseasonscentre.ca

Les Grands Ballets Canadiens de Montréal
Tel (514) 849 0269.
W grandsballets.com

National Ballet of Canada
Toronto. **Tel** (416) 345 9595, 1 866 345 9595.
W national.ballet.ca

Opéra de Montréal
Tel (514) 985 2258.
W operademontreal.com

Queen Elizabeth Theatre
649 Cambie St., Vancouver.
Tel (604) 665 3050.
W vancouver.ca/theatres

Toronto Symphony Orchestra
Tel (416) 593 4828.
W tso.ca

Vancouver Opera
Tel (604) 683 0222.
W vancouveropera.ca

SPECIALTY VACATIONS AND ACTIVITIES

The sheer variety of the massive, unspoiled landscape is, in many ways, what attracts visitors to Canada. Taking advantage of the 44 national parks, several of which are UN World Heritage sites, most specialty vacations tend to revolve around Canada's spacious natural playgrounds. The range of activities available in this single country is wide: sledding and snowmobiling with Inuit guides or cruising in the spring through the flower-filled Thousand Islands of Ontario are both possibilities. Other choices include scenic train rides through the Rockies, trout-fishing in pristine secluded lakes, and adventurous world-class hiking.

Hiking

Canada is one of the world's top hiking destinations, with excellent facilities and a wide variety of terrain for beginners and experts alike. Hiking trails range from a leisurely two-hour nature walk to several days' physically demanding trek through starkly beautiful wilderness.

The preferred starting places for hiking trails in each national park are well marked. Accommodations for longer trips are often available in cabins or yurts within a park; alternatively you can bring your own tent or rent one in a nearby town. Large-scale maps of any area, including national and provincial parks, can be obtained from **World of Maps** in Ottawa.

Most of the more popular hikes require a level of fitness but little preparation beforehand. The best-known hiking areas are found in Alberta and British Columbia,

in particular in and around the "big four parks" of Kootenay, Yoho, Jasper, and Banff, which encircle the Rocky Mountains. The variety of lands here, from the lush, gently rolling country near Calgary to craggy mountain peaks, reinforces the popularity of the area. More centrally, the prairie provinces offer a surprising variety of walking, from the arid badlands of Alberta's dinosaur country to the wilderness hiking in Prince Albert National Park. In the east the mountains resume; the steep scenery of the Quebec park of Gatineau and the untamed wilds of the eastern and central Gaspé Peninsula both have wonderful scenery.

In northern Canada the hiking is more demanding but equally rewarding. Most walking and hiking takes place from April to August, when temperatures do rise slightly, although drops to -30°C (-22°F) are not unusual. At best, the weather remains unpredictable.

Turquoise Lake O'Hara in Yoho National Park

The Chilkoot Pass is a 53-km (33-mile) trail that follows the path of early gold prospectors in the late 19th century from Bennett in northern British Columbia to Dyea in Alaska. For the area, this is a relatively easy path to follow and gives a good taste of northern scenery. More arduous, not to say dangerous, is the memorable Pangnirtung Trail through the southeast of Baffin Island, which even in the summer has a permanently frozen ice cap. Inuit guides will take hikers through the frozen wastes by arrangement.

Occasionally wildlife-watching hikes are available, and teams of husky dogs carry visitors on sleds across ice paths in the wilderness to reach remote destinations. An unforgettable experience, these tours are expensive due to their remoteness and a lack of other modes of transportation.

Hikers near Weasel River, Auyuittuq National Park, Baffin Island

Safety Measures

Training and safety procedures must be followed for any hike. Always contact the local park or provincial tourist office for their advice and route maps before setting off. Remember, however unlikely a meeting may seem, wildlife can be aggressive; following instructions on bear safety is a must *(see p304)*. While less alarming, insects are a constant irritant: take all possible measures to repel blackflies and mosquitos. However clear and sparkling it may seem, do not drink stream or river water without thoroughly boiling it first as it may contain an intestinal parasite, which can lead to "beaver fever" or giardiasis.

In the far north, freezing weather conditions place a premium on safety measures. Never go on a trip without telling someone your planned route and expected time of arrival. Consult local wardens about wildlife and routes, and take the proper equipment. Even in the summer, freezing weather changes can be sudden, so be prepared. Those venturing into little-known territory must be accompanied by a trained guide or seek local advice on dealing with the unexpected.

Equipment

Most hiking areas offer rental outlets for tents and cold-weather clothing. Nonetheless, sturdy walking boots, rain gear, and a change of spare clothing are essentials that hikers have to bring themselves, or buy in a nearby town. Appropriate medication and a first-aid kit

Rental lodge by Emerald Lake in Yoho National Park

should also be taken, in particular bug repellent, and antihistamine. Exposure, resulting in either sunstroke or hypothermia, can be guarded against by using appropriate clothes and medication. On a long trip, carry energy-giving foods such as chocolate or trail mix.

National Parks

Canada's 44 national parks cover the country's most beautiful mountains, lakes, rivers, forests, and coastline. Areas of unspoiled peace, they are the ideal destination for those seeking an outdoor vacation filled with sports, activities, or even a natural spa. The most celebrated upland areas are the "big four" parks in Alberta and BC, Kluane in the Yukon, and the arctic flower-filled tundra of Auyuittuq National Park in southern Baffin Island.

Most of the parks are administered by the government heritage body, **Parks Canada**, and each has a visitors' center or park office to welcome visitors. Here walking, hiking, canoeing, and fishing information is available, often from guides who know every detail of the terrain. These offices also issue permits for fishing, which are necessary in each park. Hunting of any kind and use of firearms are all strictly forbidden in national parks, as is feeding the wildlife and damaging any trees and plants. Most parks have camping facilities, or rustic lodges and cottages. The parks generally charge for these facilities, and most have a daily, weekly, or yearly entrance fee, but some are free. Season tickets are available from either the individual park or the Parks Canada office in Hull.

Swimmers at Radium Hot Springs in the Rockies

Canoeists on Lake Wapizagonke,
Parc National de la Mauricie

Canoeing

Native Canadians perfected the canoe to maneuver around the country's vast system of waterways for food and survival; today canoeing is a largely recreational pursuit. In provincial or national parks with many lakes and rivers, canoeists can portage (or trek) to the backwaters, getting away from the most populated areas at a gentle pace.

Over 250,000 lakes and 35,000 km (20,000 miles) of waterways in Ontario make this the most accessible canoeing destination. Rivers and lakes making up more than 25,000 km (16,000 miles) of canoe routes run through the Algonquin, Killarney, and Quetico parks. The Rideau Canal, which travels 190 km (120 miles) from Ottawa to Kingston is a favorite route through the province, taking in the capital, the sprinkling of tiny islands near the historic town of Kingston, and acres of fruit orchards by the fertile waterway. While traveling through the islands, be careful of the other marine traffic. The Canal connects with the St. Lawrence Seaway, the world's largest draft inland waterway, and shipping regulations are tight. Smaller craft may have to make way for tankers.

Most towns near canoeing routes will rent boats by the day, week, or month, and wetsuits, oars, and life jackets are usually available. Because of the popularity of watersports, Canada is an extremely reasonable place to buy fishing and canoeing equipment; many outfitters offer good-quality products at almost half European and US prices.

Whitewater Rafting

Whitewater rafting may be attempted in the national parks of British Columbia. The Mackenzie River system, which runs from the Northwest Territories, provides occasionally hair-raising rafting and canoeing. Most routes in the far north are for the experienced only. The toughest trek of all is the 300-km (180-mile) run of the South Nahanni River near Fort Simpson in the Northwest Territories. New roads here and in the Yukon have boosted the number of visitors to yet another grueling set of waterways, the Yukon River system.

Inexperienced boaters and rafters can take advantage of two-week basic training courses offered all over the country. Lake canoeing in Wells Gray Provincial Park is popular throughout the province for those seeking a more relaxing alternative.

Windsurfing in Georgian Bay Islands
National Park, Lake Ontario

Other Watersports

Although the season may be short, sailing has always been a popular summer pastime. Canada contains a large proportion of the world's fresh

Whitewater rafting on the Athabasca River, Jasper National Park in the Rocky Mountains

Snowmobiling in Ontario across virgin powder snow

water, and there are allegedly more boats per head here than anywhere else in the world. The Great Lakes are the prime sailing and windsurfing areas, as are both east and west coastal regions from May to September. Swimming is also a favorite in warm weather; beaches on Prince Edward Island and Cape Breton off the east coast offer warm waters and sandy beaches, while lakes in Ontario, such as Lake Huron, provide inland swims. Torontonians sometimes swim in Lake Ontario in the summer.

Fishing

Over three million square miles of inland waters go partway to justifying Canada's reputation as a paradise for anglers. There are countless varieties of sports fish (see p29), not to mention the charterboat ocean fishing for salmon off the Pacific coast. Almost all parks offer fishing, often in secluded, pristine lakes and rivers. Be sure to contact the park's main office to obtain a fishing license. While most visitors fish in summer, a tiny wooden structure that sits on the frozen lake makes winter fishing more comfortable. These huts sit over a hole in the ice and are often heated. It may be worth buying rods and reels at your destination; Canadian fishing equipment is very high quality, with a good choice, and is usually very reasonably priced.

Canadian snowboard

Skiing, Snowboarding, and Snowmobiling

Not for nothing is Canada known as the Great White North, and its snowy terrain provides some of the world's best skiing. In the east, the Laurentian resorts of Mont Tremblant and Mont-Ste-Anne offer excellent downhill skiing. Moving west, the resorts of Whistler, Lake Louise, and Banff provide unforgettably dramatic skiing. High in the Rockies, powder snow awaits the adventurous; heli-skiing (lifting skiers by helicopter to pristine slopes) takes place on the deserted northern peaks. Many of the runs are higher than those in the European Alps, particularly in Banff and Lake Louise. These sites have held major competitions, including the Winter Olympics at Whistler in 2010. Another advantage to skiing in Canada is the proximity of the mountains to major cities; it is perfectly possible to spend the day zipping down slopes and then dine out in town.

Cross-country skiing is available across the country, but is particularly fine on southern and central Ontario's rolling terrain and Quebec's Laurentian mountain range and Eastern Townships. Most downhill ski resorts have a network of cross-country trails, but there are also dedicated cross-country ski areas and numerous parks with trails.

DIRECTORY

Maps

World of Maps
Tel (613) 724 6776
W worldofmaps.com

Ulysses Travel Bookshop
4176 Rue St. Denis, Montreal.
Tel (514) 843 9447.
W ulyssesguides.com

Federal Maps
Tel (416) 607 6250
W fedmaps.com

Open Air Books & Maps
25 Toronto St., Toronto.
Tel (416) 363 0719.
W openairbooksandmaps.com

Useful Organizations

Parks Canada
Tel 1 888 773 8888.
W pc.gc.ca

Spinal Cord Injury Ontario
Tel (416) 422 5644.
W sciontario.org

Travel Operators

Air Canada Vacations
Tel 1 877 752 7710.
W aircanadavacations.com

Cosmos/Globus
Tel 1 800 556 5454.
W globusandcosmos.com

Grand American Adventures
Tel 1 800 872 5872.
W grandamericanadventures.com

Trek America
Tel 1 800 873 5872.
W trekamerica.com

Snowboarding has become increasingly popular in snow-sports centers across the country. All downhill resorts have a few slopes set aside for boarders.

Snowmobiles are a necessity for many living in rural areas, but snowmobiling is also a popular winter sport. Ontario has almost 50,000 km (35,000 miles) of snowmobile trails. Seasoned riders can cover up to 500 km (300 miles) in two days. Traveling in groups is advised; there are many popular pitstops en route. These "snow inns" often offer package deals.

SURVIVAL GUIDE

PRACTICAL INFORMATION

Canada is a popular holiday destination, and offers visitors a mix of urban sophistication and outdoor pleasures. Visitors' facilities are generally excellent. Accommodations and restaurants are of international standard *(see pp348–83)*, public transportation is efficient *(see pp406–19)*, and tourist information centers are found nearly everywhere. The following pages contain useful information for all visitors. Personal Security and Health *(see pp402–403)* details a number of recommended precautions, while Banking and Currency *(see p404)* answers the important financial queries, together with taxation details. There is also a section on how to use the Canadian telephone and postal services.

When To Go

Weather and geography dominate any visit to Canada. The vastness of the country means that most trips will be centered on one of the major cities, Vancouver, Toronto, Ottawa, and Montreal, although it is possible to stay in remote areas such as the isolated Inuit settlements dotted around Hudson Bay. Depending on each visitor's interests, the best time to go will be dictated by local climate and the time of year.

In general, the climates on both the west and east coasts are temperate, while harsher weather occurs in the center of the country, in Saskatchewan, Manitoba, and Alberta, where the summers are fine but the winters long and hard. Northern Canada is at its most welcoming during July and August when the land thaws, and the temperature is more likely to climb above zero.

In eastern Canada, Nova Scotia, New Brunswick, and Prince Edward Island, there are four distinct seasons, with snowy winters, mild springs, and crisp falls; summer is still the best time to visit the provinces' resorts. Quebec and Ontario have hot, humid summers and cold winters, with snow lingering until late March. Spring and fall are brief, although fall in particular can be a rewarding time to make a visit.

The northeastern province of Newfoundland and coastal Labrador have the most extreme temperatures, ranging on a winter's day from 0°C (32°F) to –50°C (–41°F) in St. John's on Newfoundland's east coast. Winter visitors to British Columbia and the Rockies can enjoy some of the best skiing in the world. This region is also noted for its temperate weather but can be very wet in spring and fall as Pacific depressions roll in over the mountains.

Entry Requirements

All visitors to Canada should have a passport valid for longer than the intended period of stay. Stricter US security regulations mean this now includes American citizens, who must show passports when returning to the US. Travelers from the UK, US, EU, and all British Commonwealth countries do not require a special visa to visit. Tourists are issued with a visitor's visa on arrival if they satisfy immigration officials that they have a valid return ticket and sufficient funds for the duration of their stay. Visitors can stay up to six

Visitors of all ages enjoying a ride on a swing carousel during SuperEx, Ottawa's annual August fair

◄ A light rail train passing through the fall forest, Edmonton, Alberta months, but to extend their stay they must apply to Citizenship and Immigration Canada in Ottawa before expiration of their authorized visit. As visa regulations are subject to change, check with the nearest Canadian Consulate, Embassy, or High Commission before travel.

Anyone under the age of 18 traveling unaccompanied by an adult needs a letter of consent from a parent or guardian. The person meeting the child also needs to have full authorization and proof of permission.

Tourist Information

Canadian tourist offices are famous for the amount and quality of their information, offering everything from local maps to hotel, B-and-B, or campground bookings. Special tours such as wilderness camping, archaeological digs, and wildlife-watching can often be arranged through the tourism service. All the provincial and national parks have visitors' centers, which generally provide maps detailing hiking trails and canoe routes.

The national Canadian Tourism Commission is the central organization, and each province has its own tourism authority. Many smaller towns also have their own seasonal tourist offices, which offer good free maps and detailed information. Each of the large cities has a main office as well as extra booths and kiosks open during busy summer months. Accommodations can usually be booked at the booths found in airports and regional offices.

Opening Hours and Admission Prices

Most museums, parks, and other attractions throughout Canada charge an admission fee. The amount can vary enormously and many sights offer a range of discount

packages for families, children, and seniors. Tourist office leaflets, brochures, and local newspapers often carry discount coupons. Some galleries and museums have free-of-charge days, evenings, or a free hour daily before closing time. Opening times vary according to the time of the year. As a rule, most of the sights are open for longer through summer but may close completely during the winter months. Many museums and galleries close one day each week, usually on a Monday or Tuesday, but not on weekends. Although many attractions are closed on major holidays, such as Christmas and New Year's Day, a surprising number are open all-year-round. School summer holidays in Canada are from late June to Labor Day Weekend, which ends on the first Monday in September. Labor Day generally signifies the end of summer. This is the weekend

Canadian Time Zones

Canada has six time zones spanning a four-and-a-half hour time difference from coast to coast. Between Vancouver and Halifax there are five zones; Pacific, Mountain, Central, Eastern, and Atlantic Standard Time, with an unusual half-hour difference between Newfoundland and Atlantic time. Every province except Saskatchewan uses Daylight Saving Time to give longer summer days from mid-March to October or November. Clocks go back an hour in October/November, forward an hour in March.

Time Zone	Hours minus GMT	Time Zone	Hours minus GMT
Pacific	–8	Eastern	–5
Mountain	–7	Atlantic	–4
Central	–6	Newfoundland	–3.5

"The Small Apple" tourist booth in Ontario

after which opening hours change over to shorter winter hours of operation. Rural sights generally have shorter hours year-round than those in cities.

Senior Travelers

In Canada people over 60 are refered to as "seniors," and are offered a wide range of discounts. Reduced rates frequently apply to the cost of movie tickets, public transportation, entrance fees, and some restaurant menus. VIA Rail reduce their fares by 10 percent for seniors. When applicable, reductions range from 10 percent to 50 percent for people aged from 55, 60, or 65, depending on the province or attraction. If discounts are not advertised it is always a good idea to inquire.

Trips with a component of lifelong learning for older adults are organized by **Road Scholar**, a non-profit organization once known as Elderhostel Canada. A typical holiday comprises morning lectures, guided tours in the afternoon, and a communal dinner.

Tourists enjoying the scenery of Niagara Falls

Traveling with Children

Although Canada lacks the numbers of theme parks of the US, its beach resorts, parks, and city centers have much to offer children and families. Most types of accommodation state whether or not they welcome children. Those hotels that do often do not charge for a child sharing a parent's room. They will also normally provide cribs and high chairs, and sometimes have baby-sitting services.

Restaurants now generally welcome children, and many offer kids' menus and high chairs, or will warm up milk and baby food. Some fast food outlets have play areas. It is best to check in advance with more upscale establishments.

Both international and internal airfares are often cheaper for children, and babies under two years old who are not taking up a seat may travel free. On public transportation children under two travel free, and those under 12 have lower fares. If you are renting a car you can reserve one or two car seats for children from your rental firm *(see p419)*.

Etiquette

Canada is very much a multicultural nation *(see pp30–31)*, which welcomes and respects people and customs from the rest of the world. Native Canadians are never referred to as "Indians"; in general they are known as Canada's "First Nations" or "Natives," while

"eskimos" are always known as Inuit *(see p35)*. In Quebec, be prepared to hear French spoken first. It is also appreciated if visitors show that they have tried to learn a few French words.

Canada's relaxed, informal atmosphere is evident in its dress codes, which tend to be practical and dependent on the climate. Canadians favor jeans and sweatshirts, and dress in layers so they can add or subtract clothing, especially when moving between well-heated malls and winter streets. However, in the cities and larger towns more formal clothing is expected, particularly in more stylish restaurants, theaters, and other formal places. Even the more humble eateries insist on proper attire, and the sign "no shoes, no shirt, no service" is frequently seen in many tourist areas. Topless sunbathing is generally frowned upon in Canada.

Drinking in non-licenced public places, such as city parks, is illegal, and it is also illegal to have opened bottles of alcohol in the car when traveling. It is against the law to smoke in public places such as on buses and trains, in taxis, in public buildings, and in restaurants and bars throughout Canada.

A service charge is seldom included in checks at Canadian restaurants. Unless it is included, the standard tip in Canada is 15 percent. Taxi drivers expect a similar tip, while barbers and hairdressers should receive about 10 percent of the total. It is customary to tip porters at airports and train stations, cloakroom attendants, bellhops, doormen, and hotel porters Can$1 per bag, and to leave something for the hotel maids. Tipping bar staff in bars and nightclubs is also expected. Anyone in charge of a large party of visitors should prepare to be generous.

Student Travelers

With an International Student Identity Card (ISIC), full-time students are entitled to substantial discounts on travel as well as admission prices to movies, galleries, museums, and many other tourist attractions. The ISIC card should be purchased in the student's home country at a **Student Travel Association** (STA) office in the nearest city. There are also a wide range of bus and rail discounts available to students,

International student I.D. card

such as the "Go Canada" Accommodation and Coach Pass, which offers both reduced-cost travel and stays in youth hostels across the country. The pass can be booked through local agents specializing in student travel. VIA Rail also offers students the "Canrail Pass," which allows a period of unlimited travel on all routes. Reasonably priced accommodations are available on university campuses in the larger cities during local student vacations. There are also comfortable hostels throughout the country, most of which are affiliated with the International Youth Hostelling Federation (IYHF). Eating out is inexpensive, so it's easy to find great food on a budget.

Electricity

Canadian electrical appliances come with either a two-prong or three-prong plug, and most sockets will accept either. The system is a 110-volt, 60-cycle system. You will need an adaptor if you are visiting from outside North America.

Batteries are universal and are readily available for all appliances. Bear in mind that bargain electrical goods purchased here will probably need modification for use in Europe.

Travelers with Disabilities

Travelers with physical disabilities can expect some of the best facilities in the world in Canada. Overall, large towns and cities offer wheelchair access in most public buildings, as well as on public transportation. Most curbs are dropped at intersections and a large number of subway staions have elevators. Check the TTC website for more information about station facilities.

Formerly the Canadian Paraplegic Association, **Spinal Cord Injury (SCI) Canada** is a great resource for those with physical disabilities. With 40 offices across the country, SCI offers disabled travelers advice on accessing major Canadian attractions. Go to the main SCI Canada website for more information about the federation and its provincial offices.

There is a wide choice of hotels with disabled facilities in Canada. Most of the big chains such as Best Western and Holiday Inn are easily accessible, as are some luxury hotels and youth hostels. The CPA also has details on the most disabled-friendly attractions.

Many of the national and provincial parks have interpretive centers, short nature trails, campsites and boardwalks that are wheelchair accessible. Call the relevant park for more information.

Conversion Chart

Imperial to Metric
1 inch = 2.54 centimeters
1 foot = 30 centimeters
1 mile = 1.6 kilometers
1 ounce = 28 grams
1 pound = 454 grams
1 pint = 0.6 liters
1 gallon = 4.6 liters

Metric to Imperial
1 centimeter = 0.4 inches
1 meter = 3 feet, 3 inches
1 kilometer = 0.6 miles
1 gram = 0.04 ounces
1 kilogram = 2.2 pounds
1 liter = 1.8 pints

DIRECTORY

Immigration

Canadian High Commission
1 Grosvenor Square, London, W1X 4AA.
Tel (020) 7258 6600.

Citizenship and Immigration Canada
Jean Edmonds Towers, 365 Laurier Ave. W, Ottawa, ON K1A 1L1.
Tel 1 (888) 242 2100.
w cic.gc.ca

Consulate General
1251 Avenue of the Americas, New York, NY, 10020-1175.
Tel (212) 596 1628.
w canadainternational. gc.ca

Tourist Information

Canadian Tourism Commission
Suite 1400, Four Bentall Centre, 1055 Dunsmuir St., Vancouver, BC V7X 1L2.
Tel (604) 638 8300.
w travelcanada.ca

Visit Canada
Tel 0870 380 0070.
w travelcanada.travel

Provincial Offices

British Columbia
Tourism British Columbia, 865 Hornby St., 8th floor, Vancouver, BC V6Z 2G3.
Tel 1 (800) 435 5622.
w hellobc.com

Newfoundland and Labrador
Department of Tourism, P.O. Box 8700, St. John's, NF A1B 4J6.
Tel 1 (800) 563 6353.
w newfoundland labrador.com

Northwest Territories
NWT Arctic Tourism, P.O. Box 610, Yellowknife, NWT X1A 2N5.
Tel 1 (800) 661 0788.
w spectacularnwt.com

Nova Scotia Tourism
P.O. Box 456, 1800 Argyle St., Suite 605, Halifax, NS B3J 2R5.
Tel 1 (800) 565 0000.
w novascotia.com

Nunavut Tourism
PO Box 1450, Iqaluit, NT X0A 0H0.
Tel 1 (866) 491 7910.
w nunavuttourism. com

Ontario
Ministry of Tourism, 900 Bay St., 9th floor, Hearst Block, Toronto, ON M7A 2E1. **Tel** 1 (800) 668 2746.
w ontariotravel.net

Travel Alberta
400, 1601-9 Ave. SE., Calgary AB T2G 0H4.
Tel 1 (800) 252 3782.
w travelalberta.com

Travel Manitoba
21, Forks Market Rd, Winnipeg, MB.
Tel 1 (800) 665 0040.
w travelmanitoba.com

Tourism New Brunswick
19 Aberdeen Campbellton, NB E3N 2J6. **Tel** 1 (800) 561 0123. **w** tourismnew brunswick.ca

Tourism Prince Edward Island
P.O. Box 2000, Charlottetown, PEI C1A 7N8. **Tel** 1 (800) 463 4734.
w tourismpei.com

Tourism Quebec
P.O. Box 979, Montreal, PQ H3C 2W3.
Tel 1 (877) 266 5687.
w bonjourquebec.com

Tourism Saskatchewan

189–1621 Albert St., Regina, SK S4P 3S5.
Tel 1 (877) 237 2273.
w sasktourism.com

Tourism Yukon
P.O. Box 2703, Whitehorse, Yukon, Y1A 2C6.
Tel 1 (800) 661 0494.
w travelyukon.com

Senior Travelers

Road Scholar
11, Ave. de Lafayette, Boston, MA 02111.
Tel 1 (800) 454 5768
w roadscholar.org

Student Travelers

STA Travel
Tel (020) 7361 6262 UK.
Tel 1 (888) 427 5639
w travelcuts.com.

Disabled Travelers

Spinal Cord Injury Canada
130 Albert St., Suite 512, Ottawa, ON, K1P 5G4
Tel (613) 723 1913.
w sci-can.ca

Personal Security and Health

With its comparatively low crime rate, Canada is a safe country to visit. In contrast to many US cities, there is little street crime in the city centers, perhaps because so many Canadians live downtown that the cities are never empty at night. However, it is wise to be careful and to find out which parts of town are more dangerous than others. Avoid city parks after dark, and make sure cars are left locked. In the country's more remote areas visitors must observe sensible safety measures. In the remote country, wildlife and climatic dangers can be avoided by heeding local advice. If a serious problem does arise, contact one of the national emergency numbers in the telephone directory.

Personal Safety

There are few off-limit areas in Canadian cities. Even the seedier districts tend to have a visible police presence, making them safer than the average suburban area at night. Always ask your hotelier, the local tourist information center, or the police, which areas to avoid. Although theft is rare in hotel rooms, it is a good idea to store any valuables in the hotel safe, as hotels will not guarantee the security of property left in rooms. Make sure you leave your hotel room key at the front desk when you go out.

Pickpockets can be a hazard at large public gatherings and popular tourist attractions, so it is a good idea to wear cameras and bags over one shoulder with the strap across your body. Try not to be seen with large amounts of cash, and if necessary use a coin purse and a wallet for larger bills. Keep your passport apart from your cash and traveler's cheques. Never hang your purse over the back of your chair in restaurants; put it on the floor beside your feet with one foot over the strap, or pinned down by a chair leg. Male travelers should not carry their wallets in their back pocket, as this makes a very easy target. Safe options for both sexes are zippered purse belts worn under clothing.

Law Enforcement

Canada is policed by a combination of forces. The Royal Canadian Mounted Police (RCMP) operate throughout most of the country, while Ontario, Quebec, and Newfoundland and Labrador are looked after by provincial forces. There are also city police in large urban areas, and some First Nations reserves have their own police forces. For the most part, the officers are noted for their helpful attitude, but it is unwise to comment on (or joke about) safety, bombs, guns, and terrorism in places such as airports, where it is possible to be arrested for an off-the-cuff remark. Drinking and driving is also taken seriously here, and remember that open alcohol containers in a car are illegal. Narcotics users face criminal charges often followed by moves for deportation.

Lost Property

As soon as something is lost, report it to the police. They will issue a report with a number that you will need in order to make a claim on your insurance policy. If a credit card is missing, call the company's toll-free number and report it immediately. Lost or stolen traveler's checks must also be reported to the issuer. If you have kept a record of the checks' numbers, replacing them should be a painless experience, and new ones may be issued within 24 hours.

If you lose your passport, contact the nearest embassy or consulate. They will be able to issue a temporary replacement as visitors do not generally need a new passport if they will be returning directly to their home country. However, if you are traveling on to another destination, you will need a full passport. It is also useful to hold photocopies of your driver's license and birth certificate, as well as notarized passport photographs if you are contemplating an extended visit or need additional ID.

Travel Insurance

Travel insurance is essential in Canada and should be arranged to cover health, trip-cancellation, and interruption, as well as theft and loss of valuable possessions.

Canadian health services are excellent, but if you do not wish to pay you will need insurance. If you already have private health insurance you should check to see if the coverage includes all emergency hospital and medical expenses such as physician's care, prescription drugs, and private duty-nursing. In case of a serious illness, separate coverage is also required to send a relative to your bedside or return a rented vehicle. Emergency dental treatment, and

Toronto policemen on bicycles

out-of-pocket expenses or loss of vacation costs also need their own policies. Your insurance company or travel agent should recommend the right policy, but beware of exclusions for pre-existing medical conditions.

Medical Treatment

A comprehensive range of treatment centers are available in Canada. For minor problems pharmacies are often a good source of advice, and walk-in clinics in the cities will treat visitors relatively quickly. In smaller communities, or in more difficult cases, go straight to the emergency room of the closest hospital, but be prepared for a long wait. In a serious medical emergency dial 911 in most areas, or 0 for the operator, to summon an ambulance.

Warning sign for motorists

Anyone taking a prescription drug should ask their doctor for extra supplies when they travel, as well as a copy of the prescription in case more medication is needed on the trip. It is a good idea to take a simple first-aid kit, especially for longer trips in the more remote or Arctic areas of the country. Generally this should include aspirin (or paracetamol), antihistamine for bites or allergies, motion sickness pills, antiseptic and bandages or band aids, calamine lotion, and bug repellent. Antibiotic creams are useful for intrepid wilderness hikers.

All the provincial capitals have dental clinics that will provide emergency treatment.

Natural Hazards

There are times when Canada's mosquitoes and black flies can be so troublesome that moose and deer leave the woods for relief. Insects are a major irritant for tourists in rural areas. They are at their worst during annual breeding periods from late spring to midsummer, and until the temperatures drop in Northern Canada. There are precautions one can take to alleviate the misery, the most effective one being the regular application of insect repellant. Stick to light-colored clothes as the bugs are drawn to dark ones, and cover as much skin as possible with long sleeves, and pants tucked into boots and socks. It might even be worth investing in a gauze mask for your head and neck if you are planning to venture into deserted areas at peak breeding times. Canada is notorious for cold winter weather, but tourists are not likely to suffer many serious problems. The media gives daily extensive coverage to the weather, and on days when frostbite is possible they offer detailed reports. Dressing in layers and wearing a hat is necessary. Sunscreen is needed in summer, even on overcast days.

Bears

Canada's national parks service, particularly in the Rockies, supplies advice on bear safety (see p304), but unless you are camping or hiking in the woods it is unlikely that you will come across them. Encounters can be avoided by following a few basic rules: never leave food or garbage near your tent, car, or

RV, do not wear scent, and make a noise (many hikers blow whistles) as you walk, as bears are more likely to attack if surprised. If you do come across a bear, do not scream or run since bears are very fast, and do not climb trees – they are even better at that. Instead, keep still, speak to them in a low voice, and put your luggage on the ground to try and distract them.

DIRECTORY

Emergency Services

Police, Fire, Ambulance
In most of Canada and in large cities call 911, elsewhere dial 0.

Consulates and Embassies

United States
Vancouver, 1075 West Pender St.
Tel (604) 685 4311.
Ottawa, 490 Sussex Drive.
Tel (613) 238 5335.
Montreal, 1155 rue St-Alexandre.
Tel (514) 398 9695.
Toronto, 360 University Ave.
Tel (416) 595 1700.
Ⓦ **canada.usembassy.gov**

UK
Vancouver, Suite 800, 1111 Melville Street.
Tel (604) 683 4421.
Ottawa, 80 Elgin Street.
Tel (613) 237 1530.
Montreal, Suite 1940, 2000 McGill College Ave.
Tel (514) 866 5863.
Toronto, Suite 2800, 777 Bay St.
Tel 416 593 1290.
Ⓦ **ukincanada.fco.gov.uk**

A polar bear approaching a tourist Tundra Buggy, northern Manitoba

Banking and Currency

Canadian currency is based on the decimal system, and has 100 cents to the dollar. Two of the most useful coins are the 25-cent, otherwise known as the quarter, and $1 pieces which operate pay telephones, newspaper boxes, and vending machines. They are also handy for public transportation in the larger cities, where as a matter of policy bus drivers often do not carry any change. It is best to arrive with some Canadian currency, around Can$50–100 including small change for tipping and taxis. Exchange bureaux are readily available in airports and train stations.

Sandstone façade of the Toronto Stock Exchange

Banks

Canada's main national banks are the Royal Bank of Canada, Bank of Montréal, TD Canada Trust, Canadian Imperial Bank of Commerce (CIBC), Scotiabank, and National Bank of Canada. These banks generally accept foreign ATM (automatic teller machine) cards, although it is wise to check with your bank first. ATMs can be found at bank branches, as well as grocery stores, shopping centers, gas stations, train and bus stations, and airports.

Banks are usually open Monday to Friday, from 9am to 5pm; some stay open later on Fridays, and a few open on Saturday mornings. All banks are closed on Sundays and on statutory holidays.

Scotiabank

Scotiabank logo

Traveler's Checks

Traveler's checks are a safe way to carry money for your vacation. It is a good idea to find out which Canadian banks charge commission for changing traveler's checks, as many have arrangements with certain issuers of checks and make no charge. The Royal Bank of Canada and TD Canada Trust, for example, charge no commission on American Express checks in Canadian dollars. A passport or other form of ID is needed to cash traveler's checks at a bank or at Bureaux de Changes offices such as American Express or Travelex.

ATMS

Automated Teller Machines (ATMs) can be found in most bank lobbies across Canada. Before you travel ask your bank which ATM systems will accept your bank card, and how much each transaction will cost, as a charge may apply. Popular systems include Cirrus and Plus, which both accept Visa and MasterCard.

Credit Cards

Credit cards are used extensively in Canada, and American Express, Diner's Club, MasterCard/Access, and VISA are widely accepted. Credit cards are often asked for as a form of ID, and for placing large deposits – most car rental companies in Canada insist on a credit card or require a substantial cash deposit. Some hotels also prefer prepayment by credit card. Credit cards can also be used to secure cash advances, but you will be charged interest from the date of withdrawal.

Wiring Money

If you run out of money or have an emergency it is possible to have cash wired from home in minutes using an electronic money service. Both American Express and Travelex provide this service, as does Western Union which has 22,000 outlets all over North America.

WESTERN UNION | MONEY TRANSFER
The world's No. 1 money transfer service

Western Union's familiar logo

Coins and Bank Notes

Canadian coins are issued in denominations of five cents (the nickel), ten cents (the dime), 25 cents (the quarter), $1 (dubbed the "loonie" because it has an illustration of the bird, the Canadian loon on one side), and the $2 coin or "toonie," which replaced the old bank note in 1996. The copper penny was removed from circulation in 2013.

Bank notes are printed in denominations of $5, $10, $20, $50, $100, $500, and $1,000. However, $100 dollar bills are sometimes viewed with suspicion as they are not used very often in small stores, or even in cafés and gas stations.

DIRECTORY

Currency Exchange And Wiring Money

American Express
Check replacement, Canada
Tel 1 800 221 7282.

Travelex
Tel 1 888 489 9901.

Visa
Tel 1 800 732 1322.

Western Union
Wiring money, Canada
Tel 1 800 235 0000.

Media and Communications

Canada has some of the most sophisticated communication systems in the world. Despite the popularity of mobile phones, there are still public payphones everywhere – in cafés, bars, public buildings, gas stations, and post offices. Most operate with coins, and while local calls are a bargain, international calls can be expensive. WiFi is also widely available in hotels and cafés.

Canada Post, the country's mail service is certainly reliable, but it is renowned for being slow. It can be quick however, if you are willing to pay an extra fee for priority handling and delivery.

Public Telephones

Public telephones operate on 25 cent coins, although there is an increasing number of phones that accept both credit and phone cards. Rates are generally cheaper between 6pm and 8am, and on weekends. All local calls cost 25, 35, or 50 cents (private subscribers have free local calls). For any call outside the local area, including international calls, the operator will tell you how much to pay for the initial period and will then ask for more money as your call progresses. It is usually easier to make long distance calls using a phone card than to have the stacks of change required.

Public roadside telephones are found countrywide

Postal Services

All mail from Canada to outside North America is by air and can take between three and seven days to arrive. If you are sending mail locally, it can also take days – not including the postal code will make the service even slower. To send mail, look for signs that say "Canada Post" since some post offices are located in malls.

Mobile Phones and e-mail

Check roaming charges with your network before you travel. It may be worth getting a pay as you go plan for your trip.

Visitors can use e-mail in the larger hotels or at one of many city-based Internet cafés.

Fax and Telegram Services

It is possible to send a fax from the commercial outlets found in most towns. Telegrams are dealt with by Canadian National Telecommunications (CNT) or Canadian Pacific (CP). There are two main services, Telepost, which provides first-class delivery, and Intelpost, which sends documents abroad via satellite.

Media

The only papers that see themselves as national publications are *The National Post* and *The Globe and Mail*, both based in Toronto. There is also a national news weekly called *Maclean's*. Most cities have their own daily newspapers and some, such as Toronto, have several. Many cities and regions have free weeklies that provide excellent coverage of local events.

Canada has a national 24-hour public broadcasting corporation (CBC), 80 percent of whose programs are produced locally. CBC also provides an excellent radio service, and can be a good source of information on local happenings and weather for visitors. They also have a national service in French.

Useful Information

Canadian Post Customer Services line.
Tel 1 800 267 1177.

DIRECTORY

Provincial Codes

Alberta - 403, 780 & 587.
British Columbia - 604, 250, 778 & 236.
Manitoba - 204 & 431.
New Brunswick - 506.
Northwest Territories - 867 (Yukon & Nunavut).
Nova Scotia & PEI - 902 & 782.
Newfoundland & Labrador - 709.
Ontario - 416, 647 & 437 (Toronto).
705 - (central and northeast).
226 & 519 - (southwest peninsula).
343 & 613 - (Ottawa region).
807 - (northwest).
Quebec - 514 & 438 (Montreal).
819 & 873 - (north).
418 & 581 - (east).
Saskatchewan - 306 & 639.

Reaching the Right Number

- For calls to another area code: dial 1 followed by the area code and the 7-digit local number. (In Toronto, dial the area code for all local calls.)
- For international calls: dial 011 then the code of the country (Australia 61, UK 44) followed by the area/city code (minus the first 0) and the number. To call the US from Canada dial **1**, the area code, then the number.
- For international operator assistance dial **0**.
- For information on numbers within your local area dial **411**.
- For information on long distance numbers call **1** followed by the area code then **555 1212**.
- An **800**, **866**, **877**, or **888** prefix means the call is toll free.

TRAVEL INFORMATION

The majority of visitors to Canada arrive by air, usually at one of the country's three largest international airports – Vancouver, Toronto, or Montreal. It is also possible to fly direct to cities such as Halifax, Winnipeg, Edmonton, Calgary, and St. John's, Newfoundland.

The size of the country makes flying between locations popular with visitors who wish to see more than one part of Canada. For example, on a short stay, it could prove difficult to see Toronto and Montreal in the east, as well as the Rocky Mountains in the west without spending some time in the air. There are other transportation choices that allow visitors to see much of Canada. The national rail network, VIA Rail, links most major cities, while long-distance bus routes provide a delightful, and often less expensive, way to see the country. There are short cruises and ferry rides that take in some spectacular scenery. Exploring Canada by car is also a popular choice, enabling visitors to get to locations that can be difficult to reach any other way.

Air Canada is the country's major air carrier

Arriving by Air

Canada is a destination for several international airlines, and the country's major carrier **Air Canada** is linked with national airlines around the world. All Europe's principal airlines fly into Toronto or Montreal, while Vancouver is a gateway for carriers such as Cathay Pacific, Qantas, and national airlines from the Far East.

Visitors who intend to see parts of the US as well as Canada can find plenty of connecting flights to such principal US destinations as New York, Los Angeles, Dallas, Chicago, and Atlanta.

International Flights

Flights between Canada and Europe take from five to ten hours; from Asia or Australia, across the Pacific, you may be in transit for as long as 25 hours. Older travelers or those with children may wish to consider a stopover for the sake of comfort (Hawaii is a popular choice, and some stop over in Hong Kong, Shanghai, or even Tokyo). It is also a good idea to plan flights so that they account for international time differences.

Canada has 13 international airports, the busiest being at Toronto, Montreal, and Vancouver. It is also possible to fly direct into airports in cities such as Edmonton, Halifax, Ottawa, Winnipeg, and St. John's, Newfoundland. All the major cities are connected with airports in the US. Several leading airlines offer special deals that allow visitors to fly to one part of North America and leave from another.

Air Fares

Flights to Canada from Europe, Australia, and the US can be expensive, especially during peak holiday periods such as Christmas, New Year, and between July and mid-September. Book as far ahead as possible and you will have a better chance of finding a

Airport	Information
St. John's	(709) 758 8500
Halifax	(902) 873 4422
Montreal (Trudeau)	(514) 394 7377
Montreal (Mirabel)	(514) 394 7377
Ottawa	(613) 248 2100
Toronto	(416) 247 7678
Winnipeg	(204) 987 9402
Calgary	(403) 735 1200
Edmonton	(780) 890 8382
Vancouver	(604) 207 7077

competitive fare. Keep in mind though that the cheapest tickets generally impose such restrictions as a minimum (usually seven days) and maximum (of 3–6 months) length of stay. It can also be difficult to alter dates of travel, and it is worth considering insuring yourself against last-minute, unforeseen delays or cancellations.

Charter flights with airlines such as Air Transat sometimes offer a cheaper alternative, with savings of 20 percent on some tickets. Round-the-world fares are increasingly popular, as are package vacations which provide a variety of choices. The kinds of deals available range from fly/drive vacations with a much reduced car rental as part

of the price of the ticket, to a guided tour, including all accommodations, transportation, and meals.

On Arrival

Just before landing in Canada you will be given customs and immigration documents to fill in. On arrival you will be asked to present them, along with your passport, to the appropriate customs and immigration officials.

The larger airports offer a better range of services, but most airports have shops, medical and postal services, foreign exchange bureaus, newsstands, and bookstores. The major car rental companies have outlets at the airport, and buses, taxis, limousines, and shuttle buses into town are available. Most terminals offer facilities for disabled travelers.

Visitors hoping to catch a connecting flight to another part of the country will have to claim and clear their baggage through customs

Roads to and from airports are well sign posted

DIRECTORY

Airlines in the UK, US, and Canada

Air Canada
Tel UK: (0990) 247 226.
CAN and US: 1 888 247 2262.
w aircanada.ca

Air Transat
Tel CAN and US: (514) 636 3630,
1 877 872 6728.
w www.airtransat.com

American Airlines
Tel UK: (0844) 499 7300. CAN and US: (1 800) 433 7300.
w aa.com

British Airways
Tel UK: (0844) 493 0787. CAN and US: (1 800) 247 9297.
w britishairways.com

before checking in with the connecting airline. Arrangements for transferring to domestic flights are usually made when you book your trip. Ask airline staff if you need more information; in large airports such as Toronto's Pearson International there are three separate terminals.

Distance from City	Average Taxi Fare to City	Bus Transfer to City
8 km (5 miles)	CAN $25	No Service
42 km (26 miles)	CAN $65	45 mins
22 km (14 miles)	CAN $40	45 mins
55 km (34 miles)	CAN $70	40–55 mins
18 km (11 miles)	CAN $30	25 mins
24 km (15 miles)	CAN $60	45–55 mins
10 km (6 miles)	CAN $25	45 mins
16 km (10 miles)	CAN $35	30 mins
31 km (19 miles)	CAN $55	55 mins
15 km (9 miles)	CAN $35	25 mins

Domestic Air Travel

Because of the distances involved, flying around the country has become an accepted part of Canadian life. There is a complex network of domestic flights, with numerous local airlines, some of which are linked to Air Canada. The smaller operators fly within provinces, and to remote locations where they are often the only means of transportation. In all there are some 125 domestic destinations. It is possible to book domestic flights with a travel agent before departure or, once in Canada, through local agents or on the internet. Domestic flights along the busier routes are becoming cheaper and discounts are often advertised in the local press. A range of pass deals are available exclusively for visitors from abroad. Light aircraft can also be chartered for fascinating but costly trips over far-flung landmarks such as Baffin Island.

Dash-7 aircraft during a trip in Canada's far north

Air Routes and Airlines

The impressive array of domestic flights available here means that most of the nation's smaller urban areas are within reach of regular services. However, you will generally have to fly to the major city in the area, principally Vancouver, Toronto, or Montreal, and then take a connecting flight.

Some of the smaller airlines are connected with Canada's major carrier, **Air Canada**, and it is often possible to book your connection through the national airline. The majority of the country's long-haul domestic routes run east-to-west, connecting the cities: from Halilfax on the east coast, through to Montreal, Toronto, Ottawa, Winnipeg, Calgary, and Edmonton to Vancouver in the west. Longer north to south flights to places such as the Yukon and Northwest Territories usually originate from Edmonton and Winnipeg. In the remote north, light aircraft are the best way to reach a destination such as Baffin Island, (which can be reached by boat only in good weather) with the exception of Churchill, Manitoba, which is connected by train.

Apex Fares and Other Discounts

There are several kinds of bargain tickets available within Canada, and low-cost airlines such as **WestJet** have increased competition and forced prices down. To take advantage of the reductions available through Apex (advanced purchase excursion) fares, you must book between 7 and 21 days in advance: the earlier the booking, the larger the discount. Each fare will have its own set of rules, which include restrictions on length of stay and time of travel (such as between certain hours or on certain days). Be aware that refunds are seldom given and it might be difficult to change your dates.

Seat sales are another bargain option whereby an airline will advertise exceptionally cheap tickets to boost travel on popular routes during quiet times of the year. There is, however, very little flexibility on these deals, and you have to fly within a specific period of time.

Air Canada offers pass deals for visitors who want to travel all over the country, as well as to the US. Most of the offers involve paying for a number of coupons, each of which represents a single flight within either the continent or a specific region. The passes also usually specify a period of time (7 to 60 days) for which they are valid.

Fly-Drive Deals

A good way to make the most of a visit to Canada is to book a fly-drive vacation. The deal invariably involves a substantial cut in the cost of the car rental. Arrangements can also be made to pick up and drop off your vehicle in different places. It would be possible, for example, to pick up a car in Toronto, tour Ontario, dropping the car off in Ottawa before flying on to Vancouver on the west coast. Known as one-way car rental, these deals may involve large drop-off fees: from Toronto to Ottawa costs around Can$200. Travel agents offer a wide range of such packages.

Baggage Restrictions

Passengers traveling economy on domestic flights should be aware that there are restrictions on the amount and weight of baggage that can be taken on board. The type of aircraft determines what can be carried, and light aircraft usually accept only hand-baggage.

In general, passengers are entitled to have two suitcases, each with an average weight of 32 kg (70 lb) per item. Hand-baggage must fit safely under aircraft seats or in overhead lockers so check the permitted dimensions with the airline. Garment bags may be carried on board some aircraft but must be soft-sided and comply with size restrictions – length 112 cm (45 in), depth 11 cm (4.5 in) – so remember to check with your airline or travel agent when purchasing your ticket.

WestJet logo

Checking In

Security is a necessity nowadays and can make the boarding procedure take longer. It is best to check with the airline, but generally for domestic flights you should arrive at the airport 90 minutes before your departure; for flights to the US and other international flights, allow at least 2 hours. If you check in online, you can usually arrive at the airport only an hour before departure, but keep in mind that long waits at security are unpredicatble and could slow you down. Visitors from other countries traveling within Canada should carry a passport to verify that he or she is the traveler named on the ticket. It is also worth noting that the daily peak periods at the larger Canadian airports are usually from 7am to 9am and from 3pm to 8pm. Passenger volume also increases significantly during the winter holiday season, March break, and the summer, so it is wise to allow extra time for parking, check-in, and security screening during these periods.

DIRECTORY

Domestic Airlines

Air Canada
Tel (514) 393 3333, 1 888 247 2262. ☑ aircanada.ca

Air North (Yukon, NWT, Alberta, and BC)
Tel (867) 668 2228, 1 800 661 0407 ☑ flyairnorth.com

Bearskin Airlines (Ontario and Manitoba)
Tel (807) 475 0006, 1 800 465 2327. ☑ bearskinairlines.com

Calm Air
(Manitoba, inc. Churchill and Nunavut)
Tel 1 800 839 2256. ☑ calmair.com

First Air
(Nunavut and NWT)
Tel 1 800 267 1247. ☑ firstair.ca

Porter Airlines (Ontario, Quebec, Atlantic Provinces, and the US)
Tel 1 888 619 8622. ☑ flyporter.com

WestJet
Tel (403) 444 2586, 1 800 538 5696. ☑ westjet.com

Principal Domestic Air Routes

Canada's major airline is Air Canada. It provides links to a number of regional carriers to form a comprehensive domestic air network, while WestJet specializes in western destinations.

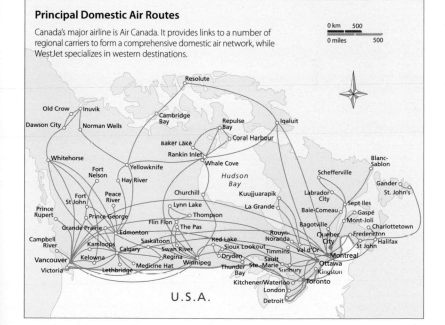

GETTING AROUND CANADA'S CITIES

Although the car is a popular way to travel in Canada, the country is noted for the fast, frequent, and efficient public transit systems of its cities. In general, the best way for visitors to explore Canada's urban centers is primarily on foot, using public transportation as a back up. The streets are clean and safe, and strolling through different neighborhoods is a pleasant way to get to know them. Most municipal transit systems are reasonably priced, with discounted multi-ticket deals and day passes. Driving around downtown areas can be daunting, particularly during the rush hour, and parking tends to be both difficult and expensive.

Most transit systems offer free maps, available at stations or tourist information centers. The following pages detail how to get around Canada's three largest cities, Vancouver, Toronto, and Montreal (see endpaper for detailed transit maps), as well as other provincial capitals and the most often visited towns and communities.

Montreal

Montreal's bus and subway network is integrated so that the stations connect with bus routes and tickets can be used on either. Be sure to get a transfer ticket, which should take you anywhere in the city for one fare. Known as the Métro, Montreal's subway is clean, safe, and air-conditioned in summer and heated in the winter. It is by far the fastest and cheapest way to get around town (see endpaper). Free maps are available at any of the ticket booths. Visitors can buy a Tourist Pass for one or three days at major hotels and at the Visitor Information Office downtown.

Driving is not recommended here, as the roads are busy and parking is severely restricted, especially in the old town. It is best to use the city's park-and-ride system. Cabs can be hailed in the street. They have a white or orange sign on the roof; the sign is lit up when the cab is available.

Many streets in Montreal now have bike lanes. The Great Montreal Bike Path-Guide is available free at the tourist office. Bikes can be taken on the Métro anytime except during rush hour, from about 7am to 10am and 5pm to 7pm on weekdays. There are some lovely bike paths, such as the waterfront trail on the historic Canal de Lachine, and those that lead through Cité du Havre and across Pont de la Concorde to the islands. There are a number of bicycle shops offering daily or weekly rental; they generally require a deposit of Can$250 or more in addition to the daily rate.

Toronto

The Toronto Transit Commission (TTC) operates a huge system of connecting subway, bus, and streetcar lines that serves the entire city. It is one of the safest and cleanest systems of its kind anywhere in the world. There are two major subway lines, with 60 stations along the way (see endpaper). The "Pick up a Ride Guide" shows every major place of interest and how to reach it by public transit, and is available at most subway ticket offices.

To ride buses and streetcars, you must have exact change, a ticket, or a token. These are available at subway ticket booths along with some convenience stores.

Toronto does not have a zone system, meaning a single, flat-fare ticket can be used for one trip, using any public transportation in the city. If you plan to connect from the subway to a streecar or bus, or if taking several connecting buses, be sure to collect a transfer pass once you have paid the fare.

A single fare for an adult is Can$3.00, while the cost for a child is just 75 cents. Savings can be made when buying multiple tokens, and a day pass costs Can$10.75, which lasts until 5:30 am the following morning. Visit TTC's website for more information on fares, maps, and schedules.

It is easy to catch a cab in Toronto; they can be hailed in the street, called in advance, or found outside hotels. Bikes are a popular mode of transport, particularly during warmer months. Some roads have cycle lanes but most don't. As a result cyclists should take care, particularly on roads busy with pedestrians and streetcars. BIXI bikes, a public rental bike system, is popular with cycling commuters. Alternatively, the

Picturesque riverside cycling route in Quebec City

Toronto taxicabs gather at a taxi stand

Martin Goodman Trail is a well-marked scenic bicycle route along the scenic waterfront.

Vancouver

Vancouver's well-organized network of light rail (called SkyTrain), bus, and ferry services is run by BC Transit. An inexpensive Transit Guide is available from newsstands and information centers. It includes a map of the city showing all routes. Driving is not the best way to see the city as congestion is heavy, and you are unlikely to find a spot to park. There is a park-and-ride system, where commuters can leave their cars at certain points around the city center.

The SkyTrain is a light rail system of driverless trains that connects downtown Vancouver with the suburbs of Burnaby, New Westminster, and Surrey. It travels partially beneath ground and partially overground on a raised track. The main terminal is at Waterfront Station at the bottom of Seymour Street. An alternative to the SkyTrain is to use the city's downtown bus routes. These are worth riding as they offer delightful tours past the city's top attractions, although it is advisable to avoid rush hour traffic. Bus services end around midnight, but there is a scaled down "Night Owl" service.

One of the best ways to get around Vancouver is by water. The SeaBus is a 400-seat Catamaran that shuttles between Lonsdale Quay in North Vancouver and the downtown terminal at Waterfront Station. The trip takes around 15 minutes and includes wonderful views of the mountains and Vancouver skyline. Aquabus Ferries connect stations on False Creek, Granville Island, Stamp's Landing, and the Hornby Street Dock.

If you want to take a cab it is best to call one of the main companies such as Black Top or Yellow Cab, as hailing a taxi in the streets is rarely successful. However, Vancouver is a great city for cyclists, with plenty of bike paths, including the 10 km (6 mile) road around Stanley Park. There is a park-and-ride service for bikes here, similar to the one elsewhere for cars.

Fares are the same for bus, SkyTrain, and SeaBus in the Vancouver area, but the price varies according to time of day and the distance you travel. Adult fares are cheaper after 6:30pm, and all day Saturday, Sunday, and holidays. There are three zones in the city, and the price of the fare depends on how many zones you cross. The off-peak adult fare in zone one is Can$2.25. There are a wide variety of discounts available: a FareSaver book of 10 tickets or a day pass are good value. Children under 4 ride free, and those between the ages of 5 and 13 pay less (as do students with a valid GoCard), and seniors over 65 also get concessions. A transfer ticket is free and lasts for 90 minutes of travel.

SkyTrain traveling over the city bridge in Vancouver on a summer evening

The scenic approach to Château Frontenac in Quebec City, best appreciated on foot

Ottawa

Fortunately for visitors, many of the capital city's major tourist attractions are within walking distance of Parliament Hill. Ottawa's sidewalks are both wide and clean, and you can do most of your sightseeing on foot, using public transportation to cover the longer distances. The region of Ottawa-Carlton operates **OC Transpo**, a 130-route bus network. OC Transpo uses a smart card system, called Presto. Passengers top up their card with credit, and then touch their card to the readers upon boarding a bus or O-train. When boarding a connecting bus, tapping the card to the reader will not charge the card again. Fares using Presto are Can$2.60 on regular routes and Can$3.90 on express routes. In contrast, standard cash fares are Can$3.30 and Can$4.65. All routes meet downtown at the Rideau Centre, and the stops are color-coded according to the route.

If you are using a car there are several reasonably priced municipal car lots – look for a green 'P' sign. Taxis can be booked by phone or hailed at stands outside major hotels. Bicycles are a good way to explore a city that has some 150 km (93 miles) of scenic paths. The Rideau Canal, that crosses the city from north to south, is bordered by delightful walking and bike paths.

Calgary

Calgary transit operates buses and a light-rail transit system known as the C-Train. For a flat fare of Can$2.25 you can transfer to either using the same ticket, although day passes for around Can$6.75 are good value for visitors hoping to see several sights in one day. The C-Train travels north to the University and airport, and south to Macleod Trail. It is free in the downtown section between 10th Street and City Hall (buses are not). Maps are available from the **Calgary Transit** offices, where you can also buy tickets. C-Train tickets can be bought from machines located on the platforms.

If you wish to travel mostly within the city center, walking and public transportation are

Logo for the C-Train in Calgary

your best options. However, the city's blocks are long, (Calgary is Canada's second largest city by area) and any trip to the outskirts and beyond requires a car. There are several rental companies, including all the major outlets. Weekend car rental rates are cheaper than weekday car rental. Cabs are expensive here and cannot be hailed on the street, but they can be picked up at hotels or ordered by telephone.

Winnipeg

Many of Winnipeg's attractions are within a 20-minute walk of one another in the downtown area, centered on the crossroads of Portage and Main Streets. **Winnipeg City Transit** operates an efficient bus system, which is also ideal for reaching farther-placed sights. There is a flat fare of Can$2.50, or you can purchase a book of 10 tickets for Can$21.50 from convenience and drug stores as well as the Transit Service Centre based in the underground concourse at Portage and Main. The center is open weekdays between 8:15 am and 4:45 pm, and offers detailed information and a free route map of the city.

There are also several pleasant bicycle paths that run through the city as well as to outlying districts.

Quebec City

The charming narrow streets of the old city are best seen on foot, especially since most of the historic sights are located within a small area of the walled city. If you need to travel farther to see one of the more distant sights such as the Musée du Québec, the bus system is frequent and reliable. Fares are cheaper if you buy a ticket before boarding and are on sale at several outlets in grocery stores costing Can$2.50 per person. There are also one- day passes for Can$5.95. The bus station is in the Lower Town on Boulevard Charest Est. Most of the main routes stop centrally on the Place d'Youville in the Old Town.

Taxi stands are located in front of the major hotels or outside city hall. Horse-drawn carriages or *calèches* may be hired for a gentle trot around the Old Town, but expect to pay Can$50 for 40 minutes.

Halifax

The compact city of Halifax is best explored on foot or bicycle, which can be hired for a half or full day. Driving around is difficult: parking is hard to come by. To reach outlying districts there is the **Halifax Metro Transit** bus system. Fares are cheap, with a flat fare of Can$2 charged downtown. It is also possible to purchase budget books of 20 tickets for Can$32. In the city from Monday to Saturday during the summer season, a free bus service called "Fred" circles the downtown area about every 20 minutes.

Charlottetown

Since the completion of the Confederation Bridge in 1997, Prince Edward Island has become easily accessible by bus and car. Travelers still use the ferry service, which runs from New Glasgow, Nova Scotia between May and November. There is a shuttle bus service from Halifax that travels to the island by ferry. The island's public transportation system is limited to a bus service in Charlottetown run by **Trius Tours**; this operates all year round. However, touring by car is most popular, and it is a good idea to reserve a car during the busiest months of July and August. Several companies offer organized bus, walking, and cycling tours.

Driving over Confederation Bridge to Prince Edward Island

St. John's, Newfoundland

In comparison to most of Canada's cities, parking is easy in St. John's. It is possible to buy a parking permit from one of many well-placed machines. They take quarters (25 cents) or dollar coins. Car rental here is less expensive than in many other Canadian cities and there is a good choice of companies.

The local bus service is run by Metrobus, and tickets cost Can$2.00 every trip. If you are planning on spending some time here it is worth investing in

a 10-ride card for Can$18.00. By riding on two routes, such as one downtown and one suburban bus, you get a bargain tour of the city.

DIRECTORY

City Transportation Information

Vancouver British Columbia Transit
Tel (604) 521 0400.

Toronto Transit Commission (TTC)
Tel 416 393 4636.
Ⓦ www.ttc.ca

Bixi
Tel 1 887 412 2494.

Montreal STCUM and AMT
Tel (514) 288 6287.

Ottawa OC Transpo
Tel (613) 741 4390.

Calgary Transit
Tel (403) 262 1000.

Winnipeg City Transit
Tel (204) 986 5700.

Quebec City STCUQ
Tel (418) 627 2511.

Halifax Metro Transit
Tel (902) 490 6600.

Charlottetown Trius Tours
Tel (902) 566 5664.

St. John's Newfoundland Metrobus
Tel (709) 570 2020.

Bus traveling over Harbour Bridge in Saint John, New Brunswick

Train Travel in Canada

The Canadian rail network is run by the government-owned VIA Rail Canada. The service has been significantly reduced since the late 1980s when many cross-country services, along with other lines, were cut. VIA Rail still provides a service on the famed 1950s *Canadian*, a beautifully restored train that travels across the country between Toronto and Vancouver, passing through stunning Rockies' scenery between Jasper and Kamloops.

Increasingly, Canadians fly long distances or use their cars to cover most of the shorter hauls. For visitors, traveling by train remains a wonderful way to see large parts of Canada (especially in those trains that have glass-domed observation cars). Smaller commuter networks around the major cities are also useful for visitors who wish to explore an area in detail.

Specialty trips on the Rocky Mountaineer travel through the Rockies

The Canadian Rail Network

Via Rail Canada Inc. operates Canada's national passenger rail service. Despite the closing of several lines there are still 400 trains every week, which cover some 13,000 km (8,000 miles) on major routes between Vancouver and Toronto, traveling on to Montreal, Quebec, and Halifax. It is possible to cross the country by train – a trip that takes five days – by connecting up with these lines. The longest continuous route remains the Vancouver–Toronto trip on board the stylish and luxurious 1950s *Canadian*, with its observation and dining cars. Places with no road link, such as the town of Churchill in northern Manitoba, rely on the railroad. Trains from Winnipeg to Churchill run on Sundays and Tuesdays and take 48 hours.

VIA Rail operates both long-haul trains in eastern and western Canada, as well as inter-city trains in the populous Ontario Corridor, from Quebec City to Windsor, passing through Kingston, Montreal, Niagara Falls, Ottawa, and Toronto. This is a fast service that offers snacks and drinks on board most trains.

It is easy to travel onward to the United States, as VIA connects with the American rail network, Amtrak, at both Montreal and Vancouver. For tickets from Montreal to Albany or New York, and tickets from Vancouver to Seattle, Eugene, or Los Angeles, you'll need to book with Amtrak. VIA Rail and Amtrak jointly run the Toronto–New York line through Niagara Falls which takes over 12 hours including a two-hour stop at the border. You can get to Chicago from Toronto via Buffalo. The VIA station in Windsor is only a few kilometers from the Amtrak station in Detroit.

Smaller Networks

Visitors should also be aware that VIA is not the only passenger rail service in Canada. The larger cities all have useful local commuter lines. Vancouver has the West Coast Express, while Toronto's Go Transit covers the numerous towns in the commuter belt as far as Kitchener, Barrie, Hamilton, and Oshawa, and Montreal has AMT *(see p413)*.

Specialty Trips

There are several lines that offer visitors the chance to enjoy Canada's best scenery in comfortable, often luxurious trains. Among the best trips is the **Agawa Canyon Tour Train** in Ontario *(see p229)*, which runs through northern Ontario's spectacular scenery. The day-trip tour runs through the stunning Agawa Canyon from Sault Ste. Marie daily from late June to mid-October. The route is particularly popular in late September and early October when the blazing fall colors are at their most intense. On Saturdays in February and early March the Snow Train makes the trip to Agawa Canyon through mammoth snow drifts and ice-covered forests.

The **Polar Bear Express** starts in Cochrane in northern Ontario and heads another (300 km) 186 miles north through boreal forest to isolated Moosonee, from where visitors can take a motorized canoe to Moose Factory. An overnight stay is recommended.

The most spectacular train ride in Canada is probably in British Columbia, where, from mid-May until early October, **Rocky Mountaineer Railtours** runs numerous excursions through the Rockies. These trips operate entirely in daylight with nights spent in hotels rather than sleeping on the train. Most routes run from Vancouver, with one starting in Seattle. You can continue all the way to Halifax with the *Rocky Mountaineer*, switching to the VIA's *Canadian* on the east side of the Rockies.

For a truly unforgettable experience hop aboard the vintage rail cars of the **Royal Canadian Pacific**. The five-star luxury service starts in Calgary and follows a loop down to Lethbridge up into the Rockies via the Crownsnest Pass and back down through Banff National Park. Nights are spent aboard in your own wood-panelled state room. Another line heads from Calgary, over the mountain passes to Vancouver.

Travel Classes

On long-distance routes there are two main classes of travel available, Economy and Business, and a variety of Sleeper classes. Economy and Business Class offers comfortable, reclining seats in cars with wide aisles and large windows, as well as blankets and pillows for overnight trips. Passengers in Economy and Business Class also generally have access to one of the onboard snack bars or

VIA Rail Canada

Maple leaf on VIARail logo

restaurants. Sleeper classes offer a range of options from double- and single-berth bunks to double bedrooms, which convert to luxurious sitting rooms. VIA services in Western Canada such as the *Canadian*, include meals.

Tickets and Bookings

Reservations for rail travel can be made direct through VIA Rail or other train operators' websites. There are a variety of discounts available if you book in advance. There are two main VIA travel passes available. The Canrailpass System covers the entire country from coast to coast and as far north as Hudson Bay. The System pass is valid for seven one-way trips over a 21-day period. Canrailpass Corridor covers the busy area from Québec City to Windsor at the border with Detroit, giving access to Montreal, Toronto, and Ottawa and all stops between. The Corridor pass allows for seven one-way trips within a 10-day

period. Both passes are available as either Supersaver, which is cheaper but has fewer seats allotted, and Discounted, which allows for more flexibility as more seats are available. It is a good idea to reserve seats in advance during the summer as there are a limited number for pass holders. Children travel for half price, there are special youth rates for those between 12 and 25, and those over 60 receive a discount too.

Principal Rail Routes

VIA Rail is the main provider of passenger rail services throughout Canada. It is possible to reach all the major centers of the country, and regional operators link up with most town's outlying districts.

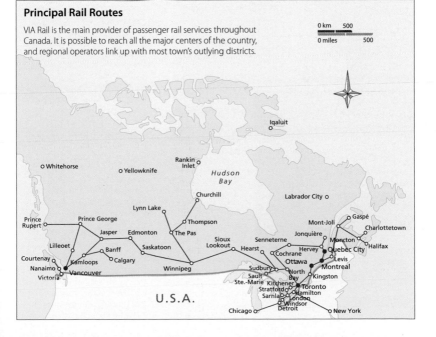

Traveling by Bus

Buses are the least expensive way to get around Canada. The majority of bus routes west of Toronto are run by Greyhound Canada, including the epic trip along the Trans-Canada Highway (Hwy 1) between Toronto and Vancouver. East of Toronto there are several smaller companies that cover most areas. Although a long bus trip can mean one or more nights spent sitting upright, the buses are generally clean and comfortable, and offer plenty of rest stops. The network is also reliable and efficient with buses usually arriving on time. In more remote regions, check timetables in advance as there may be no service or only one bus a week.

Long-Distance Buses

Long-distance buses provide a cheaper and often faster option than the railroad. The main operator, Greyhound Canada, carries more than two million passengers each year to most of the towns and cities across the country. Although Greyhound lines operate in the west and center of the country, many routes are linked to bus lines in the east, and in the United States. West of Vancouver, Greyhound links up with Pacific and Malaspina Coach Lines, east of Ottawa, with Orleans Express and Maritime Bus. DRL runs buses in Labrador and on the Newfoundland mainland. Saskatchewan has its own government-run bus company, Saskatchewan Transport Corporation, and northern Ontario communities are serviced by Ontario Northland buses since the trains stopped running in 2012. Greyhound's Express service offers a faster, highway-based service on buses that have more leg room, movies, music, and snacks.

Although smoking is prohibited, most long-haul buses stop every three to four hours so that travelers can leave the bus for a rest break. Rest breaks or driver changes take place at both bus and service stations, where you will find a variety of facilities ranging from restaurants and cafés to snack vending machines. All the buses are air-conditioned and have washrooms. Buses also offer passengers the advantage of picking up and arriving in convenient downtown areas.

Greyhound bus logo

Discounts and Passes

Greyhound tickets are cheaper when booked online over two weeks in advance. Children under 12 pay 75 percent of the full fare, and toddlers under two travel free. Seniors over 65 receive a 10 percent discount. However, the deals are better when traveling as a group or family. One person pays the full walk-up fare, and up to three people can join them at 50 percent off. High-season black-out periods may apply.

Bus Stations and Reservations

Buses from different carriers all operate from the same stations, making it easy to connect with other bus lines and municipal transit services. Reservations are not usually needed since buses are filled on a first-come, first-served basis. Passengers are advised to be there at least an hour ahead of departure time, leaving plenty of time to buy tickets and check their luggage. Do not panic if the bus fills up; it will generally be replaced with another one right away. Buying tickets in advance does not guarantee you a seat, and you will still have to line up to board the bus. Priority boarding is available at some bus stations for an extra Can$5. Go to the ticket desk no more than 45 minutes and no less then 20 minutes before your bus is scheduled to leave.

Most bus stations have a small restaurant or café where reasonably priced snacks and meals can be purchased. On long-distance journeys it is a good idea to take some food with you, otherwise you will have to rely on the sometimes over-priced, unappealing food available in service stations.

At the larger stations it is possible to rent luggage lockers, leaving you free to explore unencumbered by suitcases. In the major cities such as Toronto, you have the choice of boarding in the suburbs or in the city center. Choose the city center since the bus may be full by the time it reaches outlying districts. Always ask if there is an express or direct service to your destination; as some trips involve countless stops en route

Boarding the bus on Ottawa's Parliament Hill

Tourists on a bus trip to the Athabasca Glacier, near Jasper

and can seem very long. A small pillow or traveling cushion, a sweater (to counter the some-times fierce air-conditioning), and a good book or magazine can often help to make a long trip more comfortable.

Bus Tours

There are several tour companies that offer package deals on a variety of trips. An extensive range of tours is available, from city sightseeing and day trips to particular attractions, to expensive luxury, multi-day tours including guides, meals, and accommodations. There are specialized tours that focus on such activities as glacier hikes, white-water rafting, and horseback riding. A typical ten-day tour of the Rockies may take in everything from a cruise to Victoria, a hike in Banff, and a picnic on Lake Louise, to a trip to the Columbia Icefield, or a look at the history of gold rush country in the Cariboo region. Most companies will send you detailed itineraries in advance, and it is a good idea to make sure that there are no hidden extras such as tips, sales taxes, and entry fees, as these are often included in the price of the package. Some of the most beautiful scenery can also be seen on regular Greyhound routes, such as those in the Rockies.

DIRECTORY

Greyhound Canada Inquiries
Tel 1 800 661 8747.
W greyhound.ca

Timetable Information
(CAN & US) **Tel** 1 800 661 8747;
(UK) **Tel** 0870 888 0223.

Bookings (passes only)
(UK) **Tel** 0870 888 0223.

DRL (Newfoundland)
Tel 1 888 263 1854. W drl-lr.com

Malaspina Coach Lines (BC)
Tel (604) 885 2217.
W malaspinacoach.com

Oreleans Express (Quebec)
Tel 1 888 999 3977.
W orleansexpress.com

Pacific Coach Lines (BC)
Tel (604) 662 7575, 1 800 661 1725.
W pacificcoach.com

Bus Tour Companies

Brewster Vacations Canada
Tel (403) 762 6717; 1 877 791 5500.
W vacationscanada.travel

Great Canadian Holidays
for tours in the east **Tel** (519) 896 8687, 1 800 461 8687.
W vacationscanada.travel

Bus Routes

This map shows the main bus routes across Canada. It is possible to travel right across the country along the Trans-Canada Highway using Greyhound Canada and the bus companies that operate east of Toronto.

Driving in Canada

It is a good idea to rent a car when visiting Canada. Other modes of trans portation will get you around the cities and from one rural town to another, but once you arrive in a remote country area, a car is the best way of exploring. Tours of regions such as Quebec's wild Gaspé Peninsula *(see pp148–9)*, or British Columbia's Okanagan Valley *(see p321)* are best made by car. Several aspects of Canadian life reflect the fact that this is a driver's country: there is an excellent, well-maintained highway network, and many places have huge out-of-town malls. However, city-center traffic congestion means that visitors to the major cities of Toronto, Vancouver, Montreal, and Ottawa may find that public transportation is quicker and cheaper than driving.

Arriving by Car

Many people drive to Canada from the US. The border here is the longest in the world. There are 13 major crossing points, the two busiest being from Detroit to Windsor and at Niagara Falls. Most of the highways entering Canada connect to the Trans-Canada Highway, which is the longest highway through the country, running for some 5,000 km (8,045 miles) from Victoria, BC, to St. John's in Newfoundland. Customs control ask that visitors declare their citizenship, their place of residence, and proposed length of stay. You may be asked to show your passport and visa *(see pp398–9)*. It is a good idea to fill up with less expensive fuel on the US side. It is also possible to enter the country from the Alaska side by the famed Alaska Highway *(see pp266–7)*, which crosses the Yukon and ends in British Columbia at Dawson City.

Driver's Licenses

An up-to-date driver's license from your own country usually entitles you to drive in Canada for up to three months. There are some provincial variations: in British Columbia, Quebec, and New Brunswick your license will be valid for up to six months, in Prince Edward Island four months, and in the Yukon only one month. It is advisable to carry an International Driving Permit (IDP) with your license in case of problems with traffic officials or the police.

Insurance

Whether driving a rental or your own car you will need proof of insurance coverage, which is compulsory in Canada. If you are using your own car it is advisable to check whether your insurance is valid in Canada, as this may save money. The minimum liability cover is Can$200,000, except in Quebec, where it starts at Can$50,000. Most rental companies offer collision damage waiver and personal accident insurance for an additional charge; it is a good idea to have both. If you are driving a private car that is not registered in your own name, you will need to carry the liability insurance card or "pink slip" for that particular car. For a rental vehicle you must carry the company's official documentation for the same reason. Arranging summer rentals and insurance in advance is recommended.

A Recreational Vehicle passes mountains and forests on a trip through Banff National Park, Alberta

Car Rental

Rental cars are available just about everywhere in Canada. Most major rental car dealers such as Hertz, Avis, and National, have offices at airports and in towns and cities across the country. Among the less expensive options are booking a fly-drive package from home, or there may be discounts if you rent your car in advance. The cost varies greatly depending on the season, type of vehicle, and length of rental. Ask about hidden costs such as drop-off charges, and taxes, depending on which province you are in. When picking up your car you may be asked to show your passport and return airline ticket. The minimum age for renting a car is usually 25 or, in some cases, 21. You will need a credit card for the deposit as it is all but impossible to rent a car in Canada without one. Children under 18 kg (40 lbs) require a child seat fixed in place with a seat belt. Most companies will arrange for one with a little notice. The biggest rental companies offer a wide choice of vehicles, ranging from two-door economy cars to four-door luxury models. Most cars come with a radio and air conditioning. Bear in mind that nearly all rental cars in Canada have automatic transmission. Manual models are unusual, although cars with specially adapted hand controls for disabled drivers are available from some of the larger companies. RVs (Recreational Vehicles) or camper vans can also be rented, but they are more expensive. They should be booked well in advance if you intend to travel in summer.

Fuel and Service Stations

Fuel prices are slightly higher than in the US and half the price you pay in the UK, especially in cities and large towns, although rural areas often charge more. Unleaded gas and diesel only are available in Canada. Rental companies generally provide a full tank on departure, and give you the choice of paying for the fuel in advance or on return. Service stations are often self-service, which can be a problem if you need a mechanic. In major cities some stations are open for 24 hours, but in rural areas they often close at 6pm and are few and far between, especially in northerly regions. It is a good idea to fill up before setting off. Credit and debit cards are widely accepted.

Rules of the Road

Canada's highway system is well maintained and has mostly two-lane all-weather roads. They are all clearly numbered and signed. Most highway signs are in English, and some bilingual, except for those in Quebec where they are only in French. A good road map is essential and can be obtained from any auto club such as the **Canadian Automobile Association (CAA)**, which is affiliated with other similar clubs in the world. It is worth checking the rules of the road with them as there are numerous small provincial variations. In Canada you drive on the right. You can turn right on a red light everywhere, except in Quebec. The speed limits are posted in kilometers-per-hour (km/h) and range from 30–40 km/h (18–30 mph) in urban areas to 80–100 km/h (50–60 mph) on highways. On multi-lane highways you pass on the left for safety. Some provinces require cars to keep their headlights on for extended periods after dawn and before sunset, for safety reasons. Seat belts are compulsory for both drivers and passengers.

Driving in the north involves special procedures because the roads are extremely hazardous due to ice, and are passable only during the summer months.

Moose warning sign
on highway

Winter Driving and Safety

Canadian winters are harsh, and you should always check road conditions and weather forecasts before setting out on trips. Drifting snow and black ice are frequent hazards in winter or in northern regions. When driving in remote areas, make sure you have a full gas tank, and carry blankets, some sand, a shovel, and emergency food, such as chocolate bars, in case you get stuck. Jumper cables are also useful because extreme cold can drain a car battery quickly. Snow tires are recommended in freezing conditions and required by Quebec law in the winter months. Studded tires are also useful and are permitted in most provinces. Check with local tourist offices.

During the summer animals such as bears and moose can be a hazard, especially in parts of British Columbia. They can appear on roads when they rush out of the woods to escape the blackflies. Watch for road signs, and take extra care when you see deer or moose road signs as these indicate an area where animals are most likely to appear suddenly.

General Index

Acknowledgments

Dorling Kindersley would like to thank the following people whose contributions and assistance have made the book possible:

Main Contributors
Paul Franklin has recently completed Nova Scotia's provincial travel guide, commissioned by the Government of Nova Scotia. A writer and photographer for both Canadian and world travel guides, he lives in Nova Scotia.
Sam Ion and **Cam Norton** live and work in Burlington, Ontario. A successful travel-writing team, they contribute to newspapers, magazines, and brochures as well as their most recent work, the Ontario Government's millennium website, celebrating the province.
Philip Lee has worked as a travel writer for over a decade, and is the author of numerous articles and travel books about countries throughout the world. He has lived and traveled extensively through the US and Canada and is now based in Nottingham, England.
Lorry Patton lives and works in British Columbia, having recently been travel editor of BC Woman magazine. She currently runs an online travel magazine which includes BC, and lives on the Gulf Islands just outside Vancouver.
Geoffrey Roy is an award-winning freelance travel writer and photographer, based in Surrey, England. He has published numerous articles on Northern Canada.
Donald Telfer is a Saskatchewan-based travel writer with over 20 years' writing experience of Central Canada. He contributes regularly to a variety of Canadian and international newspapers and magazines.
Paul Waters is a Montreal-based journalist who has lived and worked in several cities in Quebec and has written extensively on the province. He is currently the travel editor for The Gazette, a popular Montreal English-language daily.

Additional Contributors
Bruce Bishop, Alan Chan, Katharine and Eric Fletcher, Helena Katz, Ffion Llwyd-Jones, Sandra Phinney, Michael Snook.

Additional Photography
Tim Draper, Bert Hoferichter, James Jackson, Alan Keohane, Gunter Marx, Ian O'Leary, Cylla Von Tiedman, Enrique Uranga, Matthew Ward, Peter Wilson.

Additional Illustrations
Stephen Conlin, Eugene Fleury, Steve Gyapay, Chris Orr, Mel Pickering, Peter Ross.

Cartography
ERA-Maptec Ltd, Dublin, Ireland.

Proof Reader
Sam Merrell.

Indexer
Hilary Bird.

Revisions Team
Gillian Allan, Emily Anderson, Claire Baranowski, Sonal Bhatt, Ilona Biro, Louise Bolton, Julie Bond, Lola Brown, Barbara L. Campbell, Divya Chowfin, Vivien Crump, Flannery Dean, Hannah Dolan, Gadi Farfour, Emer FitzGerald, Joy Fitzsimmons, Camilla Gersh, Emily Green, Mohammad Hassan, Dr. Stephen Henderson, Jessica Hughes, Marie Ingledew, Shobhna Iyer, Zafar ul Islam Khan, Steve Knowlden, Kathryn Lane, Jude Ledger, Patrick Lejtenyi, Hayley Maher, Casper Morris, Mary Ormandy,

Helen Peters, Marianne Petrou, Rada Radojicic, Mani Ramaswamy, Lee Redmond, Lucy Richards, Toby Saltzman, Sands Publishing Solutions, Azeem Siddiqui, Susana Smith, Jaynan Spengler, Mark Stevens, Anna Streiffert, Rebecca Taylor, Geordie Telfer, Helen Townsend, Vinita Venugopal, Nikhil Verma, Lisa Voormeij, Candice Walsh.

Additional Picture Research
Rachel Barber, Ellen Root, Marta Bescos

Special assistance
Canada Map Office, Ontario; Canadian Tourism Office, London, UK; Claude Guerin and Danielle Legentil, Musée d'art contemporain de Montreal; Jim Kemshead, Tourism Yukon; Wendy Kraushaar, RCMP Museum, Regina, Saskatchewan; 'Ksan Historical Indian Village &Museum, Hazleton, BC; Leila Jamieson, Art Gallery of Ontario, Toronto; Antonio Landry, Village Historique Acadien, New Brunswick; Marty Hickie, Royal Tyrrell Museum, Drumheller, Alberta; Mary Mandley, Information Office, Sainte-Marie among the Hurons; National Air Photo Library, Ottawa, Ontario; Liette Roberts, Manitoba Museum of Man and Nature, Winnipeg; Mark Sayers; Ernest D. Scullion, Aeriel Photography Services, Scarborough, Ontario; Visit Canada office, London, UK; Jennifer Webb, UBC Museum of Anthropology, Vancouver, BC.

Photography Permissions
Dorling Kindersley would like to thank everyone for their assistance and kind permission to photograph at their establishments.

Picture Credits
a = above; b = below/bottom; c = centre; f = far; l = left; r = right; t = top.

Works of art have been produced with the permission of the following copyright holders: © Bill Vazan Shibagua Shard, 1989 sandblasted sheild granite 189c.

The publishers would like to thank the following individuals, companies, and picture libraries for their kind permission to reproduce their photographs:

Air Canada: 406cla; **AKG, London:** 55bc; **Alamy Images:** Philip Bird 1c; Bill Brooks 363tl; Scott Dimond 294; Ron Erwin 343tl; Jeff Greenberg 385t; Marshall Ikonography 90-1; Gunter Marx 362cla; mediacolor's 386cla; Megapress 386tl; Rolf Hicker Photography 371cla; Don Johnston 162-3; Pictures Colour Library 11bl, 386br; Robert Harding Picture Library Ltd/Roy Rainford 8cla; Andrew Rubtsov 193tl; Stephen Saks Photography 363c; Steve Shuey 332; John Sylvester 96c; Travel Pictures 118tl; David Trevor 192tl; David Wei: 384cr; Darwin Wiggett 78, 338-9; **Auberge du Vieux-Port:** 352b; **Aux Anciens Canadiens:** 370br; **Bearfoot Bistro:** 382b; **Bell Homestead:** 222tl; **The Bison Restaurant & Terrace:** 380bl; **The Blue Door Restaurant:** 365tl; **Bryan and Cherry Alexander:** 24c, 28tr, 29cr, 30cl 35cr/br, 45tr; 59crb/cb, 161t, 328bl, 330-31, 331cr, 340tl, 345tl; **Allsport:** Jed Jacobson 41ca; Jamie Squire 43cb; Rick Stewart 40cl; **Anchorage Museum of History and Art**, Anchorage, Alaska: B74.1.25 54tr; courtesy of **The Anne of Green Gables Museum**, Silver Bush, Park Corner, Prince Edward Island: 87br; **Art Central:** Jenny Tzanakos 296tr; **Art**

Gallery of Ontario: 182tr; Edgar Degas Grande Arabesque, bronze 180bl; Paul Gauguin French 1848–1903; Lawren H. Harris Canadian 1885–1970 *Above Lake Superior* c.1922 oil on canvas 121.9 x 152.4 cm Gift from Ruben and Kate Leonard Canadian Fund 1929 © Mrs. James H Knox 168br; Paul Kane *Scene in the Northwest* (1845–46) The Thomson Collection 183br; J.E.H. MacDondald Canadian (1873–1932) *Falls, Montreal River* 1920 oil on canvas 121.9 x 153cm Purchase 1933 Acc no 2109 Photo Larry Ostrom 169tr; Henry Moore British (1898–1986) *Draped Reclining Figure* 1952 - 53 original plaster 100.4 x 160.4x 68.6 cm Gift of Henry Moore, 1974. The work illustrated on page 182cla is reproduced by permission of the Henry Moore Foundation; Robert Gray Murray (b1936) To 1963 painted aluminium, 2 units, tubular column H271.1cm planar column 275.0cm Gift from the Junior Women's Committee Fund 1966 65/60.1-2 37cb; Photographic Resources 36br; Peter Paul Rubens *Massacre of the Innocents* (1609-11) The Thomson Collection 182clb; Tom Thomson Canadian 1887-1917 *The West Wind* 1917 oil on canvas 120.7 x 137.2 cm Gift of the Canadian Club of Toronto, 1926 183crb; **Axiom**: Chris Coe 26cl, 35tc, 92cr, 209br, 241tl/cra, 243ca/bc, 251tr, 281t, 314tr, 336cr/bl, 361br. **Bard on the Beach Shakespeare Festival**: David Blue 390br; **Bata Shoe Museum**, Toronto: 187bl; **Brasseurs de Temps:** 370tr; **Bridgeman Art Library**: Emily Carr (1871–1945) *Skidgate, Graham Island, British Columbia* 1928 (oil on canvas) Gift of the J.S. Mclean Collection by Canada Packers Inc. 1990 37tl, Maurice Galbraith Cullen (1866–1934) *On the Saint Lawrence* 1897 (oil on canvas) Gift of the Reuben and Kate Leonard Canadian Fund, 1926 36cl; British Library portolan by Pierre Descaliers Canada: *from the voyage of Jacques Cartier* (1491–1557) and his followers c.1534–41 48cb, *Jacques Cartier* (1491–1557) *French navigator and discoverer of Canadian River St. Lawrence* (steel engraving after a portrait in St. Malo) 48b; Hudson Bay Company Lieutenant Smyth (19th Century) *Incidents on Trading Journey; HMS Terror Making Fast to an Iceberg in Hudson's Strait*, August 18th, 1836 167tl; medal commemorating the British capture of Quebec, 1759 (bronze) 51bl; engraving by Jean Antoine Theodore Gudin (1802–80) *Jacques Cartier* (1491–1557) on the St. Lawrence River, 1535 7; litho by Howard Pyle (1853–1911) *The Capitualtion of Louisbourg, illustration from 'Colonies and Nation'* by Woodrow Wilson, pub. in Harper's Magazine, 1901 51tl, Benjamin West (1738–1820) *Willaim Penn's Treaty with the Indians in November 1683* (oil on canvas) 34tr; Stapleton Collection engraved by Carl Vogel (1816–51) *Indian Hunting the Bison, plate 31 from volume 2 "Travels in the Interior of North America"*, 1844 (aquatint) by Karl Bodmer (1809–93) (after) 34crb, engraved by Charles Geoffroy (1832–82) *Assiniboin Indians, plate 32 from volume 2 of "Travels in the interior of North America 1832–34"*, 1844 (acquatint) by Karl Bodmer (1809-93) (after) 251bc; **British Columbia Archives**: Province of B.C. Photo 51crb. Courtesy of **Calgary Transit**: 412clb; **Cephas**: Fred R. Palmer 106tr; Pascal Quittemelle 106bl; TOP/Hervé Amiard 32bc; **CinCin Restaurant & Bar:** 360cl;, 378tr **Clayoquot Wilderness Resort**: 349t; **Bruce Coleman Ltd.**: John Cancalosi 249c; **Jean Loup Charmet**: 50tr; **Chives Canadian Bistro**: 366bc; **The Church Restaurant**: 376bl; **Colorific!**: Randa Bishop 403br; Terence LeGoubin 229tc; Black Star/Richard Olsenius 76br; Michael Saunders 107bl; Geray Sweeney 27b; Focus/Eric Spiegelhalter 325tr; **Corbis**: 33tl, 3/bc, 52cb, 54cl, 67br, 213t, 215tr, 236bl, 254bl; Craig Aurness 236-237; David Bartruff 331b; Bettman 53bl, 55cr, 56br; Bettman/UPI 207b; Alan Copson

110, 124-5; Peter Harholdt 330bl; Hulton Deutsch collection 6-7; 58fcr/bc/br; Wolfang Kaehler 330cl; Lake County Museum 237crb; Library of Congress 49tr/cb; William Manning 132; Alan Marsh 150; Wally McNamee 129cra; New York Public Library Picture Collection 48ca; PEMCO-Webster & Stevens Collection Museum of History and Industry, Seattle 55tl; Sygma/Touhig Sion 25c; UPI 39cla. **Delta Montreal**: 352tc; **Discovery Harbour**: 223b; Courtesy of **destinationlabrador.com**: 77crb; **Adrian Dorst**: 260cl, 292cr, 293cb. **Dreamstime.com**: Bcbounders 173tl; Ckchiu 389t; Jiong Dai 402bl; Songquan Deng 220-1; Tom Eagan 75cr; Fallsview 396-7; Chris Hill 210; Ritu Jethani 143tr; Wangkun Jia 13t, 20; Philippehalle 14t; Photawa 398b; William Manning 268; Paul McKinnon 40br; Meunierd 127br; Mirceax 128tr; Mkoudis 15bl; Nelugo 309-10; Norman Pogson 9b; Jason P Ross 12cr; Brandon Smith 238; Valentino Visentini 175tl; Simone Winkler 156-7; **Empics Ltd**: Sportschrome 25bl; **Robert Estall Photo Library**: 81br, 106–107, 108c, 160br; **Mary Evans Picture Library**: 51cr, 55tr, 166tr. **Fairmont Hotels and Resorts, Canada**: 199tr, 348t, 349b, 354b, 357tr, 359tr, 375br, 381tl; **Les Fougères**: 371tc; **Four Seasons Centre For The Performing Arts**: Sam Javanrouh 178tl; **P.M. Franklin**: 27tr, 29ca, 64ca, 67tr/cr, 99t; **Winston Fraser Photos**: 72br, 106cl, 107crb, 109tr, 233br, 254tl, 340br, 405clb, 407cl; Black Star 161c; Canada In Stock 223tr; Ivy Images/Don Mills 44cr, 64br, 66tr, 67tl, 76crb, 77tl, 155cr; Ivy Images/Don Mills/© Gilles Daigle 82t,/© Sylvain Grandadam 395tl; /© Tony Mihok 42br/ © Dan Roitner 85br; T.Klassen Photography 242c, 246tl, 257tc; **Fundy Restaurant**: 365br. **Genoa Bay Cafe**: 377tr; **Getty Images**: Barrett & MacKay 68, 244-5; Henry@scenicfoto.com 2-3; Yves Marcoux 102-3; mbbirdy 170; Dennis McColeman 198cl; Lisa Stokes 346-7; Superstock 276-7; Taxi/Walter Bibikow 10tr; Michael Wheatley 258-9; **Goderich**: 226bl; **Grano Restaurant Toronto**: 374tc; **The Great George Hotel**: 350bc; Courtesy of **Greyhound Canada**: 416ca; **Lyn Hancock**: 342cla, 344b, 345br, 392bl, **Robert Harding Picture Library**: 29cl, 35tl, 109cr, 262clb; Charles Bowman 111b; Jeff Greenberg 266cb; Norma Joseph Frgs 237br; Maurice Joseph Frgs, Arps 42cl, 417tl; R. McLeod 325b; Roy Rainford 184tl; Walter Rawlings 309cr; Geoff Renner 235tl; Ian Tomlinson 43t, 298bl; Dr A.C. Waltham 334b; Explorer 160tl/Patrick Lorne 148bl; Publiphoto Diffusion 28cl;/Paul G. Adam 144t;/Yves Marcoux 147t; **Hilton Hotels and Resorts**: 351tl; **David Houser**: 76tl, 77cl, 147br, 149bl; **Hudson Bay Company Archives**, Toronto: 166bl; Provincial Archives of Manitoba 166b, 167cra; **Hulton Getty Collection**: 58tl, 99cb, 108clb. **Inuit Art Foundation**, Ontario: Sarah Joe Qinuajua, Puvirnituq *A Polar Bear Meets A Woman* QC1985 Black Stone Cut 330tr. **Jasper Tourism and Commerce**: 312tr; Hugh Levy 313ca. **Wolfgang Kaehler**: 148tr, 149br; **Robin Karpan**: 23tc, 232tr, 235cr/br, 236tr, 240bl, 242bl, 247br, 248cl/bc, 249b, 250tl/c/b, 253t/b, 254cra, 255cla/cr/b, 335tl, 343br; **Joseph King**: 271br, 279t, 324bl; **Kobal Collection**: *Rose Marie*, MGM 237tr; *Anne of Green Gables*, RKO 38cl. **Frank Lane Picture Agency**: Dembinsky 28crb; Michael Gore 65crb; John Hawkins 65br; David Hosking 234clb, 264tr, 301br; Maslowski 28br; C. Mullen 147c; Mark Newman 29crb, 264cb; C.Rhodes 29bc; M.Rhode 80c; Leonard Lee Rue 29clb, 160c, 317cr; Sunset/Brake 80tl, 344cl;/T.Leeson 264bl; John Watkins 64cb; David Whittaker 264ca; Terry Whittaker 28clb; **Hotel le Priori**: 348cr; **Leisurail/VIA Rail Canada**: 415ca; **Lil' Baci Restaurant**: 372br; . **Magnan Restaurant**: 367tr; Courtesy of the

Manitoba Museum of Man and Nature: 243clb; Marcel's Bistro: 361tl, 373tc; Arnold Matchtinger: 190bl; Mccord Museum of Canadian History, Montreal: Notman Photographic Archives 57tc; Mcmichael Canadian Art Collection: Photo Arthur Goss/Arts & Letters Club 169br; A.V Jackson (1882–1974) The Red Maple, 1914 oil on panel, 21.6 x 26.9cm Gift of Mr. S. Walter Stewart 1968.8.18 168tr; Musee d'art Contemporain de Montreal: Natalie Roy Les Dentelles de Montmirail, 1995 (detail) Soutens-gorge etjupon sous acrylique et bois 32 x 300 x 35cm Denis Farley et Natalie Roy Du Compagnonnage du 2 Juin au Septembre 1999 ©SODART/DACS, 2011 120tr; Richard Long Niagra Sandstone Circle, 1981 32 pierres de gres © Richard Long 120cl; Musee des Beaux-Arts de Montreal: Laurent Arriot Teapot Photo Christine Guest 1952 DS 41 122bl; El Greco Portrait of a young Man 1945.885 123c; Harmensz van Rijn Rembrandt Portrait of a Young Lady 1949-1006 122cla; courtesy of the Museum of Anthropology, Univeristy of British Columbia, Vancouver, Canada: photo: Bill McLennan 280clb, 280b, Red Cedar Totem Poles in Great Hall, Haida and Tsimshian (Canada) 280tr; Wooden Frontlet Bella Bella, (Canada) H.R. MacMillan Purchase 281crb. National Archives of Canada: C-011371 53tc, C25739 267cra; National Gallery of Canada, Ottawa: 202cla, Davidialuk Alasua Amittu (1910– 76) The Aurora Borealis Decapitating a Young Man c.1965 purchased 1992 © La Fédération des Cooperatives du Nouveau-Québec 202; Louise Bourgeois Maman 1999 © Louise Bourgeois Trust 1999tl; Jackson Pollock (1912–56) No.29 c.1950 purchased 1968 © ARS, NY and DACS, London 2011 203tc; Francesco Salviati Virgin and Child with an Angel c.1535–1539 203crb; Tom Thomson (1877–1917) The Jack Pine c.1916–1917 purchased 1918 203ca; Natural History Photographic Agency: Brian and Cherry Alexander 65clb; Dan Griggs 27cr, 167bc; Stephen Krasemann 28bl, 64tr, 265br, 336tl, 337t, David E. Myers 22br; T.Kitchen and V.Hirst 29tr/bl, 64crb, 265ca/tr/cb, 266cla; Jean-Louis Le Moigne 265bl; Dr Eckart Pott 264bc; Kevin Schafer 64bl, 335c; John Shaw 65bl, 264br, 304bl, 324cla; NorbertWu 293cl; Naturpress: Roberto Olivas 341tl; Peter Newark's American Pictures: 46, 50–51, 50cl/bc, 51tr, 52tr, 53br, 54bl, 56t/cl, 57clb/bl, 66cl/bl; New Brunswick Tourism: 82br; Northern British Columbia Tourism Association: 316br; Num-ti-jah Lodge: 381br. Olive et Gourmando: 369bl; Opera de Montreal: Yves Renaud 391tl; Oxford Scientific Films: Tui DeRoy 65c; Breck P. Kent 65cla; Richard Herrmann 265bc. Parks Canada: Claude Picard Acadians working the fields commissioned by Canadian Heritage 66–67; PA Photos: AP/Aaron Harris 390cla; Photo Library: Robert Harding Travel/Alison Wright 345cr; Pictures Colour Library: 408cl, 411b; The Pointe Restaurant: 378br; Provincial Archives of Manitoba: neg no. CT16 53crb; Prince of Wales Hotel: 358bc; Publiphoto: 59tl; Y. Beaulieu 33c; J.P. Danvoye 145br, 149tl; Claude A. Girouard 145bl, 146bc; Jean Lauzon 58crb, 148cla; D.Oullette 146tl; M.E.F. /Boulion 145cra; S. Clement 32cl; G. Zimbal 33br. Raymonds Restaurant: 364bc; Regié

des Installations Olympique: 129tl; Retna Pictures: Steve Granitz 389bc; Phil Loftus 39b; Micheal Putland 38br; Richard Reyes 25tr; Rex Features: 39tr; Image courtesy of the Royal British Columbia Museum: 288cla/cl, 289t/cra/ crb; © Peter and Mabel Fox 288crb; courtesy of the Royal Canadian Mounted Police Museum, Regina: 236cl/br; © Royal Ontario Museum: 188cla, Man's painted caribou-skin coat, Innu, Quebec-Labradorc. 1805 188clb; David McKay 188c; Royal Tyrell Museum, Drumheller: Alberta Tourism Parks,Recreation and Culture 234cla/br, 234–235, 234tr, 235cra; 252ca/clb/br.; Courtesy of the Sainte-Anne-du-Beaupré Museum: 143bl/tl; Courtesy of Scotiabank: 404clb; Sheraton on the Falls: 356br; SKKY Hotels: 383tr; Spectrum Colour Library: 337br, 340c; Spectrum Stock: Ottomar Bierwagen 44tl; Ron Erwin 228tr/b; Henry Kalan 228c; Norman Piluke Photography 229br; STA Travel Group: 400crb; Tony Stone Images: Wayne R Bilenduke 329br, 341crb; Cosmos Condina 21b, 304br; Richard Elliot 267bl; John Edwards 177b; Suzanne and Nick Geary 418b; Sylvian Grandadam 109tl; David Hiser 257br, 331tl; Paul Souders 267tl; Jess Stock 41br. Superstock: Russ Heinl 194; Rolf Hicker 318, 326-7; Dave Reede 230-1; Swiss Hotel, Ottawa: 355tl Tate Gallery, London: The Honorable John Collier Last Voyage of Henry Hudson oil on canvas ©1988 49crb; Donald l. Telfer: 28cr, 242tr, 246br, 247tl/cr, 248tr, 249t, 256t/b; Travel Alberta: 305cr, 316tl. University of Toronto: J.B Tyrrell Papers, Thomas Fisher Rare Book Library MS Collection 26 234bl. Tourism Winnipeg: 240bl; Tuck Shop Bistro: 369; Vancouver Public Library, Special Collections: 13220 54–5; Victoria University in the University of Toronto, Canada: Lawren S. Harris Autumn Algoma, 1920 © Mrs. James H. Knox 168–169; Village Historique Acadien: 83tl/tr/bl. Courtesy of Western Union Money Transfer: 404cr; Westjet: 409c; Willensky's Light Lunch: 368tl; Collection of the Winnipeg Art Gallery, Canada: Frank H Johnston Edge of Forest, 1919 watercolour, tempera on hardboard 52.2 x 62.8cm L26 Ernest Mayer 168cl; World Pictures: 1c, 24tl, 45bl, 63cr, 65tr, 97br, 136cla, 208cl, 262br, 263tl/cla, 266bl, 305tc, 317t, 324tr, 331tr, 416bl. Yukon Government Communities: 334cra.

Front endpaper: Alamy Images: Scott Dimond Lcl; Steve Shuey Ltc; Darwin Wiggett Rcra; Corbis: Alan Copson Rtr; William Manning Rtc; Alan Marsh Rtl; Dreamstime.com: Chris Hill Lbr; William Manning Lbl; Brandon Smith Lbc; Getty Images: Barrett & MacKay Rca; mbbirdy Rcrb; Superstock: Russ Heinl Rbr; Rolf Hicker Lcla..

Jacket
Front and spine – Alamy Images: Gary Dublanko.

All other images © Dorling Kindersley.
For more information see:
www.DKimages.com

Special Editions of DK Travel Guides

DK Travel Guides can be purchased in bulk quantities at discounted prices for use in promotions or as premiums. We are also able to offer special editions and personalized jackets, corporate imprints, and excerpts from all of our books, tailored specifically to meet your own needs.

To find out more, please contact:
in the United States SpecialSales@dk.com
in the UK travelspecialsales@uk.dk.com
in Canada DK Special Sales at general@tourmaline.ca
in Australia business.development@pearson.com.au

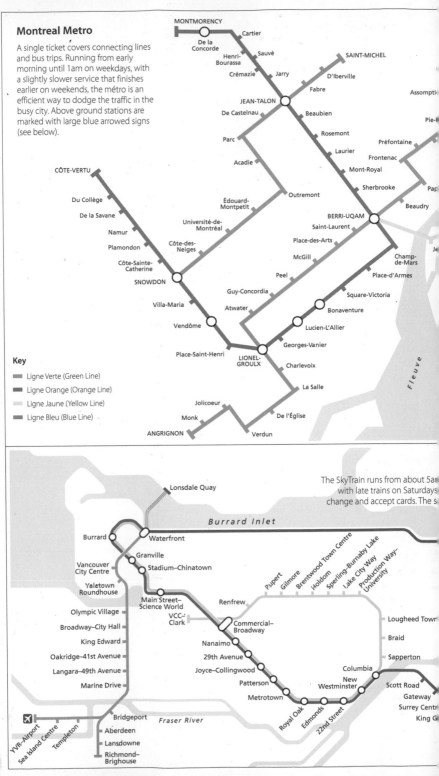

Montreal Metro

A single ticket covers connecting lines and bus trips. Running from early morning until 1am on weekdays, with a slightly slower service that finishes earlier on weekends, the métro is an efficient way to dodge the traffic in the busy city. Above ground stations are marked with large blue arrowed signs (see below).

Key

- Ligne Verte (Green Line)
- Ligne Orange (Orange Line)
- Ligne Jaune (Yellow Line)
- Ligne Bleu (Blue Line)

MONTMORENCY
Cartier
De la Concorde
Henri-Bourassa
Sauvé
Crémazie
Jarry
JEAN-TALON
De Castelnau
Parc
Acadie
Outremont
CÔTE-VERTU
Du Collège
De la Savane
Namur
Plamondon
Côte-Sainte-Catherine
SNOWDON
Villa-Maria
Vendôme
Place-Saint-Henri
LIONEL-GROULX
Jolicoeur
Monk
ANGRIGNON
Verdun
De l'Église
La Salle
Charlevoix
Georges-Vanier
Lucien-L'Allier
Bonaventure
Square-Victoria
Place-d'Armes
Champ-de-Mars
BERRI-UQAM
Saint-Laurent
Place-des-Arts
McGill
Peel
Guy-Concordia
Atwater
Édouard-Montpetit
Université-de-Montréal
Côte-des-Neiges
SAINT-MICHEL
D'Iberville
Fabre
Beaubien
Rosemont
Laurier
Mont-Royal
Sherbrooke
Préfontaine
Frontenac
Beaudry
Assomptic
Pie-N
Pap
Je
Fleuve

The SkyTrain runs from about 5am with late trains on Saturdays change and accept cards. The s

Lonsdale Quay
Burrard Inlet
Burrard
Waterfront
Vancouver City Centre
Granville
Stadium–Chinatown
Yaletown Roundhouse
Main Street–Science World
Renfrew
Olympic Village
VCC–Clark
Commercial–Broadway
Broadway–City Hall
Nanaimo
King Edward
29th Avenue
Oakridge–41st Avenue
Joyce–Collingwood
Langara–49th Avenue
Patterson
Marine Drive
Metrotown
Royal Oak
Edmonds
22nd Street
New Westminster
Columbia
Scott Road
Gateway
Surrey Centr
King G
YVR–Airport
Sea Island Centre
Templeton
Bridgeport
Aberdeen
Lansdowne
Richmond–Brighouse
Fraser River
Pupert
Gilmore
Brentwood Town Centre
Holdom
Sperling–Burnaby Lake
Lake City Way
Production Way–University
Lougheed Town
Braid
Sapperton